THE LAST KILO

ALSO BY T. J. ENGLISH

DANGEROUS RHYTHMS

THE CORPORATION

WHERE THE BODIES WERE BURIED

WHITEY'S PAYBACK

THE SAVAGE CITY

HAVANA NOCTURNE

PADDY WHACKED

BORN TO KILL

THE WESTIES

THE LAST KILO

WILLY FALCON
AND THE
COCAINE EMPIRE
THAT SEDUCED AMERICA

T. J. ENGLISH

WM

WILLIAM MORROW

An Imprint of HarperCollins*Publishers*

HarperCollins books may be purchased for educational, business, or sales promotional use. For information, please email the Special Markets Department at SPsales@harpercollins.com.

FIRST EDITION

Library of Congress Cataloging-in-Publication Data

Names: English, T. J., 1957- author.
Title: The last kilo : Willy Falcon and the cocaine empire that seduced America / T. J. English.
Description: New York, NY : William Morrow, an imprint of HarperCollins Publishers, [2024] | Includes bibliographical references and index. | Summary: "From true-crime legend T. J. English, the epic, behind-the-scenes saga of 'Los Muchachos,' one of the most successful cocaine-trafficking organizations in American history—a story of glitz, glamour, and organized crime set against 1980s Miami"— Provided by publisher.
Identifiers: LCCN 2024023837 (print) | LCCN 2024023838 (ebook) | ISBN 9780063265530 (hardcover) | ISBN 9780063265554 (ebook)
Subjects: LCSH: Cocaine industry—Florida—Miami. | Drug traffic—Florida—Miami.
Classification: LCC HV5810 .E55 2024 (print) | LCC HV5810 (ebook) | DDC 362.29/80975938—dc23/eng/20240701
LC record available at https://lccn.loc.gov/2024023837
LC ebook record available at https://lccn.loc.gov/2024023838

ISBN 978-0-06-326553-0

24 25 26 27 28 LBC 5 4 3 2 1

In memory of
Alina Rossique Falcon
1956–1992

THE NARCOSPHERE (1977–1991)

IMPORTERS/DISTRIBUTORS
Los Muchachos

Willy Falcon	Sal Magluta
Tavy Falcon	Benny Lorenzo
Tony Bemba	Justo Jay
Tony Garrudo	Ralph Linero

MONEY LAUNDERING

Panama
Guillermo Endara
Hernán Delgado
Gabriel Castro

Miami
Ray Corona
Juan Acosta

Caribbean
Shaun Murphy
Nigel Bowe
Lawrence Major

SUPPLIERS

Medellín Cartel
Pablo Escobar
Gustavo Gaviria
Manuel Garces
Carlos Lehder

Cali Cartel
Mario &
Guillermo Valencia

Guadalajara Cartel
Miguel Félix Gallardo
Rafael Caro Quintero

Juárez Cartel
Amado Carrillo Fuentes

MIAMI

Pegy Rosello
Miguel Vega
Jack Devoe
Gilberto Barrios

LOS ANGELES

Jojo Brito
Freddy Cruz
Victor Alvarez
Pepe "El Frijol"

CLEWISTON

Sermon Dyess Jr.
Butch Reddish

NYC–NEW JERSEY

Manny "Monguito" Alonso
Pacho Herrera

The exile, I know this firsthand, has lost the place
where he was and turned it into a source of myths,
the root of his longing, and the aroma of his despair.
For the Cuban, who had his exile coursing through
his blood, nostalgia is, has always been, the cradle
and grave of his passions. He cannot love without
invoking loss and he cannot sing without his mouth
filling with grief.

—*Pablo Medina, Cuban poet*

I am like any other man. All I do is supply a demand.

—*Alphonse "Al" Capone*

CONTENTS

INTRODUCTION

THIS IS NOT A BOOK about "Willy and Sal, the Cocaine Cowboys." It is the story of a criminal organization known as Los Muchachos (the Boys) that was begun by Augusto Guillermo "Willy" Falcon and thrived as a major cocaine-distribution network in the United States from the late 1970s into the early 1990s. During that period, Los Muchachos were underworld royalty. Federal prosecutors estimated that they imported seventy-five tons of pure cocaine with a street value over $2.6 billion. According to Willy Falcon, those numbers are low. He estimates that, over a fifteen-year period, he and his partners smuggled more like seven hundred tons with a street value today over $50 billion, making them the preeminent cocaine smugglers during a period when the product, if it had been a legally traded commodity, would have dominated the New York Stock Exchange.

A primary source for this book has been Falcon himself, whom I interviewed extensively from March 2021—four years after he was released from having served twenty-seven years in federal prison—to September 2023, when the manuscript was completed and submitted to the publisher.

During the period in which I communicated with Falcon, his longtime partner, Salvador "Sal" Magluta, was not available to be interviewed. He was incarcerated, serving a 195-year sentence on cocaine-trafficking, obstruction-of-justice, and money-laundering charges—the same charges that ensnared Falcon back in the 1990s.

Over the years that Los Muchachos were in operation, and then later when they became notorious in the media and in courtrooms primarily in South Florida, the focus of attention was always on Willy and Sal. The two names were linked as if they were one and the same. They were not two individuals; they were one amorphous entity. This dovetailed nicely with the prosecution's theory of the case, which held that these two men were connected at the hip; they composed a single criminal conspiracy, so that anything one of them was involved with could be used as evidence against the other. This also became a central aspect of the media's fascination with the story. Not only were the names invariably lumped together as one, but their story was told as if they were Cuban exile Siamese twins. They were both "high school dropouts," "champion powerboat racers," "Cuban exiles and anti-Castro activists," "Cuban playboys," "*narco traficantes*." Willy and Sal, Sal and Willy—the beast with two heads.

This narrative not only put forth a skewed presentation of two individual human beings with separate life stories of their own, but it also obscured the nature of how and why this cocaine operation was so powerful and lasted as long as it did. Willy and Sal were not the same person. In the end, they had separate stories to tell. This book attempts to tell the story of Falcon, admittedly one version of the Willy and Sal story. I would argue it is *the* version, given that Willy, unlike Sal, was there from the beginning. He's the one who commenced the cocaine business as part of the clandestine movement to destabilize the government of Fidel Castro, so that Cuban exiles in Miami might reclaim their country. He is the one who brought together the key players who comprised what would arguably be the most efficient cocaine importation and distribution network the United States has ever seen.

One thing Willy and Sal did share was the historical context in which the events of this story took place. Miami in the 1980s was a unique place, a confluence of forces having to do with the residue of the Cuban Revolution, the Cold War, patterns of exile and immigration, and, most notably, the emergence of cocaine.

Some have compared this era to the time of Prohibition in the United States, in the 1920s, when the sudden illegality of alcohol gave rise to a massive underworld structure of organized crime that, to an extent, still exists to this day. One major difference is that booze had been around for a long time when it was declared illegal in 1919. Most people who drank had been doing so already at the time it was banned, and therefore engaged in the illicit activity of manufacturing, selling, and consuming the product with full understanding of what it was.

Cocaine, on the other hand, was brand new to most users. When it arrived on the scene in the mid-1970s, it was as if America awoke one morning and a fresh layer of glistening white snow had carpeted the landscape. Part of what drove the era was the sense of discovery, the excitement of a new stimulant, something fresh and exciting, the ultimate party drug brought down to size and made affordable to the masses.

In 1981, *Time* magazine famously published a cover story on the cocaine phenomenon, citing its popularity:

> No longer is it primarily an exotic and ballyhooed indulgence of high-gloss entrepreneurs, Hollywood types and high rollers. . . . Today, cocaine is the drug of choice for perhaps millions of solid, conventional and often upwardly mobile citizens—lawyers, businessmen, students, government bureaucrats, politicians, policemen, secretaries, bankers, mechanics, real estate brokers, waitresses. . . . Coke is a supremely beguiling and relatively risk-free drug . . . a snort in each nostril and you're up and awake for thirty minutes or so. Alert, witty, and with it. No hangover. No physical addiction. No lung cancer.

Cocaine broke down inhibitions, and, at least superficially, made people feel sexy. It made revelers dance and get it on. For a time, Willy Falcon and those like him—major suppliers, of whom there were only a few—became stars in their own right. They were the deliverers of good times, at least until the downside of persistent cocaine use became apparent: delusions of grandeur, psychological addiction, financial ruin. Thus, the War on Drugs was born, and law enforcement came after people like Falcon and his crew with a vengeance.

IN DECEMBER 1983, WHEN THE COCAINE era was in full ascent, the movie *Scarface* was released in theaters around the United States. At the time, the organization of Falcon and Magluta was bringing in roughly $100 million annually. To celebrate their success, the core members of the organization, along with their wives and girlfriends, every year traveled from Miami to Las Vegas for a week of gambling, floor shows, and a massive New Year's Eve party at Caesars Palace Hotel and Casino.

One afternoon in late December, Falcon and eight members of his group went to see *Scarface*. The making of the movie had touched off a controversy in their hometown of Miami, where it was felt that the depiction of Cuban exiles as narcos was slanderous. Willy Falcon, following the lead of more formal exile organizations like the Cuban American National Foundation (CANF), forbid any of his gang from taking part in the production. Consequently, the movie was shot primarily in Los Angeles, using that city as a stand-in for Miami.

That afternoon in the Las Vegas movie theater, Falcon and his group found *Scarface* to be highly entertaining. They hooted and hollered during the outlandish depictions of cocaine violence and mayhem. They laughed at Al Pacino's thick Marielito accent. The movie was so cartoonish in its attempts to dramatize the cocaine business—but with enough verisimilitude that the Boys were able to identify with it—that they were even flattered. They didn't take it seriously. They thought it was a joke. But they could see that their lives were being elevated into the zeitgeist, and the movie offered the possibility of a kind of cinematic immortality.

Later came *Miami Vice*, another popular depiction of the city's narco universe. Produced by the NBC network, the show debuted in 1984 and ran for five seasons. Along with the crime stories revolving around the cocaine underworld, the show was highly attuned to surface pleasures of Miami: the pastel colors, Armani suits, sleek powerboats that were right out of the Willy and Sal story, and popular rock, R&B, and Latin music. *Miami Vice* defined cool in the 1980s and suggested that it was all an extension of the city's illicit cocaine universe.

Part of what made these works of popular entertainment so influential was that they appeared to be straight from the headlines. Movies depicting Prohibition had been popular, but they came years and even decades after the era they were depicting. *Scarface* and *Miami Vice* portrayed a phenomenon in real time, as it was happening, making those who were caught up in it feel as though they were living a dream.

In the decades that followed came many more movies and television dramas that used the cocaine universe for their storylines. Many took their cues from *Scarface*. Colombian, Cuban, and later Mexican narcos were invariably depicted as sociopaths or flat-out psychopaths in a business that politicians and people in law enforcement characterized as "evil." If there was to be a presentation of the cocaine business in entertainment or even in real life—through reports on the television news—it was invariably steeped in violence.

"Say hello to my little friend," Tony Montana's business motto in *Scarface*, was a prelude to violent mythmaking, and that seemed to be the way the American public was primed to receive any and all stories related to the cocaine business.

As is usually the case, the reality was more complicated.

For most of its existence, Willy Falcon and Los Muchachos' operations in the cocaine world involved little violence. The Boys did not seek to eliminate rivals through murder and intimidation. They did not punish their members internally with torture or killing or even the threat of killing. They did not pull out chain saws, à la *Scarface*. They did not mow down hordes of partygoers with Uzi submachine guns.

It was true that the world in which they were operating was a violent one. The narcosphere, as it was sometimes called, involved violence from top to bottom. Lowly street dealers used violence, and so did Pablo Escobar, believed in the 1980s to be the godfather of the business. And yet, the example of Los Muchachos suggests that it was possible to succeed at a high level without a reputation for murder—especially if your forte was importation and distribution, not dog-eat-dog entrepreneurship at the retail level.[1]

The story of Los Muchachos shows that it was not violence that was the dominant characteristic of the cocaine business.

It was corruption.

Dirty cops, agents, lawyers, judges, and politicians feeding off the profits of the narcosphere is what made the world go round. This existed at every level of the business, in every country, state, and city where kilos of coke passed through grubby hands on its way to and up the nostrils of the consumer. Falcon and Magluta played this game. With what seemed like unlimited resources, they bought off representatives of the system, from a county sheriff who made it possible for them to land their product at a clandestine airstrip, to a high-level money launderer who became the president of a country.

Corruption represents a human failing. It is usually practiced by people who, out of need, convenience, or necessity, choose to violate the principles by which they claim to live their lives. When it comes to corruption, greed is the most obvious culprit, stemming from a celebration of wealth, avarice, and the accumulation of more and more and more. Sometimes a person takes illegal payoffs to pay for a friend's or relative's medical costs, to deal with a family crisis, to

---

[1] After Falcon, Magluta, and eight others from their group were indicted in 1991, there were killings. There were four murders and two attempted murders of potential witnesses against Los Muchachos. It was widely speculated that these killings were related to the case of Los Muchachos, but there was never any evidence linking Falcon to any of these murders, and he was never charged. Magluta was later charged and found not guilty on all murder counts.

put a kid through college. Whatever the reason, corruption as a shortcut to the American dream became an operating principle that would turn the cocaine business of the 1980s into the most lucrative illegal endeavor on the planet.

THE NARCOSPHERE IS NOT A physical place; it is a realm of operation and a state of mind. It spans sovereign boundaries, physical space, borders, and political jurisdictions. Bolivia and Peru, where the coca plant is grown and cultivated, are parts of the narcosphere, as is Colombia, where the plant is processed into cocaine hydrochloride. For a long time, Panama City served as the central money-laundering domain of the narcosphere. The Caribbean islands, and later Mexico—which would become the preeminent region of transshipment—have been and are corridors of the narcosphere. The United States of America, the primary marketplace for the product, with more users of cocaine than anywhere else in the world, is arguably the engine that runs the entire operation. Regional players—narcos, cokeheads, drug mules, people in law enforcement, judges, politicians, distributors, dealers, citizens who look the other way—are all participants in this field of illegal commerce that still thrives in the present day.

For more than a decade, Falcon and his partners not only operated within this world but also succeeded at it to a degree that was unprecedented.

In the years since this story was in the headlines, some would rather minimize and diminish its significance to the point where one of the prosecutors of Willy and Sal, in an interview for this book, made the statement: "Falcon and Magluta were probably the most successful and biggest drug dealers in South Florida, but they weren't into importing drugs. They were receiving the drugs from smuggling gangs, and then they would distribute it, but they weren't importing."

This is a breathtakingly erroneous statement from someone who prosecuted Los Muchachos. As you will see from reading this book, Willy and Sal brokered major importation deals from around the narcosphere. In lore and legend, they have been portrayed as Cuban American playboys, high school dropouts, and amateurs who stumbled onto a hot property and exploited its popularity throughout the Dionysian era of the 1980s.

There is much more to this story than has been previously known. Partly, this is because Falcon and his closest associates have never talked about or been interviewed on the subject—until now. Back in the day, when they were facing prosecution, it was not in their interest to talk openly and honestly for the record. But the passage of time has a way of rearranging priorities. Most of these people have paid their debt to society, in many cases with long prison sentences. Over the decades, Falcon and his former partners have read accounts in the press or online, or seen documentaries on television and the internet, that present a dubious version of their personal histories. Falcon, for one, has waited a long time to give his version of what happened. His willingness to do so opened the door for many others from Los Muchachos to come forward and cooperate with the writing of this book. They represent a generation of people—mostly Cuban born or Cuban American—who got caught up in this wild era, have paid the price, and now live with the memories of their involvement in the golden age of cocaine.

It is time that this story be told from the point of view of those who lived it. Certainly, from a historical perspective, these events are significant to an understanding of the American process during a time of unprecedented crime and mayhem. But it is also important to understand that many lives, on both sides of the law, became enmeshed in the events of this time, and that their experiences—which became fodder for criminal indictments and media accounts—deserve to be recounted, preserved, and acknowledged on a human level.

History is not simply a cavalcade of big events—wars, elections, or public policies that shape the flow of human endeavor. It is also a consequence of simple people making choices—good, bad, or indifferent—that lead them on a life-altering journey, a singular adventure that maybe shapes the times in which they live. In the case of those who comprised Los Muchachos, the passage of time has shed new light on troubling personal events, unearthed deeply buried emotions, rattled the cages of ghosts, and flung open the doors of repressed recollections from long ago.

MOST OFTEN, ACCOUNTS OF THIS type are written from the point of view of those who cooperated with the government. On the street, they are called snitches, and they are the lifeblood of criminal prosecutions in American courts. Theoretically, informants are the people most able and willing to tell their story to an author, since they were likely given a plea deal to provide information and testify on behalf of the government. In the criminal world, these types of books are sometimes criticized as being the informant's version of events, and therefore suspect.

In my career as a crime writer, I have published a number of books in which the story is told from this point of view. For a nonfiction author, people who have testified for the government are often the only sources available to tell such a story. Convicted criminals are buried away in prison. Even if they wanted to submit to an interview, which is rare, the Bureau of Prisons (BOP) generally does not allow it (unless it is, somehow, beneficial to the government to do so). The common bromide that underworld history is most often told by the informants has more than a grain of truth.

This book is different. I have steered clear of sources who cooperated with the government. Not that I discount their version of events—their testimony at various criminal proceedings is readily available. For the most part, I have incorporated their version of events and relationships as they recounted it from the witness stand, or, more recently, through interviews they have done for documentaries, books, and podcasts. For some, their accounts are well known and have become the standard version of the Willy and Sal story as it exists in popular culture.

My goal with this book has been to provide an account primarily from those who did not cooperate with the government. This is the version of those who submitted to long sentences in prison rather than snitch on their friends and associates. I have also interviewed detectives, prosecutors, federal agents, and many others who played a role in taking down Los Muchachos as a criminal organization. However, the inner workings of the group—the relationships and motivations that sustained the gang for more than a decade—are here portrayed by those who did not snitch.

Theirs is a version with crazy highs and even crazier lows. For many of these people, the most astonishing fact is that they survived it, did the time, and have lived to tell the tale.

—*T. J. English*
New York City, 2024

PROLOGUE

Willy Falcon was excited to be getting out of town.

He was on his way to Miami International Airport for a flight to New Orleans for the Super Bowl, the National Football League's annual championship game. The Philadelphia Eagles were playing the Oakland Raiders. The Eagles were favored, but Willy had his money on the Raiders, the first wild card team in history to make it to the championship game. Willy loved to bet on the underdog.

Most of Falcon's crew was already in New Orleans with their wives and girlfriends. In the last three years, it had become a tradition for the inner circle of Los Muchachos to attend the Super Bowl in whatever city it was being held. It had become a cherished trip to celebrate their business successes and to revel in their brotherhood as fellow Cubans. Los Muchachos, as led by Falcon, was one big extended family of exiles—spouses, parents, grandparents, uncles and aunts, cousins—most of whom had been transplanted from their homeland after being uprooted by El Diablo Grande, Fidel Castro.

Falcon was driving with his wife, Alina, in their Mercedes convertible. While he was working through traffic, Willy's car phone buzzed. The phone was the ultimate status symbol, a rarity at the time except for international businessmen, political operatives, and narco bosses. Willy picked up the receiver: "Hello."

"Get over here right now." It was his father, fifty-two-year-old Arsenio Falcon.

"What's wrong?"

"Just get over here immediately."

Willy was alarmed by the urgency in his father's voice. He hung up, turned the car around, and drove toward his parents' house. He was going to miss his flight, and therefore the Super Bowl, but he could tell this was something serious. And in his business—the international cocaine-smuggling business—"serious" could mean any number of things, often not good.

Driving toward his father's house, a couple of blocks away, he came upon an unexpected sight: his mother walking intently in the direction of her and Arsenio's house. Her usual forthright demeanor was slightly askew, her hair mussed, her face flushed. She was holding a piece of cloth in her hand. At the age of fifty-two, Marta Falcon was not the type to go for walks in the neighborhood. She preferred to drive in an air-conditioned vehicle. Willy pulled over and said, "*Mima*, what are you doing out here by yourself?"

She got into the car and answered, "Just drive. To the house." Willy was getting a sinking feeling from his parents' mysterious commands. Then his mother blurted out, "I was kidnapped! They blindfolded me"—she held up the piece of cloth—"with this."

"Kidnapped!? By who?"

Her answer was something Willy found hard to comprehend. "The police," she said.

Willy was so startled that he drove the remaining few blocks to his parents' house without saying a thing.

At the house, people had already gathered. Willy's younger brother, Gustavo, known to all as "Tavy," was there, as were other family members and friends of his parents.

Arsenio Falcon had a weathered face from years in the sun, and a gravelly voice that, whether speaking English or his native Cuban Spanish, carried with it a lifetime of experience. He told Willy what had happened: Marta Falcon, while out driving, had been pulled over by what appeared to be two Miami police officers. They told her she was being stopped for a traffic violation, but then they cuffed her and put her in the back of a squad car. They blindfolded her and took her to a house. They tied her to a chair, called her husband, and had Marta speak into the receiver, telling him she was alive and okay. The kidnappers grabbed the receiver; they told Arsenio that they were demanding $500,000 for her release. They warned the elder Falcon that if he mentioned the kidnapping to anyone, including his son, they would kill Marta. Then they hung up.

Arsenio felt his mind racing and heart pumping like an overheated engine: suck, squeeze, bang, and blow. This was exactly the kind of thing he had feared ever since his son became involved in the cocaine business. He knew he had to do what the kidnappers said, or they would kill his beloved Marta. Even when he'd seen Willy that morning, Arsenio said nothing. He waited until his son left the house, then he extracted the money from a large stash of cash that Willy kept hidden in the ceiling of the laundry room. (Willy had thought his parents didn't know about it.) The old man paid the ransom. When he was informed that Marta had been dropped off on an anonymous street corner near their house, he then called Willy.

Willy Falcon was stupefied. The ransom payment meant nothing. In the larger scheme of cocaine profits, it was chump change. But there was something else at work, something ominous and diabolical, a dark cloud blowing in from a dark place.

Maybe this was it: the chickens coming home to roost. In the four years that Falcon had been in the business, he and his organization had lived a privileged existence; they had never really been challenged or made to suffer. The coke business in Miami had exploded with violence in recent years: shootouts, kidnappings, and brazen executions. Rivalries and competition among factions fueled a crazed, bloody atmosphere that rivaled Gangland Chicago during the peak years of violence in the Roaring Twenties. And yet, Los Muchachos—what federal authorities would soon refer to as "the Falcon DTO (Drug Trafficking Organization)"—had, up until now, remained above it all. Willy and his partners believed this was because they were local boys, admired and protected by all, including the cops.

Now they were being directly challenged in an audacious kidnapping of Willy Falcon's mother. It was an insult almost too outrageous to comprehend.

A month earlier, a business associate of Falcon's had experienced a similar trauma: a family member was kidnapped by cops or gangsters pretending to be cops—maybe these same kidnappers. They had taken the man to a house, demanded a ransom. When the business associate dragged his feet making the payment, they murdered the kidnap victim, cut his testicles off, and stuffed them into his mouth. The risks were real, and they could be brutal.

Marta Falcon sat on the sofa, looking glum. She had not been physically harmed, but she was rattled. The darkness of the narco world had been visited upon them. In recent years, deep down she and her husband had suppressed their fears, but now they knew they would never be safe. They would never be free.

Arsenio Falcon's anguish was such that his sons worried about his blood pressure. "*Tranquilo, Pipo, tranquilo,*" Tavy said to his father. "It's all over now."

But it wasn't over, not by a long shot. For Willy Falcon and Los Muchachos, the nightmare had only just begun.

I
THE PROMISED LAND

1

FREEDOM FLIGHT

THE ROAR OF THE ENGINE, two thousand tons of horsepower propelled forward at a speed of 125 miles an hour, along with the force of the powerboat's fiberglass hull as it skimmed along the surface of the ocean, made Willy Falcon feel as if the rumbling and bouncing would rock the fillings from his teeth. He remembered the first few times he ever piloted a machine like this. Back then, his whole body tightened up—his jaw clamped so hard that it was sore for hours afterward, and his sphincter muscle squeezed so tight that he probably could have held a fifty-pound cast iron weight dangling from his anus. What he had learned over the years was that to handle the speed and discombobulation while behind the wheel of the boat, you had to channel the controlled energy of a Zen master. Total relaxation was required—the ability to maintain physical and mental equilibrium even while the world zipped by all around you at speeds rarely tested by man.

Cocaine also helped. There were few highs as invigorating as snorting a line of yeyo before turning over the engine and hitting the blue horizon. Bend and sniff, the burning of the nasal membrane, a rush of ectoplasm to the head and through the body like liquid protein, the heart pumping strong and steady, the sometimes-frenetic effect of the white powder crystalized into laser beams of concentration. It was the kind of tunnel-vision effect that allowed a person to feel only the rumbling of the boat as if it were an intrinsic internal mechanism of the human body. Nirvana on the high seas.

Down the homestretch, Willy was feeling good. These were waters he knew well, through previous competitions as part of the Seahawk racing team, and as a teenager growing up in Miami. In his career as a trafficker, Willy had also mastered the sea and used it to facilitate his business. In some cases, his organization had used these same high-speed powerboats to transfer kilos of cocaine under cover of darkness.

Falcon crossed the finish line three lengths ahead of the nearest boat. His partner, Sal Magluta, had won a couple of competitions before, but this was Willy's first.

That night, Willy and the rest of Los Muchachos partied in the spirit of the hit song by Prince—like it was 1999. Willy was there with his beautiful wife, Alina; his brother, Tavy; his partner, Sal; and dozens of other partners and revelers. On the *dance floor, Falcon looked out over the crowd of mostly Cuban exiles like himself and thought, "Look at us. See how far we've come from having lost everything. Watch us soar. Watch us soar like a flock of falcons."*

Recently, Willy had given as a gift to his inner circle of partners a pendant on a gold chain, a diamond-studded figure of a falcon with its wings spread wide. The falcon represented the organization, but it was more than that: the pendant also represented the strength of their bond as blood brothers. They wore those pendants with pride.

Given the fortune amassed by Los Muchachos in the years since starting their business—which commenced with cocaine but had branched off into a half dozen other ventures, including the Seahawk powerboat racing empire—Willy could be forgiven for thinking his victory on the open seas was part of his destiny. Falcon and Los Muchachos, all they did was win. They won at everything, and the money flowed in—cash that was sometimes stored in shoeboxes, pillowcases, suitcases hidden away in closets, in an underground vault, and in secret offshore bank accounts. In Miami, it seemed as though Falcon, Magluta, and their crew were loved by everybody—friends, partners, even the city at large—and that the flow of good times and prosperity would never end.

January 1967

Arsenio Falcon sat his son down in their domicile in Havana, Cuba, and said, "Get all your things together, *hijo*. We are going to the United States."

"To visit?" asked eleven-year-old Willy.

"No. To live with our relatives."

Young Willy felt a rumbling in his gut, as if his whole being were experiencing a *terremoto*, an earthquake. In the months leading up to this moment, he had sensed something catastrophic was coming. The signs were everywhere: the consternation on the faces of his parents and other adults; the long speeches on black-and-white television by the surprisingly young, bearded *líder máximo*, who talked for hours—using apocalyptic language—without coming up for air; the military personnel, also mostly young and bearded, pulling up to houses in jeeps, armed with rifles and handguns, sometimes rousting neighbors out of their homes and taking them away. It was like a tropical depression, only the dark clouds were not blowing over: they were gathering in a way that was ominous even to a youngster like Willy Falcon.

Even so, the arrival of this moment was abrupt, like the passing of an elderly relative. Yes, there had been signs of diminishing capacity, but this person had been such a vital presence—for so long—that it seemed life would always be this way.

Born September 1, 1955, in the town of Alquízar—a one-hour drive southwest of Havana—Falcon had enjoyed an idyllic early childhood. When he thought about it years later, it felt as though he had been born into a tropical paradise. With a population of five thousand inhabitants, located in what was known at the time as La Habana Province (now Artemisa Province), Alquízar was bucolic, with ubiquitous palm trees, tobacco plantations, and small farms.

The family business was agriculture; the Falcons grew, harvested, and sold produce. They owned a ranch that was about sixty acres, with cows, horses, a few donkeys, and many chickens. Willy's father, Arsenio, was the boss. Marta's brother Mongo owned a transportation company of ten to twelve trucks; they made a decent living delivering produce and sugar from area farms to markets in Havana. Altogether, the Falcon family's commercial ventures employed thirty to forty field laborers, truck drivers, and handymen.

Even as a child, Willy liked to act as if he were an integral part of the family business—he helped pick the tropical fruits and harvest the vegetables and load and unload trucks. He took a special interest in engines, whether they were trucks or tractors or even the family car.

When Willy wasn't at school or being made to feel as if he were a useful worker on the family farm, he played baseball. He loved the sport more than anything. A natural athlete, he spent his afternoons on the ball field near his school, and on weekends, he played from sunup to sundown. Willy excelled at the sport, playing center field, second base, all the positions that required speed and dexterity. He was good enough to fantasize that when he grew up he might play professionally for the Cuban national team, or, better yet, make it to the Major Leagues in the United States, just like Minnie Miñoso, the great Cuban outfielder who, by the time Willy was learning the game, was an all-star outfielder in the American League. Miñoso had been born in Perico, in the province of Matanzas, and first played in the US Negro leagues with the New York Cubans.

Along with playing baseball, Falcon spent much of his time at his uncle Mongo's cockfighting arena, or *valla*, as the campesinos called it. Cockfighting in the provinces was a national pastime and a rite of passage for boys on the journey to adolescence and manhood. The cockfights could be bloody; some youngsters were known to recoil in horror. Willy was drawn to the ritual and sense of tradition that surrounded all aspects of the endeavor.

At the age of seven, Willy attended his first cockfight. It was held at a *valla* on his uncle's farm. Uncle Mongo's nickname was *ventaja*—which meant "advantage"—because he was always looking for an edge in life and business. His edge as a *gallero*, or cockfight empresario, was the special spurs that he had flown to Cuba from Spain. They were extra sharp. One day, Willy watched as his uncle fitted the spurs on one of his prize roosters. The boy held one of the spurs and lightly tapped it with an index finger. Instantaneously, a bead of blood appeared on his fingertip; Willy was so fascinated by the process that he ignored the pain.

His uncle Mongo was known to have the best roosters in town. On a small farm, he raised and trained his birds with loving care.

At the cockfight, the roosters ferociously attacked one another. Mongo shouted, "El Pinto! El Pinto is fighting back." Willy assumed that El Pinto (black bean) was his uncle's bird, and so he started shouting as well, "Go, El Pinto, get him!" After the fight was over—after El Pinto had his eye poked out of its socket and was shredded to death in the ring—Willy learned that El Pinto was not Mongo's bird. He had been rooting for the wrong cock all along.

In April 1961, an event occurred that made it clear to Willy for the first time that his beloved homeland was going through something that was out of the ordinary. On the southern coast of the island, there was a massive invasion attempt in an area known as Bahia de los Cochinos, the Bay of Pigs. The invasion was thwarted by the Cuban army, which had advance warning that a band of anti-Castro Cuban exiles, backed by the US government, had set out from training camps in Central America. In a violent confrontation, the invaders had been stopped, but the repercussions lingered on for days and weeks. Especially for Cubans who lived in the area, it was a time of fear and chaos. For a young child like Falcon, it was terrifying. A lifetime later, he remembered:

The location where the invasion occurred was not too far from Alquízar. I remember the sirens going off for days afterwards. For months, the schools were closed, and I was not allowed to go outside and play. Looking out the window of our house, I saw soldiers dressed in green uniforms and wearing heavy black boots, carrying their rifles with long bayonets, screaming and threatening people. I asked my father, "Dad, why are we afraid and what did we do wrong?" "Just go to your room and stay out of trouble," he answered, without ever giving an explanation.

Within months, young Willy figured it out.

Down the street from the Falcons' house was the province police station (El Cuartel de Policía). Many afternoons, like clockwork, the sound of gunshots rang out. This was the sound of neighborhood people, or prisoners held at the station, being taken out and executed by firing squad.

Willy watched as his mother, Marta, and his aunts gathered in the house. They wept and lit candles on a homemade altar in honor of those who were being executed. They held rosary beads between their fingers and said prayers under their breath. Their novenas were a clandestine act. To be seen mourning those killed by the authorities could rouse suspicion among compañeros who were loyal to the regime of El Comandante Fidel Castro.

After the invasion and the executions, things changed dramatically. It seemed as though each day brought startling new pronouncements from the revolutionary government. In late 1961, in a speech on television, Castro announced that all private industry and family holdings would be seized and owned by the government. It didn't matter if you were for or against Castroism; your businesses would now be under the control of military personnel. Citizens were expected to run their businesses as before, but any proceeds generated by the business were distributed according to the dictates of the regime.

The response of many Cubans vacillated among shock, anger, and sometimes volatile acts of resistance. In return, the Castro regime clamped down hard. The executions continued. Increasingly, some among the business class in Cuba made the difficult decision to leave their homeland and go into exile. Others—those who had been supportive of the previous government before Castro took over—were forced out.

In the midst of all this, Willy Falcon's brother, Gustavo, or Tavy, was born on July 25, 1961. Arsenio and Marta Falcon now had two young boys. Willy was excited. Within the family, there was new life, but outside it seemed the world was in turmoil. Willy could see the effect it was having on his parents, his uncles, and all the adults in his world. People they knew were being arrested, taken away, thrown in prison. There was much fear and paranoia.

The political transformation was granular, affecting daily life in Cuba on every level, but the conflicts were also international. The revolutionary government hadn't seized only the holdings of average citizens, it had also appropriated all foreign businesses operating in Cuba. This meant that major companies owned by corporations from Spain and France and, most notably, the United States were placed under government receivership. Companies like AT&T, the Hilton Hotel chain, United Fruit, and others lost everything as Cuban banks became nationalized. In the United States, CEOs of major corporations applied political pressure on senators and congressmen to do something about the situation.

In February 1962, President John F. Kennedy proclaimed an embargo on trade between the United States and Cuba. For decades, the United States had been Cuba's primary trading partner. On the island, the embargo's effects were felt almost immediately. Basic goods such as soap, gasoline, oil, and medicine became scarce. Food products disappeared from the shelves of local markets. Even daily necessities such as milk, eggs, produce, and poultry were hard to come by under the weight of regulations and controls. Sugar, a product that had sustained the island from its inception as a nation, was now primarily reserved for export.

The country was starving, and the only solace that Castro had to offer was that sacrifice was now the destiny of the Cuban people. El Comandante rarely passed up an opportunity to take to the airwaves, on radio and television stations owned and controlled by the government, to extoll the virtues of the revolution.

In the spring of 1962, in response to the embargo, Castro gave yet another mammoth public address. In this one he denounced the United States as an imperialist nation and capitalism as an oppressive system that depended on the exploitation of labor, and he declared that Cuba was now a Communist government.

The idea of Cuba becoming a Communist gulag was yet another shock. Some who had been supporters of the revolution, including men and women who had fought alongside the Castro brothers as rebels and lived on paltry food rations, horsemeat, watery coffee, and cigars while hiding out in the Sierra Maestra mountain range, saw this as the ultimate betrayal. The anti-Castro movement was energized, leading, in counter-reaction, to the creation of the

Dirección General de Inteligencia (DGI), an information-gathering apparatus of the Cuban government designed to seek out and destroy enemies of the state.

In October 1962 came the Cuban Missile Crisis. Through covert overhead intelligence photos, the Kennedy administration discovered that the Soviet Union was storing missiles in a series of silos on the island of Cuba. Over a period of thirteen days, a game of brinksmanship between Castro, Russian president Khrushchev, and Kennedy ensued, bringing the hemisphere to the edge of annihilation. The missile crisis was resolved, but as a consequence, all commercial flights between Cuba and the United States were discontinued. Cubans dissatisfied with the new revolutionary government were now trapped on the island, seemingly without recourse.

For the Falcons and others who were trying to subsist as they had before, daily life devolved into a state of depression that became the norm. Some citizens crossed the threshold of despair. Willy's uncle Mongo, who had acclimated the youngster to the ways of the fighting cocks, had been able to flee the island to the United States before the missile crisis, as did other extended family members and neighbors. Arsenio and Marta Falcon were left behind. They held on, until one day, when Willy was ten years old, he came home wearing the red scarf of the Young Pioneers around his neck.

The government called it a Communist education program, but those among the resistance saw it as brainwashing. All school-age preteens were required by the government to take part in what was an indoctrination program, conducted with quasimilitary marching exercises as the kids shouted revolutionary slogans and pledged fealty to the leaders of the new regime. In the classroom, the Young Pioneers were introduced to the principles of Marxism and warned that Yankee capitalism, as practiced in the United States, was an existential threat to an island nation like Cuba.

Arsenio and Marta Falcon were mortified. They immediately pulled Willy out of school and sent him to live with an aunt near the coast.

In 1966, the Falcons moved to a house in Havana where Uncle Mongo had been living before he left the country. It was there, after several months, that Willy's father told him, "Muchacho, it's time to go. Get your things together."

That year, the administration of President Lyndon B. Johnson announced that it had negotiated a "Memorandum of Understanding" with the Cuban government whereby close relatives of Cubans already in the United States would be allowed to immigrate to the country. Cubans who were fortunate enough to have relatives in South Florida could be sponsored and granted a special visa that allowed them to live in the country.

Every day, flights sponsored by the US government left the airport in the resort town of Varadero, east of Havana. "Freedom Flights," they were called by the exiles and the US government. Nearly every flight was filled.

The day that the Falcons left was one Willy would always remember. Once their visas were approved, they prepared to leave immediately. At the airport, soldiers and customs officials taunted the Falcons and other families, calling them "traitors" and "Yankees." Young Willy stood at the top of the airplane stairs, looking back at his home country for the last time. "I knew I could never come back to this place as long as Castro and his regime were in power," he remembered.

As the flight took off, with the wheels of the plane lifting off the tarmac, the occupants erupted in cheers and applause. But soon after an eerie silence descended over the passengers. Those near the windows looked down as the tropical island of Cuba became smaller and smaller, and the future, though it loomed large, was hazy and uncertain.

FOR ELEVEN-YEAR-OLD WILLY FALCON, WHAT followed was a time of disruption for him and everyone around him. From the time of the revolution in 1959 to 1973, when Castro put a stop to the Freedom Flights, three hundred thousand Cubans came to the United States. They settled mostly in and around Miami, which at the time was a medium-size resort town that catered primarily to tourists in the winter. Miami had a climate much like Cuba's, but a culture that seemed impenetrable to a child. There was a new language to be learned, an unfamiliar system of currency, streets that were forbidding, and a school system that had not been designed to suddenly take in planeloads of kids, most of whom did not speak English.

The Falcons stayed with relatives in a crowded apartment in a small building at 2001 SW Sixth Street, in a neighborhood that had only recently taken on the name "Little Havana." A four-square-mile area in the city's southwest section, Little Havana was not physically attractive. Calle Ocho (Eighth Street) was the neighborhood's main thoroughfare, with store signs in Spanish and restaurants, coffee stalls, and cigar shops that seemed as though they had been transported there directly from Cuba. Among the new citizens with special refugee visas that allowed them to stay in the United States, the talk was not of assimilation or "How do I fit in?" It was, rather, "How do I make a living for me and my family?" and "When do we kill Fidel, overthrow his regime, and return to *la patria* [the homeland]?"

Willy was put into a special program at Shenandoah Elementary School that included Cuban kids of varying ages who did not yet speak English. There he met other boys and girls living in Little Havana. There was no shortage of refugee children. They were human cargo born of desperation, the consequence of a brutal though unavoidable choice to get the children out so they might have a shot at a decent future in a country with an open economic system. Many adults stayed behind on the island, with the idea that maybe they could escape later.

One day Willy came home from school and there was a kid sitting on a bench outside his apartment building on Sixth Street. The kid had been locked out of his family's apartment and was waiting for someone to come home to let him in.

"Hey," said Willy, "I've seen you on the bus going to Shenandoah. You live here?"

"Yes," said the kid.

"Me, too. My name is Willy Falcon."

"I'm Tony Garcia. Everybody calls me Tony Bemba."

Willy smiled. The word *bemba* means "lips" in Cuban Spanish. The kid was tall and gangly, with curly black hair and yes, plump lips.

Garcia had been born in Havana in 1956; he was nine months younger than Willy. He and Falcon got to talking and discovered that they had much in common. Garcia's family had gone into exile one year before Willy's, in 1966. Willy asked Tony, "You live here with your parents?"

"With my grandparents, my aunt and cousins," said Tony. "My father is back in Cuba. He is being held in prison by the government."

Tony told Willy the story of his family, how his father owned a small butcher shop, and his youngest uncle had been a police officer in the time of Fulgencio Batista, the military dictator of Cuba before Castro. Tony loved his uncle, age thirty or so, who used to arrive at their grandparents' house in his police car.

He would turn on the car's flashing lights, which Tony and other kids in the neighborhood loved.

The fact that the uncle had been a police officer under the Batista government made him a figure of suspicion, an acolyte of the oppressor and a potential enemy of the pro-Castro generation.

One evening, the uncle was working a police checkpoint in Havana. It was a rule of the new regime that all cars would be stopped and searched while passing through various checkpoints around the city. The uncle, doing his job as a police officer, stopped a truck driven by an old man. He searched the vehicle and found the shank of a pig wrapped and hidden in the back of the truck. The meat was illegal. The Castro regime had begun to clamp down hard on anyone who violated the weekly rationing regulations for meat, which had become a prized commodity. The uncle told the old man, "Hey, *viejo*, you got to be careful. There are searches going on everywhere. Get rid of that meat, eat it or whatever, or you're gonna get into big trouble." The uncle let the guy go with this warning.

Farther down the road, the old man got pulled over at another checkpoint. The police searched his truck and found the pig. The old man pleaded, "Oh, but the policeman at the previous checkpoint let me through."

That night, Tony's uncle was arrested. Except no one knew he'd been arrested; he simply disappeared, which was disconcerting, since citizens under suspicion were being snatched off the street and out of their homes by the police on a regular basis.

Willy Falcon, listening intently to this narrative, asked, "What happened? Where did they take him?"

"I don't know where they took him," said Tony Bemba, "but a few weeks later two military policemen showed up at the house with my uncle's clothes. They handed them to my grandparents and said, 'He was executed this morning for having violated the laws of the revolution.'"

Willy's mouth hung open in disbelief.

"They killed him," said Tony, "because of the guy with the pig in the back of the truck."

"*Coño*," said Willy.

Tony explained that after the death of his uncle, his father became active in the underground anti-Castro movement. He went to meetings where plans were devised to resist the government; he distributed counterrevolutionary pamphlets from a hole in the floorboard of a car, so that they littered the streets; he took part in the stockpiling of weapons in expectation of the day when he and like-minded fellow insurgents might attempt to overthrow the government by force.

Eventually, Tony's father got caught and thrown in jail. On Friday nights young Tony, barely six years old, and his mother and grandparents made the trip to Batabanó, a port city on the coast. At midnight, they boarded a boat for the arduous five-hour trip across the ocean to the infamous Isle of Pines prison. Routinely, there were tropical storms and even hurricanes in that part of the sea. Little Tony often became seasick and had vomited several times by the time he arrived at the prison to see his father.

Nothing made the kid more depressed than to see his father locked away behind bars.

In 1966, Tony Garcia, then ten years old, fled Cuba with his grandparents on a Freedom Flight and came to the United States. Every day, Tony expected to hear news from contacts back in Havana that his father had been executed. "I wish I could go there and get him out of prison before the government has him killed," Tony said to Willy.

The two young boys nodded their heads in agreement. From that day forward, Willy and Tony were best friends.

As dramatic as Tony Bemba's story was, it was not uncommon among the Cubans who had settled in Little Havana. Fathers, uncles, brothers, and sometimes women also were rotting in prison on the island, victimized by a despot and his grand revolutionary schemes, their suffering the natural inheritance of a generation of exiles that would not rest until this gaping wound was cauterized.

IT WAS LIKE A CUBAN version of Charles Dickens: *el mejor de los tiempos y el peor de los tiempos* (the best of times and the worst of times). On Sixth Street, where the Falcons lived, Cuban kids far outnumbered the adults. In the streets and parks and playgrounds, they played basketball and baseball all day long. These may have been sports that originated in the United States, but in Little Havana the language that accented these games—the shouts of encouragement and camaraderie—was almost exclusively Spanish. Maybe in school you were required to speak the language of American radio announcers, but at home and on the playground, the *R*s were rolled, the question marks inverted, and the Castellano roots of the language were given a staccato, rough inflection that was uniquely from the Caribbean.

Willy Falcon emerged as a prince within his world of teenage Cuban strivers. He was, according to most everyone, handsome and appealing. The Falcons of Cuba had Spanish blood, but they also had indigenous blood from the Taíno, an Arawak Indian people whom Christopher Columbus had encountered when he first landed in the port of Baracoa in 1492. It was a pleasing combination, reacting well to the sun. By the age of sixteen, Willy had a muscular, sinewy physique, luxurious hair, and a killer smile that could light up a room. He had a generous spirit and a way of welcoming friends into the inner circle of his group, making them feel as if they were chosen for something special. Whether it was at neighborhood basketball games in Little Havana, or during extracurricular activities at school, or dance parties sponsored by various community organizations, Willy stood out. He never sought to promote himself as a leader; his ego was such that he let the kids come to him. Soon, as a teenager, he was part of an inner circle of boys who would later become the nucleus of Los Muchachos. This group included Willy, Tony Bemba, Justo Jay, Ramiro Moedano, Jojo Brito, and Sal Magluta, neighborhood kids who grew up within a small radius of a few blocks.

One person who was not yet a member of this group was Tavy Falcon. Six years younger than Willy, not yet a teenager, Tavy might as well have been an embryo still in his mother's womb. Says Tavy:

> They called me *mojón*, which means "little turd." On Sixth Street, where we lived, my parents wouldn't let me cross the street. There was too much traffic. But I could take my bike and ride around the block to watch them play and hang out on Fifth Street. These were the guys who I wanted to be with. They're six years older, they're cool. They have girlfriends, they have cars. Back then, this was all I wanted to be. I didn't hang around with friends my age; I watched Willy and them and dreamed about being part of their group one day.

For the most part, the work ethic around Little Havana and the rest of Miami was startling to the Americans who lived there. At the time, in the

1960s and into the early 1970s, Miami was a sleepy little town, nothing like the major Latin metropolis it was soon to become. Like many immigrants in the United States, Cubans banded together to form business associations and commercial enterprises that did business mostly with other Cubans. The struggle for survival created an ethos of solidarity. The inhabitants of *el exilio* worked long hours, often at more than one job at a time.

A law signed by President Lyndon B. Johnson in November 1966 called the Cuban Adjustment Act allowed the exiles the opportunity to "adjust" their legal status so they could become American citizens. To the average American— John Q. Public—this was presented as an act in keeping with the Cold War tenor of the times, a repudiation of communism and an extension of American freedom at its most benevolent. But because it created a special dispensation for Cuban immigrants, US critics of the policy referred to it as a double standard.

Some recently arrived Cubans intuited that the gringo population in Miami, and maybe beyond Florida and around the United States, resented that they were being given privileged immigration status. This led the Cubans to turn inward and also, as a result, to work harder than anyone else, to prove their worth to the larger American public.

At the age of sixteen, Willy and Tony Bemba went to work for a small construction company owned by a fellow Cuban exile. Willy learned carpentry skills and Tony installed drywall. Sometimes they switched roles and did other jobs as laborers and handymen. It was hard physical labor, with the constant pounding of nails and carrying of heavy work materials, and long hours from early in the morning into the evening. In some ways, the boys worked hard as a tribute to their parents, who had endured so much. What could be a greater act of revenge than to rise above the hardships of exile and make it in America? To succeed in a way and at a level that would never be possible under a Communist system?

The city of Miami was growing rapidly, alive with the newfound energy of a displaced population determined to create a new reality for itself. On construction sites from Miami Beach to Hialeah, downtown Miami to Key Biscayne and all around the city, Willy and Tony marveled at the beautiful natural environment. Miami had not yet been fully exploited, with towering glass high-rises and narco-mansions along the city's many beaches and tropical waterways, but the process was underway.

One day, while on lunch break at the construction site for the Brickell Bay Club, a massive thirty-one-story condominium on the water that would set the standard for future building, Willy and Tony took in the view. Seated on the balcony of an upper floor, they looked out over Biscayne Bay toward downtown. Noted Tony, "Willy, look at those buildings that weren't even there a couple months ago. Miami is growing so fast."

"Yes, and think about it, Tony—here we are in the middle of it, helping to construct this new city with our own hands."

It was a grandiose observation for a teenager, one that would take on even more expansive implications once Falcon, Tony Bemba, and others were to construct the largest cocaine importation and distribution network the country had ever seen.

AS MUCH AS THE NEW generation of exiles was falling in love with Miami, there was an ever-present dichotomy. They also dreamed of returning to Cuba. As Willy put it, "I loved my new country. I love the United States. I love the system, freedom, justice and all. But my dream, my idea was always to go back to my roots, go back to Cuba, ninety miles away. My mind was here in the US, but my soul never left Cuba."

As a result, Willy, Tony, and others they knew became actively involved in the anti-Castro movement that was so fervent in Miami among the exiles. The desire to displace Castro and take back Cuba became the number one dream— even bigger than the dream to make it in business.

By the time Willy and Tony became involved in the mid-1970s, the movement had already gone through permutations. Since the disastrous Bay of Pigs invasion fifteen years earlier, the effort to kill Castro and install a new government in Cuba had mostly gone underground. Public support for this movement was still a highly visible aspect of the community. Willy, Tony, and others of their generation attended massive rallies and demonstrations in Bayfront Park, at Dinner Key, and in Little Havana. The speakers at these events were often members of the 2506 Brigade, who had survived the Bay of Pigs invasion and spent a year and a half in prison in Cuba until their release was negotiated by the US government.

People like Tony Bemba, who still had a father locked up in prison in Cuba, were treated like royalty at the rallies; their names were mentioned, and they were cited as the reason *la lucha*—the struggle to take back Cuba—was a flame that could never be allowed to grow dim.

After the rallies, the crowds marched into the streets chanting slogans, hoisting placards in Spanish and English, and, sometimes, burning in effigy crudely made puppets of Castro, Che Guevara, and other "luminaries" of the revolution. In response to these displays, which were sometimes videotaped by television crews and broadcast on news programs around the world, Castro publicly derided the exiles, referring to the Miami counterrevolutionaries as "*gusanos* (worms)."

Willy and Tony attended these rallies on a regular basis—so much so that esteemed leaders of the movement, who were always on the lookout for fresh blood, began acknowledging them by name. Both these youngsters had dropped out of Miami High School so that they could work full time in the construction business. They were diligent workers, from families that were known to be staunchly anti-Castro, and they were devoted to the cause. They were the kind of young men who seemed destined to play a role in the ongoing struggle to free Cuba.

Construction work in Miami was seasonal; in 1976, there was a lull in activity, and both Willy and Tony were temporarily laid off from their jobs. This gave them more time to devote to the anti-Castro movement.

On April 19, 1976, they attended a rally to commemorate the fifteenth anniversary of the Bay of Pigs invasion. After the rally, they were approached by three men who were revered operatives in the anti-Castro movement: Isaac Padron, Armando Lopez Estrada, and Rafael "Chi Chi" Quintero.

Quintero and Estrada, in particular, were legendary counterrevolutionaries. Quintero, thirty-five years old when he approached Falcon and Garcia (who were now twenty and nineteen respectively), had been a member of the Bay of Pigs invasion as a covert operative living in Havana in the months before the invasion. If the attack had been successful and Castro removed, Quintero was designated to serve as a high-ranking representative of the new ruling junta. After the invasion was crushed, he became stranded in Cuba and lived for a time as a fugitive from the Castro regime. He escaped by boat and settled in

Miami, where he became not only a counterrevolutionary but a contract agent with the US Central Intelligence Agency (CIA).

In 1962, Quintero became an important participant in Operation Mongoose, a top secret initiative, instituted by US Attorney General Robert F. Kennedy and the CIA. Put into operation in the wake of the Bay of Pigs' soldiers being released by Castro and returned to the United States, the program was steeped in skullduggery and Cold War espionage that gave rise to innumerable CIA-facilitated plots to assassinate Castro. Quintero was not only an active participant in these plots, but was credited within the Kennedy administration–CIA axis with having devised some of them.

Armando Lopez Estrada, who like Quintero was Cuban born, had also been involved in the invasion as a soldier who was lucky enough to have escaped death or capture. Like so many who had taken part in that seminal event, it became the motivating factor in a life devoted to the overthrow of Fidel. Estrada, like Quintero, also worked covertly with the CIA and, in July 1976, met secretly with leaders of the anti-Castro movement at a gathering in the Dominican Republic.

Many in the movement felt that efforts to kill Castro and take back Cuba had become factionalized over the years. This meeting in the DR resulted in the creation of a new governing body of militant *exiliados* in the United States that would be called the Coordination of United Revolutionary Organizations (CORU), of which Armando Lopez Estrada became a ruling member.

By the time these two veteran leaders of *la lucha* met with Falcon and Garcia, the counterrevolution had adopted a slightly different strategy. More than a decade had now gone by with anti-Castro Cubans and the CIA trying to assassinate the Cuban leader, with nothing to show for it. Under the new presidential administration of Jimmy Carter, the US government had officially disengaged from efforts to destabilize Cuba or take out Fidel. The militants would not give up entirely on efforts to assassinate Castro, but it was time to shift focus to take on Castroism, which was in danger of taking root south of the US border in Central America.

In recent years, Chi Chi Quintero had become involved in a new initiative. Working again with the CIA, he had been assigned a leadership role in establishing guerrilla military camps in Honduras. The agency had intelligence revealing that Castro, emboldened by nearly two decades in power, had begun to export his brand of Marxist communism to other Latin American countries. Specifically,

Castro had sent Cuban military advisers to Nicaragua, which borders Honduras, to help train the Sandinista National Liberation Front (SNLF), a rebel group that was currently at war with the ruling government of Nicaraguan president Anastasio Somoza.

At secret camps in Honduras, and later, in El Salvador, Cuban exiles stockpiled weapons and trained for guerrilla warfare on a number of fronts, including Nicaragua. The demand for arms, equipment, and financing for operations was ever present. The exiles could count on wealthy, right-wing donors in the United States—Yankee industrialists and rich Latinos who had been chased out of Cuba by Castro. But militant Cubans also needed to create their own lines of financing and supply.

Quintero saw a role for Falcon and Tony Bemba. At a motel near Miami International Airport, where he kept a room for secret rendezvous with militant exiles, CIA agents, political mercenaries, and arms dealers, the Bay of Pigs veteran met with the two young Cubans. He explained to Willy and Tony, "*La lucha* is a hydra with many heads. Right now, the primary theater in the war to stop Fidel is in Nicaragua, with the Sandinistas. We must stop the Communists. We have the support of the CIA, which has pledged to facilitate this covert war of aggression. But we need weapons, and weapons cost money."

Quintero explained that *los exiliados* had contacts in Honduras who would sell them cocaine at a wholesale rate. The idea was to import the cocaine into the United States, sell it, and use the proceeds to purchase large shipments of armaments—guns, ammunition, and explosives—which would be transported to the camps in Honduras and El Salvador.

A sense of awe came over Falcon and Garcia as they grasped what was being asked of them. Seated in that anonymous motel room, it seemed as though destiny had come knocking. Some of the most esteemed leaders of the anti-Castro movement were telling them that they needed their help. And that the commodity that would facilitate their needs was cocaine.

At the time, there was no great stigma attached to the white powder. Yes, it was illegal, a Schedule II controlled substance as designated by the US government, the possession or sale of which was a felony crime. But no one yet saw it as the scourge of society. For militant Cuban exiles caught up in a self-justifying liberation struggle, it was believed to be downright ingenious to use cocaine in this way.

Willy and Tony Bemba's role was to receive the cocaine shipments in the United States and, most important, to sell the product as quickly as possible. "You're young and well connected in the community," Quintero told them. "You must know or should be able to create clientele for this product."

Cocaine was not an unknown commodity in Miami in 1976–77, but no one was yet smuggling it in large quantities. Mostly, what entered the United States came from Bolivia or Peru, strapped to the bodies of housewives and college students traveling to and from South America and the Caribbean. There was no such thing as a "cartel" in Colombia or anywhere else.

There were older Cuban exiles who had made the transition from smuggling marijuana to smuggling coke, in small amounts, to finance *la lucha*. The benefits were obvious; the powder was less bulky, didn't smell, and had a profit margin that was many times greater than weed. But as of yet there did not exist a system for smuggling large shipments, partly because, given the price, no one knew if there was a consistent market for the product.

This was where Willy and Tony came in: by approaching these young Cuban hustlers, Quintero and the leaders of the movement were looking to create a new clientele, to foster a demand among a new generation of users, the profits from which could be used to help finance their covert political agenda.

The two young exiles did not hesitate: "We're in," they said.

Remembers Tony Bemba: "We felt like this was our opportunity to be seen as heroes. We were being asked to play a role in the liberation of *la patria*, that's how we saw it. We wanted to be heroes."

Concurred Willy: "I was flattered that these individuals came to us. . . . If we could help defeat the left-wing Sandinista Communist rebels in Central America, then we were helping to defeat Castro."

And then, yes, there was also the money.

Quintero explained that in the next couple of days they would receive sixty-five kilos of pure cocaine by plane at a remote location in Kissimmee, Florida. Willy didn't know exactly how much Chi Chi and the others paid for the cocaine shipment, but it was agreed that Willy and Tony would pay $45,000 per kilo (on consignment, the money fronted by Quintero and his people), which they would sell on the open market for $55,000 to $60,000 per kilo. That was a profit of $10,000 to $12,000 per kilo for Willy and friends. On a shipment of sixty-five kilos, Willy and Tony stood to clear $700,000.

Two days later, Willy and Tony made the two-hour-and-forty-five-minute drive north on I-95 and Florida's Turnpike to Kissimmee. They arrived under cover of darkness at the predetermined location: an open field with a dirt road. They brought a small two-way box radio that they could tune to a frequency that allowed them to communicate directly with the pilot. Around nine p.m., they heard over the radio, "Listen, I'm half an hour away. Be ready." They mounted some fluorescent lights used by night fishermen onto their van. Once they heard and then saw the small plane flying overhead, they placed flares on the ground to create a clandestine landing strip along the dirt road. The plane landed and they quickly unloaded three US Army duffel bags filled with bricks of cocaine. Then they headed back to Miami.

It was exciting as hell. Willy was now a professional smuggler, and he had to admit, it was invigorating. Only now he had sixty-five kilos of pure cocaine that he needed to sell as quickly as possible—a tall order.

He had already been asking around. At $55,000 to $60,000 a kilo, the product was not cheap. Willy was not looking to sell the coke in gram increments; he wanted to find people who could handle purchasing at least a kilo or more at a time.

A friend of Willy's who owned a nightclub was one obvious contact. Though he had never handled a shipment of this weight, the club owner made the leap; with Willy fronting the product, he was good for a half dozen kilos. This friend led him to other possibilities. These were dealers who were looking to sell to other dealers, in a roundelay of offloading product that would become a way of life in Miami and other American cities in the decades ahead.

The nightclub owner introduced Willy to a friend who owned multiple women's beauty parlors. It turned out that women liked to use cocaine as much as or more than men; the beauty parlors were an excellent outlet for product.

Willy met a woman who was able to sell kilos via flight attendants for various US airlines, who distributed the product to buyers in cities from coast to coast.

He approached a lawyer he knew, thinking he might have other lawyer friends with disposable income who might be interested in investing in the cocaine business. *Bingo!* Not only was the lawyer interested, but he had recently represented a chapter of the Hells Angels in a criminal case. The lawyer brokered a major coke deal with the Hells Angels who, with chapters in cities large and small around the United States, proved to be a major early source for kilos supplied by young Willy Falcon.

It took one month to unload sixty-five kilos.

The second load went off much as the first, only this time Willy and Tony also played a role in loading the guns that were the flip side of their coke-for-arms deal. At Clark Aviation, a flight school based at Opa-Locka airport in northwest Miami, they lifted duffel bags filled with rifles, machine guns, handguns, and ammunition onto a plane that would leave for Honduras that afternoon and then return to Kissimmee the following morning loaded with cocaine.

With each shipment, the number of kilos increased. The second load was one hundred kilos, brought to Florida in the same manner. Willy enlisted into his operation three more lifelong friends from the neighborhood, Antonio Garcia Perez (whose nickname was "El Guajiro"), Ramiro Moedano, and Justo Jay. They all took on logistical and bookkeeping duties and received a 15 percent cut of every load.

In early 1977, as they prepared for a fourth coke-for-arms shipment, comprising 140 kilos, Tony Bemba broke his leg in a pickup game of basketball. Consequently, Willy reached out to another neighborhood buddy, Sal Magluta. No one recognized it at the time, but Sal replacing Tony as Willy's most visible partner would be, for many, the official commencement of the cocaine era in Miami.

Willy had known Sal since childhood. Unlike some in the group, Magluta did not have matinee-idol good looks that made the girls swoon. He had wooly hair—a modified Jew-fro, which made sense since, even though he was Cuban, he also had Jewish blood on his mother's side. As a kid, Sal was a sometimes awkward combination of shy and cocky. He was scrappy and fearless and ready for anything. Willy and Sal grew up together playing sports, a proclivity that continued at Miami High School, where they both starred on a school football team that contended for a state championship. Willy was also an all-star center fielder on the school's baseball team.

Despite their excellence in sports, Willy and Sal were both indifferent students who could not see how graduation from high school and, presumably, entrance into college was going to enhance their financial standing in the world. Both dropped out of Miami High around the same time early in their senior year. Eventually,

Sal took the General Education Development (GED) test and passed, achieving graduate equivalency. He even briefly attended community college to study, of all things, law enforcement.

At the time Willy went into the construction business, Sal worked as an accountant at a bank. They were both hard workers but restless—until Willy was given the opportunity to try his hand at the cocaine business.

Sal had skills that Willy admired. He could handle the budding organization's financial ledgers, and he was a good organizer, which, even Willy would agree, he was not. Willy was more of a motivator, a keeper of the group's morale and an inspirational leader.

The group's fourth cocaine-for-arms shipment took place in March 1977. By now, the boys had established a distribution network that became more streamlined and robust with each shipment. They were stunned by how quickly they had discovered an insatiable demand for their product. They weren't just offloading keys in Miami. At least 30 percent of their clientele were buyers from out of town, who were purchasing cocaine from Willy Falcon and taking it back home to Atlanta, New York, Houston, Los Angeles, and other places.

The profits were mind-boggling. On the fourth shipment, when they met to go over the books, Willy asked Sal, "How much did we clear?"

Sal smiled and said, "Over two-point-five million dollars." They all laughed. For a group of guys who were only a few years removed from having dropped out of high school, working at remedial jobs and dreaming of a day when they might return to Cuba, it was almost impossible to comprehend.

Along with veteran anti-Castro operatives like Chi Chi, Estrada, and Isaac Padron, Willy and the boys were working with a professional crew of smugglers. Chi Chi made the introductions. Many of the pilots were gringos with CIA connections who made regular gunrunning flights to Central and South America. They composed a network of rogues, mercenaries, and adventurers, most of them ex–US military, put into action by the CIA in clandestine operations that most US citizens knew nothing about.

Willy was especially fascinated by one of the pilots, Jack Devoe, who had been born in Miami but had the cool energy of a California surfer dude. Though he was six years older than Willy, he was youthful and unpredictable like a wild, untamed horse. He reminded Willy of a movie star—Steve McQueen or Paul Newman. Despite the blue eyes and mercurial personality, Jack was no wimp. Like all the pilots, he took major risks flying cocaine and gun shipments through foreign airspace, touching down at makeshift landing strips in sometimes hostile territory. For this reason, Willy gave major props to Jack Devoe and the other pilots.

One morning at the Clark Aviation hangar at Opa-Locka airport, as Willy, Tony Bemba, Sal, and Devoe were loading armaments onto a plane for the freedom fighters in Honduras and El Salvador, Chi Chi Quintero approached. "I got some bad news," he said.

"What?" asked Willy.

"Isaac Padron was killed yesterday. He died in a plane crash." Quintero explained that his Cuban militant partner and two others had been flying supplies from one of the border camps in Honduras into Nicaragua and their plane had crashed in the mountains. Their bodies had been found that morning.

They were all saddened by the news but sanguine: it was the price of doing business.

Willy wondered what he should do with Isaac's portion of the most recent cocaine shipment, close to $1 million in cash. He and Sal talked about it, and they decided they should seek out Isaac's wife and give her the payment. It was the right thing to do. They also wondered about Isaac's two Navajo propeller airplanes that they had been using to make their shipments of cocaine and guns. The planes were sitting in a hangar at Opa-Locka.

Willy and Sal dressed themselves up nicely in suits and ties and drove to the house of Isaac Padron's wife, in suburban Miami. They knocked on the door. The wife answered, and after they explained who they were, she invited them in.

They sat in the kitchen, drank Cuban coffee, and ate some guava *pasteles*. After some obligatory chitchat, they explained to the wife why they were there. They presented her with a valise filled with close to $1 million in cash. "This belongs to you," they said. "It's Isaac's share of our last transaction, undertaken on behalf of the struggle to free Cuba, for which your husband gave his life. He died with his boots on."

The woman looked at the cash, and her eyes filled with tears.

"One more thing," said Willy. "Your husband's airplanes, those two Navajos in a hangar at Opa-Locka, we'd like to make an offer to buy them from you."

Isaac's widow thought about it; she looked at these two fine young Cubanos and said, "You know what? Not many people would have done what you just did, sought me out to pay me the money that was owed to my husband. You could have taken that money and disappeared. You are good boys. Heroes, just like my husband was. I want you to have those airplanes, and you don't have to pay me a thing."

Willy and Sal left that house with a bounce in their step. On the drive back to the city, Willy said to Sal, "You know, Sal, *mi hermano*, we now have probably the best cocaine-distribution operation in all of Miami. Our client base is growing, and now we got our own airplanes." Added Willy, "If we could find a regular supplier and purchase the product directly from sources in Colombia, we could cut out the middleman and have our own independent operation. Imagine the money we could pull in. We'd have enough for Chi Chi and his people and still we could make two or three times what we make now."

It didn't take much convincing: Sal, who would become known as the smart one in the organization, got it right away.

They drove back to Miami mostly in silence, as they pondered their future. The seed for Los Muchachos had been planted.

2

ALINA

WHEN SIGMUND FREUD, WORLD-RENOWNED NEUROLOGIST, medical doctor, and founding father of modern psychoanalysis, first began studying cocaine, he wrote a letter to his beloved wife, Martha. The date was June 2, 1884. Freud, born in Austria, was twenty-eight years old. His wife had written him with news that she was recovering from an illness during which she had grown pale and lost her appetite. While away on a research trip, the doctor wrote back:

> Woe to you, my Princess, when I [return], I will kiss you quite red and feed you till you are plump. And if you are froward [*sic*] you shall see who is the stronger, a gentle little girl who doesn't eat enough or a big wild man who has cocaine in his body. In my last severe depression, I took coca again and a small dose lifted me to the heights in a wonderful fashion. I am just now busy collecting the literature for a song of praise to this magical substance.

Among other things, Freud was fascinated by cocaine's power as an aphrodisiac.

> The natives of South America, who represented the goddess of love with coca leaves in her hand, did not doubt the stimulative effect of coca on the genitalia. . . . Among the persons to whom I have given coca, three reported violent sexual excitement which they unhesitatingly attributed to the coca.

Freud was most interested in the physiological use of cocaine and its effects on the human psyche. He was hopeful about the drug's therapeutic potential, and in his writings, he noted that already there had been experiments that showed that cocaine had tremendous value as an anesthetic, especially when topically applied directly to the surface of the eye during surgery on the cornea.

Freud spent nearly a year using cocaine, off and on, and recording his re-actions. His findings, at the time, were unprecedented. Though the coca plant and its use by indigenous people in the Andes region of South America went back centuries, medical science in Europe and America had mostly ignored the plant.

As an enthusiastic advocate for this new "discovery," Freud made sweeping statements about the long-term effects or consequences of its sustained usage, stating that, as far as anyone could tell, it was not addictive or detrimental to a person's health. Later studies showed otherwise: excessive use of cocaine led to exhaustion, emaciation, and moral and spiritual depravity and an overriding apathy toward everything not connected with the enjoyment of the stimulant. In later years, after cocaine became illegal, Freud backtracked on his early, unbridled advocacy. But much of what the renowned doctor put forth about the drug in the 1880s—free of Judeo-Christian moralizing or the doomsday pandering that became the foundation for a punitive reaction to the drug— stands today as a refreshingly clearheaded appraisal of the plant and its effects.

Part of what captured Freud's imagination was the epic role of the coca plant and its alkaloid byproduct (cocaine) in the development of the human species. *Erythroxylum coca*, the leafy, six-foot-tall bush grown most expeditiously on the eastern slopes of the Andes, had been in use as a cultural talisman before the Spanish Conquest. The leaves of the plant, when masticated or made into a tea, were first used by the Inca in religious ceremonies and for medicinal pur-poses. As Freud wrote in "Über Coca," the earliest of his published articles on cocaine, "Legend held that Manco Capac, the divine son of the Sun, had de-scended in primeval times from the cliffs of Lake Titicaca, bringing his father's light . . . and the knowledge of the gods, taught them the useful arts, and gave them the coca leaf, this divine plant which satiates the hungry, strengthens the weak, and causes them to forget their misfortune."

After it was discovered that the plant could be dried, pulverized, alkalized, and bleached into a pristine white powder that isolated its most powerful qual-ities, a new day dawned. By the time Freud discovered cocaine, it had become an object of desire for rich people. The process of transforming it from a plant into an easily stored and transportable powder substance was costly. In the decades that followed, it acquired a certain cultural cachet in Europe and the United States.

In 1890, it was turned into a sugary soda drink called Coca-Cola, which was a major commercial success all around the industrialized world. Cocaine was viewed as a harmless stimulant, much like caffeine. At the end of the nineteenth century, you could enter pharmacies in the United States and buy cocaine to sniff, chew, smoke (in cigarettes), gargle, rub on as an ointment, or insert as a suppository. Since its manufacture was expensive and minimal, it was used primarily as an additive. At the turn of the new century, few consumers were snorting it directly or using it in large quantities.

The popular use of cocaine as an additive was banned with passage of the Food and Drug Act in 1910. Coca-Cola and other soft drinks were forced to supplant coca with caffeine. In December 1914, with passage of the Harrison Anti-Narcotics Act, the drug was declared illegal—except when prescribed by a doctor—throughout the United States.

This did not bring to a halt the demand for cocaine, but it did increase the price. Somehow, the white powder remained viable. Jazz musicians sang about it, and it was furnished to movie stars, entertainers, and international playboys. By the 1960s, marijuana may have been the drug of choice, rising from the counterculture into the mainstream, but coke served a practical purpose that grass did not. Weed was great for getting stoned, but it diminished motor skills to the point where a person was barely functional. In the frenetic, stressful, achievement-oriented back alleys of the Great American Hustle, now more than ever, there was the need for a drug that could get you high but not reduce you to a Cheech and Chong stereotype.

In the early 1970s, the entertainment business became the driving force behind a burgeoning cocaine clientele. You could snort coke and remain functional on a movie set, or at least that was the rumor. And if that was true, then it also had a place in the boardrooms among the so-called Masters of the Universe, and in the offices of adventurous doctors and lawyers. Yes, it was expensive, but those folks could afford it.

Unbeknownst to Willy, Tony, Sal, and the rest of their crew of young Cuban exiles, this cultural volcano was on the verge of eruption. As the status of the drug rose, so did the demand. Cocaine was becoming more and more visible at nightclubs in Miami. From the beginning, as Willy and Sal entertained the idea of branching off from their anti-Communist militant partners and launching their own independent operation, they knew the key was to establish clientele above and beyond Miami. There was a market to be exploited from Miami Beach all the way north to New York and Chicago, and west all the way to California. The boys were thinking big.

What had started as an effort to assist those who hoped to kill the bearded dictator and liberate Cuba was about to become the white powder avalanche that changed America.

WILLY FALCON FIRST LAID EYES on Alina Rossique at Citrus Grove Junior High School in Miami when he was sixteen and she was fifteen. From the beginning, he knew they were going to marry. She was the most beautiful girl he had ever seen—blond, petite but shapely, with an air of class and sophistication. At the time, Willy had nothing; nor did Alina. They were kids, the children of Cuban exiles struggling to get by. But Willy and Alina both saw their budding romance within the context of a fable or fairy tale. They both believed they could help make each other's dreams come true.

Alina's younger sister, Ileana, adored the sister who, from the day they had left Cuba as children, protected and looked out for her:

Ever since we were little girls, she was the most beautiful. Everybody wanted to be like her, including me. At first, it was just the two of us, and because she was three years older than me, she felt it was her job to protect me.

Alina was born in 1956; Ileana in 1959, the year Castro rolled into Havana atop a tank. In later years, the sisters learned that their father had suspected from the start that Castro's arrival was the beginning of a Communist dictatorship. The new regime was cagey at first, not proclaiming its Communist agenda until the government began seizing private businesses and jailing anyone who spoke out against the regime.

Almost immediately, José Rossique, Alina and Ileana's father, began looking for a way off the island. He moved family money through bank transfers out of Cuba to Spain, a fortunate move since the government soon began seizing bank accounts and prohibiting financial transfers of any kind. This was before the period of the Freedom Flights. For the average citizen, getting out of Cuba was complicated. José befriended an ambassador from Curaçao, an island in the Dutch Antilles, located off the northern coast of Venezuela. The ambassador provided the Rossique family with visas so they could leave.

They pretended they were going on vacation; that was the only way the revolutionary government would allow them to leave. They carried with them a minimal amount of clothing, leaving behind a fully furnished home in central Havana. They fled first to Curaçao, where they lived for two months, and then continued to Madrid, Spain, where José Rossique's sister lived outside the city.

All along, the plan was to get to the United States, but Alina and Ileana did not know this. At the ages of eight and five, they settled into their new home in Madrid as if this were their permanent station in life. With the money that had been smuggled out of Cuba, Alina and Ileana were put into a Catholic boarding school in Madrid. On her eighth birthday, Ileana received the holy sacrament of communion. Boarding school was exciting, but she didn't always get along well with the nuns.

At dinner in the cafeteria, they put in front of me a bowl of white rice slathered with ketchup. There was no way I was going to eat that. The other girls ate it and were excused. Eventually I was there all alone. They told me, "Think of all your fellow Cubans starving in Cuba because they don't have enough food." Nothing they said could make me eat it. So eventually they brought in my sister. They told her to convince me to eat the rice. She said to me, "Please Ileana, you have to eat it or they will kick us out of the school." My sister tried, but I wouldn't budge. The nuns dismissed her. I remember seeing Alina standing in one of those huge Spanish doorways, a door from the floor to the ceiling. She turned around, looked at me, and began to cry.

Ileana felt terrible. Her sister was her protector, and she had broken her spirit with her stubbornness. It was something she never forgot.

Tears were not uncommon for a generation of Cubans who had been thrown asunder. For Alina and Ileana, the transition was not difficult; they were children, and it was all a big adventure. But they could see the toll it took on their parents. One incident that Ileana would always remember was when the family received word that José's father—her grandfather—had passed away back in

Cuba. José Rossique was devasted, and he wept like a child. "I had never seen a grown man cry before," remembered Ileana. "It was traumatic."

José held himself responsible, as if the decision he made for his family to flee Cuba had devastated his parents. Perhaps the sadness had caused his father to have a fatal heart attack. Such was the guilt and remorse of a generation forced to make life-altering decisions brought on by the unnatural consequences of exile.

After a few years in Spain, José Rossique became concerned about life under the dictatorship of Francisco Franco. He was especially worried about how patriarchal the society was for women. He was a man with four daughters (the fourth, Leslie, was born in Spain) and another child on the way. He felt that there was no future for them under such a misogynist system.

In 1967, he was able to secure visas for the entire family, and they made the move to Miami.

They stayed with José's aunt Angelina—his father's sister—in what was designated an "adult-only community." Angelina and her husband did not have children, which were prohibited in the community. Alina, Ileana, and the other girls had to walk on eggshells and be quiet at all times. If it was discovered that there were children in the house, they would all be kicked out.

The girls loved Miami, and they adapted quickly. They learned to speak English, advancing rapidly from level one to level two, and so on. On Sundays, they went to the park to roller-skate. They remained blissfully unaware of the turmoil back in their home country of Cuba, which seemed to be the only thing their parents and other adult exiles ever talked about. Ileana remembers her father saying, more than once, "If there's one thing I did good in my life, it was getting my girls out of Cuba."

Ileana was twelve years old when, one day, Alina brought home her dreamboat of a boyfriend. His name was Willy Falcon, and he was already known around Little Havana for his reputation as a student athlete, and for his good looks. He owned a used red Thunderbird that he had bought with his earnings from the construction business. The cocaine business was four years in the future, but even then, he had swagger. When Alina's parents met Willy, they liked him, but they thought he needed to cut his hair. The hair was extravagant. In keeping with the style of the times, Falcon's hair was long and wild. Eventually, in the 1980s, he would bring it under control. Hair became a well-manicured aspect of Los Muchachos in general; Willy had his trimmed and coiffed on a regular basis.

Alina and Willy were married September 22, 1973. The ceremony was held at the Cathedral of Saint Mary's, the seat of the archbishop of the Roman Catholic Archdiocese of Miami, located on Second Avenue and Northwest Seventy-Fifth Street. Their honeymoon was delayed because Willy could not get time off from his construction job.

They lived for a time in a duplex next door to Willy's parents, then moved to an apartment building at Seventy-Second Avenue and Second Street. In 1975, their first daughter, Aileen, was born. One year later, when Willy got laid off from his construction job, the family finances became problematic. That all changed when Falcon and Tony Bemba first started in the cocaine business. It was like they hit the jackpot. The money rolled in.

With Willy and his crew taking in hundreds of thousands of dollars—and eventually millions—on those initial shipments for the anti-Castro underground, Falcon went on a spending spree. He bought two new cars, a Cadillac Coupe DeVille and a Mercedes convertible, and a vacation house in the Keys. After their second daughter, Jessica, was born in 1979, they moved into a house in Coral Gables, one of the city's most prestigious neighborhoods. Alina knew better than to ask questions. She knew that Willy and his friends were actively involved in *la lucha*. In Little Havana, this was a subject often spoken about in whispers, as it involved smuggling arms and explosives, and other illegal acts.

In the mid-1970s the movement had veered into acts of terrorism. On September 21, 1976, a Chilean ambassador who had publicly met with Castro was blown up in a car bomb on Embassy Row in Washington, DC. It was a carefully planned assassination carried out by a Miami-based underground exile group known as Alpha 66. Two weeks later, on October 6, a Cubana de Aviación jetliner traveling from Barbados to Havana was bombed out of the sky; seventy-three innocent passengers and crew members were killed, including the entire Cuban fencing team. Anti-Castro operatives had planted the bomb.

These acts shocked many exiles, even those who were vehemently anti-Castro. But the struggle continued, and in Little Havana, it was understood that the counterrevolution was a kind of holy war.

Alina knew that Willy was meeting and doing business with men like Chi Chi Quintero, a hero in the community. He was doing his duty as a Cuban exile.

If somehow his business with the anti-Castro movement was also proving to be highly remunerative for her husband, this was a blessing. Every Sunday she went to church at Saint Mary's and thanked God that their financial lives had taken a sudden turn for the better.

WILLY AND SAL WERE UNLIKELY innovators. Sal had mostly taken over the role first filled by Tony Bemba. Tony was still involved as an accountant for the group, but Sal quickly assumed the role of coleader along with Willy. Their skills complemented one another, and to the underlings who worked for them, they were a dynamic team.

Like most Miami Cubans of his generation, Magluta had his own epic origin story to tell. He had come to the United States in 1961, at the age of seven, as a member of Operation Pedro Pan. Of all the epic sagas of exile from the island, the clandestine Pedro Pan flights held a special place in the hearts of many exiles. Devised and sponsored by the Catholic Church, Pedro Pan (Peter Pan) was the name given to a series of covert flights, between 1960 and 1962, filled with unaccompanied minors ages six to eighteen. They were sent by parents who feared that the Communist party in Cuba was planning to take their kids away and place them in Communist indoctrination centers. It was, at the time, the largest exodus of refugee minors in the Western Hemisphere. Once the kids arrived in the United States, they were taken in by Catholic orphanages, where they lived until their parents or other family members were able to get out of Cuba, come to the United States, and claim them.

Sal was ten years old by the time his parents arrived. Up until then, he lived with his aunt and uncle in Little Havana, playing basketball and baseball, two sports he later excelled at alongside Willy Falcon at Miami High.

Now that Willy and Sal had branched off on their own by initiating cocaine deals that were independent of the anti-Castro movement, they were, to a degree, making it up as they went along. The cocaine business was burgeoning; at the street level, there were more dealers than ever before. But for importation of large quantities—"weight"—there was no tried-and-true system in place. Sal and Willy had to create one.

Willy and Sal had a vision from the beginning: they dreamed of a national distribution network, based in Miami, that brought the product to big cities around the United States. Miami would be ground zero for a national market-place.

They had lined up a major supplier, George Ordoñez, a Colombian from Medellín living in Miami. Ordoñez was twenty years older than Willy and Sal. He was well connected in Colombia, a country that had, in the late 1970s, emerged as the world's premier exporter of cocaine.

Working with Ordoñez, Willy and Sal brought in two major shipments of cocaine hidden inside the engine blocks of heavy equipment such as Caterpillar-brand bulldozers and cranes. The equipment arrived on cargo planes at Miami International Airport. After the cargo cleared customs, Willy and his crew met the shipment at the airport with an invoice. They offloaded crates containing the engines, moved them to a warehouse outside the city, and unpacked the cocaine. This route continued for a year, with a new load arriving every month. Some of these shipments were brought in by air, and some entered via Miami harbor. The product needed to be transported and stored. Then there was the cash, huge amounts from major transactions that needed to be kept in a "stash house."

Security was paramount. For this, the boys leaned on the local community in Little Havana.

Because of the subterranean anti-Castro movement, Cuban exiles were accustomed to the idea of clandestine activity that needed to be kept secret. Through trusted relatives and friends, they stored cash in everyday middle-class homes. They brought carpenters into these homes to create a "clavo." In Spanish, the word *clavo* means "nail," but in Cuban slang it refers to secret hiding places in attics and basements, or in special compartments beneath floorboards and behind walls. The occupants of these homes—average citizens, not narcos—were paid anywhere between $50,000 and $100,000 per month. They were tutored on how to not spend the money lavishly and attract attention.

These stash houses existed throughout Little Havana and Hialeah, another neighborhood where recent Cuban exiles settled. There were two kinds of stash house: one for money and one for product—never together under one roof, in case of police or nosy neighbors.

The cash came in various denominations—tens, fifties, one-hundred-dollar bills, and higher. It was stacked neatly, bound in rubber bands and stuffed in shoeboxes, duffel bags, or suitcases. The product came in a compressed brick, tightly bound in polyurethane plastic. Some Cubans called the merchandise *yeyo;* others called it *perico* (parakeet), because when the white powder strafed the nasal passage and hit the brainpan, the verbal logorrhea was sometimes repetitive and came forth in a torrent.

The houses were monitored by security personnel in automobiles or nearby abodes, which were purchased and modestly furnished by the organization.

The person in charge of overseeing the locations was Justo Jay, Willy's friend from childhood and the old neighborhood. Justo was one of the group's few Afro Cuban leaders. He was trusted like a brother, which was a requirement to be a member of Willy and Sal's operations.

By late 1977, the organization consisted of three bosses who split the proceeds as follows: Falcon, since he initiated the business, received 50 percent; Tony Bemba, 25 percent; Sal, 25 percent. Justo Jay and others were paid a percentage of each shipment in which they played a role.

In the spring of that year, someone came up with the idea that after the product surreptitiously passed through customs, each individual brick of cocaine would be stamped with the name "Los Muchachos." Everyone liked this as the name for their organization. Willy thought that stamping the product with the name of the group was a brilliant stroke of branding.

At least two shipments of more than two hundred kilos each came into Miami and were stamped "Los Muchachos." They arrived as hidden cargo on a huge tanker, and were then offloaded to warehouses and stash houses, to be broken down and sold at roughly $50,000 a kilo. After a while, someone noted, "Uh, do you think it's a good idea to have the name of your organization advertised on the product? If these loads ever get intercepted or busted, it's gonna be pretty easy for law enforcement to figure out whose loads these are."

True enough. Reluctantly, they stopped stamping the loads with the Los Muchachos brand. Many were sorry to see it go, especially Willy.

The branding was gone but the name was not. Members of the group continued to refer to themselves as Los Muchachos. It had a nice ring to it, and it seemed to capture the spirit of their endeavor: a group of young capitalists—boys—seeking to alter the trajectory of the universe through guile, ingenuity, and lawlessness.

THE LATE 1970S WERE A difficult time for the city of Miami. The municipal budget was in arrears, and political corruption scandals seemed to dominate the news. And then there was the violence. The earliest inklings of the cocaine craze hit the city like a tsunami. Not many had seen it coming. The era became characterized by a litany of savagery that unfolded like a sun-blasted, palm tree–laden version of the Dark Ages:

A dealer shot to death in a remote field in Dade County; a dead body dumped in a fashionable neighborhood; a narco gunned to death on the greens of the Miami Springs Golf Course; a cokehead shot to death in the back of the head in a South Dade citrus grove; a low-level narco driven off the road after leaving a shopping center and killed in front of his family in the belief that he was an informer; the maid at the home of a Miami drug boss strangled to death during a home invasion; a narco beaten and tortured to death as vengeance for the maid's murder; two rich cocaine clients shot to death inside their posh condominium on Biscayne Bay while they slept; a dealer found shot to death in a trash dump; a cokehead gunned down inside a Latin disco; an entire family wiped out in a drive-by shooting, narco related; an unidentified body shot in the head, execution style, the corpse left floating in a canal in southwest Dade County half eaten by an alligator.

All these killings—and many more—took place during an eighteen-month period from late 1977 to mid-1979. Learning about these acts of violence in small snippets in the *Miami Herald* or sixty-second reports on the TV news, as many citizens did, was like trying to deconstruct Japanese haiku. The details were sparse and obtuse, which left everything to the imagination. If you closed your eyes, you could almost see the blood splattered on the walls and floors; smell the bodies decomposing after being dumped in the Everglades; gag at the sight of a body bludgeoned to death, wrapped in plastic and stuffed in a trunk. There was rarely any context in the reporting. Who were these sorry hoodlums? Why was this happening? Who or what was behind the carnage?

For the most part, local cops were simply overwhelmed. Pat Diaz joined the South Miami Police Department in 1976 and switched to Miami PD a few years later. "It was insane," he says of that time. "Dead bodies in barrels, decomposed, throats slit. I was twenty-two years old. 'What the hell is going on out here?' There was one scene at 220th Street and US 1. The car was left on the road, guns left scattered on the road. The people are dead on the road, a shootout at a traffic light. I mean, that's the Wild West. I think we averaged seven murders a night. There wasn't much we could do. We just went from case to case."

Al Singleton joined the Miami police force in 1973. Originally from Ohio, he had to catch up on the local culture. "On-the-job training," he remembers. "I was transferred to Homicide in 1978, right when the killings were getting out of hand. We didn't close a case before another one popped up. We didn't always know what was going on."

Willy, Sal, and the Boys knew full well what was going on. They may not have known who or what was behind every hit, but they knew that the business, at the street level, was descending into madness. In one sense, they were inoculated from the mayhem, which was the consequence of competition among low-level dealers. What Willy and Sal were attempting to create was an importation, transportation, and distribution network that was a few steps removed from the craziness. Even so, the time had come to arm and provide firearms training for everyone in the organization.

The leadership of Los Muchachos talked about the violence. It was agreed they would use their weapons to protect themselves and their families, but as a business policy they had no intention of resorting to wanton violence, as was becoming common in the streets. Partly, this was a consequence of the type of people who had begun to coalesce around Los Muchachos. They were not hardened criminals or men with violent histories. Yes, they were exiles, which was another word for refugees, but they lived in a community that was solid and self-supporting. They did not come into the business in a state of abject desperation. Their intention was to run their cocaine operation as a seemingly legitimate import/distribution business, and to stay out of the mayhem business, if that was possible.

It would involve constant maneuvering in and around a world that was becoming increasingly explosive.

One of the main prerequisites for a safe operation was to be careful with whom you chose to do business. They were clearing multiple millions in revenue every month with the Colombian, George Ordoñez. The problem was that Ordoñez, who had become a major cocaine importer in Miami over the previous year, was also doing business with Griselda Blanco, a rare woman

Colombian cocaine boss, who had turned the narco business upside down in Miami, New York, and Medellín, Colombia, through her wanton use of violence as a business strategy.

Raised in the slum neighborhood of Barrio Antioquia, in central Medellín, Griselda was often said to have more cojones (balls) than the average male. Among her more outrageous smuggling operations was the $40 million worth of cocaine that she secured on a Colombian ship, *La Gloria*, a forty-foot "tall ship" sailing vessel that was invited by the US government to take part in the bicentennial celebration of 1976. The ship sailed into ports from Miami to New York and Boston along with other tall ships from around the world—only this ship surreptitiously offloaded bricks of cocaine.

Griselda's penchant for murder was legendary. She had virtually invented the concept of the *sicario*, desperate ghetto youth on motorcycles with machine guns who mastered the grisly technique of the drive-by shooting. As Max Mermelstein, one of her American partners, put it, "She ordered murders like some people order pizza."

By the late 1970s, Blanco had become a liability in the trade. Being in business with anyone who was in business with her was problematic. Not only that, but on a few occasions socializing with George Ordoñez, Willy had noticed that he had a fierce cocaine habit.

Los Muchachos certainly had no problems with cocaine use. Willy, Sal, and nearly every member of the group used "tootie," as they called it, while partying, having sex, or during pickup games of basketball. Cocaine had become so common in some Latin circles that it was like having a beer in other cultures. But Ordoñez was smoking *basuco*, which was cocaine paste before it was processed into a white power. *Basuco* was like smoking crack, before crack was invented. The deterioration that came from using the drug this way was accelerated.

Between the *basuco* and Ordoñez's associations with Griselda Blanco, Willy began to feel that this particular Colombian narco was more trouble than he was worth.

A solution was suggested by an underling whom Willy and Sal had hired to do their taxes. Jorge "George" Valdés was a former honor student who had dropped out of college to go into the cocaine business. Willy felt that George was overly flashy and full of bravado. He drove a 1977 silver Corvette with silver interior and wore silk suits, lots of jewelry, and carried around wads of cash. He may have been reckless, but he was a crafty accountant, and he did have excellent contacts in the business.

"I have someone you should meet," George told Willy and Sal. "You don't know his name, and I'm sure you've never heard of him, but he is one of the pioneers of the modern cocaine business. Trust me. I file his federal income tax return every year and help him wash his money through various US companies. He's a smuggler of contraband going back decades, and he can connect you to suppliers in Colombia at the highest levels of the business."

Willy and Sal made an appointment to meet the man. George Valdés may have been blowing smoke out his ass, as he sometimes did, but it was worth exploring. In a way, they were doing what diligent dealers do, attempting to move up the chain of supply, away from reckless partners and the mayhem of the streets. If they could buy their product directly from suppliers in Colombia and arrange their own methods of transport, it would put them on a level in the United States that was unprecedented at that time.

In June 1977, Willy and Sal met with Manuel Garces, by all appearances an elegant, well-appointed Colombian businessman. They met at Victoria Station restaurant, near Miami International Airport. It was love at first sight.

Garces, born in 1928, was twenty-seven years older than Willy and Sal. He found it charming to be dealing with a couple of Cubans who were so young. "You two remind me of myself when I first began in the smuggling business," he said.

Willy and Sal were in awe as the Old Man (Willy later referred to Garces as El Padrino, "the Godfather") gave them a thumbnail sketch of his career: He had started in the contraband business in the early 1960s, smuggling alcohol, Marlboro cigarettes, household appliances, rare fabrics, and coffee. He worked primarily from Colón, the famous free-trade zone located on the Atlantic coast of Panama. Garces traveled from Medellín, his home base, and lived in Panama City for three months at a time, at the Carleton Hotel. Every day, he went to work at a warehouse in Colón. With an invoice in hand, he organized the merchandise for shipments to Medellín or Bogotá, or to Colombia's coastal port cities, Cartagena or Buenaventura, for shipment overseas.

Colombia had a long tradition of contraband smuggling. Some of this was a consequence of geography. With two separate coastlines, one on the Pacific Ocean and another on the Caribbean Sea (connected by the Panama Canal), the country was well situated as a launching pad for illegal products from South America to all points north.

Manuel's partner in the business was Alfredo Gomez Lopez, the godfather of Colombian smugglers, also known as El Hombre Marlboro for his having cornered the underground cigarette market in Latin America. According to Garces:

> At that time, being a *contrabandista* may have been illegal, but it was respectable. Nobody carried weapons or anything like that. We were gentlemen providing a service to the marketplace, or at least that's how we saw it. If necessary, we paid off people in law enforcement or politics to help make things happen. Rarely were there arrests, or anything like that. Technically, it was an illegal activity, but many people saw it as a semilegitimate form of commerce.

Around 1970, Garces returned to Medellín. At that time, the entire underground economy in Colombia was transitioning to the smuggling of marijuana. El Hombre Marlboro was approached by a consortium of smugglers from the region of La Guajira, on Colombia's Caribbean coast. Garces knew the group only as "Los Guajiros." They told Gomez and Garces, "We have the connections, but we lack money. Invest in us and you will make millions."

Marijuana was the new craze. The product could be grown right there in Colombia, particularly in a northern region of the country known as the Greater Magdalena, which was arid and lush. From there, it could be shipped from Riohacha, the primary port city in La Guajira.

It was through smuggling marijuana that the Colombians first established connections in the Caribbean islands, particularly in Aruba and Curaçao. Because of its bulkiness and noticeably pungent aroma, the product could not be smuggled in large amounts directly from Colombia to the United States and Europe. It needed to be offloaded and stored in the islands, parceled out and distributed to suppliers mostly in North America. These connections would lay the foundation for the smuggling of cocaine, which was to begin in earnest in the next few years.

As Garces remembers it, he and El Hombre Marlboro were approached by a major contraband smuggler from Bogotá, whom he knew only as El Profesor (the Professor). The Professor said to them, "Why are you doing this with marijuana? Let's start doing it with cocaine. Less quantity, less bulk, way more profitable. You will make 200 percent more with the white powder."

The Professor already had a system in place. He was smuggling kilos of cocaine from Bogotá. There were no "processing labs" in existence at the time. Cocaine paste was crudely processed into white powder in warehouses, garages, or people's basements. It was a slow process that could produce only two or three kilos at a time.

Garces and El Hombre Marlboro met the Professor's pilot, an American named Billy, married to a Colombian woman, who had served as a fighter pilot during the Vietnam War. Billy told them, "I have a contact so we can fly the cocaine to the Bahamas. There we can transfer it to commercial fishing boats and smuggle loads into the US." The maximum amount they could ship was twenty to thirty kilos.

And so, the Colombians became involved in the cocaine business. It was slow at first. One of the problems was establishing buyers in the United States who had sophisticated-enough operations that they were able to buy directly from suppliers in Colombia. This was why Garces had wanted to meet with Willy and Sal. He was especially impressed when he heard they had their own planes and pilots who could pick up the product in Colombia and transport it to the United States. Offering to make the purchase at the source and take all the risks—this was almost unheard of in the cocaine business at the time.

Garces told the Boys, "I have major contacts in Medellín and in Cali. Between those sources, you will have access to more cocaine than you ever dreamed of."

Afterward, Willy and Sal went for a drink and discussed the situation. They were in awe of the Old Man, who was a smuggler with a long history. He could connect them at the highest levels in Colombia.

"You know," said Willy, "it's almost like destiny is leading us in this direction. First, being approached by Chi Chi and the freedom fighters. Then, Isaac's widow gave us those planes. Now, out of the blue, we meet this guy, the Godfather. Everything is falling into place. Like it was meant to be."

THE MANUEL GARCES CONNECTION STARTED paying dividends right away. The Old Man connected them to major suppliers in Medellín and Cali, and the shipments commenced. Loads of 250 kilos, with a street value close to $15 million, were not uncommon. The Boys sent their pilot Jack Devoe, who had been working with them since the coke-for-arms shipments to Honduras, and another pilot on runs deep into Colombia, where they landed at secret airstrips in the jungle, loaded the product, and flew back to the United States. An ingenious technique, pioneered by Devoe, was to fly low, below the radar, so the flights would not be detected. Sometimes they sent up an identical decoy plane, so that if the original cocaine-laden plane was detected by aviation officials and ordered to land, the empty decoy plane would land in its place. They never lost a load.

The money coming in was almost beyond comprehension. One day, Sal told Willy, "We need to create a legitimate financial infrastructure, and we need to do it now. Or we're going to lose everything."

The first order of business was banking. Willy had a family friend he knew named Ray Corona, who was in the banking business. He had met Corona through Alina, his wife, who had worked for a time as a loan manager at the Bank of Miami, located downtown. Corona was the bank's vice president (his father, Rafael, was president). Willy and Alina, and Ray and his wife, began socializing together. One night, over drinks, Willy hinted that he was involved in something that required sudden deposits and withdrawals of cash in the multiple millions of dollars.

Up until then, Willy and his crew were still counting money by hand, which was an insanely slow process susceptible to error (they counted the money by weighing it on a kitchen scale). Willy asked Ray, "You know what I need? Counting machines, like those ones they use at banks. Do you think you could order a couple of those for me?"

"Consider it done," said Ray. He ordered for Los Muchachos two state-of-the-art counting machines that, overnight, changed their way of doing business.

The counting machines were only the beginning. In 1977, Corona came to Willy and Sal with a proposition. He wanted to buy in as majority owner and president of Sunshine State Bank, a state-chartered commercial savings and loan business. If Willy and Sal were to lend him $5 million, he could become a majority shareholder at the bank and do whatever he wanted.

By then, Corona was fully aware that Willy and Sal were kingpins in the cocaine business. One day, the three of them got together over drinks and came up with a plan. The two young cocaine merchants would give Ray his loan; in return, they would make unregistered deposits of millions of dollars in cash—cocaine proceeds—at Sunshine State Bank. The bank would then "loan" money to business entities created by Willy and Sal. It was clever on a couple of levels: it allowed Willy and Sal to launder their proceeds and gave them financial cover to explain large amounts of capital that was being used to finance their other legitimate businesses.

As the legend of Willy and Sal began to take shape, no incident was more renowned than the time the Boys showed up at Corona's Sunshine State Bank with more than a dozen duffel bags filled with over $100 million in cash for deposit.

Among the first legitimate businesses Willy established was the construction company he bought that laid him off from work back in 1976.

He and Sal also got into the real estate business, constructing and selling condominium apartment buildings around the city, a business that was managed by their fathers, Arsenio Falcon and Manuel Magluta. Willy also set up his father in the clothing business.

By far the most cherished enterprise devised by the Boys was the Seahawk Marine boatbuilding company, which they based out of offices and a warehouse on North Miami's renowned Thunder Road. This area was the center of powerboat culture in the United States.

Offshore powerboating was as crucial to the identity of Miami as football was in Dallas or Green Bay. Boating, in general, was highly popular due to the area's many spectacular waterways, but offshore powerboating was a fiercely competitive sport. A high premium was placed on the design of the boats, which were constantly being refined to enhance the machine's sleekness and hydrodynamics.

It was Willy's brother, Tavy, who first got the group interested in racing the boats. Tavy was then nineteen. Just like his brother, he had dropped out of high school at the age of seventeen. Through a friend of his, he had raced powerboats a few times and loved it.

Tavy told Willy, "I wanna buy a new Phantom boat." Willy said he would help with a loan. Unbeknownst to Willy, the person Tavy was buying the boat from was a longtime friend. In fact, this person had arrived in Miami from Havana on the exact same day as Willy in 1967.

The guy called Falcon and said, "Willy, my old friend, I have a boat company. I own three molds—twenty-six, twenty-eight, and thirty-one feet long. The business is kicking my ass. How about you buy the whole company?"

And so, for $1 million, Willy bought the company. He and Tavy were both copresidents of the company, which they called Impulse Marine Inc. Later, they changed the name of the company to Seahawk Marine Inc.

At first, it was not Willy's intention to race boats or enter them in competition. It was simply an advantageous business investment, and he loved being in on the design of the boats. The business took off immediately. In addition to the three molds Falcon purchased, his company added one more, a mold for the granddaddy of them all, the thirty-eight foot Seahawk, which was a thing of beauty.

It was Tavy who first took Willy and Sal out on the water and showed them the rudiments of the sport. They were hooked. Powerboat racing was the ultimate Miami endeavor, and the fact that they were major players in the boat business was a boost to the ego. With the cocaine biz, they had to hide their involvement, but success in the boat business was something they could declare far and wide.

What does it take to race powerboats? Two things, according to Falcon: "Balls, and you have to be crazy."

There was no training course. You learned the sport by racing in small local races, accumulating points until you were eligible to take part in races sponsored by the American Powerboat Association (APBA). Powerboat racing had its dangers. The boats were explosive pieces of machinery that could malfunction, causing fires, and racing at speeds over one hundred miles an hour could be terrifying. If a boat flipped, as they sometimes did given the speeds and choppy waters, the pilots could be seriously injured or killed.

In 1978, Seahawk entered a few boats in the professional circuit of the APBA, which sponsored fourteen races a year in different cities around the United States.

That year, Willy, Sal, and Tavy all took part in the races. During a race, the boat was run by a three-man team that included a navigator, a throttle man, and a pilot, or driver. Willy and Sal were drivers in two separate boats, while Tavy served as throttle man.

Equally important was the pit crew. Two mechanics, Ralph Linaris and Fernando Gonzalez, were part of that team, as well as Benny Lorenzo (also known as "Benny B."), whom Willy first met when Benny was still a student at Miami High.

At first, Willy's crew raced under the name "Cougar," and Tavy's crew—for which Sal was a driver—raced under the name "Seahawk," but after the first season both crews raced exclusively under the company name.

Los Muchachos did not win any major races in 1978, but the group activity of preparing for and then actively participating in the sport was an incredible thrill for all involved. There was the camaraderie and sense of accomplishment, and the pure joy of racing at high speeds on the pristine waters of South Florida and elsewhere around the United States. The powerboat culture was also highly conducive to the selling and using of cocaine. Few things were more adrenaline inducing than to have a toot (or two, or three) while keeping the boats functioning at peak performance. To be part of a piloting team and maintenance crew during a race was a powerful bonding activity for those involved, and to do it while buzzed on yeyo made a person feel as if he truly was a Master of the Universe.

More than anything else, activities surrounding Seahawk came to symbolize the unbridled success of Los Muchachos. There were races nearly every month. Wives, kids, cousins, friends, and mistresses all attended. It was an exciting communal activity, a gathering of the tribe. After every race was a major party, financed by Willy and Sal. They were spreading goodwill and enhancing their reputations as the providers of good times.

Seahawk built the boat's hull, but it did not build the engines. The big boats required two 500-block engines, which were constructed by Mercury Racing Performance, a company based in Wisconsin. Every month, Willy, Sal, and other Seahawk employees traveled to Wisconsin to test-run new engines. Mercury was the best engine-building company in the world. Willy was envious; he had been fascinated by the inner workings of engines since he was a kid.

In 1978, Willy approached Mercury's two best mechanics—Keith Eickert and Milton Morizumi—who had been building engines for Seahawk for two years. "Whatever Mercury is paying you," Willy said to the mechanics, "I will pay you twice as much to come work for me."

Willy and Sal wanted to start their own engine company. The mechanics thought it was a great idea. But they said to Willy, "We're small-town people. We don't want to live in a big city like Miami." Eickert suggested that he had a friend and former boat racer in Saint Augustine, Florida, who had some land he might be willing to sell.

Located on the state's Atlantic coast, roughly three hundred miles north of Miami, Saint Augustine claimed to be the oldest municipality in the United States. Founded in 1565—fifty-five years before the Pilgrims landed at Plymouth Rock and forty-two years before the British colonized Jamestown—Saint Augustine had been established by Spanish colonialists. By the 1970s, much of the town's original architecture had been lovingly preserved. It was a remote though popular tourist destination, low key, with a couple of beautiful beaches and a modest though diverse year-round population of barely ten thousand people.

Willy, Sal, and the mechanics met with Eickert's contact in Saint Augustine. The two Cubans had never been there before. Both Willy and Sal were taken by the town's charm and beauty. They made the purchase of ten acres of waterfront property and went to work.

Four different buildings were constructed on the property. One warehouse was to build the parts for 350-block to 500-block engines; the second was to assemble the engine blocks together, along with the pistons, carburetors, and wiring; the third was to connect the engines to diagnostic equipment for calibration of RPMs or measuring of horsepower; the fourth building was to mount the engines inside the boats with the final touches.

Building 4 also included a suite of offices and a gym on the second floor that overlooked the warehouse, and, through a separate plateglass picture window, a view that took in both the boatyard and the majestic bay. Eickert and Morizumi were encouraged to hire their own crew, the best workers in the business. The office was staffed with friends and local people, so that the company would blend seamlessly with the local business fabric of Saint Augustine.

They called the company KS&W Offshore Engineering. The *K*, *S*, and *W* stood for Keith, Sal, and Willy.

Financing the company required some fancy financial footwork. Willy and Sal inaugurated a shell company in the Virgin Islands called Motores Marinos.

They sent $2 million to a bank account in the islands, then transferred the funds into the account of Motores Marinos. The shell company then loaned the money to KS&W Offshore Engineering to purchase the land and construct the facilities.

The company was another major coup for Willy and Sal. With Eickert and Morizumi as their lead mechanics, KS&W quickly became one of the most in-demand engine companies in the world. By the early 1980s, the company was building racing engines for 25 percent of the professional racers in the United States and building engines for some of the most successful teams on the racing circuit in Japan and the United Kingdom.

It seemed as though Willy and Sal had the golden touch. Not only were they premier traffickers of one of the most desired illegal commodities in the world, but they were also learning the art of money laundering and corporate diversification, with business entities that were highly successful in their own right, bringing in more money, esteem, and notoriety to the operation's technically nonexistent parent company, which could have been called Los Muchachos Inc.

3

MAKIN' IT

ALINA FALCON KNEW THAT HER husband was cheating on her. All the indicators were there. Since he first started working in the anti-Castro movement, and then full time with the cocaine business, he was spending more and more time away from home. There were trips to the Caribbean islands—to Aruba and the city of Freeport, in the Bahamas—and weeklong trips to Los Angeles for "business." Even at home in Miami, he sometimes stayed out all night or didn't make an appearance around the house for days. Miami felt like a small town. For Cuban exiles who grew up there, went to high school there, everybody knew everybody. Willy was seen at such and such nightclub with a group of young women, or at The Forge restaurant in Miami Beach with one woman in particular; it always got back to Alina.

Eventually, it became an issue. She said to Willy, "How dare you disrespect me like that. I'm here with our child, raising our child, and you are out fucking everything that moves."

"Listen," he answered, "I'm out there making a living for both of us. I'm hustling every day. You know full well how we make our living. It's a dangerous fucking profession. Sometimes, I need to unwind."

"You can unwind at home with your wife and your daughter. You don't have to be sleeping with those bitches and whores."

"Come on! You're being paranoid."

Willy never did come right out and deny that he was sleeping around. In his world, he secretly believed that it was his right as a Cuban male, and as a highly successful criminal. In a way, it was as though the rules did not apply to him, both in his professional and his personal life. He was an outlaw, and outlaws lived by their own rules. Maybe Alina did not understand that, but eventually she would. It was his job to break her in.

So much had changed in their lives. When they had first married four years earlier, Willy was a struggling high school dropout with no money. The effort it had taken to establish his business in recent years was insane: making deals, monitoring shipments, overseeing cash transactions in the millions. Willy was a workaholic. The fact that they had achieved this ungodly level of financial success so quickly was unheard of, and he felt that he was not being given credit by his wife for how he had created a good life for his family.

The bit about creating a good life was a diversion, and Alina knew it. "We're not talking about that," she said to Willy. "I know you work hard, and I give you full credit for that. I'm talking about you feeling the need to put your dick in everything that moves."

Exasperated, Willy shrugged and gestured: *What do you want from me?* "My obligation is to put food on the table, put a roof over your head, make sure you have all the comforts of life—a car, house, nice clothes, jewelry. Do I not do that?"

She knew he was grandstanding and would not give him the satisfaction of an answer.

"I take care of business. After that, I'll do what I want."

The arguments usually ended with a series of threats. "If you don't stop," said Alina, "I'm going to take our child and move out of here. I'll move in with my mother and divorce you."

Willy believed that the threats of divorce were an act of gamesmanship on Alina's part. He never believed she would do it.

"You do what you gotta do," he said, then slammed the door and headed out into the night.

NIGHT.

That was part of the problem. Nights in Miami were filled with possibilities. The women were out in the nightclubs, shiny, barely dressed, and overheated. The clubs had begun to establish themselves as the pot at the end of the rainbow, the logical receptacle of consumption in a process that began far away in the Amazon basin, passed through Colombia for processing, sailed or flew to the United States courtesy of Willy, Sal, and the Boys, and made its way up the eager, fertile nostrils of patrons at clubs and bars throughout South Florida and the rest of the country.

In Miami, there were a few clubs known for drugs, music, dancing, and good times, but few could compete with the Mutiny, which straddled Biscayne Bay Boulevard.

The Mutiny first opened in 1968 under the name Sailboat Bay Apartments in what had already been declared the Coconut Grove Historic District. Coconut Grove had emerged from being a bucolic, sleepy community to being one of the city's most vibrant neighborhoods. Thick tropical vegetation, many beautiful homes, and an idyllic harbor dotted with sailboats made "the Grove" one of the city's most iconic settings.

The Mutiny name was first associated with a private club on the property, which overlooked the bay. In 1976, when the venue's apartments were converted to hotel units, it became the Mutiny Hotel. The club on the ground floor became the major draw. By 1977, the Mutiny had become a nexus for the city's burgeoning cocaine and disco universe. Willy and Los Muchachos were the club's silent partners, having invested $1 million through the owner, Burton Goldberg.

The club became known for the cliques of celebrities that came into the place: the Miami Dolphins had a regular table. Since the Democratic National Convention had been held in Miami in 1972, the club had a following in the political realm. Ted Kennedy had been there, former presidential candidate George McGovern, former first lady Jackie Onassis. When Paul Newman was in town shooting a movie, he was there. And, a few years later, when the movie *Scarface* was filmed partly in Miami and the hit television show *Miami Vice* came to town, Al Pacino, Don Johnson, and others from these productions were regulars at the club.

The music industry was especially well represented. The Bayshore Recording Studio was in the building next door; musicians and record producers spilled over into the Mutiny, making the scene feel like an East Coast version of Sunset Boulevard, or Hollywood. The Eagles recorded an album at the studio; Crosby, Stills, and Nash wrote a song called "Mutiny," and funkmaster Rick James often strolled in with an entourage of spangled, hip-hugging, cornrowed creatures of the night.

The scene was fueled by Andean marching powder. In the club itself, with its many booths and roped-off VIP areas, saucers of cocaine were out on the tables. It wasn't even necessary to disappear into a bathroom to do a line. At the Mutiny, sooner or later someone was going to put a miniature spoon made of silver or gold up to your nose, and if you were so inclined (and why wouldn't you be, it was the Mutiny), you took a hit.

Everyone loved the club's staff, especially the Mutiny Girls, who worked in various capacities as hostesses, waitresses, and servers. There were Latinas, but the club's owner, Goldberg, seemed to prefer the corn-fed, all-American look, the more innocent the better. The women received gratuities and did favors beyond the call of duty. Cash was like wallpaper at the Mutiny; waitresses and bartenders were the primary beneficiaries.

Mollie Hampton, who started working at the Mutiny at its peak of popularity, was a naive church girl from Tampa when she was hired as a server. "I'd never even heard of cocaine," she said. "I was wondering how these girls stayed up all night, because I was exhausted by five in the morning after a long shift." Eventually, a fellow waitress put a couple of lines down in front of her. She didn't want to do it at first, but once she did, it was love at first sniff.

The first time Willy Falcon was in the club, he was underage and had to be sneaked in through the club's kitchen. He was an impressionable twenty-year-old at the time and not yet in the cocaine business. The club made such a powerful impression that when he, Sal, Tony Bemba, and others from Los Muchachos started being treated like royalty at the Mutiny, he knew they had arrived.

Tony Bemba was most impressed that the club's chef, Manny, would make for them a large chocolate soufflé. "He used to come to our table and say, 'I made something special for you guys.' We'd go in the back room off the kitchen and he'd present us with the soufflé." To Tony and the other young exiles, all of whom had come from Cuba under dire circumstances, it was an act of kindness that could bring them to tears; the soufflé was irresistibly luxurious.

The scene at Willy and Sal's table was the ultimate example of mixing business with pleasure. There were phone jacks at selected tables; you could have a phone brought over to make and receive calls. From their vantage point at the Mutiny, Willy and Sal monitored coke shipments. When they received word that a shipment of yeyo had arrived safely, they had a ritual. Carlito, the club's DJ, was instructed to play "Makin' It," a current disco hit by David Naughton. When the song blasted over the sound system, the patrons went wild and took to the dance floor. Everyone knew that it meant a new load of the white powder had landed in Magic City. They flocked around Willy's table: "Hi, Willy, how are you doing? How is it? Is it good quality? Is it the same as the last one? Same price? Same discount? Where can I pick it up?"

Said Falcon, "Right there, you knew you had the market in the palm of your hand."

The anti-Castro movement's elite were especially welcome at the Mutiny. The club's director of security was Fernando Puig, a rotund former member of the 2506 Brigade and political prisoner in Castro's gulag. He made sure that veterans of the brigade felt like royalty in the club.

Table 14 on the club's poop deck was the place where the esteemed activists sat. Willy, showing his respect, often sent bottles of Dom Pérignon to their table, which included local legends such as Ricardo "Monkey" Morales, a Bay of Pigs veteran who had been working as a spy for the CIA since the early 1960s. Morales's legend was fostered under a dark cloud of intrigue; he was a revolutionary, counterrevolutionary, mercenary, confessed murderer, bomber, informer, and cocaine dealer. At the Mutiny, his entourage sometimes included Detective Raul Diaz, who was the head of CENTAC, the Miami PD's renowned homicide squad.

Across the table from Morales was Bernardo de Torres, another veteran of the invasion who became a CIA asset, taking part in many covert operations. De Torres had once been part of President John Fitzgerald Kennedy's security entourage. He was believed to have an inside track on who really killed the president, and his own involvement was a source of speculation and rumor. This was a rumor that Bernie himself, high on coke and champagne, spread at the Mutiny.

Also often at table 14 was Carlos "Carlene" Quesada, a midlevel coke dealer who had emerged as a rival to Willy and Sal. Some considered Carlene to be suave, with an entourage of younger women (another prominent feature of the Mutiny) even though he was, at age thirty-seven, older than many and no one's idea of an Adonis.

Table 14 represented the Knights of the Round Table, the acknowledged stars of the anti-Castro movement in Miami. But even they knew that Willy Falcon and his group were the wave of the future, because they were the ones generating the cocaine revenues that made everything possible.

ALONG WITH THE WHITE POWDER, the other main feature at the Mutiny was sex. In an era before AIDS, a generation of Americans was shedding the inhibitions and hang-ups of their parents. New York City had Studio 54, which was also awash in cocaine at the time. The scene at the Mutiny was, if anything, more comprehensive.

The first floor of the hotel, directly above the club, consisted of a series of plush, thematically designed rooms that were available for rent by members of the club. There was the highly popular Bordello Room, with red wallpaper adorned with voluptuous cupids, gilded molding, a canopy over the bed with flounces of moiré fabric, and a ceiling mirror. The Arabian Nights room was distinguished by boldly striped fabric bedspreads, with the same material riding up to a canopy, reminiscent of a sheik's desert tent, enclosing, of course, a mirror over the bed. The Isis Room was based on the ancient Egyptian goddess of motherhood and fertility. The Safari Room was decorated with African masks, spears, and authentic animal hides. It also had a mirror on the ceiling.

Each suite had a king-size bed, a fully stocked bar, a large shower, a video cassette player for watching porn, and end tables with smooth glass tabletops, ideal for snorting lines of blow. Some of the suites had connecting doorways, so you could have a party that spread through multiple rooms and out into the hall.

The club at the Mutiny was not open to the general public. There was an annual fee of $75 and a metal membership card embossed with a mustachioed pirate that made you a member at the Mutiny. To acquire a key card to one of the theme rooms cost extra. These suites seemed to have been designed for sex parties and orgies, which were not uncommon for regulars at the club.

Mollie, the waitress, was sometimes invited to one of the rooms for champagne and yeyo. When regular members from table 14 like Carlene Quesada, Bernardo de Torres, and Rodolfo "Rudy Redbeard" Rodriguez Gallo discovered that she was a lesbian, they got wide eyed and started breathing heavy. "It drove them crazy with excitement," Mollie recalled. "They wanted to watch me with other women and would pay almost anything for it."

In *Hotel Scarface*, a book about the Mutiny by Roben Farzad, there is a description of the time Quesada put Mollie to work:

In a suite at the Mutiny, Carlene Quesada called down to the club and asked Mollie to take a break and head upstairs. "Girl, watchooo doing? Come over!" He introduced her to his mistress, Teresita, and asked if she'd initiate the shy, crucifix-wearing brunette into her sapphic ways.

"I want you to be with her," he said, his rapid-fire voice slowing to a quiver. Quesada watched, seemingly traumatized, while Mollie undressed and made out with someone she'd literally just met—a woman who had never kissed a woman, no less.

Another waitress was called upstairs to have sex with twin sisters from the Dominican Republic.

Hostesses and waitresses went along with these overtures at their own discretion. It wasn't required of the job, but the money was often absurdly remunerative. And there was usually lots of coke involved, free of charge.

It is perhaps not surprising that the Mutiny was a sore subject with Alina Falcon, who viewed the scene there as a smorgasbord of temptation that had led her husband astray. Mollie remembered a few times when Alina was in the club. At the Mutiny, Friday nights were for wives, and Saturdays were for mistresses. Mollie's impression of Alina was that she was "crazy."

"She was very territorial with Willy, making a big deal of every woman he spoke to. Willy was a very friendly guy, he spoke with everybody, and most people felt comfortable approaching him. But [Alina] wasn't having it."

IN EARLY 1977, ALINA REACHED the end of her rope. The final straw was that Willy had a regular mistress named Yolanda, whom he paraded around. But really, it was all the Yolandas.

Alina made good on her threats: she took two-year-old Aileen and moved out of the house. She moved in with her parents and filed for divorce, which was granted. She and Willy were no more.

"I don't think she was done with the relationship," said Ileana. "I think she wanted to put a scare in him, to shock him into realizing he could lose his wife and child. She was teaching him a lesson."

Not many people knew that they had divorced, but everyone knew that they were now living separately. It was a shock to many in their tight-knit circle of friends. Willy and Alina were like the couple on top of the wedding cake, the Cuban Barbie and Ken. People had a hard time accepting that they were not together.

Willy was shocked but also outraged. No one was going to tell him what to do. Arsenio, his father, came to him and said, "Willy, you need to reconcile with Alina. You need to reach an understanding with her and get the marriage back together." Already, Willy was having a hard time with his father, who was losing control over his oldest son and didn't like it. Not only did Willy refuse to reconcile with Alina, he doubled down, declaring, in so many words, *I'll show her.* He moved into a penthouse apartment at the Mutiny and continued sleeping around. The field was large, and he picked fruit from many trees. Most were one-night stands or occurred on weekend business trips to the islands and to Los Angeles, where he was laying the groundwork for a major expansion. Occasionally, he settled in for a dalliance that lasted a few months.

Karen DeLayne Jacobs, known as Laney, was a gringa who had been making a name for herself in the city's Latin narco circles. She was a platinum blond who exuded "class," with a slight southern accent that was a holdover from her childhood in Alabama. Since coming to Miami, she had married and divorced one Cuban and had her sights on others. She craved glamour, fancy cars, men who were powerful and handsome, and loud dance clubs. She was a knockout, just Willy's type (he dated only blonds), and she was open to sexual liaisons, especially those that would give her entrée into the cocaine business.

Willy first met Laney when she became his client, recommended to him by a well-known and highly respected criminal defense lawyer in town.

By the time Laney and Willy became an "item," she had already established herself as one of his most valuable clients. Her mode of operation was ingenious. She had established a network of nearly a dozen flight attendants and airline workers who acted as couriers, purchasing cocaine from her in Miami and delivering it to destinations all around the United States. Remembered Falcon, "I sold to her between one hundred twenty-five and one hundred fifty kilos every month. She had no trouble unloading it."

Like a true entrepreneur, out of her palatial six-bedroom house at 6660 SW 125th Avenue in Coral Gables, Laney conducted business. On nights when Willy slept over to have sex with Laney, the next day her stewardess clients would arrive one by one. Laney had prepared a package for each, a travel bag packed with up to ten kilos of coke that the stewardesses, as employees of an airline, did not have to submit to inspection when they boarded their planes. The stewardesses always kept the bags within eyesight, storing them on the plane in a compartment reserved for employees. Dallas, Chicago, Saint Louis, Seattle, Los Angeles, and Honolulu—once the stewardesses' flights landed, they would go to a hotel, where they would be met by local clients. The terms of the deal had already been negotiated; they delivered their contraband to the local dealers, who peddled it on the open market in their cities and towns.

After these transactions were consummated, the stewardesses also brought back cash in the same manner as their deliveries, arriving at Laney's house with suitcases filled with hundreds of thousands of dollars.

On days when Willy was there, he would sit in his robe, sipping coffee, as Laney did business with her crew of attractive kilos-and-cash couriers, women of varying ethnicities who worked for the country's most prestigious airlines.

Laney had other talents. She was older than Willy by eight years and more experienced in the ways of the world. As they spent time together out in public, she took on Willy Falcon as a kind of project. Willy had gone from being a country bumpkin in Cuba to a street guy in Miami without ever learning the niceties of high society. He didn't know the so-called correct way to hold a fork, a door, or a chair for a lady, or how to leave a tip for the hired help without being ostentatious about it. His manners were crude. Laney showed him that if he planned on interacting with powerful people in high society, he needed to know how to play the role. Willy loved it; sometimes, he would deliberately commit an obvious social faux pas just to see if Laney would catch it.

Eventually, Laney started bringing up the subject of marriage. Willy made it clear that wasn't going to happen. He was aware that she was extremely ambitious and possibly using him as a stepping stone in the cocaine business (she quickly married and divorced another Latino narco not long after they split up). Plus, deep in his heart, Willy had not given up on the idea that he and Alina would get back together.[1]

---

[1] The saga of Laney Jacobs did not end when she split from Willy Falcon. She became romantically involved with Milan Bellechasses, who was a cocaine client of the Falcon organization. Bellechasses helped set Laney up as a major dealer in Los Angeles. Laney had always dreamed of getting into the movie business, and by the early 1980s she was supplying coke for some major Hollywood players, including the producer Robert Evans. Among the people Laney befriended in LA was a New York–born producer named Roy Radin, thirty-three years old. Using as an investment seed money from Laney's cocaine business, Radin and Robert Evans partnered on a movie project, in which Laney believed she was also an equal partner. Evans owned the option on a script about the famous Cotton Club nightclub in Manhattan and was seeking to make it into a movie directed by Francis Ford Coppola (together, Evans and Coppola had created *The Godfather*, the highest-grossing movie of all time). When Radin and Evans set up the project at a major studio, Laney was cut out. She became enraged, and, in May 1983, hired a team of hit men to murder Roy Radin. The case went unsolved for years, but eventually Laney was found guilty of second-degree murder and kidnapping. This verdict came at a time when she was the suspect in another murder—the killing of her most recent husband, a cocaine smuggler named Larry Greenberger. For the Radin murder, Laney Jacobs Greenberger was sentenced to life in prison with no parole.

As Willy made the rounds in Miami's social circles with an assortment of blonds on his arm, Alina did not sit idle. She also was dating during this period.

That summer, Alina briefly dated a Miami cop. Many suspected that this was a strategy to rock Willy and his world. Willy was startled but acted as if he wasn't bothered. That relationship soon ran its course; Alina and the cop split up. The next person Alina began dating was even more of a shock.

Some people thought of Carlene Quesada, one of the regulars at table 14 at the Mutiny, as a rival of the Falcon organization. Willy did not. In terms of weight, Quesada was small time compared with Los Muchachos. But he had an outsize reputation in Miami Cuban circles as a wheeler and dealer. He lorded over table 14 at the Mutiny, and he had a crew of younger bodyguards and dealers who thought he was a prince of the city.

No one knows when Alina first connected with Quesada, but word of their pairing sent a ripple of concern through the Cuban narco world. Dating someone who is considered a rival of your ex-husband in what was becoming viewed increasingly as a volatile and violent business seemed like a risky undertaking. Plus, Quesada was nobody's idea of a physically beautiful specimen. He was older, with thinning hair and a look that did not draw attention in a crowd. Why would Alina Falcon, a woman known for her attractiveness and stature, be hanging out with an average-looking, middle-aged man like Carlene Quesada?

Many people heard the rumors and didn't believe it. Alina and Quesada were cautious enough to keep it out of the Mutiny or other clubs where their being a romantic item would ruffle feathers. On the other hand, they didn't hide it. "They were definitely together," said Humberto "Bert" Becerra, who was Quesada's bodyguard, business partner, and roommate. "I sometimes would pick her up and bring her to our house and take her back to her car. She didn't want to be seen pulling up and parking in front of the house."

Quesada and Becerra lived at 1725 SW Sixteenth Street in a house they dubbed Casa Lola. It was a modest two-story structure that had become a crossroads for all kinds of political and criminal shenanigans, as well as late-night parties that continued into the wee hours of the following morning. Alina Falcon was rarely at these parties; her relationship with Carlene was more of a surreptitious affair that took place behind closed doors.

Some suspected that Alina, by having a romance with Quesada, was simply attempting to make Willy jealous. Others believed that in the arms of an older man she was able to confide in, she found levels of maturity and support that were comforting.

From friends, Willy heard about the relationship. Another thing that he heard about, from contacts in law enforcement, was that Quesada's house—Casa Lola—was under surveillance by detectives from the Miami-Dade drug task force.

As part of his divorce settlement, Falcon had the right to see his daughter on weekends. It was on those occasions that he and Alina had their only contact. One Saturday, when Willy came by Alina's parents' house to pick up his daughter, he told her, "Hey, you better be careful with that new boyfriend of yours. His house is under twenty-four-hour surveillance. You don't wanna be there when a raid goes down."

Alina said nothing, but she got the message.[2]

Willy and Alina's dating life both fascinated and saddened their social circle. Why were these two beautiful people, junior high sweethearts who clearly belonged together, torturing each other with a parade of inferior mates? Even they, eventually, tired of their antics.

At one Sunday brunch at a restaurant in the Grove, Willy was there with a date, and, purely by chance, Alina was there with her latest suitor. They glanced at one another as if they couldn't care less, but really, they both suffered in silence every time they saw or heard about the other's love life. It was part of a charade that had been ongoing for months.

Willy got up to use the bathroom. When he came out of the men's room, unexpectedly, Alina was there. Suddenly, she grabbed him by the balls and whispered, "When are you gonna stop this bullshit and come back to your wife and daughter?" She let go of his balls and went back to her table.

Not long after that, in December, they went to City Hall and remarried—no ceremony, no party, no announcements to the public. It was as if the divorce had never happened. They had been apart for less than a year.

---

[2] Beginning in 1981, as part of an investigation that included surveillance of Casa Lola—a case that became known as Operation Tic-Talk because agents planted a listening device in a wall clock at Quesada's home—Carlene was convicted on charges of cocaine trafficking and sentenced to twenty years in prison. He later became an informant and witness for the government. Quesada passed away from natural causes in 2019.

THE DEMAND FOR COCAINE WAS such that the business never let up. Willy and Sal now had roughly one thousand kilos coming in every month, and it was barely enough to satisfy their clients. The market seemed as though it was bottomless.

More and more, Willy found himself leaning on Jack Devoe, who was a pro with many valuable connections. Willy had made a multimillion-dollar investment in Jack so that he could open Devoe Aviation School, a pilot school, in a hangar at Opa-Locka airport. The school was mostly a front for Devoe's various covert activities, which included, along with smuggling loads of cocaine from Colombia to South Florida for Falcon, shipments of arms to Central America on behalf of the CIA. Like many experienced pilots in the coke business, Devoe believed that serving a dual function as a CIA asset gave him cover if he ever got busted.

Jack had a crew of four pilots, one of whom was Profullo "Prof" Mondal, a former Air Force navigator and Vietnam veteran who also had been involved in numerous CIA smuggling campaigns.

Devoe and his crew were top notch, but they were also party boys. At the Mutiny, Jack was a regular at a table designated for pilots and aviation people, but he was also welcome any time at the Los Muchachos table.

One afternoon, Willy, along with Justo Jay, met with Jack in an office at his aviation school. Willy liked to check in with Devoe to find out if his needs were being met. To Willy, the pilots were the superstars of the entire operation, and he listened carefully to their suggestions.

Jack said to Willy that it was time for Los Muchachos to expand their piloting capabilities. He suggested that they buy two new identical Piper Navajo planes. Willy agreed. Jack also mentioned that he was looking to buy a house in the Florida Keys, at Ocean Reef Resort, which had a landing strip and storage facilities where they could offload product.

At the time, Devoe was bringing in loads of five hundred kilos a month from a remote airstrip in Llanos, a barren region of southeastern Colombia. From these shipments alone, the organization netted $20 million per month, before operational expenditures. Devoe cleared close to $1 million profit every month.

As they continued talking, they both agreed that the ultimate dream would be to have their own large-scale landing area, somewhere in the interior of the state, away from Miami or the Keys. Willy told Jack that he would look into it.

In 1978, not long after Willy and Tavy launched the Seahawk boat racing venture, Willy hired a real estate agent to hunt for property near the town of Clewiston, Florida, in a part of the state once known for sugarcane production. The area was ninety-five and a half miles north of Miami, remote, in an area known as South Okeechobee because of its proximity to the mammoth Lake Okeechobee. The area was tree laden, which was ideal for laying down a landing strip that would be shielded from prying eyes.

The realty company consisted of two men, Butch Reddish and Tony Perez, both locals who knew the area inside out. Before long, they had a piece of property in mind. Willy and Sal made the drive north, through the cane fields. There was a time—when sugarcane was still harvested by human toil and sweat—that the fields would have been occupied by workers, mostly immigrants imported on special work visas from Haiti, who labored twelve-hour shifts in the hot sun. The workers lived in shacks on the property in a kind of indentured servitude, at a time when sugar was the state of Florida's primary cash crop. Now it seemed as though cocaine was in a position to emerge as the most lucrative product in the state, though it was an imported commodity rather than something that rose out of the local soil.

They drove along Route 27 (a.k.a. the Sugarland Highway) to South Okeechobee. After some twists and turns, Willy and Sal arrived at the property on the outskirts of Clewiston, a town of barely three thousand people. To Willy, it reminded him of where he had grown up in Cuba. The area was rural and in the middle of nowhere, far removed from the tropical energy of Miami, without a Cuban in sight.

The Boys were assured that the land was ideal for agriculture. They planned on operating the property as a legitimate farm, with citrus groves and livestock. They purchased five hundred acres. They installed a double trailer home and built twenty-six stables for horses and five hundred heads of Brahma cattle.

One month later, Butch Reddish contacted Willy and told him he had found another piece of land. This property was four times bigger, with some of the most fertile soil in the area for agriculture, and it had its own airstrip. Not only that, but it was adjacent to the lot they had already purchased, so it could be incorporated as one large estate.

Purchasing the property required the usual financial sleight of hand. Willy and Sal had a front company—one of many—called Leachville Investments Co., based out of the Netherlands Antilles in the Caribbean. On business records in the Antilles and a few other islands, it was not necessary to list the names of primary shareholders, the owners of what were known as "bearer shares" of companies. This was greatly advantageous for narcos or others wanting to hide ill-gotten gains in offshore accounts. Which was why, over the next few years, the islands would be awash in cocaine profits.

Willy and Sal worked with an accountant named Shaun Murphy, who was establishing himself as the premier financier for laundering narco profits. Working out of an office in Tortola, British Virgin Islands, Murphy received cash and wire transfers of dollars from narcos and helped them establish fraudulent companies in banks throughout the Caribbean. Handling these transactions for Willy and Sal on the Miami end was an attorney named Jim Molans.

Officially, the entity that purchased the Clewiston ranch was called Eveready Investment Ranch, Inc. The price tag for the property was $3 million. The purchase was financed by a loan from Leachville Investments in the Antilles.

Immediately, Willy and Sal developed plans for the property, which included a ten-acre mansion, separate quarters for a staff of ranch hands, copious stables, and barns for storing product that would be flown into the property's one-mile-long landing strip, a road covered with grass, making the strip nearly undetectable to the naked eye.

To fly in product on a semiregular basis presented problems. Willy felt that they needed a local contact who could feed them inside information on the monitoring of local airspace and the activities of local law enforcement. It just so happened that one of the partners in the Clewiston real estate company that had brokered their deal for the Eveready Ranch was Earl Sermon Dyess Jr., the son of longtime Hendry Country sheriff Earl Sermon Dyess Sr., who was a local legend. In fact, Sermon Jr. was himself a deputy sheriff believed to be in line to assume his father's job one day.

Carefully, Willy broached the subject of making an under-the-table payment to the sheriff's son. The offer was made through Dyess's real estate partner, Butch Reddish. The payment was for "protection." All Dyess Jr. had to do was keep his mouth shut about what was happening at the ranch. The offer was $700,000, plus much more on future endeavors. Said Dyess, "I wasn't given an amount that I would receive, just that I would make more money than I had ever seen in my life."

The sheriff's son agreed and took the offer.

December 1978

The time had come for a trip to Colombia.

If the Boys were to make the most of their new ranch, with its landing and storage facilities (still under construction), they first needed to arrange for the increased delivery of product. To Willy and Sal, cocaine was a people business. No matter how bullish and international it might become, Willy wanted to know personally those from whom he was buying his product. The Colombian Manuel Garces had connected him with major players in Cali and Medellín. Willy spoke over a shortwave radio transmitter with these people, but there was, in the view of Willy and Sal, nothing better than looking someone in the eye and taking his measure as a man.

They would first meet Manuel Garces in Medellín. Already, in Miami, Garces had introduced them to the Valencia brothers, Mario and Guillermo, based in the city of Cali. There was no such thing as the Cali Cartel yet in existence, but the Valencia brothers would be founding members of that organization in a couple of years.

In Medellín, Willy and Sal were to meet a person Garces had known since he started in the smuggling business. In fact, this person had gotten his start as a bodyguard for the organization of Garces and El Hombre Marlboro back in the 1960s. His name was Pablo Escobar.

The name meant little to Willy and Sal, except that Escobar had risen to be recognized as the current premier narco boss in Medellín.

They traveled to Colombia under false identities. In Miami, an international city with an emphasis on South America and the Caribbean, the making of false IDs was a booming business in the underworld. Willy was introduced to a barber who had a barbershop on Calle Ocho. The barber had once worked for the US government and still had contacts who could supply him with everything from birth certificates and passports to voter registration cards and social security numbers.

Using false identities had become a necessity. Earlier that year, Willy had heard from a contact inside the Dade County police department that the drug task force, headed by Detective Raul Diaz, had obtained warrants to plant a recording device at a stash house of Willy and Sal's in the neighborhood of Fontainebleau Park. Supposedly, Diaz was on to Willy Falcon as one of the city's biggest suppliers of cocaine. As a result, the Boys became more cautious. They changed their stash houses and used different company cars. They used only public phones and beepers, until they transitioned to a two-way radio communications system, so that they weren't using public phones either. They rented new apartments under an assortment of false identities.

Willy and Sal traveled to Medellín under the names Wilfredo Vargas and Angelo Maretto. Neither of them had traveled outside the United States since their arrival as Cuban exiles. The trip felt like a monumental adventure, in which they were possibly taking their cocaine business to new and unprecedented heights.

They brought with them a member of the crew named Tony Fandino. A cousin of Sal's wife, Tony fit the definition of family, which is how Willy preferred to structure his business. In theory, family could be trusted.

Tony was a long-distance shortwave radio fanatic. He was the one who had designed a communications system for Los Muchachos. Using different radio frequencies, Willy and Sal were able to communicate overseas without being tracked by law enforcement. A week earlier, Willy had shipped shortwave radio equipment to Medellín, where he, Sal, and Tony Fandino intended to deliver the equipment to their partners in Colombia and show them how to use it.

They arrived at Medellín international airport and were met by Manuel Garces and a Colombian customs agent. The agent stamped their passports and led them through customs, bypassing any and all lines. It was two o'clock in the afternoon when they arrived at the Continental Hotel in Medellín. They dropped their bags and went to Garces's business office, where they retrieved the shortwave equipment they had shipped earlier.

Willy, Sal, and Tony Fandino hooked up a portion of the radio equipment right there in Garces's office. Fandino went to the roof of the building and set up an antenna; then, back in the office, he placed the receiver on a desk and calibrated the frequencies. Fandino called his brother, Ray, back in Miami. Immediately, his brother's voice came over the frequency, loud and clear. Manuel

Garces was impressed. This mode of communication did not yet exist in the narco business in Colombia.

"Pablo is going to love this," he said to the Boys. Then he cautioned them, "Remember, don't tell Escobar that you're doing business with the Valencia brothers in Cali. And don't tell the Cali people that you're doing business with Escobar." Manuel had explained to Willy and Sal that it was better that the two major cocaine groups believed they were engaged in an exclusive arrangement with the Cubans from Miami.

That evening, Manuel took them to a fancy restaurant in an affluent part of the city. Everyone seemed to know Manuel Garces; they greeted him with welcomes and hugs. After a lavish meal, Manuel took them back to the Continental and said, "Get a good night's sleep. I pick you up at eight a.m., then we go meet Pablo and his cousin, Gustavo Gaviria."

The next morning, in Pablo Escobar's office on an upper floor of a tall building, with an expansive view of downtown Medellín all the way to the city's infamous *barrios bajos* (slums), Manuel Garces introduced Escobar and Gaviria to "Los Muchachos," Willy and Sal. (Tony Fandino sat in an outer room until it was time to show off the shortwave radio equipment.)

For a while, the Cubans and Colombians made small talk, trading comments on the weather, the local cuisine, and the finer qualities of Colombian versus American women. To Willy, Pablo seemed laid back and friendly; he liked him right away. Gaviria was more serious, more business oriented.

Escobar was a man on the rise. Though he had chosen a life of crime from early adolescence (one of his first rackets was stealing tombstones, sandblasting them clean, and reselling them), he entered public life with the pretense of being a civic-minded citizen—a politician or legitimate business leader. In 1975, at the age of twenty-five, he ordered the murder of Fabio Restrepo, one of Colombia's earliest cocaine bosses, and took over his business. The following year, in 1976, he was arrested for the first time, on charges of having smuggled thirty-one kilos of cocaine. He attempted to bribe a judge to secure his release, then ordered the murder of the police investigator who arrested him. Bribery and murder, "*plato o plomo*" (silver or lead), became the motto of his burgeoning cocaine empire.

In Pablo's office, Willy, Sal, and the Colombians talked about the regular loads that they had been shipping to Miami inside the engines of Caterpillar-brand tractors and other heavy equipment: two hundred kilos per month at $50,000 per kilo (the price in Miami). It was a nice arrangement for Escobar because Willy and Sal were selling the product in the States, of which half— one hundred kilos—belonged to Escobar. Every month, after those kilos were sold, Los Muchachos delivered to Pablo $5 million in profit.

Willy was pleased to hear that Escobar no longer wanted to use George Ordoñez as a go-between. Pablo called Ordoñez a "low life" because of his flagrant use of *basuco* and his associations with the "unreliable" Griselda Blanco. "You no longer need to have any communication with that man," said Escobar. Willy had already terminated his relationship with Ordoñez and was relieved to hear that he and Pablo were on the same page.

Already, Willy had informed the Medellínistas that he was building a private landing strip that would make it possible to bring planeloads of product directly into Florida (at the time, Los Muchachos were receiving planeloads from Cali but not Medellín). They were in the process of acquiring more planes. Escobar and Gaviria were encouraged. "Whatever you think you can handle," said Pablo, "we will supply. We control everything here in Medellín and most of Colombia."

The Cubans and the Colombians agreed that any transaction conducted between them would be split on a fifty-fifty basis.

Willy called Tony Fandino into the room to set up and explain the shortwave radio equipment. The Colombians looked on in fascination as Tony explained the different frequencies. He contacted his brother in Miami; the brother's voice was so clear, it was better than a telephone connection. Willy explained how the frequencies were changed each day of the week, to throw off anyone seeking to monitor their communications. In addition to that, on the radio they always spoke in code—"Martinez" was the word for cocaine and "Betty" the word for money.

Willy explained, "Tony's brother, Ray, is paid to be on call by the radio from eight in the morning until ten at night. If you have to contact us, you call Ray and we will receive your communication almost immediately."

Pablo was impressed: the Colombians had not had this capability until now. Tony Fandino set up a shortwave receiver right there at Pablo's desk, so he could monitor shipments and talk with Willy and Sal while he had his morning coffee in the office.

Escobar said to Willy, "From now on I'm going to call you Doctor, because you have solved all our problems." They all laughed. Willy loved the nickname, and from then on he tried to get his people to refer to him as "Doctor" or "the Doctor," though not everyone went for it.

That evening, they all went to another nice restaurant for dinner, and later, a nightclub at the Continental Hotel. They commandeered the champagne room, ordered numerous bottles of Dom Pérignon, gathered a dozen or more beautiful women at the club, and partied into the night. At one point, Pablo said to Willy, "Doctor, I think maybe tonight we have altered the course of history."

Willy thought, *Damn, this guy, Pablo Escobar—he's no joke.*

Willy, Sal, and Tony Fandino said goodbye to Pablo and his cousin Gustavo. They left the club around two a.m. and headed back to their hotel.

The following day, around noon, they gathered the remainder of their shortwave radio equipment and headed to the airport, where they met Manuel Garces. The Old Man led them to a private plane, where they flew a short forty-five-minute flight from Medellín to Cali.

The Valencia brothers did not meet them at the airport. Garces and the Boys did not want the Cali people to know that they had flown from Medellín. As far as they knew, Willy, Sal, and the others had arrived that morning all the way from Miami.

The origins of what would eventually be known as the Cartel de Cali, or Cali Cartel, was, like much of the smuggling business in Colombia, rooted in marijuana. The Cali organization was smaller than that of Medellín, but it was highly organized into cells with a governing body like a board of directors. Whereas Medellín-based narcos would eventually revolve around the central authority of one man—Pablo Escobar—many in Cali had no idea who the leaders of their group were.

The Valencia brothers, Guillermo and Mario, were not yet high-ranking leaders, but they had established themselves as traffickers on the rise. Guillermo was fifteen years older than Mario, who was roughly the same age as Willy and Sal, in his midtwenties. Falcon and Guillermo Valencia had met once before, in Miami, so they got right down to business. Guillermo mentioned that the only thing holding them back from total domination of the international cocaine business was the quality of the product. The Valencias wanted to improve quality control over their product by building their own processing lab in the Valle del Cauca region, a few miles north of Cali.

There were only two known labs in the country that processed nearly all the cocaine then being produced. They were located in remote jungle regions and sometimes susceptible to the activities of the Fuerzas Armadas Revolucionarios de Colombia (FARC), the leftist rebel group in Colombia that was at war with the government. The FARC sometimes sabotaged the facilities and kidnapped workers and managers, holding them for exorbitant ransom payments. The Valencia brothers wanted to create a state-of-the-art processing facility that they owned and controlled through multimillion-dollar payoffs to the Colombian military, which would serve as security.

Guillermo said to Willy and Sal, "Would you be willing to cofinance this proposition? Fifty-fifty, you and us? It would cost you four million dollars to help purchase the land, just to get it started. If you agree to invest money with us here in Cali for construction of the lab, I could produce five hundred kilos, and we could go fifty-fifty on the airplane transactions. If we own our own lab, the cost of each kilo would be three thousand dollars. It would be the best quality pure cocaine ever produced."

Willy and Sal looked at each other; they didn't even need to discuss it. They were in.

That settled, Willy indicated for Tony Fandino to set up the shortwave radio system. The Valencia brothers were, if anything, even more flabbergasted than Escobar and Gaviria had been. Since most of their product was being shipped by planes, the radio system was revolutionary; it allowed the Valencias to communicate with their pilots on a private frequency. It also greatly improved their ability to communicate with all aspects of Willy and Sal's operation.

After the meeting was over, a secretary brought a bottle of aguardiente and shot glasses into the room. They raised a toast. "To the continuation of a beautiful relationship," said Manuel Garces. They all drank their shots of the cane liquor.

WITH THE CONNECTIONS THEY HAD made in Colombia, Willy, for the first time, felt pressure. It was time for him and Sal to raise their game.

Los Muchachos were already sending cocaine shipments to the West Coast. Fifty to one hundred kilos every six weeks, driven by car from Miami to Los Angeles and San Francisco. Cash from these transactions was also transported by car back to Miami. It had always been their intention to increase the number of kilos. Los Angeles felt like a logical destination and hub for distribution. The entertainment business was centered there, with rock stars, movie stars, and the sports world—all areas where the proliferation of cocaine set an example, and standard, for desirability and prestige.

Willy hired two old friends from the neighborhood, including Randy Sosa, to make the cross-country drive to Los Angeles. On one trip, Sosa's codriver couldn't make it. Being a hands-on boss, Willy offered to make the trip.

It was a leisurely drive along Interstate 10, through Louisiana, Texas, New Mexico, and Arizona, among other states. One hundred kilos were loaded into a compartment in the back of the vehicle. They never drove above the speed limit, made illegal turns, or did anything that would give police a reason to pull them over. They carried false IDs, in case they were stopped.

In LA, they stayed at the recently constructed Bonaventure Hotel, a glass tower located downtown. From a floor high in the hotel, Willy looked out at one of the least impressive downtowns of a major American city. LA sprawled as far as the eye could see. Willy liked the place—the weather, the women, the beaches. But he could not stand that the city closed down around 1:30 a.m. Even so, in LA, people started using their coke early in the day. Since he had been coming there over the last year, Willy had begun to realize that the City of Angels was an important marketplace for his product.

At the time, Los Muchachos had ten clients in Los Angeles and two in San Francisco. Willy met with his primary client in California, an old friend he had gone to school with back in Miami who had relocated to LA. The client had clients of his own in Southern California and north in the San Francisco Bay Area who could hardly keep up with the demand.

Willy returned to Miami, realizing that the West Coast connection was being underutilized. He and Sal had a conversation about it and decided that the smart move would be to enlist a trusted associate—in this case, Jojo Brito, a Cuban homeboy from Little Havana—and relocate him to Los Angeles. Jojo (pronounced by the Cubans as "Yoyo"), born in Santiago de Las Vegas, Cuba, had worked with Willy in the construction business as a teenager, busting his butt to make a modest living. He was ready to move up in the world.

Jojo's move west would be financed by the organization. He was to find a nice place to live, buy a car or two, and get to know the area. It was a tried-and-true strategy of the American underworld: expand your reach by sending forth operatives to gather intelligence and make friends. Initially, Jojo wouldn't even be involved in the selling of cocaine. He was merely an emissary whose job it was to establish a beachhead in LA, so that when Los Muchachos made the Big Move, started importing major weight, Jojo would be their local expert, with an understanding of the lay of the land.

Meanwhile, there was work to be done closer to home. Plans for Eveready Ranch in Clewiston were moving full steam ahead. Willy and Sal constructed an eight-bedroom, twelve-room house on the property. It included a built-in pool and recreational facilities for dirt-bike riding, a shooting range for target practice and arms training, an obstacle course, and plenty of land for horseback riding and hunting on the property. The landing strip and storage facilities were ready to go. All that remained was a concrete, binding deal with Sermon Dyess Jr., the sheriff's son, who was the key to making sure the Boys could receive loads by air and conduct activities on the ground without being bothered by local authorities.

Already, Dyess had taken a $700,000 under-the-table payment. This gave the Boys reason to hope that he could be enlisted in a more involved way as a troubleshooter, facilitator, and local overseer—a partner, basically, with skin in the game in the dirty business of cocaine smuggling.

4

VIVA LAS VEGAS

THE VIDEO CANARY CASE WAS a hoot. In April 1979, law enforcement threw out a net so broad that it roped in all manner of shellfish, crustaceans, octopi, sharks, viperfish, firefly squid, stingrays, and square grouper. All in all, seventy-two people were arrested across the city of Miami and charged with conspiracy to distribute or sell cocaine. Among those indicted were Willy Falcon and Sal Magluta.

The investigation had been spearheaded by the Miami/Metro-Dade police and was the result of numerous wiretaps, including one at a Los Muchachos stash house at the Fontainebleau Park apartments.

Willy was arrested at his home in Coral Gables by Detective Raul Diaz. He knew Diaz well from the Mutiny, where the detective sometimes sat at table 14 with Monkey Morales, who turned out to be one of his informants.

Falcon was taken to the Dade County jail and arraigned that afternoon. He pleaded not guilty to the charge of conspiracy to distribute cocaine. He was released on $25,000 bond.

Afterward, the nucleus of Los Muchachos gathered at Willy's house. Ramiro Moedano, who had been with the group from the beginning, asked Willy, "What are we going to do now?"

"We are going to continue doing the same thing," said Falcon.

The arrests made the front page of the *Miami Herald*. For the first time, the names of Falcon and Magluta were in the media associated with the cocaine business. Willy felt that it was important to show everyone connected with his organization—workers, clients, and even partners in Colombia—that everything was okay and no one was going to panic.

At the time of Willy's arrest, Sal was in Panama, where he had been exploring a new route to smuggle product from a source in Bolivia. After talking with Willy and being assured that he would likely be released on bond, he flew back from Panama to Tijuana, Mexico, where he crossed the border into the United

States. Together with Randy Sosa, he drove back to Miami and turned himself in. He was released on $20,000 bond.

The case seemed like a fishing expedition on the part of Detective Diaz, who was busy on other major investigations at the time. The sheer number of defendants guaranteed that the prosecution would lack focus, and that many of the accused would slip through the net. Besides, the indictment contained no indication that law enforcement understood the role of Falcon and Magluta as overseers of a massive smuggling operation. They were facing a maximum sentence of ten years.

The most significant aspect of the case, for Willy and Sal, was that they enlisted as their attorney Melvyn Kessler, a renowned criminal defense lawyer in Miami with a list of former clients that included Meyer Lansky, the legendary financier of the Mob and one of Miami Beach's most notorious residents.

Kessler assigned to the case fellow lawyer Shelby Heighsmen, a patrician WASP and former circuit court judge. As Willy and Sal arrived in court on the day of sentencing, they were told by the lawyer, "I was able to convince the prosecutor that if you plead no contest, you could get fourteen months' imprisonment and five years' probation. You will also have the luxury of remaining free on bond until the process of your appeals has been exhausted."

Willy responded, "Okay, I think we can live with that."

Heighsmen smiled and said, "I know the prosecutor from my time as a judge. Sometimes these kinds of relationships come in handy."

Willy and Sal stood before Dade circuit judge James Jorgenson and made their plea. The judge imposed the sentence. They were free to go, pending an appeal that, in the hands of crafty criminal defense lawyers, might stretch on for years.

That night, to celebrate, the Boys invited the lawyers Kessler and Heighsmen to join them for dinner at the Mutiny. Kessler was a veteran of the Mutiny whom some had even nicknamed "Mutiny Mel," but Heighsmen had never been.

Willy pulled out all the stops: Driving his Rolls-Royce, he first stopped by Shelby's home to deliver his $500,000 legal fee in cash. They continued on to the Mutiny, where Manny the chef prepared a special dinner of Maine lobster, with much champagne, and a chocolate soufflé for dessert.

The resolution of the case had been instructive. Yes, they would need to be more cautious in the future to avoid tails and wiretaps. But they had faced prosecution without missing a beat, and they were still free men. All in all, they came away from it with a belief that when it came to law enforcement and potential prosecutions, they could handle whatever was thrown their way.

THE TRUTH WAS THAT REALITY could intrude at any time. The possibility of indictments, arrests, and convictions was a hazard of the trade. As if that weren't enough, there were other forces that might intrude—political or cosmic forces that were beyond the control of the average narco.

That summer, as Willy and Sal were dodging a reckoning in court, the unthinkable came to pass. The Sandinistas toppled the long-running dictatorship of Anastasio Somoza. It was both a blow and a boon to the anti-Castro Cubans who had been helping train the Nicaraguan National Guard in the art of anti-guerrilla warfare.

More than two years had passed since Willy Falcon first took part in cocaine-for-arms shipments on behalf of Chi Chi Quintero and his group of freedom fighters in Honduras. Since then, efforts to stop the Sandinistas had been an abject failure—at least that's how it appeared. In July, as Sandinista rebel forces advanced on the capital city of Managua, Somoza deserted the country and fled to Miami. The Somoza family, in one form or another, had ruled the country for forty-four years in an authoritarian dictatorship. And now they were out.

For Cuban exile sympathizers in South Florida, and anti-Communists throughout the US government, it was a shock akin to the Cuban Revolution. In the eyes of the world, Somoza's defeat was Castro's victory. To see Daniel Ortega, a member of the new ruling junta in Nicaragua, meeting with President Jimmy Carter, was an insult to the exiles. Ortega had been trained in Cuba under the tutelage of the Castro regime. He spoke of Fidel as a mentor.

The Sandinista victory may have been a defeat, but in revolutionary conflicts—as many Cubans understood from their own personal history—defeats were sometimes motivation for renewed resistance. With the Sandinistas now in power, the tables had been turned. Cuban exiles no longer were supporting a corrupt regime in power, they were supporting an opposition movement of the aggrieved and the displaced. Counterrevolution—the principle of using the techniques of revolutionary warfare to counteract a revolutionary government—was the central artery of *la lucha*. Militant Cuban exiles had been living in a state of counterrevolution at least since 1959, when Castro came into power. Opposition to the new ruling government in Nicaragua, like opposition to Castro, was a cause they could understand—emotionally, spiritually, and tactically.

Since the fall of Somoza, opposition to the Sandinistas' avowedly Marxist government had been vociferous and chaotic. Some former National Guardsmen from the Somoza regime fled to Honduras and joined the anti-Sandinista camps established by Cuban militants and others. Eventually, the many counterrevolutionary aggregations coalesced into an organization known as the Fuerza Democrática Nicaragüense (FDN). More commonly, the entire movement in opposition to the Sandinistas became known as "the Contras."

Cuban exiles and the CIA had been playing this game, in relation to Cuba, for decades. Entire careers had been launched by militant operatives who were determined to shape the world in their image, on the grounds that it was good for capitalism and the United States. The fact that it was an underground movement in which participants felt empowered to violate international law, bypass the tenets of civil society, and, as operatives, spies, and counterspies, engage in all manner of skullduggery was the stuff of action-adventure stories and James Bond movies.

The ascension of the Sandinistas energized Cuban exile militants, who commenced fundraising and gathering arms on behalf of the Contras.

Falcon had never given up on the cause. Though he no longer took part in cocaine shipments on behalf of anti-Sandinista rebels, those shipments were still ongoing. Others picked up the slack. In the meantime, Willy supported the movement through cash donations to his boyhood friend Antonio Garcia Perez, a.k.a. El Guajiro, who had emerged as a major player in the anti-Castro movement. Like Tony Bemba, El Guajiro had family still in prison in Cuba. For him, *la lucha* was personal.

In late 1979, in the wake of the Sandinistas' stunning rise to power, Falcon and Magluta made a donation of $150,000 to their longtime friend. Antonio Garcia was involved in the creation of Contra training camps in South Florida, particularly in the area of Homestead, forty miles south of Miami. Homestead had played an important role in the launching of the 2506 Brigade and other activities related to the anti-Castro efforts.

Antonio was on the lookout for new training territory. At a café in Little Havana, he asked Willy and Sal, "That new ranch of yours in Clewiston, is it big enough for training purposes?"

"It's over three thousand acres," said Sal.

"What kind of terrain?"

Said Willy, "There's a canal out behind the main property that's like a man-made lake. You could simulate an entire beach landing if you wanted to. Plus, there's a shooting range and an obstacle course. It's perfect for training."

The following weekend, Willy, Sal, and Antonio loaded two large vans in Little Havana with nearly two dozen militants. Among the group were activists from two well-known militant cells, Omega 7 and Alpha 66. They drove to Clewiston. The mansion at Eveready Ranch had only recently been completed. The leaders from the militant groups, including two gringos who Willy and Sal believed were CIA agents overseeing the training, stayed at the house. Other rank-and-file operatives stayed overnight at local motels.

Early the next morning, they gathered for training. Inflatable rafts were used to stage a beach landing. The trainees waded through water and fired live rounds at mounted targets. Smoke bombs and M-80 firecrackers were used by the trainers to disorient the militants, some of whom were experienced paramilitaries while others were rookies. That afternoon, the militants utilized the obstacle course and firing range.

Willy himself took part in the landing simulation. He slogged through the water, holding a rifle over his head, and crawled in the mud on his belly. The trainers were rigorous taskmasters. Falcon found the process invigorating. It was easy to imagine that it was a live situation. For those involved in the struggle against Castroism, the thought of doing something—landing on a beach in Nicaragua, or, better yet, going toe to toe with Castro's army somewhere in Cuba—was a fantasy come to life.

That night, pleasantly exhausted from a long day of drills and training, the exiles gathered in the backyard at Willy and Sal's brand-new rural mansion. They roasted suckling pig on a spit and drank beer and rum, assuring one another that they would defeat Castroism in Nicaragua or anywhere else it reared its ugly head, and that one day, they would devise a way to eliminate Fidel from this world. And then, under a full moon and a sky filled with stars, they would return to Cuba, free their family members and friends from bondage, and restore the island to its former glory.

THE APBA POWERBOAT RACING CIRCUIT was in full swing. By now, Seahawk Marine had established itself as a major player in the trade. The fact that Willy and Sal had been charged and later pleaded no contest on cocaine conspiracy counts did not damage their reputations. Powerboat racing was a sport with a long history of shady characters—Ben Kramer, perhaps the biggest marijuana smuggler in the United States, was a powerboat champion out of Miami; Don Aronow, who invented the lean, fast Cigarette boat, had Mafia connections from Miami to New York City. Willy and Sal were merely the latest rogues to enter the trade.

There were four different classes on the circuit: the Open Class, the Sport Class, the Modified Class, and the Production Class. Seahawk had five boats racing in the different classes. They won a dozen major races on the circuit in 1979.

Willy and Sal both piloted boats in the Open Class, which showcased the biggest boats and was considered the most prestigious. Many felt the key to their success was Tavy Falcon, expert throttle man, who raced as part of Sal's piloting crew. The throttle man operated the boat's accelerator and determined the speed.

Willy, Sal, and Tavy were profiled in industry publications of the APBA and frequently interviewed on television before and after the races. The Seahawk brand had taken the sport by storm; Falcon and Magluta were local celebrities.

If that weren't enough, in 1979 Willy and Sal also inaugurated a softball team that became a source of camaraderie and good times for Los Muchachos. The modified-pitch softball league played a season of twenty games every summer, followed by a vigorous playoff tournament based in different cities around the United States.

Unlike powerboat racing, in which it took the Boys a year or so before they mastered the sport and began winning races, in softball they dominated the league from the beginning. Both Willy and Sal were star players. And they had a habit of hiring former professional players to be part of the team. It was against the rules to do so, but Willy and Sal knew other teams were doing it. Seahawk had unlimited resources and was willing to pay "ringers" more than they might make if they were playing on a professional minor-league team.

The desire to win at all costs was paramount among this community of Cuban exiles. If cutting corners would lead to that goal, they were willing to do it. Winning was a zero-sum game. In sports, as in life, someone came out on top, and someone lost. The exiles had been taught this lesson through revolution and trauma. They knew the humiliation of defeat, and they were determined to control their destinies so that could never happen again.

Boat racing and softball games became the central activities in a busy social calendar that continued throughout the year. But, by far, the most convivial time of year, when the families came together in a spirit of celebration, appreciation, and camaraderie, was the week leading up to and including New Year's Eve, which culminated with nights of gambling, feasting, partying, and taking in floor shows and concerts at the casinos in Las Vegas, Nevada.

Willy had discovered Sin City as a wonderfully appropriate reward for their successes in the cocaine business earlier that year. On a brief trip to Vegas with his main client from Los Angeles, he met Mandy Campo, who was an accounts manager at Caesars Palace Hotel and Casino. Campo was a Cuban in his fifties who had come to Las Vegas immediately after Castro took over in 1959. Many Cubans who had worked at the casinos in Havana in the 1950s fled the island and found casino-related work in Las Vegas, which was emerging as the gambling mecca of America.

Willy hit the gaming tables hard on that trip. Campo recognized that he had a high roller on his hands. He made some phone calls to friends in Miami and determined that Willy Falcon was a special kind of customer. Falcon and his friends were staying at the Aladdin Hotel; Campo invited them to transfer to Caesars.

Willy and his entourage took the Cuban up on his offer. When they arrived at Caesars, Campo was there waiting for them. "Give them the new villas by the pool," Campo told the desk clerk. "These are my friends. If they ever come to this hotel and I'm not here at the time, make sure you call me at my house. Let the other clerks know. I want to be notified that my friends are here."

Willy later spent some time with Campo in his office off the casino floor. After they got to know one another, Willy asked Mandy, "Do you snort cocaine?"

Said Campo, "I have no other choice, because when the holiday season arrives, the week between Christmas and New Year's, I sometimes have to work eighteen and twenty hours per day. To keep myself awake and able to perform my duties accommodating our VIP customers, I snort cocaine."

Willy reached in his pocket and pulled out a small vile of white powder. "Do you want to try some?"

Mandy smiled and took the small bottle, which had a miniature spoon attached to it. He took a hit of coke, then another. "The quality is excellent," he said. "I can feel the energy immediately."

Willy told Mandy to keep the bottle. "There's plenty more where that came from."

From then on, Willy was treated like royalty at Caesars. That night, he went to the Paul Anka show at the casino and sat in the VIP section. Afterward, he was introduced to the singer at a private party. On the casino floor, it seemed as though all the dealers and croupiers had been told who he was. They lavished him with courtesies and attention.

For Falcon, then twenty-four years old, it was a dream come true to be given VIP treatment at a famous casino in Las Vegas.

It was Campo who told Falcon, "Willy, you should consider bringing your family and friends here to celebrate New Year's Eve. It's the best time of year at the casino, and I'll make sure your entire group is given special treatment at the hotel. You'll get our best suites and tickets to all the best shows. All expenses will be covered by our VIP program here at Caesars."

Willy returned to Miami, but he never forgot Mandy's offer.

There was a lot to do before the trip to Vegas. Los Muchachos had three major shipments of kilos in the works, and it was Willy's intention to complete those transactions before the Christmas holidays.

One load involved corrupt retired Venezuelan air force colonel Frank Ocando Paz. Smuggling a load of two hundred kilos from Pablo Escobar's Hacienda Nápoles in Medellín to an airport in Caracas, Venezuela, Ocando was flying a brand-new Beechcraft Super King Air 200 twin turbo craft plane purchased by the organization. Another load—this one involving five hundred kilos—was being flown by a different crew of pilots, Ralph "Cabeza" Linero and Nidio Cruz. Ralph and Nidio were guided to Hacienda Nápoles, where they picked up their shipment and set out for Opa-Locka airport. And finally, two days later, Jack

Devoe and his partner, Prof Mondal, flying a Piper Navajo aircraft, made a flight to the Valencia brothers' ranch in Cali. They picked up five hundred kilos destined for the Eveready Ranch in Clewiston.

All three of these shipments would be unfolding in the days leading up to the holidays. Willy would be in constant contact with the players involved, both in the United States and in South America, to make sure everything was in place.

At the same time, it was party season for Los Muchachos and their families. It all began with Alina Falcon's birthday on December 24, which would be celebrated with a large-scale party to be held at Willy's parents' house in Coral Gables. Then there was Christmas Day, with the unveiling of lavish presents from Willy to his wife, daughter, and selected friends. On December 28, there was another party for the birthday of Sal's wife, Isabel. Everyone was invited—more food, booze, and presents.

All of this was a prelude to the main event, when the families of Willy, Sal, and Tavy would depart on December 28 for Las Vegas to celebrate the new year. And if all that were not enough, on January 4 they continued from Vegas to Vail, Colorado, for a week of skiing, saunas, shopping, and relaxation at a condominium they had purchased for the occasion.

It all began with a shopping spree on Willy's part. At Le Trianon Jewelry in Miami, Falcon purchased a necklace and diamond ring for Alina that totaled $125,000. He also bought gifts for his parents and daughter totaling another $70,000 or so.

For the trip to Vegas, Willy needed to pick up a tuxedo and various suits from the Franco B Miracle Mile clothing store in Coral Gables. He always ordered weeks in advance—five Brioni suits with matching shirts, ties, shoes, and belts. The tuxedo was custom fit and would be worn one time at the New Year's Eve party, then stored in a closet. The following year, Willy would likely purchase a whole new tuxedo.

Preparations for Alina's party started in early December. It was supposed to be a surprise. Plotting with his parents, Willy arranged for four different smoking pits in the yard to cook the *lechon*. There would be unlimited amounts of food and drink, and party gifts for everyone. For entertainment, Willy hired the band of Hansel and Raul, two Cuban singers from the New York band Charanga '76 who had recently relocated to Miami and established themselves as one of the city's best party bands.

With all the shopping and preparations, Willy still found time to duck into the shortwave transmitter room he had established in his house. On the radio, he communicated with Gustavo Gaviria in Medellín and Mario Valencia in Cali, who were overseeing the cocaine shipments on their ends. Willy was in constant communication with Jack Devoe and Ralph Linero, his pilots, following up on every little detail, acting as a go-between and coordinator for all parties involved.

On December 17, Willy received word from Frank Ocando Paz that the shipment from Caracas had landed safely at Opa-Locka airport. Willy immediately dispensed Justo Jay to pick up the product and move it to a safe house.

Two days later, Willy heard from Ralph Linero that the five hundred kilos from Colombia had arrived.

The following day, Jack Devoe informed Willy that he was leaving to pick up the 550-kilo shipment from the Valencia brothers in Cali. Willy contacted Mario Valencia by radio and delivered the message by code: "On way to pick up Martinez. Betty soon to follow."

At the same time, Willy had to make sure the financial side of these transactions was completed. He liked to deliver the money himself: the personal touch.

On December 23, the day before Alina's birthday party, Willy and Justo Jay visited Jack Devoe at his aviation school offices at Opa-Locka. Jack had delivered his recent shipments and was owed $1 million. Usually, the payments took longer, but Willy wanted to make sure his pilots were compensated before the holidays.

At the office, Willy had Justo Jay present Jack with a large box. Said Justo to Jack, "The Doctor has a present for you" (Jay was one of the few Muchachos who had adopted Escobar's preferred nickname for Willy).

Devoe opened the box, and his eyes lit up at the sight of all that cash. "How much?" he asked.

"One million," said Willy. "You earned every penny of it. Merry Christmas and happy New Year. I'll be in touch mid-January after I come back from vacation."

"I'll be ready for the next load whenever you are," said Jack.

Willy and Justo next visited Ralph Linero at his apartment. Willy had special affection for Ralph, who was known to all as Cabeza because of his big head. Ralph, like Willy, loved engines, and he was a crucial partner at Seahawk, where he served as a navigator during the races. Cabeza was a wild man and an entertaining raconteur, with outrageous stories about his career as a pilot and smuggler of contraband.

Ralph was thrilled to receive his $1 million before the holidays. He and Willy wished each other well and pledged even bigger and better things for the new year.

The trip to Vegas was one for the ages. Mandy Campo rolled out the red carpet for Willy and Los Muchachos, who arrived in Vegas by private jet and were picked up at the airport by limousines sent by Campo.

They checked into the hotel using false names and fraudulent passports, but when Willy and Alina arrived at their suite, written in light and projected onto the room's curtain were the words: WELCOME TO CAESARS PALACE, WILLY FALCON.

Upon arriving at the hotel, Willy received the exciting news that they would be joined by none other than Pablo Escobar and his wife, Maria Victoria.

Willy had invited Escobar months earlier, but Pablo had been unsure whether he would be able to make the trip. Willy was excited. Pablo's presence showed a major level of commitment to his partnership with the Cubans from Miami.

Not many people in the United States knew anything about Pablo Escobar. Willy explained to Mandy Campo that Escobar was an important "business-man" from Colombia and should be accorded all of the many courtesies Campo had bestowed on Willy, Sal, Tavy, and their companions.

Campo got the message. He put Escobar and his wife in an executive suite on the same wing as the others.

The usual routine during the day was that the wives would go shopping and the men would hit the gambling tables. Willy had an account at the casino with a balance of $500,000 under the name Martin Costaño. He played mostly baccarat and blackjack and was up $125,000 after the first day. Pablo did not gamble much, but he liked to watch and take in the atmosphere.

At night, they ate at the best restaurants on the Vegas Strip and went to numerous shows: Wayne Newton, Gladys Knight and the Pips, Kool and the Gang, Siegfried and Roy.

At first, Pablo was reticent. "I don't think he likes us," Sal said to Willy.

"Naw," said Willy, "he likes us. He's just shy."

Eventually, Escobar began to warm up to the Cubans. Every day around noon, they met at the hotel sauna for a steam, shave, detox, and a massage. They talked about many things: business, sports, and politics. Willy learned that Pablo was very ambitious: the Colombian talked about using his riches to improve the plight of poor people in Medellín. "With all this money," he said, "maybe we can make a difference." Willy was impressed; Escobar seemed to have a plan for what to do with his newfound power and riches.

Escobar talked about his massive new processing lab called Tranquilandia, located in the Amazon basin region of Llanos. Cocaine base was flown in from Bolivia and Peru; Tranquilandia had its own landing strip and the capacity to churn out more bricks of cocaine than any other lab yet constructed. Pablo also talked enthusiastically about his new home, Hacienda Nápoles, located on nearly eight square miles of land in the department of Antioquia, in the middle of the country. On the property, Escobar had built a Spanish colonial estate, along with a Formula 1 racetrack, a private bullring, and a zoo stocked with wild animals from different continents around the world, including elephants, antelope, giraffes, and a hippopotamus.

The New Year's Eve party at Caesars Palace was outstanding. Food, drink, and dancing until seven in the morning. Willy stumbled from the party back out onto the casino floor. He was hooked on baccarat, a game he had only recently learned. This time, he didn't do so well, losing most of what he had won—and then some. He didn't care. He was having a great time.

On January 2, Pablo and his wife headed back to Medellín. Willy and Sal concluded that the trip had been invaluable bonding time for them and the man who had emerged as the single-most-significant cocaine supplier in the world.

Later that day, Willy was approached by his brother, Tavy. Throughout their days in Vegas, Tavy had been cut out of most of the business conversations. Willy, Sal, and Pablo would go off to the sauna to talk turkey and Tavy was expected to accompany the women on their shopping sprees. Tavy took it as an insult and let his brother know.

"Willy, you know I work hard at KS&W and Seahawk, keeping the books, staying on top of everything. Don't you think it's time I was rewarded and given a partnership in Los Muchachos?"

Willy sighed. He and Tavy had had this conversation numerous times before. "Tavy, I told you, I made a promise to our parents that I wouldn't get you involved. *Pipo* told me, 'Your mother could not live with two sons being sent away to prison.' I promised them."

It was a sore subject. Sal, who felt that Tavy should be brought in on the business, had already used Tavy to oversee certain things, such as the stash houses. When Willy found out, he was upset. He had a conversation with Sal about the promise he had made to his mother and father about not letting Tavy get involved. "This is a nonnegotiable subject," he told Sal.

At Caesars, when Tavy saw that Willy was annoyed, he backed off. No sense in spoiling the fun. But he was determined that this would not be the last time he broached this subject with his brother.

WAS HE OR WASN'T HE? Only Sermon Dyess Jr. knew for sure. It was time to kick the tires and find out if the deputy sheriff was road ready. Time for a test run.

The ideal occasion had arrived. The Houston Livestock Show and Rodeo, in Houston, Texas, was a hoedown of epic proportions. Since purchasing their ranch, Willy and Sal had become unlikely cattle barons. They expanded the herd on their property in Clewiston to more than three thousand Brahma cattle and two thousand heads of Black Angus cattle. They had acquired so many cows and bulls that they purchased an additional piece of property, which they called the International Ranch. It was a few miles away from the Eveready Ranch. The Boys began crossbreeding Brahma and Angus cattle to create a new breed known as Bramgus, which was highly sought after for public consumption. Selling the semen of Brahma cattle to other breeders was a highly lucrative investment.

Among the animals they purchased and kept on the property was a rare Brahma bull, for which they paid $350,000. The animal was a behemoth, powerful and fierce. They named the bull Elefante. It was Willy's intention to enter Elefante into competition at the Houston livestock show.

Being a good ol' boy from South Okeechobee, Dyess was pleased to accept an invitation from Willy and Sal to join them at the legendary event.

On February 9, 1980, Willy and Sal, along with Manuel Garces, Ramiro Moedano, and Jorge Valdés, joined Sermon Dyess Jr. on a flight to Houston.

They landed in Texas and all checked into the same hotel near the Astrodome, where the event was being held.

Over three days, there was a busy schedule of rodeos, barbecues, cattle shows, exhibits, and horseshoe-tossing competitions. It was traditional for participants at the Houston show to dress in classic western garb. Willy and Sal hired the most expensive tailor in town to take their measurements and create the clothes. They wore eel skin cowboy boots and matching eel skin belts with enormous gem-encrusted buckles. Sal went for the desperado look, all black, with an authentic six-shooter in a holster around his waist. Willy, who had grown up watching American western movies on television and at the theater, chose the John Wayne look, with a suede vest and ten-gallon hat that looked like a chandelier on his head.

To Jorge Valdés, Willy said, "How do I look, hombre?"

Valdés looked him up and down, and, in reference to Willy's indigenous bloodline, said, "Amigo, you still look more Indian than cowboy."

They both laughed so hard they almost fell out of their boots.

At the time, Valdés was experiencing the downside of being a narco. In the years since he had been hired as a tax accountant for Willy and Sal, he lived the high life. To say he was flashy only told half the story. He stood out in a crowd. As Deputy Sheriff Dyess put it, when asked how, upon first meeting Valdés, he knew he was a narco: "All you had to do was look at him."

The previous year, Jorge had been on a plane loaded with cocaine flying from Bolivia—the shipment's point of origin—destined for an airport in Macon, Georgia, where the smugglers had bribed an air traffic controller to look the other way. But the plane never made it to Georgia; it crash-landed in rural Panama. Miraculously, no one was hurt, but the occupants were arrested on smuggling charges. Valdés spent a week in a dungeon in Panama, where, he later claimed, he was tortured by Panamanian military officials who were looking to curry favor with their CIA advisers.

Willy and Sal put superlawyer Mel Kessler on the case. Kessler checked with contacts in Panama, who told him that Valdés was on a fast track for extradition. Within days, Jorge was back in the United States, in a federal holding cell. He was put on trial in the Middle District of Georgia, and, in November 1979, he was convicted on possession and smuggling charges. While at the Houston livestock show, he was out on bond awaiting appeal on the charges. It seemed likely the appeal would not be upheld, and he would be going to prison for an extended period.

Jorge's predicament created a valedictory mood at the cattle show for Willy and Sal, and for Manuel Garces, who had been introduced to the Boys by Valdés.

Even so, the main event was the deputy sheriff. To Willy, all indications were that Dyess was on board. In fact, the deputy sheriff seemed to be going out of his way to indicate to the Cubans that he was ready to take part whenever they were. His enthusiasm made Sal nervous. As Dyess put it years later: "I think the issue was that Sal didn't trust me. I was a lawman."

At age thirty-nine, Dyess was fourteen years older than Willy and Sal. He looked like the actor Glenn Ford, with a crew cut and a no-nonsense manner. He appeared to be a straight arrow, which made his willingness to play ball difficult to gauge.

Dyess had been married to his high school sweetheart for twenty years. After spending three years in the US Navy, he followed in his father's footsteps by joining the Hendry County Sheriff's Office. There were only five or six members. Sermon Jr. quickly rose to the rank of captain. Even that position afforded barely enough income on which to live. By the mid-1970s, Dyess had three children and a mortgage. He supplemented his income by starting a small contracting company and applying for and receiving a real estate license.

After years of struggling to pay the bills, Sermon Dyess had arrived at a place in his life where he was willing to stretch the boundaries. If having a badge gave him an edge, so be it. He was ready to dance with the devil.

But could he be trusted? Willy and Sal argued about it. Willy believed that since Dyess had already taken a $700,000 payment, he was on the hook. Said Sal, "Yeah, but what if that's all a trick to set us up?"

As with many public displays of camaraderie by Los Muchachos, the trip to Houston was a kind of seduction. Willy and Sal would use the product to find the answer they needed.

On the last day of the cattle show and rodeo, Willy and Sal's prize bull, Elefante, took first place in the main competition. They took pictures with the trophy. The two Cuban narcos from Miami were proud as could be.

After the competition, they all gathered at a nightclub to celebrate. They met some women at the club and invited them back to their hotel suite to continue the party.

In the room, Willy dug into his luggage and pulled out a half ounce of coke he had brought with him. The women hardly waited for Willy to pour some white powder into a large ceramic ashtray before they were cutting it into lines and snorting it off the coffee table. Other partygoers stepped forward and did the same. Willy did a line, then sat back and watched Dyess.

He and Sal watched out of the corners of their eyes, not wanting to be too obvious.

Dyess sat forward. With a sense of purpose, he reached into his back pocket and took out a wallet. He removed a crisp hundred-dollar bill and rolled it into a tight little straw. The Hendry County sheriff's son leaned forward and did two hefty lines, one for each nostril. He then sat back with a smile on his face.

Willy and Sal glanced at one another: *Did you see that?* They had Sermon Dyess Jr. right where they wanted him. His willingness to do coke in front of everyone seemed designed to deliver a message: Open for business.

SONNY'S REAL PIT BAR-B-Q, LOCATED on the Sugarland Highway in Clewiston, was famous to residents of South Okeechobee. A classic barbecue venue with wooden picnic tables, booths for two along the walls, and heaping portions of food, the place first opened in 1968. Sonny's advertised its style of slow cooking as "feel good barbecue," and everyone seemed to agree. The place did good business for brunches, lunches, and dinner most every day of the week, but especially on Sundays, as Pentecostal parishioners streamed into the place after church.

Willy was there to meet Sermon Dyess Jr. and his partner, Butch Reddish. It was six p.m. on a Sunday evening. There were mostly families in the place, with youngsters running around and parents settling in for some serious smoked ribs cooked in the southern style—succulent, tender, with the meat falling off the bone.

They were met by Tony Perez, the local Realtor, partner of Reddish, whom Willy and Sal had hired to serve as manager of their two local ranches.

There was a sense of urgency to the meeting. Willy and Sal had just finalized arrangements for two shipments of five hundred kilos each coming in from their people in Medellín and Cali. Jack Devoe and Prof Mondal would be flying the planes. Willy wanted to land the two planes almost simultaneously at the Eveready Ranch.

They all said their hellos and sat at a table. Willy kicked off the discussion: "First off, Sermon, if you don't want to do any of the things that I'm asking of you, all you have to do is tell me, and we'll let it be. I get the feeling that you've been wanting to take part in our operations for a while and make some money. I will give you the opportunity to make more money than you ever dreamed of if you can provide protection for what I am about to do at my ranch."

Sermon said, "Willy, I'm interested in any type of proposition that you want to run by me."

Willy explained that he had two planes loaded with multiple kilos of cocaine coming in from Colombia the very next day. He could have set up these deliveries without the knowledge of local authorities, but, Willy explained, out of respect for the Dyess family name and what it represents to local law enforcement, he wanted to offer Sermon an opportunity to make some money on the transaction.

Dyess saw this meeting with Willy as a way to finally establish a relationship that would be ongoing. He seized the opportunity to pitch Falcon on what he could offer, how he could make calls and monitor state and federal law enforcement activity in the area. He could be Willy's eyes and ears in Hendry County. Said Sermon: "I will protect you and the planes at all costs, even if I have to tell my father that the planes loaded with coke are mine. I will do so to protect you and the load."

Between chomping on the ribs and licking his fingers, Willy nodded. He asked, "What would be your fee for all this?"

"Oh, I don't know," said Sermon. "Let's say, one hundred fifty grand."

Willy wiped his hands with a napkin. He had come to dazzle the deputy sheriff, which meant maximizing the bribe. "I'll tell you what: if you can do those things you offer, protect the loads at all costs, I'll pay you two hundred thousand for each shipment."

Sermon licked his fingers, wiped his hands, and extended a hand for Willy and him to shake on it. "You got a deal," he said.

Immediately afterward, Willy called Sal in Miami to tell him the good news. "Contact Jack and Prof, let them know there's been a change in plans. They will be landing at the ranch."

Everyone was excited that they would finally be using the ranch for its intended purpose.

That night, even though Willy had advocated for the use of Sermon Dyess and helped consummate the deal, he was unsettled. Going outside their circle of Miami Cuban exiles was not something he did lightly. Yes, they occasionally—though rarely—used other non-Cubans, notably the pilots Jack Devoe and Prof Mondal. But they were professional smugglers with a history in the trade. Dyess was an active lawman.

In bed, Willy tossed and turned. His dreams were filled with apocalyptic imagery signifying betrayal and disaster. He did not sleep well. The following day, he prepared for the delivery with a nagging sense of trepidation.

On his end, Dyess had only one goal: to prove to Willy that he could deliver and therefore increase his chances of future opportunities to make money.

THE NIGHT AFTER THE MEETING at Sonny's, on a warm May evening, Sermon drove by Butch's 7-Eleven convenience store on the Sunshine Highway. There he met Butch and purchased some Coca-Colas and beer and crackers. Then he and Butch hopped into Butch's Blazer. They headed out on Route 27 and turned south on Highway 832 toward the Eveready Ranch. They drove by the ranch just to check and make sure everything looked okay. That day, Dyess had called around to the Florida Highway Patrol and the local DEA on the pretext of "checking in." If anything had been up, they would have informed him, as a representative of the preeminent Hendry County law enforcement organization.

Sermon knew that Butch Reddish had history with the narcos. Two months earlier, Reddish told Dyess the story of how he and Tony Perez had traveled to Colombia carrying hundreds of thousands of dollars in cash to make a coke deal. The money was stuffed inside nylons they were wearing underneath their clothing. At an airport in Colombia, the money was discovered by security. Butch and Tony were taken into a room by police. The cops stole half the money and let them go. Tony called Willy and Sal's contact in Colombia; given that no one was harmed, they thought it was funny. Butch told Dyess, "It didn't bother them at all that they lost one hundred fifty thousand dollars."

Sermon wasn't sure he believed the tale. He knew Butch to be a bullshit artist who often exaggerated his stories.

Sermon and Butch drove by the ranch and headed down a gravel road that took them to the Lykes Brothers Bridge, a wooden structure that spanned the L-1 Canal on the back perimeter of Willy and Sal's property. They pulled over on the side of the road near the bridge, an elevated area that afforded them an expansive view of the Eveready Ranch. Sermon had brought along a department radio receiver so they could monitor all local police communications.

They sat and talked and sipped some beer: they were killing time until the planes came in.

Much to their surprise, an announcement came over the radio that a plane had landed. Sermon and Butch were startled because they had seen no such plane. Butch cursed and said, "Wait a minute. That wasn't the plan."

In less than a minute, another message came over the radio—a 10-22, code for a message to disregard the previous message. The plane had already been on the ground and was not landing: "I repeat, that's a ten-twenty-two. There is no unauthorized plane landing."

Butch took a deep breath. Sermon gave him a look and said, "What in the world is wrong with you, boy?"

Said Butch, "If that had been our plane, I was supposed to kill you."

"Are you crazy?" responded Sermon.

"No, sir, I am not. They ordered me that if anything went wrong with the shipment, if the plane got caught, I'm supposed to kill you. And if I don't kill you, then they are going to kill me and my family."

Sermon glared at his partner: either Butch Reddish was lying—which was possible, given what Sermon knew of Butch as a fabulist—or the Cubans from Miami were far more treacherous than he imagined.

Dyess decided to put his trust in Willy Falcon. That night, he watched as two planes loaded with coke landed at Willy's ranch. In the months ahead, he took responsibility for dozens of incoming cocaine shipments and made millions in bribe money.

Along with clearing the way for the plane arrivals two or three times a month, Sermon acted as Los Muchachos' eyes and ears in Hendry County.

One day, Willy and his anti-Castro partner Antonio Garcia Perez, along with a crew of militants, spent a long afternoon engaged in tactical rebel training. Willy was surprised to see the deputy sheriff arrive at his door, wearing his brown sheriff's uniform with a cream-colored cowboy hat. Willy and a couple of others were sitting on the porch, some drinking, some smoking cigars. "Sheriff Sermon," asked Willy, "what brings you here?"

"Well," said the sheriff, "I wanted to let you know that we had complaints from a couple of your neighbors. They said they heard gunshots and the sound of explosives coming from your property."

Willy smiled. "You know how that is. One day Cuba will be liberated. We are in training to be the tip of the spear."

"Yes, sir, I know all about that. And I wish you Godspeed in your efforts. I'm with you 100 percent. But given all that you have going on here, you may want to keep the noise level down so as not to attract attention, know what I mean? Consider it a friendly suggestion."

Willy thanked the sheriff and asked him to say hello to his family.

From then on, they would see to it that their armed training sessions to invade Cuba and kill Fidel Castro did not disturb the neighbors.

5

MIAMI RISING

MEL KESSLER KNEW HOW THE game was played. Since first being admitted to the Florida State Bar in 1961, he set about familiarizing himself with Miami's unique criminal landscape. He was among the first criminal defense attorneys in the city to be associated primarily with narcotics cases. By the late 1970s, his most famous client was Ben Kramer, the marijuana king of Florida and the owner of the Apache powerboat racing team that dominated the sport—until the Seahawk team came along. Kessler also represented members of the Black Tuna Gang, a group of marijuana traffickers who smuggled five hundred tons of weed into Miami over an eight-year period.

In the courtroom, Kessler was an adequate legal representative, but he had one quality that placed him in the upper 1 percent: he was charming as hell.

L. Mark Dachs, a young attorney from New York City, two years out of law school, began working for Kessler's firm in 1978. "He was one of the most charming individuals I've ever met," said Dachs. He said this many years after their first meeting, with much water under the bridge, including convictions and prison time for both men on separate legal transgressions.

Kessler was steeped in the lore of Miami. He had graduated from Miami Beach High School in 1953, the University of Miami in 1959, and the University of Miami School of Law in 1962. He loved speedboats, which may be how he entered the orbit of Ben Kramer. He awoke early every Sunday morning to get fresh bagels for his wife and children.

There was a rumor in criminal defense circles that Kessler was shady. This was an accusation that dogged many criminal defense lawyers, and in some cases it turned out to be true. Specifically, there was a story about Kessler and his dealings with a client named Marty Levy. Kessler had represented Levy on numerous criminal counts; the client was willfully delinquent paying his fees. When Kessler received an anonymous tip that Levy had just been murdered in his house, the lawyer immediately went to Levy's and cleared out all money and valuables before the killing was even reported to local police.

The story may have been apocryphal. Kessler adopted the persona of a free-wheeling riverboat gambler. The thought that he might be viewed as a hustler did not cause him to lose sleep at night.

In the courtroom, some lawyers were pious. Not Mel. He once said to a jury during closing argument, "When you retire to the jury room, have lunch first. It's free."

On another occasion, when a US district judge presented to counsel instructions on an insanity defense, Kessler said, "Put that one in for me. I haven't been paid yet for being here."

Willy Falcon first met Kessler at the time of their Video Canary case, and he was impressed. He had read a recently published nonfiction book called *Easy Money: The High-Rolling, Superflying, Drug-Powered World of the Spanish and Black "Mafias"* (Farrar, Straus and Giroux, 1978), by Donald Goddard. It was partly the story of a cocaine dealer in Miami named George Ramos. Kessler, who represented Ramos, was described in the book as "tough, businesslike, and human. No bullshit." Willy had never met someone he had just read about in a book; it didn't seem possible.

Kessler took a liking to Falcon. Having been raised in Miami, he understood how the politics of the anti-Castro movement, with its connections to the CIA and the Republican Party, dovetailed with certain criminal activities such as drugs and the smuggling of guns. To Kessler, Falcon was a man of action, but he was amazingly uninformed as to the nature of US law. Said Falcon:

> Kessler schooled me on things like conspiracy, the application of different laws, how the judicial system operated in the United States. Later, when we got to know each other better, he instructed me on what to do with my money to avoid being charged for tax evasion by the Internal Revenue Service.

When Jorge Valdés returned from his ordeal in Panama—his release from custody in the United States having been negotiated by Kessler—Willy and Jorge stopped by the lawyer's office to make payment for services rendered. No fee had yet been discussed, so they weren't sure what they were in for. At the time, Falcon was experiencing one of the business's periodic cash-flow slowdowns. The laundering of money through fraudulent accounts in the Caribbean islands had not yet worked its way through the pipeline. If Willy were to make a large-scale cash expenditure, they did not, at the moment, have adequate coverage to explain where the money came from.

Jorge had a solution. Seated in Kessler's waiting room, he said to Willy, "Why don't you pay him in cocaine?"

Falcon was startled bordering on shocked by the suggestion. To him, offering the lawyer payment in cocaine was possibly a show of disrespect. Cocaine was an illegal product. Paying the lawyer with an illegal product—which was, irrefutably, a criminal act on both their parts—could be considered outrageous. Willy felt that he didn't know the esteemed lawyer well enough to assume he would be on board for something like that.

"Listen," said Jorge. "I know Mel Kessler. I think he'll go for it. And even if he doesn't, what have you got to lose? He's your criminal defense lawyer. What's he going to do, report you to the authorities? I don't think so."

The two Cubans were called into the office. At first, they all made small talk about some recent offshore powerboat races that Kessler had attended. The conversation soon got around to the subject of Kessler's fee.

Said Willy, "Mister Kessler—"

"Stop that. Call me Mel."

"Mel. We were wondering. How about if we were to pay your fee in product? Is this something you could agree to?"

"Hmm. That's an interesting proposition."

Willy explained the company's cash-flow issues, but more important, he suggested, he thought it was a good idea because he wanted to put Kessler on an ongoing retainer. "What we are looking for, basically, is someone who can serve as our lead counsel. Someone who is there for us whenever legal matters come up. Someone who can handle cases or refer us to other lawyers if you aren't available for a particular case. We're looking for a trusted adviser. Let's face it, there's nobody better than Melvyn Kessler."

Kessler knew when smoke was being blown up his ass, and he liked it.

"How about ten kilos off the top for every shipment we bring in?" said Willy. "Pure. Uncut. Straight from the jungles of South America. Right now, those kilos sell on the street in Miami for fifty-five thousand a key. That's a lot of money. In exchange, you work only for us." They discussed what that might involve: From that day onward, anybody from Los Muchachos who got arrested, in Miami or anywhere in the United States or the world, would have legal representation in less than twenty-four hours. This would be a local legal representative from that jurisdiction who knew the lay of the land. That lawyer would visit the client and take care of their needs, get them to a bond hearing before a judge, and have them back out on the street as quickly as possible. It would be Kessler's job to oversee all of this.

The lawyer smiled. "You know what? I just happen to have a friend, a bail bondsman, who has a side business as a dealer. He could move those ten keys without too much trouble."

Willy and Jorge sat in silence: Sometimes, for a legitimate citizen, it took them a while to figure out the obvious. Patience was required.

"Okay," said Kessler. "I think we can make that work."

In the legal profession, taking payment in kilos of coke was a relatively new phenomenon, even in Miami. Willy thought about it later. It was like when the deputy sheriff also succumbed to the power of the White Lady and the concurrent riches that it implied.

In the beginning, Willy surmised that he was simply dealing an illicit product like stolen cars, guns, weed, or whatever. But clearly, cocaine was different. Cocaine was more like gold, diamonds, or some other precious gem. Apparently, it was the holy grail, something so timeless and valuable that it made people tremble or brought them to their knees. To say that cocaine had the power to corrupt, to make people do things they might not otherwise do, was like saying that sex was an aphrodisiac. The thing itself defined its own terms. As the ancient Incas knew, the plant was a gift from the gods, and to later generations, its alkalized offshoot created an alternate reality of euphoria and the promise of riches that could turn a person inside out and reduce them to a shadow of their perceived self. You didn't have to use cocaine to be controlled by cocaine. It was a force of nature, a kind of sacred totem, an emblem of desire that had a power far beyond its chemical properties as a stimulant, or its expanding status as the most coveted forbidden substance in the world.

THE TRAVAILS OF JORGE VALDÉS in Panama had opened a door for Los Muchachos. Sal and Randy Sosa had traveled to Panama with $250,000 to bribe Jorge out of custody. They connected with a couple of powerful local lawyers in Panama City, who they hoped might be able to pull some strings. The lawyers had not been able to make it work; Valdés had already been extradited back to the United States to face trial in Georgia.

The lawyers in Panama were Guillermo Endara and Hernán Delgado, who headed a prestigious law firm. Endara, in particular, was a well-placed attorney who was also active in politics. Many felt that he was positioning himself as a rival of the country's de facto leader, General Manuel Noriega, and could possibly be president one day. Sal met directly with Endara. He felt that the lawyer could be a highly useful contact for them in Panama. In fact, he left the $250,000 bribe money with Endara as a kind of retainer.

This was pertinent because Willy and Sal had a pressing problem with their financials. Rumor was that the Netherlands Antilles, where they based their many fraudulent shell companies, was about to institute new restrictions that would have a direct effect on their accounts. Under international pressure from United States and European law enforcement, all the Caribbean island protectorates were being compelled by law to reveal the names of all bearer shares of companies with holdings at local banks. In other words, these accounts would no longer work as fronts for people like Willy and Sal. It presented a major conundrum.

In a lunch at the Mutiny with Mel Kessler, Willy and Sal talked it over. While attempting to spring Valdés from custody in Panama, Mel had been in contact with Guillermo Endara. Among other things, Endara mentioned that the country of Panama was not bound by changes in the law that required full disclosure of bearer shares holders on private accounts. Willy and Sal were free to move their money to Panamanian banks and leave their names off the accounts. In fact, Endara told Kessler, his law firm could handle such an arrangement because it was one of their areas of expertise.

"We need to do this as soon as possible," said Sal. As the accountant for Los Muchachos, he bore the responsibility to protect their assets.

At the Mutiny, Kessler noted that he was a criminal defense lawyer, not a "financial guy." He told Willy and Sal, "You need a local attorney with expertise in tax law and overseas accounts." They thought about it and realized that they already knew the perfect person, a lawyer named Juan Acosta whom they had met through their banker, Ray Corona.

The next day, Willy and Sal met with Acosta in his modest law office at 4100 NW Ninth Street. At fifty-three years old, Acosta, like so many lawyers in Miami, had built his practice around the narco trade. He had chosen not to be a trial lawyer and instead worked behind the scenes in financial law. Money laundering was the backbone of the modern cocaine business. Acosta would never have the notoriety of a Melvyn Kessler, but the remunerations could be tremendous—especially if you had clients like Willy and Sal, who paid a percentage of their business profits for services rendered.

Acosta listened as the Boys explained how they needed to move their dummy companies and accounts from Tortola, in the Virgin Islands, to Panama. Acosta said that he could handle the legalities of these transactions on the US side, but to establish the companies in Panama they needed to meet face-to-face with Endara and Delgado in Panama City. "There are certain matters that need to be discussed in person, if you know what I mean," said Acosta.

Willy and Sal understood. It was agreed that Acosta would handle legal matters pertaining to the companies on the US side of things, and that the Boys would make further arrangements in Panama with the Endara Firm.

Together with their private banker, Ray Corona, Willy and Sal flew to Panama City. Since they were both still on bond pending their appeal in the Video Canary conviction—which meant they were prohibited from leaving the country—they traveled using false passports and identities.

As with their trip to Colombia to meet Escobar and the Valencia brothers, this was another landmark adventure for the two dropouts from Miami High. Both sensed that this move—the transfer of their financial infrastructure from the islands to Panama—was more than just a bookkeeping matter. Though, presently, they barely knew the depth of what they were getting into, they knew they were heading into a brave new world, in yet another foreign land, with a new set of characters, which would take them deeper into the narcosphere, a world unhindered by borders and unrestrained by international law.

Though neither of them said the words, it was understood: they were pioneers. What they had set up in Colombia, and what they were seeking to do in Panama, had not been done before—at least not on this scale. They were expanding the parameters of how to structure a major cocaine enterprise.

Upon landing in Panama City, Willy, Sal, and Ray all checked into their rooms at the Hilton Hotel, in the city's business district. They were met at the hotel by Hernán Delgado. "Welcome to Panama City, gentlemen," said

Delgado. "I know we have much to discuss, so, if you feel you are ready, let's go to the office and meet Guillermo."

"El Gordo" is a nickname used often in the Latin world. It fit Guillermo Endara, who weighed somewhere around 280 pounds and moved with the lumbering gait of a water buffalo. In his fifties, he resembled the Argentine comic actor and television host Jorge Porcel, who presided over a popular late-night variety show viewed throughout the Spanish-speaking world on the Telemundo network. Porcel was known as "El Gordo de América" (America's Fat Guy). His show was called *A la cama con Porcel* (In Bed with Porcel), and he was beloved by those with a taste for bawdy humor and risqué jokes.

From his plush office, with lighting that reminded Willy of Don Corleone's office in *The Godfather*, Endara listened carefully as Willy and Sal explained the situation. "You've come to the right place," he said.

The lawyer explained how Panama, unlike countries in the Caribbean, was not likely to change its banking laws any time soon. The promise of anonymity was at the core of the system. Not having to list the names of primary shareholders of companies had been established as a way to protect wealthy industrialists, so that they would not be kidnapped and held for ransom by terrorist rebel groups such as the FARC in Colombia and the Sendero Luminoso (Shining Path) in Peru.

There was work to be done. In total, Willy and Sal were shifting close to $250 million. The various shell companies were:

- Pilea Marine Services: This company was being used to finance Willy and Sal's construction companies.
- Copane Marine Services: Willy and Sal's recently purchased condominium in Vail, Colorado, and many other real estate ventures, were financed through this company.
- Motores Marinos de Panamá SA: The parent company of Seahawk Marine and KS&W Offshore Engineering in Saint Augustine, Florida.
- Southern Farm Inc.: The parent company of Willy and Sal's two properties—the Eveready and International Ranches—in Clewiston.
- Hassid Enterprise SA: A company designated for Falcon's personal assets in the United States.
- Enterprise Ramadan: Likewise for Magluta's personal assets.

Willy's and Sal's names would be listed nowhere in the ownership of these companies. Guillermo Endara would be listed as president, and Endara and Delgado would be codirectors of the company's board of directors. The sole financial entity behind these shell companies would be the Endara Firm of Panama City, Panama.

It was a staggering transaction involving loyalty and trust. Endara sensed as much and said, "My friends, after you've had a chance to go back to your hotel and freshen up, I hope you will accompany me as my guest for dinner tonight."

At the restaurant that night, Endara was in a jovial mood. He discussed with the Cubans his political career. Though it had not yet been publicly announced, he was planning on running for president of Panama in the next election. He would be running against the current president, who was a puppet of General Noriega.

Said Falcon, "Aren't you concerned that the general will resist your candidacy?"

Endara answered, "Yes. No doubt he will. That's why I've been cultivating important relationships within the American government. With the United States openly on my side, there's not much Noriega can do about it."

The next day, the Boys lined up another important meeting. Through Ray Corona, they were introduced to Gabriel Castro, who was the chief of the Panamanian Public Forces (PTJ), which was the equivalent of the FBI in the States. The PTJ was part of the Ministry of Public Security and operated under the motto *"Dios, Honor y Patria"* (God, Honor, and Country). Falcon had an idea for smuggling cash into Panama, to be deposited in the accounts of their shell companies. He wanted to run it by the boss of the Panamanian FBI.

The idea was this: drywall.

Having worked in construction, Willy was very familiar with the packaging of drywall for building projects. A stack of drywall from the factory normally has thirty sheets, four feet by eight feet, in each stack. The stacks are bound together as tightly as possible with metal strips. Willy's plan was to cut the metal strip and remove the middle twenty sheets in the stack, leaving alone the top five and bottom five sheets. They would then cut a three-by-seven-foot hole in the middle sheets. That hole would be loaded with banker boxes filled with cash in large denominations. The unaltered sheets of drywall would then be put back into place on the top and bottom of the stack. The entire stack would be tightly rebound with metal wiring and look exactly as it had when it left the factory.

Willy and Sal's plan was to ship ten containers of drywall on a commercial freighter from the Port of Miami to Panama. "What we would need," Willy said to the chief, "is for someone to provide protection. You would meet the shipments at the port of entry here in Panama, retrieve them from the cargo company, and store them in a safe place. We would pay you 5 percent of every shipment."

Said the lawman, "That's a great idea." What we will do, he continued, is open a construction company in Panama. This front company will place drywall orders, making the transaction look totally legit. "The only thing I would need," said Castro, "is notification from you of the day the freighter with the money will be arriving at the port."

They all shook hands on the arrangement. Willy and Sal headed back to Miami and immediately put this plan to the test. Using a legitimate import-export business owned by a friend of Willy's, they loaded multimillion-dollar shipments of cash into the drywall and sent them by freighter to Panama, where they were picked up by the construction company. There was legitimate paperwork for every step of the transaction.

The shipments to Panama tickled Willy and Sal. It seemed as though they were devising new innovations on nearly a daily basis.

Already, they had created a transportation system for moving cash and product around the United States by using tractor trailers, also known as semitrucks, or semis. The organization had purchased two semis at a price of $100,000 each. No longer were members of Los Muchachos driving kilos of coke and cash stuffed in gym bags and in the trunk of cars. Now product, and multimillion-dollar loads of money, were hidden in double-wall compartments inside huge tractor trailers. Often, the trucks were loaded with produce from legitimate companies to disguise the shipment.

The semis made their operation far more mobile. The number of kilos being sent to LA increased, and Willy and Sal had begun to maximize their operation in the New York–New Jersey area. They had seven major clients in New York whom they serviced monthly to the tune of one hundred kilos, with a profit of $10 million.

The larger they became, the more it challenged their imaginations. Nearly every innovation paid off with huge dividends.

As the new decade of the 1980s arrived, Willy, Sal, and the inner circle of the group would gather at the Mutiny, or farther down Bayshore Drive at Monty Trainer's restaurant in the marina (where Willy kept his recently purchased fifty-four-foot Bertram Jamapa yacht), and raise a toast to their accomplishments. In three short years, they had achieved a staggering level of success. It seemed as though every doorway they pushed through opened into a new world of wonder and possibilities.

So far, there had been few lost loads or significant hitches in the flow of product.

THE US DRUG ENFORCEMENT ADMINISTRATION (DEA) was created in 1973, during the presidential administration of Richard M. Nixon. The idea behind this new agency was to combine the responsibilities of previous narcotics agencies under one powerful entity that existed within the labyrinthian corridors of the Justice Department. At the time, the primary concerns were marijuana, psychedelic drugs like lysergic acid diethylamide (LSD), and heroin. Along with creating a new bureaucratic organization to address the drug problem, the administration proposed newer and more stringent laws to punish those who possessed or sold these illegal substances. The Controlled Substance Act, passed in 1970 but not fully implemented until the DEA was created, established classifications to grade various drugs and create a hierarchy of punishment. Cocaine was categorized as a Schedule II controlled substance, separate from Schedule I (which includes heroin, marijuana, LSD, peyote, and other drugs) because of its medical value as an anesthetic. Sentencing guidelines for each categorization were equally severe.

The DEA had some significant early successes. Special agents everywhere wanted to reproduce the notoriety of the French Connection case, which resulted in the seizure of 402 kilos of heroin, made headlines around the world, and became the subject of an Academy Award–winning movie. Popular culture set the tone. The challenges for law enforcement were formidable: since the 1960s, drug trafficking was pervasive and respect for law enforcement was fractured. If the efforts of cops and special agents could be made to appear daring or worthwhile (as in *The French Connection* and other movie and television dramatizations), perhaps the forces of government could level the playing field.

As with cocaine, heroin was derived from a plant that had likely been around longer than the human species. In some quarters, its usage was part of an ancient ritual. By the 1960s, the locus of its growth and cultivation was in Turkey, where the poppy plant flourished. The business side of the heroin trade was controlled by the Corsican mob in Europe. Heroin was smuggled from Turkey to Marseille, France, where it was processed into powder and shipped around the world. In the United States, heroin was purchased and distributed by the Italian Mafia.

By the time the DEA emerged from the alphabet soup of federal law enforcement (FBN, ATF, FBI, etc.), major routes for the drug had been discovered and disrupted. Since Nixon first declared the War on Drugs, in a 1971 speech, law enforcement budgets for narcotics investigations had skyrocketed. The competition among agencies and agents to make cases was formidable. In the view of many federal agents, local law enforcement agencies could not be trusted. Given the money involved in the cocaine trade, lowly paid cops were prone to bribes and corruption. The easy cash was tempting to local authorities like Deputy Sheriff Sermon Dyess Jr. of Hendry County.

In 1980, David Borah, age twenty-seven, had been serving for four years as a cop in Louisville, Kentucky. Though there was cocaine—and other drugs—circulating in Louisville, the city was far removed from the major centers of usage in Miami, Los Angeles, New York, and other big cities.

Borah was a local product, having graduated from the University of Louisville in 1974. The only thing he knew about the War on Drugs was what he saw on the television news or read in the newspaper. It was a stretch to think that one day he could be a federal agent in the government's highly touted War on Drugs. But David Borah, to those who knew or had worked with him, was unusually diligent and ambitious.

One afternoon while on the job, Borah's department was visited by a recruitment representative from the DEA. Federal agencies may have feared corruption among local cops, but when it came to recruitment, local law enforcement was still the most likely pool from which to draw prospective agents. The DEA had a rigorous screening process. The theory was that it could skim from the top the best local candidates for the job and reject the rest.

The recruitment rep stood before a handful of Louisville cops and local sheriffs, including Borah, and explained the situation. There were in the DEA at the time 1,964 special agents. The rep suggested that these numbers were sure to increase (over the next decade they would nearly double). The average agent was paid a yearly salary of approximately $50,000. The average FBI agent made slightly more, but it was the contention of this DEA rep that those numbers were going to change. Drugs, and especially cocaine, were a growth industry in the United States. The trajectory showed the likelihood of increased trafficking activity and the need for more special agents. Now was the time for those who were interested to get in on the ground floor of the most exciting federal law enforcement agency currently in operation.

For Borah, the soil had been tilled. Four years would pass before he filled out an application and made the leap to federal law enforcement. Meanwhile, he educated himself about the subject of national narcotics trafficking, an avenue of study that, once he was able to apply his knowledge in the field, would bring him directly into the orbit of Los Muchachos.

MIAMI WAS BOOMING. THE MEDIA fixated on the violence. Murders had gone from 243 in 1978 to 320 in 1979, and the early months of 1980 suggested that number would climb. One mass slaughter that captured the attention of citizens was the Dadeland Mall shooting of July 1979. In the middle of the day in a popular shopping area, gunmen emerged from a delivery van bearing the inscription HAPPY TIME PARTY SUPPLY. With a .380 automatic handgun and an automatic rifle, they entered the Crown Liquors store at the mall and opened fire, with bullets shattering glass and bystanders ducking for cover. The two intended targets were killed in a hail of bullets, and many others were wounded. It was a gangland hit characterized by chaos and terror. Said the chief of the Dade County Public Safety Department, "What we have here is a bloody power struggle among different groups in which no quarter is given. These people stop at nothing. They have already shot at law enforcement. They'll throw hand grenades next and nobody's going to be safe anymore."

More killings followed—stabbings, shootings, asphyxiations, beheadings.

The violence did not deter tourists from visiting, or people from moving to South Florida, or companies and rich individuals from investing in local real estate, or thrill seekers from populating nightclubs where narcos sometimes did pull out guns and open fire on one another.

It was common knowledge that Miami was awash in cocaine and craziness. It seemed to be a big part of the draw.

All around the city, glass towers were rising. Condominiums became the new palm trees. These buildings, and many other budding construction projects, were the direct result of narco dollars washing over the city like liquid gold. As Miami became the gateway to South America and the Caribbean, the city began to resemble Panama City, another money-laundering mecca where narco dollars gave rise to a high density of glass skyscrapers.

At times, it seemed like a carefully orchestrated siphoning off of dirty money. In 1980, as the cocaine business was exploding, the savings and loan industry was deregulated, so real estate developers with little experience were encouraged to invest. A year later, the federal income tax code was revised in favor of real estate investment as a tax shelter. Shell companies for narco operations in Colombia and elsewhere in South America, as well as homegrown narco operations in the United States, began funneling money into Miami real estate.

Willy and Sal were in the middle of it, investing in condominiums, shopping malls, public parks, start-up businesses owned by associates, and pet projects that only a narco could love.

It was a unique characteristic of the cocaine business. Heroin traffickers were not known to have invested in large-scale public works projects. Marijuana dealers rarely reinvested their profits in buildings or parks. The narcotics business as a form of large-scale reinvestment, or philanthropy, was a new concept. The belief that cocaine profits were a legitimate foundation for business investment, civic awareness, and even the funding of political candidates would become an operating principle in Miami-Dade County in the years ahead.

Willy and Sal made campaign contributions to local district and political leaders. These contributions were usually made via cash stuffed in a shoebox or a gym bag, depending on the size of the graft.

Bribe money was often helpful in clearing the way for construction projects. With their money safely buried away among various shell companies in Panama, Willy and Sal were not shy when it came to investing. In 1980, they commenced construction on two eighty-unit condominiums in Hialeah. They were the secret financiers behind a series of companies: World Land Investments, Bright Construction Corp., and Ridgewood Development Corp., at which Arsenio Falcon and Manuel Magluta—Willy's and Sal's fathers—held executive positions. Eventually, these companies would construct three apartment complexes consisting of eighty units each in the Fontainebleau Park area (one of which was bugged by local police as part of the Video Canary case).

Shopping centers were major sources of investment. Starting in the late 1970s, Willy and Sal single-handedly increased the number of large-scale shopping centers in Miami from three to seven. Within those malls were dozens of businesses owned or partly owned by Los Muchachos: pharmacies, grocery stores, flower shops, coin laundries. Said Willy, "Believe it or not, the coin laundries were great for laundering money. We owned fifteen coin laundries. You declare two million dollars a year. As long as you're paying taxes on it, who's going to say anything?"

For Willy, it was a matter of pride. Miami was his hometown—"first Cuba, then Miami"—and to see it grow and take on the stature of a major American city was gratifying. And it wasn't only buildings or businesses. Willy and Sal were always on the lookout for community-related projects to boost. They broke ground on a new park with baseball and soccer fields in Hialeah. The Seahawk company invested over $200,000 to install lights on the baseball field of Florida International University. Sure, the Seahawk softball team wanted to use the field for its practices, so there was an ulterior motive, but they also built a scoreboard, a new outfield fence, stands for patrons, and dugouts. Willy and Sal took special pleasure in outfitting the Miami High School baseball team, for which they once played, with new uniforms and equipment.

In a sense, it was all a ploy to curry favor with the citizenry. Willy and Sal were positioning themselves as the Robin Hoods of Miami, stealing from the rich and giving to the exiles.

In 1980, Los Muchachos purchased what, among family and friends, would become known as their signature piece of property. The two-acre ranch, located at 12000 SW Forty-Ninth Street in a suburb of Miami known as Horse Country, was nothing to look at. There was a single-level, five-bedroom house and accompanying horse stables, all of it surrounded by a stone wall and gate. The property was purchased for $190,000 under the name of Isabel Magluta, Sal's wife, and her sister-in-law. Later, they purchased two smaller lots behind the house and expanded the property.

The Boys had big plans for the location. They hired a crew to clean the property, gut the house, and they began from scratch, turning the location into the clubhouse, or man cave, or fitness center, that they had always wanted but had never gotten around to constructing until now.

Inside the house was a full gym with free weights, dumbbells, and bench presses; universal weight machines; five treadmills; five StairMaster machines; heavy bags for punching; and various workout mats. In addition, there were two saunas, two steam rooms, and two large whirlpools. Outside was a full-size basketball court, with lights so they could play day or night. Also on the premises was a gaming room, with pool tables, pinball machines, and various TV monitors. There were big sofas and chairs around the room, a fully stocked bar and kitchenette, and a dining area.

Finally, and most important, Tony Fandino had installed a shortwave radio antenna on the roof of the house. Inside, the Boys created a separate communications room to send and receive messages from pilots, or their contacts in Colombia, or elsewhere.

Almost immediately, what they called the CMM Ranch became the de facto headquarters for Los Muchachos Inc. Willy arrived there around ten a.m. most mornings, and other members of the group trickled in to work out or conduct business, or both. They had official meetings there twice a week to discuss business: ongoing shipments, payments due and cash delivered, legal issues, client control, or whatever.

The creation of the man cave fostered a further sense of camaraderie. The organization had now grown to fifty or so people. Disparate members of the operation, from far-flung divisions of the business—pilots, stash house people, paymasters, transportation people, secretaries, etc.—came to CMM Ranch and met each other, some for the first time. Before, Los Muchachos had seemed like a gaggle of disconnected people doing business together. Yes, they met at the Mutiny and other nightclubs, at Alina's annual birthday party or community and family gatherings, but this was different. Now they had a place for the inner core of Los Muchachos to meet on a regular basis to conduct business, snort cocaine, shoot hoops, snort some more cocaine, and partake in other male bonding rituals that were essential to the esprit de corps of a large-scale, community-based racketeering enterprise.

THE POINT OF IT ALL was to enjoy life. What good was money if you couldn't spread it around? Sometimes, spreading it around could be serious business, like the financing of the anti-Castro movement, which was ongoing. The movement was being waged on two fronts: (1) the efforts to infiltrate Cuba and bring down Castro, and (2) the mandate to support with arms and supplies the Contras in Nicaragua. Antonio Garcia Perez, Willy's main contact in the movement, met with Willy and Sal every two months or so at the man cave in Horse Country to give updates regarding covert activities on both fronts.

The immediate issue was the Contras. Several times that year, Willy and Sal made cash donations of $500,000 or more to Antonio, to facilitate the many Contra training camps in the Everglades. When it came to the movement, Willy was a soft touch. He always said yes.

Another way he used his money was to celebrate life.

In a way, the success—and all the material trappings that came with it—was for Willy and his fellow exiles a rebuke of the Communist system. At least that's what they told themselves. In Castro's gulag, under communism, you could never achieve economic freedom or advancement. Ambition was not rewarded. What Willy and Sal created with the coke business was the ultimate expression of capitalism. To Los Muchachos, the fact that their success was based on what was deemed to be a criminal activity was incidental. What mattered were the results.

There was liberation, and sometimes a touch of desperation, in the feverish celebrating that became a central part of the lifestyle, as if partying, somehow, could make it all right.

One night at the Mutiny, the scene at Los Muchachos' table was even wilder than usual. "There must have been ten or twelve beautiful ladies with us," said Willy, "and all the guys were there—me, Sal, Benny, Jay, Tony. Near closing time, four a.m., I tell one of my guys to retrieve two customized vans that belong to the organization. I say to the women and guys, 'Hey, let's go to our ranch in Clewiston. We've got the pool. We can go horseback riding. We can slaughter a cow and cook some steaks.'"

With high heels clacking on the pavement, women giggling, and the men slapping each other on the backs, they all climbed into the vans, some carrying bottles of champagne and flute glasses, others additional bottles of wine and rum. And, of course, there was plenty of yeyo to go around.

At that hour of the morning, there was little traffic. On I-75 north to the Sugarland Highway, driven by two trusty chauffeurs, they traveled under a starlit sky through citrus groves and sugarcane fields. Seventy-five minutes later they were at the ranch.

Willy stepped out to unlock the front gate. But he had forgotten to bring the key. Somebody handed Falcon a .357 Magnum, and—*boooom*—he shot the lock. The sound of the gunshot woke the caretaker, Heriberto, who lived on the property in a trailer home with his wife and family. He came out and asked, "Willy, what are you doing here?"

Standing before his group of coke-addled friends and women in skimpy dresses, tight jeans, and catsuits, Willy announced, "I brought some friends from the Mutiny so we could continue our party."

And so they did. The women and some men stripped down and jumped in the Olympic-size pool. As the rising sun began to lighten the horizon, they did some coke, drank some champagne, and did some more coke.

Heriberto showed up to ask Willy if there was anything he needed. Willy figured the real reason Heriberto was there was to see the half-naked women. He laughed and said, "Yes, my friend. Saddle up some horses and bring them around."

The women, and some of the guys, climbed up on the horses and rode them around.

The sight of a beautiful, club-ready blond or brunette or redhead riding in a skimpy cocktail dress in the morning light was not one normally seen on the ranches of Clewiston.

Afterward, Willy asked Heriberto to kill one of the Brahma calves, slice it up, and have it ready for a barbecue later that afternoon.

After the horseback riding, it was around noon, and even cocaine couldn't keep them going. The men and women paired up and crashed in one of the house's many bedrooms.

The next day, they arose from the dead, blinked, rubbed their eyes, stretched like cats, showered, and enjoyed a barbecue of the finest beef in Hendry County.

Sometimes, it seemed like one long, ongoing party with no end in sight.

II
IN THE KINGDOM OF YEYO

6

NEW SHERIFF IN TOWN

ALINA FALCON WAS ATTEMPTING TO adapt to a new reality. By 1980, her world involved prosperity, luxury, a certain kind of status, and material riches too numerous to mention. She lived in Coral Gables, shopped at Miracle Mile (the Rodeo Drive of Miami), wore the best jewelry given to her by her husband, and ate in the best restaurants.

Since the birth of her and Willy's second child, Jessica, in 1979, she was determined to not succumb to one of the dangers of motherhood: the loss of personal identity. She loved the children and took her role as matriarch seriously but sensed that her happiness—her sense of fulfillment—required that she stay active outside the house. After she and Willy remarried in late 1977, they talked about this: Willy's success in the business, the constant demands on his time, made Alina feel left out. Willy was having all the fun. Sure, he could bring her along to the Mutiny and the other clubs, include her in celebrations surrounding the boat races and the softball team, but that wasn't the same as her having her own duties and responsibilities, or an endeavor she could call her own.

"What is it that would make you happy?" asked Willy.

"My own fashion business," she said.

In 1980, Alina Falcon opened Scruples, a women's clothing and fashion boutique at Twenty-Seventh Avenue and Southwest Eighth Street, in the First National Bank building. A year later, the store moved to Miracle Mile. Alina lived in the area and now had her own business alongside jewelry stores, the best salons, and boutiques with the latest fashions from Europe and South America.

Part of running the business involved going to fashion shows in Milan, Madrid, and Paris. Her sister Ileana was her constant companion on these journeys to Europe (the trip to Madrid was emotional, as it brought back memories of their time there as young girls). Ileana recognized how important it was for Alina to have her own thing; it gave her a feeling of accomplishment separate from Willy's reputation as the cocaine king of Miami. They took full advantage of the luxuries provided by an affluent lifestyle—they flew first class, stayed in the best hotels, and enjoyed all the trappings of prosperity. They lived the good life.

Willy was proud of Alina's accomplishments. He saw how much the business meant to her, and he was supportive, especially financially. Scruples, and Alina's other ventures related to the fashion business, were subsidized by the cocaine trade.

Willy may have been proud of his wife, but that did not stop him from sleeping around with other women. Since the remarriage, he had at least been making an effort to cover his tracks. "I liked to go fishing at night," said Willy. "Ever since me and Alina were married, I would go out with friends on boats to fish, sometimes as late as midnight. So I started to use this as an explanation for why I was out late. I would come home with fishing equipment, sometimes with actual fish that I claimed to have caught."

The need to have sex with other women was like a compulsion for Willy. Deep down, he felt he would be less of a man if he did not seize on this opportunity to make the most of his power and stature. On the other hand, he loved Alina Rossique Falcon. She was, in many ways, his dream woman, and he believed that, in his own way, he honored her role as the mother of his two young girls.

According to Ileana, Alina likely knew what Willy was up to, but she chose to look the other way. "Women put up with all kinds of difficulties in a marriage," said Alina's sister. "Who knows why? She loved Willy. And she was committed to being his wife no matter what." As for Willy's philandering, said Ileana, "she never talked about it."

THE COVERT WAR BETWEEN CASTRO and *los exiliados* was a never-ending battle that went through cataclysmic permutations. In the view of many Cubans in the United States, the presidency of Jimmy Carter, a Democrat, was a disaster. Carter was weak, and he seemed determined to open up relations with Castro and perhaps end the embargo. There were a series of political concessions by the US government that rankled the exile community. It all culminated with the biggest crisis among *los exiliados* since the disastrous Bay of Pigs invasion.

On April Fools' Day 1980, in Havana, five Cuban citizens crashed a bus through a fence into the Peruvian embassy. There was a shootout with Cuban security personnel that resulted in one dead guard. Castro demanded that the Cuban refugees be released for arrest and prosecution in the death of the guard. Not only did the Peruvian government not turn over the five men, they granted them the status of political asylum.

In recent years, as the Cuban government dealt with a barely functional economy and a lack of necessities due to the embargo, the Cuban people were pushed to the breaking point. Since Cuban citizens were not allowed visas to leave the country unless they had relatives overseas, many found illegal means by which to flee. The most common vehicles of transport were rafts and rickety, homemade vessels by which refugees set out to sea and often perished in the unforgiving waters of the Straits of Florida.

The crisis had been mounting. With the incident at the Peruvian embassy, desperation took over. An estimated ten thousand Cuban citizens swamped the Peruvian embassy seeking asylum. Peru and several other countries announced that they would take in Cuban refugees in limited numbers. This angered Castro, who felt that Western countries in South and North America with economic ties to the United States were seeking to humiliate Cuba.

On April 13, President Carter issued a statement proclaiming that, under the emergency authority provided by the Refugee Act of 1980 (signed by Carter one month earlier), the United States would admit up to 350,000 Cubans. Carter called on Castro's government to "facilitate the prompt, safe, and peaceful exit of the Cubans" from the island.

Castro's response was to announce that any Cuban who wanted to leave could do so. "Those who have no revolutionary genes, those who have no revolutionary blood . . . we do not want them, we do not need them," he said in a speech. For many Cubans, this announcement came as a shock, as it was contrary to Cuba's heretofore closed emigration policy. Prospective refugees flooded to the port of Mariel, a town forty miles west of Havana, where, Castro announced, anyone could leave if they could arrange for a boat to come pick them up.

What followed was an international chess match, with the Cuban people serving as pawns. Castro took the opportunity to release an undetermined number of convicted criminals from prisons and mental patients from psychiatric facilities. He had them transported to the docks of Mariel. The scene at Mariel was chaotic. Most of the boats arriving to pick up what became known as the "Marielitos" were piloted by Cuban Americans from Miami. They were arriving to pick up family members who desperately wanted off the island. But Cuban military and police officials saw to it that for the Americans to pick up relatives, they also had to take a number of strangers who were being allowed to leave. Along with legitimate family members and friends, the boats were overloaded with riffraff from prisons and sanitariums.

In South Florida, where most refugees were headed, the Mariel Boatlift created a humanitarian crisis of staggering proportions. From April to October, when Castro discontinued the policy, 125,000 Cubans fled the island. At first, Cuban Americans and the Carter administration welcomed the refugees, on the principle that it made the United States look like a beacon of freedom. For those opposed to the Castro regime, it had the added benefit of showing just how desperate people were to leave Cuba and its failed revolutionary society.

In South Florida, nearly everyone was affected in some way. For Los Muchachos, it created an immediate crisis that needed to be dealt with.

The many boats coming from Cuba (an estimated 1,700 over six months) were met at sea by the US Coast Guard and directed to dock at a massive, makeshift detention facility in Key West. This scenic, Rabelaisian tourist town at the far end of the Florida Keys, best known for Hemingway, daiquiris, deep-sea fishing, and some of the most beautiful sunsets in the Western Hemisphere, became overrun by refugees. Authorities attempted to contain the multitudes in camps and military facilities until they could be processed. Most were being given special emergency visas that allowed them to stay as US residents. Many of the refugees simply walked off or escaped the detention camps and disappeared into the Cuban diaspora of South Florida.

By land, there was only one way out of Key West: the long, picturesque Overseas Highway (US 1) that ran through the Keys all the way to Miami. US customs and immigration personnel established an armed checkpoint along the highway to stop each and every car, truck, and bus heading east out of Key West.

For Los Muchachos, the problem was that they had a sizable stash of kilos at the home of Jack Devoe in Ocean Reef, a town located near the entrance to the Keys. The Boys made payoffs to authorities at a landing strip that was part of Ocean Reef Resort. They sometimes landed loads of cocaine at the airport, unloaded them, and then stored them at Jack Devoe's property. In fact, the very day the roadblock was established they had received from Escobar and Gaviria in Medellín a shipment of five hundred kilos with a street value of $27.5 million. Those kilos were still sitting in the airplane parked in a hangar at Ocean Reef Resort.

It was Justo Jay, whose job it was to oversee the unloading and transportation of those kilos, who called Willy and said, "Doctor, we have a problem."

"Okay," said Willy, "*dime.*"

Jay explained that a heavy load of merchandise at Ocean Reef was trapped behind enemy lines. US Customs had put up a roadblock to apprehend Marielitos. They were stopping and searching nearly every car that passed along that highway. Plus, US immigration agents were searching the area. "We need to get those kilos out of there before they are discovered," said Jay.

Willy wanted to see the situation for himself. He and Justo Jay drove to the location, parked, and monitored the roadblock. Sure enough, a team of thirty customs agents were stopping and searching most of the cars leaving the Keys. But they were not searching every car. The checkpoint guards were engaged in flagrant racial profiling. Cars with Latino passengers were being stopped and checked, but cars with only gringo passengers were being waved through.

Willy thought about it and said to Jay, "Find me the three most gringo-looking people we have in our organization. Blond hair, blue eyes, if possible. We divide the kilos into three loads and load them in the trunk of three separate cars. Hopefully all, or at least some of the kilos, will make it through the checkpoint."

It was a kamikaze mission for anyone transporting the coke through the checkpoint; if they were caught, they would be arrested on the spot.

That evening, Willy had invited Deputy Sheriff Dyess and his sidekick Butch Reddish to dinner at the Mutiny. Before meeting the boys from Clewiston, he stopped by the man cave in Horse Country to communicate with his partners in Colombia. The crisis of the Mariel Boatlift was having a direct, residual effect on the business, and he needed to keep his partners up to speed. On the shortwave radio, he contacted Pablo Escobar and told him what was happening. Then he called Mario Valencia in Cali. Valencia insisted that the next load be picked up and delivered as scheduled, as he was going on vacation and wanted to clear his "to do" list before he left town.

"Okay," said Willy. "I'll take care of it."

The flow of product was a raging river that stopped for no man. Clients all around America were expecting their deliveries to arrive. If the kilos became caught in some kind of bottleneck, it would have a domino effect. People could die; wars could be touched off at the street level. Willy knew that he had to get those kilos out of Ocean Reef Resort.

That night at the Mutiny, Deputy Sheriff Dyess drank copious amounts of alcohol and gawked at the parade of attractive women at the club. He had "never seen anything like it," he said. Every time a shapely woman walked by, he let out a "yeee hawww," like he was at a rodeo.

Later, Willy told Sermon and Butch that they were too drunk to drive back to Clewiston. Willy booked a room for Sermon on the second floor in one of the theme rooms; he set him up with a woman who would be paid by the organization. Before Willy departed, Sermon pulled on his coattail and asked if Willy could leave him some cocaine, as he and the woman were going to need it.

Willy took a small vial of coke from his pocket—his own personal stash—and handed it to Sermon. The deputy sheriff's eyes lit up like a demon, and he hurried back to his room at the hotel.

Willy watched him go: layer by layer, the real Sermon Dyess Jr. was being revealed. Now that he had let go of the side of the pool, Dyess was splashing in the water like a happy whale. He was a man without moorings. It occurred to him that the deputy sheriff's gleeful descent into corruption could have negative consequences, but he buried those thoughts. He had committed to Dyess as a partner and needed to facilitate the relationship. In for a penny, in for a pound.

The next day, Willy met with Sal, Justo Jay, and a few others at the man cave to discuss what they needed to do. In an attempt to retrieve their five hundred kilos in the Keys, they had assembled what they felt were three non-Latino-looking drivers who would, in separate cars, transport the coke to the government checkpoint, with the hope that they would be waved through.

The last of the three vehicles to attempt passage through the checkpoint would be driven by Richard "Blondie" Passapera, whose duties with the organization involved transporting product to and from the stash houses. Blondie was a natural for the job—a Cuban with German blood who, they believed, could pass for a gringo.

At Ocean Reef Resort, Justo Jay loaded approximately 165 kilos into three separate cars. The drivers had been told to meet Jay at Alabama Jack's, a fish shack restaurant on Card Sound Road, a couple of miles outside the gate of Ocean Reef. They were to have a meal by themselves, then go outside to the parking area, where their car would be waiting for them with the keys hidden under the front floor mat. One by one, ten minutes apart, they would leave Alabama Jack's and attempt to drive through the checkpoint.

Jay monitored the operation from a distance, with binoculars. He watched as the first two cars made it through, no problem. But the third car, a Buick LeSabre driven by Blondie, was waved to the side of the road. The customs official opened the trunk of the car and discovered nine gym bags stuffed with multiple kilos of pure cocaine.

Willy was driving with Alina in their convertible Mercedes when the car phone rang.

"*Que pasa?*" said Willy.

On the phone, Jay explained the situation.

"Fuck," said Willy. This was a serious predicament. The bust would bring heat to the entire area. They had a shipment from Cali scheduled to arrive the following day. A member of their organization had been arrested and would be facing serious charges. Willy took it as a personal responsibility on his part to make sure his people were taken care of. Whatever the charges, he wanted to see to it that Blondie could post bond and not have to spend a night in jail. If Los Muchachos could not take care of their own—if they could not provide legal succor in a time of need—what good were they?

Willy said "okay" to Jay and hung up.

Alina said, "Something serious?"

Willy groaned. At a red light, he picked up the phone receiver and punched in the number for Mel Kessler.

August 17, 1980

Earl Sermon Dyess Sr. was the spitting image of his son, Sermon Jr. The only difference was the hair; Senior had more of a pompadour, or a greaser look, a holdover from his young adulthood in the 1950s. He went by Earl, and in the thirty-plus years he had served in the sheriff's department of Hendry County (twenty as sheriff), every two years he ran for the position of top dog in mostly uncontested elections. According to those who worked with him, Earl brought a Bible to work every day. He was a God-fearing man, respected and beloved by his South Okeechobee community.

On a blustery Saturday night, the sheriff was home with his wife, Dorothy, in their modest house at 547 East Sagamore Avenue in Clewiston. Sagamore was one block south of the Sugarland Highway, not far from the southern edge of Lake Okeechobee. Around eleven p.m., Dyess heard a noise that could have been a gunshot coming from the alleyway behind his house. He went out back to check it out.

At the age of fifty-nine, he was not armed. It didn't seem possible that there could be a legitimate perpetrator in his yard, but occasionally, the used car lot on the other side of the alley from his house attracted assorted riffraff.

As he walked into the dimly lit alley, Dyess encountered two teenagers, an eighteen-year-old boy and his fifteen-year-old stepbrother. The older of the two boys held a .22-caliber pistol.

Dyess announced himself as Earl Dyess, sheriff of Hendry County. "I'm gonna have to ask you to give me that gun," he said to the kid with the firearm. He stepped forward and grabbed the teenager's arm. A tussle ensued between the sheriff and the boy.

Suddenly, the stepbrother lunged forward with a bowie knife and stabbed the sheriff in the heart. This initial puncture likely killed the sheriff, but the fifteen-year-old stabbed the sheriff twice more.

The two boys ran, leaving Earl Dyess to bleed out in the alley behind his house. The revered lawman was gone.

As news of the tragedy spread throughout local law enforcement circles, somebody said, "Has anyone told Sermon yet?" A deputy sheriff was sent to the house of Sermon Dyess Jr. to deliver the horrendous news.

The following afternoon, Willy Falcon was met at his house in Coral Gables by Justo Jay, who had just come from making a $200,000 payment to Sermon Dyess in Clewiston. "Willy," said Jay, "you're not gonna believe this. Last night Earl Dyess Sr., Sermon's father, got stabbed to death in the alley behind his house."

Said Willy, "*Coño.* Do they know who did it?"

"They arrested two local teenagers. The one who stabbed the sheriff was fifteen."

The following morning, Willy called Dyess and said, "Sermon, my condolences to you and your family. I'm still in shock. You must be devastated."

Said Sermon, "I just came from the burial. Everyone was there, including the county commissioner. He informed me that I am being appointed interim sheriff as of today."

"Congratulations," said Willy. "What does this mean for us?"

"Nothing changes for us, except that I will have even more power and influence to call the shots."

"Excellent," said Falcon.

"Willy, there is one thing. The election for the sheriff's position is in November. Of course, I'm going to run. My old man's legacy, and the fact that I'm running as an incumbent, puts me in a strong position. But I know at least two other deputies who will be running for the job. People here take these elections seriously. I was wondering if you'd be willing to make a campaign contribution."

"Of course," said Willy. "We'll have Jay add an extra one hundred thousand dollars to what you are owed. That should help with the campaign."

Over the next few weeks, two sizable loads of coke were flown from Colombia and landed at Eveready Ranch, with Sermon and Butch Reddish running interference. As Willy and Sal received the loads, and throughout the fall, people in Hendry County talked about the upcoming election. SERMON DYESS JR FOR SHERIFF signs were all over town.

To show his appreciation for the campaign contribution from the Boys, Sermon began supplying the organization with a county sheriff's escort to guide their truckloads containing kilos and cash out of town.

To the citizens of Clewiston, it was a curious sight. A large semitruck with three Hendry County police vehicles in front and on both sides, cherry-tops flashing, sometimes a siren wailing, as the truckload of cocaine was escorted to the county line.

In October, the Boys had a party at the ranch to support Sermon's campaign for sheriff. They hired a local band and laid out a massive spread of food and drink. Sermon gave a speech to the crowd thanking "our friends from Miami" for their support.

Sermon liked to party; he drank and, occasionally, sneaked off to the bathroom to do some coke. Later that evening, when everyone was tipsy and high,

Sermon came up to Falcon and put a hand on his shoulder. "Willy," he said with a grin, "I own this damn county. We can do anything we want here."

As the party wound down, someone suggested they go to Duffy's Pub, the only bar in Clewiston. Sermon insisted on providing Willy and his friends a police escort to the bar. When they arrived at the bar, the sheriff cleared customers out of the way to make room for Willy's group. Willy watched as Sermon strutted his power as a local potentate, keeper of the Dyess family tradition.

Noted Willy to himself: *Sermon doesn't seem too distressed by the death of his father.*

In November, Sermon Dyess Jr. was elected sheriff by a landslide.

THE HOLIDAY SEASON FOLLOWED THE usual routine: Alina's birthday (her twenty-fifth) and the attendant party; Christmas presents and family dinners; Isabel Magluta's birthday party; then the trip to Las Vegas for New Year's Eve; and finally, two weeks in the snow in Vail. This time, for transportation, Willy and Sal rented a private jet, which made it possible for them to bring more members of their crew. In addition to Tavy and his longtime companion, Amelia, Ileana Rossique brought her boyfriend, a Cuban exile named Antonio "Tony" Garrudo. Benny Lorenzo came with his girlfriend. Jack Devoe, the pilot, was there with a couple of employees from his aviation school. Justo Jay and Ralph Linero made the trip. And, once again, Los Muchachos were honored by the presence of Pablo Escobar and his wife from Medellín.

Willy came home from Vail after three weeks of vacation feeling like a new man. The next event on the social calendar was the Super Bowl, which a contingent from Los Muchachos had made a point of attending for the last few years. This year the big game was being held in New Orleans. Willy was looking forward to it, which was why the events that took place on the day before the Super Bowl were such a shocker.

The kidnapping of Marta Falcon had reverberations throughout the city's underworld. Though no reporting on this crime appeared in the local media, it was on the mind of everyone connected to Los Muchachos. *Willy Falcon's mother was kidnapped and held for ransom!? She was kidnapped by cops? How could such a thing take place?*

From the day Marta was kidnapped, some within the group's inner circle wanted to strike back immediately. Though it was not the usual pattern for Los Muchachos to react in that way, Willy understood the impulse. He wanted to make whoever committed this act pay dearly for the transgression. Death to the kidnappers was not beyond the realm of possibility. But, in truth, no one knew for sure who was behind it. First, they needed to get to the bottom of things.

That night, Willy, Sal, Tony Bemba, Ralph Linero ("Cabeza"), and Justo Jay, among others, gathered at Willy's house in Coral Gables to discuss strategy. Jack Devoe stopped by; he remembered seeing guns everywhere, including a gun that Willy, from that point onward, always kept strapped to his ankle. Willy's parents were brought to the house and grilled on every little detail they remembered about the day, from before the kidnapping until the present moment. At one point in her ordeal, Willy's mother—as she was being transported to the house where she was held—saw some landmarks out of the corner of the blindfold, a street sign and some other buildings she recognized. Maybe she could reconstruct where she had been taken.

The next day, Willy hired two private investigators, and they began to canvass the underworld. They were able to determine that there had recently been at least three other kidnappings using the same modus operandi: local cops, a traffic stop, blindfolding, apprehension, and then the ransom demand. Specifically, a person Willy knew—a major marijuana smuggler who, by chance, owned property near Willy and Sal in Clewiston—had been kidnapped by this same crew. There was also a Colombian narco who lived in Miami; his son was kidnapped by a crew of cops. And finally, a Miami businessman who owned a popular chain of shoe stores; his brother was kidnapped.

That kidnapping had ended in death, with the brother's testicles severed and stuffed into his mouth. The body was dumped in the Miami River.

The shoe store owner wanted revenge: he wanted to find the kidnappers and have them killed.

A week after Willy's mother was snatched, they all met at one of the shoe store owner's shops, in a mall on West Flagler and Northwest Seventy-Second Street. Willy was there with his parents, his private investigators, and everyone who had been kidnapped or had a family member kidnapped by this crew of cops. The victims traded details about what they knew. Eventually, a portrait started to emerge.

Based on this information, they were able to find the house the cops were using to hold their victims. The private investigators put a twenty-four-hour stakeout on the house. They witnessed police cars coming and going. Sometimes, the cops stayed there overnight.

After a week of stakeouts, Willy put together a crew. This crew included the owner of the shoe stores, who insisted on being there. Everyone was armed. They raided the house. Only one person was there from the kidnapping crew. Willy and his people tied the guy to a chair. They tortured him until he told them everything they needed to know.

It was a crazy story that would be hard to believe in almost any city other than Miami. A crew of police officers, led by a recent "officer of the year" in the suburban Medley Police Department, had devised a scheme to kidnap people and hold them for ransom. The cop's name was David Earl Rogers. One of Rogers's partners was Jose Prieto, who had been employed as a cop in several police departments in Broward and Dade Counties. Mostly, Rogers, Prieto, and their crew kidnapped people from the criminal world—or related to the criminal world—so that the victims and their families would not likely go to the police.

Having lost his brother in a brutal murder, the shoe store owner wanted to see the dirty cops pay with their lives. Willy thought about that; his mother was still alive. In fact, Marta Falcon told Willy how the kidnappers had treated her well and even checked her blood pressure at one point to make sure she was not having a panic attack. Willy could see that the shoe store owner wanted the ultimate restitution and had every intention of following through. Willy decided to step aside and let street justice take its course.

Eventually, the cops got busted. Rogers and Prieto, both thirty years old, were arrested separately in April by Miami homicide detectives and charged on various counts of kidnapping and extortion. At the time of their arrest, it was also announced in the press that they were suspected in three murders.

Rogers was released on $25,000 bond. One month later, his body was found floating in the Miami River. He had been shot in the head. Prieto, who was still in custody, was moved from the general prison population to an isolated cell—for his own protection. It was likely the only thing keeping him alive—for now.

The kidnapping of Willy's mother changed everything for Los Muchachos. Willy hired bodyguards for his parents, his kids, and whoever in the organization felt they needed protection. He hired his own bodyguard, William "Bubba" O'Leary, a brawny former Miami cop who now accompanied Willy almost everywhere he went, including to the Mutiny, the gym, restaurants, and so forth.

Most everyone in the Los Muchachos universe had come to believe that the most outrageous aspects of the cocaine business—intimidation, violence, death—did not apply to them. Somehow, they were the chosen ones who had been cast out of paradise (Cuba) and were now experiencing cosmic restitution, a life of good times and riches, with no downside. After Marta Falcon's kidnapping, everything changed. Los Muchachos were vulnerable, perhaps even more susceptible than most to danger because they had achieved success on such a grandiose level. Their success made them a target—a realization that tended to take the fun out of things. All the members of the group, including wives, girlfriends, and extended family members, familiarized themselves with the use of handguns. They signed up for martial arts classes and learned to be vigilant—watch every unfamiliar car or person while out in public. Never answer the door unless it was someone you knew. Trust no one, including—or in this case, especially—the police.

To some, the thrill of being part of the narco universe would never be the same. In later years, some would even surmise that the kidnapping of Willy's mother, and its dark aftermath, was the beginning of the end.

JACK DEVOE WAS CONSIDERED A star of the operation. Willy Falcon, for one, viewed Jack as an essential partner. Jack had been there from the beginning, when they were still smuggling coke and weapons for what eventually became the Contras in Nicaragua. With his CIA pedigree, Devoe was a swashbuckling character to Willy. He praised Jack all the time, boosted his ego, and took it upon himself to make sure he was well compensated for his labors. He referred to Jack as "*hermano*," which is the highest praise that a Hispanic male can give to a gringo. Theirs was a bromance in a universe where bromance was the ultimate form of flattery.

In the spring of 1981, Falcon hadn't seen Devoe in a while. Earlier that year, Jack told Willy that he was going on vacation. He said that his duties were being left in the very capable hands of Prof Mondal and also Bob Colquitt, a pilot he had hired fifteen months earlier. Colquitt was a former US Marine who had worked as a Cessna distributor out of Denver. He had been flying loads on behalf of Los Muchachos as part of Devoe's crew for the past year.

One night at the Mutiny, Willy saw Jack Devoe for the first time in many weeks. In the week or so since Jack had returned from vacation, Willy heard reports, from Justo Jay and others, that something was wrong with him. He looked terrible—gaunt and pale, with raccoon rings around his eyes. The rumor was that he was hooked on *basuco*.

Willy found it hard to believe. To him, Jack was the consummate professional. He was CIA, for God's sake, a disciplined operative of numerous covert campaigns. Jack was the last person he could conceive of as a drug addict.

When he saw Jack, he was stunned. Everything he heard was true: Jack looked bad. Among other things, he had lost an alarming amount of weight.

Willy embraced Jack. He pulled him aside and said, "What the hell is going on with you?"

Jack played dumb. "What do you mean?"

"Well, for starters, you've lost a lot of weight. You don't look healthy."

Devoe claimed that he had a stomach virus from his travels that caused him to lose weight.

Willy wasn't buying it. He said to Jack, "Listen, *hermano*, you need to get your shit together. We depend on you. *I* depend on you. You're our best pilot. Plus, you're a good-looking guy, the ladies go crazy over you. And now you are ruining your looks. I mean it. You need to straighten up. *Entiende?*"

"Willy, I hear you," said Jack. "You don't need to worry about me."

Over the next few weeks, Willy kept his eyes on Jack, and he didn't like what he saw. He became most alarmed when Jack requested that one of his cocaine loads from Colombia include a kilo of *basuco*. Jack claimed that he knew a client who had requested it. Willy suspected otherwise, but he kept his thoughts to himself.

A week later, Jack disappeared. Willy couldn't reach him on the phone. No one at Devoe Aviation had seen Jack or been able to get ahold of him. Jack Devoe was AWOL.

Willy was concerned because Mario Valencia from Cali was on the radio wanting to know when Devoe would be arriving to pick up the next five-hundred-kilo load.

Willy called a cocaine client of his who he knew was a good friend of Jack's. The client informed Willy that Jack had been involved in a plane crash in his Cessna. He said that Jack was okay, but he was pretty banged up. He was recuperating from his injuries at the house in Ocean Reef Resort.

Willy called the house—once, twice, three times. No answer. So he contacted Randy Sosa, one of their drivers, and said, "We're going to the house at Ocean Reef. I gotta see for myself what's going on with Jack Devoe."

In the last month, the Mariel Boatlift crisis had finally subsided, and the Keys were no longer the battleground they had once been. The immigration and customs checkpoints had been discontinued, and life in the Keys mostly returned to normal. Elsewhere in Miami, the crisis was ongoing. Most of the Marielitos who did not have family in the area were held at the Krome Detention Center in the Everglades. Built in 1965, Krome was a former military base that had closed down and now, with emergency funding from the federal government, reopened as a holding center for undocumented Cubans. Negotiating the end of the crisis was one of Jimmy Carter's last acts as president. The legacy of the boatlift would continue to haunt Miami for generations to come.

At the house in the Keys, down a private road, surrounded by tropical foliage, Jack Devoe was recovering from a fractured leg, a concussion, and multiple contusions. He had stitches on his forehead, and bruised ribs. It hurt when he breathed.

Some of the injuries came from a plane crash. He had, in fact, fallen asleep at the controls of his plane. This was because he had been up for three days freebasing cocaine.

In the last month, Jack had been on a cocaine bender that was likely one for the record books. He had picked up the habit of freebasing *basuco*, smoking it in a small water pipe. Freebasing *basuco* was like injecting the drug straight into your cerebral membrane. The effect was instantaneous, and the high thunderously powerful. The high did not last long, and the comedown from the high could be debilitating. Devoe had crash-landed his plane while nodding off.

His injuries from the crash were not that bad. The Cessna was wrecked, but Jack walked away with little more than bruised ribs, a slight concussion, and a cut on his forehead that was stitched up at a local hospital emergency room. He went to a friend's house to recuperate, hiding out from Willy, Sal, and his other partners. He didn't want anyone to see him until he was healed.

It turned out the crash was only the beginning of Devoe's descent. While recuperating at his friend's condominium, he continued to freebase. One afternoon, after three days of hitting the pipe without sleep, he turned on his friend and said, "They're after us. They're coming to get us."

"What are you talking about?" said the friend.

"Don't you understand? Are you blind? They're coming to get us."

"Jack, you're high. You're all fucked up, and you're not making any sense."

Devoe was in the midst of a psychotic episode. He pushed his friend out of the way and ran outside. He started screaming, and, somehow, he was able to climb up on the roof of the next-door neighbor's house, where he continued shouting, "They're coming to get us."

The neighbor came out of his house and shouted at Jack, "If you don't come down from there I'm going to call the police."

So Jack jumped off the roof. It was a thirty-foot drop. He hit the ground and shattered his leg.

The neighbor called for an ambulance and the cops. On a fractured leg, Jack tried to run away through the tropical foliage. He didn't get very far before the police arrived and took him away.

By the time Willy arrived at the house in Ocean Reef, Jack had been released from a hospital and had retreated into a cocoon. Willy banged on the door and peered in the window. "Jack, I know you're in there," he shouted.

Eventually, Jack came to the door. He looked terrible. He was bruised and battered, with a cast on his leg.

"Jack, what the fuck happened?" asked Willy.

Devoe blamed it all on the plane crash, leaving out the part about the psychotic episode and the roof dive.

Willy and Randy Sosa entered the house. The place was a mess. "When was the last time you ate something?" asked Willy.

"It's been a while. I can't really walk, and I can't drive."

"Are you still smoking that shit?"

Jack sat in a chair. Tears came to his eyes. He looked utterly defeated and hopeless.

Willy turned to Randy and handed him some cash. "Go to the market and buy some groceries. Eggs, bread, milk. Get some protein—beef, chicken."

Jack protested: "I can't keep anything down. It's gonna make me sick."

Said Willy, "Jack, you're gonna eat something. I'm gonna stay here with you. You're gonna stop smoking that *basuco*, and you're gonna eat. Then you're gonna sleep, like a normal person. You can't live like this anymore."

Jack slumped into silence. Willy nodded for Randy to go.

Jack was ten years older than Willy, but he was like a baby in need of help.

When Randy returned, they unpacked the groceries. Willy said to Randy, "You go ahead back to Miami. I'm gonna stay here with Jack for a couple days." Randy drove back to Miami.

For the next three days, Falcon stayed at the house. He cooked for Jack scrambled eggs and toast with coffee, until his stomach could handle more substantial fare—a piece of steak, pasta, chicken salad.

Willy scoured the premises for powder cocaine, *basuco* paste, a pipe, and any other paraphernalia he could find; he threw it all in the garbage.

At night, Jack, in a cold sweat, cried out in agony. His cravings for the pipe were severe. Willy put a damp hand towel on Jack's forehead (on top of the stitches and bruises) and told him everything was going to be okay.

Eventually, Jack started to regain his strength. He came out from under a *basuco* bender that had gone on for weeks and months. One afternoon, as they both sat sipping coffee, Willy asked Jack, "You went to Miami High, right?"

"Yeah, just like you and Sal."

"College?"

"I went to Mississippi State for two years, then I dropped out."

"What were your dreams that you were hoping to accomplish with your life?"

Devoe explained how he had always wanted to be a commercial pilot. He got his pilot's license when he was twenty years old. That's why he dropped out of college—to become a pilot.

Jack explained that as part of his application with Pan American airlines, he was required to undergo a physical exam. On his EKG, it was determined that he had an irregular heartbeat. Devoe was rejected for this reason. At first, he was stunned: this was not something a person could change. An irregular heartbeat was a permanent condition. Jack felt defeated, in the cosmic sense.

Then he realized, no, what this is, is a problem that needs to be solved. So, he applied again to another airline. This time he used a friend's EKG and submitted it as his own: a fraudulent act applied to an implacable situation, perhaps the beginning of a mentality that would lead Jack Devoe to the other side of the law.

The airline determined that the EKG results were fake. They not only rejected Devoe but also threatened to press charges, though they eventually let him go with a warning to never show his face around those parts again.

Jack Devoe's dreams of being a commercial pilot were over. He returned to Miami and embraced an alternative dream as a smuggler of contraband. His initial cargo was marijuana, then guns, then cocaine. At one point he signed a contract with the US Marshals to transport convicted criminals from one jurisdiction to another. Then he fell in with the CIA, Cuban exiles, and the Contras.

Willy listened to all this with fascination, and he helped nurse Jack back to health. After a few days, Devoe was eating and sleeping regularly. He seemed to be on the road to recovery. Said Willy to Jack, "I'm gonna go home now. You seem much better. Jack, stay away from that bullshit *basuco*. You have so much going for you. Don't fuck it up."

Jack said thanks and reassured Willy that he would not backslide again.

IT HAD BEEN A ROUGH year, with the kidnapping of Willy's mother and the near loss of Jack Devoe as an essential cog in the machine. Los Muchachos needed some good news, and they got it that November when Blondie Passapera went to trial.

His arrest at the roadblock in the Keys had been another setback. Willy enlisted their house counsel, in the person of Mel Kessler. Mel would not be available to try the case in court, but he assigned two highly capable legal professionals: Joe Oteri, an attorney from Boston who was now handling narco cases in South Florida, and L. Mark Dachs, the young lawyer from New York who now worked as Kessler's partner.

From the beginning, the decision to go to trial was a calculated risk. Blondie had been caught red-handed—or so it seemed. The prosecution claimed that Richard Passapera was a professional cocaine smuggler, though they had no evidence other than his being caught with a car trunk full of kilos. They even brought bricks of cocaine into the courtroom and stacked them on the evidence table, like a game of show-and-tell. They assumed that would be enough for a jury.

Passapera's defense was that he had traveled from Miami to Key West to visit a friend. When his friend never showed up, he decided to hitchhike back to Miami. Two Latino males picked him up. Not far from the roadblock, they stopped. The two Latinos met with a couple other people they knew. One of the Latinos came back to the car and said, "Friend, we're going to stay here with these people we know. We were wondering if you would go ahead and drive the car to Miami for us. We'll pick up the car from you once we get back there."

Blondie agreed to drive the car. He had no idea what was in the trunk.

It was a wild defense, specious, to be sure, but with a kernel of truth. Because of his blond hair and gringo appearance, he had been used as a cocaine courier, just not in the way he described it from the witness stand.

Improbably, he was found not guilty. It was like a Hail Mary pass that worked.

Willy, Sal, and others from the Los Muchachos family were in the courtroom when the verdict was announced: everyone erupted in cheers. The judge banged his gavel and called for order, but there was little he could do to curb the reaction.

That night at the Mutiny, they had a party to end all parties. Willy rented the entire second floor of the club. "I told Jay to bring a couple ounces of my exclusive crystalized rocks that I personally would use on special occasions," said Willy.

All the lawyers were there, and most of the essential members of the organization. The club's disco ball twirled—with twinkling shards of light that glistened off the faces of sweaty dancers. The music throbbed, and the champagne flowed. At one point, Willy raised a glass and said to everyone, "In our business, every opportunity we have to celebrate a big victory, we have to take advantage of these opportunities. Because you never know when it could be your last celebration."

Everyone cheered and drank the champagne, though the toast felt cautionary. Since the kidnapping of his mother and the paranoia it had instilled in the Los Muchachos universe, the gang's sense of immortality had been punctured.

These feelings, which had crept into the ethos of the group, were based on actual events that rattled morale and left some people unsettled, but they did not involve a diminution of the massive flow of product. Even with the occasional setback, like the seemingly minor loss of a couple hundred kilos in the trunk of Blondie's car, the desire for product was as solid as one of Willy's carefully curated crystal rocks.

The cocaine era had arrived.

7

WAR ON DRUGS

TIME MAGAZINE WASN'T THE ONLY US publication to make note of the cultural ascendance of cocaine in 1981. That year, the *Washington Post*, in an article on the front page of the newspaper, exalted the white powder as America's "drug of choice." Noting that "street sales of the drug may have reached $35 billion . . . outselling marijuana by $11 billion," the article quoted an esteemed pharmacologist who referred to cocaine as "the Mercedes Benz of the drug business." A DEA spokesman reported that "we estimate as much as fifty metric tons of cocaine were brought illegally into the U.S. last year. We think it's running a little more this year." Fifty metric tons was 110,000 pounds of cocaine.

The prevalence of the product was startling. People from all walks of life were sporting coke spoons and embossed razor blades for cutting up the chunky white powder. Celebrities were at the vanguard. That year, there would be a scandal in the National Football League as players began to admit to cocaine use and addictions. In the US Congress, a right-wing Southern California politician let an undercover narcotics detective pose as a member of his staff; the narc claimed that six current and three former members of Congress had used cocaine. In the entertainment world, the scandals came fast and furious: In June 1980, comic actor Richard Pryor set himself on fire while freebasing cocaine. Less than two years later, John Belushi died from an overdose after injecting a "speedball," a cocaine-heroin mixture.

The most prevalent locale for usage remained the nightclubs. From Los Angeles to Chicago, San Francisco to Houston, Miami to New York City, the clubs were under the thrall of blow.

These were the obvious locations to purchase and use, but the *New York Times*, in an April 1981 article titled "Trade in Drugs Thriving in Office-Tower Shadows," noted that Manhattan during the day had become a blatant drug market. Customers came in all shapes and sizes. A detective from the NYPD's narcotics division was quoted as saying, "They're all kinds, all classes. From mail-messenger types to three-piece junior executives." The highest volume of street sales was around Wall Street, at Chase Manhattan Plaza, where every weekday (and especially on Fridays before the weekend), mostly white people surreptitiously copped small $40 glassine bags of cocaine.

Street sales among the worker bees were far removed from the world of Willy and Sal. There were many levels to the trade. Los Muchachos were not operating at the level where the white powder was purchased and diluted, or "cut," using baking soda, laxatives, or other additives to maximize profits. They were not peddling grams and dime bags to the proletariat. And they were not vying with midlevel dealers to control territory or outhustle competitors.

Explained Falcon:

> We didn't have no competitors. Not really. You have to understand, mostly the cocaine business is based on consignment. At the top, Colombian bosses like Escobar front the product to midlevel dealers—other Colombians, Mexicans, Americans, whatever. Then those people sell it to other dealers or at the street level. There's a lot of pressure, because the Colombians— Pablo, the Valencia brothers—they want their money. They expect to get paid. That's where all the violence comes in. Somebody is late on a payment, or they got ripped off or busted. But with us, we owned our cocaine. We bought it outright from the point of production, in the jungle labs. We never took anything on consignment.

The fact that Willy and Sal owned their cocaine meant that they could set their own price. Oftentimes, they deliberately undercut the market price. Since their access to product was unlimited, they never had to worry about profit margins. They could control the market.

With their direct line to what was now becoming known as the "cartels" (Escobar and Gaviria in Medellín, Guillermo and Mario Valencia in Cali), competition at the street level or even midlevel did not matter. What did matter was a reliable system of distribution.

> For example, John in San Francisco. Let's say we make a deal for ten kilos. He'll pay me for five up front, and then the other five I will give to him on credit. He'll drive the cocaine from Miami to San Francisco.

It can take a week to get there, a few days to sell the merchandise, then another week to drive back. Too much time. So, it's my job to make it easier for John. We had the cars and later the semitrucks. I said to him, "Here's what I'm gonna do. I'm gonna give you the ten [kilos] up front, and I'm going to transport the cocaine to San Francisco." I facilitated the transportation, made it easier for my client. That's why everybody wanted to work with us.

At the time, law enforcement had little idea of the dimensions of the business. Compared with heroin and marijuana, large-scale cocaine shipments were transacted quickly. The DEA did not know much about how the product was distributed around the country, but it did know how—and where—it was coming into the country. Together with the FBI, the US Customs Service, the ATF, the IRS, the US Marshals, and US attorney's offices around the country, it was determined to do something about it.

On January 20, 1981, Ronald Reagan was sworn in as the fortieth president of the United States. He had not talked much about the War on Drugs during the campaign, preferring to focus on bread-and-butter issues, but within his first year in office as president he seized on the issue. Standing before cameras in the White House Rose Garden, the former Hollywood actor, star of *Bedtime for Bonzo* and other movies, addressed the press and the American people:

Drugs already reach deeply into our social structure, so we must mobilize all our forces to stop the flow of drugs into this country . . . to erase the false glamor that surrounds drugs. . . . We can put drug abuse on the run through stronger law enforcement. . . . We're rejecting the helpless attitudes that drug use is so rampant that we're defenseless to do anything about it. We're taking down the surrender flag that has flown over so many drug efforts; we're running up a battle flag. We can fight the drug problem, and we can win.

By January 1982, the Reagan administration was ready to announce its most grandiose initiative in this newly reinvigorated drug war. The South Florida Drug Task Force was an acknowledgment that the bulk of cocaine was coming into the United States via the Caribbean islands and South Florida. Under a staggering budget of $1.2 billion—approved by Congress—the idea was to create a framework for full cooperation among all federal law enforcement agencies, especially when it came to gathering and sharing intelligence.

The task force would be led by Vice President George H. W. Bush, a former director of the CIA. The effort would combine nearly two hundred agents from the DEA and FBI and draw support from the US Customs Service, the ATF, and the IRS. On the executive board of the task force were representatives from the departments of State, Treasury, Defense, Justice, Transportation, and the White House Drug Abuse Policy Office.

The primary goal of the task force was the interdiction and stoppage of drugs from entering the country, but there was also recognition that drug organizations—and drug profits—were being funneled through financial institutions. Vice President Bush, on announcing what was an unprecedented commitment on the part of the federal government to put teeth behind the War on Drugs, noted that prosecution of bankers, lawyers, and businessmen would also be a priority. "White collar criminals will not be given a free lunch," he said.

If anyone doubted the overall seriousness of the effort, within the creation of the task force was an amendment to the Posse Comitatus Act of 1878. For more than a century, the country had banned the military from involvement in civilian law enforcement activities. Not anymore. Although military personnel could still not participate in search and seizures or arrests, the amendment allowed for technical assistance such as transport, intelligence support, surveillance, training, and the use of military vessels and equipment.

Before, it had been a war on drugs in name only. Now, the entire infrastructure of American law enforcement, with the assistance of the US military—Army, Air Force, and Coast Guard—were being marshalled to go after smugglers like Willy and Sal, and organizations like Los Muchachos.

The war was on.

TAVY FALCON'S MARRIAGE TO AMELIA Rosello, his childhood sweetheart, was a long time coming. They had known each other since they were children at Henry M. Flagler Elementary School. Amelia was ten years old, two years behind Tavy, when she first laid eyes on him in the school hallway. He was two years older than her and tall for his age, with a sweet disposition.

Even at that age, Amelia couldn't stop thinking about Tavy. "Remember how in the afternoon, at grade school, they would have you put your head down on the desk to nap?" she said. "I used to do that and say to myself, 'God, I want to marry this guy.'"

At first, Tavy hardly noticed her; she was so young. But by the time she turned fourteen, he noticed. Amelia's dream came true when Tavy asked her if she wanted to be his steady girlfriend. She said yes.

At the age of sixteen, it was clear that Tavy and his friends were making lots of money. As soon as he got his driver's license, Tavy was driving a Porsche Carrera. He also had a Camaro that turned on by itself. Amelia was flabbergasted: "Can you imagine? A car that turns on by itself? At sixteen!" Tavy's brother, Willy, had even more cars, boats, and houses. Amelia went on trips to Vegas and Vail. She had a vague idea that they were involved in the construction business, and that they made money from boats and engines. She didn't ask questions. It wasn't until the kidnapping of Tavy's mother that she realized that perhaps her boyfriend was in the cocaine business. Now when they went out, they had special drivers and bodyguards. Caution and paranoia were the rule of the day. When they talked about "the business," they did so in whispers.

The two young lovebirds always wanted to get married, but Tavy's parents cautioned against it. They wanted Tavy to wait until he was twenty-one, the legal age of adulthood in the state of Florida. But Tavy and Amelia couldn't wait that long. On January 31, 1982, they tied the knot. Amelia was eighteen, Tavy was twenty.

The wedding was a spectacle. In many ways, it was a kind of coming-out party for Los Muchachos in the community and city. Willy wanted Tavy and Amelia's ceremony and party to send a message that, even after the kidnapping, they were not in hiding. Though six hundred people were invited, nearly one thousand showed up: political figures, business leaders, local celebrities, on top of extended family members and everyone who worked for the organization. Said Tavy, "The wedding wasn't even about my wedding; it was more like a political statement."

Amelia did most of the planning herself; it was a big undertaking. The wedding ceremony took place at Little Flowers Catholic Church in Coral Gables, standing room only. Afterward, a caravan of Rolls-Royce limousines took the wedding party to the Omni Hotel, a glass tower with views overlooking glistening Biscayne Bay, the newest and fanciest hotel in downtown Miami. In the same ballroom where the internationally famous actress Sophia Loren had her wedding reception a month earlier, a diverse gathering of the city's movers and shakers were in attendance. Tables and seats were designated for those with invitations, but it was soon apparent that there were dozens of crashers. Said Amelia, "The hostess kept telling me, 'They say they're friends of Willy's. What should I do?'" The cream of the city's narco world would not take no for an answer. More chairs and tables were added.

The entertainment was provided by Hansel and Raul, Willy Chirino, and Gloria Estefan, who was the lead singer for a group called the Miami Sound Machine. Estefan's father had fought in the Bay of Pigs invasion, making her royalty in the anti-Castro exile community. Tavy's wedding marked the first time Gloria Estefan was hired to perform at a Los Muchachos event, but it would not be the last. Separately, she and Chirino—a singer who was also hugely popular among the exiles—became regular performers at weddings and other events sponsored by Willy and Sal.

Willy picked up the tab for the event, and he spared no expense. The food, champagne, and entertainment were lavish. Cocaine use was not out in the open; that was restricted to bathroom stalls or out in the car.

It was Tavy's wedding, but Willy was a center of attention. In recent years, Willy had emerged as a kind of godfather in the community. Mostly this had to do with the money and stature that Willy and Sal had accumulated through the cocaine business, but also the offshore powerboat scene, the softball league, the anti-Castro efforts, and various business ventures around the city. Seahawk had become known for acts of altruism and philanthropy in the city's Cuban community. Between Willy and Sal, Willy was viewed as the more approachable and friendly. At Tavy's wedding, a nonstop flow of people pulled on Willy's tuxedo coattails with business propositions, favors they wanted, requests, praise. Willy was only twenty-six years old, but already they treated him like a wise elder. Sometimes, he found it embarrassing. He recognized the importance of having a godfather-like figure in the community; his wealth and success afforded him a level of respect that was humbling. On top of his other responsibilities and obligations, it sometimes seemed like a burden.

The musical acts took turns taking the stage, and the dance floor was lively until well into the early hours.

As the evening turned into morning, and the festivities wound down, Willy was approached by Tavy, who wanted to talk. Willy hugged his brother and told him how proud he was. "Today, on this day, you are now truly a man."

"That's what I wanted to talk to you about," said Tavy.

They found a quiet spot away from the remaining revelers. Tavy explained to his big brother how his life would be changing now that he was married. Already, he and Amelia had broken ground on a new house they were having constructed from scratch. It was going to cost millions. They were planning on children—two, maybe three. "Willy, the time has come. I'm asking you to cut me in as a partner in the business."

Up until now, Willy and Sal had been paying Tavy an annual salary of $100,000 (equivalent to over $300,000 in 2024) as a bookkeeper with KS&W and assorted other tasks. Occasionally, he was paid a percentage on cocaine loads that he had unofficially assisted in some way. To be brought in as a partner with Willy and Sal meant he would be given a percentage of the *entire business*. Willy and Sal were raking in at least $300 million a year, which they split fifty-fifty. Tavy stood to net tens of millions annually if he became a partner.

Willy acted as if he were tired of hearing about the subject, but really he was hiding a smile. He said to his younger brother, "All right, all right. I spoke with Sal. We both agree—it's time. You're in. To start with, your cut is 20 percent. Eventually, you'll get the same cut as us—equal partners."

Tavy was ecstatic.

"But, hey, *meida*, listen to me. You cannot tell *Pipo* and *Mima* about this. You understand? They will kill me if they know about this. It has to be kept secret."

Tavy nodded and gave Willy a big hug. As far as he knew, this was the beginning of a new life of unimaginable prosperity. He had no way of knowing it would take him and his family down a path toward near-total oblivion.

AT THE CMM RANCH, OR man cave, in Horse Country, Willy, Sal, and others associated with Los Muchachos liked to work out and watch TV at the same time. While on a treadmill, working up a sweat, they watched the nightly news, which those days was dominated by reports on the US government's War on Drugs. Reagan and Bush had called on the American people to rally their support around what Reagan described as "the gravest threat to our national security" since the onset of the Cold War.

To Willy, there was an element of hypocrisy to the whole affair. Vice President Bush, who had been selected to spearhead the effort and give it an air of gravitas, had served as director of the CIA from 1976 to 1977. He had been director of the agency when Willy and Tony Bemba first began smuggling cocaine and weapons to fight the Sandinistas in Central America. This was commonly recognized, by Willy and others, to have been a CIA covert operation. Chi Chi Quintero had been a CIA asset for years, as were other Cuban exiles from the Bay of Pigs generation. Willy met many gringos who were introduced to him as CIA. No, he did not ask to see their identifications, but these were, in some cases, veteran agents with a long history of anti-Castro-related activities.

In Willy's mind, George Bush had to have known these covert operations involving cocaine were underway. Likely, there was no paperwork to prove that these activities were known about or sponsored by the agency, much less Director Bush. So what? A good deal of what the CIA had been doing since the beginning of the Cold War was not committed to paper.

Willy believed that when he was smuggling coke and guns for Chi Chi and his CIA contacts, he was doing his patriotic duty on behalf of the United States. Chi Chi told him as much. Was smuggling cocaine patriotic when you were doing it for the government and a horrible crime when you were not?

There was a duplicity to this war on drugs that Willy and other Muchachos found hard to swallow. Even so, they knew they needed to treat it seriously, because the government was clearly launching a counteroffensive against the cocaine business that was unprecedented in scope.

One of the initial acts of the South Florida Drug Task Force that affected Los Muchachos directly was the use of the US military's Tethered Aerostat Radar System. Aerostats are helium-filled fabric envelopes that can be tethered to a rope and flown as much as fifteen thousand feet above the ground. This technology made it virtually impossible for planes to fly below radar without detection, as Jack Devoe and other pilots had been doing for years. For Los Muchachos, it was a big problem.

In a meeting with Willy, Sal, Tavy, and the pilots at the offices of Devoe Aviation, they discussed the issue. It was no longer safe to fly loads directly into the United States, as they had been doing for the last few years. The flights into Clewiston would have to be discontinued. It was not an easy decision. Seventy percent of their loads were coming into the United States this way. They had spent many months cultivating Sermon Dyess Jr. He had only recently been elected sheriff, which made him unassailable in Hendry County. Terminating that relationship was not something they did lightly. Not to mention the fact that in cutting Dyess loose, there could be repercussions. Tony Perez, manager of the Clewiston properties and a longtime friend of Sermon, was assigned the task of breaking the news to the sheriff. The plan was to tell him that flights into the ranch were being put on hiatus for a while. "Don't tell him that they are being discontinued altogether," said Willy. This way, Sermon would keep his mouth shut in expectation that his services might be needed down the road.

If sizable loads of cocaine were no longer going to be flying into Clewiston, this meant that Los Muchachos would be redoubling shipments by sea. There were still mouths to be fed, clients who demanded product on a regular schedule. Creativity was an essential aspect of any delivery system. Willy, Tavy, and Sal took it as a challenge to move under or around and through any obstacle that law enforcement might construct.

The kilos from Colombia would now be flown to the islands—the Bahamas, Aruba, the Lesser Antilles—where they would be offloaded, stored, and then reloaded onto boats from Seahawk. The kilos would then be brought ashore in the Keys.

There was nothing new about this method. Smugglers had been using the Caribbean islands, boats, and the South Florida shoreline since the time of pirates and buccaneers. Seahawk's fleet of high-speed powerboats put Los Muchachos in a position to maximize shipments and dominate the waterways in the same way they had the skies. Once the product was brought ashore, they could, as before, capitalize on the organization's superior systems of transportation, distribution, and clientele.

TO SHORE UP OPERATIONS IN the islands, Willy, Sal, and Tavy commandeered Willy's yacht, with Tavy as captain, and set sail for the Bahamas. On the island of Bimini, which is part of the Bahama islands, they arrived to meet Nigel Bowe, an attorney who worked directly with the prime minister of the

Bahamas, and a person introduced to the Boys as Lawrence Major, an assistant commissioner of the Royal Bahamas Police Force.

Major was no ordinary cop. In 1979, Assistant Commissioner Major had spearheaded a raid on Norman's Cay, which had at the time been literally taken over by a Medellín Cartel boss, Carlos Enrique Lehder Rivas, who was Pablo Escobar's man in the islands.

Major had been celebrated as perhaps the lone incorruptible cop in the Bahamas willing to take on the cocaine cartels. His presence at this meeting, and the role he would play in future endeavors with Los Muchachos, suggested that his public reputation was far removed from his personal behavior.

Nigel Bowe was a contact of Jack Devoe's, who had been using the Bahamas as a smuggling route before he ever met Willy and Sal.

The Miami Cubans headed to Bimini Big Game Club marina, docked their yacht, and went to the restaurant, where they met with Bowe and the assistant commissioner.

Frederick Nigel Bowe was from a prominent Bahamian family, with substantial investments and holdings in real estate in the Exuma islands region of the archipelago. A stout, elegant Black man graying at the temples, with a well-groomed mustache and a somewhat affected British accent, he immediately brought up his close relationship with Sir Lynden Pindling, the prime minister of the Bahamas. Bowe assured the Boys that Pindling was a partner and received a percentage of every illegal transaction on the island.

After drinks and small talk, they got to the point: Willy told Bowe that they were looking to step up their operations on the island. His plan was to bring in a shipment of 750 kilos direct from Colombia and land it on one of the islands. If Bowe could protect this shipment and make sure it was not disturbed, Willy would pay $1,000 per kilo—a total of $750,000 for the load. Plus, this was only the beginning; there would be much more where that came from.

As a drop-off location, Bowe and Major suggested the landing strip at Great Harbour Cay, the northernmost outpost in the Berry Islands, a beautiful chain of small islands in the Bahamas.

In Cali, Mario Valencia was ready to send the shipment immediately. This load would be flown by a Colombian pilot in a turboprop Twin Commander 1000 airplane. Los Muchachos pilot Ralph Linero would be on the flight to direct the plane to the proper landing location.

Willy, Tavy, and Sal stayed overnight at Great Harbour Cay. The next morning, they took Willy's yacht offshore and dropped some fishing lines into the water to look like tourists doing what tourists do while in the Bahamas: fishing and getting some sun. From the yacht, they were able to spot the Commander 1000 as it came in low and disappeared behind the tree line, headed for the airport. On a shortwave radio, they contacted Mario Valencia to let him know that the kilos had arrived. They informed him that once the transaction was complete and the shipment secured in Miami, the multimillion-dollar payment for the load would be shipped to Colombia via the drywall method.

From the airport at Great Harbour Cay, the kilos were offloaded and transferred to a commercial fishing vessel. That night, two speedboats from Seahawk would meet the fishing vessel a few miles offshore, and the transfer would be made.

These were no ordinary speedboats. Seahawk had outfitted a half dozen boats for this purpose. This particular run involved a Midnight Express powerboat and a thirty-eight-foot Cigarette boat. Both boats were painted black and hollowed out for the purpose of storing carefully wrapped kilos. The boats had a special device implanted in the engine drive to muffle the sound of the 500-horsepower engines. They had a special dimmer switch for the lights. The boats skimmed the ocean's surface at night, under cover of darkness, without being seen or heard.

The man in charge of Willy and Sal's powerboat operations was a fellow Cuban exile, Bernardo Gonzalez, a.k.a. El Venado (the Deer). Willy called Venado on the radio and told him to have the speedboats meet the fishing vessel in the waters off Grand Harbor Island at eight o'clock that night.

From the yacht, the Boys monitored every step of the action over their two-way transmitter. Meanwhile, they continued onward to the island of Aruba to meet with their other Colombian partner, Pablo Escobar.

The Boys had arranged to meet with Pablo, his partner Gustavo Gaviria, and the notorious Carlos Lehder.

Lehder was a heavyweight in the narco business. Born in Armenia, Colombia, he was from a well-off German Colombian family that was suspected of having collaborated with the Nazis during World War II. Lehder's parents separated when he was fifteen; Carlos was raised by his mother in New York City. He started his criminal career as a car thief, a crime for which he did prison time in the United States before returning to Colombia and becoming involved in cocaine smuggling.

Since 1978, Lehder had been operating as the Medellín Cartel's overseer in the islands. He had established Norman's Cay, in the Bahamas, as his base of operations. On Norman's Cay, he owned the airstrip, the marina, and the local yacht club. The cay had become the Caribbean's main smuggling hub, and Lehder was well known to drug investigators in the United States and around the world.

After Lehder's compound was raided as part of an operation led by Assistant Commissioner Major, Lehder was allowed to return to the island and resume smuggling cocaine. Some wondered why. According to Willy Falcon, it was because the assistant commissioner was paid off by Lehder: "I know this for a fact because Major became a crucial partner of ours in the Bahamas."

Carlos Lehder was six years older than Willy and Sal, with shaggy hair and a mercurial personality that made some people believe he was mentally unbalanced. Others revered Lehder, as he had donated millions of dollars for schools and housing in his hometown of Armenia.

The previous November, Lehder had escaped a kidnapping attempt in Colombia. A squad from the terrorist group M-19, a Marxist guerrilla movement even more anarchic than FARC, snatched him off the street, put a hood over his head, and drove off. Somehow, Lehder escaped from the car and ran off. As he fled, he was shot in the back, but he survived and got away. Later that month, M-19 did succeed in kidnapping Marta Ochoa, the sister of the Ochoa brothers, Jorge and Fabio, two cocaine partners of Escobar.

Willy and Pablo had talked about it at the time. Willy, whose mother was kidnapped earlier that year, was concerned that kidnapping for financial or political ends was becoming commonplace. "We're going to take care of it," said Pablo.

Taking care of it meant creating a private antikidnapping squad called Muerte a Secuestradores (Death to Kidnappers), or MAS. The role of this small army was to find and kill M-19 kidnappers.

Manuel Garces, the veteran Colombian smuggler who had introduced Willy and Sal to Escobar, had attended the infamous meeting where MAS was first created. All the major Colombian narcos were there—Pablo, Gustavo Gaviria, Lehder, Mario and Guillermo Valencia, and many others. At the meeting, over two hundred businessmen from all over Colombia pledged their support for MAS. Some donated money; others supplied hit men. Garces, who had advocated nonviolence, came away from the meeting fearing that the cocaine business was about to descend into mayhem and murder.

A week later, at a soccer stadium in Cali, an airplane dropped on the attendees a communiqué drafted by MAS that read in part, "Kidnapping by guerrillas seeking to finance revolution through the sacrifice of people who, like ourselves, have brought progress and employment to the country, will no longer be tolerated. . . . The basic objective will be the public and immediate execution of all those involved in kidnappings, beginning from the date of this communique." The guilty parties "will be hung from the trees in public parks or shot and marked with the sign of our group—MAS. Kidnappers in jail will be murdered. If that is not possible then our retribution will fall on their comrades in jail and on their closest family members."

The people braced for the worst: a wave of killings followed, much of it carried out in the tradition of La Violencia (the Violence) that had plagued Colombia for decades. The Colombian Necktie (in which a victim's throat is cut and the tongue is pulled out through the slit) and the Flower Vase Cut (in which severed limbs are stuffed inside a mutilated torso) were used as common modes of execution. Within six weeks, over one hundred members or suspected members of M-19 had been murdered. On February 17, 1982, Marta Ochoa was released unharmed.

When Manuel Garces returned to Miami, he met with Willy and Sal and said, "Be careful with Pablo. He seems to have embraced violence and killing as the solution to all his problems."

In the cocaine business, you did not always get to choose your partners. From everything Willy knew about Escobar, he was honorable and professional to deal with. He seemed intelligent and rational. Willy felt that he had no business telling Pablo how to run his operations in Colombia—especially since the whole reason he and Sal and Tavy were having this meeting in Aruba with Pablo was to ask a favor.

"I'm having an issue with my plane routes," Willy told Pablo. Now that federal authorities were cracking down on trafficking by air, it was creating problems. Los Muchachos could send pilots to Colombia to pick up loads of cocaine; those pilots then landed those loads in the Bahamas. The pilots then flew back to Florida with no cocaine. It should have been no problem. Except that for the pilots to make the flight from Florida to Colombia in the first place, they had had to attach backup fuel tanks, known as "bladders," which made it possible for the small planes to make the long flight. When the planes reentered US airspace, they were searched upon landing. Customs agents who spotted these bladders knew, or suspected, that the plane in question was smuggling narcotics, which they reported to the South Florida Drug Task Force. Once the plane was in the system, it was effectively no longer usable for smuggling.

Willy explained that it would be highly advantageous if Pablo could supply planes and pilots for the delivery of product from Colombia to the islands.

It was a reasonable request, but a request, nonetheless. Pablo might have said, "This is not my problem." Instead, he said, "Doctor, we are brothers in this business, and we have to help each other out when we can. I will supply the pilots and planes on my end, no problem."

That night, after dinner and drinks, the six of them retired to the casino at the hotel. Willy watched Pablo at the baccarat table betting coup after coup. Whether he won or lost didn't seem to matter. He had the fever. Willy, Sal, and Tavy also bet heavily that night, drinking and gambling into the morning hours.

For narcos, gambling was a tonic. The risk and thrill involved in wagering money was a metaphor for what they did as smugglers. You took a leap of faith, and if you were lucky (and had skills), you reaped the reward. In Las Vegas on New Year's Eve, in Aruba and other islands where casino gambling was legal, the narcos couldn't help themselves. Life was one big game of chance.

ILEANA ROSSIQUE'S HUSBAND, TONY GARRUDO, had a nickname. "El Cuño" (short for *cuñado*, or brother-in-law) is what Willy called him. Ever since Ileana and Tony were married in 1982, in one of those massive, spare-no-expense extravaganzas that the organization was becoming known for (price tag: $10 million; entertainment: Gloria Estefan and the Miami Sound Machine), they were ever-present members of the tribe.

In Spanish, the word *cuño* has a duel meaning. As well as "brother-in-law," it also translates into English as "wedge." A wedge is something you use to jimmy your way out of trouble, a tool or implement that is used as a last resort. A wedge can be a secret weapon. It works when everything else has failed.

In the universe of Los Muchachos, and especially to Willy, Tony Garrudo was El Cuño, the Wedge.

It hadn't always been that way. When Tony and Alina's sister first started dating in 1977, Willy kept his distance. He knew Tony Garrudo from the neighborhood of Little Havana, where he had arrived in 1968. As far as Willy knew, Garrudo was a jack-of-all-trades; he was a diesel mechanic, an electrician, a plumber. He was also a marijuana dealer. Willy didn't approve. One of the first conversations they had was when Willy said, "The weed business is for lowlifes. If you're smart, you'll get out of that business." He didn't tell Garrudo he was a cocaine trafficker, and he wasn't offering him a job (not yet anyway), but it seemed to Tony that Willy was taking an interest in his welfare.

Tony had come to Little Havana like all the others, in a state of hardship and trauma. He had been born and raised in the city of Santa Clara, in the province of Las Villas, in the center of the island. Tony's father owned and managed a Ford automobile dealership and made a decent living. He had four children, Tony being the oldest.

When the revolution happened, the new government seized the old man's dealership and the family's bank account. They told the father he could still operate the dealership, but it was now owned by the government. They would pay him a small salary.

Said Garrudo, "My father told them to fuck off. He had no intention of working for a Communist government. He made it clear that his intention was to leave the island. The government had a rule that you could leave, but you first had to work for two years in a work camp during the sugar harvest. So they took him away."

As Tony approached the age of sixteen, he was faced with mandatory induction into the Cuban military. The father said to Tony, "You're my firstborn son. I'm not going to leave you here to get killed in Angola, or somewhere like that. I want you to come with me to Spain."

Leaving behind the rest of the family, father and son fled to Seville, Spain, where Tony's grandfather lived.

Both father and son worked at menial jobs and lived in a tiny one-room *piso*, or apartment. Tony worked as a waiter, then he pumped gas. It was at the gas station that he became a jack-of-all-trades. He was especially good with engines of all types.

Eventually, Tony's mother and three siblings were able to get out of Cuba and come stay with them. It was now six people crammed into a tiny room. It was a hard life. Tony was usually broke; what money he made was contributed to the family's central fund to pay for rent and food. His father, like many of the Cubans in Spain at the time, worked in a sugar mill.

When Tony was seventeen, he wanted to go on a date for the first time. He asked his father if he could borrow five dollars to take a girl to a movie. "How can you ask me that?" said the father. "You see how hard I work to take care of the family." After that, Tony held back some of his pay so he'd have a little something for himself.

After a few years in Spain, the entire family moved to Miami.

In Little Havana, Tony was aware of Willy, Sal, and many others who would come to compose Los Muchachos. As kids, they played ball at the same playground and in the same streets. They all eventually wound up at Miami High, which is where Tony first met Ileana. At the time, Ileana's sister Alina was already involved with Willy Falcon.

Tony and Ileana dated for five years before they married. In that time, Tony was around the Rossique family often, at meals, family gatherings, and other events.

Though Willy never came right out and told Tony that he was a cocaine kingpin, eventually the brother-in-law figured it out. You would have to be an idiot to not know. The entire family went to restaurants and public events in a chauffeur-driven Rolls-Royce Silver Shadow. Tony's first time at the Mutiny was like being invited to sit at the throne of King Louis XIII. "It was a snow-storm in there," said Tony, referring to the white powder. "And people treated Willy and Sal like they were royalty."

Tony knew that Willy was checking him out, waiting for the right opportunity. As Willy put it, "I knew [Tony] had certain skills. I was interested to see what he could do for us. But at that time, he was just a boyfriend. I didn't know how long he was going to be around. It wasn't until they got engaged that I felt it was time."

After the wedding, Tony was El Cuño. He was family.

One day, out of the blue, while at Willy and Alina's house, Tony was approached by Willy, who said, "Cuño, I'd like you to come with me on something. We have to go see somebody."

Without asking questions, Tony said, "Sure." He got in Willy's car, and they drove off. As they were driving, Willy said, "You got your piece on you?"

"Always," said Tony. He kept a gun in an ankle holster.

They drove to a house and met a guy. They were there to pick up some kilos. The guy told Willy that the kilos were in the trunk of his car in the garage. He handed the keys to Willy, who handed them to Tony to go retrieve the product. Which Tony did. Duffel bags filled with kilos that Tony loaded into the trunk of Willy's car. Later, Tony delivered these kilos to a safe house.

Over the next couple of weeks, he made that same run—by himself—on several occasions. Tony went to the house, picked up some kilos, and transferred them to a stash house. He never asked why. He never asked if he was going to be paid. He knew that he was being tested. "I just do what I have to do," said Tony. "No questions. After that, and a few other little jobs I did for them, Willy said to me, 'I think your time has come.' I was a member of Los Muchachos."

Eventually, there was a big job.

By then, Willy had known Tony for a few years. He knew that he was the kind of guy who could solve problems. That's how he got his nickname—the Wedge.

Willy explained the situation: Recently, Los Muchachos had begun smuggling cocaine loads from Caracas, Venezuela. This route was the product of Willy and Sal's usual serendipity in the business. It started when they hired a former major-league baseball player they knew to play on their softball team. They paid him $100,000. The guy was thrilled. One day, when he and Willy were sitting in the dugout during a game, the guy told Willy that he had an uncle who was close friends with a retired colonel in the Venezuelan air force named Francisco "Frank" Ocando Paz. The retired colonel was a smuggler of contraband. The baseball player was certain that, if they wanted to, Willy and Sal could smuggle product from Venezuela, and the colonel, with his connections, would protect the entire shipment.

Falcon arranged a meeting with Colonel Ocando Paz in Miami. Frank, as he preferred to be called, was a man in his fifties, tall and well-built, who, at the time Willy met him, had a fastidious mustache. Ocando told Willy he was aware that he and Magluta were involved in the cocaine business. He explained that he was getting product directly from a Bolivian supplier, but his contact was able to supply him with only thirty kilos a month. He needed someone like Willy and Sal, who could supply him with "more weight."

Willy told the colonel, "I will discuss your proposal with my partners and get back to you."

It was a promising offer, but it needed to be checked out. Immediately after the meeting, Falcon launched a full intelligence investigation of Colonel Ocando. Sal and Tavy were dispatched to Venezuela to confirm that the details of Frank's story were true, including the identity of his cocaine supplier in Bolivia. In Miami, Falcon hired a private investigator to run a full check on Ocando. Said Willy:

> When you are bringing new people to work with your organization, believe me, you have to be extremely careful. Because this guy could be working undercover for law enforcement. You need to take every precaution; you're not only putting yourself at risk but also everyone in your organization.

The colonel's story checked out. Willy and Sal decided that if they were going to work this new route with Ocando, they would do so with their partners in Medellín, Escobar and Gaviria. The Colombians had recently established at Pablo's Hacienda Nápoles ranch a hidden landing strip, which would be ideal for shipping product to Caracas.

Willy and Sal arranged for a sit-down among themselves, the Colombians, and the retired Venezuelan colonel. They met on the island of Aruba, which had become a favored location for these kinds of gatherings. The weather was nice, the scenery ideal, lots of eye candy in bikinis, and, of course, twenty-four-hour legal gambling in the hotel casinos.

At the meeting, Escobar introduced to Ocando his personal pilot, Rodrigo Ortíz, who was instructed to guide the Venezuelan in his Beechcraft Super King Air 200 to the Hacienda Nápoles landing strip to pick up two hundred kilos. The operation was up and running in a few weeks.

It was a good route, because the planes they loaded in Caracas, bound for Miami, were regularly scheduled charter flights filled with tourists. The narcos lined the side panels of the plane's interior with two hundred kilos of cocaine. It was a short trip from Caracas to Opa-Locka airport, where the plane cleared customs as a legitimate commercial flight.

With the first couple of loads, Justo Jay oversaw receiving the product. Then Tony Garrudo came into the picture.

El Cuño was assigned to do the task along with a partner of Frank Ocando's. After a couple of runs (they would eventually do three a week), Tony thought, *This is a disaster in the making.* "First of all," he told Willy, "Frank's partner is weak, he's a fucking *mariconcito* [a little faggot]. You can't go on a mission like this with someone who is scared." The other problem was that the plane landed and parked in a hangar that was exposed. They were being asked to unload the kilos right out in the open where they could be clearly seen from the flight tower.

Tony said to Willy, "It's no good. The way we're doing it, we're gonna get caught."

"Okay," said Willy, "what do you suggest?"

"First of all, get rid of the *mariconcito*; I can't work with him."

"Okay. The *mariconcito* goes."

"Here's the plan: What's the first thing that happens once a plane lands and the passengers get off and leave the plane? The plane's interior gets cleaned by a crew. Well, that's gonna be us. I'm gonna put together an airplane-cleaning service. Totally legit. A van with the name of the business on the side. Jumpsuits with our logo on the front. All the best cleaning equipment. And you know what? That plane is going to get the best cleaning in the business. For real. We will leave the interior shining like new. And at the same time, we get those kilos and load them into our van."

It worked like a charm. Tony's four-man crew showed up in two vans marked AVIATION CLEANERS. They left one person at the gate as a lookout with a walkie-talkie. They parked the vans in such a way that they blocked the view of people in the flight tower. Within thirty minutes, they stripped the plane clean of its kilos, vacuumed and cleaned the interior, and were back in the vans and on their way.

After that, Willy began to rely on Tony. He was fearless and loyal. A few years later, when the television show *MacGyver* came on the air, Willy started calling Tony "MacGyver" after the main character on the show, who was a master at coming up with solutions to problems: that was Tony G.

JACK DEVOE HAD COME TO the end of the line. For a while, he seemed okay. Since those days when Willy babysat Jack and nursed him back to health,

Jack's friends and partners were hopeful that he had stopped smoking *basuco*. And he had—for a while. But by late 1982, he was back to disappearing for weeks at a time. He was back on the pipe. When he didn't show up one day to pick up a load at the Ocean Reef location, that was it for Willy; he'd had enough.

He took El Cuño with him to Devoe Aviation to meet Jack. They brought along a payment of $600,000 that was owed from a previous shipment. Jack was pleased to receive the money. He had no idea that it was a farewell payment.

Willy didn't even bother to ask Jack why he had missed the pickup at Ocean Reef. He said to Devoe, "Jack, I have people depending on me. Everything is based on being responsible about your business obligations. I don't see the level of commitment from you that I used to see. Your heart has to be in your work, or eventually you become a liability."

Jack sensed what was coming. "Willy, I'm trying to straighten things out. I'm going into rehab next week."

"That's good, Jack. I'm glad to hear that. But I've got to keep going. You're the pilot, you're bringing in the load. You got to do your side. If not, I got to find someone else."

It was awkward. Willy never came right out and said, "Jack, we're finished. I can't use you no more." But Jack knew; he got the massage. Jack Devoe and Los Muchachos were finished.

On the drive home, Willy said to Tony, "That's fucked up. I liked Jack. He was an inspiration to me."

"You did the right thing," said Tony. "I just hope he doesn't become a problem for us in the future."

In another kind of group, Devoe's life might have been in danger. In the Mafia, and especially in the narco universe, when a member of a gang falls afoul of the group, they wind up dead. They know too much. As an outsider, Devoe was a threat to Los Muchachos. Among the hardened and the merciless, it would have been preferable to make him disappear. In the underworld, murder was sometimes the first and most obvious option.

Tony Garrudo looked at his brother-in-law expecting a response, but Willy said nothing. He was saddened by the loss of Jack. He was driving, and he kept his eyes on the road.

8

PABLO IN DISNEY WORLD

THE PROCESSING LAB IS WHERE the alchemy takes place.

In Peru and Bolivia, where the plant is grown, local harvesters, known as *raspachines*, strip the leaves from the stem. *Raspachines* work long hours for modest pay, but still, it's good money for rural laborers with little education or opportunity for steady work. Entire swaths of the Andean region are given over to the growing of the coca plant; the crops are protected by armed guards, and, in some cases, military personnel who have been bought off by the narco bosses.

The harvested leaves are turned into mulch, stored in barrels, and shipped to labs around Colombia for processing.

The reason Colombia became the dominant producer and distributor of cocaine in the 1970s and 1980s is because it developed a monopoly on the refinement of the coca leaf into powder. "Lab," or "laboratory," is a fancy word to describe what is a rustic and even primitive operation. Wooden sheds and shacks are thrown together to provide cover as the process is underway. The labs are set up in remote areas, usually in the jungle, far from civilization. They are often located near rivers or waterways to absorb overflow from a messy process that spews toxic chemicals and effluvia. A good-size lab might employ thirty or forty people, making it necessary to create modest housing, sanitation, a water source, a food supply chain, and space for recreational activities for the workers and their families. All of it is usually protected by a heavily armed security force.

The very nature of what defines a "cartel" is an organization that controls the creation of the product. The godfathers of cocaine in Colombia—men like Gilberto and Miguel Rodríguez Orjuela, José Santacruz Londoño, and the Valencia brothers in Cali, and in Medellín, Fabio Ochoa and Jorge Ochoa Vásquez, José Gonzalo Rodríguez Gacha, and Escobar—understood that unless you controlled the means of production, you were just a dealer, and dealers were a dime a dozen. Although the Cali and Medellín cartels were structurally dissimilar, they each operated as an international corporation with ultimate control over its slice of the market.

Willy and Sal were among the biggest suppliers in the United States, and, like many of their generation, were recreational users of the drug, but they knew little about how it was produced. Which was why, on one of their semi-regular visits to Cali to go over the books with the Valencia brothers (which they did every six months), when Mario Valencia asked, "Would you like to visit our lab in the Valley of Cauca?"—they jumped at the chance.

By late 1982, the number of cocaine processing labs in Colombia had grown from two to over one hundred. Most of them were in the region of Cauca, in the western part of the country near the Pacific coast. Recently, the area had become a war zone, with the FARC warring with the cartels and local authorities over coca plantations and processing labs. The Cali Cartel had staked out a large swath of the region by creating its own security force, led by former leaders of MAS. Two brothers, Fidel and Carlos Castaño, working together with Colombian military forces, used their right-wing paramilitary organization to enforce security in the area.

Willy, Sal, Mario Valencia, and two armed guards with machine guns slung over their shoulders flew in a helicopter over the valley on a clear day. Brooding mountain forests with lush tropical vegetation, clusters of Quindío wax palm trees, some as much as two hundred feet tall (unique to the humid forests of the Andes), and the majestic Cauca River (which would soon be nicknamed the River of Death because of the narco violence) spread out beneath them in various shades of green, brown, and blue.

They landed the copter at a makeshift landing pad near a series of sheds outfitted with mosquito nets and warehouses with corrugated tin roofs. Mario led the way. He introduced Willy and Sal to the lab's managing director, Ivan Urdinola Grajales, a compact hombre in his twenties with a furrowed brow and permanent scowl. Urdinola's nickname was "El Enano" (the Dwarf); he was a midlevel manager in the Cali Cartel who would eventually branch off, with others, to start his own group called Norte del Valle Cartel.

Urdinola introduced the Boys to a local *cacique*, or tribal leader of the indigenous population, that lived in the area and whose members were among those working at the lab. The Boys were not introduced to the security personnel, who were ever present around the property, mostly young men in their twenties with machetes and machine guns.

As Urdinola showed the visitors around the facility, Willy and Sal were dumbstruck. With all the cocaine they had handled in recent years, rarely had they stopped to consider the process of creation that gave birth to the product that had turned them into millionaires on their way to being billionaires in only a few short years. Their guide took them through the process: After the coca mulch arrives at the labs, it is first soaked in gasoline inside the drums. Then sulfuric acid is added, forming a layer of gasoline-and-acid mixture on top that is removed. Sodium bicarbonate of ammonia is added to the solution, creating cocaine base. The base is then removed from the drums, filtered through a cloth, and allowed to dry.

Most of these steps took place in different sheds on the property, with workers moving drums and buckets of solution with wheelbarrows and hand trucks.

The next stage is when the base is dissolved in a solvent of ether and then heated in a hot water bath called "*baño maria*." Concentrated hydrochloric acid is added to the boiling water, which results in the crystallization of cocaine hydrochloride. The cocaine is then put through a hydraulic press and a microwave oven, where it is hardened into a brick for packaging and distribution.

With all the chemicals and unusual smells in the air, Willy and Sal had to cover their noses with handkerchiefs, which made the workers smile. They were used to seeing the rare visitor to the laboratory have this reaction. Some visitors even vomited. Most of the workers were immune to the aromas.

One thing that affected Falcon was that almost all the workers in the lab were indigenous men, women, and youngsters. These were, no doubt, families who had been making their living from coca cultivation and processing going back generations. There are those who would look at this reality and see exploitation—poor indios slaving away in fields and laboratories for narco bosses, terrorists, and cartels—but Willy saw it as an example of how coca from this part of the world had sustained these people since ancient times. This plant was part of a sacred tradition going back to the beginning of civilization in this area. As Willy took in the sights and smells of this system, with the various brown-skinned hues (not unlike his own) of the workers, it made him feel connected to the human process. He found it incongruent that the byproduct of all this, which he was witnessing at its point of creation, would be the white powder that went up the noses of oblivious North Americans in places like the Mutiny and elsewhere. It gave Falcon a deeper appreciation and understanding of the product he was trafficking.

Urdinola, Valencia, and the Cubans discussed a recent issue: The chemicals used to concoct cocaine hydrochloride were purchased in Germany and shipped to Colombia. Since the Reagan administration had announced the South Florida Drug Task Force, one of the effects was that the US government was putting pressure on nations that were seen to be enabling the coke business. Specifically, the United States let it be known that Germany needed to stop allowing for massive shipments of calcium chloride, acetone, and potassium permanganate, the main ingredients in the cocaine alkaloid process. The banning of chemical shipments was creating problems for the cartels, yet another legal battlefield that had emerged in the newly reinvigorated War on Drugs.

On the plane back to Miami, Willy and Sal talked about what they had seen and experienced. Both came away from it with a sense of awe. The riches of the coke biz were one thing, but the history, traditions, and labor that went into the creation of the merchandise made them feel as if they were part of something larger than themselves.

In the previous few years, as they had undertaken many adventures together as the public face of Los Muchachos, Willy and Sal's relationship had deepened. Willy respected Sal's business acumen, and Sal appreciated—and perhaps even envied—Willy's people skills.

In the beginning, it was supposed to be Willy and his childhood friend Tony Bemba. They were the ones who organized the cocaine-for-guns shipments on behalf of the anti-Castro militants. When Tony broke his leg in 1977, he was out of the loop for a while, and when he returned, Sal had usurped his role in Los Muchachos. Over time, Tony became disenchanted. He told Willy and Sal he wanted out of the business. They tried to talk him out of it, but he was insistent. Tony was given a buyout of $8 million, which he thought would last him the rest of his life. He remained within the social circle of Los Muchachos—he was one of Willy's oldest and closest friends—but he was no longer part of the cocaine business.

For a time, Sal had been merely a high-level partner of Willy's, one of a few key members of Los Muchachos. It wasn't until 1980 that Willy cut Sal in as a fifty-fifty partner.

Because of the offshore powerboat races, the softball league, the real estate and construction businesses, and other highly visible public endeavors, Willy and Sal, as a duo, were ubiquitous. Many members of Los Muchachos thought of them as one and the same. Fernando Garcia, who worked for the gang in the cocaine and boat businesses and had known Willy and Sal since they were all kids together in Little Havana, said, "Willy and Sal were so close that sometimes I thought they were gay."

They were not gay. They had—at least publicly—cultivated a bond that was meant to serve as a powerful example of brotherhood to the rest of the group. Willy was just as likely to spend time with Tony Garrudo, and he was also close to Justo Jay. His brother, Tavy, was blood, which put him on a higher level than Sal. But Willy and Sal were business partners, and in the Cuban exile community, business partners were sometimes more inextricably bound than husbands, wives, and family members.

AFTER THE VISIT TO THE Cauca Valley to see the cocaine-creation process up close, Sal became taken by the idea that they were the equivalent of CEOs of a Fortune 500 company. He suggested that they create an actual office that would give their business the imprimatur of a legitimate corporation. The man cave, as fun as it was, did not meet Sal's idea of a serious locale to promote an image of business gravitas.

At an office building named Executive Tower 1, on Seventy-Second Avenue near Miami International Airport, the Boys rented a series of offices. In this space, they linked together some of their front companies. They created an office for Ressa, Inc., which was their import-export company. Ralph Linero, who, now that Jack Devoe had been banished from Los Muchachos, was the group's premier pilot, had an office for his commuter airline company. A couple of Willy and Sal's construction companies were also based at Executive Tower 1. Willy and Sal had their own separate corner offices with large picture windows that overlooked the main runway at the airport.

Another essential business with offices on the premises was HoneyComb

Paging, a company whose front man was Eddie Lezcano, Sal's brother-in-law. There was also a cell phone company called Cell Enterprises.

The pager and cell phone businesses were more than a front. As the organization expanded, with different divisions covering differing aspects of the business, communications were essential. Telephone landlines were almost never used, given law enforcement's ability to listen in. Pagers were the primary manner of contacting one another, but by the early 1980s cell phones were the latest technology. Los Muchachos needed to have a limitless supply of beepers and phones. Every truck driver was assigned a cell phone, often more than one. Phones were supplied by Cell Enterprises, under false names, so they could not be traced. For security reasons, they were often trashed and replaced by new phones.

Willy and Sal carried four or five phones each, with different numbers. Willy knew who was trying to get ahold of him by which phone was ringing.

One thing Willy and Sal did not do very often was hang around the office at Executive Tower 1. Sal's intention of creating the illusion of a legitimate business setting, where they would assemble like CEOs working a nine-to-five job, never did catch on. They were either at the man cave shooting baskets, or on a boat somewhere, or in the air, or at the Mutiny, or tending to the flow of kilos. They were not the kind of guys to sit at a desk twiddling their thumbs.

CONSPICUOUS CONSUMPTION WAS A BIG part of the narco lifestyle. Boats, planes, cars, motorcycles, houses, jewelry for wives and girlfriends, expensive clothes and shoes, hair salons and spa treatments for the women that might stretch on for days—it was all a way to revel in their success and make a statement that the United States truly was the land of opportunity. Even if an expenditure was beyond the means of the average Muchacho, there was always another major cocaine load just around the corner. As soon as you heard "Makin' It" being played at the Mutiny, it was time to start shopping for a new house, car, or boat.

There was a belief among some in the group that maybe they shouldn't be so flashy. Just because they could afford to buy all these toys and trinkets didn't mean they should. Justo Jay, for one, tried to counsel the younger members of the group to not be so obvious with their wealth. He spoke with Pedro "Pegy"

Rosello, Amelia Falcon's little brother, who had begun running errands for the Boys when he was sixteen. Pegy used to hand-wash their cars—the Lamborghinis, Benzes, Corvettes, and the Rolls-Royce—for twenty-five dollars a wash. By the time he was twenty, he was running kilos. Pegy was a fun-loving kid, talkative, popular with the girls, a fellow traveler who was dazzled by the money, the coke, the thrill of it all. He was especially close to Tavy Falcon, who would eventually initiate him into Los Muchachos. By the time Pegy was twenty-one, he was a millionaire, and Justo Jay's words of caution were like admonitions from the parish priest—they fell on deaf ears.

"Were we flashy?" said El Cuño, Tony Garrudo. "Yes. We were the flashiest guys in town, and we make no apologies for that. The point of having the money was to spend it. Because that's our way of life."

Certainly, Willy and Sal did not hold back. They lived the high life as an example to everyone else—not only to those in the organization, but also to the Cuban exile community at large, the city of Miami, the region of South Florida, and the entire United States of America.

In April 1982, Willy purchased the gang's biggest trinket of all—a Learjet. Willy and Sal had fantasized about it for a while. Ever since they had started renting private jets for their annual trips to Las Vegas for the holidays, they had thought, "Hey, we need to get one of these."

The Lear 55 was the premier jet manufacturer's latest model. Willy and Sal had put their names on a list so that they would be among the first to purchase the plane when it came onto the market. To avoid US Internal Revenue Service tax liability, they made the purchase in the name of Francisco Ocando Paz, the retired Venezuelan colonel who facilitated their cocaine shipments from Caracas. The plane cost $8 million.

At a hangar at Miami International Airport on Thirty-Sixth Street, Willy, Sal, and Tavy were given a tour of the plane and taken on a test flight. The interior cabin of the Lear 55 was like a private lounge, with leather upholstery, marble countertops, a thick shag carpet, and lots of headroom. The bathroom was large enough for a woman to spread out her makeup and hair spray and turn the place into a mini salon. The Boys joked about how their wives were going to love it.

In the cockpit, they watched as the pilot showed them a series of maneuvers; the jet was remarkably smooth and responsive. After ninety minutes flying over the beaches, swamps, and waterways of South Florida, they landed back at the airport.

In the first month they owned the plane, Willy and Sal were constantly thinking up reasons to go for a ride. The pilot was on call twenty-four hours a day, seven days a week. The major consideration before takeoff was what type of food they wanted for the flight. Using their favorite catering service (owned by Magluta's cousin), they ordered lobsters, filet mignon, and fine bottles of wine or champagne to be ready and available on the flight.

One of their first trips was to Vegas for the Larry Holmes–Gerry Cooney world championship heavyweight bout at Caesars Palace. Willy took Alina on a trip to New York for Fashion Week. Willy, Sal, and Tavy flew to the finals for powerboat races in Wisconsin and New Jersey. Nearly the entire softball team loaded onto the plane for a semifinals game in Spokane, Washington.

On one of their trips to Aruba to meet with Escobar and Gustavo Gaviria, Pablo saw the plane and fell in love. He had his own jet, but he didn't have a Lear 55. Escobar said to Willy, "I've been meaning to take my family on a vacation to Disney World in Orlando. Do you think I could borrow this plane for the trip?"

"Well," said Willy, "I tell you what: I think my wife and two girls might enjoy a trip like that. How about I have the pilot come and pick you up, and we'll all go to Disney World together?"

"That's perfect," said Escobar. He had been to Disney World for the first time in 1981, when he brought his wife and kids. The rides, exhibits, amusements, and overall carnival-like atmosphere—Pablo found it all enchanting.

A few days later, Willy, Alina, Aileen, and Jessica kicked back on the jet as it flew down south to pick up the Escobar family in Medellín, and then north to Orlando.

It was a wonderful day at the world-famous amusement park, as the wives and kids went on the rides while Falcon and Escobar—two of the most preeminent narco traffickers in the Americas—strolled among the crowd, surrounded by Dopey, Goofy, Sleepy, and other grown adults dressed up as beloved Disney characters.

Pablo seemed to be in a state of controlled agitation. Recently, he had become obsessed with Colombia's 1979 extradition treaty with the United States, which he saw as a violation of the country's national sovereignty. The idea that he or other members of his cartel could be sent to the United States for prosecution and incarceration was offensive to Escobar, as it was, according to public opinion polls, to a majority of the Colombian people. To Willy, Pablo used a phrase that would become his clarion call as he took up the issue of extradition: "Better a tomb in Colombia than a prison cell in the United States."

As Escobar stepped into the arena of public discourse and advocated for his cause, he was denounced by political rivals and some in the media as a narco murderer. This was after he had spent years cultivating an image as a Robin Hood by building parks, soccer fields, and housing in the city's worst *comunas*, or slums. Pablo told Willy, "No matter what I do, the political establishment turns against me." He considered his opposition to be part of an organized campaign of harassment. To fight back, he was considering running as a delegate for the national congress so that the government would have to deal with him as a legitimately elected official.

When he heard that, alarm bells went off in Willy's head. He questioned Escobar, "What do you know about politics?" Pablo explained how he had studied political science at the University of Antioquia. He had dreamed about a career in politics before he ever got involved in the cocaine business. "One day," he said, "I want to be president of Colombia so I can help the poor people."

Willy played devil's advocate, telling Pablo that his running for office or getting involved in politics would "create a lot of enemies" and bring a level of intense scrutiny.

"If I'm the president, nobody can touch me," said Pablo.

For Willy, it was an ominous sign. He hoped that Pablo was not serious, but a couple of months later, in a conversation with Pablo over the shortwave radio, the narco king told Willy that he was officially running to be a representative in the Colombian congress.

On July 20, 1982, Escobar was elected as an alternate deputy representative to the Chamber of Representatives of Colombia's congress.

Willy was committed to his partnership with Escobar, and so he hung in there. That summer, as Pablo assumed his new role in congress, Falcon and Magluta offered to introduce Pablo to their money managers in Panama City. They would be highly beneficial for Escobar, who was having a hard time moving his billions around without attracting scrutiny. Willy explained to Pablo how they were transporting millions in cash every month through their drywall shipments to Panama. Willy told Pablo, "Look, we're already shipping our profits to Panama City, where our people deposit it into our secret accounts. We could just as easily send our payments to you through this same system. You could deposit the money right there in Panama. We'll introduce you to Guillermo Endara, our man there. He's powerful and well connected. He'll take care of you."

Pablo liked the idea, so they all rendezvoused in Panama City (any excuse to use the jet). Willy and Sal checked into a room at the Hilton Hotel. They had the meeting right there in their suite. Pablo and Gustavo Gaviria from Colombia, along with Guillermo Endara and Hernán Delgado, and Gabriel Castro, the leader of PTJ, the Panamanian FBI.

Willy introduced Pablo and Gustavo to the Panamanians as "our partners from Medellín." He explained that they wished to set up a similar system to what he and Sal had been utilizing: cash smuggled in through the fraudulent import-export company, to be deposited in a series of dummy corporations. Everyone seemed pleased; it was Problem Solving 101, narco style.[1]

Two weeks later, Willy and Sal were back in Panama City, this time with Mario and Guillermo Valencia from Cali. Once again, Willy explained to Guillermo Endara how they intended to use their accounts in his bank as a central financing system for payments to the Cali Cartel.

Later, over drinks at a private club, in a penthouse high above the city, Willy and Sal looked out over the Pacific Ocean and the city's busy port. Endara, who seemed to know everyone in the place, explained to the Boys how, because of his girth, he had his suits handmade by the best tailor in Panama City, a place well known for its expert couturiers. "Feel the fabric," he said to Willy, extending his arm.

Willy touched Endara's sleeve. "Amazing," he said. "Very high quality and craftsmanship."

Guillermo raised his glass. "You two have been tremendous clients. I had no idea."

---

[1] What Willy and Sal did not know was that Escobar and the Medellín Cartel were already in deep with the leader of Panama's military—and Endara's political rival—General Noriega. In mid-1982, through an underling of Noriega's, Escobar negotiated a deal to smuggle cocaine shipments into Panama. The general was paid between $100,000 and $250,000 per load of cocaine. In addition, Noriega permitted the cartel to establish a processing plant in the province of Darién, in La Palma, near the border with Colombia.

Said Magluta, "The feeling is mutual, Guillermo. We like the way you do business."

Under his breath, Willy said to Sal, "Look around the room."

Magluta looked around at the assortment of Latin American power brokers, men, like Endara, in finely tailored suits, with snifters of cognac, puffing on cigars, the smoke wafting overhead.

Said Willy, "We're the youngest guys in here."

It was true. The Boys were pioneers. Since they first met Endara, Willy and Sal had contributed mightily to the further flowering of Panama City as the preeminent international money-laundering center for Cocaine Inc. By the end of the year, the Medellín and Cali cartels were separately sending between $16 million and $25 million a month through Guillermo Endara's matrix of bank accounts and shell companies. For the Endara Firm, which received 10 percent of every transaction, the commissions were luxurious.

November 17, 1982

Air Force One, the official jet of US presidents, touched down at Miami International Airport on a mild Wednesday morning. The president's jet, a Special Air Mission 27000, was bigger than Willy and Sal's Lear 55, but it lacked some of the amenities. For one, the ladies' bathroom was small, with none of the counter space for laying out makeup and hair products or long lines of cocaine to be snorted at thirty thousand feet above the blue horizon.

President Ronald Reagan and his attorney general arrived in Miami that day to a throng of national media, who for the last year had been reporting on the "War on Drugs." There had been massive arrests and seizures, along with dramatic drug raids using the latest technology in planes, boats, and surveillance equipment. New laws had been enacted to combat what Reagan and Vice President Bush had both been referring to as "the drug menace," which was "a threat to our way of life." The full weight of the presidency and the US Justice Department was being used to rally the American public to the cause.

Reagan had a busy schedule that Wednesday, though he was there for one reason only: to call attention to the efforts of the South Florida Drug Task Force.

He was first taken aboard the Coast Guard cutter *Dauntless* and introduced to some of the crew, who were credited with having made over one hundred arrests in recent months. He was shown the boat's state-of-the-art tracking equipment and given a peek at the crew's arsenal of guns and explosives.

After lunch with Republican senator Paula Hawkins of Florida, the president was taken to a hangar at Homestead Air Force Base, where he was shown the fruits of the task force's busy year. Laid out on tables was a display of seized evidence: dozens of machine guns and handguns, bales of marijuana, $4 million in confiscated cash, and neatly stacked kilos of cocaine valued at $5.9 million.

Against the backdrop of drug-chasing planes and helicopters, Reagan stood to give a prepared address to a large gathering of federal prosecutors and agents. He was there to congratulate the troops for their efforts. Cocaine seizures in South Florida, he claimed, were up 56 percent in the last ten months. His trumpeting of his administration's "unprecedented success" sounded suspiciously like a victory lap, though he stopped short of declaring that the War on Drugs had been won. On the contrary: Reagan announced that he would ask Congress for an additional $75 to $100 million to finance the task force for the upcoming fiscal year.

In his speech, Reagan said to the audience of lawmen and media people, "Our goal is to break the power of the mob in America and nothing short of it. We mean to end their profits, imprison their members, and cripple their organizations."

There was a built-in flaw in the president's assessment. Yes, seizures of merchandise, guns, and cash profits were up. And new laws were being passed to aid law enforcement in its efforts. But whether the US government was making a dent in the massive flow of kilos into the country was a far murkier equation. That year, the US General Accounting Office announced that, despite the seizures and successes touted by Reagan, the amount of cocaine imported had increased from forty to forty-four tons, with a street value in the hundreds of millions of dollars.

The number of users in the United States was on the rise. The Reagan administration's policy experts had come up with a strategy to deal with that issue. As part of the War on Drugs, the administration devised an initiative to address matters of consumption. Spearheading the effort was First Lady Nancy Reagan, whose campaign to combat drug use was distilled down to a pithy, cogent, and widely ridiculed slogan: "Just Say No."

The slogan was a denial of reality. Never mind the social and psychological issues that had given rise to the use of cocaine as a stimulant, a crutch, a panacea, and a floodwall against the frenzied shallowness of a soulless culture. Never mind the thorny subjects of dependence and addiction. Ignore all that, because none of it was relevant. All you had to do was say no.

JACK DEVOE HADN'T LEFT THE business. Since being dumped by Willy Falcon, he had moved on to other suitors. It was far from easy. Starting up with new partners was problematic. Devoe did not have his own sources for cocaine, and so he came to Willy Falcon one day at the man cave in Horse Country. "Willy," he said, "I'm sorry for everything I put you through, the irresponsible behavior. That was the *basuco*, but I'm over that now."

"That's great, Jack," said Willy. "Glad to hear it."

Jack explained that he had an opportunity he wanted to present to Willy. "Nigel Bowe, in the Bahamas. Do you know him?"

"Yes."

"Well, he's got a connection for us. A Colombian named José Cabrera Sarmiento."

"I know him, too. A very responsible person and highly capable of supplying you with merchandise. What do you need me for?"

"I'm broke. I've got some property but no currency. I need you to let me borrow two hundred fifty grand for part of the money to purchase two planes so I can transport the cocaine shipment for Pepe."

Willy was annoyed by the proposition: he was not happy that Nigel Bowe was dealing with other Colombians behind his back. He made a mental note that it was time to cut off all relations with the Bahamian lawyer turned narco.

"Unless you want to take over this deal yourself," added Jack.

"Jack, I told you: I'm retired." Saying he was retired was Willy's way of telling Jack that he did not want to do business with him anymore.

"How about the money?" asked Jack.

"I'll have Jay drop off two hundred fifty grand tomorrow at your aviation school."

"Thanks, Willy. I appreciate it. I will pay you back, I promise."

Jack exited; Willy was happy to have him out of his hair.

Months later, he heard some information about Jack that made his knees buckle. On a phone call, Ralph Linero informed him that, through a law enforcement source of his, he had heard that Jack Devoe had been arrested at Palm Beach International Airport. DEA and customs agents had gone to Little Darby Island in the Bahamas and confiscated two planes and other equipment Devoe was using to smuggle cocaine.

The pilot had run a total of six shipments for Bowe. The whole operation was conducted under the auspices of Carlos Lehder.

Willy didn't know much about Jack's coke operation with Bowe, José Cabrera, and Lehder, but he did know one thing: Jack Devoe was a junkie, and he was weak. If Devoe cracked and decided to cooperate with government prosecutors, he could do a lot of damage to Willy, Sal, and their entire operation.

Willy, Sal, and Tavy met to talk it over. Their immediate concern was shipments they were currently running through the Bahamas. With Devoe's arrest, and future investigations sure to come, the islands had suddenly become a dangerous smuggling route. US authorities seemed to be focusing on the connections between Colombia and the Caribbean as a transshipment route for cocaine destined for the United States. It was Sal who said, "The islands are too hot. We've got to come up with something else."

Once again, it was time to improvise.

For a while, Willy had been thinking about Mexico. A few years earlier, when he had made the drive with Randy Sosa from Miami to Los Angeles to deliver coke and bring back millions in cash, they pulled off Interstate 10 near El Paso, Texas, and stopped to fill their gas tank. Willy had been standing at the pump on a sweltering hot afternoon when he looked on the other side of a nearby gully at a dense thicket of impoverished shacks on a hill. "What is that?" he asked Sosa.

"That's Mexico," said his underling.

Willy was stunned at how close it was; you could practically throw a rock over there. Way in the back of his mind, a thought was hatched: bringing kilos of cocaine across that border—via *la tierra*, the land—has got to be easier than transporting it by air and by sea.

In late 1983, as they prepared for their customary holiday galivanting in Las Vegas and Vail (all of it made much easier by the availability of the Learjet),

Willy and Sal received a special guest at the man cave in Miami. Mario Valencia was in town from Cali to conduct business and check on the Boys. Willy told the Cali Cartel coleader about their problems with the Bahamas. "This war on drugs is hitting close to home. DEA is focusing on the Bahamas and on South Florida. We've got to find another way. I've been thinking about Mexico."

"Yes," said Mario, "I agree." Valencia explained how, just before he caught his flight to Miami, he had stopped in Armenia, Colombia, to see Juan Ramón Matta-Ballesteros. "You remember him?" he asked Willy.

"Yes, I think he helped us out when we were smuggling kilos for the Contras based in Honduras at the time."

"That's him. He remembers you. It was his pilot that brought you your very first load of cocaine in Kissimmee, Florida. I told him the problems we were having working through the Bahamas. And without me even saying anything, he said, 'Mario, you should meet my friends in the Guadalajara Cartel in Mexico. They've been smuggling marijuana into the US for decades.'"

Matta was a pioneer in the earliest stages of the relationship between the CIA and anti-Communist militants in Central America. Born in Tegucigalpa, Honduras, with a history of occasional drug incarcerations in the United States and Mexico (where he was suspected of having murdered two inmates), he had smuggled arms to various rebel camps in Honduras and El Salvador on behalf of the CIA since the mid-1970s. He was an expert covert operator and narco trafficker.

Mario Valencia explained to Willy and Sal that when he returned to Colombia, he would contact Ramón Matta and ask if he could arrange a meeting with "his Mexican friends."

One month later, after they returned from their holiday excursions in Vegas and Vail, Willy and Sal made a trip to Mexico City. They checked into the Camino Real Hotel, in the upscale Polanco neighborhood. They were met there by Mario Valencia, who flew in from Colombia.

In a suite at the hotel, they all came together: Willy, Sal, Mario Valencia, Ramón Matta, and Matta's Mexican contact, Rafael Muñoz Talavera. After some small talk between Falcon and Matta about the halcyon days of smuggling cocaine for arms in Central America (an activity that was still ongoing with a new cast of characters), they got down to business.

Said Willy, "Rafael, what we want to know is whether or not you can assist us in smuggling cocaine from Colombia into Mexico and then across the border into the United States. You would be doing this on behalf of the Falcon-Magluta organization."

Muñoz, born in El Paso, Texas, and raised in Ciudad Juárez, was a midlevel manager in the Guadalajara Cartel. To Falcon's proposition, he said, "I don't see why not. We have a well-established route for smuggling marijuana. Smuggling cocaine should be no problem, maybe even easier because it's less bulky." He added, "We have a landing strip in Jalisco that you can use to bring the merchandise into the country from Colombia."

Sal suggested to the Mexican that they start with a trial run of five hundred kilos. They would pay $6,000 per kilo, for a total of $3 million.

Willy added that if the trial run went according to plan, Muñoz could expect much larger shipments in the future.

Muñoz shrugged. "You can send as many kilos as you want to Mexico. We have total control here." He explained that once the shipment landed, it would be brought across the border to a drop-off point near Los Angeles, where the Cubans could pick it up.

Willy said that they would send, by commercial airline, one of their pilots to Jalisco. If they could show him where the landing strip was located, then he would be ready to go.

On their way back to Miami, Willy and Sal were feeling those familiar butterflies in the stomach. Once again, it seemed as though they had pulled a rabbit out of the hat. If this played out as they hoped, it could be a whole new era in cocaine smuggling. Using Mexico as a transshipment point would be costly; the Mexicans would receive a percentage far higher than what they paid in the Caribbean, but it was well worth it. Once the kilos were in Mexico, the Mexicans would take charge of bringing it into the United States through their own systems. In some ways, this was a far less labor-intensive method than what the Boys had been doing for the last few years.

Back in Miami, they made preparations to receive the shipment in LA. At the man cave in Horse Country, Willy met with Victor Alvarez, one of the key Muchachos who had been handling their shipments to the West Coast. "Victor," said Willy, "we got a load of five hundred kilos coming from Mexico in the next few days. Can your people in LA handle this?"

The cocaine-distribution business was based on devising a set system in which everyone knew the routine. Alterations to the system were usually not well received. For a couple of years so far, Los Muchachos had been sending a manageable amount of cocaine (one hundred kilos every two weeks) from Miami to Los Angeles via the eighteen-wheel tractor trailers. Victor had some concerns about initiating an entirely new route. "With the product coming from south of the border," he noted to Willy, "we're going to have to start from scratch. I mean, we don't even know these people. We'll have to decide on a safe transfer location. And then things like storing the kilos until we can move them. Normally, I would have them presold before our Miami shipments even arrived, but this is much more than we ever received all at one time."

"Well, Victor, let's get moving," said Willy. He told his underling that he needed to go to Los Angeles immediately, rent a house with a double garage, then purchase a cargo van and a car. "If this goes well," said Willy to Victor, "you won't be traveling back and forth anymore. You'll be living in LA full time."

The following day, Victor called Willy and said, "Okay, boss, I've got a flight to Los Angeles tomorrow night."

"Good," said Willy.

That night, around seven p.m., Willy received a call from his Mexico connection: "The shipment has passed through Mexico and is waiting to be picked up in Los Angeles as soon as possible."

Coño. That was fast.

Willy called Sal and said, "You won't believe this, but that five hundred kilos from Mexico arrived in LA today."

"Shit. Already?" said Sal.

"Listen, I'm gonna go out there myself. This is too important to leave it to others. Can you have our guy book a flight for tomorrow morning for me and Victor and Benny Lorenzo? Earliest flight we can get."

"Willy, you don't have to go. That's what we have our people for. I mean, for all we know, this could be law enforcement."

"*Hermano,* this thing has to work to perfection. I'm gonna supervise the entire transaction. There's always that chance it could be the law, but this is a risk I'm willing to take." Willy and Sal both knew that this was possibly the beginning of something monumental. For generations, the Mexicans had been smuggling marijuana loads as big as ten thousand pounds. They had devised a system utilizing two thousand miles of border from Texas to California, picking and choosing where they wanted to cross. For Willy and Sal, it was the new frontier. Said Falcon to his partner, "This could be our future right here."

The next day, Willy, Victor, and Benny Lorenzo rose early and boarded a seven a.m. flight for Los Angeles. As the jetliner rose into the air and settled into its altitude, Willy heard Sal's warning in his head. It had been a while since Willy had been on the front lines of a shipment, as he had been back in the days of smuggling cocaine and arms as part of *la lucha*. What if Sal were right? What if he and the others were walking into a sting operation?

Fuck it, he told himself. Nobody said that cocaine trafficking was supposed to be easy.

THE REASON WILLY BROUGHT BENNY B. along was because he wanted to break him in. Benny, born in Las Villas, Cuba, in 1958, was a few years younger than Willy and Sal. Recently, they had given him the responsibility of overseeing shipments of cocaine from Freeport on Grand Bahama Island. Benny organized the offloading of shipments by air from Medellín, and then coordinated the pickup at sea between Boston Whaler fishing boats and the specially retrofitted Seahawk powerboats.

There were some who believed Benny was part of the group because he was a pretty boy. Benny's grandparents were both from the Canary Islands. He was good looking, with thick black hair and bedroom eyes. Even Willy would admit that the reason he and Sal recruited Benny into Los Muchachos was because he was a "chick magnet." But he was also smart and had balls. Willy felt he might be someone who could rise in the group, but he was green and needed to be tested.

They arrived at LAX after a six-hour flight across the United States. At the airport, they rented a van and a sedan, both of which they drove to the Bonaventure Hotel, where Willy had stayed on previous trips to LA. After they checked in, Willy called the phone number he had been given by the Mexicans. He had been told to ask for "Pepe." Willy's code name was the Doctor.

Pepe gave the Doctor the address of a café in San Bernardino. Willy had no idea where that was, so it was decided that he would take a taxi and the others would follow: Victor in the van and Benny in the car.

There was no time to waste. It was a one-hour drive east of Los Angeles. A brown haze of smog ringed the city. They arrived at the small, nondescript café just off the highway. Benny waited in the car, while Willy and Victor entered the café. Willy had been told to look for a Mexican wearing a green windbreaker. Right away, he saw the guy sitting in a booth with another guy.

Willy walked over and said, "Hello, are you Pepe? I'm the Doctor."

Pepe said, "You know the Doctor?"

Willy explained, "No, I am the Doctor."

Pepe was impressed; he had not been expecting the main guy. He asked Willy to sit. There was no small talk. Pepe told Willy to give him the key to their van. He would take the van to go get the product, which might take ninety minutes. He would return to the café, park the van, lock it, and leave the keys on top of the left front tire.

Willy gave Pepe the keys and said, "Nice meeting you. If I don't see you again today, hopefully we do more business in the future. Victor here is going to be handling these transactions with you from now on."

The Boys from Miami decided to rent a motel room directly across the street from the café. Their room gave them a great view of the location. They waited there until Pepe returned with the van and left. They retrieved the van, and in their two vehicles they drove back toward the Bonaventure in downtown LA.

First, they stopped and purchased a half dozen large suitcases. When they got to the hotel, in the parking garage, they transferred the five hundred kilos to the suitcases and took them up to their room. Then Willy called Jojo Brito.

Jojo had been waiting two years for this moment. Ever since he moved from Miami to LA at the behest of Los Muchachos, he had been told there would one day be a major expansion of their cocaine business in the City of Angels. After a year learning the city (in the days before GPS, the *Thomas Street Guide to Los Angeles & Orange Counties* was his bible), Jojo began selling kilos to his own small stable of clients, which included Gordy, a recent graduate of Stanford University who lived in Marin County and sold coke in the Bay Area. Gordy had a gringo client named Craig who distributed coke in Oregon and Seattle.

Jojo lived in Malibu, in a house with an ocean view, and he also had a home in Encino. He owned a high-end automotive repair shop, tending to Mercedes, Ferraris, and Lamborghinis. BSC Automotive was not a front; Jojo liked to tinker with engines, and the business was successful in its own right.

Willy also contacted Gilberto "Veci" Barrios, who was their man in charge of organizing the semitrucks that transported merchandise. Barrios's nickname derived from the word for neighbor—*vecino*—which was shortened to Veci. He lived in both LA and Miami. Barrios owned a trucking company and had a fleet of drivers who were on call twenty-four seven.

Veci was a pro, but he was also a beast. Once, Pegy Rosello, Tavy Falcon's brother-in-law, was with Barrios, unloading a truck, and he saw him capture a lizard with his bare hands.

"Cool," said Pegy.

Then Barrios held up the lizard by its tail, dropped it into his mouth, and ate it.

"Damn, you're rich," said Pegy. "You don't need to be eating lizards."

In Los Angeles, Barrios sat attentively alongside Jojo, Victor, and Benny B. in the bar/lounge of the Bonaventure Hotel. "Our entire operation is shifting to LA," Willy told the men.

They were five Cubans, born on the island, every one of them in exile from Castro's revolution, now cocaine millionaires in the United States.

Willy explained that not only would they be servicing their clients in California and in the west, but that Los Angeles would now likely become the primary point of entry for their product.

Barrios, whose role became exponentially more important as the organization expanded geographically, asked Willy, "You mean, we're going to be receiving product in LA and driving it across the country to Miami?"

"Among other places, yes," said Willy.

Barrios laughed; he thought that was great. "Driving cocaine from LA to Miami, instead of the other way around. Nobody would suspect that."

That night, to celebrate, Willy ordered two limousines to take them to Dodger Stadium for a baseball game. The Cubans loved baseball. It may have been America's game, but it reminded them of their homeland. Willy was partial to the San Francisco Giants, his second-favorite team after the New York Yankees, but he was thrilled to be at Dodger Stadium for the first time.

Los Muchachos (the Boys), all grown up. *From left to right*: Tony "Bemba" Garcia, Tavy Falcon, Roberto Solis, Willy Falcon, Sal Magluta, Benny Lorenzo, Frank Ocando Paz, Tony "El Cuño" Garrudo.

At left, Tavy (*standing*), with Sal and Willy. (Falcon Collection)

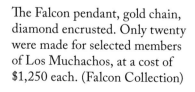

The Falcon pendant, gold chain, diamond encrusted. Only twenty were made for selected members of Los Muchachos, at a cost of $1,250 each. (Falcon Collection)

The island of Cuba, with its fierce tropical beauty, lived on in the imagination of the exiles. (T. J. English)

Willy and Tavy Falcon as children. (Falcon Collection)

FREEDOM FLIGHTS: From December 196? to December 1973, an estimated 300,000 Cubans fled to the United States, including the Falcon family. (National Museum of the American Latino)

EL BARBUDO ("THE BEARDED ONE"): In 1961, Fidel Castro visited the United States to give a speech before the United Nations. Plots to kill Castro had become a cottage industry and would continue for decades to come. (Wikimedia Commons)

...rsenio and Marta Falcon, *seated*, with Tavy, Sal, and Willy standing behind them. (...alcon Collection)

In the hills of Peru, *raspachines* harvest the coca plant in its organic form, working long hours in the hot sun. The leaves are gathered in bales and shipped to cocaine labs in Colombia. (Getty Images)

At a rustic lab in Colombia's Cauca Valley, the leaves are treated with powdered lime, the first step in an elaborate process that transforms the leaves into pure powder cocaine (Getty Images)

Wedding day for Willy Falcon, age nineteen, and his bride, Alina Rossique, age eighteen, on September 22, 1973. (Falcon Collection)

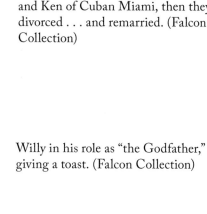

Alina and Willy were the Barbie and Ken of Cuban Miami, then they divorced . . . and remarried. (Falcon Collection)

Willy in his role as "the Godfather," giving a toast. (Falcon Collection)

Willy and Sal pioneered a cocaine distribution network in the United States that was second to none, with hubs in Miami, Los Angeles, and the New York City area. (Falcon Collection)

THE WAR ON DRUGS: President Ronald Reagan scowls at bags of confiscated cocaine while appearing at an event in honor of the South Florida Drug Task Force. (Getty Images)

The Dadeland Mall massacre, a shootout between rival narco factions in Miami, occurred July 11, 1979. It had no direct relation to the operations of Willy and Sal, but it set the tone for the cocaine business in the city for years to come. (HistoryMiami Museum)

Los Muchachos were as much a family as they were a criminal organization. *From left to right*: Ileana Garrudo, Tony Garrudo, Amelia Falcon, Tavy, Willy, Alina, Isabel Magluta, and Sal. (Falcon Collection)

Seahawk racing boat, aluminum Cougar Cat, thirty-eight-footer, fuel-injected 2,000 horsepower engine. (Falcon Collection)

THE CREW, *from left to right*: Juan "Recut" Barroso, Sal, Willy, Tavy, and *seated*, Ralph "Cabeza" Linero. (Falcon Collection)

Willy Falcon after the race. (Falcon Collection)

THE MUTINY: Fueled by cocaine, the disco era flourished in Miami, especially at the Mutiny, seen here in a rare photo taken inside the club. (John R. Lawrence)

Willy with Lourdes Castellon, his mistress and mother of his twin boys. (Lourdes Castellon)

THE CITY THAT COCAINE BUILT: Miami circa 1980 had a modest skyline, with little urban development. (Library of Congress: Carol M. Highsmith Archive)

For every kilo of cocaine seized, thousands more reached the marketplace. (HistoryMiami Museum)

By the early 2000s, the city was transformed. (Wikimedia Commons)

NARCOS: Colombians Pablo Escobar and Carlos Lehder pioneered cocaine smuggling in the late-1970s. (Edgar "El Chino" Jiménez)

The entrance to Escobar's estate, Hacienda Nápoles, in Medellín. (Wikimedia Commons)

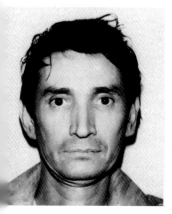

THE MEXICANS, *from left to right*: Félix Gallardo and Amado Carrillo. (AP Photos)

Vice President George Bush meets with General Manuel Noriega. (Wikimedia Commons)

President Bush gives his infamous crack speech on national television. (Getty Images)

Noriega is apprehended in Panama City and booked in Miami on cocaine smuggling charges. (Wikimedia Commons)

Guillermo Endara is all smiles after being installed as President of Panama by the Bush Administration. (Getty Images)

DRUG WAR TROPHY:
Pablo Escobar (inset) was killed by Colombian military police on a rooftop in Medellín. (Wikimedia Commons)

THE TRIAL, *from left to right*: attorney Roy Black, attorney Marty Weinberg, Sal and Willy (in cuffs), attorney Bobby Wells, attorney Albert Krieger. (Netflix)

The family of Willy Falcon, with Alina, Jessica, Will Jr., Willy, and Aileen. This Polaroid, taken in 1992 in the visiting area at the Miami detention center, is one of the last photos taken of Alina before she was killed. (Falcon Collection)

THE PROSECUTORS: AUSA Pat Sullivan (striped tie) walking into court. Courtroom sketch of AUSA Chris Clark. (Pat Sullivan)

Willy Falcon on a private jet in November 2018, after having been deported twice, once from the United States and once from the Dominican Republic. (Sandra Osorio)

Willy Falcon being interviewed by T. J. English at an undisclosed location in May 2021. (Sandra Osorio)

Tavy Falcon, in a 2023 photo, holding his newly born twin grandchildren. He is wearing the same Falcon pendant he has owned since the mid-1980s. The cocaine era has passed, but the memories linger. (Amelia Falcon)

Over the next couple of days, they put down roots. Through a local real estate agent they knew—Cuban, of course, originally from Miami—they rented a series of domiciles they would use as stash houses for product and money. They purchased several cars to be used for company business. They contacted their telecommunications people at HoneyComb Paging and Cell Enterprises in Miami and had them ship a couple dozen beepers and cell phones, which would be especially important in LA, a city known for its urban sprawl. Finally, they rented two primo town houses at the Marina City Club in picturesque Marina del Rey: unit 109, on the first floor, and unit 215, located directly above on the second floor. The rooms had a beautiful view of the boat marina and, beyond that, the glistening blue Pacific Ocean, which danced in the afternoon sunlight. They purchased furniture for the two town houses and the other stash houses they were renting.

The City Club was in a private community, with an electronic gate and twenty-four-hour security. This would be Willy and Sal's place of residence whenever they were in LA.

When Willy and Benny Lorenzo were finally ready to return to Miami, Willy called for their Learjet to come and pick them up.

It had been a whirlwind adventure, with all the things you might want from the cocaine business: a secret rendezvous with a Mexican named Pepe, the always adrenaline-pumping transfer of kilos, the promise of riches yet to come. By shifting the importation of product through Mexico and into Southern California, the Boys were, in a sense, redirecting the entire cocaine business in the United States for years to come.

9

"IT'S A BOY(S)!"

LOURDES CASTELLON HAD COME TO Miami from New Jersey when she was a young girl. All her life, people told her that she was beautiful. Her face was composed of clean lines and elegance, like the actress Ali MacGraw, who was a big movie star in the 1970s. Both of Lourdes's parents were born in Cuba and had fled the revolution. They lived a humble, working-class life. By the age of fifteen, Lourdes was being recruited to sign a modeling contract. In Miami, that meant spending a lot of time at the nightclubs, where the beautiful people hung out. Her older sister chaperoned her at the clubs, since she was underage. Older men cruised the clubs looking for fresh young faces, those that stood out in a room full of beautiful faces, the human ritual in its modern form, with antecedents that likely went back to caveman times.

One night when she was seventeen, she was at Faces in the Grove, a relatively new club, seated with a group of friends. A waiter came over to Lourdes's table with a bottle of champagne and said, "Excuse me, this is from the gentleman over there." The waiter nodded toward Willy Falcon, seated with a group of people. "He says he would like to meet you."

Lourdes looked past the waiter and saw Willy, who nodded. She said to the waiter, "Tell him thanks for the champagne, but I'm here with my friends."

One of her friends elbowed her sharply. "Are you crazy? Look, you wanna go over there."

The waiter smiled at the situation. He also was young. He said to Lourdes, "I think you wanna meet him. That guy is very nice. Trust me, he's a gentleman."

Lourdes knew who Willy was, sort of. She had a good friend who had dated Sal Magluta, so she was familiar with the lore of Los Muchachos.

She went over to the table, and Willy said, "Please, have a seat. My name's Willy Falcon."

Lourdes was not exactly Willy's type. She was a brunette, for one thing. But she was tall, with long legs and a seductive smile.

Lourdes sat down. It was as if everything else in the room faded away, and their eyes focused on one another like they were looking through the long end of a telescope. Lourdes said to Willy, "I know who you are."

"How? I'm pretty sure we never met. I would remember."

"No, we never met. But a girlfriend of mine, Marilyn Bonachea, she used to date a friend of yours. Sal Magluta."

"Small world," said Willy.

She got the impression he knew everything she just told him, but he was polite enough to make it seem as though he were receiving new information. They chatted for a while. Noted Castellon, many years later, as an older and wiser woman, "He was very respectful, very nice, very sweet, charming, funny. He made everybody laugh. He had this thing about him, I guess you'd call it charisma."

People were coming and going at the table. Willy said, "You wanna go somewhere else? Let's go somewhere else."

In a chauffeur-driven limousine, they drove to Cats (located in the same space as Faces in the Grove, which had closed months earlier), and then on to Alexandre at the Omni Hotel. Everywhere they went, Willy was treated like a star by the doormen and owners. (As Willy put it, "Many of the club owners were friends and even clients of mine. It meant a lot if I showed up with my people. Los Muchachos were very well known in the club scene. It was good for their business if we hung out there, so we often made the rounds at these places.") At the end of the night, Willy kissed Lourdes on the forehead and said goodbye.

They didn't see each again for a long time—maybe three or four months. In that time, Lourdes had her eighteenth birthday, which made her a legally consenting adult in the eyes of the law. Then, out of the blue, Willy contacted her and invited her on a trip to Aruba. For Willy, it was a business trip, but there was also lots of time for pleasure: tootie, drinking, gambling at the hotel casino, swimming, and lots of sex. After five days alone together in Aruba, Lourdes was in love, and Willy was in lust.

Willy treated all his women like queens to be bestowed with gifts. He gave Lourdes a Rolex Presidential watch and later a diamond necklace. When they went gambling together in Aruba and won $150,000, though Willy did most of the wagering, he let her keep all the winnings.

Inevitably, Alina Falcon found out about Lourdes. Alina had many spies operating in the universe of Los Muchachos. It wasn't like Willy was trying to hide the affair. He invited Lourdes to boat races and softball games. She was on the Learjet more than once. She got to know some of the Boys, who treated her with respect.

One time, Willy, Sal, Benny Lorenzo, and a few others included Lourdes on a semiregular trip to Wildlife Ranch, a wildlife refuge in Comal County, Texas, where, for a sizable fee, visitors could hunt and shoot live animals. She was the only woman in a group of Muchachos. Though Lourdes had never held a gun before, with a rifle she shot and injured a wild deer. Willy and the others were all impressed by that. (Someone else finished off the deer by shooting it in the head.)

Even before Willy started the affair with Lourdes, he and Alina had once again been struggling. They had even begun living separately.

For a time, Willy, Alina, and their two girls had been living in a brand-new penthouse condominium at a sleek building located at 2025 Brickell Avenue. Falcon and Magluta purchased apartments number 1 and 12 on the top floor. The building was officially known as Atlantis. Designed by the renowned Miami architecture firm Arquitectonica, the views from the patio were panoramic and spectacular, and the building lobby was itself a work of art. (One day, not long after moving into the place, Willy noticed that they were shooting a movie at one of the other penthouse apartments. Among the crew and other personnel hustling about, he spotted the actors Al Pacino and Michelle Pfeiffer. They were shooting a scene from *Scarface*, with the Atlantis building serving as the apartment of Frank Lopez, Tony Montana's boss in the movie.)

Two years later, Falcon purchased two more penthouse apartments in Brickell Key Tower 1, located at 520 Brickell Key Drive. Alina took charge of converting these two units into one large suite by breaking down walls and retrofitting the entire space. The penthouse had five bedrooms, a large living room, a game room with a bar and pool table, and a dining room with a big oak table that sat twelve people. Everything was high tech: dimmer lights, central air-conditioning, and electric curtains. The master bedroom was converted from what used to be three bedrooms, with a circular bed and a sliding wooden door that opened into the master bathroom, which included a jacuzzi and a steam room.

Alina selected the artwork and décor for the entire penthouse—paintings and sculptures purchased at art auctions in New York, Madrid, and Paris.

Willy's philandering caused Alina to move out of the condo at the Atlantis and make the Brickell Key Tower suite a permanent residence for her and the girls. She told Willy, "You will never have that boy you want so badly, because I'm having my tubes tied."

Alina and her sister Ileana were busy with Scruples, their couture clothing store on Miracle Mile. But Alina's business responsibilities did not stop her from obsessing about her cheating husband. Some worried that the situation was eating away at Alina's sanity and emotional health. She had already tried divorcing Willy, which had worked, but only temporarily.

She knew that Willy had one-night stands, and, to an extent, had been willing to tolerate that. But when he spent more than three days with a woman, showing her off in public, Alina became enraged. The only thing that could have been more disrespectful, she believed, was if he were to get one of his mistresses pregnant.

At the world championship boat racing finals in 1983, in Key West, it turned ugly. Alina was not there, but many of the wives and girlfriends of other members of the group turned on Lourdes. "They were a bunch of bullies," said Lourdes. As Lourdes remembered it, Willy had to straighten them out: "He told them, 'Hey, back off, she's with me, and that's the way it's gonna be.'"

After that, Alina began to wage what Lourdes remembered as a campaign of harassment against her. One night she was at the popular nightclub Cats with friends, and Alina showed up. She saw Alina speaking with the manager, whom Lourdes knew. "The manager came over and said, 'Look, you girls are gonna have to leave.'" One of Lourdes's friends started arguing about it, but Lourdes said, "Hey, no problem, man. I'm outta here." "I never fought it. I didn't want to cause a scene."

Another time, Lourdes came out of her apartment to discover that both front tires of her car had been slashed. Then, somehow, Alina got her phone number and started making vaguely threatening calls. It was beginning to get exhausting.

And then, thunder clapped, the clouds parted, and Lourdes got pregnant. In fact, she had been pregnant for a while but didn't know it.

When Lourdes first told Willy, it had been a while since they had seen one another. Willy was having brunch with a group of friends at Sundays on the Bay, a popular waterfront bistro in Key Biscayne. Willy was drunk. Lourdes tapped him on the shoulder and asked to speak privately. They stepped away from the table, and she said, "I'm pregnant."

Willy was stunned, but he shouldn't have been. They had not been using contraceptives. They spoke for a few moments, and both agreed there would be no abortion. Lourdes would have the baby.

"Is it a boy?" asked Willy.

"They don't know yet, but we will soon."

No one knows how Alina found out. Willy never told her, and he had no plans to do so, but she heard that Willy's "whore on the side" was with child, and Willy was the father.

Around this time, Falcon received a call from his brother-in-law Tony Garrudo: "Willy, I'm calling you from the hospital. Alina tried to commit suicide. She swallowed something like thirty Valium."

"Oh my God," said Willy.

"Yeah. The doctors are pumping her stomach right now. She's going to be okay, but she's completely out of it. She will be here in the hospital at least overnight, maybe longer."

Willy couldn't believe what he was hearing. He felt guilty and depressed. As soon as Alina was discharged from the hospital, he moved into the Brickell Key Tower 1 condominium to be with his daughters and to help nurse his wife back to health. It was a time of reconnection. They talked in a way they hadn't in a long time. There had always been that issue between them that Willy wanted to have a boy, but Alina did not want another child. A year earlier, she had her tubes tied through tubal ligation surgery. In a peace offering to Willy, she now submitted to another surgery to have her tubes untied. The doctor told her there was only a 50 to 80 percent chance that she would get pregnant. On the other hand, after having the reversal procedure, if she were to get pregnant, it would likely happen right away.

As soon as Alina recovered from the surgery, she and Willy made love for the first time in months.

Willy Falcon was not yet over his season of surprises. While at one of the Seahawk softball team's games, somewhere in Michigan, he received a cell phone call from Lourdes. "Are you sitting down?" she asked.

"Yeah, I'm in the dugout. Here for the big game."

"Well, I thought you should know right away. You're gonna have a boy."

"Wow. That's amazing."

"In fact," she added, "you're gonna have two boys."

"What!?"

"Yeah. I'm pregnant with twins."

Two weeks later, Willy learned that Alina was also pregnant. The doctors told her it was a boy.

Falcon had always wanted a boy. And now, in a matter of weeks, he learned that he was having three from two different women.

LIFE CAN BE A CAVALCADE of happenstance, or it can be a brutal game of cause and effect. Illness, death, and the gift of life sometimes takes place according to its own logic. Willy Falcon's seemingly sudden and unexpected status as a father-to-be was not exactly an unpredictable act of God. Willy liked to gamble, to take chances. He had been engaging in the ancient art of fornication, as it is called from the church pulpit, and he didn't always use protection. Now he had to deal with a reality for which he knew of no rule book or source of wisdom that might help soothe the roiling waters. He was on his own.

On the other hand, Willy was not the one who was pregnant. For Lourdes and Alina, the issue was not only metaphysical, but also physical. Lourdes was three months ahead of Alina, and she was pregnant with twins. Though she was young (now nineteen years old), she was dealing with back pain, headaches, and hot flashes in the middle of the night.

Alina hadn't bothered her in a while. Apparently, the suicide attempt, recovery, and subsequent pregnancy was keeping her busy. Willy had been good about stopping by Lourdes's place to make sure she was okay. Though they both knew that they would never be together as man and wife—a circumstance Lourdes claimed she never wanted in the first place—Willy promised her that her boys would never want for money. He would take care of their financial security.

One night, when she was nine months pregnant and ready to give birth any day, her doorbell rang. At the time, Lourdes was living in Brickell Estates, in a condo that Willy had purchased for her. She was there with her mother, who had moved in to help her in the latter stages of her pregnancy.

Lourdes waddled over to the door and opened it. Standing there was Alina Falcon, who was herself six months pregnant, with a noticeable baby bump.

The two women stared at one another, and then Alina said, "I had to see for myself whether it was true."

"Yeah," said Lourdes, "it's true, so I guess you'll just have to get used to it."

"You know, you can be the mother of his child, but you'll never be his wife. Always remember that."

Two pregnant women in a state of exhaustion, overheated, bodies aching—neither of them needed a confrontation like this.

"Why exactly are you here?" said Lourdes. "What are you trying to prove?"

Lourdes's mother had come up behind her and asked, "Who's there? Who is it?"

Alina asked, "Is that your mother?"

"That's none of your business. Listen, I never disrespected you. I've never bothered you. You have no right coming over here and causing a scene in front of my mother. You have no right."

Alina pointed a finger at Lourdes and, raising her voice, proclaimed, "He will never love you the way he loves me, you understand? You will never have what we have."

"Go away," responded Lourdes, adding in exasperation, "You have no right to be here. Can't you see I'm about to give birth?"

Alina turned and walked away. Lourdes shut the door. The two women never saw one another again.

The very next day—June 22, 1984—Lourdes Castellon was rushed to the hospital and gave birth to two healthy baby boys. She named one of them Angelo and the other William, or Willy, after his father. As a surname, she used Castellon, not Falcon, out of respect for Willy's family.

Three months later, Alina gave birth to a boy that she also named William, or Willy, after his father—though he would most commonly be referred to by the family as Will Jr.

WILLY NOW HAD THREE NEWBORN babies in his life, which was miraculous and sometimes joyful. But the cocaine business was not designed to seamlessly accommodate the whims and fancies of a conventional life. Falcon's idea of being a father was to make sure his children, and their mothers, were taken care of financially. At the same time his family was expanding, his business had become one large battlefield, with legal assaults that ate away at the edges of Willy and Sal's empire.

From late 1983 into 1985, there were a series of major criminal indictments that, though they did not hit directly at the Falcon-Magluta organization, seemed to suggest that federal law enforcement was beginning to develop a picture of how the cocaine business was run in the United States. Some of those indicted were people who had been, or still were, mentors and partners of Willy and Sal.

In mid-1984, Manuel Garces, Willy's initial Godfather in the cocaine business, was indicted on trafficking and money-laundering charges related to the Great American Bank, which he helped to create as a vehicle for laundering Colombian narco profits in the United States. Garces knew the indictment was coming and fled to Colombia. The US Justice Department was attempting to have him extradited. Garces was held in prison in Bogotá until November, when the president of Colombia authorized his extradition to the United States to face charges.

In December 1984, Ray Corona and his father, Rafael, were arrested and charged as part of a thirty-count indictment involving drug smuggling and money laundering. Unlike Garces, who Willy and Sal believed would never crack and cooperate with the government, they worried that Ray Corona, in order to protect his sixty-three-year-old father, might cut a deal. His testimony would be problematic, if not devasting, as he had helped launch Willy and Sal in the business through his ownership of the Sunshine State Bank of Miami. Ray Corona was also the one who introduced them to Guillermo Endara in Panama, and to Gabriel Castro, the head of Panama's FBI, who helped them establish the fake import-export company for shipping millions in cash.

Attorney Mel Kessler, who had been an adviser to Willy on matters of criminal law, was another of their associates facing trouble. The DEA had its sights on Kessler for years, even before he became Willy and Sal's lawyer. In a 1983 case, the US Customs Service targeted Kessler; his name came up in at least twenty drug-smuggling cases. According to a customs report (case #GFGS-81-4011), "In May 1979, Kessler was suspected of arranging the shipment of 200 kilos of cocaine from Bolivia to the United States." In December 1980, he was suspected of financing a smuggling venture from the Caribbean islands to San Juan, Puerto Rico. More recently, he had become involved with Ben

Kramer, the championship powerboat racer and marijuana kingpin, smuggling tons of marijuana through the Isle of Man. An indictment was imminent.

Of all the pending legal cases, the most ominous was one involving Jack Devoe. After Devoe's arrest at the West Palm Beach airport in 1983, rumors circulated that he was cooperating with the government. It seemed he was headed in that direction in November 1984, when he testified before the President's Commission on Organized Crime in Washington, DC. Later, in 1985, he went to trial. After he was found guilty on cocaine-trafficking charges, it became official that Devoe was cooperating with the US Justice Department.

All these legal developments were potentially perilous for Los Muchachos, but Jack Devoe becoming a "snitch" caused some immediate concerns. Devoe knew a lot. First and foremost, there was his knowledge of the Clewiston ranch landing operation.

With Mel Kessler under the cloud of indictment, Los Muchachos now had a new team of lawyers that included L. Mark Dachs, Joe Oteri (who had represented Blondie Passapera at his trial), and Marty Weinberg, another Boston-based lawyer whom they met through Oteri. In a meeting with the lawyers, it was explained to Willy and Sal that due to new drug-seizure laws instituted as part of the War on Drugs, prosecutors now did not even need an indictment to seize properties of those suspected of having attained the properties through narcotics profits. Said Dachs, "They will seize everything you own, and there's not much you can do about it."

"Damn," said Sal, "that's not fair."

Replied Dachs, "You need to take a hard look at your assets. If there are things you can sell, you better do it now, before the government can take it away from you. This way, at least it won't be a total loss."

For Willy, it was hard to bend his mind around the idea that the Clewiston ranch had to go. Much time and money had been invested in making it a seemingly legitimate business enterprise. There were their many hundred heads of cattle and an agricultural business they had launched less than a year earlier. They had even begun growing turf and selling it to the Florida state highway system—a highly profitable side business. Now it all had to be sold quickly, even at a loss if necessary.

An even bigger problem was they had more than $25 million in cash buried in a five-hundred-gallon septic tank on the property. The first thing they needed to do was retrieve those millions, pack it in drywall shipments, and send it to Panama.

Reluctantly, Willy and Sal began the process of selling Eveready Ranch. "The sooner the better," Dachs told them.

All these legal matters were considerable, but they were nothing compared with the shitstorm that had been unleashed by their partner in Colombia, Pablo Escobar.

Since being elected as an alternate delegate to the Colombian congress, things had not gone well for Pablo—as Willy had feared. The justice minister of Colombia, Rodrigo Lara Bonilla, had launched a crusade against Escobar to expose him as a narco. When first elected, Escobar had successfully expunged from his record the fact of a 1976 cocaine conviction. After Lara brought that conviction to light, Escobar was forced to resign from office. It was a public humiliation for Pablo that would compel him to turn against Colombia's political establishment for the rest of his life.

The narco boss held a particular animus toward Lara, who did not stop with Escobar's resignation. The justice minster advocated for Escobar's extradition—and the extradition of *all* narcos—to face trafficking charges in the United States.

At the same time, DEA agents, working in conjunction with Colombian National Police, had placed a satellite tracking device on tanks of ether, a primary component in the processing of coca paste into cocaine hydrochloride. The ether was created at a chemical plant in New Jersey and delivered by an export company called Arbron Miami International Distributor. The barrels were delivered to Tranquilandia, the Medellín Cartel's processing compound in southeastern Colombia. On March 10, 1984, a massive raid of the lab took place, during which the facilities were destroyed, and 13.8 tons of cocaine seized, with a street value over $1 billion. The raid was authorized by Justice Minister Lara.

Seven weeks later, on April 30, Lara was seated in the back seat of an official state limousine when the sound of motorcycles caught his attention. His entourage, which included security vehicles in front of and behind him, was driving in broad daylight. Two young assassins on separate motorcycles ambushed Lara, riddling the limo and the justice minister with a torrent of gunfire from MAC-10 submachine guns. He was killed instantly. One of the assassins was killed in a shootout with authorities and the other captured. Eventually, the captured sicario admitted what everyone suspected: the execution had been ordered by Escobar, who had paid the killers $20,000 each.

It was a heinous act, unprecedented, and also very risky. The Colombian government came after Escobar with everything it had, raiding his home at Hacienda Nápoles. Pablo narrowly escaped and disappeared deep into the narcosphere.

Willy heard all of this through Gustavo Gaviria, Pablo's cousin and partner. They spoke over the shortwave radio. In a coded conversation, Gaviria told Willy and Sal, "Pablo did [the Lara murder] on his own. Most of us argued against it. But now, what's done is done. Pablo has gone underground. You're not going to hear from him for a while. But our business together does not change. No matter what happens, your loads will continue to arrive on schedule."

At the time, Willy and Sal had three major shipment routes coming into Miami from the Medellín Cartel: one was the kilos hidden inside the tourist charter planes coming by way of Venezuela, another was a shipment of two hundred kilos hidden inside spare tires that were being shipped into Miami, and a third was monthly flights coming from Colombia into the Bahamas. All told, close to two thousand kilos every six weeks, with a value close to $60 million a month. A lot was at stake.

Willy had grown close to Pablo. Their time together in Vegas, the trip with their families to Disney World, and even an unexpected rendezvous in Madrid, Spain, the previous year, when Willy was there on a trip with Alina, and Pablo just happened to be there on business—the relationship between them had evolved beyond trafficking into a friendship. In a sense, they were all in it together. And now, with these latest developments, there was a feeling, perhaps for the first time, that the closeness between them—the interdependence—was something that could bring them all down.

Willy said to Gustavo, "If you talk to Pablo, tell him that we love him like a brother and hope to see him, or at least speak with him, in the near future. Please tell him that."

"Yes, Doctor, I will tell him."

WILLY AND SAL WERE CLOSER to Escobar than they were to the Valencia brothers. Though the Valencias were closer in age to the Cubans, they had not been invited to Las Vegas or on the Lear 55 to Disney World. Conversely, it was with the Cali Cartel—not Escobar—with whom Los Muchachos had chosen to open up a route through Mexico. Willy and Sal said nothing to Pablo about this, nor did they intend to. All this time, the Boys had managed to do business with the two biggest Colombian cocaine cartels in the world without either of them knowing that Los Muchachos had been double-dipping.

In the beginning, no one would have thought anything of it. There was no real competition among cartels from different parts of Colombia. In the late 1970s, when the Medellín and Cali groups first made inroads into the US market, they agreed to a division of spoils: Medellín had exclusive rights to Miami, Cali had New York, and they both shared Los Angeles. By the mid-1980s, those terms mostly held tight.

Mexico, on the other hand, was wide open. All those years that smugglers from Colombia used the Caribbean islands as their primary transshipment locale—because it had always been that way—nobody thought to consider what it would be like if they used a massive, powerful conduit. With its long tradition of corruption and physical proximity to the largest cocaine market on the planet, Mexico could energize the flow of kilos across the border and add a layer of intrigue to the business.

In the summer of 1984, Willy and Sal had a second meeting in Mexico City with their Mexican connection. This time, it was not a midlevel narco but three of the most powerful traffickers in the entire country.

After arriving at the Camino Real Hotel in Mexico City, Willy and Sal checked into their room. Sal called the front desk and asked to be connected with the room of Oscar Martínez, which was the name Mario Valencia used when he traveled on narco business.

"We're here," said Sal.

"I'll be right over," said Mario.

A few minutes later, Valencia arrived at the door. He entered, and everyone embraced. "They should be here in thirty minutes," said Mario.

In the ensuing small talk, the name of Pablo Escobar came up. Mario was angry about the Lara Bonilla murder, which was creating problems for narcos everywhere. "Escobar is a madman," said Mario. "He is going to ruin the business for all of us." Mario seemed to be fishing for information from Willy and Sal; he maybe suspected or had evidence to suggest that the Cubans were doing business with the Medellín Cartel. Willy and Sal were cautious; they revealed nothing.

Mario's position about Escobar echoed the official position of the Cali Cartel, whose "chairman," Gilberto Rodríguez, was quoted saying in the press, "Mister Escobar is sick, a psycho, a lunatic . . . he thinks that a criminal can win a war against the state. I think that is absurd."

There was a knock at the door. Rafael Muñoz Talavera, whom they had met at the previous Camino Real meeting, introduced Willy, Sal, and Mario to his three companions.[1] Each in his own right was a luminary in the Mexican narco universe.

Miguel Félix Gallardo, born in 1946, was a cofounder of the Guadalajara Cartel in the mid-1970s. A former Federal Judicial Police agent, he was known to some as El Jefe de Jefes ("the Boss of Bosses"). Rafael Caro Quintero, six years younger than Gallardo, was another cofounder of the cartel who presided over the city of Guadalajara through violence and fear. Ernesto Fonseca Carrillo, at age fifty-four, was the eldest of the three. Fonseca was a legend in Mexican smuggling circles. Known as Don Neto, he was one of a group of traffickers who created and operated El Búfalo (the Buffalo), a ranch in the state of Chihuahua with arguably the largest marijuana plantation in history.

Though these three men were notorious in Mexican narco circles, Willy and Sal did not know much about them. They had been told by Mario Valencia that they were the top echelon of the Guadalajara Cartel, which was the most powerful smuggling operation in Mexico. That was good enough for Willy and Sal. They would learn the backstories of these men as the relationship unfolded; in the ensuing years, events would occur that put all three of them front and center in the media and on most wanted lists in the United States, Mexico, and Colombia.

Willy told the Mexicans that the cocaine test run of five hundred kilos had gone well. They were ready to do more.

Said Félix Gallardo, who seemed to be the boss, "That is good to hear. We have been meeting among ourselves to discuss this new direction. For the longest time, our main business has been *mota* [marijuana]. We are planning to transition to cocaine."

---

[1] As with many narcos Willy and Sal met in their cocaine-smuggling careers, Rafael Muñoz rose in the cartel hierarchy—until 1998, when, at the age of forty-six, he was found in an abandoned Jeep Cherokee in Ciudad Juárez with three bullet holes and a plastic bag over his head, and cigarette burns and bruises on his body. "Muñoz's body bore the signs of a classic drug hit," said authorities (Molly Moore, "Mexican Drug Lord Found Slain," *Washington Post*, September 12, 1998).

Said Don Neto, the elder statesman, "The Guadalajara Cartel controls most of the drug trafficking in Mexico, especially along the border corridors. We provided the money for our government to improve the roads into Jalisco, where we maintain our landing strips. We make regular payments to DFS [Dirección Federal de Seguridad, Mexico's national intelligence agency] to protect our operations. It doesn't matter if your group is sending one plane or ten; we pay the same amount to DFS for protection. The more airplanes you send to us, the better it is, because we all make more money that way."

Said Willy, "Don Neto, we are in the process of buying another Twin Commander turbo airplane. Once we do that, we'll be sending two airplanes with one thousand two hundred kilos each. We will try to accommodate your wishes to find a way to bring more cocaine in each transaction."

They talked about money. On the previous test run, Los Muchachos had paid the Mexicans $6,000 for each kilo. "We prefer to pay a percentage of the loads that we are smuggling together," said Sal. They talked numbers. It was a civil conversation among men, an intermingling of Cuban, Colombian, and Mexican Spanish with one intention: to maximize profits for all involved.

They all agreed that the Cubans would pay the Guadalajara Cartel 33 percent of every load.

"The shipments from Colombia will be arriving by plane in the next three or four days," said Mario.

After the meeting was over, they all went to a nearby restaurant to eat and socialize. Félix Gallardo raised a toast: "To the new partnership between our different groups—the Valencia brothers from Colombia, the Guadalajara Cartel here in Mexico, and the Falcon organization in the United States. To the future."

They all said, "To the future," and downed their drinks.

The following day, on their Learjet, Willy and Sal flew back to Miami. Falcon immediately reached out to Gilberto Barrios, their trucking organizer. At a meeting at the man cave in Horse Country, Willy told Barrios, "This whole thing hinges on you, *entiende*? We will be dropping the price of a kilo in LA, to stimulate the market. We will be doubling the number of kilos we bring in every month. Your drivers will be transporting loads across the country to Miami and also New York City and everywhere else we do business."

Barrios indicated that he was ready.

Two days later, they filled the jet with fuel and took to the skies.

Now that the kilos were in motion, there was the issue of how to manage the resulting cash flow. Willy and Sal flew to Panama City primarily to meet Guillermo Endara. But first, they met with Gabriel Castro, the head of PTJ, to let him know they would now be sending much more cash. The drywall shipments were great, but they might have to develop additional methods to accommodate all the money that would be in play. Castro said he would formulate some ideas and get back to them. Then they headed to the offices of the Endara Firm to meet with Guillermo and Hernán Delgado.

Endara was in a good mood. The corpulent attorney told the Cubans that he had recently been appointed as the minister of planning and economic policy in Panama. This, said Guillermo, would give him tremendous power over banking regulations. In addition, the position would serve as an excellent launching pad for his planned run for the presidency of Panama. "It's definitely happening," he told the Boys. "Of course, this would be tremendous for our relationship. As president, I would have access to all intelligence and law enforcement activities not only in Panama but in the entire region." Endara cleared his throat and asked the question foremost on his mind: "If I do decide to run for president, can I count on you to support my campaign?"

Willy and Sal glanced at one another: *Here we go again with one of our partners dreaming of presidential glory.*

The Endara situation was different from Escobar's. Guillermo had always been involved in politics. From the beginning of their relationship, it was understood that he might one day seek the presidency. The Boys thought maybe he was delusional to think there was a path to the top office without the backing of General Noriega, but Endara was looking for an opening.

They all agreed that the prospect of a President Guillermo Endara of Panama was a wonderful concept.

On the way back to Miami, Willy asked to be dropped off in Aruba. He felt a strong urge to hit the gaming tables. He arranged to be met there by Francisco Ocando Paz, the Venezuelan ex-colonel, who had become his preferred gambling companion.

On the island, he checked into the Concorde Hotel and Casino. He showered and then called the director of the casino, who oversaw taking care of players with VIP status. Willy asked the director, "Has Frank Ocando arrived yet?"

"Yes. As soon as he walked into the hotel, he went straight to the baccarat table and began playing."

Willy took the elevator down to the casino and seated himself next to Frank, who hardly noticed him. It was nine p.m. According to Falcon:

> The next day came and we were still sitting gambling at the baccarat table. I was up close to three million dollars. It was one of those times when I couldn't lose. If I put money on the bank, the bank would win. If I put money on players, the players would win. It was at a time in my gambling career where I didn't mind losing, but I just couldn't lose. All the luck in the world was in my favor.

Willy and Frank Ocando stayed in Aruba gambling for three days. When it was time to go, Falcon was still up $3 million. Frank had managed to lose $2 million. Willy paid the colonel's debt and took home a check for $1 million, written out to one of his fake passport names.

RALPH LINERO, A.K.A. CABEZA, HAD been with Willy and Sal almost from the beginning. He was a mechanic and navigator with Seahawk and an airplane pilot who had gone on many daring missions for Los Muchachos. On one of those missions, in 1980, Ralph was transporting marijuana. He was flying high—in more ways than one. He liked to toot while in the air; it made the trips go faster. However, if he went many hours without sleep, he became inattentive, which was why he hadn't noticed that the fuel tank in his DC-3 airplane was low.

This happened sometimes while flying in Colombia; the humidity caused condensation that seeped into the fuel bladders and diluted the supply. Ralph was forced to dump his three-thousand-pound marijuana load into the ocean and make an emergency landing somewhere in the northern part of the country. Military police spotted his plane coming down, and Ralph, coked out of his mind, was arrested and thrown into prison somewhere outside Barranquilla.

Linero was allowed one phone call, so he called his girlfriend, Holly, and told her to contact Willy Falcon. Holly showed up at the Seahawk offices and explained the situation to Willy.

"I'll take care of it," he told her.

Back in Barranquilla, Ralph came down from his cocaine high in a dank holding cell surrounded by assorted Colombian riffraff. Eventually, an administrator opened the cell door, and Ralph was told, "You can go." He walked outside into the morning light and there was the man himself: Pablo Escobar.

Ralph had met Pablo once before, at the gambling tables in Aruba.

"You good?" Escobar asked Ralph.

"A little stiff," said Ralph.

Pablo said adios, and Linero made his way back to Miami. It all made for a great story to be told at CMM Ranch and the Mutiny. (To Falcon, the moral of the story was, "No more marijuana loads. Ever. From now on, if you're with me, yeyo only.")

By mid-1984, Ralph began to feel as if the cocaine piloting business was passing him by. Though he had taken over from Jack Devoe as lead pilot of Los Muchachos, it had happened at a time when Willy and Sal appeared to be transitioning to land transport from Mexico across the US border. Increasingly, his services were not needed. He was still running the occasional load from Colombia to Freeport in the Bahamas and to other islands, but not nearly as often as before. He was thinking it was time to end his pilot career and transition into something else.

Ralph had been fascinated by planes since he was ten years old. Back in Cuba, his father had been a commercial airline pilot; he used to take his son on plane rides. Ralph had gotten his own license when he was seventeen. Flying was what he knew best.

That summer, Linero arranged a meeting with Willy at his penthouse condo in Brickell. They hadn't seen each other in a while. Ralph asked his partner, "Willy, I need two keys. Do you think you could front me that?"

"Really?" said Willy. "What do you need two kilos for?"

"Well, I got a guy who wants to buy two keys."

"Oh, okay." Willy gave it some thought. "How much money you going to make on the transaction?"

"Well, this guy is my cousin. I'm going to make, like, five thousand with the two keys."

Willy stood up and walked over to a closet. His disappeared into the closet and returned with a stack of cash. Dropping the money into Ralph's lap, he said, "There's five grand. It's not a loan, it's yours to keep."

Ralph didn't know what to say.

"Don't be an asshole," said Falcon. "You're a pilot, not a dealer. That's not you. You fly. And don't ever come back to me asking for merchandise."

Ralph said thanks. He left the place with five grand and tears in his eyes. To Ralph Linero, Willy Falcon was everything:

That's why I'm with him. He always said, "Whenever we have a problem, somebody didn't pay or whatever"—his philosophy was, "Okay, so the guy didn't pay, he owes us five kilos. So we're going to go and kill him? Why? We can't take his body to the bank. And now we've got a fight with his brother." You know what Willy would do? He would call the guy and say, "Here's two more keys. You go and sell it and pay me back." That guy would be kissing Willy's feet. I know at least two occasions where people advised him, "Let's fucking hit them. Let's make 'em pay." And Willy would say, "Nope, nope, nope. Bring them over here. We're gonna kill 'em with kindness."

IN DECEMBER, WILLY SAID TO Sal, "I'm moving to LA. I'm going to go out there and oversee our operation on a daily basis. We now have more kilos per month coming into California than we do Miami. It's time we show everyone that we are giving it our highest priority." He added, "You can stay here and remain our guy in Miami. You can come out there any time you want. With the jet, it's more like a commute than a big journey."

Sal thought it was a good idea. Alina was not nearly as enthusiastic. "Is this move really necessary?" she asked when Willy told her.

"Yes. I don't have no other choice. Somebody has to take care of business, right?"

"What about the children? They are in school here. Are they moving, too?"

"No, that's not necessary. I'm just moving there temporarily to see how things are running. You can visit me any time you want. All you have to do is call one of the pilots and have them fly you on the jet. You are gonna love Los Angeles. They have their own fashion style over there."

Five days later, Willy left for LA in the Learjet. He brought some wardrobe until he could buy clothes in his new place of residence. After touching down at

LAX, he went straight to the condo at Marina City Club. The place was fully furnished and outfitted with a portable shortwave radio for communications with designated contacts in the narcosphere.

The next day, Willy received a call on the radio from Pepe the Mexican, whose code name was "El Frijol" or sometimes "the Guy with the Big Hat," a reference to the stereotypical image of a Mexican with a broad-brimmed sombrero. Pepe called to tell Willy that the latest load had arrived: 2,400 kilos were accounted for and secured at the stash house. Willy arranged for Victor Alvarez to come over to the marina apartment, to discuss strategy. They sat out on the patio overlooking the sailboats and catamarans and drank cocktails. Willy called Barrios, his truck transportation guy—the guy who liked to eat lizards—and told him that he should dispatch a couple of semitrucks to Los Angeles as soon as possible.

Los Muchachos were now receiving 2,400 kilos from Mexico every six weeks. Fourteen hundred were held in Los Angeles and one thousand sent to Miami.

The key delegates for the organization in Los Angles were Jojo Brito and Freddy Cruz, both exiles from Little Havana. Jojo handled the product and Freddy handled the cash. They took pride in running a seamless operation. "Security was important," said Jojo. "Every time we move merchandise or cash, we have a car in front and a car behind. Countersurveillance. In case we're being followed. It never happened, but we did it anyway, as a precaution."

The trucks were never loaded at a stash house. The kilos or cash would be brought by van to a produce company that served as a front for Los Muchachos. A semitruck would back into a loading dock. Only Barrios, boss of the truck drivers, was allowed to do this. The other drivers had no idea where the transfer location was located.

The shipments of cash were always transported the same way: drywall. The kilos were buried within a variety of products, including piñatas, electronic equipment, and, sometimes, actual produce. Onions were best; on long journeys, they tended to sweat and emit a pungent aroma. Every truck driver was given an official invoice for the load for when they stopped at weigh stations while en route, or if, for any reason, they were pulled over by the highway patrol.

According to Jojo, Willy was a "micromanager." Falcon took an active role in the importation and distribution of merchandise, but that was not the main reason he came to Los Angeles. Successful cocaine operations revolved around leadership, and Willy wanted not only his people but also the entire underworld of Los Angeles to know that the Miami Cubans had arrived in a big way. Part of establishing a presence was to socialize, to be conspicuously present at sporting events, nightclubs, and places where the rich and famous (potential cocaine clients) hung out.

Typically, if Sal or others from the Miami crew were in town, they would put on their Brioni suits, call Mr. T, their limousine driver (Jojo told Willy, "In this town, you drive a Ferrari or you got a limo, otherwise you are a nobody"), and make the rounds. They tended to stay away from the famous clubs on Sunset Strip—the Rainbow Bar and Grill, Whisky a Go Go, or the Roxy—holdovers from the 1970s with potheads and hippies. This was the disco era, with the spinning disco ball and overheated dance floor. Willy's favorite dance club was Voila, in the Beverly Center on La Cienega Boulevard. The celebrity quotient was high, with movie, music, and sports star–sightings at all the clubs.

Whatever club they chose, the one hit song that filled them with pride was "Conga" by Gloria Estefan and Miami Sound Machine. In 1985, the song rose to number ten on the national charts, and it became a virtual theme song at discos from Miami to LA and New York. Estefan was a fixture at Los Muchachos celebrations. She performed at their weddings and birthday parties even before she was known to a mass audience. Whenever the song kicked in, with the opening lyric—"Come on, shake your body, baby, do the conga/I know you can't control yourself any longer"—the Cubans hit the dance floor. It was as if the song was proclaiming their right and destiny as kings and queens of the disco era, which was another way of saying cocaine royalty.

While in Los Angeles, Willy went by the name Tony. Most of the Cubans used fake IDs and false names. Jojo went by George Barnet. Sometimes, it seemed as though they were living in an alternate reality. Willy liked being anonymous. Nobody in Los Angeles knew who he was, so they weren't asking for gratuities or favors. Sometimes he traveled with his bodyguard, Bubba O'Leary, whom he brought out from Miami, but Willy didn't feel like he even needed a bodyguard on the West Coast.

For Willy and the Boys, a major part of their social life in the city was the Los Angeles Lakers, who played their home games at the Forum. This was the team of Kareem Abdul-Jabbar, Magic Johnson, and James Worthy. The team was enormously popular, and getting tickets was nearly impossible, but Willy was able to find a way. He purchased a ten-person booth for all home games that season. The cost was $14,000 per seat, for a total of $140,000, which included hockey games and boxing events.

Purchasing the booth included invitations to VIP parties sponsored by the Lakers' management. Willy, Sal, Benny B., Jojo, and the rest of their group partied with the likes of Jerry Buss, the owner of the team, and celebrities such as Jack Nicholson and others. It was known that they were the "Cubans from Miami," which was another way of saying they were the ones who made it snow. At a time when the product was booming in Southern California, that put them in the elite of the city's social universe.

And still, they had time for Vegas.

New Year's Eve 1984–85 was special. Los Muchachos were scattered by then, with underlings in Miami, Los Angeles, New York, and elsewhere. The annual gathering in Vegas was something of a reunion for everyone.

With his contacts at Caesars Palace, Willy and his crew were invited to all the big parties. Diana Ross, Barbra Streisand, and Donna Summer were just some of the celebrities they met. Whoever was headlining at a major casino in town, Los Muchachos were likely to get an invite. The introductions were made by Mandy Campo, their contact at Caesars, who usually did so with a wink and a smile, letting it be known to the celebrities that if blow was needed, these were the Boys.

Los Muchachos also met Frank Sinatra, Sammy Davis Jr., and Dean Martin. Through Campo, Willy had the audacity to invite the three megastars out to dinner. To Willy's surprise, they accepted the invite. Turned out Willy and his group were part of a larger contingent that was having dinner with the stars, but still, it was an auspicious occasion.

At the time, likely no one thought about the historical implications of this confab, but for the narcos, it would be remembered as the night Los Muchachos met the Rat Pack. To those in the know it was an example of how, in America, fabulous wealth—no matter how it was acquired—might logically bring you into the orbit of some of the most famous people in the world.

10

LA BLUES

WILLY AND SAL WERE ON their way to meet Pablo. This was far more complicated than it used to be. Since the murder of Justice Minister Lara, Escobar and many others in his organization had been forced into hiding. In Panama, General Noriega—for a price—had allowed Escobar safe refuge at a private estate in Panama City. There, surrounded by massive security, Pablo hunkered down with his wife and kids and his primary partners: Gustavo Gaviria, Carlos Lehder, and José Gonzalo Rodríguez Gacha.

The flow of kilos from Colombia continued as before. The raid and unprecedented bust at Tranquilandia, a joint Colombia-DEA operation, had slowed things down until other jungle labs were able to pick up the slack. Within months, business was back to normal.

In July 1984, a federal grand jury in Miami indicted Escobar, Lehder, and four others on drug-trafficking charges. The US State Department simultaneously announced that it was seeking the extradition of these men, in accordance with the extradition treaty that had been instituted by the Colombian government five years earlier.

By the time Willy and Sal headed to Panama to meet with Pablo, the issue of extradition was foremost on everyone's agenda. Escobar had been waging an aggressive and violent propaganda war with various Colombian social institutions, most notably the government and the media. The six major narcos who had been indicted in the United States banded together to form a consortium they called the Extraditables. Initially, it existed primarily as a propaganda apparatus that placed ads in newspapers with jeremiads against extradition. They even created a logo, under which they sent out press releases by fax to media outlets and government offices, as if they were a legitimate political lobbying group. But soon, much like MAS before them, the Extraditables became part of the Medellín Cartel's war of terror against Colombian society.

On July 23, 1985, just a few days before Willy and Sal arrived in Panama, a superior court judge who had played a role in the recent indictment of Escobar and Lehder was gunned down in the street by motorcycle sicarios: a brutal midday assassination. It was part of a strategy announced by the Extraditables. Judges, politicians, and law enforcement personnel who in any way enabled the extradition process would be executed. In a communiqué to the public, the Extraditables announced, "Blood will run freely through the streets of Medellín, Bogotá and other Colombian cities."

Willy and Sal had been watching all of this from afar. At times, it gave them pause. The violence and terror wrought by Escobar were anathema to the way they ran their business in the States. They were startled by the Lara murder and concerned about the assassination of the judge. In a perfect world, they might have distanced themselves from Escobar. They were making plenty of money with the Cali Cartel. Leaders of that cartel were referred to as "the Gentlemen of Cali." Seemingly, they were more circumscribed in their narco killings, more like a traditional Mafia organization. Pablo was becoming a major problem.

When Willy and Sal landed in Panama City, they were met by Gabriel Castro of PTJ. Castro escorted them through the airport, bypassing Panamanian customs. Once they were in Castro's car, it was suggested that, to make sure they weren't being followed, they drive around awhile before going to see Escobar.

Driving through the streets of Panama City, Willy was startled by how fast the city had grown in the five years since he had commenced his relationship with the Endara Firm. Tall glass skyscrapers dominated the financial district, which is where the banks and financial offices were located. These modern structures represented the central banking system for the entire narcosphere, including riches accumulated by the Medellín and Cali cartels, and Los Muchachos, which was by now the largest distributor of cocaine in the United States.

Panama City was a metropolis engorged on narco profits, and the ubiquitous skyscrapers were the consequence of a nefarious system seemingly unhindered by international law.

Thinking about all this wealth had a strange effect on Falcon. Being escorted around the city, making frequent left, right, and U-turns as a diversionary tactic, Willy wandered in his mind back to his earliest years in Little Havana. Neither Willy nor any of his friends had a nickel to his name. Now here he was, surrounded by more wealth than anyone could imagine, dwarfed by the physical monuments to money laundering, surrounded by limousines, Mercedes, and other expensive cars.

"Hey, Sal," said Willy, "remember that time when we were kids and we found that abandoned '57 Chevy?"

Sal had to think about it, access his memory bank. "Yeah," he said, "I do remember that."

They were maybe fourteen years old at the time. Willy, Sal, and their friends—Ramiro, Tony Bemba, and Justo Jay—found a 1957 Chevy all by itself in a gravel parking lot. The car's body and tires were in decent shape, but there was no engine in the vehicle. The boys claimed it as their own. Willy got behind the wheel, Sal in the front seat next to him, and the others pushed the car through the streets. Eventually, they came to an incline, and the propulsion of the vehicle left Ramiro, Tony, and Jay panting in the background. Of its own volition, the Chevy picked up speed and headed near downtown, a part of the city unfamiliar to Willy and Sal. The engineless Chevy cruised the streets, and the boys looked out the windows as if they were on a magic carpet ride.

It was all so long ago, in a time of innocence, before the boys from Little Havana had taken on their identities as international narcos.

Finally, after driving around for ninety minutes, they arrived at the compound where Escobar and his people were living. Escorted by armed guards, they were led through the house to an expansive back patio. Willy approached Pablo and Gacha, who were sitting in a cabana. Gacha was smoking a Cuban cigar. Nearby, Carlos Lehder and Gustavo Gaviria were playing tennis at one of two courts side by side on the property. They stopped their tennis game and came over to the cabana. Everyone greeted each other. Drinks were brought to the table.

"It looks like you have a nice life here," said Willy. "I'm thinking of going on the run myself; maybe I could join you guys." They all chuckled at that.

After the pleasantries, Pablo got down to business. He seemed to feel he needed to explain a few things, starting with the killing of Rodrigo Lara. Without ever coming right out and admitting he ordered the murder, he told Willy and Sal, "This guy was trying to put dirt on my name and end my political career. I tried many times to warn him, but he continued to taint my name. He dug up information on my conviction from years ago and sought to ruin me. He was also responsible for that big raid at Tranquilandia. We lost fourteen thousand kilos on that raid."

Said Willy, "Well, Pablo, that's your business. But you better be extra careful now because, as you know, Lara had his supporters in the government, and they are going to come after you now."

Pablo nodded; he knew this fact very well. As for the judge who was murdered, he told Falcon and Magluta, "We are at war," adding, "Wars are not for the squeamish. Prepare yourself for more of this."

Changing the subject, Willy mentioned that the latest one-thousand-kilo load from Colombia, which had been hung up temporarily because of delays in the Bahamas, had that morning arrived in Miami.

"Good," said Pablo. "We need to do something fast to make some money because of our situation."

Sal asked, "Do you feel secure here in Panama?"

Said Escobar, "For now, yes. But let me tell you, I don't trust Noriega." Pablo explained how, in a show of acquiescence to the US government, the Panamanian military had shut down the Medellín Cartel's processing lab in Panama. They also seized—or, more accurately, stole—$2 million in cash. Through back channels, Escobar cursed out Noriega and told him if the $2 million wasn't returned, he would be killed. Noriega took the threat seriously and returned the money. As a further courtesy, Escobar and his people were allowed to hide out in Panama City. "That fucking general, he may kill me, torture me, or have me extradited to the United States. He is a *puta*, and I will take care of him in due time."

Asked Willy, "But you're still able to use the country for transshipment, yes?"

Pablo stood, stretched, and indicated for Willy to follow. Separate from the others, they strolled around the property. "I have a proposition I wanted to ask you about," said Escobar. "Recently, I've begun talks with the Sandinista government in Nicaragua. I'm thinking of transitioning from Panama to that country. I may even establish Nicaragua as my base of operations. The government there wants to do business with us."

Willy did not like what he was hearing. The Contra movement was still going stronger than ever. Willy and Sal set aside money on a regular basis for Antonio Garcia Perez, whom they trusted to direct it to the anti-Sandinista cause. Taking down the Sandinistas was a holy crusade, one that Willy had been supporting since his earliest days in the cocaine business.

Said Willy, "Pablo, you have your own business decisions to make. That's up to you. But I cannot do business with those Communist sons of bitches. They bow down at the altar of Fidel Castro. They are my sworn enemy. I'm sorry, Pablo, but I can't do business with the Sandinistas. No fucking way."

Escobar sighed. "I thought that might be your answer. Do me a favor, think about it. What I'm suggesting here has nothing to do with politics. It's business. Think about it for a few days, then let me know."

Willy said he would. Two days later, he and Pablo spoke on the radio. "I've thought about it," said Willy. "I can't do it, Pablo. I can't work with no fucking Sandinistas."

It was the first time Willy said no to Pablo Escobar.

THE APBA BOAT RACING SEASON was like a lifeline for Willy and Los Muchachos. No matter what was going on in the cocaine business, the boats were a source of joy and gratification. The Seahawk crew always felt that if they really put their hearts and souls into it—if they focused on the task at hand and applied high levels of dedication and discipline—they were unbeatable.

The finals for the world championship regatta were held that year in Point Pleasant, New Jersey, located on the Jersey Shore, sixty-four miles from New York City. From the Seahawk boatyard on Thunder Road in Miami, the power-boats had to be shipped via the eighteen-wheel tractor trailers. They were stacked side by side and driven carefully, as they were for all the races on the APBA circuit, which were spread out in locations all around the United States.

The race at Point Pleasant Beach was shaping up to be a mega-event, with coverage on national television and a media contingent larger than anything the Boys had seen before. Both Willy and Sal had boats in the race. Willy was racing in a thirty-eight-foot aluminum Cougar Cat, with two 500 aluminum-block fuel injected engines, and 1,000 horsepower in each engine. Sal's boat had similar specs, except his boat, at thirty-six feet, was shorter and lighter.

So far that season, Willy had been experiencing mechanical issues with his boat. Consequently, his qualifying point totals on the circuit placed him at the back of the pack. Magluta, on the other hand, was leading all boats in points and had guaranteed a place for himself in the world championship race later that fall.

From the beginning, Willy was feeling it was time to go for broke. "That entire season had been frustrating, and I wanted to make up for it with a good showing."

It was a windy day, with swells from two to four feet. Sal's boat took command early and stayed out front. Willy kept pace, and in the last quarter mile, he indicated to Justo Jay, his throttle man, "*Go for it! Throttle to the metal!*"

The engines roared, and the boat sliced through the waves like a razor blade chopping the contours of crystal rock. Falcon's Cougar Cat crossed the finish line, with the official checkered flag indicating that he had won the race. Sal came in a close second. Both of them would be advancing to the championship race in Key West.

That night, they celebrated with a party at a club not far from the racing area. To perform at the party, Willy had hired Carlos Santana. His band was flown in from California for the event and would be paid $100,000 for the private gig. If you were as rich as Willy and Sal, that's what you got to do: hire your favorite band of all time for your own personal events.

After the race and party were over, Alina Falcon flew into Newark Airport. Willy had promised Alina a week in New York City. He picked her up at the airport, and they drove into the city and checked into the world-renowned Plaza Hotel, which faced Central Park South and the upscale shopping district of Fifth Avenue.

Willy contacted Raymond "Manny" Alonso, also known as Monguito, or Mongui, a young hustler who had been organizing the Boys' cocaine routes in New York. Willy asked Manny to dip into one of his local stash houses for $50,000 in cash that he wanted to give to his wife for shopping.

That night, Manny showed up with the money. Willy gave the cash to Alina and told her, "If you need more than that, just put it on the credit cards."

Since Alina had given birth to Will Jr. the previous October, she and Willy had been attempting to honor their roles as husband and wife, and as parents. For this trip, their three kids had been left back in Miami with Alina's mother and father.

Willy was still having sexual liaisons with other women whenever he felt like it. Alina may or may not have known. It was impossible to keep up with Willy's schedule, since he was constantly traveling on trips that Alina was told about only on a need-to-know basis. It's possible that she had accepted some version of a détente that allowed Willy to have his flings. Willy bedded down with many paramours, including Lourdes, the mother of his twin boys. In early 1986, Lourdes got pregnant again. This time, they decided that she would have an abortion—a fact they kept secret from everyone, even the inner circle of Los Muchachos.

For Alina, the trip to Manhattan was a major excursion. She had a close friend in New York who accompanied her on shopping sprees, while Willy and Manny took the time to get to know each other better.

The New York City metropolitan area had always been a complicated market for Los Muchachos. The Medellín Cartel had no presence in New York. By agreement with Escobar, New York and New Jersey were strictly a Cali operation. In the 1970s, the cartel had established as leader in the city a young narco boss named Francisco Hélmer "Pacho" Herrera Buitrago. Born and raised in the Cauca Valley, metaphorically, and, at times, literally, Pacho Herrera had cocaine in his blood. Among other things, he was the only known gay narco—at least openly so—in the upper echelons of the cartel hierarchy.

Los Muchachos had always been a little intimidated by New York. It was a massive cocaine market, maybe the largest of all. Since the ethos of their organization was based on family connections, in New York they only dabbled in the business. Willy realized that this meant that they were likely selling themselves short in New York. He had been on the lookout for a trusted overseer of their New York operation. Both he and Sal had concluded that Manny Alonso was their man.

Born in 1961, Alonso was six years younger than Willy. He had been raised in a part of New Jersey—Union City, Bergen County, West New York—that had the highest concentration of Cuban exiles outside Miami. In the 1970s, Bergen County had a vibrant Cuban underworld. The anti-Castro movement was active, with underground cells and covert operations that rivaled South Florida's. The largest illegal numbers-betting operation, known to Latinos as *bolita*, was based in Union City. The Godfather of *bolita*, a Bay of Pigs veteran named José Miguel Battle, was a local legend.[1]

---

[1] In the mid-1980s, Battle moved to South Florida. He maintained his *bolita* empire from New York–New Jersey to Miami through an organization known as the Corporation; he was also a cocaine client of Falcon-Magluta.

Manny got his start at a club called Lucero Cubano, located on Forty-Seventh Street off Bergenline Avenue in Union City:

> It was a Cuban social club. On the third floor were rocking chairs; old people used to go there to play dominos. And on another floor, they used to have dances and wedding receptions, shit like that. But in the basement, there was an illegal baccarat table. They used to open it Thursday, Friday, and Saturday all night until early in the morning. . . . All the Cuban bookies and *boliteros* hung out at that place. Man, there were some characters. There was a guy they called Goldfinger who had a long gold fingernail on his pinkie finger that he used to snort coke. He also had a gold-plated gun, gold-rimmed eyeglasses, and he wore a gold crown. There was another guy who looked just like Superfly. You know Superfly? You should have seen the gold chains on him, with the diamonds. And then there was El Morro, the Arab who owned the baccarat concession at Lucero. He was a skinny old man, always dressed in white, with a white hat and white shoes. He lived in a fifth-floor apartment with no elevator. He used to be on welfare, but the fucking guy, he would reach in his pocket and pull out the biggest wad of one-hundred-dollar bills you ever seen. And he was on welfare.

As a teenager, Manny ran errands for the older gamblers at the club. One person he befriended was Felipe "El Chino" Magluta, who was the uncle of Sal Magluta in Miami: "El Chino was a heavy gambler; he had a serious problem. He would gamble away milk money for his daughter. But he was like a father to me. If he had five dollars in his pocket, and you needed it, he'd give it to you. That's the kind of man he was."

In 1981, Felipe told Manny all about his nephew, Sal, and Willy Falcon, who were becoming cocaine kingpins in Miami. Felipe introduced Manny to two local Cuban truck drivers who made regular runs for Felipe down to Miami to pick up product from Willy and Sal, to be sold in New Jersey and New York. One time, Manny was at the home of one of these guys. The guy was bragging about his Miami connections. He pulled out of the closet a stack of five kilos. "Here," he said to Manny, "why don't you see what you can do with that?" The guy was joking, but Manny said, "Okay. What the fuck. I'll take it."

In two weeks, he sold the cocaine, paid off the guy, and made a little something for himself. The guy said to Manny, "Say, so you want to go to Miami?"

In Miami, Manny stayed at the Holiday Inn. He was introduced to Sal, but not to Willy Falcon. Sal made no promises. He liked the fact that Manny was close with his uncle Felipe ("He says you're like the son he never had," Sal told Manny), but he was not ready to make Manny a member of Los Muchachos just yet.

It took two years. In 1983, when the Seahawk team made a previous trip to Point Pleasant for the powerboat race, Manny finally met Willy Falcon. The meeting took place at one of the crew's epic postrace parties. Seahawk had rented out the entire top floor of a hotel at the beach.

Falcon warmed up to Manny right away: "He seemed very responsible, smart, a serious young man. I was curious to see what he could do if we really put him to work."

Back in Miami, Willy suggested to Sal that they give Manny a chance.

Said Manny, "I began receiving shipments every six weeks by truck from Miami. I remember, the driver was a Marielito. He smelled awful when he arrived because he would drive for days without a shower. This was his hustle. He'd only been in the country—what?—a year or so, and he was making hundreds of thousands of dollars."

Manny already had a few clients of his own; now, Willy and Sal were asking him to service their clients as well.

Manny turned out to be highly adept at organization. He maintained eight stash houses—four for merchandise, and four for money—all located in middle- or upper-middle-class neighborhoods spread out around North Jersey—Union City, Jersey City, Fort Lee. His client base was mostly in New York—Queens, the Bronx, Manhattan.

Once Willy and Sal realized how efficient Manny Alonso could be, they enabled his operational capabilities. Willy contacted Mario Valencia of the Cali Cartel and suggested that he supply Manny's crew with worker bees, young ghetto males who were paid to service the organization. Their families back home had houses bought for them and were well taken care of by the cartel. These workers, who were referred to as "secretaries," arrived in New Jersey with instructions to do whatever it was that Manny wanted them to do.

Manny treated them as family. They lived in groups of three and four in rented homes in nice neighborhoods. Manny enrolled them in English-language school and made them learn the language. He bought them nice suits to wear so they looked like young professionals. He maintained a fleet of Buick Century automobiles for the young men to drive around in style. They were outfitted with fake identities and the appropriate IDs to back it up: driver's license, legal residence visas, social security and credit cards. The secretaries didn't even know Manny's real name. They called him "the Professor." They managed the daily flow at the stash houses. They delivered the product. They ran errands.

Willy and Sal were management, regularly supplying Manny with product, but the Cali Cartel was the home office, sending worker bees all the way from Colombia to do the grunt work.

Willy explained to Manny that most of the product would now be coming from Los Angeles, not Miami, in partnership with the Cali Cartel and the Mexicans. "What you've been doing here is incredible," Willy told Manny, "but—guess what?—we're going to step it up."

They were seated in the Oak Room at the Plaza Hotel, an establishment with velvet chairs and brass railings, reeking of Old World wealth. The patrons were mostly in suits and ties, well off, a mix of European visitors and Americans trying to look like European visitors. White people.

Willy explained, "The shipments coming from California will be partly ours and partly for Pacho Herrera and the Cali Cartel. Barrios will be sending our trucks from LA, and you'll be receiving at least twice what you've been getting up till now." Point blank, Willy asked Manny, "Do you think you can handle it?"

"Of course," said Manny. "I can handle whatever you send me."

"Good," said Willy.

The only problem Manny could see was loading and unloading cash and kilos. Right now, he and his secretaries were moving product at truck stops off the Jersey Turnpike, and in the parking lot of a Howard Johnson's. At the diner, Manny once stood on the back end of a truck as they shifted kilos from a semitrailer to the trunk of a luxury sedan. Through the window of the Howard Johnson's, he could see a couple of New Jersey state troopers sitting in a booth drinking coffee and eating donuts, oblivious to what was going on. Manny thought, *There's got to be a better way.*

Willy told Manny how, in Los Angeles, they had created a produce business and warehouse to disguise and facilitate the flow of kilos and money.

Manny's eyes lit up. "Yeah, that's a great idea."

Later, after Willy left New York and returned to his apartment in Los Angeles, Manny began looking for a suitable location to establish a produce market. It took many months. It was a big job. Manny had his sights on the Hunts Point Produce Market in the Bronx.

The Hunts Point market was a massive, forty-acre facility that first opened in 1962. It was the largest food-distribution center of its kind in the world. Thousands of delivery trucks passed in and out of the facility on a weekly basis. The price to rent a location at the market was $1 million. Manny thought he could do better. Through a friend, he found an old Cuban guy who owned a space at the market that he wasn't using anymore: "So I gave the guy one hundred thousand dollars. We bought a couple vans. We put a new name on it, and we started buying bananas, yucca, all kinds of vegetables. We started to give produce to local bodegas on credit, so that it appeared we were doing legitimate business."

Manny established two more stash houses, in Queens, not far from the market. He rented an apartment in Manhattan, in a building overlooking the entrance to the Queens-Midtown Tunnel. He kept his ledger books at that location, and his New York girlfriend (as opposed to the New Jersey and Miami girlfriends). By then, he was a rich man, and getting richer by the day.

By the time the produce business at the Hunts Point market was up and running, the trucks from LA arrived every six weeks. With a safe and nearly undetectable location to unload the containers of cocaine and cash, Los Muchachos were able to double the size of their shipments. No one in law enforcement would have been able to bend their mind around the concept: a cocaine operation based in Miami, importing cocaine into Southern California, sending it by truck to New York City. It defied all logic.

IN AUGUST 1985, FALCON RECEIVED A call on the radio transmitter from Escobar. He had not seen or spoken with Pablo since he and Sal visited the Colombian narco boss at his hideout in Panama City. Willy was concerned because he had said no to Pablo's proposition about running kilos through Nicaragua. There hadn't seemed to have been any fallout from that; shipments from the Medellín Cartel to Miami continued to flow. Escobar had gone ahead and, in conjunction with the Sandinistas, smuggled shipments through Nicaragua anyway. As far as Willy was concerned, that was Pablo's decision to make. No harm, no foul.[2]

But now Escobar was contacting him with another scheme. This one involved a trafficking partner even more problematic than the Sandinistas. Pablo was suggesting that they smuggle sizable shipments of cocaine through, of all places—Cuba.

Willy was so startled that he had to hear it again: "Excuse me, what did you say?"

"Cuba," Escobar repeated.

It had occurred to Willy that since Pablo was now in business with the Sandinistas, it was possible that he might go into business with the Castro regime. But it never dawned on him that Escobar would ask him and Sal to also get in bed with Castro. "Pablo, you know I love you like a brother. But those people are Communists. You can't trust fucking Communists."

Pablo was anticipating resistance on Willy's part. "Hear me out," he said.

Escobar explained: A month earlier, he had moved from the compound in Panama City; Gustavo Gaviria and Gacha had the others moved back to Medellín. Pablo moved on to Nicaragua, where he was granted political asylum by the Sandinista government. In Nicaragua, he was introduced to General Arnaldo Ochoa Sánchez. Ochoa was a high-ranking Cuban military official who had been assigned by the Cuban government to liaise with the Sandinista military. Ochoa oversaw the training of the Sandinista army on how to deal with a guerrilla insurgency such as the one currently being waged by the Contras.

Escobar and the general hit it off. He asked Ochoa if he could broker a deal for weapons—guns, rocket launchers, explosives. Since Escobar had gone on the run, he anticipated that he might be going to war with the Colombian

---

[2] Using Nicaragua as a transshipment point did cause problems for Escobar. In 1986, a DEA surveillance photograph surfaced of him, and others, loading kilos into the cargo hold of an airplane in Nicaragua. President Reagan seized on the issue in a nationally televised address, saying, "I know every American parent concerned about the drug problem will be outraged to learn that top Nicaraguan government officials are deeply involved in drug trafficking. This picture, secretly taken at a military airfield outside Managua, shows . . . a top aide to one of the nine *comandantes* who rule Nicaragua, loading an aircraft with illegal narcotics, bound for the United States. No, there seems to be no crime to which the Sandinistas will not stoop." American parents might also have been interested to know that the US government, in the guise of the CIA, was trafficking cocaine to raise money and procure weapons for the Contras. This was something that would not be known for another three years, after Reagan was out of office.

government, the United States—whoever. He was stockpiling weapons for whenever this day might arrive.

Ochoa said yes. Over the next few weeks, he served as middleman in a $10 million transaction. Escobar bought a cache of weapons from the Sandinista armed forces. General Ochoa received a nice piece of the action for serving as broker. Afterward, he said to Escobar, "You know, we could do this with cocaine. Ship it through Cuba. I could protect the shipments. Facilitate the whole thing."

Escobar loved the idea. Because Cuba had no diplomatic relations with the United States, American law enforcement had no jurisdiction on the island or the surrounding waters. Escobar asked Ochoa, "What about the Castro brothers?"

"Let me handle that," said Ochoa. "I guarantee you there will be no interference from Fidel Castro. As for Raúl, the defense minister, we've been best friends since our days together in the Sierra Maestra during the revolution."

What the general was offering was hard to resist. Escobar could land his kilos at Varadero Airport, located on the island's northern coast. Varadero was a popular beach resort, with lots of tourist activity. From Varadero, the shipment would be transferred to Cuban gunboats, which would sail out to the international demarcation line at sea. This is where Los Muchachos came in.

"We need your boats," Escobar told Willy. "You've got the best fleet of powerboats in the business. We need your people to pick it up and bring it ashore in the Keys."

Willy thought about it: it wasn't much different from what they were doing already through the Bahamas. Every six weeks, Escobar sent five hundred kilos to one of the Bahamian islands. Willy's boats picked up the shipment at sea, always under cover of darkness. It was a few hours from the transfer point to the Keys. The Coast Guard tried, but they could not keep up with this operation. Even if they managed to spot a boat, which—given that the powerboats were painted black, with the lights dimmed and the crew outfitted with night vision goggles—was rare, the Coast Guard boats were at a disadvantage. They could not traverse shallow waters in the way the speedboats could; all the narco boats had to do was hug the shoreline to evade capture.

Willy told Pablo, "Let me look into it. I will check out this General Ochoa to see if he can be trusted."

In a way, Falcon felt sorry for Escobar. He seemed desperate to create new routes. He was seemingly at war with the world, and he was asking his friend Willy to throw him a lifeline. As much as the idea of running cocaine shipments through Cuba offended him, he promised Escobar he would check it out.

He consulted with three people: his partner, Sal; Antonio Garcia Perez (El Guajiro), who was his longtime contact in the anti-Castro movement; and George Morales, a renowned Colombian-born, Miami-based powerboat champion and a smuggler of weed and cocaine.

Willy was aware that Morales had been smuggling shipments of contraband through Cuba for years. Willy, on a trip to Miami, met Morales at a restaurant on Thunder Road, where Seahawk and other powerboat companies maintained offices and dry-docked their vessels. Morales told Willy, "You can trust the general. He seems to have total control in Cuba. He can deliver."

"Well," said Willy, "what I need to know is, what about the two snakes, Fidel and Raúl, do they know about it, and, if so, do they get a piece of the action?" Falcon's main concern was that, if he did partner with the general, would he in any way be contributing to the Castro dictatorship?

Morales told him, "Well, you know, Ochoa and Raúl Castro are not only friends, but as defense minister, Raúl is basically Ochoa's boss. I can't say for sure, but I don't see how any of this happens without Raúl signing off on it." Also, Morales added, he'd heard that General Ochoa was disenchanted with the leadership of Fidel Castro and was possibly planning a military coup d'état to overthrow "the snake."

Willy found the whole thing unsettling but also fascinating.

Sal felt the same way about it as Willy. Doing business with Cuba was mind-blowing but possibly a lucrative opportunity. Willy then approached Antonio Garcia Perez, from whom he sought counsel on all matters relating to anti-Castro activities. Antonio listened carefully as Willy laid out the details of the scheme. Antonio said, "I love it. It's a tremendous intelligence-gathering opportunity."

"That's true," said Willy.

"But here's the best part. By smuggling the merchandise through Cuba, you would be raising money that we would then redirect back into the anti-Castro efforts. Basically, the bastard would be helping to finance his own demise. It's brilliant."

That night, Willy got on the shortwave radio and told Escobar that he was in. Pablo was pleased to hear it. "Let's meet face-to-face to iron out the details," said Pablo. "The general is excited to meet you. He's told me that many times."

"Pablo," said Willy, "I'll do the deal, you can count on me. But I'm not going to meet with that general."

"But Willy, why?"

"I don't like Communists."

They agreed that Willy and Sal would send Antonio Garcia Perez to represent them at a meeting with General Ochoa. The meeting took place in Panama a week later. Afterward, Antonio called Willy and said, "It's all set. Willy, I know you have your reservations, but I think this is going to be good for us. This guy is disgruntled with Fidel. This could be a major breakthrough for us."

Weeks later, the cocaine transaction in Cuba went off without a snag. With the general in control, and the threat of US law enforcement interference eliminated as an issue, it was almost too easy to be true.

Over the next three years, there were ten more shipments. Then it stopped. Escobar got sidetracked by his mounting war with Colombian society, and the general was arrested in Cuba. It all ceased as suddenly as it began.[3]

Willy Falcon, for one, was relieved to see the shipments through Cuba come to an end. "I never felt good about it," he said. "It went against my principles, my ethics, to have anything to do with Cuba while it was under the control of the Castro regime."

BY THE SUMMER OF 1985, the price of a kilo in Southern California had dropped from $32,000 to $19,000. Partly, this was a calculated strategy by Willy and Sal. The affordability of the product created a frenzy on the street, where the white powder became like sand at the beach, granules of artificially

---

[3] In early 1989, General Ochoa was put on trial in Cuba for narcotics smuggling. Knowing that the US government was preparing to invade the country of Panama and apprehend General Noriega on narcotics charges, Castro was concerned that President George H. W. Bush would attempt the same thing in Cuba. The Cuban government used Ochoa's military tribunal for its propaganda value: Ochoa was found guilty and given the death penalty. This was no small matter: Ochoa, a hero of the revolution, was Raúl Castro's dear friend. After Ochoa's execution, Raúl allegedly went into a deep depression and began drinking heavily, to the point where he was reported to have become inebriated and soiled himself in public on multiple occasions (Julia Preston, "Cuban General Said to Admit Crimes," *Washington Post*, June 27, 1989; Robert Pear, "Cuban General and Three Others Executed for Sending Drugs to U.S.," *New York Times*, July 14, 1989; Juan O. Tomayo, "Arnaldo Ochoa—A Problem for Castro Brothers 25 Years Ago," *Miami Herald*, June 22, 2014).

stimulated joy, the elixir behind LA's vaunted reputation for hedonism. It was like Miami had been five years earlier, when cocaine first blanketed the nightclubs and contributed to an ethos of seduction that was embraced by many.

Business was so brisk that Willy and Sal summoned other members of Los Muchachos to LA to help with the operation. Tavy Falcon came out west and rented an apartment with his brother-in-law, Pegy Rosello. As they had back in Miami, they oversaw the stash houses, which were the central nervous system of the organization. Pegy was also being trained by Tavy to do the bookkeeping.

Los Muchachos had two separate bookkeeping mechanisms—Sal and his ledgers, and Tavy with his, to cross-check numbers and make sure there were no disputes with partners in Medellín, Cali, or Mexico.

Tony Garrudo, El Cuño, made frequent trips to Los Angeles to sell kilos to one of his clients on the West Coast. Benny B. moved into one of the condos at the marina with Sal and others. He was in Los Angeles to receive the shipments from the Mexicans. As with the others, to Benny life in California was like being on vacation. The Miami exiles used the city as an occasion to party. Sun, booze, sexual freedom, and enough Andean marching powder to deviate more than a few nasal septa.

In the clubs of Los Angeles, the Boys were viewed as cocaine elite. Benny remembered one time when their services were enlisted, at a club called Vertigo, as judges in a bikini contest. It was tough work, but somebody had to do it.

There were those among Los Muchachos who felt that discipline had become lax in Los Angeles. El Cuño, for one, had concerns. One evening, he visited one of the apartments in Marina del Rey. Willy was not there, but Benny B. and some of the others were having a party. There were stacks of cash, kilos of coke, and guns out on the table. The Boys had procured a couple of local escorts for the occasion. Tony didn't like what he saw: having cocaine, cash, and guns together at one location was a no-no. And inviting strangers to the apartment, with everything out on display, was a rookie mistake. Tony told Willy about it. Willy said he would take care of it, but he never did.

That same week, Alina and Sal's wife, Isabel, flew on the jet to Los Angeles, as they did at least once a month. On this occasion, they brought their own private hairdresser along. Once they landed and got settled at the apartment in the marina, the women went on a shopping spree to Rodeo Drive in Beverly Hills and returned with enough bags and packages to fill the jet.

On the night of October 29, Willy, Sal, and the wives prepared to go out to dinner. When Willy saw Alina dressed in the gown she had purchased for the occasion, her hair styled by her personal hairdresser, he was thunderstruck. "Baby," he told her, "if any Hollywood movie producer were to see you right now, he might cast you to a leading role in one of his movies."

Alina laughed. After all their years together, she still appreciated being flattered by Willy for her beauty.

They went out to a fancy dinner, and afterward they went to Voila, their favorite club in LA. Alina and Isabel were scheduled to return to Miami the next day, but at the club they heard about an upcoming Halloween party to be held at Voila. They decided to stay a couple of extra days so they could attend.

The next day, they looked through the phone book and found several stores that sold Halloween costumes. They went to a costume warehouse in Hollywood and found a couple of costumes they liked. Alina bought herself a Cinderella outfit, and Willy bought a mask, bandolero hat, and fencing sword to dress up as Zorro.

That evening, Willy heard partying going on in the apartment downstairs. It reminded him that, considering what El Cuño told him about the visibility of coke and guns, he meant to talk to Benny B. about being careful. He had not done so yet, but he figured he would later.

That night, in preparation for the Halloween party the next day, Willy and Alina turned in early. At about eleven p.m., they were awakened by the sound of a banging noise from downstairs. Then they heard someone shout, "Police! Police! Police!"

Willy said to Alina, "It's the cops. I'm gonna run."

He quickly pulled on his pants and ran to the balcony. It was his intention to jump the twelve feet or so to the ground level. But when he looked down from the balcony, he saw three police officers pointing their guns at him.

He turned and ran back into the apartment. By now, three or four more lawmen had burst into the room. They were wearing jackets that had MARINA DEL REY SHERIFF emblazoned across the back. They placed Falcon under arrest, cuffed him, and led him downstairs to the police cruiser. Lights were flashing, and there must have been a half dozen police vehicles. Willy looked and saw Alina in the back of one of the cruisers. His heart sank. Seeing his wife in police custody made him feel awful.

Benny B. and Jorge Lopez, a.k.a. Fat George, a chubby member of Los Muchachos from Miami, were all arrested that night, along with Willy, Sal, Alina, and Isabel. A small amount of drugs and some cash were confiscated.

Willy was able to make one telephone call—he called Tony Garrudo, El Cuño. He told Tony that they were being held at a Los Angeles County jail. He and Sal had been arrested under their false identities. Willy told Tony to check around and see if anyone else in the organization had been busted, or if any of their stash houses had been raided. He told Tony to contact their lawyer Mark Dachs in Miami and have him recommend some local attorneys and a bondsman to post bond immediately and get them out of jail.

Around five o'clock that morning, a local lawyer and a bondsman came to see Willy and Sal at the jail. They informed the Cubans that they had posted bond at $250,000 apiece. They had also posted bonds of $75,000 apiece for Alina and Isabel. Said the lawyer, "They likely have already been released, or will be shortly."

A couple of hours later, Willy's and Sal's fake names were called over a loudspeaker. A guard came to their holding cell and escorted them downstairs to retrieve their belongings. Their fake driver's licenses and cell phones were returned to them. "We called Tony and had him come pick us up," said Willy. "We got out of there ASAP before they realized that we had given them fake names, and even made bond on these fake names."

Tony had rented hotel rooms for everyone at the Marina Ritz-Carlton, where he was staying—a few blocks away from the Marina City Club, site of the raid. The wives were already there, recovering from the shock of their arrest. Willy saw Alina and said, "*Mi amor*, I am so sorry that you had to go through this." They embraced. Alina seemed to be okay.

Jojo Brito and two other local Muchachos, Gus "G-Man" Posada and Victor Alvarez, showed up at the hotel. Willy sent them over to the City Club to assess the damage at their apartment rooms. When they returned, they told Willy and Sal that the rooms had been turned upside down. Their shortwave radio equipment had been confiscated. The cops had broken into a safe and taken their ledger books and $500,000 in cash.

Jojo reported that none of the organization's stash houses had been raided. There was no indication that the police knew anything about their operation beyond what they had seized at the apartment at the marina.

The following day, all the leaders from the Los Angeles operation came to the hotel, and they had a summit meeting. Willy told everyone that business would go on as before, with a few changes: Everyone would be receiving new phones and beepers; the ones they had been using would be destroyed. The stash houses for merchandise and cash would be moved to new locations. The kilos from south of the border would continue to flow.

Then came the arraignment, the following day. Willy and Sal were relieved that the charges against their wives were being dropped. Alina and Isabel were free to go. As for Willy and Sal, they were indicted on charges of possession and distribution of cocaine. One thing they both found curious: on the police affidavit detailing their arrest, it was noted that from a safe in their room, $150,000 was confiscated and vouchered as evidence. That left $350,000 unaccounted for.

The Boys were perplexed. They had been arrested by the Marina del Rey sheriff's office, not the Los Angeles Police Department—whatever that meant. If this raid had taken place in Miami, Willy and Sal would have known everything about it within twenty-four hours. But they were in LA, where they did not have the contacts or sources of information within the system. Was this part of a larger investigation? Or was this a band of rogue cops looking to score? Did Willy and Sal need to be worried that their operation in LA had been compromised? It was all a mystery.

One thing they did know: Los Angeles was no longer a hospitable environment in which to live. Business would continue, but it would go on without Willy Falcon living at the marina and overseeing the operation on a daily basis.

That night, on a red-eye commercial flight leaving from LAX, they headed back to Miami. At seven a.m., Willy arrived in Miami and took a taxi to his penthouse apartment in Brickell Key. He dropped his bags and looked out the window at the wide expanse of Biscayne Bay—the glistening water, the soaring seagulls, and the morning traffic along the causeway to Miami Beach. It felt good to be back home.

AS AN INFORMANT, JACK DEVOE was all in. He had miscalculated by going to trial and being found guilty on charges related to his smuggling operation with Nigel Bowe, José Cabrera Sarmiento, and Carlos Lehder. Now, even though he was agreeing to cooperate, the government held all the cards. The most he could hope for was a reduced sentence from a judge in exchange for his full cooperation, and a journey deep into the bowels of the federal witness protection program (WITSEC). Devoe would be strip-mined by a series of agents and prosecutors looking to make cases on information provided by the renowned narco pilot. In the halls of justice, he was the darling of federal prosecutors, for all the wrong reasons. They had him over a barrel.

By early 1986, Devoe was being prepped for two major trials at which his testimony would be crucial—a case against disgraced lawyer Mel Kessler, and another against Carlos Lehder, the Medellín Cartel's man in the islands.

There was a monotony to Devoe's current predicament: six days a week, he was picked up from the military compound where he was currently being held. He was escorted by US Marshals to the federal prosecutor's building in downtown Miami. They sat him in a room, with a cup of coffee, where Devoe was met by a succession of special agents and prosecutors who were there to squeeze him like a sponge. One of those people was Special Agent David Borah of the DEA.

It had been two years since Borah left the Louisville police department and joined the DEA in 1984. He was joining the nation's premier drug-interdiction agency at a time when the War on Drugs was becoming a national obsession in the law enforcement community. The Reagan administration had made its position abundantly clear. Funds for the drug war were being routinely approved by Congress without much resistance from either side of the aisle. For a federal agent looking to advance his or her career, there was nowhere better to be than on the front lines of the US government's crusade against cocaine trafficking.

With his very first assignment, Borah was fortunate. He was sent to the Miami/Fort Lauderdale office, ground zero in the War on Drugs. As part of the South Florida Drug Task Force, Borah was given an auxiliary role in the forensic lab. He let it be known that he felt his skills would be better served working as an investigator in the field.

One Friday, he was called in to his supervisor and was told, "On Monday you report to operations. They got a special investigation. You will probably be there for about thirty days."

Borah reported to operations. He would be there for the next six years.

It turned out the investigation he was being assigned to had to do with Jack Devoe. The pilot had cut a deal with the feds, and he was being debriefed, or interrogated, on an ongoing basis. Borah was the junior man in the interrogation unit. He was invited along to look, listen, and take notes.

Jack Devoe seemed bored with it all as a succession of agents asked him variations on the same questions. Borah studied Devoe carefully. Like many informants, Devoe seemed to know more than he revealed; he wasn't going to give anything up unless he was asked specifically about a subject.

Devoe was talking about flight routes to Colombia when he said something about "the Cubans." Borah had never heard anything about Cubans in relation to Colombian trafficking. He asked Devoe, "Cubans? What about the Cubans?"

Jack smiled. "They call themselves Los Muchachos, the Boys. You'll never catch those guys. Willy Falcon and Sal Magluta. They run the operation." Devoe gave a thumbnail description of the operation, how the Cubans owned their own planes and boats and smuggled their merchandise through a variety of means. It was a highly disciplined group, said Jack. Mostly, they only used other Cuban exiles in their operation—family members, cousins, brothers-in-law. Few of them were professional criminals with records, so they would be difficult to build a case against.

"How much weight are they moving?" asked Borah.

"You have no idea—tons," answered Jack. "They are probably the biggest importers and distributors of cocaine in the United States, and nobody knows about them."

"Where do they meet, how do they communicate?" asked another agent in the room.

"They are big on the powerboat racing circuit. The APBA. They're championship boat racers. They have regattas every couple months. That's the only time you'll see them together as a group, far as I know."

It was getting late. The agents finished their debriefing of Jack Devoe. The junior agent, Borah—the southerner from Kentucky—couldn't stop thinking about what the pilot had said. In an almost offhand way, he declared that this group—Los Muchachos—was impenetrable and could not be brought down. They were being described, in a sense, as the holy grail, an object of unattainable glory in the War on Drugs.

What better challenge was there for a combatant in that war than to go after a group of traffickers who were considered untouchable? For Borah, it was like a call to arms—a pipe dream, perhaps, for an agent with only two years in the DEA, but from that day forward it was his goal to bring a case against Falcon, Magluta, and their organization.

III
GREEN EYES

11

WHITE DUDE WITH A CAMERA

THE LAST DRINK WILLY FALCON ever had at the Mutiny was on the night of his thirtieth birthday. It was also one of the last nights that the club was in operation. Burton Goldberg, the original owner, sold his piece of the club in 1984 to a group of investors for $17.5 million. Willy and Sal did not recoup their $1 million contribution. Goldberg was not remembered fondly by many employees or customers, but he had fashioned the club into something remarkable—especially if you liked cocaine, sex, and hearing Madonna's "Like a Virgin" five or six times a night.

In a way, Falcon was doing the club a favor by having his birthday party there. The Mutiny's popularity had been waning for years. The incident that turned the tables occurred in 1982, when a young model and hostess at the Mutiny was brutally murdered. Margarita Eilenberg was a Dominican-born model who fell into the trap that many young women did when they worked there. Rich narcos with underworld connections presented themselves as movie and television producers. Mind you, there were often legitimate theatrical producers of one type or another in the club, so it was an easy ruse for which to fall. Margarita fell for a suitor who was a smooth psycho killer. It ended for the model and hostess when her body was found near mile marker 105 on US 1, near Key Largo. She had been injected four times with lethal amounts of cocaine: once in the leg, twice in one arm, and twice in the jugular vein. The dead body of twenty-three-year-old Margarita Eilenberg was wrapped in a pink woolen blanket that came from a room at the Mutiny Hotel.

The murder was a shock to the women who had worked with Margarita at the club, but the party slogged on. Eventually, the notoriety had a negative effect. When the movie *Scarface* was released in late 1983, with a club depicted in the movie based on the Mutiny (it was called Club Babylon in the film), tourists started arriving from around the country. The Mutiny became almost a parody of itself, with a reputation for danger and sleaze.

For his birthday party, Willy had one request. Even though she no longer worked at the club, he requested the return of Esmeralda Ochoa. Esmeralda was a harpist who sat on the club's terrace wearing a G-string and no top, glitter mascara, and multicolored fingernail polish while she played her instrument. Some paid little attention to Esmeralda and her harp; she was a subtle grace note in a club known for bombast. Others, like Willy, were mesmerized by her near-naked body and the heavenly sounds she produced.

Willy's birthday bash was a celebration like many others that Los Muchachos had experienced over the years. Caseloads of Dom Pérignon were imbibed, everybody danced, and the perico was plentiful.

As for the Mutiny, its days were numbered. In November 1985, the owners who had taken over after Goldberg filed for bankruptcy. The club closed down, but the hotel continued until 1989, when the entire enterprise went out of business. Later, in 1997, the property was purchased, refurbished, and reopened as a midlevel hotel, with no nightclub. It retained the name—Mutiny Hotel—but the ghosts from the cocaine era had long since moved on.

WILLY AND SAL WERE NEVER truly able to find out who or what was behind the raid in Los Angeles. They did learn that one of the escorts hired that night had been serving as an informant for the police. She was the one who told the Marina del Rey sheriffs about the cocaine, guns, and cash. As far as the Boys could tell, the raid was a one-off and not connected to any larger investigation. Since their arrests had been under false names, there was no indication that prosecutors in LA County had any idea of their true identities.

Meanwhile, back in Miami, they took stock of their operation. One thing Willy and Sal noticed was that they could control its parameters: the kilos flowed when they wanted them to flow. By the summer of 1986, they were receiving 1,000 kilos every six weeks from Escobar, via the Bahamas. From the Valencia brothers, a staggering 4,800 kilos were being shipped, via a fleet of four Twin Commander 1000 airplanes, to the landing strip in Jalisco, Mexico. From there it was smuggled by Pepe (a.k.a. El Frijol) across the border into the United States. In LA, Jojo and Freddy kept 3,250 kilos for West Coast clients. Of that, 1,500 was sent to Miami for East Coast clients. In addition, every six weeks, Jojo was sending 1,000 kilos from LA to New York City.

Their system of importation and distribution was a juggernaut, with airplanes, semitrucks, stash houses, and billions in cash. The big cities—LA, Miami, New York—served as hubs for other cities, with layers of clients below Los Muchachos working out their own deals to distribute the product into the hinterland—a matrix of cocaine that had literally taken the country by storm. For Willy and Sal, to meet the demand, the operation almost ran on automatic pilot. At this stage, it would have been harder to make it stop than it was to keep it flowing.

What Los Muchachos could not control was the larger framework of the narcosphere. Starting with production of the coca plant in South America and the massive smuggling network that facilitated its delivery to the marketplace, the business was vast, with nooks and crannies in different countries, and operational decisions in one jurisdiction affected other aspects of the pipeline. Willy and Sal could control their own operation, but they could not control all the variables that dictated its success. Other people were involved, people with egos, fickle temperaments, delusions of grandeur.

Pablo Escobar may have been on the run, first in Panama and then Nicaragua, but this did not stop him from wreaking havoc in Colombia. Mostly, this had to do with his war against institutions of social and political power. In November 1985, the country experienced what seemed like a culmination of the atrocities that had been ongoing. In the middle of the day, a group of armed guerrillas from M-19 staged an explosive attack on the Palace of Justice in Bogotá. The siege lasted for twenty-six hours. In the ensuing slaughter, ninety-five people were killed, including eleven Supreme Court justices. Many court documents, including all pending extradition requests, were set on fire and destroyed.

It was later revealed that Escobar had financed the attack.

In December 1986, Escobar ordered the assassination of the editor in chief of the newspaper *El Espectador*, who frequently wrote editorials in favor of stiffer penalties for drug traffickers.

Pablo's war against civilized society horrified the world. He was killing people left and right and seemed to be daring proponents of the War on Drugs by declaring, *You wanted a war, so now you've got one.*

In the United States, the Reagan administration realized that along with huge seizures of product, arrests, indictments, and the beginning of a process that would become known as "mass incarceration," a restructuring of the system was in order. In October 1986, President Reagan signed the Anti-Drug Abuse Act, a massive omnibus drug bill that appropriated $1.7 billion to fight the drug crisis. From it, $97 million was allocated to build new prisons, and $200 million for "drug education," which really meant a propaganda war in which Just Say No was merely an opening salvo.

Amongst the narcos, no one knew where all this was headed. For Falcon and others in his position, it created an air of uncertainty. If Pablo didn't get his way, he seemed willing to take the entire narcosphere down with him—which, even though the business was thriving and the money rolling in, tended to take the fun out of things.

In a conversation with Gustavo Gaviria over the shortwave radio, Willy asked, "What the hell is going on with Pablo? Something tells me this is about more than just extradition."

Gaviria explained that lately Pablo was in an especially foul mood. "Ballistic and delusional," Gustavo called it. Much of it had to do with how the Cali Cartel leadership had responded to his war against extradition. He felt they were undermining the effort and showing weakness. "His hatred for the Cali people is so intense that he's not thinking rational at times," said Gustavo.

The problem, noted Pablo's partner and cousin, was that his mistress—the renowned Colombian journalist Virginia Vallejo—was going behind Escobar's back and having an affair with Gilberto Rodríguez, a leader of the Cali Cartel. The mistress was going back and forth between the two men, "pouring gasoline on the fire." Keeping Pablo from exploding with rage and making rash decisions had become, for Gustavo, a full-time job.[1]

Around the same time Willy was having these conversations with Gaviria, he was on the radio with Mario or Guillermo Valencia getting their side of the story. There were some among the Cali Cartel leadership who felt that Escobar should be killed. It was understood that if the "Gentlemen from Cali" undertook such an act, it would likely bring about a kind of nuclear Armageddon in the narco universe. In lieu of total annihilation, the only alternative was to try to talk sense into Escobar. "Doctor," said Mario Valencia, "we know that you

---

[1] On August 11, 1990, Gustavo Gaviria was shot multiple times and killed by a Search Bloc (*Bloque de Búsqueda*), a unit of Colombia's National Police. According to those who knew Escobar, Gaviria's death had a profound impact on the narco boss, pushing him deeper into his psychosis ("Key Cocaine Cartel Member Killed by Colombia Police During Raid," *Los Angeles Times*, August 12, 1990).

are doing business with Pablo. That is your business, and we would never seek to interfere with that in any way. We are pleased to be doing business with you and Sal. Especially with this route we've opened up with the Mexicans, the future is bright for us. But this situation with Escobar seems to be headed in a very bad direction. Would it be possible for you and Sal to speak with him? He's your business partner; maybe he will listen to you."

For a while, Willy and Sal had suspected that the Valencia brothers likely knew about their relationship with Pablo, but the request to intercede on their behalf caught Willy completely by surprise. He didn't like the idea at all. He told Mario, "My friend, I greatly value our partnership. It's an honor to be doing business with you. But I'm not going to get in the middle of this. I think it would cause more trouble than it's worth."

Sal was also on the radio. He spoke up. "If it's okay with Willy, I'll talk to Pablo. Maybe I can talk some sense into him."

Willy kept his mouth shut, but he didn't like it. From what Gustavo had told them, bringing up this subject with Pablo was only going to get him riled up. Willy was convinced that the best course of action for them was to stay out of this dispute. But if Sal thought he could play peacemaker, let him go ahead and try.

A few days later, Willy asked Sal how his conversation went with Pablo. "Not too good," said Sal. "Gustavo was right. Pablo can't be dealt with on this subject right now."

Willy was not surprised. His only hope was that Sal hadn't made matters worse by giving the impression they were taking sides on behalf of the Cali Cartel.

IN LATE 1986, DEA SPECIAL Agent David Borah opened a case against what he designated the Falcon-Magluta Drug Trafficking Organization (DTO). The big break had come one year earlier, when the agent had received a call from, of all places, Scotland Yard. An agent with Scotland Yard informed Borah that they had recently closed a major bank robbery case in England. Part of that case had involved investigators tracing the deposits of stolen proceeds to accounts in the Virgin Islands, as part of a money-laundering scheme.

The agent told Borah, "We were able to trace the money transactions from the bank robbery to an accountant on the island of Tortola. His name is Shaun

Murphy. He's very well connected in the islands, with clients in government and business. When we told Murphy that he was a target of our investigation, he folded right away and agreed to cooperate. He gave us the name of a Miami lawyer—Jim Molans—who he was working with to open accounts for cocaine dealers."

Borah was intrigued. He made plans to travel to Tortola in the Virgin Islands, to debrief Shaun Murphy. He brought along Agent Donna Sigers from the investigative division of the Internal Revenue Service.

Shaun Murphy was everything an investigator might have hoped for: an accountant who had never done time in prison and had no intention of doing so. Murphy explained everything to the agents, why and how modern-day narcos used the Caribbean islands to launder their money. He explained how, through the Miami attorney Molans, he had opened twenty-five separate shell companies for US clients. Four of these companies—Mid Valley, Aminton, Matridge, and Leachville—had assets and businesses in the United States that could be traced directly to Falcon and Magluta.

Borah returned to his office at the DEA Group 13 field division in Fort Lauderdale and continued the hunt. It was a game of connect the dots. Through Murphy and his connection to Molans, the investigators were able to uncover a vast network of assets, including, among other holdings, construction companies and real estate properties. One of these properties was the 3,600-acre ranch in Clewiston, which had been purchased by Leachville.

For Borah and IRS Agent Sigers, it was a laborious process but also a major breakthrough that made it possible for the DEA and IRS to officially open a joint case against Falcon and Magluta. They could see the Boys' financial empire, but it was, in a sense, a case of the cart before the horse. Borah still had much to learn about the structure of Los Muchachos and the specific cocaine transactions that might have laid the groundwork for their various accounts and assets.

Most of what he did know was based on a deposition from Jack Devoe, with whom Borah conducted several debriefings. The former pilot for Los Muchachos provided the agent with names, but since few had criminals records or were listed in law enforcement databases, the first order of business was to place faces with names.

Borah had been told that Willy and Sal were coleaders, and that Tavy Falcon, Tony Garrudo, Justo Jay, Benny Lorenzo, and a few others were what could be called underbosses. There were a host of underlings who worked with the boat crews who were also part of the Los Muchachos organization.

In the summer of 1987, Borah and a fellow agent attended two races at two different locations, one in Atlantic City, New Jersey, and another in Fort Myers, Florida.

The race in New Jersey was sponsored by a well-known real estate mogul and casino owner named Donald J. Trump. His name was plastered all around the racing site on banners and advertising for the event.

The race in Fort Myers was traditionally one of the most popular on the circuit. Seahawk boats always did well at this race, as the water conditions in this stretch of the Atlantic Ocean were familiar to the crews from South Florida. Which is why everyone was surprised when Sal Magluta's boat overheated and caught fire. Sal, Tavy, and their team were forced to abandon ship by diving into the water, where they were met by an emergency rescue unit.

It was a strange sight to see Magluta and his crew in a state of distress. As Willy watched from the shoreline, along with other family members and fans of the Seahawk team, it was hard not to see the disaster as a harbinger of things to come.

The incident cast a pall over the day's events. Later in the afternoon, Willy and Justo Jay were at the Seahawk trailer, which the team used as a central office or gathering place on the day of the race. The day was winding down, with people milling about the grounds. Jay said to Willy, "See that guy over there? That guy with the camera?"

"Where?" said Willy.

Jay pointed. "That white dude over there. That guy's been following us around all day."

Willy looked at the guy. Normally, Willy would listen to Jay, who was one of the group's most diligent members: levelheaded and cautious, but not paranoid by nature. On the other hand, cameras were common at the boat races. Media people, or just interested observers, constantly snapped photos so often that you hardly noticed they were there.

"He's just a guy with a camera. What's the problem?"

"I've been watching him. He's only taking pictures of Seahawk. I think he's a cop."

Willy scrutinized the guy: five foot ten, sandy blond hair, built like an athlete, seemed to be in his thirties.

"I'm gonna go over there," said Jay.

"Go ahead," said Willy.

Jay headed off toward the man with the camera. Willy went inside the trailer, grabbed a beer out of the refrigerator, and sat at a kitchen table. He watched through a window as Jay walked up to the guy and started talking. At first, the conversation seemed to be civil, then Jay pulled out his wallet, extracted some cash, and tried to get the guy to take it. He reached for the guy's camera, but the guy pulled away. The exchange became more heated. The guy took out some identification and showed it to Jay. Through the window, Willy saw Jay curse at the guy, and then he walked back to the trailer.

Willy stepped out onto the grounds.

"Fucking *puto*," said Jay. "I knew it."

"What?"

"I offered him one thousand dollars for the film in his camera. Who would say no to that, right? Only a cop. When I reached for his camera he got all scared. He took out his badge and showed it to me."

"Did you catch the name?"

"I didn't see the name, but I saw the agency he works for—DEA."

"Fuck," said Willy. "The feds."

The Boys did not worry too much about local cops; they always figured they could buy them off. But federal authorities were a different animal.

It was like the drip of a leaky faucet that could not be turned off. Los Muchachos kept hearing about investigations, arrests, and grand jury hearings that seemed to be nibbling away at the edges of their business. They knew Jack Devoe was cooperating with the feds. Then there was Ray Corona, their initial banker. In 1985, Ray and his father had gone on trial for their involvement in a major marijuana-smuggling enterprise; that ended in a hung jury. But then they were retried and, in December 1986, found guilty on multiple counts. Willy heard that Ray Corona subsequently had flipped; he was testifying at secret grand jury hearings.

It seemed apparent that the feds were investigating Los Muchachos.

Two weeks after the incident at the Fort Myers race, Willy was at the KS&W offices up the Florida coast in Saint Augustine. It was rare for Falcon to visit KS&W, but usually around tax time, he flew by jet to the facility and spent two or three days going over the books with an accountant. He enjoyed getting away from Miami for a couple of days.

On this particular visit, he was in a gym that they had built on the top floor of their office complex. Willy had just come out of the sauna and was drying his hair with a towel when an employee from downstairs entered and said excitedly, "Willy, the DEA and IRS are on the property. They're here with a search warrant. The warrant says they have the right to search our files regarding Seahawk and KS&W."

"Holy shit," said Willy. "They're here now?"

The guy nodded.

"How many?"

"I don't know. I saw three or four. A lady and three men."

"All right, all right. Just go back down there. I'm gonna stay here. Just because they have a warrant to search for documents doesn't mean they get to search the entire premises." The guy went back downstairs.

For the next few hours, Willy stayed put in the gym. Occasionally, he peeked out the window to see the various agents moving boxes and other materials from the KS&W office to their car and back. One of the agents caught Willy's attention: it was the same guy they had seen at the race in Fort Myers, the guy with the camera who was confronted by Justo Jay. He seemed to be the one in charge of the search team.

Finally, after the agents packed up and departed, Willy headed downstairs. "Jesus," he said to the office workers, "they took their time. What were they looking at?"

"Financials. Transactions. Tax records. That kind of thing. The lead agent left a business card." The worker handed the card to Willy.

It was the standard-issue federal law enforcement card, this one embossed with the insignia of the Drug Enforcement Administration. The name on the card was David Borah.

FALCON WAS NOT SLEEPING WELL. The dark cloud of the DEA had entered their world. And then there was Sal's racing accident, the image of the boat giving off black smoke, with Sal and Tavy having to flee for their lives. Ominous signs created stress, and stress led to somnambulant anxieties, images from childhood, the trauma of exile as visual signifier. In his dreams was the memory of Tato, one of Willy's earliest clients in the cocaine business. Back in 1977, Tato was murdered in a public execution. It wasn't the murder that Willy remembered, it was the funeral, the sad faces, and the overwhelming feeling of loss.

It was around this time that Willy made the decision that he would retire from boat racing. He would still maintain ownership of the company; he enjoyed the business. But at the age of thirty, after close to sixty races as a boat pilot on the circuit—with one world championship—he was done with the rigorous schedule of training for and taking part in the APBA races.

LATER THAT SUMMER, WILLY AND Sal made another trip to Mexico City. Flying in on the Lear 55, Willy took in the dingy sprawl of the city, the endless humanity of a metropolis that seemed to wheeze and cough like *un viejo asmático*, an old man with a respiratory ailment. As they descended, the carpet of buildings—houses, condos, slums, and shacks—made Willy wonder how many of those inhabitants were users of the white powder. Since getting involved in the business, Los Muchachos had seen the product expand its reach to become a global phenomenon. As their system of distribution in the United States became more efficient, the price per kilo dropped dramatically, so that it was more affordable to the masses. Cocaine was in demand all over Europe and especially in Latin America. It altered the chemistry of the mind and body, until, temporarily, everything seemed fresh and exciting. It was a glorious illusion that appealed to all classes and races and nationalities.

Willy and Sal stayed, as they always did, at the Camino Real Hotel. They anticipated meeting with Mario Valencia, from Cali, and with the three leaders of the Guadalajara Cartel. Mario was present, but when the Mexicans arrived at the room, it was only Félix Gallardo. Conspicuous in his absence was Rafael Caro Quintero.

Gallardo explained: the previous year, in February 1985, a DEA agent named Enrique "Kiki" Camarena was kidnapped, tortured, and murdered at the behest of the Guadalajara Cartel.

As Willy already knew, the murder caused a furor in the US law enforcement community, and in the media. The torture and murder of a federal agent was a new low. The DEA came after Caro Quintero, who fled and hid in Costa Rica for nearly a year. For a time, he considered shifting his entire narco operation there. Eventually, Rafael Caro Quintero was apprehended by authorities and brought back to Mexico, where he was being held at a prison compound.

"How is he doing?" asked Sal.

"He's good," said Félix. "He has everything he needs—the best food, the best women. You know how Rafael is—long as he has women and tequila, he will be fine. And we'll make sure he has the best legal representation in Mexico."[2]

Once again, the Boys found themselves having to deal with the consequences of their partners' actions. In some ways, the narcosphere was a fragile organism. A major criminal act in one jurisdiction had reverberations. The murder of DEA Agent Kiki Camarena was their problem also, whether they liked it or not.

Félix explained how the situation with Caro Quintero was affecting his business: "I am by myself running this operation, and I have been insanely busy. I have thousands of hectares of sinsemilla marijuana plantation to take care of, and also the handling of the shipment of these large sums of marijuana into the United States." And then he added, "For me to continue receiving planeloads of cocaine from Colombia—for it to be worth it to me and the Guadalajara Cartel—you will need to send at least seven planes with twelve hundred kilos each. The reason is that I pay huge amounts of money for the protection to the police commanders in Jalisco, where the shipments land. And then I pay a percentage to the people in the Baja border region, which gets a piece of all loads crossing the border into the US. For me to afford this, we need to increase the size of the loads. *Entienden?*"

Willy, Sal, and Mario Valencia all looked at one another. This was an unexpected request. Said Willy, "Félix, if you don't mind, we need to discuss this among ourselves in the other room."

---

[2] The saga of Rafael Caro Quintero would span decades. After being sentenced to forty years in prison for his role in the murder of DEA Agent Camarena, Caro Quintero was released in August 2013. Though he had served only twenty-eight years of his sentence, a Mexican state court ruled that he had been tried improperly. The US government expressed outrage and sought his arrest on still-pending murder and trafficking charges. The aging narco boss went into hiding but was eventually captured. In January 2023, at a prison in Ciudad Juárez, he escaped as a part of a violent attack on the facility by heavily armed gang members. Seventeen people were killed (ten guards), and twenty-five inmates escaped. In July 2023, Caro Quintero was recaptured. The US State Department requested that the narco, now in his early seventies, be extradited to face criminal charges in the United States.

Gallardo nodded. They filed into another room in their suite and shut the door.

Said Sal, "Can we do this? We've only got four planes."

Mario answered, "I think we can do it. Pacho Herrera, our partner, he has at least two Commander 1000s ready to go. He'd be happy to participate, I'm sure."

Added Willy, "We can buy a seventh plane. We might not have it in time for the next shipment, but we can have it by next month."

They all agreed. They went back into the next room and explained the situation to Félix.

"Okay," he said. "On the understanding that you will add a seventh plane for future shipments, I think we can agree on this."

They retired to a nearby restaurant and celebrated the continuation of their partnership. It seemed unusual to Willy that Félix Gallardo was so relaxed. The murder of the DEA agent was having reverberations that would soon lead to the disillusion of the Guadalajara Cartel as an organization. He had to know that his group was facing a grave existential threat. And yet he seemed totally relaxed, even jovial. To Falcon, it was a lesson on how a narco boss was supposed to handle his business.

SINCE BEING CUT IN AS an equal partner in the business, Tavy Falcon had been busy. It wasn't just bookkeeping. By now, he was functioning as a high-level manager and organizer. His skills at overseeing the stash houses and as a financial bursar, making sure payments were made and that money due was received and accounted for, became a big part of his role. Tavy may have been a high school dropout, but he was good with math. Also, he had an even temperament. He seemed to always be in control. Though he was younger than both Willy and Sal, in some ways he was more mature, or at least more stable in his home life. He was not out partying and bedding down with assorted women, as was his brother. His marriage to Amelia, his childhood sweetheart, was rock solid.

Though neither Tavy nor Willy said anything to their parents about Tavy's higher profile with Los Muchachos, their father, Arsenio, knew what was going on. Said Tavy:

This was always a problem, since I was a teenager. "What your brother is doing," he would say, "don't go down that road." Nonstop, he would say that. Later, when the money was rolling in, when we had the house and the cars, he would say, "I never expected this from you. From your brother, yes, but not from you." One time, he saw I was driving a new Mercedes. I had it parked in front of his house. "Why are you driving that car? Why are you calling attention to yourself like that? What are you thinking?" I didn't even try to explain it. Whatever I said, he wasn't going to understand it anyway.

More and more, Tavy's wingman was Pegy Rosello, his wife's brother. Some thought Pegy was not too swift, but he was a blood relative and therefore trustworthy—according to the philosophy of Los Muchachos, and to Tavy.

Underneath Pegy was a midlevel worker whom Tavy would come to trust more and more. Wilfredo "Mata" Pino was a Cuban exile from Camagüey, Cuba. His girlfriend and future wife was a cousin of Amelia's. Mata first met Willy Falcon in the construction business before Los Muchachos existed. At family parties and gatherings, he got to know the Falcons, both Willy and Tavy, and he longed to be part of their circle. He knew they were in the cocaine business, and that there was money to be made.

The word *mata* means "shrub" or "tuft of earth," something persistent but often overlooked.

It was Tavy Falcon who first realized that Mata could be valuable to the group. He assigned Pegy the job of training Mata to organize the stash houses.

Mata was astounded by the suitcases filled with more cash than he ever dreamed he would see in one place. Even more than the money, he was impressed by the camaraderie of Los Muchachos. As with others in the group, his father had been a political prisoner in Cuba. Mata had gone through the difficult and humiliating process of exile. In Miami, he struggled to make a living and doubted he would ever achieve the kind of American dream he saw on television and in the movies. Then along came the Falcon brothers, and Sal Magluta. Within weeks of going to work for Los Muchachos, he was bringing home hundreds of thousands of dollars.

Said Mata, "To me, the group was like my family. Tavy was my brother. I feel like I finally found a place where I belong."

Eventually, as Tavy's role as manager of the organization broadened, with frequent business trips to Houston, El Paso, Tucson, and other far-flung destinations where the product was coming in from Mexico, Tavy brought Mata along as a bodyguard. Mata was small but tough, like a bantam rooster. He was a black belt in karate, and eventually a martial arts instructor with his own school.

Loyalty and physical confidence: Wilfredo "Mata" Pino was Tavy's Doberman pinscher, and a welcome addition to the club.

MARIO VALENCIA FELT THAT WILLY and Sal needed to meet Pacho Herrera. The cocaine trade was a people business at its core. In many ways, the cartels in Colombia and Mexico were Old World business operations. They thrived on personal connections, face-to-face contact. Pacho Herrera may have been unknown to the public at large, but in the narcosphere he was another of those legendary pioneers in the business who inspired respect and curiosity.

Like Escobar and Lehder of the Medellín Cartel, Herrera had spent considerable time in his youth in the United States. Born in 1951, he lived in New York City in his twenties and made a living as a jeweler and a broker of precious metals. By the mid-1970s, he was selling cocaine. He was twice arrested on possession and distribution charges. In 1982, he negotiated the deal with Escobar and the Medellín Cartel that ceded New York City to Pacho and his group.

Willy and Sal had heard that there was some sort of dispute between Pacho and Pablo Escobar. Later, they would learn that it had to do with Herrera's unwillingness to kill a narco who Escobar believed had killed one of his people. It's also possible that Pablo's animosity toward Herrera had to do with his own latent homophobia. Willy and Sal were vaguely aware that by going into business with Pacho, they might be stepping on Pablo's toes. But in the cocaine business, it was believed that business trumped personal histories. They were sure that Pablo would accept the business imperative involved—though, as it would turn out, they were wrong.

To meet Pacho Herrera, Willy and Sal flew to Aruba. They arrived a day before the scheduled meeting so they could take in the beautiful setting at the Concorde Hotel and Casino, the pristine white sands and gentle waters of the Caribbean Sea lapping at the shoreline. Willy lay at the beach for a while under a hot sun and allowed himself to get dark, like a true indio.

The following day, Mario Valencia arrived with Pacho Herrera. They met at Willy and Sal's suite. The Boys from Miami were fascinated by Pacho. It was known that he was gay, which was a novelty in the business. They were half expecting a Colombian Liberace, with spangled clothing and flamboyant gestures. Pacho was the opposite. Some Latin narco bosses were crude country bumpkins, and some were cultured, erudite sophisticates. Pacho was the latter. His linen suit was beautifully tailored, and his manner was calm, respectful, and businesslike.

Pacho had already agreed to supply additional turbo planes for the shipments from Colombia to Félix Gallardo and the Guadalajara Cartel. He complimented Willy and Sal on the operation they were running in New York City, which was Pacho's primary sphere of distribution.

Said Sal, "That's Manny Alonso, Monguito, our man in New Jersey. He has done a great job organizing our system in that area."

Los Muchachos were charging Pacho 50 percent of the load they were smuggling for him through Mexico, and also $500 for every kilo they transported via semitrucks from Los Angeles to New York City. Willy informed the Colombian that they would have to raise that to $1,000 per kilo, because of additional costs and expenses.

The narcos rarely argued over money. The profit margins were so extravagant that you would have to be a miser (there were some) to haggle over nickels and dimes. Usually, when someone announced they were having to raise the price, the typical response was the one Pacho made to Willy: "I have no problem with that, but can we increase the loads, bring in more product?"

Willy smiled. "I think so. Let me check with Félix Gallardo. I'd say as long as we have the Commander 1000 airplanes, we should be able to accommodate almost any size of load."

After they were done with their meeting, they all retired downstairs to the gambling casino. Baccarat, of course: the cards dealt from the shoe; the dealer burning the first card, face up; the croupier calling out the totals to the player and the banker; the distinctive feel of the green felt tabletop; the silent swish of the baccarat pallet, shaped like a wooden paddle; the quiet expectation before a wager. High rollers are drawn to baccarat, their demeanor serious and elegant.

The ladies gather around, bronzed and golden, with low-cut dresses. The minimum bet is $500. It is not a game for the cowardly or cheap.

In honor of their successful meeting, all four of them—Willy, Sal, Mario, and Pacho—gambled throughout the night and into the early hours of the morning.

THE COCAINE BUSINESS WAS SOMETIMES like a revolving convention, a series of sit-downs in hotel rooms, bars, offices, and restaurants. The narcosphere was subterranean but social; there were deals to be made, and partnerships needed watering like temperamental houseplants. Willy and Sal did not need to be present for the consummation of every deal, or monitor every transaction, but they were adherents of the personal touch. Meet, shake hands, raise a toast, and hug it out.

From Aruba, they flew to Panama City to meet the man who had become their financial guru. They had a shipment of $35 million in cash hidden in drywall shipments arriving in the Panamanian capital that day. It was their single largest shipment of cash so far. They wanted to make sure the money was received and expeditiously deposited into their hidden account at Banco Aleman-Panameno, so they could pay the Valencia brothers for the most recent shipment of product through Mexico.

Guillermo Endara, the corpulent banker, lawyer, and money launderer for some of the most powerful narcos in the world, sat in his office. Standing aside his desk was Hernán Delgado, his partner at the Endara Firm. As Willy and Sal were ushered through the door, with deep tans from their days in Aruba, Endara didn't even wait for them to sit. "Well," he said, "it's official. I'm running for president of Panama. We will be making a public announcement next week."

"That's amazing," said the Boys, almost in unison.

Delgado, who would be serving as Endara's campaign manager, explained to the two Cubans that General Noriega had already handpicked his candidate, Carlos Duque, a former business partner of the general. "We can beat Duque," said Delgado. "We've created a new party, the Democratic Alliance of Civil Opposition, which is a coalition of parties opposed to the Noriega dictatorship."

"Good," said Willy. "Noriega reminds me of Fidel Castro. He thinks he is God."

Endara stood and let the full immensity of his three-hundred-pound frame make its own statement: "When I'm elected, we will have total access to the banking system, free of regulation. I will be able to place friends in high positions of government. We will have access to the Panama Canal to load and unload money and facilitate shipments of your product to the United States. I intend to appoint one of our law partners to head the intelligence service of Panama. This way we will have constant oversight of any law enforcement activity in the region."

"That sounds almost too good to be true," said Sal.

Furthermore, Endara explained how his people had been in contact with Vice President George Bush, who, in October 1987, announced that he would be running as Reagan's successor for president in the upcoming US election. Bush assured Endara that if he could show that he had a legitimate shot at winning, the Bush administration would endorse his campaign for the presidency of Panama.

"There's only one issue," said Delgado. "Money. The only way we beat Noriega's candidate is with a massive campaign effort—television advertising, newspapers, magazines, billboards all around the country. Would you gentlemen be willing to make a campaign contribution?"

It was like Sheriff Dyess Jr. of Hendry County all over again—corrupt partners soliciting narco dollars to make their dreams come true. "How much do you need?" asked Willy.

Said Delgado, "We will leave that up to you. Whatever you think you can spare for this effort would be greatly appreciated."

Willy and Sal looked at one another, and Willy said, "How about ten million dollars?"

Endara and Delgado appeared to be amazed. Said Delgado, "With ten million dollars, Guillermo could probably beat George Bush for president."

They all laughed.

THE CRIMINAL CASE AGAINST WILLY, Sal, and the others in Los Angeles was an annoying piece of business that would not go away. In August 1987 they were scheduled to appear in Los Angeles Superior Court for a status conference on their case. Three days before their appearance, their lawyers in LA received a phone call from the LA County prosecutor's office: "We know the real names of your clients—Sal Magluta and Willy Falcon."

The lawyer was surprised; he didn't even know those names. He had agreed to represent Angelo Maretto and Wilfredo Vargas.

The way the authorities discovered the real names was the equivalent of a left-handed bank shot. It transpired on a Sunday afternoon that summer, when the APBA powerboat races in Atlantic City were broadcast live on ESPN television. During that broadcast, between races, a correspondent interviewed members of the Seahawk crew. One of the people they interviewed was Sal Magluta, who was identified by name on the screen.

In Los Angeles, one of the sheriffs who arrested Magluta under the name Angelo Maretto happened to be watching the powerboat races on ESPN. He saw the guy being identified as Sal Magluta and thought, *Wait a minute. That's the guy I arrested at the Marina City Club. His name was not Sal Magluta, it was Maretto.* The sheriff picked up the phone and called the LA County prosecutor's office.

When Willy heard about this, he thought it was strange: *Why would the prosecutors tell us that ahead of time? Why wouldn't they wait until we showed up for the status hearing, and then spring it on us then?*

Ever since DEA Agent David Borah and the IRS had come into the picture, Willy was feeling paranoid. He and Sal discussed whether or not they should even show up for the status conference in LA. Maybe it was a trick to lure them to court, revoke their bail, and take them into custody. They seriously considered jumping bail and going on the run. It was decided that they would appear in LA County court, but they would bring their experienced duo of lawyers— Joe Oteri and Marty Weinberg—in case the feds tried anything tricky at the hearings.

Willy and Sal flew on a commercial flight to Los Angeles and checked into the Bonaventure Hotel. The next day, they arrived early to meet Oteri and Weinberg, and their Los Angeles–based lawyer, Scott Furstman, in the courthouse cafeteria before their scheduled ten a.m. appointment in court. Willy and Sal were both nervous. The whole thing felt suspiciously like a setup to them.

As they were having their coffee and a bagel with the lawyers, what appeared to be the prosecution team entered the cafeteria. The prosecutors did not notice them in the crowded cafeteria. Willy froze: among the group was David Borah and the woman IRS agent who had executed the search of documents at the offices of KS&W in Saint Augustine. Borah was pushing a cart that contained legal boxes exactly like the ones they had used to remove files from KS&W.

Sal saw the look on Willy's face and realized something was up. They looked at each other: without saying a word, they realized that a moment of reckoning had arrived.

Said Willy to the lawyers, "Hey, me and Sal need to step out for a minute. We left some important papers in the car. We'll be right back."

As soon as they were in the hallway, Willy said to his partner, "It's the feds, just like we suspected. DEA and IRS. We need to get the fuck out of here. Now."

They didn't even have time to think about it. It was time to flee.

The car they were using was a rental. They drove back to the Bonaventure Hotel. They realized that since they were using their real names on this trip, the authorities could trace the rental or be waiting for them at LAX for their return flight to Miami. Without even gathering their things at the hotel, they called for a taxi. "Please take us to the airport in San Diego," they told the driver.

On the drive to San Diego, past an endless stream of fast-food restaurants and freeway diners—Denny's, McDonald's, IHOP—they discussed the situation. The day had arrived: they were officially on the run.

At the San Diego airport, they booked a small, commuter flight to Las Vegas. At the same time, they called Tavy Falcon in Miami. They told him to load a million dollars into suitcases, secure the Learjet, and meet them at Caesars Palace Hotel in Las Vegas.

Traveling through the airports, arriving in Vegas, and checking into the hotel, they eyeballed everybody: Were they a cop? A bounty hunter? A US Marshal?

On the flight, Willy closed his eyes and kept seeing the face of Borah, the DEA agent.

From the hotel room at Caesars, Willy called Alina and told her what was happening. She was stunned, bordering on hysterical. Said Willy, "There's a lot we need to talk about, but not on the phone. In the next couple days, I'll have Tony Bemba come and get you."

The adrenaline was pumping. Willy and Sal had talked about the possibility of this occurring, and now it was happening.

Willy and Sal purchased suitcases, toiletries, and some clothing items. How do you plan for a life on the run? Would it be for a week or a lifetime?

They checked into separate rooms. After Tavy and Tony Bemba arrived, they gathered in Willy's room. They ordered food and drinks from room service. For hours, they discussed the situation. They decided that the first thing they needed to do was have a summit meeting with the inner circle of Los Muchachos. Said Willy to the others, "We'll meet in Orlando. Nobody would expect to find us there. Day after tomorrow. I'll call Mario Valencia and tell him to be there." Willy told Tavy to contact the essential Muchachos in Miami: Justo Jay, Tony Garrudo, Benny Lorenzo, and Miguel Vega, the group's paymaster. Also, he instructed Tavy to contact Jojo Brito and Freddy Cruz in Los Angeles, and Manny Alonso in New York. Also Gilberto Barrios, who was in charge of the truckers. Everybody. In two days, they would meet at the Polynesian Hotel near Disney World in Orlando. There, they would discuss the future of the organization.

IN WILLY'S EXECUTIVE SUITE AT the hotel in Orlando, the primary members of Los Muchachos arrived, along with Mario Valencia of the Cali Cartel. The faces were somber. They had heard gossip about what was happening, but they had gathered to hear it directly from their leader. Willy explained the situation: "Me and Sal are now fugitives from the law. As of today, don't even use the names Willy Falcon and Sal Magluta. Those names no longer exist. As for the business, nothing changes. We are still on call twenty-four seven, just as we have always been. Your duties and responsibilities with the organization haven't changed. In some ways, you may find that me and Sal are even more available to focus on our business. No more boat races or softball games to distract us. We are available to you whenever you need us."

Willy explained that he was in the process of locating and purchasing places to hide out in Manhattan, Fort Lauderdale, and Santa Monica, California.

These places were regionally situated so Falcon could monitor their primary spheres of business even while he was in hiding.

After this meeting, Willy met separately with Mario Valencia. Speaking on behalf of the Cali Cartel, Valencia was concerned that Willy and Sal would be in constant fear of arrest. "You should come live in Colombia," said Mario. "You could live in splendor, free from any problems with the law."

It occurred to Willy that Mario really had no idea of the full scope of the Los Muchachos operation. He explained that there was no way he and Sal could leave the country. With all the moving parts of their importation and distribution system, it required hands-on vigilance. They needed to be close to home. "Between your organization and ours, I assure you, nothing changes," said Willy.

The meeting in Orlando was an exercise in crisis management. After the members of the organization returned to their various cities, Willy, Sal, and Tavy remained in Orlando with their wives and children, who were staying at a separate hotel located inside Disney World.

Willy and Alina discussed the situation. Where were they going to live? Was Willy's family still going to be a part of his life?

There was no blueprint for living a life on the run. It was going to be difficult for the children. They realized they would be making it up as they went along.

Within days of their deciding to become fugitives, while still in Orlando, Willy and Sal learned of another major complication. Apparently, once the state of California realized that Falcon and Magluta had chosen to flee, it triggered further investigation. Among other things, it was brought to the attention of prosecutors in Miami that the two narcos had never been held accountable for their plea deal in the Video Canary case, which was now seven years old. In that case, they had been sentenced to serve fourteen months in prison. They had long ago exhausted all appeals. Somehow, the case had slipped through the cracks. They owed the state of Florida fourteen months in prison, which meant they were now wanted in two states, California and Florida.

Moreover, Willy and Sal were aware that they were the focus of federal grand jury hearings in the US District of South Florida. The DEA and IRS were building a case against them that could possibly lead to an indictment.

Though they told themselves—and their underlings and partners—that nothing had changed, it was an exercise in magical thinking. In truth, their life of liberty and leisure, boat races, softball championships, and late nights at their favorite club, was becoming like their early lives in Cuba, a distant memory bathed in nostalgia and tinged with joy, wonder, and regret.

Before they left Orlando, Willy pulled Tavy aside and said, "Look, who knows when it will be safe for me or Sal to return to Miami. You're the man now. People will be looking to you for direction. I'm putting you in charge down there."

Willy's brother nodded and said, "I'll take care of it."

Willy and Tavy didn't always agree with each other. As Tavy would say, "I sided with Sal on many things." All three of them had a way that they communicated that came from boat racing.

Back in the day, on a powerboat going at full speed, the noise was overwhelming. Seahawk spent hundreds of thousands of dollars trying to come up with a system that solved this seemingly insurmountable communications problem. They tried an earbud audio system, like the one used at NASCAR races, in which team members talk into headsets. It was still too loud; the static of the boat's engines drowned out everything. They tried an intercom system, which was even worse.

Eventually, they settled on the most low-tech communications system: signs. Sometimes that meant hand signs, but mostly it meant reading each other's nonverbal expressions. Said Tavy, "When you are in a boat going that fast, the fear in your eyes, nothing will hide it. When you're scared, you're scared. You see the expression of your partner in the boat, you know what he's going to do, and then you know what you should do."

Willy looked at Tavy, and Tavy looked at Willy. Their plan of action was understood.

They embraced and went their separate ways.

12

NEW YORK STATE OF MIND

THROUGHOUT THE SUMMER OF 1987, as Willy Falcon was coming to terms with his legal predicament, an event unfolded on national television that gnawed at the edges of his consciousness. The impact of this event made itself felt most notably in airports, where news of its unfolding reality droned on televisions mounted in waiting areas, and on the car radio, where it was the subject of special bulletins, or at home, where it led off broadcasts of the nightly news. To the public at large, it was known as the Iran-Contra hearings, a congressional investigation that attempted to make sense of a covert government operation involving armaments illegally smuggled to the Contras in Central America. To Willy, this public scandal was a fascinating though horrifying train wreck of revelations and testimony that came alarmingly close to exposing aspects of his introduction into the cocaine business.

In the end, it was not the disaster it could have been. The Iran-Contra committee called witnesses and solicited testimony on the Reagan administration's efforts to bypass a law passed by Congress—known as the Boland Amendment—that prohibited sending financial or military aid to the Contras without congressional approval. In a covert plot authorized by CIA Director William Casey and spearheaded by Lieutenant Colonel Oliver North, the agency secretly used Israel as an intermediary to sell guns to Iran on its behalf. The money from this transaction was diverted to covertly help finance the procuring of weapons for the Contras. It was an arrangement that involved a cesspool of spooks, Cuban exiles, pilots, arms merchants, and other misguided patriots the likes of whom had been swirling around anti-Castro efforts since the days of the Bay of Pigs invasion.

Willy watched the hearings with a pending sense of doom. Chi Chi Quintero, Juan Ramón Matta-Ballesteros, and others whom Falcon knew from his days in the anti-Castro movement were prominently mentioned. In the early days of the hearings, it appeared as though links among the CIA, the anti-Castro underground, and the Contras might be blown wide open, but the proceedings ultimately steered clear of the Contra-cocaine connection.[1]

For Willy, the testimony was a cautionary tale. This was the murky world that had drawn him into the cocaine business in the first place. These were the political entanglements that defined the lives of certain Cuban exiles who were caught up in the anti-Castro movement. Falcon, Tony Bemba, Justo Jay—half of the originators of Los Muchachos got their start smuggling cocaine as part of what they were told was a US government–sponsored initiative. They believed that they were exercising their patriotic duty. Now, other agencies of the same government were after them and trying to put them behind bars on cocaine-smuggling charges. It felt like a cruel joke of cosmic proportions.

The Iran-Contra hearings passed. Willy and Sal were in the same predicament as they were before the hearings: they needed to figure out the next phase of their lives as high-flying narcos and fugitives.

THEY WERE NOW FUGITIVES WANTED by the law. It was like the John Wayne movies from their youth that they loved so much, only they were not Duke Wayne, with his cowboy hat and six-shooter. They were the *hombres malos* whose faces were on wanted posters at the sheriff's office and in the town square.

Sal moved to a house in Houston and took on Benny B. as his roommate. His wife and kids stayed behind in Miami. After one month, Sal got bored and lonely, so he moved to a massive house and compound on La Gorce Island, on Miami Beach. At first, not many Muchachos knew that he had moved back home. It seemed like a crazy thing to do. Sal and Willy were wanted men, with warrants out for their arrest. Sal's argument was that La Gorce was a private island, highly exclusive. As long as he stayed on the compound, allowing Benny B. to run errands for him, he would be as safe there as anywhere.

Willy, on the other hand, took the opportunity to live in a place he had always wanted to experience: New York City.

---

[1] The subject of drugs and the Contras eventually did come under scrutiny as part of an investigation by the US Senate Subcommittee on Terrorism, Narcotics and International Operations, chaired by Senator John F. Kerry of Massachusetts. These hearings received scant attention in the media, and the committee's final report, issued in April 1989, received even less. No government officials have ever been held responsible for the likelihood that CIA-enabled shipments of cocaine to help finance the fight against communism in Central America may have played a significant role in inaugurating the entire cocaine era of the 1980s.

In a large four-bedroom apartment on East Seventy-Fourth Street and Fifth Avenue, directly across from Central Park, Willy and Alina set up shop. Willy lived under the name Antonio Barrios, with a United States passport and the necessary IDs to back it up; Alina maintained her actual identity. Life as a fugitive was not an ideal situation, but Willy and his wife were both excited about being in Manhattan.

One hard part had been deciding what to do with the children. They decided to leave the daughters in Miami with Alina's parents. The daughters had school and friends that made it difficult to leave. Three-year-old Will Jr., who was not yet in school, came with them to New York.

In a way, it gave new life to their relationship. Willy and Alina felt like newlyweds with a toddler and a fresh life in front of them.

It took Willy a while to get used to the new reality: no more time-consuming preparations for the boat races, no more softball practices and games, no more late nights at the Mutiny. Without the distractions from their extended community of friends and family in Miami, Willy became hyperfocused on the cocaine business.

To accommodate communications with his partners in Colombia and Mexico, he flew Tony Fandino to New York and had him outfit a newly purchased Chevrolet Astro cargo van with a shortwave radio transmitter:

It was amazing. We had all the latest equipment, which had advanced greatly since we first started using this system. The interior of the van was designed almost like a lounge, with a sofa, a small refrigerator, a small TV, and excellent sound system. There were no windows in the back, so nobody could see inside. All you had to do was turn on the power supply and connect the transmitter to the radio. There was an antenna that rose and lowered automatically. The sound quality on the transmitter was extraordinary. We could talk to people in Colombia and Mexico like we were all in the same room.

On days when Willy wanted to spend significant time on the shortwave, he would have his chauffeur—one of the "secretaries" from New Jersey who worked for Manny Alonso—drive around New York while he talked narco business in the back of the van.

After he had been in Manhattan for a month or so, Willy heard from Pablo Escobar for the first time in a while. Willy, Pablo, Sal—they were all fugitives now, which sometimes inhibited communication.

Willy thought Pablo would be curious about their respective living situations now that they had been forced to go on the lam, but that's not why he had called.

"Doctor," said Escobar, "I've heard something that disturbs me greatly." Sal was also on the line, having tuned in to their frequency on his equipment at La Gorce in Miami Beach.

"What is it?" asked Willy.

"I am hearing from a friendly source that you are using Mexico to transport the cocaine into the United States."

"Yes, my friend, we are. Is there a problem with this?"

"Not with Mexico, no. But I hear you are doing this in partnership with my archenemy, that *maricón*, Pacho Herrera. Is this true?"

Willy and Sal knew that Escobar despised Pacho Herrera, and, for that matter, the entire Cali Cartel. But they didn't know why. "Pablo, out of curiosity," said Willy, "I ask you, why are you so upset with these people?"

Escobar launched into a tirade about the Cali Cartel that lasted for ten minutes, increasing in volume as he spoke. He cited chapter and verse on every dispute that he had with Cali going back to the kidnapping of Marta Ochoa, dealings with the M-19 rebel group, his efforts with the Extraditables, and, more recently, a vigilante group in Colombia that called itself Los Pepes, which had declared war on Escobar. Pablo believed that Los Pepes were being secretly financed by the Cali Cartel.

"Pablo, you are our friend, and we would do anything to assist you. We've been doing business together for a long time. But you have to take into consideration that me and Sal started with the Valencia brothers, and they are from Cali. If Mario Valencia, who is my partner, decides that we need assistance from Pacho Herrera, I am not going to tell Mario that we won't work with Cali people because my friend Pablo says so."

"I'm not saying that," Pablo responded. "Of course, I know that you and I go back a long way. Look . . ." Pablo sighed. "I don't mean to involve the Doctor and the Accountant [his nickname for Sal] in this. This is a situation that I'm having to deal with, and it makes me angry. What I really wanted to say is that if you could include me with those transactions you are doing through Mexico, I would really appreciate it."

Money, of course: the bottom line.

"Pablo, I will see what I can do for you."

Later, Willy and Sal spoke over the transmitter about "the Pablo problem." Truth was, they didn't really need Escobar and the Medellín Cartel anymore. They were importing more kilos than ever with the Cali Cartel and the Mexican connection. Their allegiance to Pablo was mostly sentimental; they had started in the business with him and felt a sense of loyalty. Loyalty meant everything to the Cubans. But it was possible that a time would come when Escobar was more trouble than he was worth. Then they would have to tell Pablo that they were "retired." In the narco business, telling a major partner that you were retired was another way of saying the relationship was finished. It was a situation that could—and sometimes did—end badly for everyone involved.

THE ARREST IN LA HAD been a source of inspiration to Special Agent Borah and his investigators. Willy and Sal were on the run; this created a scenario in which mistakes could be made. The idea was to continue to apply pressure and flush them out of the woodwork.

In late 1987, both Tony Bemba and Justo Jay were arrested in the state of North Carolina on cocaine-trafficking charges. This was a coke deal that Tony and Justo Jay had undertaken on their own. When he heard about it, Willy was beside himself:

> In our organization, people were allowed to make their own deals on the side. Me and Sal never tried to restrict our people. Once I heard about Tony and Jay, I realized that was a mistake. By allowing our people to make their own deals, we were giving them the rope to hang themselves. And eventually their legal problems were going to come back on us.

One way it affected Willy and Sal was that it added fuel to the DEA investigation. Along with a number of associates who were now cooperating with the government—Jack Devoe, Ray Corona—they heard that the lawyer Juan Acosta, who had helped them set up their accounts with Endara in Panama, had been subpoenaed to testify at the grand jury.

All of this underscored the fact that the government was likely to be coming after their assets. Already, they had sold Eveready Ranch and the smaller International Ranch in Clewiston for $15 million. This included their thousands of heads of cattle. The sale price was likely low, but they were happy to have made the sale. Now other items had to go. Like the Learjet.

Having to sell the jet was a heartbreaker. Everyone loved the jet; it had become a kind of talisman of their success. But it was also one of the more obvious assets they owned. Even though it was not in their name, it wouldn't be difficult for investigators to link it to Los Muchachos. It had to go.

Willy and Sal discussed other properties and holdings that the feds were likely to be coming after—the Seahawk company, KS&W, the condos in Brickell Key and Vail, Willy's yacht, the CMM Ranch (a.k.a. the man cave), and so forth. It was a long list. It was unfortunate to have to liquidate in this manner, but for Willy, it made him feel as though at least he was in control of his destiny. He and Sal were in survival mode now. They were in the central matrix of the War on Drugs. If getting rid of their holdings was necessary for their continued existence, then so be it.

LIFE IN NEW YORK CITY was yet another clandestine adventure. Willy got his false identifications from a Cuban across the river in Union City, New Jersey. He was a good friend of Sal's uncle who went by the name Culito, which meant "Little Ass." Culito had contacts in New York who, for a price, could provide a complete set of New York State IDs: driver's license, birth certificate, social security card. The IDs cost $25,000. The false IDs made it possible to get credit cards under the fake names, based on bank accounts that were also established under false identifications.

Willy and Manny Alonso spent a lot of time together in New York. Whenever Willy needed cash, he would have Manny bring it from one of their many New Jersey stash houses—thirty or forty thousand at a time. They went on shopping sprees; Willy once bought three pairs of shoes for $12,000 at a luxury boutique in Midtown Manhattan. In the evenings, Willy and Manny frequently went to New York Yankees baseball games together, and when the Yankees weren't in town, they went to Shea Stadium to see the Mets.

Falcon and his wife took walks in Central Park with Will Jr. Sometimes, Alina's sister Ileana would fly into town and stay at one of the guest rooms in their apartment. They would go shopping and take in fashion events. In the fall of 1987, they all went to Fashion Week together. Willy enjoyed watching Alina in her element; she scouted out new fashions for her boutique in Miami. Seeing her business acumen, and how she presented herself among the glitterati in Manhattan, Willy was reminded of what first attracted him to Alina Rossique Falcon. She made him shine, and he felt proud to be in her presence.[2]

Every month, Willy and Alina flew back down to South Florida and reunited with their daughters at their compound in Fort Lauderdale. The daughters knew only that their father was away on business (what business that was, they didn't know for sure). Aileen, the oldest, was now twelve. The fact that she had eaten foods like caviar and sushi did not seem strange until one of her friends asked how her parents could afford that. She answered, "They are very successful at what they do and make lots of money." Ever since the kidnapping of Willy's mother, Aileen and Jessica had bodyguards pick them up at school or at ballet practice, but the girls never thought of them as bodyguards, only as "business associates" of their father.

In Fort Lauderdale, at the waterfront estate at 1247 Seminole Drive, they lived a fantasy life. Not seeing their parents for a month at a time, and then being reunited with them, was a loving ritual. They were happy to see each other, and the bond was rekindled. Eventually, Willy also bought a beach house in Fort Lauderdale. Life, it seemed, was like a series of vacations, with their parents flying in and out of their lives like mysterious characters—or dignitaries—from

---

[2] Willy did not completely cease his life of philandering. In November 1987, under a false identity, he traveled to the West Coast to check up on cocaine operations in LA and San Francisco. This was Falcon's first time in LA since his court appearance there months earlier, when he and Sal decided to skip bail. In the City of Angels, Willy secretly met with clients to reassure them that the business would not change even though he and Magluta were on the run. While there, Falcon attended a Lakers game at the Forum and then headed on to San Francisco. John, his primary Bay Area client, had been receiving kilos from Willy almost since he first entered the business in the late 1970s. They reminisced about how, in that time, the price of a kilo had gone from $60,000 to $12,000. In SF, John introduced Willy to his wife's cousin, a woman named Mary, whom Falcon described as a "knockout." Willy and Mary had a torrid five-day affair that included much sex, unlimited cocaine, and a trip to many of the city's most notable tourist attractions, including Alcatraz prison, where Falcon, given his current predicament as a wanted fugitive, could not help but ponder the possibility of incarceration.

another world. To anyone else it might have seemed unreal, but to the children of Willy and Alina Falcon, it was the only life they knew.

ONE THING WILLY AND ALINA both enjoyed about life in New York was checking out the nightclubs. Willy's favorite club was the Red Parrot, located on West Fifty-Seventh Street. Alina's was Limelight, which was an old nineteenth-century church on Sixth Avenue that had been converted into a club. Though Willy and Alina were both in their thirties, in New York they partied like they were twenty-one all over again.

One night, they decided to go to Tunnel nightclub with a couple of their Miami friends who now lived in New York. Tunnel was a club on Manhattan's West Side in the Chelsea neighborhood. It was in an old train terminal building, where the New York Central Railroad used to maintain a freight line.

Through Manny, Willy had a chauffeur in New York who was well connected at all the clubs in the city. On the night that Willy, Alina, and their friends arrived at Tunnel, there was, as usual, a long line behind a velvet rope. The chauffeur pulled some strings, and the Falcon group was let into the club without having to wait.

Willy had a .38-caliber PPK handgun strapped in an ankle holster, and he was carrying plenty of cocaine. His group immediately went to the VIP lounge located in the basement of the club. They ordered drinks and did some blow. While they were taking in the scene, Willy's friend Joe, who seemed to be the highest of the group, noticed three guys in suits who were looking their way. "Willy, those fucking guys over there haven't stopped looking at us since we sat down."

"Where?" said Willy.

Joe nodded toward the three men.

While on the run, paranoia was like a low-grade fever that would not go away. Anything could touch it off. Willy looked at the three guys. He was determined not to let the paranoia ruin his night. "They're probably just checking out our women," he said. But he kept an eye on these guys. They were dressed somewhat formal, in suits and ties, when most club patrons wore a mix of casual and Manhattan chic.

Said Joe, "I'm gonna go to the men's room and do some blow."

"I'm good," said Willy. "I'll wait here for the ladies."

Joe went off to the men's room, and the women returned. As far as Willy could tell, the three suspicious guys had gone elsewhere.

When Joe returned, his eyes were wide as two golf balls. He sat down and said, "Willy, you're not gonna believe this. I was in a stall having a toot. I peeked out through the crack of the door and there were those guys. One of them took his coat off and he had a gun in a holster. Those guys have to be law enforcement."

Now Willy's adrenaline was pumping, but he didn't want Joe to know he was concerned. He acted like it was no big deal. For the rest of the night, he kept track of where those guys were in the club. At one point, the guy who Joe said had the gun peeled off and headed to the men's room.

Willy figured it was time to confront the situation. He unbuttoned his ankle holster for easy access. Then he went into the men's room. The guy was in a stall, and there were others coming in and out of the room. Willy splashed water on his face and watched the stall through the mirror. Club music throbbed beyond the doorway and got even louder when people entered and exited. The guy came out of the stall and walked over to the sink.

Said Willy, "Hey, you know, you better be careful carrying that gun around. It's not legal in New York to carry a piece without a license."

The guy said, "Oh, I have a license. I carry a weapon because I own a jewelry store here in the city. We've had robberies."

Willy said, "Jewelry, huh? My wife will want to know about your store. Do you have a business card?"

The guy took out a card and handed it to Willy. "Come by the store sometime. I'll give you a good deal." Then he left the men's room.

The rest of the night, Willy's paranoia lingered like smoke from an overheated oven. The next afternoon, he called the number on the business card. A secretary answered. Willy asked for the guy whose name was on the business card. The guy came on the phone. He was friendly and guaranteed Willy that if he came by with his wife, he'd give him a discount.

Willy never went by the jewelry store. He was reasonably certain that the guy was not law enforcement and that his story was legitimate. But when you were on the lam, you never could tell: you had to worry about everything and everyone.

IN NEW YORK, MANNY, A.K.A. Monguito, was in charge; he liked to show off his operation to Falcon. He took Willy to the Hunts Point Produce Market, where the shipment of 4,800 kilos arrived from Los Angeles every six weeks. At the same time, it was a fully functioning market with incoming and outgoing produce and more than a dozen employees. Willy was impressed. He said, "Monguito, we've come a long way since you were unloading kilos in the Howard Johnson's parking lot off the New Jersey Turnpike."

Manny took Willy to dinner at Victor's Café on Fifty-Second Street, near Times Square. Victor's was a cultural center of the Cuban universe in the New York area.

Manny was unusually diligent about the cocaine business. By now, in his late twenties, he was a major distributor in the area, but hardly anyone knew who he was. He took pride in his work. For a hustler, he had achieved great success, and his hope was to keep building his business.

One day, he was driving in Manhattan. He was there to monitor a transaction that was currently unfolding. That morning, Manny had delivered a 2,400-kilo shipment to Pacho Herrera's people. One of Manny's secretaries, a young Colombian named Monito, had just picked up payment for the load. Monito was driving a blue Buick Century, and in his trunk was $5 million in cash.

Around four thirty in the afternoon, Manny received a call on the car phone, a portable Motorola that he kept stuffed underneath the front seat. The call was from Monito: "Hey, Prof, I'm being followed, man. I'm being followed."

Said Manny, "Are you sure? Where are you?"

"I'm on First Avenue at Sixty-Fifth Street."

"Okay, I'm gonna catch up with you. Drive over to Second Avenue and head south. But drive slow. I'm not far away." Manny stayed on the phone with Monito until he came within a block and saw the blue Buick. "Okay, I see you."

"All right," said Monito. "You see that gray sedan a couple cars behind me? They been following me since I left the Bronx."

They all stopped at a red light. "Yeah," said Manny, "I see it."

Manny was watching the sedan. There were two guys in the front seat. Suddenly, the one in the passenger seat rolled down his window and placed a police cherry-top on the roof of the car. The spinning light was not yet activated, but clearly the sedan's occupants were getting ready to move in and make an arrest.

"Oh, yeah, Monito, you're fucked, brother, you're fucked," said Manny. "Listen, whatever you do, don't go to the stash house."

"Fuck, Prof, what do I do?"

"Don't panic. I'm gonna stay on the line with you. Here's what we're gonna do: You're gonna take a left on Fifty-Seventh Street, go back over to First Avenue, and head north. You're gonna get on the FDR Drive heading north to the George Washington Bridge. Okay? Just do that for now. I'm gonna be behind you the whole way. I'm watching these cocksuckers as they follow you."

As Manny was watching Monito make these maneuvers, he pulled out his flip phone and called Willy. He said, "Doctor, we got a fucking problem."

Willy was in Central Park playing with Will Jr., as he sometimes did in the late afternoon. Manny explained to him what was going on. "I'm leading Monito back to New Jersey. We're gonna have to ditch the vehicle."

"Fuck," said Willy, "that's a load of five mil, right?"

"Yeah, but we have no choice. If he gets pinched, it'll be worse."

"You're right." Willy thought about it and said, "I'm gonna stay on the line. Where are you now?"

Manny interrupted himself to get back on the phone with Monito. They were at the bridge: "Okay, what you're gonna do now is, you're gonna go to Route Four, Paramus mall. Understand? You're gonna drive to the mall and park as close as you can to the mall entrance. Get out of the car and enter the mall. Just leave the Buick behind." Manny was watching the sedan following Monito, staying a few cars behind. The cops—if that's what they were—had no idea that Manny was eyeballing them. "When you get inside the mall, walk around like you're shopping. Make sure nobody is following you, and then exit the mall far away from where you entered. You got that?"

"Yeah, I got it."

"You're doing good. I got you. I'm right behind these fucking cops. I'm following the followers."

In Central Park, Willy watched his child on the swing set. "Manny, you there?"

"Yeah, I'm here. We're gonna ditch the car in the mall parking lot and see what happens. I wanna get my guy out of there so he doesn't get arrested."

"Good," said Willy.

Rush-hour traffic was slowing things down. Time inched along. Monito crossed over the majestic George Washington Bridge, with early-evening sunlight reflecting off the Hudson River, and made it to the parking lot for the Paramus mall. He found a spot near the entrance, parked the car, locked it, and headed into the mall.

"Okay," said Manny, "stay on the phone. And be cool. Act like nothing's happening."

From inside the mall, Monito said to Manny, "Prof, one of these guys is still following me."

Said Manny, "Okay, lead him through the fucking mall. You're gonna exit way on the south side of the mall."

By now, Manny was parked with his eyes on the Buick. "Willy, you there?"

"Yeah, I'm here."

Manny could hear kids playing in the background. "Okay, I'm here in the parking lot. I've got my eye on the sedan. They've pulled up behind the Buick. Oh, shit, wait—" At that moment, two more cars pulled into the lot behind the Buick.

Said Willy, "Just make sure it's real cops and not a rip-off by somebody else, okay? If it's the law they'll have the DEA jackets."

A half dozen people exited the various vehicles and approached the Buick. Three of them were wearing jackets with DEA emblazoned on the back. One of them was on the phone, and another was giving instructions. One of them pulled out what looked like a crowbar. He began to jimmy the trunk of the Buick until it popped open. All the lawmen gathered around.

Manny was on the phone narrating all of this for Willy. "Fuck, they got it, man. They got the money. They got the five million dollars."

"That's a fucking tragedy," said Willy. "But listen, focus on your guy. Make sure he gets out of there. We don't leave nobody behind on the beach. I'm gonna call Pacho Herrera and find out what the fuck happened."

Meanwhile, on the phone, Monito was relieved: "Hey, Prof, I just exited the mall way on the other side. I don't see the guy, maybe I lost him in the store. How do I get the fuck out of here?"

Said Manny, "What's around you there?"

"I see a bus at a station."

"Where's it going?"

"I'll ask the driver." Monito stuck his head in the bus and asked the driver where he was going. The driver said the Port Authority bus station in Manhattan.

"Take it," said Manny. "Take the bus. Get off at Port Authority. Make sure no one is following. Check into a hotel around there and I'll come get you in the morning."

Willy called Pacho Herrera. They hashed it out. Both were concerned that this might all have been part of a larger investigation, though it seemed more likely that the agents had stumbled onto something they knew nothing about. The Buick was licensed under false identification and could not be traced to anyone in the organization. The only loss was the money. Five million dollars, up in smoke. To some, that was a lot of money. To Willy Falcon and Pacho Herrera, it was the price of doing business.[3]

WHILE LIVING IN NEW YORK, Willy was exposed to something he hadn't really thought about before. To much of American society, it was a full-blown crisis, a conundrum bordering on hysteria. In New York, it dominated a media universe that was more multilayered and in-your-face than anywhere else in the United States. The entire phenomenon was encapsulated in one word that dominated newspaper headlines and was uttered by TV reporters and co-anchors with ominous overtones: crack.

By the mid-1980s, crack had emerged as a more affordable version of cocaine hydrochloride. Willy heard about it first in Miami and Houston, and then later in Los Angeles. By the middle of the deacde, crack had seized New York like a virus, with a level of desperation by users and street dealers that seemed even more depraved than the city's heroin phase of the 1960s and early 1970s.

Ever since cocaine became prevalent, there had been attempts to create a cheaper, faster version of the coke high. Cocaine paste had been used primarily by people in the business, but *basuco* was not sold in bulk and therefore rare to the average user. A more popular cocaine derivative was freebasing, a technique

---

[3] As it turned out, this incident *was* part of a larger investigation. In December 1991, the DEA announced the arrest of Ramiro Herrera, the brother of Pacho Herrera, along with ninety-seven other people in the New York City area. The feds seized more than $14.6 million in cash, including, presumably, the $5 million in Monito's trunk. By the time the arrests were announced, the investigation had been underway for nineteen months. Robert C. Bonner, chief of the DEA, called the arrest of Ramiro Herrera "the most significant arrest of a Cali head in the United States in the last two and a half years" (Michael Isikoff, "Drug Raid Nets a U.S. Leader of Cali Cartel," *Washington Post*, December 7, 1991).

for ingesting coke that became trendy in the late 1970s. Freebasing involves smoking cocaine in a pipe with an additive such as ether; the substance was smoked with a powerful lighter or even a blowtorch, a heat source that was highly combustive. The popularity of freebasing diminished greatly after the comedian Richard Pryor accidentally set himself on fire while freebasing and nearly died.

Whoever could come up with a less lethal version of the same turbocharged high as freebasing, but without the potential for self-immolation, was bound to strike it rich.

Nobody knows who invented crack, but among street-level chemists and narco entrepreneurs it became as commonplace as the electric popcorn maker. The process was simple: If you mixed cocaine with a household substance such as baking powder, you could cook it over a stove into a solid substance. That substance was then dried out. It hardened into rock, at which point it could be chipped into smaller pieces, or rocks—little white chunks of concentrated coke that were smoked in a pipe. One hit sent a rush of adrenaline directly to the central nervous system. The effect was at least ten times more powerful than the average hit of straight white powder. For users, the high was orgasmic, but it was also tantalizingly brief. Twenty minutes later you craved another hit off the pipe.

Crack—its existence and popularity—was an odd and unfamiliar phenomenon to Falcon, Magluta, and most anyone associated with Los Muchachos. Willy had never done crack and was pretty sure he didn't know anyone who had, certainly not on a regular basis.

The production, sale, and distribution of crack created a separate business ecosystem from what Willy and Sal had created. In the beginning, Willy and Tony Bemba got involved in cocaine smuggling for political reasons, to aid and abet the anti-Sandinista movement, which they saw as an extension of the effort to take out Castro. Later, when Sal Magluta came into the picture, Falcon and the others realized that the white powder was their ticket to the American dream, a phenomenon that could make them all rich. Cocaine was the ultimate party drug in nightclubs from Miami to the West Coast and beyond, a facilitator of sex and good times. Los Muchachos sold their product—uncut—to a limited number of clients. What their clients did with it was their own business.

As high-level suppliers, Los Muchachos were insulated from the mayhem in the streets. Now that violence was being driven by the wholesale arrival of crack, which could be smoked for as little as five to ten dollars a rock.

Willy was learning about crack; what he knew came almost exclusively from the media. In New York City's many daily newspapers and numerous television news programs, crack as a news item was unlike any crime story since the days of Prohibition in the 1920s. The New York City tabloids—the *Daily News* and the *Post*—routinely ran front-page stories with blaring headlines referring to crack as an "epidemic" and a "plague." The drug was portrayed as being instantly addictive. The newspapers wrote luridly about ghetto mothers who sold their bodies on the street for one hit of the drug, and "crack babies" who were born already under the sway of addiction to a drug they had never used. Though these reports were highly anecdotal and, in the case of crack babies, totally without scientific or biological merit, they shocked the public into believing a full-scale catastrophe had been visited upon the populace.

Newspapers weren't the only outlets caught up in the frenzy. The nightly television news routinely led off programming with reports of the latest crack atrocity. The highest concentration of stories was in New York, which was considered the epicenter of the crisis, but by 1986 the phenomenon had gone national. In the month of July alone, the three major TV networks presented seventy-four evening news segments on drugs, half of these about crack. National newspapers and magazines published roughly one thousand stories calling attention to crack; that year, *Time* and *Newsweek* each devoted five cover stories to the crisis.

The media coverage may have peaked in the fall of 1986, when the CBS newsmagazine show *48 Hours* presented a segment titled "48 Hours on Crack Street." The show was previewed by Dan Rather on the *Evening News*: "Tonight, CBS News takes you to the streets, to the war zone of an unusual two hours of hands-on terror." The program earned the highest Nielsen ratings of any similar news show in the previous five years—fifteen million viewers.[4]

---

[4] As with the story of the cocaine-Contra connection, the crack era has come into clearer focus in retrospect. A small library of books, essays, and academic papers exist on how and why the phenomenon of crack happened in the first place. One of the best of those studies, a book titled *Crack: Rock Cocaine, Street Capitalism, and the Decade of Greed* (Cambridge University Press, 2019), by David Farber, posits the theory that the crack era was a ghetto version of Reagan's "It's Morning in America" campaign slogan. Since the Reagan administration proudly gutted most social programs, with unemployment among young African American males at 40 percent in the mid-1980s, crack became an opportunity for those with few options.

Willy Falcon saw "48 Hours on Crack Street," and while living in New York City in 1987 and into 1988, he couldn't help but be alarmed by the staggering level of media attention. Notable to Falcon was how crack was portrayed as a moral abomination. Most Americans knew nothing about crack other than from the media, where it was portrayed not only as a health, crime, and public safety threat, but also as an activity that was evil and unpatriotic. This reporting drastically changed the tenor of how cocaine was viewed by the public. The white powder was no longer just a party drug used in nightclubs by young professionals and rock stars; it was the basis of a demonic scourge that threatened to emerge from the ghetto and infect the entire nation.

Throughout his time on the lam in Manhattan, Willy spoke frequently with Sal. They talked over the radio transmitter, with Willy in the back of his van and Sal in his radio room at the mansion on La Gorce Island in Miami. Both expressed concern about how all the media attention about crack was bound to bring down an even greater level of heat from law enforcement.

"Did you see that Congress just passed a new bill allotting eleven billion to the War on Drugs?" said Sal. "That's in addition to the forty-seven billion they already spent."

"It's insane," said Willy. "If they spent half that much on the space program, the United States would have a colony on the moon by now."

Increased scrutiny from law enforcement was one thing; equally alarming to Willy and Sal was how the demonization of cocaine was affecting their public image. More than ever, cocaine traffickers were more likely viewed as merchants of death and destruction—and un-American to boot!

The War on Drugs had entered a new phase: it wasn't just cops and agents breaking down doors and seizing product; it was an orchestrated propaganda war, with the media serving as a crucial partner in a concerted effort to turn the public against cocaine.

For the first time, Willy and Sal began to tentatively discuss the idea of get-

---

Writes Farber: "In a de-industrializing America in which market forces rule, service industries abounded, and entrepreneurial risk-taking was celebrated, the crack industry was a lucrative enterprise for the self-made men—the 'Horatio Alger boys' of their place and time—who were willing to do whatever it took to improve their lot in life." As for the resultant violence, this also, Farber surmises, was part of an American process, a Wild West mentality combined with gangster capitalism: "Crack kingpins had to be ready to use violence against competitors, against deadbeat customers, against unsatisfactory employees, against arrested compatriots who threated to turn against them, against unguarded suppliers, against thieves and robbers, against community members who challenged their business, and even—though rarely—against law enforcement personnel who got in their way."

ting out of the business. The crack cocaine phenomenon was spoiling the party. "Maybe it's time to cash out," Willy said to Sal.

"Well, *hermano*," said Sal, "think about that. It's not as easy as it sounds."

In the previous ten years, Willy and Sal had created a business juggernaut that nearly ran on automatic pilot. Hundreds if not thousands of people in Colombia, Venezuela, the United States, and now Mexico were financially dependent on the regular flow of product and cash. The activities of Los Muchachos generated billions of dollars on an annual basis.

The spigot could not simply be shut off without immediate and dire consequences. Their efforts fed many mouths, people whose entire reason for being was a product of the cocaine business. To pull the plug would result in many deaths, not to mention unforeseen consequences and repercussions beyond anyone's imagination.

"Okay," said Willy, "but we need to start thinking about it. Maybe we can do it slowly, over time. I'd rather find a way out of this, on our terms, before it ends badly for everybody."

Sal sighed. "Of course, you are right, my friend. We both know you are right. Let's give this some thought, and we can discuss it later."

"Okay, my brother, enjoy the sunset there in Miami Beach. Keep your eyes open and take care."

"You, too. If you go out tonight to one of those famous clubs in Manhattan, don't have too much fun without me."

Willy chuckled and said, "Okay." He scrambled the frequency and shut off the transmitter and receiver.

FOR THE EXTENDED FAMILY OF Los Muchachos, the crack era had become a major downer. With incessant print and broadcast reports on the violence and degradation, it was hard to avoid the negative implications of the business. It was no longer about speedboats, women in bikinis, disco balls, and Gloria Estefan singing "Come on, shake your body, baby, do the conga." The good times had taken a dark turn. The predominant feeling had become that if you were peddling the white powder, whether you were a crack dealer or not, you had blood on your hands.

For those in the extended circle who enabled the business—family members and friends who partook of the product and openly took pride in the successes of Los Muchachos—it left a bad taste in the mouth. All along, they had labored under the belief that Willy and Sal ran a clean operation, with no gratuitous violence. They did not target the underclass and would never have sold crack. But now, the line between coke and crack was like a line of the product itself: now you see it, now you don't. The tide had turned: in the public eye, coke was increasingly seen as a destructive force. And not only that, if you were a supplier or dealer, the perils of doing business had risen exponentially. Even casual observers of the trade could see that cocaine merchants did not normally make it to retirement: they either wound up dead or in prison for an extended sentence, or they became snitches.

To the family members of Los Muchachos, it was a cautionary tale. As the War on Drugs elevated to new levels, they were the ones faced with losing a husband, son, father, or brother-in-law to imprisonment or something worse.

For some within the circle, there had been reservations all along. Though Los Muchachos certainly had a broad base of support among their generation of Cuban exiles, some detested how the narcos among them accumulated their status and wealth. It was especially difficult for the parents, who had left or been forced out of Cuba with hardly a nickel to their name. Some had arrived in the United States via Spain or some other circuitous route, laden with young children or other family members, with few connections other than equally destitute recent exiles. It was called *la lucha*—the struggle—for a reason. Life in exile was not meant to be easy. For most Cuban Americans, it was a burden they bore because they had no choice; this was the hand they had been dealt by fate. And sometimes, fate was a *puta*.

Even so, the average exile was not immune to the pleasures or righteousness of success. Most had arrived in South Florida with nothing, and a phenomenal number of Cuban exiles had advanced in America. In a decade or two, they achieved unparalleled levels of accomplishment in business, sports, and the arts. In Miami, they had created their own empire, where you didn't even need to speak English to succeed. You could speak Cuban Spanish and do business only with other Cubans it you wanted to. Unlike most other ethnic groups, which assimilated into American culture, Miami Cubans were able to create their own version of Cuba in the United States. They didn't need to assimilate, or if they did, it would be on their own terms, not that of the larger culture.

For that first generation who fled Castro's gulag, this was all a point of great pride. Success was meant to be hard-earned. There were no shortcuts. Okay, so cocaine had presented an opportunity for their children's generation that they did not have. It provided a pathway to success. But at what cost? The money came too fast and too easy. It was, in some sense, a trap. In the United States, free from the horrors of communism, you could acquire riches, but you could also lose your soul and possibly your freedom.

Oddly, this was a point of contention that found its symbolic core with that most American of status symbols: the automobile.

As members of Los Muchachos accumulated their wealth, many of them derived special gratification by purchasing gifts for their family and friends. In the late 1970s, when Falcon first started taking in millions, he bought a new car for his father-in-law. Willy was reasonably certain that José Rossique knew how he made his living. When Alina's father refused the car, citing the fact that it was purchased with *dinero sucio* (dirty money), it caused a strain between the two men that lasted for years.

Benny Lorenzo had a similar experience:

> When I started making money, I bought my dad a new car. A Dodge, a real American car. I parked it in front of the house where my father still lives. I left it there with no explanation. When he came home from work, he called me and said, "Hey, what's this all about?" I said, "Dad, I bought you a new car." He was quiet for a second, then said, "Come over here and pick it up, get it out of here. Man, I don't need this shit. I don't need a new car." He already had a Dodge Polara, which was old with many miles on it. In a way, his refusal hurt my feelings. But he was old-school, that's the way he was. So I fixed him up with some new watches. Those he took.

AS A MEMBER OF LOS Muchachos' inner circle, El Cuño, Tony Garrudo, had been taking in millions since at least the early 1980s. He lavished money on his family—his sister, his brother (he bought them both houses), his parents, and his friends. "The whole reason I went into the business," he said, "was to make a comfortable life for my parents, especially my father, who had sacrificed so much for me." Unlike Willy and Benny B., Garrudo's father did not turn down the gifts, even the car Tony purchased for his dad on his birthday. Tony's father understood that his son's generosity was a consequence of a bond between them. Tony was trying to make up for lost time, and to make it all better. At times, the father seemed uneasy with his son's lavish gifts, but he never said anything, because he understood that Tony needed to take care of his parents for his own reasons.

In mid-1987, Tony and his wife, Ileana, became the proud parents of their first son. It was around this same time that Willy and Sal were forced to go on the run. In the media, every day there were reports on crack and the cocaine wars. It was a disturbing juxtaposition: Willy and Sal under indictment and in hiding, and the demonization of cocaine in the media, with reports and images of carnage that made it seem as though anyone at any level of the business was a monster. For some Miami Cubans, the shame and guilt were real, and it appeared as though everything was building toward a climax.

One afternoon, Alfonso Garrudo asked if he could speak with his son and daughter-in-law. They all sat down at Tony's house. The elder Garrudo said to Ileana, "You have made me very proud. You've given me a healthy, beautiful grandson; it's more than I ever could have asked for." To his son he said, "We went through some difficult times in Cuba and in Spain. We both know, it was not easy. And now, the way you take care of your parents and your family makes me feel like I raised you the right way. I am proud of you also."

Said Tony, "Thanks, *Pipo*. I think you know how much we both love you—" He looked at his father. "What is it?"

"It's time for you to quit what you are doing," said the father, "because you already have enough. *Muchisimo*—that's what life has given you. But everything has an end—"

"We know," interjected Ileana.

The father raised his hand: "Listen to me. Hang up your gloves, son, while you are a champion and not later."

Said Tony, "Yes, of course, I agree with you. But you need to understand, a person can't just walk away. It takes time."

"Why? Why can't you end it now? If you don't, it will catch up with you, and you will be made to pay a big price."

"Look," said Tony, "I have many people who depend on me. I agree with you that we have more than enough. I agree that we need to start thinking about getting out. I promise you, within a year I will be out of the business. I will transfer everything to my hydraulic company and everything we do will be 100 percent legitimate."

The father was not satisfied. "Listen, once they capture Willy and Sal, they will come for you. Maybe sooner. And the only thing I want in my life, let me tell you, is that when it's time for you to pay, you stand up like a man. You understand?" Tears came to his eyes.

"Of course," said Tony.

"I don't want to be ashamed in the street and have somebody tell me, 'Your son is a fucking rat, and he didn't know how to be a man.' You understand? This would kill me."

"I'm shocked you would even say that. You didn't raise me to be that kind of animal."

The elder Garrudo sniffled and wiped his nose with a hanky. "Because it will come, believe me, son. The time to pay will come."

For days and even weeks afterward, El Cuño was shaken by this conversation with his father. As with many within the orbit of the gang, it was dawning on him for the first time that the good times came with an expiration date, and that date was possibly fast approaching.

13

SAL AS ZORRO

IN EARLY DECEMBER 1987, WILLY AND Sal received an urgent communication from their narco partners in Mexico. Their presence, without delay, was requested by the leaders of the Guadalajara Cartel. They were not informed of the details, but in the narcosphere, when a partner requests an immediate meeting, you know it's something serious.

Given that Willy and Sal were currently living in separate states, the rendezvous required some coordination. This was the first time since the two had gone on the lam that they would be traveling out of and back into the country. They had their false passports and backup identifications, but they needed to give some thought to what might be the most secure means for traveling to Mexico City.

They agreed to meet in El Paso, where they would cross the border on foot into Ciudad Juárez. From there, they would take a taxi to the airport and book a flight to Mexico City. "Travel light," Willy told Sal. "One small bag. That's it."

They both arrived on commercial flights and booked separate rooms at a Holiday Inn in downtown El Paso. Willy and Sal had not seen each other since their group meeting in Orlando, when they first informed the rest of Los Muchachos that they were going on the run. In the lobby of the Holiday Inn, they embraced like long-lost brothers.

Sal had a deep suntan from the days at his compound hideaway at La Gorce Island in Miami Beach. Willy was paler than usual from living most of the time in New York City.

"You look like life on the lam has been treating you well," said Willy.

Replied Sal, "You look like you put on a little weight."

The next morning, they crossed the Bridge of the Americas into Juárez, made their way to the airport, and traveled on a commercial flight to Mexico City.

In the Mexican capital, they checked into their usual suite at the Camino Real Hotel. Willy picked up the phone, called the desk, and asked to be connected to the room of "Oscar Martínez." Mario Valencia answered the phone. "We're here," said Willy.

"Okay, come to my room," said Mario.

At the room of Mario Valencia, the Cubans and the Colombian were met by Félix Gallardo. As always, Félix was dressed elegantly in a tailored suit with an open-collared dress shirt.

It was different from their previous meetings: for one thing, Rafael Caro Quintero and Ernesto Fonseca Carrillo were both currently incarcerated, as part of the joint US-Mexico investigation into the murder of DEA Agent Kiki Camarena. Since, in the absence of his primary partners, Gallardo had assumed sole control of the cartel, he had been dealing with one crisis after another. This latest crisis directly affected his business with Willy, Sal, and Mario Valencia.

Félix explained: "Through our intelligence contacts in the Federal Judicial Police, we have learned that the DEA has become aware of our shipments from Colombia into Jalisco. They are lying in wait to seize our next load. We have to change our method of transportation."

Said Mario, "Are you certain the DEA has this information?"

"Absolutely," answered Gallardo. "Our source of information is impeccable." He continued, "What I would suggest is that we transport the shipments by sea. Bring the product up the Pacific coast on fishing boats; there they can be offloaded at sea and brought ashore in Baja California. Do you have the means to do this?"

"Well," said Willy, "at the moment, I can't answer that question. I will have to talk to other people I know that are in the marijuana business that transport their pot in fishing boats. And I'll need to talk with others in my organization that would assist us in transporting the cocaine from Colombia. We will get back to you as soon as I find solutions to these problems."

Félix nodded. "Gentlemen, I regret the inconvenience, but due to these current circumstances, I'm sure you understand. I simply can't guarantee protection for your pilots and cocaine loads as before."

They all nodded. "We'll figure something out," said Falcon.

Gallardo left the room. Said Mario Valencia to Willy and Sal, "I'm going to order some food for the room. We will stay here until we can devise a new strategy."

On the face of it, it had the makings of a catastrophe. Los Muchachos had been smuggling massive loads of kilos by air into Jalisco, and then across the border into Southern California. And now that was all out the window. It was time for the Boys to roll up their sleeves and once again engage in Narco Problem Solving 101.

WHEN PEGY ROSELLO WAS A young boy, he was visited by an alien spaceship. As he put it many years later:

> We were driving back from Clewiston on Route 27. I was, like, seven years old. Me, my sister, China (Amelia Rosello Falcon's nickname), my mom, and my dad. We were coming down 27, back to Miami. It wasn't nighttime, it was dusk. My dad's driving. This thing came down, a shiny light that slows down to a stop, stays right there for fifteen seconds, and then it takes off. . . . People don't believe this until it happens to them. I don't like to talk about it, because people think you're crazy.

Over the years, as a teenager and then a young adult, Pegy mostly kept this spaceship sighting to himself. He had come to believe what few others did, that aliens live among us, and we are not alone.

Who knows how this affected his life choices, but those who knew Pegy say he was often in a state of being startled. He laughed awkwardly at times and seemed not to comprehend things that were obvious. Benny B., who worked with Pegy in the cocaine business, said, "I always thought the kid was a little retarded; he was goofy."

Some believed that Pegy's stature in the gang came from his close relationship with Tavy Falcon. Seeing as Pegy was the baby brother of Tavy's wife, he was undeniably in a privileged position. More likely, his acceptance in the group came from his relationship with Justo Jay.

Pegy often told stories of how Jay looked out for him. After Pegy had become part of the gang and was making hundreds of thousands of dollars a year, he dropped out of Miami High School in the middle of his senior year. For his birthday, he purchased a brand-new Corvette. When Jay heard that Pegy dropped out, he came to Pegy's house with a screwdriver and removed the license plates on the front and back of his Corvette. Pegy was stunned. "Why would you do that?" he asked Jay.

"You gotta go back to school," said Jay. "Soon as you graduate, I'll give back the plates and you can drive."

At first, Pegy thought it was a joke. But Jay was serious. After trying to think of ways he might get his plates back from Jay, he called Willy Falcon: "Willy, how am I supposed to do business for the organization when I have no car. This is crazy!"

Within an hour, Jay returned the plates to Pegy, who never did graduate from high school.

Since Willy and Sal had first fled Los Angeles the previous year, Pegy had risen from being Tavy and Jay's sidekick to a primary representative of Los Muchachos in Southern California. In Los Angeles, he did business under the name Luis Mendez, with the prerequisite false IDs supplied by the organization. He oversaw the books, the stash houses, and the transfer of cash for various and sundry business expenses. Before long, he got himself into trouble with the law when he began dealing kilos on the side. He did so with Victor Alvarez and Gus Posada, who were both veterans of the organization. While living at the Muchachos' safe house in Santa Monica, they were all charged with possessing and selling cocaine.

For the next year, with Willy Falcon living in New York City, Pegy bounced back and forth between Miami and Los Angeles, where his presence was required at a series of pretrial hearings. The case against "Luis Mendez" was weak, and eventually the charges were dismissed by a judge. (Victor Alvarez, on the other hand, was found guilty on misdemeanor possession charges and spent a year in jail.)

On the day Pegy returned to Miami for good, members of Los Muchachos— including Willy, Sal, and Tavy—were present at a party they threw in his honor. Pegy had faced criminal charges like a man, and he had not snitched. His new stature as a "stand-up guy" was, in the eyes of the group, something to celebrate.

Pegy's reputation in Miami ascended. With Willy and Sal in hiding, and Justo Jay and Tony Bemba facing criminal charges, to some, Pegy became the new face of the organization. Twelve years younger than Willy and Sal, he could strut into a club with the full weight of the organization at his disposal.

Public attitudes about cocaine may have changed in the larger culture, but in the pulsating, high-adrenaline universe of Miami nightlife, a well-connected mover of flake was more esteemed than a professional athlete.

Since the Mutiny closed, the center of the city's social scene had shifted from Coconut Grove to "the Beach"—Miami Beach—and its glamourous, neon-tinged collection of clubs, restaurants, and sexy cocktail lounges. Still in his early twenties, Pegy was a prime age to ride this wave. He had full, free-flowing hair, a perennial tan, and a body honed by daily workouts at the gym and enhanced by steroid supplements. At Club Nu, which opened in 1987 and immediately became the hottest nightclub in South Beach, Pegy was a star. He had a preferred "bottle girl" named Terry, who kept the champagne flowing, and a bodyguard named Mancha. When he rose to go to the bathroom or leave the club, Mancha cleared a pathway, like the parting of the Red Sea, and outside the entrance on Twenty-Second Street, a valet had his latest high-performance vehicle waiting at the curb.

Usually, Pegy had two or three women from the club trailing along with him. They piled in the car, or hurried to their own cars, and met him in Brickell. Since Sal was on the lam at La Gorce Island, Pegy was allowed to use his penthouse at the Arquitectonica-designed high-rise on Brickell Key Drive as his own private crash pad. Pegy called the place "the Scarface building" because that's where several scenes from the movie had been filmed. With gorgeous views of the city skyline and the surrounding bay, he and the girls screwed all night and into the morning hours.

It was good to be a Muchacho.

In early 1988, at his trial in North Carolina, Justo Jay was found guilty on cocaine-trafficking and conspiracy charges. Under new federal sentencing guidelines—a product of the War on Drugs—Jay was hit with a life sentence. Everyone in the gang's orbit was saddened, including Pegy, though it benefitted his standing in the group. Pegy took Jay's spot in the organization behind Willy, Sal, Tavy, Tony G., Miguel Vega, and Benny B.

To most everyone who knew Pegy Rosello, he was a likable kid. But there was a flaw that some did not see or chose to ignore. Pegy was a child of the cocaine business; it was all he knew from his days as a preteen, when he used to wash cars for Willy and Sal and dream of being a narco just like them. It was the money, clothes, women, and accoutrements of success that activated his adolescent libido and gave him a white powder hard-on. The money was not only a representation of the lifestyle he desired, but also a reflection of the value system he wholeheartedly embraced.

Willy used to refer to it as "green eyes." He would say to his partners, "The women love us because we got green eyes. Money. They look into your eyes, and they see money."

But green eyes had another meaning also. Having green eyes meant that you had an instinct for the financial bottom line. When Willy said that he had green eyes, he meant that he could see the value of a deal in ways that others could not. He had a nose for making money.

Pegy had green eyes, which, in his case, meant that money was all he could see, and all that he valued.

Having green eyes could make you rich, but it could also blind you. If money was all that you valued, what else was there?

IT DIDN'T TAKE LONG FOR Willy, Sal, and Mario Valencia to come up with a new strategy for smuggling kilos through Mexico. In fact, as soon as they left their meeting with Félix Gallardo at the Camino Real Hotel in Mexico City, they flew to Colombia for further discussions about how they could make things work. As can sometimes be the case when faced with adversity, out of the ashes of their aborted route via the landing strip in Jalisco they came up with a new plan, something so grandiose and seemingly airtight that it had the potential to increase the volume of kilos into the United States to unprecedented levels.

It was Pacho Herrera, in Cali at the time, who came up with the first piece of the puzzle. At a meeting among the narcos, he told Willy and Sal, "I have a new method of transportation for you. I have a friend who owns a DC-7 airplane. The plane can fly a very long distance without needing to refuel. It can also airlift several tons of cocaine to the Pacific Ocean and drop the duffel bags stuffed with kilos to the Mexican fishing vessels at a designated area."

Asked Willy, "How many kilos can this plane carry?"

"Well," said Pacho, "my friend uses this plane to airlift as much as twenty thousand tons of marijuana. The plane has a cargo door that makes it easier to airdrop the bales of marijuana, or, in this case, duffel bags of cocaine. The sky's the limit."[1]

Willy and Sal began to spitball a plan. Said Willy, "We can first send a pilot to Mexico to meet with the fishing captain so they can map out latitude and longitude coordinates for an airdrop at sea."

"Right," said Sal, "then we have the DC-7 fly to that location and drop the load, where the fishing vessels will be there to pick it up and bring it ashore."

"The main thing," added Willy, "is that the kilos inside the duffel bags are tightly wrapped in rubber coating so there can be no water damage."

"It's risky," said Sal, "but once we get the shipment on land, we can use our usual importation methods with Pepe, El Frijol, to bring it across the border into California."

They were convinced that it could work. At Mario Valencia's house in Cali, over a shortwave radio, they contacted Félix Gallardo in Mexico and told him the plan. The very next day, they would send their designated pilot of the DC-7 via a commercial flight to Mexico, where Félix would arrange a meeting with his personnel. Said Gallardo to Falcon, "Doctor, I think we can do this."

Feeling good about themselves, Willy and Sal booked a flight together back to the United States, landing at Dallas International Airport, where, using their false passports, they entered the country and caught a commuter flight to West Palm Beach airport in Florida. From there, Willy went to his palatial house in Fort Lauderdale, and Sal continued on to his mansion at La Gorce Island in Miami Beach.

It was late December, and the holiday season had arrived. It was usually a time of vigorous partying and celebrating for Los Muchachos, who, for ten years now, had been using Christmas and New Year's—not to mention both Willy's and Sal's wives' birthdays—to bring everyone together. This year, it seemed, things would be different. Willy and Sal were wanted by the law, and nobody was supposed to know where they were.

---

[1] Pacho Herrera's days were numbered. In September 1990, a team of gunmen dressed in police and military uniforms (believed to have been hired by Escobar) opened fire on a crowd at a soccer stadium where Herrera was seated. Eighteen people were killed, but not Pacho; he escaped unharmed. Eight years later, after he had turned himself in to Colombian authorities in exchange for a relatively light sentence on trafficking charges, he was gunned down in the prison yard by a hit man who had entered the facility posing as an attorney. ("Final de un capo que empezó como mandadero" ["End of a capo who began as an errand boy"], *El Tiempo*, November 6, 1998.)

Willy decided that he would still have the annual birthday party for Alina, but it would be a more sedate affair. They did not have it at his parents' house, as they normally did, but at a restaurant, where they rented the entire place for their private party.

As for the annual New Year's Eve trip to Las Vegas, Willy and Sal talked about it and decided that it was important that, for the morale of the organization, they did not hold back. They would still have their gathering at Caesars Palace and then, after that, their two weeks in Vail for snowboarding, skiing, and general good times with the family in the fresh mountain air.

Two weeks earlier, Willy and Sal had found a buyer for their Learjet. At $3.3 million, the bid was less than half what they paid for it. But it was $3.3 million they wouldn't have if the jet was seized by the feds. The deal had not yet been finalized but would be soon. This trip to Vegas would likely be the last time Los Muchachos got to use the jet and travel in a style to which they were accustomed, making that year's celebration extra special.

While Willy prepared for the festivities—with the usual rounds of shopping for Christmas gifts for the children, jewelry for Alina, and new Brioni suits and a tuxedo fitting for himself—at the same time he monitored the upcoming shipment of product. Everything was in place to ship the kilos via the DC-7 airplane up the Pacific coast of Mexico to the Baja Peninsula. There, at a designated location far out at sea, the shipment would be dropped. Fishing vessels from Mexico would retrieve the bundles and bring them ashore.

Since this was a new route never used before, they decided the first shipment would be a test run. They would send six thousand kilos. If everything went as planned, they would increase the loads tenfold.

The day after Christmas, Willy was on edge. For the last forty-eight hours, he had been glued to the transmitter. An underling of Los Muchachos had driven the Chevy Astro cargo van from New York to Fort Lauderdale. Willy kept it parked in the carport outside the house. As his wife and children opened gifts alongside their Christmas tree (the girls received rollerblades), Willy routinely ducked outside, until his daughter Jessica asked, "Daddy, what's in the van?"

"Never mind that," said Willy, adding, "Hey, do you like your rollerblades?"

"I love them," said Jessica.

On the transmitter in the van, Willy was able to tune in the frequencies of the pilot of the DC-7 and also the Mexican fishing vessels. He was able to monitor every stage of the transaction. To airdrop the kilos, the pilot had to make numerous passes over the drop zone, dropping fifteen duffel bags at a time. It took hours. Eventually, after the entire load had been dropped, Willy heard from Mario Valencia: "It's going to take the fishing vessels some time to retrieve the loads. Go to bed. I will contact you tomorrow."

The next morning, Willy gathered his children together and headed to the new roller-skating rink in Fort Lauderdale. Rollerblading was the latest craze, with youngsters and adults of all ages crowding the floorboards. The scene was part disco, part children's playground. Falcon took pleasure in the squeals of joy from his kids as they learned to skate for the first time in their young lives.

Afterward, back at home, Willy ducked into the cargo van and called Mario. "What's the latest?" he asked.

"Well," said Mario. "It didn't go so well." He told Willy that the fishing vessels were able to retrieve only four thousand of the six thousand kilos. Apparently, the duffel bags—which had been fastened together with bungee cords—separated on impact and dispersed in different directions. They were scattered all over the ocean. "Some of the boats are still out there searching," said Mario, "but it's unlikely they will find anything more. What do you want to do?"

Willy sighed. "Listen, it's the holidays, and we are going to shut down business for the next few weeks anyway. We'll let this sit for a bit, think about it, and come up with something new. I'll contact you soon as I return from out west."

The airdrop system was not viable, but Willy had another idea. While in Colombia, he had spoken with his old mentor Manuel Garces, who was living in Medellín fighting extradition to the United States, where he was wanted on money-laundering charges. Willy and Sal had been exploring all options, and Garces had suggested that he knew an ex-navy captain with contacts in Chile. Maybe they could send the kilos by freighter from Chile up the coast and not have to airdrop the product. At the time, Willy and Sal opted for the airdrop method because the various pieces for that plan were already in place. Willy reminded himself to check back in with Manuel Garces after the holidays.

That year's trip to Vegas for New Year's was tinged with a new kind of mania. Since Willy and Sal were on the lam, and they were using the Learjet for the last time, and their entire operation was on hold until they straightened out their delivery method through Mexico, everyone seemed on edge. They partied a little harder than usual—more drinking, more yeyo, and nonstop gambling. Said Willy:

> Our first night in Vegas, the wives were tired from jet lag, so the boys—me, Sal, Tavy, and Benny Lorenzo—we gambled until five in the morning. We were sitting at the baccarat table. I had one of my worst nights gambling ever. I lost half a million dollars. I would bet my money on the bank side, and the player would win. And if I would bet on the player side, the bank would win. Baccarat is the only game in the casino with a fifty-fifty chance of winning. It is sort of like flipping a coin for heads or tails. When I would bet heads that night, tails would win, and vice versa.

Sitting next to Willy at the baccarat table was Pepe, El Frijol, their Mexican contact from Los Angeles. Given that Willy was on the lam, he had been worried about the transfer of large amounts of money, so he had entrusted Pepe and a member of Los Muchachos, Jorge "Fat George" Lopez, to drive from Los Angeles with two briefcases filled with $1.5 million in cash. When they arrived in Vegas, Pepe and Lopez deposited the money in the casino account of Willy and Sal (the account was under the name "Wilfredo Vargas").

At the baccarat table, Willy's luck was so bad that he started letting Pepe place the bet. Still, they lost every time. Finally, Pepe said to Willy, "Doctor, our luck is so bad that if we decided to buy a circus, even the midgets would grow. That's how bad our luck has been."

Willy laughed. Pepe added, "Let's concentrate on what we do the best, and that is smuggling cocaine."

When Willy and the boys turned in for bed, the dawn light was on the horizon.

Though the holidays were meant to be a break from business, the fraught nature of their legal situation guaranteed complications. On New Year's Day, still hungover from the big New Year's Eve party, Willy received a call from his attorney, Mark Dachs. The lawyer had some disturbing news to report. From a source within the office of the US attorney for the Southern District of Florida, Dachs learned that not only were Willy and Sal under investigation, but that there was a sealed indictment in their name.

A sealed indictment was an indictment that had been filed but was being kept under wraps as grand jury hearings remained ongoing. The feds were still gathering evidence, but the indictment was a fait accompli. Eventually, the indictment would be unsealed; it was only a matter of time.

Dachs reiterated what he had been saying for many months: Willy and Sal needed to liquidate their accounts in the United States, and they needed to sell off their properties. Already, earlier that year, the feds had seized the CMM Ranch, their man cave in Horse Country. Though the property had been purchased under the name of Sal's sister-in-law, when she was subpoenaed to appear before a grand jury, on advice from her attorney, rather than answer questions she claimed her Fifth Amendment privilege thirty-seven times. The property was seized by the US government.

Under new federal laws, the government was allowed to sell the property, which it did at public auction. Unbeknownst to them, the person who bid highest and was awarded the property was a surrogate for Los Muchachos. The gang had literally purchased the property back from the government without its knowing about it.

It may have been a clever ploy, but paying twice over for the property did little to stem the group's mounting financial complications.

The problem for Willy and Sal was that if they closed out all their US accounts and moved the money to Panama, they would have no cash. The bulk of their money—over $400 million—was already tied up in Panamanian accounts. To draw from or close those accounts required a signature from Guillermo Endara of the Endara Firm. Liquidating the accounts involved financial disclosure, and Endara, who was gearing up for a presidential run, might be loath to associate himself with anything related to Falcon-Magluta. They would have to wait to see how that played out.

As the holidays wound down, Willy, Sal, Tavy, and their wives flew on the Lear 55 back to Miami. They raised a toast to what was to be their last trip in Learjet splendor.

IN EARLY 1988, AFTER COMPLETING the terms of their one-year lease, Willy and Alina gave up their apartment in Manhattan and moved full time to the house on Seminole Drive in Fort Lauderdale. As far as Willy could tell, life on the lam was manageable. It required diligence; you had to always be on the lookout for law enforcement tails or everyday situations in which someone might recognize you. Mostly, you stayed inside, which was not a major problem for Willy and Sal, as they were both living on large properties with swimming pools, home gyms, big yards, and the beach a short drive away. Somehow, they were still able to live the good life even though they were wanted by the law.

After speaking over the transmitter with Manual Garces in Colombia, Willy was excited that they might have an alternative plan for smuggling kilos. But they would need to travel to Medellín to meet the ex-navy captain who Garces believed could help them out. While on the lam, Willy and Sal wanted to keep overseas travel to a minimum. They were leery of passing through US Customs, even with false identifications. Their actual names and faces were likely prominent as wanted fugitives in law enforcement databases from Florida to California. Even so, the flow of kilos, which was the lifeblood of the narco-sphere, took precedence.

Leaving from Fort Lauderdale airport, the Boys flew to El Paso, where they once again crossed the border into Juárez and then booked a flight to Medellín.

It had been years since they'd seen Manuel Garces, who had served as an essential conduit for Willy and Sal when they first entered the business. It was Garces who introduced them to both Pablo Escobar and the Valencia brothers. Manuel was their Godfather. The meeting was bittersweet, since Garces was facing extradition and criminal charges that would eventually land him in prison. Still, to Garces, Willy and Sal were his cocaine godsons, and he was touched to see them after many years.

They met at Garces's home. Mario Valencia traveled from Cali and was also in attendance.

Said Manuel, "Gentlemen, I want you to meet my good friend, navy captain Carlos Zuluaga."

The men all greeted one another and got down to business.

Captain Zuluaga was a Colombian in his forties who maintained his physical bearing from his time with the Colombian navy. During his military years, Zuluaga was also a smuggler of contraband. Eventually, he was arrested and sentenced to three years in prison. While incarcerated in Colombia, he met a Chilean fishing captain who was doing prison time for smuggling cocaine. The fishing captain worked for a Chilean businessman who owned a shipping company in Chile. The fishing captain told Zuluaga, "Cocaine. That's the future. Way more profitable than marijuana. Once we get out of here, we should do business together."

Postincarceration, Zuluaga stayed in touch with the fishing captain and eventually met his business partner. That's how it worked in the underworld—contacts from prison became business contacts on the outside, a self-sustaining criminal universe of the damned.

Zuluaga's meeting with Willy and Sal was fortunate, even monumental in a way, because what Zuluaga was suggesting was the largest cocaine-smuggling scheme in the history of the United States.

They still needed to confirm details with the Chilean, but this was the plan: Specially designated kilos of cocaine would be manufactured at labs in the Valley of Cauca. They would be transferred to the nearby port city of Buenaventura. There, the narcos would establish a fishing company with a fleet of boats that would send the kilos out to sea.

Meanwhile, in Valparaíso, Chile, using money supplied by Los Muchachos and the Cali Cartel—a fifty-fifty split of expenses—the Chilean businessmen would create an import-export company, with at least two large freighters. This company would be staffed with management and a crew of twenty-eight people responsible for loading shipments and operating the vessels. The company would be partly legitimate, exporting from Chile bananas, vegetables, and other produce for which the country was famous.

Every member of the management and crew would be carefully chosen; many were ex-inmates whom the Chilean captain had recruited while in prison. They were all "in on it," professional smugglers who, by becoming employees of the company, were enlisting in a massive cocaine operation.

At the port in Valparaíso, a freighter would be loaded with dozens of large cargo containers. Some of these containers would be loaded with produce, others with tons of zinc in the form of sand-like particles that filled the container. The freighters would head up the Pacific coast to Colombia, where they would be met far out at sea by the Colombian fishing vessels. The kilos of cocaine would be transferred from the boats to the freighter, where they would be buried inside the containers filled with zinc.

The freighters would then continue north all the way to the Baja Peninsula, on the Mexican coast. There, miles offshore, they would be met by a fleet of Mexican fishing boats with crews that would offload the shipment and bring it ashore in the city of La Paz. From there, it would be transported via semitruck to Tijuana, then brought across the border into the United States.

No airdrop, no kilos scattered on the high seas.

Given the size of the Chilean tankers, the loads could be massive. As a test run, Mario Valencia suggested twelve thousand kilos of the best that Cali could provide. As for future loads, as Mario liked to say, the sky was the limit.

Willy pulled Sal aside. Under his breath he said, "This could be it."

"What?" said Sal.

"This could be our way out. After a number of these loads, given the size and money, we can retire."

There were still details to discuss and introductions to be made. Willy and Sal wanted to meet the Chilean businessman and organizers of the Colombian fishing fleet; Carlos Zuluaga was asking for an initial commitment of $5 million to buy two freighters. Willy and Sal suggested that everyone connect later in the week to finalize the deal.

The Boys parted ways with Manuel Garces, thankful that the legendary *contrabandista* had once again opened the door for them all to make millions. Days later, they flew back home: Willy into the arms of his wife and children in Fort Lauderdale, and Sal back to his private compound at La Gorce Island in Miami Beach.

ON THE SHORTWAVE RADIO, WILLY received a call from Pablo Escobar. Pablo was mad as a hornet—this time for good reason.

In January 1988, while Willy and Sal were still in Colorado, a thunderous explosion occurred outside Escobar's apartment building in Medellín (coincidentally, the building was only a few blocks away from the home of Manuel Garces). Someone had planted a car bomb containing 150 pounds of dynamite. The explosion killed two security guards, injured ten people in neighboring buildings, and left a twenty-five-foot crater on the grounds in front of the building. Escobar was not present at the time of the explosion, but his wife and children were. His daughter, Manuela, was left deaf in one ear from the attack.

Various leftist political groups had called authorities to claim credit for the bombing, but Pablo thought he knew who was behind it: the Cali Cartel.

"Those fucking motherfuckers!" Pablo shouted through the radio transmitter. "I will make them pay." For the next ten minutes, the Paisa (Medellín native) narco baron ranted about his enemies from Cali. Willy had never heard Pablo like this. This was the Pablo whom Gustavo Gaviria had told him about, a man who could not be reasoned with. Eventually, Willy was able to butt in and say, "Pablo, my brother, how can we help you? Is there anything we can do?"

Escobar stopped hyperventilating and calmed down for a minute. He explained how being under siege from the Colombian government and now the Cali Cartel was exhausting his resources and affecting his business. He felt like he needed new smuggling routes. He told Willy flat out, "I asked you before about your Mexican contacts; can you help make those connections for me?"

It was a touchy subject. Willy and Sal were just getting ready to launch their new route via the Chilean freighters. This operation was jointly financed by Mario Valencia and the Cali Cartel. It was not realistic that the Cubans could cut Escobar in on this operation.

"Pablo," said Willy, "let me further explore the possibility of something. Okay? I promise you I'll get back to you. How is everything else, okay?"

Escobar explained that after two years on the run from Colombian authorities, he was now in negotiations with the administration of President Virgilio Barco Vargas to surrender to the government. Talks among various representatives were top secret and ongoing. Escobar was skeptical that he could get the terms that he wanted. In the meantime, he did not stop his campaign of violence against Colombian society. The bombings and assassinations of journalists, judges, police officers, and community activists continued unabated.

OWEN BAND WAS A MIDLEVEL cocaine dealer in Miami with a taste for the nightlife. He got his start as a narco while working as a bartender at Alexandre, the popular nightclub located at street level of the Omni Hotel, where cocaine might as well have been listed on the food menu. After his shift ended at Alexandre's, he often made his way to the Mutiny, where all the major players gathered.

At the Mutiny, Owen befriended Bernardo de Torres, at least twenty-five years his senior. As a veteran of the 2506 Brigade who had become, like many of his contemporaries, a CIA asset, Bernardo was a man of mystery and an operative of considerable local notoriety. In his early sixties, he was a big man with a bad comb-over, and he spoke Spanglish with a comical accent. But no one made fun of Bernie to his face.

Of the many rumors about Bernardo de Torres, his role as a former member of JFK's security entourage put him at the center of many theories about the president's assassination. Some suggested he had been one of the gunmen on the Grassy Knoll. Which was odd, given that Bernardo had worked as an investigator for Louisiana state attorney Jim Garrison on his infamous case claiming that the assassination was the product of a Deep State conspiracy. De Torres did not seek to demythologize his past; on the contrary, he preferred to let the rumors swirl at the Mutiny, or at Versailles restaurant in Little Havana, or in Domino Park on Calle Ocho, or anywhere else where the lore of the brigade was a favorite topic of conversation.

The reason for Owen Band's close relationship with Bernardo was simple: he was the older man's coke supplier.

Circulating in the clubs and the cocaine universe of that era, Band knew Willy and Sal. His relationship with someone as esteemed as Bernardo de Torres meant that he was treated with respect by everyone, including the Boys. Though Band was Jewish and originally from Newark, New Jersey, he mixed well with the Cuban exiles in Miami. He had the perennial suntan and disco attire, the wide-collar shirt open to midchest, the fancy Rolex, the tiny coke spoon on a chain around his neck, all of which was a kind of uniform for Miami in the 1980s. Owen had gone to Boston University and later applied to Harvard Law School. It was clear to many of the Cubans that he was smarter than the average coke dealer. Band would later claim that both Willy and Sal tried to recruit him for their organization, but Owen felt it was best to operate as a freelancer. Sometimes he purchased his cocaine from Los Muchachos, sometimes from other suppliers in South Florida. He established his own clientele in Atlantic City, where he sold the bulk of his product.

In 1986, he went to Los Angeles to explore the possibility of moving there and establishing a client base. As a Miamian and veteran of the Mutiny, he connected with members of Los Muchachos whom he knew from the club. He purchased a kilo of cocaine and began peddling the product among people he knew from Miami who had relocated to the West Coast.

Among those people was Rick James, the notoriously slick, multiplatinum funkmaster who, back in the day, had been a regular habitué of the Mutiny. James's coke habits were legendary. He often rented one of the rooms above the club, had wild sex orgies, and engaged in crack benders before crack was even a thing.

In consort with a couple of local hoodlums, Owen Band's client list included James, who remembered Band from Miami. Said Band:

> Rick was living in North Hollywood. He had a place with a jacuzzi. We entered his place and made the transaction. He saw that we had additional stash in the gym bag from which we gave him his coke. He invited us all out to the jacuzzi. There were a couple ladies in bikinis. There was a small cabana for us to change into bathing suits. We left our clothes and gym bag in there, went out, and got into the jacuzzi. After a while, James says he had to go get something. My companions have their eyes on him. They see him go into the cabana where we left our things. He comes back out, gets back into the jacuzzi, acts like nothing strange is going on. My partner gets up and goes into the cabana, he comes out with the gym bag and says, "You motherfucker, you stole our coke."

Watching all this, Band took a deep breath. Rick James, the king of funk, had just tried to rip them off.

> James got out of the jacuzzi and said, "No I didn't, what are you talking about?" And my partner starts pistol-whipping Rick James. Broke his skin, there was blood. I got up and stopped the guy; I said, "He'll give us our coke back and we'll leave." James returned the coke to us and we got out of there. He doesn't know how lucky he was.

Band remembered it as the night he saved Rick James's life.

A year later, Band returned to Miami. He kept up with the latest news in the cocaine universe, which included stories about Willy and Sal on the lam. He hadn't seen either of them in years and figured he never would, since they were wanted fugitives. Which is why he was surprised when, at a Halloween party at Club Nu in Miami Beach, there was Sal Magluta. He was dressed up in a Zorro outfit, with a black hat and mask, but it was unmistakably Sal.

At the time, Club Nu was the most popular club at the Beach. It astounded Band that Magluta, who everyone knew was a wanted man, would circulate openly in a popular nightclub.

Owen went over to Magluta and said, "Hey, Sal."

"Owen," said Sal. "Long time no see. How you been?"

"Sal, what the hell are you doing here, man? You don't think there could be feds in this place right now?"

Said Magluta, "They'll never recognize me. I'm Zorro!"

Remembered Band, "He laughed. I thought it was a crazy thing for him to be there out in the open like that. It was the last time I saw Sal."

In his time living at La Gorce Island, Sal had become cavalier about his life as a fugitive. There were rumors that he was out and about. People repeated stories about how they'd seen him at a well-known restaurant or club. Benny Lorenzo, who lived with Sal and was supposed to look after him, could see that Magluta was becoming lazy and not taking the necessary precautions; he was often going out on his own. Benny said to Sal, "Let's get out of here. We can go back to Houston. We have a place waiting for us there. You can go out whenever you want in Houston."

Sal's answer was always something along the lines of "my people are here. I'm safe in Miami."

Benny sometimes complained to Willy about it. Falcon was concerned, but he didn't feel comfortable confronting Sal. Truth is, except when they traveled on business, or at their meetings once a month to go over the financial ledger books at Sal's place, the two rarely spent time together while on the lam. It was better to not be seen together in public, especially in Miami, where they were viewed as minor celebrities.

After months of planning, the first shipment using the Chilean freighters had gone perfectly. The test run of twelve thousand kilos had arrived in Los Angeles. After the transaction was complete, on an afternoon in October,

Mario Valencia contacted Willy from Cali. He wanted to increase the next load to sixteen thousand. Willy tried to connect on the transmitter with Sal, as they always did when talking with Mario, but Sal was not responding. "Listen," Willy said to Mario from the Astro van at his house in Fort Lauderdale, "I'm sure it will be okay, but I need to consult first with my partner about the size of the load."

"Let me know," said Mario. "I will be on the radio at six p.m. on Friday. We have to make a decision so I can inform the lab how many kilos we are going to buy."

All day, Willy tried beeping Sal and calling him on his various cell phones. Nothing. No answer. Which was unusual. Willy contacted Benny. "Where the fuck is Sal? He's not returning my calls."

Said Benny, "I don't know where he is. I've been beeping and calling him all afternoon. He doesn't return calls."

Both Willy and Benny called around the Muchachos' network trying to find anyone who had seen Sal that day. No luck. Finally, at ten p.m., Willy received a call from Isabel, Sal's wife: "Willy, Sal got arrested. He was at an office supply store and some local detective recognized him. He's being held at the county jail."

"*Coño*," exclaimed Willy. "Look, I will call the lawyers. We're gonna do everything we can to have him released."

Willy phoned Joe Oteri, one of their attorneys on call. He told Oteri, "We need to get him out of there ASAP, before the feds realize he's there and pick him up on a federal warrant. If that happens, we'll never get him out."

Said Oteri, "First thing in the morning, I'll see what I can do."

For those who were in the loop, it was a sleepless night. The following morning was tense. Willy got on the phone and started making calls. The fact that Sal was being held at the Metropolitan Correctional Center and not the federal detention center provided a window of opportunity. Los Muchachos had friends in the system, people who knew people. It was possible that they could find someone within the jail system who, for a price, could get Sal released.

Around noon, Willy heard from Isabel. "The feds already know he's there," she said on the phone. "Last night he was transferred to the South Florida Reception Center. He was visited by a DEA agent named Borah. He refused to talk to the man. He said the US Marshals were coming to pick him up and take him away later today."

Willy continued making calls. Eventually, he was told by a contact of his who worked in the system, "Willy, I think we got it covered. We have a clerk who works for the county. It's possible that we can do something."

Four hours later, much to his surprise, Willy heard from Sal: "He was whispering on the phone that they had released him due to the paperwork saying he had already completed his fourteen-month sentence of imprisonment." Sal was riding on the I-95 expressway, heading north, with Isabel driving. "I don't know how you guys did it," he said to Willy. "Another hour and the feds would have snatched me up and I'd be gone for good."

"Well," said Willy, "the Lord works in mysterious ways."

Willy met Sal at an anonymous roadside motel, where he and Isabel stopped so that Sal could gather himself and figure out what to do next. Meanwhile, Willy had dispatched members of the group to monitor the house at La Gorce. Sal was certain that the house was still safe. At Dolphin Office Products at 300 Northwest Twenty-Seventh Avenue, he had been spotted by a former high school classmate of his who was now a Miami detective. It was purely a stroke of bad luck and had nothing to do with any kind of local investigation. According to Benny B. and other gang members who canvassed the area, there was nothing amiss at the house—no surveillance or questioning of neighbors, or anything like that. It appeared the coast was clear.

Said Willy, "Sal, you need to lay low. No going to the clubs or running errands around town. You have Benny and others for that. You need to stop that shit. We dodged a bullet here, you understand?"

Sal nodded vigorously, giving the impression that he most definitely understood.

That Friday, at six p.m., Mario Valencia called from Cali. Willy took the call inside his van communication center; Sal was on the same frequency at his home at La Gorce Island. The Boys did not tell the Colombian about the drama of Sal's arrest. They agreed that their partner in Cali did not need to know. It was as if nothing had happened.

Said Mario, "Okay, Muchachos, what is your position on the next load of product?"

Willy let Sal do the talking, to show that all was right in their world. In coded language, Sal said to Mario, "We agree with you, my friend. Let's increase the load to sixteen thousand kilos. The sky is the limit."

After Mario left the frequency and it was just the Boys, they spoke about the state of the business. "It's incredible," said Willy. "Here we are on the run from the federal government, hiding underground, and we've never done better. We are receiving large shipments and making more money than ever before. We are very lucky guys."

"It's not luck," said Sal, "it's Miami. Think about it. Here, we have friends, we have family, we have contacts at every level of the system. Here, we're untouchable. Willy, that's why I stay here and don't go to Houston or anywhere else. We have protection here. There's no place like home."

Willy thought Sal may have been overstating the case, but he was right. In South Florida, they could cover their ass and continue to generate billions.

14

MEXICAN HAT DANCE

WHEN CHRISTOPHER "CHRIS" CLARK FIRST came to Miami from his home state of Wisconsin, the city was just establishing its reputation as the cocaine capital of the universe. The year was 1984 and the TV show *Miami Vice* had debuted with decent ratings and much fanfare in the media. Like much of America, Clark watched the show. The flashy cars, Armani couture, and glamorous South Beach aesthetic did not have much to do with his new job as a prosecutor in the Florida state attorney's office. But it was fun to watch, and the idea that his work as a local prosecutor brought him into the center of a world that was being dramatized on television as chic and exciting was of great interest to Clark's friends and relatives back home in Wisconsin. If he were paid ten dollars every time somebody asked, "Hey, is it just like it is on *Miami Vice*?" the young prosecutor might have doubled his modest salary.

In Wisconsin, at Marquette University and later Marquette Law School, Clark knew he wanted to be involved in criminal law. After he graduated from law school, his brother, who was a criminal defense lawyer in Milwaukee, told him he should check out Miami, which was becoming known as the crime capital of America. Chris liked the idea; he drove a 1975 Pacer, known locally as a "Kenosha Cadillac," all the way to Miami and applied for an internship at the US attorney's office. He was interviewed for the position by US Attorney Janet Reno, who was a local legend, the only woman US attorney in the country.

Clark—twenty-five years old at the time—got the job. It was required that he serve a three-year apprenticeship in the state attorney's office. He lived in a frat house at the University of Miami. It didn't take long before he realized that drug cases were the lifeblood of local prosecutions.

Clark had always envisioned himself as an assistant US attorney (AUSA), and when a position opened in 1988, he jumped at the opportunity.

He was hired for the job by US Attorney Dexter Lehtinen, a controversial local figure who had left the Democratic Party to become a Republican stalwart in the Reagan administration's War on Drugs. After serving three years in the Florida State Senate, Lehtinen was appointed by US Attorney General Edwin Meese to serve as the US attorney for the Southern District of Florida. As part of his mandate, Lehtinen increased the number of prosecutors from ninety to two hundred, making South Florida the largest prosecutorial division in the entire Justice Department.

Upon Clark's arrival in the US attorney's office, major cocaine cases comprised the bulk of the daily docket. There had been a slew of high-profile cases that set the tone for the Justice Department's role in the drug war. Prosecutors in Miami knew what many in law enforcement were not willing to admit: cops and federal agents from DEA, FBI, ATF, US Customs, and the Coast Guard made the busts and the arrests, but the bone marrow of the War on Drugs— the ability to secure indictments and put cases together in court—was the purview of the US Justice Department. And when it came to the international nature of major cocaine conspiracies, the heavy artillery was supplied by the US attorney's office.

In 1988, grand jury hearings in the case against Falcon and Magluta were ongoing. Federal grand juries are allowed to serve for eighteen months at a time, and an assistant US attorney had been assigned to the case. That prosecutor, Diane Fernandez, became pregnant and left the case on maternity leave. Chris Clark had been in the US attorney's office less than two years when he was assigned to the case. He was told that he was there "to carry the water" until Fernandez could return. Her pregnancy became complicated, and she never did return to the case.

By the time Clark took over *US v. Falcon-Magluta*, the case was into its second grand jury phase. The key evidence so far consisted of depositions from Jack Devoe and Ray Corona, which detailed cocaine trafficking and money laundering. They also had Shaun Murphy, the banker from the US Virgin Islands who initially helped Willy and Sal set up their offshore accounts. After being convicted in a criminal case in the United Kingdom, Murphy was cooperating with authorities in exchange for a sentence reduction. Melvyn Kessler, the high-flying criminal defense lawyer, had been convicted at trial on trafficking and money-laundering charges and was being pressured to give up information on Falcon and Magluta. It seemed likely that he would roll over.

Also that year, Jorge Valdés, Hendry County sheriff Sermon Dyess Jr., and his partner, Butch Reddish, were all indicted on cocaine-trafficking charges.

After Los Muchachos sold their ranch in Clewiston and parted ways with Dyess Jr. and Reddish, Valdés returned to South Florida after serving five years in prison. The three men hatched a plan to smuggle kilos from Colombia into the state of Georgia. After being caught, they all three pleaded guilty, and it was hoped that they could be compelled to cooperate with the investigation of Willy and Sal.

With all of these possibilities in some stage of development, the case was coming together, but prosecutors were still not ready to unseal their indictment. What was missing was a cooperating witness who was a member of the gang, someone inside the organization who could detail the way it worked—its internal structure—and how decisions were made.

From the beginning, DEA Special Agent Dave Borah had been told that penetrating the core of Los Muchachos was impossible. He hadn't really believed that until the fiasco with Sal Magluta.

Long after Sal had been released, Borah still became angry about it every time the subject came up. Not only had Borah gone to see Magluta when he was in lockup, he was the one who, along with half a dozen US Marshals, showed up at the South Florida Reception Center to have Magluta transferred to federal prison. When he was told by a clerk that Magluta had been released earlier that morning, he was dumbfounded. How could that be? Borah had just seen the man a day earlier.

It was a humiliating turn of events that made them all look like fools. Borah and his supervisors at the DEA demanded an immediate investigation to find out who had altered Sal Magluta's paperwork. The investigation was ongoing, but it was possible that the screwup was buried deep within the bureaucracy, and the truth would never be known.

Clark liked Borah, which was preferable but not always guaranteed when men and women were thrown together on major criminal cases. Their rapport was based on the fact that Borah had been on the case for two years by the time Clark came on board. Among other things, Borah had recently worked on a couple of prosecutions that were important ancillary cases for understanding the world of Willy and Sal: the Mel Kessler case and a major trafficking prosecution involving the powerboat champion Ben Kramer.

Clark had much to learn, and Borah was the one who had been strip-mining this quarry and understood the priorities.

First among those priorities was the dream of cracking the inner sanctum of Los Muchachos. In that regard, there had been a couple of potential breaks. Justo Jay—who had once confronted Borah when he was taking photos of Los Muchachos' members at the powerboat race in Fort Myers—was recently convicted, sentenced, and serving a life term with no possibility of parole at Marianna Federal Correctional Institution in the Florida Panhandle. Also convicted that year was Tony "Bemba" Garcia, who had been given an eighty-year sentence on cocaine-smuggling charges.

Clark and Borah first approached Justo Jay in prison and made an offer for his cooperation. Jay was told, "Cooperate with us and we will go before your sentencing judge and make a recommendation that your sentence be reduced. You could possibly get out of here one day." Jay told them that there was no way he would ever testify against his friends. The next step was to drag Justo in front of a grand jury that the prosecutors had empaneled in Miami. He was asked a series of questions about Willy and Sal. Jay had been counselled by his attorney to claim his Fifth Amendment privilege on every question.

The assistant US attorney who prosecuted Jay was quoted telling a reporter, "The thing that is surprising and disappointing to me is that Jay is in his early thirties, with a wife and two young kids, and he chooses to serve a life sentence without parole rather than cooperate. It is misplaced loyalty and a perverted sense of honor."

The same thing was done with Tony Bemba. For a while, Jay and Tony Bemba were held at the same facility in Miami, then they were both moved so that they could be used against one another. Prosecutors told each of them that the other was cooperating and would be testifying against them in court, which Tony Bemba knew wasn't true. The value of not snitching against each other was an honored principle among Los Muchachos.

In 1989, Tony Bemba was approached by Clark and Borah. It wasn't the first time he had been approached in this way. Immediately after his conviction, he had been approached by Diane Fernandez, the previous prosecutor on the case. The same pitch was made to Tony that was made to Jay, but with Bemba the prosecutors had leverage. Even though he had been given an eighty-year sentence, with "good time" considerations there was a possibility he might see a release date before he died. So they threatened Tony with contempt of court. They were going to drag him in front of the same grand jury as Jay, and if he didn't cooperate, they would cite him for contempt. (Diane Fernandez had even told Tony Bemba that if he didn't cooperate, they were going to go after his father, who had only recently been released from prison in Cuba and immigrated to the United States.)

Clark and Borah used the same approach, threatening Tony Bemba with a contempt charge. The Cuban narco was respectful with the prosecutors:

> I tried to tell them that for me it was a principle to not say anything against my friends, the people I grew up with. They are like family. . . . Also, I had a daughter, she was five. I said to them, my daughter will grow up. I don't ever want her to go out and have somebody say to my daughter, "Your dad is a piece of shit snitch motherfucker." I don't want that to happen. The other thing was my father. If I became [a witness against my friends], my dad would never speak to me again. That was the way it was.

Tony was put in front of the grand jury. He was asked a series of questions and repeated the line, given to him by his lawyer, that he had spent hours memorizing: "I refuse to answer on the grounds it might incriminate me." Bemba was cited for contempt of court, adding two additional years to his sentence.

For Clark and Borah it was a show of power, and a fruitless exercise.

Borah told Clark, "I'm beginning to understand what Jack Devoe meant when he told me, 'You will never crack those guys. They're not just a criminal organization. They're a family.'"

WITH THE PRINCIPAL DEFENDANTS IN their case still at large, whereabouts unknown, one strategy the prosecutors did have at their disposal was asset forfeiture. In 1984, as the War on Drugs kicked into overdrive, Congress passed the Comprehensive Crime Control Act, one of numerous pieces of legislation, passed with bipartisan support, designed to facilitate the government's ability to take down narco organizations. Passage of the law led to the Justice Department's creation of an assets forfeiture fund. For the first time in US history, money and properties seized by the government were put into a fund that could be used by agencies within the Justice Department to finance their own special operations. In the 1980s, both civil and criminal asset forfeiture were to become effective—and controversial—tools in the War on Drugs.

In 1988, as part of the Justice Department's case against Willy and Sal, the US attorney's office in Jacksonville, Florida, launched an investigation of KS&W Offshore Engineering. The company had been a source of pride for Willy and Sal, who often noted that they would be millionaires on the legitimate financial success of KS&W alone (failing to mention that the company would not have existed in the first place were it not for narco profits). Hearings in front of a federal judge in Jacksonville led to Keith Eickert, the president of the company, being issued a subpoena to testify. Federal prosecutors offered Eickert an immunity deal if he were willing to testify about his relationship with Willy and Sal.

Eickert's attorney was Mark Dachs, whose legal fee was being paid by Willy and Sal's organization. When it came to the government's offer to Eickert—or any client, for that matter—Dachs had a standard speech that he gave. Said Dachs: "My philosophy on how I represent people, I tell them they have three choices: Go to trial, plead guilty, or you cooperate with the government. Sometimes, that might be a client's best decision. And that's fine. But I'm not having anything to do with it. I've actually given money back to clients so they can hire attorneys to replace me. Because I don't represent anyone who wants to cooperate. There are lawyers that will, but I'm not one."

Rather than face a contempt charge, Eickert did get a new lawyer and answered questions in front of a judge at the asset-forfeiture hearings in Jacksonville. Eventually, a case by prosecutors in the Middle District of Florida was filed: *United States of America v. KS&W Offshore Engineering and Milton H. Morizumi.* Eickert testified against his former partner. It was ruled that KS&W was a financial byproduct of Willy and Sal's cocaine business. Since KS&W was basically the financial overseer of Seahawk, that enterprise was also seized by the government.

Even while on the run, the Boys were regularly in contact with Dachs and their other lawyers. News that they had been "betrayed" by Eickert and that KS&W and Seahawk were no longer their property was a major blow. The way they saw it, the problem was that they had not been able to get Guillermo

Endara, whose firm was the sole financial entity behind the Panamanian shell companies, to release funds from their accounts. Their inability to access those funds had hindered their ability to make key financial decisions. It was time they got to the bottom of things.

TECHNICALLY, ENDARA WAS NOT A narco. He was not a party to the shortwave radio communication system, which the narcos used to bypass bugs or other forms of electronic surveillance that the feds might put in place. They could call Endara, but conversations about secret accounts were not something that could be discussed over the phone. There was only one way: in person, at a secret location.

In May 1989, Willy and Sal traveled to Panama City to meet their banker. They probably should have made this trip earlier. To an extent, Endara had been ducking them while he campaigned for public office, and the Boys had let this problem metastasize to the point where if they didn't act immediately, they might lose all of their Panamanian holdings.

At the time, the name of Guillermo Endara was possibly the most prominently mentioned name in the Panamanian media—except for that of Manuel Noriega.

On May 7, Endara won the Panamanian presidential election. His margin of victory was 71.2 percent to 28.4 percent for his opponent. The election was certified by international monitors from the Roman Catholic Church in Panama and former US president Jimmy Carter. But Noriega refused to accept the results. Recently, he had released his private police, known as Dobermans because of their uniform logo of a Doberman pinscher, to beat and intimidate pro-Endara partisans in the street.

On May 9, Willy and Sal arrived at the Hilton Hotel, where they usually stayed while in Panama City. There were police and military soldiers everywhere in the streets and in front of the hotel. Through their contact Gabriel Castro, chief of the PTJ, they were told that it was not certain whether Endara and Hernán Delgado would be able to meet with them. The day before, there had been some sort of confrontation in the street between Endara, his supporters, and "Noriega's thugs." Willy and Sal were told to stay in their hotel room and remain on standby.

The following day, Willy and Sal received news that Endara would meet with them. He was on his way over to their hotel.

He arrived with an entourage of bodyguards. On his head, Endara had a large gauze bandage. He was ushered into the room by Delgado, while outside the room—in the hallway—armed men stood guard. Willy noticed that some of the bodyguards were gringos, and they spoke English.

"Gentlemen," said Endara, "I heard from our friend Castro that you were in town and wanted to see me. With everything that is going on, I almost didn't come. But I felt you deserved an explanation."

Said Willy, "Guillermo, what the hell is going on?"

Endara told Willy and Sal that after the election, Noriega unleashed his goons. "He finally has gone off the deep end," said Endara. Two days earlier, as Endara and a group of supporters marched through the streets to celebrate their victory, they were set upon by a group of hired thugs whom Noriega referred to as his Dignity Battalion. Endara was hit in the head and knocked unconscious. Endara's running mate in the election was beaten bloody, an image that would appear on the cover of *Newsweek* magazine in the United States. Endara wound up in the hospital, where he received six stitches and told reporters, "I won't back off one inch in the fight. Noriega stands for everything bad in Panama. He has to leave."

After the attack, explained Endara, he was contacted by representatives of the recently elected administration of President George H. W. Bush. "They immediately provided me with bodyguards," said Endara, nodding toward the door, where his security detail stood guard out in the hallway.

"Gentlemen, I'm going to tell you something that nobody is aware of. This is top secret. But I've been told by the Bush people that if Noriega doesn't leave Panama immediately, they are going to invade the country and topple his regime. That comes straight from the US president."

Willy and Sal glanced at one another—what Endara was telling them was astounding, but as they received this information, they both felt a sinking feeling in the pit of their stomachs. With all this political chaos, the chances of their getting Endara's full cooperation regarding their accounts was getting slimmer by the hour.

Endara explained: "I have been told to remain calm. In the coming weeks and months, the Bush administration will build their case in the US Congress and among the American people to get the approval to invade if Noriega does not leave voluntarily."

Said Sal, "That is good news."

"Yes," said Willy. "I wish they would do the same thing in Cuba. Guillermo, this is what it's like to live under a dictatorship. You are getting a taste of what we have experienced for decades."

Said Endara, "Well, Willy, listen. Maybe this is the beginning of all that. Maybe the experience of deposing Noriega will give the United States the courage to take on Fidel Castro."

They all shook their heads in unison. Endara got up to leave. "My friends, let's keep all of this between us. These are difficult times. Let's maintain our composure till this plays out and we see where we stand." With that, Guillermo Endara was ushered from the room.

His law partner, Delgado, stayed behind. He said to Willy and Sal, "Listen, I know you are concerned about your accounts with the Endara Firm. We have a slight problem with this." That morning, Delgado explained, as a representative from the US State Department met with Endara, they told him that, for the United States to support Guillermo as the man to succeed Noriega in power, he must appear to be above reproach. They told Endara that they were aware that he maintained "certain business relationships" and financial accounts that could be problematic. They recommended that, for the time being, he make no effort to alter, close, or even acknowledge those accounts. The eyes of international monitors and media organizations would be all over his movements in the months ahead. It was better that he made no moves that might call any attention to any "problematic alliances."

"I'm sure you understand," Delgado said to Willy and Sal. "We can't go anywhere near those accounts right now. Maybe later, but not now."

After Delgado departed, Willy and Sal sat in their hotel room as if they had just been kicked in the groin. Delgado had just told them that the United States government had warned Guillermo Endara not to go anywhere near their accounts, which meant those accounts were effectively frozen.

"I got a headache," said Sal, rubbing his temples.

"Yeah," said Willy.

It was a thorny predicament: they were cocaine rich, and cash poor.

IT WASN'T THAT THEY WERE completely broke. They had accounts under false names in the United States that contained millions. They had cash in stash houses from Miami to Los Angeles and New York–New Jersey. They had money tied up in real estate and ancillary businesses that they probably didn't even know they had. They were billionaires many times over.

But the accounts in Panama represented a massive nest egg. That was the money that would make it possible to retire and still have enough for everyone in their extended family circle. It was the reason they had stayed in the business, to make sure that their parents and children and their families would be taken care of in perpetuity. It was their ticket to a life of freedom and prosperity, a huge middle finger to Fidel Castro, Che Guevara, and anyone who sympathized with those Cuban symbols of communism and oppression. Now their access to that dream was complicated by world events, and Willy Falcon was not sure when or how they would be able to free themselves.

They had another problem. Shortly after their meeting with Guillermo Endara in Panama City, they received word that Félix Gallardo had been arrested in Mexico City. It wasn't exactly a shock. In the last few years, the investigation into the notorious torture and murder of DEA Agent Kiki Camarena had become a sinkhole that had taken down the entire upper echelon of the Guadalajara Cartel. Gallardo was only the latest. For Willy and Sal, it was a major complication. Félix had been their contact as they devised the shipping of kilos through Chile on cargo freighters up the coast of Mexico to the Baja Peninsula. Félix was the one who paid off Mexican authorities and took responsibility for the shipments. His expertise had been invaluable.

But the entire purpose of a cartel—the lives that were lost in its creation, the corruption that facilitated its growth, the riches that it dispensed to huge swaths of the underworld—was its elasticity. Individual leaders might be taken down, but the ship continued to sail. That was the idea, anyway. A cartel was supposed to be larger than any one leader.

The arrest of Gallardo necessitated a series of sit-downs in Mexico City among the Boys and a confederation of representatives from the various Mexican narco organizations. Along with Willy and Sal, Tavy Falcon was present for at least two of these meetings.

Félix Gallardo's greatest accomplishment as leader had been to establish this alliance and maintain its cohesiveness while he was in power. There was concern about what might happen now that Félix was incarcerated. All the various leaders understood that the cocaine shipments coming by freighter from Chile, put in motion by the Cali Cartel and Los Muchachos, was an important operation. The Mexicans pledged their support in continuing these shipments.

It was at one of these meetings that Willy and Sal first met Amado Carrillo Fuentes, who was similar in age to Willy and Sal. Amado was the nephew of Ernesto Fonseca Carrillo, Don Neto, whom Willy and Sal had met in their initial meeting with leaders of the Guadalajara Cartel. (Don Neto had also been arrested and charged in the Kiki Camarena murder conspiracy.)

Amado Carrillo was an earthy character, originally from Sinaloa, with ambitions to consolidate power in *la frontera*, the borderland area in the American Southwest connecting Mexico and the United States. Amado's operation was known as the Juárez Cartel; its base of operation was Ciudad Juárez, across the border from El Paso. In recent years, Amado had accumulated a fleet of 707 jets that he used to transport marijuana and cocaine shipments, which earned him the nickname "El Señor de los Cielos" (Lord of the Skies).

Amado was introduced to Willy and Sal as a willing participant in the consortium that Félix Gallardo had created. He was receiving a piece of the shipments on the Chilean freighters, as his organization provided invaluable support as the product was transported across the border. But Amado had plans of his own. He befriended Willy and Sal and invited them to come visit him in his home city of Juárez.

As hustlers, Willy and Sal were open to any and all partnerships (as long as they didn't involve Marxist Nicaragua or Communist Cuba). A few weeks after meeting Amado in Mexico City, they traveled the route that had lately become a semiregular commute: they flew together from Fort Lauderdale airport to El Paso and crossed the border on foot into Juárez.

Amado met Willy and Sal at the Holiday Inn, where they were staying. The Lord of the Skies was gregarious and demonstrative, a brash operator with a big black cowboy hat and a thick black beard. Immediately, with hat in hand, he made his pitch to Willy and Sal. "You know, we don't need the others to make this operation work. We can cut out the middlemen. With my fleet of 707 jets, my people could fly to Colombia, pick up the cocaine shipment, and transport it to my locations on *la frontera*. I own the borderland, my friends. Believe me. I will charge you 50 percent of the load."

Willy and Sal smiled. Said Willy, "Well, Amado, we like the idea of doing business with you. But you should know, the Guadalajara Cartel is only charging us 33 percent of the loads we are smuggling by freighter to La Paz, on the Baja Peninsula."

Amado jumped to his feet. "Listen, I'm not trying to cheat you. I have expenses that they don't have. You think I'm trying to cheat you?"

Said Sal, "No, *señor*, of course not."

Willy noticed that when Amado got excited, he had a slight twitch in his right eye.

The cartel *jefe* calmed down and said, "Anyway, in this business, everything is negotiable, as you know. If you want to do business, we can do business." He put on his hat. "Now let's go to the Red Zone and have some fun."

In the pantheon of border towns—free-commerce zones with bars, strip clubs, prostitution, drugs, alcohol, and all manner of carefully curated debauchery—Ciudad Juárez was renowned and revered. Amado took his Cuban visitors along Juárez Avenue, "the Strip," past the old-school neon signs, peddlers and street hustlers, souvenir stores selling counterfeit Rolex and Gucci watches. There was music coming from nearly every bar and club, doormen at the clubs, taxi drivers, *policía*, and mostly young American tourists who crossed the border for a good time. Amado took Willy and Sal to the Kentucky Club, which on its awning was billed as world famous. Opened in 1920, the bar was not only a favorite spot for smugglers, bootleggers, crooked cops, and gangsters, it served celebrities such as the boxing champ Jack Johnson, John Wayne, Steve McQueen, Marilyn Monroe, and Jim Morrison of the Doors. Framed photos memorializing their visits lined the walls.

Drinking at the Kentucky Club and walking around La Zona de Pronaf, the city's commercial district, Willy felt that it was only right that he and Sal found themselves in this slightly sleazy border town. They were smugglers, after all, from a long line of smugglers who brought illegal contraband into the United States from elsewhere. Juárez was one of those places, a more old-school, run-down, funkier version of Panama City, or Medellín, or even Miami Beach, where being a hustler or a *traficante* was a badge of distinction. It reminded Willy of the stories he had heard from Manuel Garces, their Colombian Godfather, who told them of a time when being a *contrabandista* was a respectable profession, and there was no shame in being a denizen of the black market.

Willy and Sal said goodbye to Amado and promised they would give serious consideration to his pitch.

A WEEK LATER, BACK IN Fort Lauderdale, Willy received a call from Pablo Escobar. Sal was also on the shortwave frequency from his home on La Gorce. It had been a while since Pablo spoke with the Boys. In the last year, the renegade narco boss had continued his assault on Colombian society. It was Pablo against the world. The most recent atrocity was the outrageous assassination of Luis Carlos Galán, a candidate for president who had been speaking out in favor of extradition. Galán was riddled with machine gun fire at an outdoor campaign rally in front of thousands of traumatized witnesses. Afterward, President Virgilio Barco Vargas issued an emergency decree reinstating the policy of extradition. In response, the Extraditables, led by Escobar, commenced a bombing campaign that was still ongoing.[1]

To some, the issue of extradition may have seemed simple, but it wasn't. Colombia's justice system was under siege and therefore incapable of bringing to justice major narcos who were guilty of crimes against humanity. This was the argument of the United States government and many in the Colombian ruling class. But the alternative view was equally as powerful. It wasn't only Escobar who noted that to give up Colombian citizens to another country to be put on trial was a violation of a nation's sovereignty. It was an admission on the part of the Colombian citizenry that the country was incapable of applying justice and taking care of its own business. It was not something to be taken lightly, and the debate—which Escobar no doubt hijacked and inflamed to suit his own needs—touched at the core of Colombia's view of itself as a functioning society.

Over the shortwave radio, Pablo said to Falcon, "Doctor, I have some good news. I have established my own contact in Mexico. We have agreed to ship

---

[1] The most depraved act occurred on November 27, 1989, when Escobar ordered the planting of a bomb on a commercial jetliner, Avianca Flight 203. It was a domestic flight leaving from El Dorado International Airport in Bogotá to Cali. The plane exploded in the sky, killing all 107 passengers and crew, and three people on the ground. Two Americans were among the dead; President Bush demanded retribution. Nine days later, another atrocity occurred: a car bomb outside the headquarters of the Administrative Department of Security (DAS) exploded at seven thirty a.m. Fifty-seven people were killed and 2,258 were injured. The bombing, ordered by Escobar, was an attempt to kill DAS Director Miguel Maza Márquez, who escaped unharmed.

kilos from our labs to various locations in Mexico, where they can be brought across the border into the US."

"Okay," said Willy, "that's great. Who is your contact?"

Said Pablo, "Amado Carrillo Fuentes, the Lord of the Skies."

Willy was silent.

"Doctor, are you there?"

"Yes, *hermano*, I'm here."

Continued Pablo, "I would like for you and the Accountant to come in with me on this. I want you two to meet Amado in Ciudad Juárez. He's a good man; you are going to like him. Meet him there and make whatever arrangement you need to import the product. This is going to be very lucrative for all of us."

When Pablo hung up, and it was only the two of them on the shortwave frequency, Willy and Sal almost had to laugh. Escobar thought he was fixing them up on a blind date, but they had already smoked this cigar.

Willy and Sal marveled at the fact that even though they were on the lam, under indictment, they were more in demand than ever. "Think about it," Falcon said to his partner. "We are at the top of our game. Who else is able to work together with the Colombians and the Mexicans in harmony? Who else does that? We create new routes and use cutting-edge technology, the best equipment. We have a fleet of boats and trucks. If things go wrong, we always devise a backup plan. We are invaluable to the cartels. They need us more than we need them."

Said Sal, "You got that right, *mi hermano*. We are the ones who make it happen."

Later, on his cell phone, Willy called Amado, who said enthusiastically, "Doctor, how are you doing, my friend? I just saw you a couple weeks ago, and now here we are talking again."

"Yes," said Willy. He pictured the Mexican in his black cowboy hat. "Nowadays, I am seeing you even in my soup. I guess we are in great demand lately."

They set up a date for the three of them—Willy, Sal, and Amado—to meet in Juárez at the same hotel as before. It was, as the renowned baseball player Yogi Berra once said, "déjà vu all over again."

At the Holiday Inn, they worked out the details. When they had ironed everything out, Willy said to the cartel boss, "One thing, Amado, if we are to do this, I ask that you say nothing to our partners from Cali and the Guadalajara Cartel about this deal with Pablo Escobar."

"Why is that?" asked Amado.

"Because the Cali and Medellín cartels are at war with each other," said Willy.

"Okay, but why can't we say anything to the Guadalajara people? Why can't they know?"

"Listen, Amado, respectfully, this is the way we need it to be. We have our reasons."

Amado was silent for a second, then he said, "Okay."

Willy noticed that his right eye started to twitch.

September 5, 1989

President George H. W. Bush had been on the job for eight months when he decided to give his first national address from the Oval Office. The speech has gone down in history as an insidious moment in the War on Drugs. The president held up a cellophane baggie filled with chunks of white powder and solemnly announced to the nation, "This is crack cocaine." It was "seized a few days ago in a park across the street from the White House." The president looked into the camera and declared:

> Our most serious problem today is cocaine, and in particular, crack. . . . Tonight I am announcing a strategy that reflects the co-ordinated cooperative commitment of all federal agencies. . . . I am proposing that we enlarge the criminal justice system across the board. . . . We need more prisons, more jails, more courts, more prosecutors. . . . Our message to the cartels is this: the rules have changed. . . . We will intensify our efforts against drug smugglers on the high seas, in international airspace, and at our borders. . . . We will pursue and enforce international agreements to track drug money to the front men and financiers. And then we will handcuff these money launderers, and jail them, just like any street dealer. And for drug kingpins, the death penalty.

The president's speech was the culmination of a policy he had instituted from his first day in office. Earlier that year, he created a new branch of the federal bureaucracy called the Office of National Drug Control Policy.

As leader of this agency—a position known as the drug czar—President Bush appointed the conservative firebrand William J. Bennett.

A Washington, DC, attorney who was both a two-pack-a-day cigarette smoker and a gambling addict, Bennett was determined to move the government's public policy away from viewing drugs as a health issue and to focus on morality. As drug czar, he sought partnership with Christian fundamentalist leaders and even the televangelist Billy Graham. Illegal drugs, Bennett said in a speech that May, "obliterate morals, values, character, our relations with each other, and our relation to God."

The US government had been fighting the War on Drugs for more than twenty years. Despite the billions spent, the millions incarcerated, the ineffectual river of rhetoric from political leaders, drugs were cheaper, more potent, and used by more teenagers than when President Nixon inaugurated the policy. The number of cocaine dependents had grown (though crack use was down since 1987, when it peaked). Street violence, which was uncommon when the war began, was now commonplace in many US cities. Drug combatants were killed daily; the number of innocent bystanders slain in shootouts among rival street dealers, or with law enforcement, had tripled in the two years prior to Bush's inauguration.

Rather than evaluate the social costs of the policy, Bush and his drug czar doubled down—more money spent, more aggressive law enforcement, more punitive laws.

At congressional hearings to pass the National Drug and Crime Emergency Act, Los Angeles police chief Daryl Gates suggested that "casual drug users should be taken out and shot." Even casual drug use, he said, was "treason." A congressman from Georgia suggested that drug offenders be rounded up and shipped to penal colonies on the "extremely remote" Pacific islands of Midway and Wake. "There's not much chance they're going to get anything but rehabilitated on two small islands like these," said the congressman. "You can't go anywhere. . . . You won't be interrupted by families that come visiting every weekend."

On the popular television talk show *Larry King Live*, Drug Czar Bennett suggested that beheading drug dealers was "morally plausible" if "legally difficult." When King pressed Bennett on the subject, asking if he was serious, he said, "Yeah. Morally I don't have any problem with it."

The more the War on Drugs failed—the higher the costs to the American people—the more bellicose and outrageous the rhetoric became.

By the time President Bush gave his national address, after months of his strategizing with Bill Bennett, administration narco policies had become entangled with another issue: General Manuel Noriega. Initially, the argument against Noriega had focused on his control of the Panama Canal, which had been a favorite saber-rattling issue for Republican Party politicians since Ronald Reagan first used it to get elected eight years earlier. Now, as Bush prepared to depose Noriega with an invasion, if necessary, he shifted the pretext to narcotics smuggling.

It was an argument fraught with historical land mines. Manuel Noriega had been an asset of the CIA going back to a time even before Bush was director of the agency. As an informant for the CIA in Latin America, supplying information on Salvador Allende in Chile, the spread of Castroism in Latin America, the rise of the Sandinistas, and any other political movement that the United States considered problematic, the general was paid hundreds of thousands of dollars by the US Central Intelligence Agency.[2] Back when George Bush was vice president, he had met with Noriega and publicly declared that he was an ally in the War on Drugs. But now he was a narco kingpin and money launderer who needed to be removed by military force.

The president's national address was an effort to bypass congressional overseers and go straight to the American people.

It was, on multiple levels, a duplicitous act. For one thing, the centerpiece of Bush's presentation—the bag of crack that had been purchased across the street from the White House—was agitprop. In an article in the *Washington Post* two weeks after the speech, it was revealed that the sale and purchase of crack in Lafayette Park was orchestrated by DEA agents on behalf of the Bush administration. A young street dealer had been lured to the park, where he was told a sale could be made. The dealer was skeptical; when told that the site of the transaction was across from the White House, he reportedly said "Where the fuck is the White House?" The president's men chose the location for its potential to outrage, illustrating that the peddling of crack was pervasive. After

---

[2] In 1991, at his cocaine-trafficking and money-laundering trial in the Southern District of Florida, lawyers for Noriega claimed that, over the years, he had been paid $11 million by US intelligence.

making the sale to an undercover agent, the dealer was arrested. His product became exhibit A in the president's pitch to the American public.

The whole thing had been a setup, a stunt, the latest shady act of prestidigitation in the American government's ongoing War on Drugs.

September 18, 1989
It was one of those Monday mornings, humid and seemingly routine. Attorney Juan Acosta, age sixty-two, parked his car and entered his office building at 4100 Northwest Ninth Street in Miami. Acosta owned the building where he had maintained his law office for more than a decade. His office was on the second floor. Thankfully, his secretary, Elizabeth Rodríguez, was already there and had turned on the air-conditioning. Acosta said good morning to Rodríguez, poured himself some coffee, and headed into his office.

It was thirteen days since President Bush had given his crack cocaine address to the nation, which was watched by an estimated twenty million Americans. The drug war, and particularly its connections to events in Panama, was on Acosta's mind these days.

For a few years now, Acosta had been serving as a legal liaison between numerous narco organizations, including that of Willy and Sal, and the law firm of Guillermo Endara in Panama City. It was a business that had made Acosta rich, as, along with his legal fees, he received a commission on each transaction he brokered. The relationship with Willy and Sal had been tremendous. Not only had Acosta played a role in helping the cocaine kingpins set up their accounts with Endara, but he had also benefitted from an expanding universe of clients. Representatives of the Cali and Medellín cartels, thanks to recommendations from Willy and Sal, also relied on Acosta to broker the transfer of funds from the narcosphere to accounts in Panama to banks in the United States. It was a money-laundering empire that made it possible for the upper echelon of the cocaine business to flourish.

A problem for Acosta was that he had been outed by Ray Corona. Earlier that year, the convicted banker, now cooperating with federal investigators, had named Acosta as a key figure in the Boys' money-laundering operations. Acosta had been subpoenaed to testify before the grand jury. For more than a year, he had been engaged in a legal battle to avoid having to appear before the grand jury. The situation had caused him great distress. By September 18, Acosta had exhausted all remedies and was scheduled to appear in two weeks.

The question was: What would he be compelled to testify about? He had lawyers negotiating with the US attorney's office attempting to limit the nature of his testimony, but the time had come: he would testify about his dealings with Falcon and Magluta, or he would go to jail.

At noon, a woman who identified herself as Sandra Gomez arrived at Acosta's office along with two young men for a scheduled appointment. The woman had called numerous times the previous week asking if the lawyer could advise her on her divorce. Even though his specialty was real estate law—he was not a divorce lawyer—he had agreed to meet the woman. Her companions that day were both Hispanic males; the woman identified one of them as her husband and the other as a friend.

Acosta's secretary, Elizabeth Rodríguez, led the woman and her "husband" into Acosta's office. She introduced everyone, then sat down and pulled out a notepad, to take notation.

After speaking for a few minutes, Acosta said to the woman, "The first thing is that you will need one hundred fifty dollars to pay a filing fee." The woman said she needed to go to her car to get the money.

As soon as she left the office, her so-called husband pulled out a gun. "All I remember was a black gun, and it was very large," Rodríguez said later in a deposition. "The next thing I remember, Acosta tried to give him his watch. I think he thought it was a stickup, and he had a gold watch on, and I remember him beginning to take the watch off. And he had his hands up."

The gunman shot the lawyer six times, using a gun equipped with a silencer. The coup de grâce shot was a bullet in the head at close range. "The next thing I remember was Mister Acosta on the floor bleeding."

Rodríguez stood paralyzed as the two men fled the office to a getaway car and driver waiting outside at the curb.

The secretary called 911. By the time paramedics arrived, it was too late. Acosta was already gone.

Willy Falcon was at his home in Fort Lauderdale when he received a phone call from Richard Passapera, a.k.a. Blondie: "Doctor, turn on your television and go to the six o'clock news station. Somebody shot Juan Acosta."

Willy turned on the news and there it was: images of Acosta's office, where Willy and Sal had met the lawyer years earlier, and a photo of the victim. A correspondent said that detectives did not yet know who or what was behind the killing.

Willy's mind started racing: Acosta had handled all six of Willy and Sal's major accounts that had been set up through Panama and the Endara Firm. Once investigators were able to access Acosta's files, both his physical ones and those on computers, it was likely they would untangle the matrix of connections among Acosta, the narcos, and Endara. And once that happened, it could be narco Armageddon. Endara didn't just represent Willy and Sal. The Boys had also introduced Endara to Mario Valencia and Pablo Escobar. The Endara Firm managed hidden accounts for all these entities—the Medellín and Cali cartels, and Los Muchachos. And Juan Acosta was only a step or two removed from all of it.

Furthermore, when Endara first announced that he was running for president, Willy had convinced Pacho Herrera of the Cali Cartel and José Gonzalo Rodríguez Gacha from the Medellín Cartel to make a campaign contribution as an investment. If Endara became president, Falcon told them, it would be "good for all of us."

One week after the death of Acosta, in late September, Willy called Hernán Delgado in Panama City. "Hernán, this killing of Acosta could be a problem for us." As if he'd never brought up the subject before, Willy added, "One of the reasons that I wanted to speak with you is concerning the corporations that we have with you that were represented by Acosta in the United States. You and Guillermo are in control of those companies. You are the incorporated attorneys and treasurers, and I would like to move as fast as possible trying to sell the assets that those companies have here in the United States. With this murder investigation, if they put the pieces together, they will eventually figure out that we are the owners of the properties. You can be sure that they are going to know your law firm represents the foreign owners of companies that are purchasing our assets here in the US."

Delgado sighed. "Willy, we talked about this. In the current political climate, Guillermo Endara can't go near those accounts."

"Yes, Hernán, but things have changed. This murder investigation could expose us. The US government is going to find out, and how is that going to look for Guillermo?"

Said Delgado, "The Bush administration already knows about those accounts. They are the ones who told us to back off and not do anything that will create a scandal." Delgado continued, "Right now, the US military has troops in Panama doing military exercises; they're trying to lure Noriega into a confrontation that will serve as a pretext for an invasion. It's a very delicate situation."

Willy and Delgado talked back and forth; it was clear that their priorities were different. Willy could see Delgado and Endara's position, but that didn't solve his problem. He and Sal were in danger of losing half their fortune.

And then another disaster struck. On September 28, Willy received a call from Freddy Cruz, one of their key organizers in Los Angeles. Cruz had just seen a special bulletin on the local television news reporting the largest cocaine bust in history. At a warehouse in Sylmar, a northern Los Angeles neighborhood, a law enforcement team of DEA, LAPD, and SWAT officers conducted a raid that uncovered twenty tons of cocaine, with a street value of $7 billion. They also seized $12 million in cash (in twenty- and one-hundred-dollar denominations). This was the largest bust since the 13.8 tons of cocaine seized in the Tranquilandia raid in Colombia.

"Is that ours?" Willy asked Freddy.

"I think it is, but I need to check."

It turned out that it was partly theirs; the warehouse at Sylmar included twenty thousand kilos that Pablo Escobar had shipped in his arrangement with Amado Carrillo Fuentes of the Juárez Cartel. Los Muchachos were part owners of the shipment, together with Escobar and the Colombian cartel boss José Gonzalo Rodríguez Gacha. Los Muchachos were supposed to pick up those kilos and distribute them as part of their distribution network.

Willy made a rare visit to Sal's house on La Gorce Island to discuss the situation. It was a huge loss, but they both knew that this was the price of doing business. The US Department of Justice and the local police in Los Angeles were touting the bust as a major success, but it seemed that they had little evidence outside of a warehouse full of kilos. There was nothing—yet—that connected the operation to Los Muchachos.

Willy and Sal still had their semiregular shipments (every six weeks) coming via the freighters from Chile. The total of those loads had been increased to 24,000 kilos. The latest shipment was on its way in November. They hoped to have that shipment fully received and distributed by early December, in time for their annual holiday vacation.

With the various murders and busts that had occurred, Willy and Sal, for the first time, made a rare concession to their status as fugitives. It was decided that it was too risky to go to Las Vegas that year. Instead, they would go to Lake Tahoe, Nevada. Willy called his contacts at Caesars Palace in Las Vegas to book them at the Caesars in Tahoe, making sure that his group would be afforded the same special privileges (limos at the airport; rooms, meals, and shows comped by the house; VIP treatment in the casinos) that they were in Las Vegas. Falcon reserved connecting suites for friends and family.

After leaving Sal's house, Willy was feeling a little down about not going to Vegas for the first time in more than a decade. He decided to compensate by going on a birthday-and-Christmas shopping spree for Alina and his daughters.

He was driving a new Audi, wearing a baseball cap with the Dallas Cowboys logo and Ray-Ban aviator sunglasses. Willy considered this a disguise, of sorts. He drove to his preferred jewelry store, located at the old Zayre shopping center on Thirty-Seventh Avenue and Seventh Street Northwest, in the middle of the city.

He had a list that he'd been carrying around for days. After parking his Audi, he entered the store and greeted Alfredo, his friend and jewelry consultant for years. "Willy, oh my God. So great to see you. Come into my office before someone recognizes you. Why don't you send someone to do your shopping, it's too risky for you to do this."

"There are some old habits I just can't shake. If I don't get Alina her birthday and Christmas presents, then I'm gonna be in real trouble." Willy lowered his voice and said, "Forget the law, the only thing I'm scared of is my wife."

Alfredo laughed.

"I've got a list," said Willy, looking at his piece of paper. "I overheard my wife and her sister raving about the new Cartier women's watch. I'm going to surprise her with that. I also need a four-carat diamond ring. I know she'll fall in love with that. Get me a tennis bracelet for Aileen, my daughter, and get my daughter Jessica a nice chain with a heart pendant on it. Also, a nice pearl necklace for my mother, Marta. My dad I'm getting a Piaget watch. And for Los Muchachos, I'm gonna need six Presidential Rolex watches."

The bill was over $100,000. All items were separately gift wrapped. Said Willy, "Happy holidays, Alfredo. Hopefully, I will see you again next year."

On his way home, Willy was feeling nostalgic. He decided to drive into Little Havana and stop at his very first place of residence in America. The building at 2001 Southwest Sixth Street looked the same, though everything seemed smaller, almost like a toy re-creation of the home as he remembered it. He parked and got out, stood on the sidewalk in front of his building. He buzzed the intercom for his old apartment, and explained that he used to live there, could he come in and look around. The current occupant allowed him entry:

The apartment was extremely small, a living room, a small kitchen with two chairs, a tiny bathroom, one single bedroom in the back where me, my father, my mother, and my brother all slept in the same room. My current walk-in closet I had in Fort Lauderdale was bigger than the bedroom I shared with my entire family. Wow. I realized how far I had come.

Willy went back outside and drove his car to Twenty-First Avenue and Fifth Street Southwest. Again, he parked and got out. This was the area where, at the age of eleven and twelve, he spent much of his time once school was out. Stickball and touch football in the street with Tony Bemba, Justo Jay, Sal, Tavy, and Ramiro. Willy felt the memories wash over him. Those had been innocent days, a much simpler time.

Suddenly, he realized that standing alone in the street could attract attention from someone who might call the cops. He got in his car and drove forty-five minutes home to Fort Lauderdale.

By the time Willy got back to the house, Alina was angry. "Where have you been?" she said.

"I was at Sal's."

"Your nose is going to grow big from lying like that. Sal called here looking for you two hours ago."

Willy didn't want to tell her he had been at the jewelry store buying her presents; that would spoil the surprise. But he could tell by the twinkle in her eye that she knew. "Were you with another woman?" she said.

"Woman, let's go upstairs to the bedroom so I can prove to you I wasn't with someone else."

They went upstairs and made love. Afterward, while Alina was in the bathroom freshening up, Willy called Sal and told him about his little trip down memory lane at the old neighborhood. "Reminiscing like that, remembering your childhood," he said to Sal, "it's so powerful. It gives me strength."

After hanging up, Willy put on some clothes and headed downstairs and out to the garage. He opened a safe and took out a 9 millimeter that he kept in his waistband. He retrieved a .38 Special that he kept in a holster on his left ankle. Finally, the MAC-10 semiautomatic machine gun, which he kept under the front seat of the Audi with at least three magazines.

He wasn't going anywhere, but after a day of reminiscing and lovemaking, it was time to come back to reality.

15

TIGER BY THE TAIL

THE KILLING OF JUAN ACOSTA was a troubling demarcation line for Los Muchachos. It didn't take long for reporting on the crime to merge with the story of Willy and Sal. Only occasionally in their careers as cocaine kingpins had the Boys' names been mentioned in the media for any reason other than the powerboat racing circuit. It had been years since Seahawk or Falcon and Magluta had been a major news item in Miami. Now, whenever their names appeared, it would invariably be in relation to the cocaine business.

Throughout the holiday season, as Falcon monitored the local police investigation of the Acosta murder, another major event dominated his attention.

On December 20, not long before Willy and Alina headed to Lake Tahoe for their vacation, the United States invaded Panama. It had been coming for some time. After a coup attempt by Panamanian miliary leaders earlier that year, which Noriega squashed, he had declared that Panama was at war with the United States. American troops were already in the Canal Zone awaiting orders to commence military action. When a US Marine was shot dead during a routine stop at a Panamanian military roadblock, President Bush gave the order.

The invasion was dubbed Operation Just Cause by the administration's public relations apparatus. In the following two weeks, 516 Panamanians were killed in military confrontations, including 314 soldiers and 202 civilians. Twenty-three US soldiers were killed, along with three US civilians. The UN General Assembly and the Organization of American States condemned the invasion as a violation of international law.

From his room at Caesars Palace in Lake Tahoe, Willy watched a report about the invasion on the television news. Of particular interest was video footage of none other than Guillermo Endara at a US military base being sworn in as president of Panama.

Later, at a bar inside the casino, Willy, Sal, and Tavy talked about the events of that day. They were all excited by the invasion. They couldn't help but equate what had happened in Panama with what they had always hoped would happen in their home country of Cuba. Said Willy, "Maybe now the United States will grow a pair of balls and do the same thing to Fidel."

Falcon and Magluta had maintained their connections to the anti-Castro movement, even while on the lam. They still met regularly with Antonio Garcia Perez, a.k.a. El Guajiro, their primary contact in the movement. That spring, at the restaurant Sundays on the Bay in north Miami Beach, El Guajiro filled them in on the latest, which was that a tight cadre of patriots had created a new paramilitary organization called Partido de Unidad Nacional Democratico (PUND). At this meeting, El Guajiro introduced Willy and Sal to Frank Sturgis, the notorious Watergate burglar who had been a CIA operative since the time of the Cuban Revolution. (Falcon had been concerned about meeting with Sturgis, since he and Sal were wanted by the law, but Guajiro assured him, "Believe me, this guy can be trusted.")

Guajiro and Sturgis laid out their plan for a final and comprehensive effort to overthrow Castro. The timing was essential. Sturgis explained that he had confidential intelligence straight from the CIA that predicted the Soviet Union was soon to fall. Cuba would be losing its financial support from Russia and would therefore be highly vulnerable to attack. They needed to move fast to beef up their secret antigovernment cells in Cuba and their training facilities in the Everglades. They needed guns, explosives, and tactical equipment. Guajiro was asking for $2 million for PUND.

As always, Falcon and Magluta gave them the money and even agreed to have a representative from Los Muchachos meet with them every three months, to assess the situation, and to give them another quarter of a million dollars. It was the least that they could do.

These days, Willy's focus wasn't so much on Cuba; it was on Panama and the tumultuous events that were dominating the news.

With their personal banker and money launderer being handpicked by the United States and sworn in as president, Willy was cautiously optimistic. The last time he spoke with Endara by phone, the president-to-be assured him, "I always take care of those who have been reliable friends. That is the way I am." The gloom Willy had felt earlier when Endara was physically attacked in the streets and Panama descended into chaos was replaced with new hope that once Noriega was captured and order restored, the Boys would be in a good position to salvage their accounts.

Noriega, however, wasn't making it easy.

As a young man, Noriega had spent months taking courses at the School of the Americas, then located at the US Army base in the Canal Zone. He also took a course in psychological operations at Fort Bragg in North Carolina. Noriega liked to think that when it came to a war of wills, he could not be defeated. Like many dictators, he was delusional. As the US military seized control of Panama City, Noriega took sanctuary in the Apostolic Nunciature, the Holy See's embassy in Panama. Prevented by treaty from invading the embassy, US soldiers from Delta Force surrounded the building. A standoff ensued that lasted for days. Eventually, the general was flushed out and surrendered after being bombarded, over loudspeakers, with the heavy metal music of Van Halen and other headbanger bands.

While all this was unfolding, Willy Falcon moved on from Caesars Palace in Tahoe to the condo in Vail, where he frolicked in the snow with his children. Jessica, Aileen, and Will Jr. loved being in Colorado and were blissfully unaware of the international complications that were having significant impact on the family business.

One morning, Willy and the children were outside making a snowman. Willy played with the kids, putting the eyes of the snowman in the wrong place. The kids laughed and said, "You're silly." When he put a carrot at the belly-button level of the snowman, rather than as the nose as he was supposed to, they howled with laughter.

Watching his kids in a state of ecstatic joy, Willy felt a wave of sadness wash over him. Both he and Sal were aware that with their pending indictment, it was likely they could be arrested at any time. No doubt they had a mammoth legal fight on the horizon. If you thought it through, as the Boys had many times, a future of serious incarceration was not beyond the realm of possibility. Willy had always thought of this in terms of his own personal freedom and how that would be affected. Now, as he watched his kids enjoying some carefree time with him, he wanted to cry. If he were incarcerated for a long stretch, they were going to lose their father. They would grow up without a dad, and they would shoulder the stigma of his being branded a notorious criminal.

That day, January 3, as he and the kids came inside from the snow, he saw on a television in the lodge a report of General Noriega turning himself in to US authorities. A reporter announced that the former dictator would be put on a plane and immediately taken to federal prison in the District of South Florida. He was facing multiple counts of cocaine trafficking and money laundering, and his trial would take place in Miami.

It did cross Falcon's mind: If the US government could do that to a person as powerful as Manuel Noriega, what could they do to him and Sal?

GIVEN THAT THEIR FUTURE WAS in question and their organization was under scrutiny, 1990 was an amazingly lucrative year for Los Muchachos. The shipments by freighter from Chile were increased with each load, until eventually they were trafficking thirty thousand kilos per load. These were perhaps the largest loads of cocaine to enter the United States in the history of the country.

Smuggling the product into the United States from Mexico was not difficult. For a time, the smugglers were aided greatly by a secret tunnel that had been constructed in the town of Agua Prieta, in Sonora, that led across the border to a false drain inside a warehouse in Douglas, Arizona. The tunnel was three hundred feet long and had electrical lights and a motorized rail system for carts. When it was discovered in May 1990, it was estimated that close to three thousand pounds of cocaine had been smuggled through it.

DEA and US Border Patrol agents touted the tunnel's discovery as a major blow in the War on Drugs, but for the cartels and Los Muchachos, it was little more than a temporary diversion. Afterward, Gilberto "Veci" Barrios, organizer of the semitrucks for Willy and Sal, was more likely to dispatch drivers to Laredo, Texas, or El Paso, or Tucson, Arizona, or Houston. Whereas cocaine for years had been making its way primarily from Miami or Los Angeles or New York to American cities from coast to coast, it now made its way from the southwestern borderland up through the middle of the country to Denver, Chicago, Detroit, and Cincinnati. Despite all the money and manpower expended by the US government to stop the flow of cocaine, as the new decade dawned, there was more white powder circulating around the United States than ever before.

SINCE COMING ON AS LEAD prosecutor in the case against Falcon-Magluta et al., Chris Clark was feeling overwhelmed. He had a stack of motions filed by attorneys representing different players in the Boys' criminal organization. Justo Jay and Tony "Bemba" Garcia had been represented by two experienced and highly skilled attorneys based out of Boston, Joe Oteri and Marty Weinberg. Their fees were paid for by the organization. The defense lawyers were filing appeals of their clients' convictions on various grounds, and those appeals needed to be contested in court. Seizures of properties owned by Willy and Sal, the most successful and effective aspect of the investigation so far, were contested by lawyers representing Falcon and Magluta. That alone might have required a team of prosecutors with expertise in appellate law, but Clark was on his own. "At the time, I was mostly a one-man band, young and ignorant," said Clark.

One person the neophyte prosecutor did have at his disposal was DEA Agent David Borah. If Clark was a one-man band, then Borah was the instrument by which they hoped to hit the high notes. His main priority at this point was attempting to turn informants into potential witnesses. It was a specialized skill, and the fact that Borah's supervisors had him working as a lone agent on the case was a testament to their belief that he was the right man for the job.

In his effort to find "snitches," Borah had already been rebuffed by Justo Jay and Tony Bemba. These were veteran members of the Falcon-Magluta group who would have been impressive witnesses at trial. Their refusal to cooperate was a setback, but as the investigators were learning, the Falcon organization had been in operation for more than a decade; it had many moving parts and many participants, some of whom had left the gang and gone on to their own criminal activities. Some had gotten busted and were facing significant time in prison. These types of criminals were the most likely to be open to making a deal.

In the summer of 1990, Borah approached Jorge Valdés, who he had heard was an early partner of Willy and Sal's in the cocaine business. For years, Valdés had been going around in Miami—and during his time in the prison system—telling people that he was the one who staked Willy and Sal to thirty-one kilos of cocaine that started them in the business. "At the time, they were selling grams at the disco," said Valdés. This wasn't true. Falcon had been smuggling product for Chi Chi Quintero and the anti-Castro underground for more than a year before he ever met Jorge Valdés. What was true was that it was Valdés who introduced Willy and Sal to Manuel Garces, the Colombian Godfather who, in turn, introduced them to the Valencia brothers and Pablo Escobar.

Jorge Valdés had sacrificed a lot for the Boys. He had crashed in the jungle in a plane carrying their cocaine in 1978, been tortured by military police in Panama, and still not given up the names of Willy and Sal.

In the early 1980s, Valdés went to prison on smuggling charges (one of his last social forays before imprisonment was his attendance at the Houston cattle show with Willy, Sal, and Sermon Dyess Jr.). He was away for five years. When he returned, he reconnected with Dyess Jr., who had become sheriff of Hendry County, and Butch Reddish on a cocaine-trafficking scheme that landed him in prison again. He was being held at a county jail in Mobile, Alabama, when he was visited by David Borah.

Valdés had built up considerable resentment and perhaps jealousy toward Willy and Sal. In jail, he had found Jesus and would eventually become a Christian minister. Though he still had fond feelings for Sal Magluta, who had been a family friend since he was a child, he sometimes derided Willy Falcon as "stupid." Most of all, Valdés blamed Falcon for having usurped his relationship with Manuel Garces, who had become an invaluable patron of Los Muchachos.

Borah introduced himself to Valdés and explained why he was there. Since Valdés had recently found Jesus, he had concluded that he needed to be honest and "come clean" with God. Part of that involved cooperating with David Borah and his investigation. Years later, in a published memoir, Valdés wrote, "When David Borah left that day, I felt that I had found another friend within the government system. Eventually, I wrote a poem with David Borah in mind and titled it, 'My Enemy Became My Friend.'"

Another prospect for the investigators was Juan "Recotado" Barroso. *Recotado* means "sawed off," a reference to Barroso's diminutive stature. Some called him Reco, for short, or even Recut, the English-language translation. Another Cuban-born exile whose family had fled Cuba and settled in Little Havana, Barroso had known Willy and Sal since 1969 from the neighborhood and, later, Citrus Grove Junior High and Miami High School.

Starting in 1983, Barroso was instrumental in piloting boatloads of kilos from the islands—especially the city of Freeport in the Bahamas—into the Florida Keys. At the same time, he was a crucial element of the Seahawk powerboat racing team, where he often served as Willy's navigator during the races. He accompanied the Boys on the APBA racing circuit to Fort Myers, Sarasota, New Orleans, New Jersey, Michigan, and other locations.

As a smuggler, he worked under a crew of powerboat pilots that was overseen by the Deer (El Venado), Bernie Gonzalez, who managed that aspect of the business for Los Muchachos.

In the mid-1980s, when Los Muchachos stepped up their trafficking operation in Los Angeles, Barroso drove kilos from Los Angeles to Miami in a cargo van. He was paid $60,000 per shipment. When the gang purchased their semitrucks and upgraded their land transportation system, and the vans were no longer needed, Barroso returned to Miami and continued his role running kilos by boat into South Florida locations.

In November 1990, Barroso was transporting a load of 220 kilos from the Bahamas via a thirty-eight-foot Mirage boat. The kilos had been given to him by another group of drug smugglers, who transferred the cocaine at sea from one boat to another. Barroso and a partner steered back toward Miami. While still out at sea, their boat broke down. They unloaded the kilos by simply dumping them into the ocean. Then they called the US Coast Guard, hoping for a tow ashore. The Coast Guard never showed up. They fired off some flares, and eventually a salvage boat towed them ashore. There, they were met by a Coast Guard vessel, and officers placed Barroso and his partner under arrest for cocaine smuggling.

Barroso was able to get released on bond, but he had other problems. Shortly thereafter, he was indicted again on smuggling charges, on a case based in the state of South Carolina. Cumulatively, he was facing charges that could put him away for life.

In the federal detention center in Miami, Barroso was approached by David Borah and Chris Clark together. They laid it out for Recut. He was going away for life unless he cooperated. He would have to reveal everything that he knew about the operation of Willy and Sal, or he would never again see the light of day outside prison walls.

Barroso had some personal concerns. He had a son who had been born with the AIDS virus, which he had inherited from his mother. Barroso had divorced the mother and was living as a single parent with his son. He was concerned about what might happen to his son if he was sent to prison for a long sentence, much less life. Then there was his sister, who lived in Los Angeles. She had allowed for her house to be used as a stash house for Los Muchachos. Maybe, if the prosecutors were willing to give his sister immunity from prosecution, he might sign a cooperation agreement.

Thus began a negotiation. The investigators were in no hurry. Let Recut stew behind bars for a while. Let him approach us.

They had as witnesses peripheral though important figures such as Jack Devoe, Ray Corona, and Jorge Valdés. They had accomplice witnesses such as Sermon Dyess Jr., Butch Reddish, Shaun Murphy, and others. That was all good. But they weren't Juan Barroso. If they got him—powerboat smuggler, Seahawk team member, cocaine courier, and all-around errand boy for Los Muchachos—Recut would be the first bona fide insider to flip and become a snitch.

IN LATE 1990, WILLY HEARD from his attorney Mark Dachs that the US attorney's office had finally moved in on all their properties. They seized the condos in Vail, which were owned on paper by one of their Panamanian shell companies. This meant that investigators had likely learned through Juan Acosta's legal files about Falcon and Magluta's various holdings and accounts. There would be no more post–New Year's vacations in the snowy mountains of Colorado. No more making snowmen with the kids. Those days were over.

Willy had sold his fifty-four-foot Bertram Motor Cruise yacht the previous year, but he kept the smaller thirty-five-foot Sports Fisherman Bertram. The government came for the yacht with a SWAT team and helicopter that scared the hell out of two or three mechanics who were working on it at the time. With a helicopter circling overhead, DEA agents and local Miami-Dade officers showed to the mechanics, and also employees of the Brickell Key Marina, drawings of Willy Falcon as he might look in different guises, with long hair, a mustache, a shaved head. Everyone said they had never seen the guy.

To Willy, it was almost as if you could hear the footsteps of the law getting closer and louder.

One afternoon, Tony Garrudo, El Cuño, came over to Willy's Fort Lauderdale house in a state of agitation. He had just come out of a liquor store when he ran into Tony Posada. A low-level cocaine dealer in Miami, Posada had stepped on a lot of toes. Willy remembered one time when Tony Posada had the audacity to rip off Mario Valencia of the Cali Cartel by telling him that a plane he had been using to transport kilos malfunctioned, and they had to drop the load into the ocean. It turned out to be a lie. Valencia had wanted to kill Tony Posada, but Willy talked him out of it.

Said El Cuño to Willy, "His eyes were bugging out of his head. He said someone planted a bomb in his car and he almost got blown to pieces. Then someone tried to shoot him. He believes that it was either you, Sal, or Mario Valencia. He says you guys better back off because he has already contacted the FBI."

"This fucking *pendejo*," said Willy. "If it wasn't for me, he would have been dead a long time ago."

"He says he had a conversation with Jorge Valdés from prison. Jorge says you guys have a hit list of potential witnesses and you or the Colombians are going to start killing people."

"See that, the rats are already starting to get together to feed on their own paranoia. They're already spreading lies amongst themselves."

Willy went on a mini rant about the underworld code of honor. "When you go into a business like ours," he said to his brother-in-law, "there's an old saying: You are given two bags, one is for the money you make from your illegal activities, and the other is for the time that you could be facing if you get arrested. If this happens, and you get stuck with that bag of time, that's tough luck. But you don't betray the code of loyalty. You go to prison and do the time. If you can't accept the pressure and handle the consequences of doing time, then it's best for you to find another profession. Maybe a car salesman, or work in an office, or do anything you want that's not illegal."

"Well, I thought you should know right away about this guy Tony Posada," said Tony.

"You did the right thing," said Willy.

That afternoon, while Tony was still at the house, Sal came by, as he sometimes did to work the shortwave radio with Willy. They would sit in the back of the Astro van and communicate with Mario Valencia in Cali, or Pablo Escobar wherever he was hiding out, or the Mexicans in Jalisco and Juárez, or Freddy Cruz in LA, or Monguito in New York City.

With Sal that day was Jorge "Fat George" Lopez, his sidekick who had moved from Los Angeles and, along with Benny B., was living with Sal in the mansion at La Gorce. Lopez was a 260-pound hanger-on who had attached himself to Sal Magluta. He had once acted as a cash courier, delivering, along with Pepe (a.k.a. Frijol), a couple of briefcases filled with millions from Los Angeles to Las Vegas, where the Boys would gamble it all away. In Miami, Lopez was not trusted by some Muchachos. Tony Garrudo, for one, did not like Fat George and said so to Willy. Falcon was perturbed that here was this acquaintance at his house for the first time. He pulled Sal aside and said, "What the fuck is he doing here?"

"Who? George? He lives with me."

"Sal, there are exactly four people who are supposed to know where I live. You, my wife, El Cuño, and my bodyguard, Carlos. Okay, also my kids, who have been trained to say nothing to nobody. My brother, for his own protection, I do not burden him with knowledge of where I live. Now you bring this asshole over here who I don't even trust? That's a violation of my security."

It was unusual for Willy and Sal to have words. In their entire time together, it happened maybe two or three times. Sal seemed surprised by how angry Willy was; maybe the pressure was getting to them. Maybe everybody was a little bit on edge. Sal knew he was at fault, but he did not apologize. He merely nodded his head and said, "Okay, okay, I get it."

IN APRIL 1991, WILLY AND SAL had their first conversations with Justo Jay and Tony Bemba since the two had been—separately—convicted and sent away to prison. Both had recently been transferred from different states to the Metropolitan Correctional Center (MCC) in Miami, where they were part of a large contingent of inmates in the prison system who had been brought to the city to appear in front of the latest grand jury investigating Willy and Sal.

Willy was nearly in tears as he took the cell phone from Miguel Vega, the Los Muchachos member who took the call from Jay. They were at Sal's house on La Gorce.

"My brother," said Falcon, "how are you doing?"

"Under the circumstances, Doctor, I'm not doing too bad," said Jay

Jay explained the reason for his call. In the MCC, where he was being held, dozens, if not hundreds, of inmates had been brought by the federal prosecutor and DEA agents to be interviewed as potential witnesses in the case against Willy and Sal. Jay had spoken with some of these people, and they all shared similar stories of how they were being encouraged to trade information and coordinate their stories, to give "evidence" whether it was true or not. "I've had people come up to me and offer to pay me money if I'd give them stories about you and Sal in the coke business," said Jay.

Later, they heard from Tony Bemba. He was calling by phone from the MCC, where he was being submitted to the same scenario as Jay. "I've had people who I've never met in my life tell me they were part of Los Muchachos and are looking to score a deal with the prosecutors," said Tony Bemba. He warned Willy and Sal that the unsealing of their indictment must be imminent, given the way the government was trolling for witnesses against them.

Talking with Jay and Tony, who were both now serving long sentences, was an emotional experience for Willy and Sal. These were their blood brothers, friends, and partners whom they had known since childhood. They wanted to help them out in some way but felt powerless.

After speaking with Jay and Tony, Sal said to Willy, "Hey, let's go to CMM Ranch in Horse Country." He said it almost as a challenge. Willy said, "Yeah, let's do it."

Willy called Tony Fandino, who years earlier had traveled with them to Colombia to meet Escobar and the Valencia brothers for the first time. Fandino had been serving as a caretaker of the ranch. He had the keys. They told him to meet them at the house.

They stepped outside, got into Willy's Audi, and drove south.

By then, most of their properties, businesses, and toys had been seized by the government. The CMM Ranch, their man cave, had also been foreclosed on, but Los Muchachos had surreptitiously reclaimed it at auction. The property just sat there; the Boys felt it was too risky for anyone to show their face at the ranch. Other than Tony Fandino, no one had been there in years.

When Willy and Sal drove up to the property, it looked as though it were frozen in time. Nothing had changed. Sal still had the remote control for the garage door. He opened it, and they parked the car, closing the door behind them.

Willy and Sal exited the garage and walked toward a building behind the main house that had served as a gym. Sal peered in the window and said, "Damn, it's exactly the same as it was when we left it three and a half years ago." They went next door to a homemade basketball court, outdoors, but with an awning and sidewall that blocked viewing it from the street. Willy picked up a basketball and they began shooting baskets, as they had done many times back in the day.

Tony Fandino approached. "You guys are crazy. You know you shouldn't be here. I've seen police cars come by here many times. I even saw one parked on the corner like they were waiting for you guys to show up."

Said Willy, "We looked. There's nobody out there. We made sure nobody saw us pull into the garage."

They walked over to the batting cage that they had installed on the property. Sal turned on the automatic pitching machine. They filled it with softballs, grabbed a bat, and took turns hitting pitches from the machine. Willy told Fandino, "Hey, go get us some beers, will you? We're gonna be here for a while." Tony drove to the market and returned with a six-pack of Michelob Light. Then he positioned himself to serve as lookout as Willy and Sal hung out and reminisced about old times.

"Remember that time . . ." became the common intro to their many stories about Jay, Ramiro, Benny B., Tony G., and all the rest. There was a time when they met at this location multiple times every week to play games, do lines of coke, work out, eat, and strategize about their business. Those were good times, and it seemed as though they would never end. Where had the years gone? Although their cocaine business was still generating more money than ever before—somewhere around $1 billion—those days of camaraderie had been disrupted and driven underground. Now it felt more like they were hunted animals, and every day of freedom was a reprieve, or a gift from God.

Whacking softballs, shooting baskets, and sipping beer from a can, they considered their options. "We could go live in Tijuana," said Sal, "run the business from there."

"We have an open invitation in Colombia," said Willy. "Mario's been trying to have us move there for years."

They both knew it was unlikely they would go into hiding in another country, leaving behind their wives, kids, and extended family.

"There is another option," said Sal. "We could try to work out a deal with the government, negotiate a settlement where we turn over money, plead guilty to some charge lesser than the continuing criminal enterprise. If we could negotiate a sentence less than fifteen years, we'd be out one day and still have a life with our families."

There was a time, not long ago, when they never would have considered such a proposition. But now it felt like an option worth exploring. Said Willy, "Let's run it by the lawyers and see what they say."

Willy took a swing at an incoming pitch and fouled it off.

The next day, Willy and Sal had Mark Dachs and Joe Oteri contact the office of the US attorney for the District of South Florida. The offer was as follows: Willy and Sal would pay $25 million in cash, they would forfeit all real estate holdings, and they would lead federal agents to one thousand kilos of cocaine in storage. In exchange, their sentence would be in the fifteen-year range.

Weeks went by before they heard anything in return. At Sal's mansion, they spoke on a conference call with the attorneys. Joe Oteri told them at first representatives from the US attorney's office seemed interested. They said they needed to discuss it with higher-ups. Then they came back to the lawyers and said, "Look, for us to even discuss the terms of something like this, Falcon and Magluta need to first turn themselves in. Then we can talk about a plea deal. And you should know that any deal, no matter the length of the sentence, would involve Falcon and Magluta cooperating with the government in other criminal cases we are investigating."

"That means snitching," said Willy.

"Correct," said the lawyer.

"Fuck that," said Sal. "That's something we'd never agree to."

"They got the wrong guys," said Willy. "We're not built like those weak punks they've been rounding up to testify. We come from another type of cloth. Forget about us cooperating with any kind of law enforcement. They can come and get us."

"Okay," said the lawyer, "I will let them know."

They hung up the phone. Willy said to Sal, "Well, partner, at least we tried."

May 17, 1991

It was around ten a.m., and Willy had just rolled out of bed. The phone rang. Cautiously, Willy answered it. On the other end of the line was Ileana Garrudo. She was upset bordering on hysterical. "Willy, DEA, FBI, US Marshals, and a bunch of local police raided our house in the Gables at five o'clock this morning. They arrested Tony and took him to prison on account of the indictment against you and Sal, which I guess they have now unsealed. They had a search warrant for the house. They searched everything and destroyed my place."

"That is terrible," said Willy. "I am so sorry."

"They confiscated everything they claimed was related to you guys. The safe, the jewelry, and everything else. They searched the house for five hours before they finally let me, my kid, and the nanny back inside. I'm calling you right now on a public pay phone. I drove to Seven-Eleven to call you."

"Listen, Ileana, we will deal with this. We will get Tony out of there."

"Willy, they showed to me and the nanny computer sketch drawings of you with long hair, a goatee, and from different angles. They tried to force the nanny to identify you. They asked her questions like if you ever visit the house, has she seen you at all, especially lately. I felt bad for her."

"Ileana, listen to me, this is important: Call the criminal attorney Frank Rubino and make sure he handles Tony's case. Tell him to try and get Tony out on bond at his arraignment tomorrow. I'll call Frank also to make sure that he goes to visit Tony in jail immediately. Anything that you need, just let me know. And call me back if you hear from Tony."

Willy hung up and immediately called Sal. He explained the situation and had Sal call around to their people and tell them to "be on point" and stay away from their homes. Apparently, the indictment had been unsealed, and the shit was going down.

Willy called Frank Rubino. Of all the hotshot criminal defense attorneys in town, Rubino was in the upper echelon. A former Secret Service agent who once protected Richard Nixon in Key Biscayne, Rubino had represented Carlos Lehder Rivas of the Medellín Cartel, and, most recently, he had become lead counsel for General Manuel Noriega, who was in a local prison awaiting trial in Miami. Rubino was already on it. He had obtained a copy of the indictment, hot off the presses. Said the lawyer, "Send one of your people over to my office and I'll give you a copy."

After getting their hands on the indictment, they all met over at Sal's compound on La Gorce. One of the most alarmed was Benny B., who discovered that along with Willy, Sal, and Tony Garrudo, he also was listed as a defendant. There were six others: Luis "Weetchie" Escobedo, Victor Alvarez, Dominique

Gonzalez, Pedro "Pegy" Rosello (whom they had indicted under his alias Luis Mendez), Juan Barroso, and Gustavo "Tavy" Falcon.

Right away, Willy received a call from Vega informing him that Willy's father had called and asked him to relay a message. That morning, a large squad of US Marshals, DEA officers, FBI agents, and all kinds of police officers raided Tavy's home. They spent six hours turning the place upside down. But Tavy, his wife, Amelia, and their two kids were nowhere to be seen. They got away.

The leadership of Los Muchachos took stock of the damage: Tony Garrudo, Juan Barroso (who was already incarcerated), and Weetchie Escobedo had all been arrested and charged on various counts of cocaine smuggling, and, in some cases, money laundering. Willy's brother-in-law Dominique Gonzalez was also indicted, but he fled the country to Mexico City and would not be captured until 2002. In the indictment, Willy and Sal were charged on twenty-four counts for having imported seventy-five tons of cocaine totaling $2 billion in proceeds. They were also charged with being the leaders of a continuing criminal enterprise, which, if proved, carried a natural life sentence in prison.

Pegy Rosello had evaded arrest, but he would be found and arrested within the next few weeks. Willy, Sal, and Benny were hunkered down and still hiding out. The feds did not know where they were. Tavy, it seemed, had, for the time being, escaped into the wind.

The main thing was for Willy and Sal to secure legal representation for all their people. There were wives, girlfriends, and extended family members who needed to be reassured that their loved ones would be taken care of, to the extent that they could be now that they were under indictment.

Other than that, for Willy, Sal, and Benny, little changed. The day after the arrests, Willy received a call on the transmitter from Monguito in New York. He advised the Boys that he had just received three semis with a total of 4,500 kilos at the Hunts Point market in the South Bronx. All the kilos were accounted for at the stash houses. Willy told Monguito to deliver 3,500 kilos to Pacho Herrera's people in New York and to distribute the other 1,000 kilos to their various clients in the city.

Willy called Jojo Brito in Los Angeles and asked, "Hey, Jojo, do you have that twenty million in cash ready to send to Miami?"

"Almost," said Jojo. "It's here, all I need to do is finish counting it first, then I will send it with the semi as soon as possible."

"Good," said Willy. "With all the lawyers and everything, we're gonna need that money."

Just to be safe, that summer Willy rented a private house at the beach in Fort Lauderdale that nobody knew about—not even Sal. Willy had plenty of time to spend with Alina and the kids, and he could take care of narco business on the transmitter in his van, which was always kept nearby.

On long, sunny days and warm, sultry nights at the beach house, Willy did what he had been doing for nearly four years now, mastering the life of a fugitive on the run, drinking wine, the occasional toot, working out at the home gym, and monitoring the ominous forces that seemed to be taking shape on the horizon.

Since the arrest of Pegy, Willy was on the phone constantly, trying to get him bonded out of jail. The attorney they hired for Pegy was Vincent "Vinny" Flynn, another seasoned member of the city's high-flying criminal defense bar. Flynn had been arguing Pegy's case at various bond hearings, but it didn't seem likely that Pegy would be released from jail before a trial took place. This concerned Willy, Sal, and especially Benny B., who thought that the kid was weak and even "retarded," or "goofy."

In early October, Willy heard from Vega, who had become the group's primary communications intermediary. Vega told Willy that he had just heard by phone from Vinny Flynn, who told him that when he tried to visit Pegy that morning in the North Dade jail that houses federal prisoners, Pegy declined his lawyer visit.

For a few seconds, Willy felt a sense of vertigo, his world turning sideways. "I don't like the sound of that at all," he said.

He called Sal and told him the news. "That is not a good sign, my brother. Pegy knows about your house on La Gorce. You should move out of there for at least a month or so till we know what's happening with this kid."

"I'm going to play it by ear," said Sal.

Willy hung up.

October 15, 1991

That morning, Benny Lorenzo took the car and went to run some errands. At the time, he was driving a Honda because it was an inconspicuous vehicle that would not attract attention. Storm clouds were gathering, and it looked like it was going to be a rainy day. After running errands, Benny stopped at a gas station near the compound on La Gorce to tank up:

> While I'm pumping gas, I see a car with tinted windows just sitting there. Whoa. I didn't like that at all. I put the nozzle back, pay up, and I leave. I drive around in a circle for a while, to make sure I'm not being followed. When I get to our place, I drive up to the gate, as always. There was a guard in the booth who was there nearly every day, the same guy. But today it was somebody different, a Black guy.

It all made Benny uneasy. He relayed his concerns to Sal.

"Come on, Benny, you're just freaking out, like you always do," said Sal.

For years, Benny had been telling Sal that it wasn't safe for them to be there. Occasionally, Sal would agree, then he would become comfortable and change his mind. One thing that Benny never stopped harping on was the fact that Sal kept the gang's ledger books in a safe on the premises. Everyone told Sal that wasn't good enough. The ledger books should be kept somewhere else, in a separate location, so if there were ever a raid, they would not be sitting there waiting to be found. Sal would respond as if he shared the concern, then he wouldn't do anything about it.

Benny figured he would go work out at their home-built gym, in a small house behind the main house on the property. By then, it had started raining a bit, and it felt like it was going to turn into a torrential downpour. As Benny approached the gym, he noticed there were two guys working on a satellite dish up on the roof. Benny felt a shudder through his body. Everything that day seemed off. Everything felt ominous and out of the ordinary. But it was also true that he had been on the run with Sal for so long that it was easy to dismiss concerns and worries: he had had them many times before, and they always turned out to be nothing.

Benny opened the gym door and entered. As soon as he did, he heard a loud bang like an explosion from somewhere outside, then the sound of helicopters and voices shouting. He stepped outside.

Two helicopters were hovering overhead and coming in low. From the perimeter of the huge yard, Benny saw what looked like soldiers holding guns coming out of the bushes. It was hard to tell because it was raining, and it was also smoky with what turned out to be tear gas. Many of the soldiers were wearing gas masks.

Benny ran for the main house and burst through the door. He shouted, "Sal, Sal, it's the cops!"

WILLY WAS GETTING ANNOYED WITH Sal. They had arranged to be on the transmitter with Mario Valencia at six p.m. They were all supposed to call in on the usual frequency at that hour. Willy and Mario were on the line, but Sal was not. Mario was looking to raise the next shipment on the Chilean freighters to forty thousand kilos.

Said Willy, "Let me see if I can find him. We will meet back here on the transmitter at seven thirty p.m. Okay?"

Mario agreed, and they signed off.

Willy called Sal's cell phone twenty times. No response. He called Sal on his beeper and left their agreed-on emergency code—17. Still no response. Strange. It was an understanding they had that when either of them called, the other responded right away. If one of them didn't respond—like the day Sal got pinched at the Dolphin Office Products store—it was invariably a bad sign.

At seven thirty, Willy called Mario on the transmitter: "He's not responding."

Said Mario, "Well, what should I do?"

"Go ahead and order the kilos and I will handle it."

Alina had made reservations for them at eight p.m. at a new Chinese restaurant in Fort Lauderdale that was getting great reviews. They drove there in their black convertible BMW. After leaving the car with the valet, they entered the restaurant and were shown to their table. Years later, Willy remembered:

> The restaurant was excellent. I had a big snapper, baked snapper, with the caramelization on top. The Chinese put that slightly sweet sauce on there. That was fantastic. I could really taste that fish. I guess I knew it was the last one I was going to eat in the free world for a long time.

SAL HUNG FROM THE BALCONY on the second floor of the house at La Gorce, and he dropped to the ground. It was on the only side of the house where there were no cops. The noise was incredible. Helicopters, dogs barking, sirens, and smoke wafting in the air. The rain was coming down now—a tropical rain, warm and humid. Sal ran into the bushes and looked for a place to hide.

Inside the house, Benny had nowhere to go but up. He knew they were surrounding the house, so he raced up into the attic and bolted the door shut. He heard someone shout over a bullhorn: "You are under arrest! Do not try to hide! Do not run. Come out with your hands raised!"

He started destroying all his communications devices. He smashed his various cell phones and tried stomping on his beeper until it was obliterated.

By then, the invaders had set off tear gas canisters in the house. The smoke quickly rose upward. Benny could see it seeping in under the door. He tried rolling up a blanket and putting it at the base of the door, but soon he was coughing, his eyes watering. He could barely breathe.

He pulled the door open and headed downstairs, his hands raised high. "I'm unarmed. Don't shoot!" he shouted as he descended the stairs.

It was a surreal scene, almost like a science-fiction movie. The SWAT team members were all dressed in black, wearing gas masks and bulletproof vests, and carrying high-powered weapons. As soon as Benny came down the stairs, they grabbed him and ushered him out the front door.

At least he could breathe. Cops were swarming the yard. They pushed him down on the ground. "Face down, on your belly!" somebody shouted. "You're under arrest."

The rain was persistent. All Benny could see was feet everywhere, the SWAT team's boots and the black patent leather shoes of federal agents. Benny heard someone walking on gravel toward him. The person stood over him, reached down, and grabbed Benny by the hair. He pulled Benny's head up so that Benny could see him. It was DEA Agent David Borah, who smiled and said, "Benny B. How are you?"

Benny looked up at the guy.

Said Borah, "You saw what happened to Justo Jay. You saw what happened to Tony Bemba. If you don't help me, the same thing's gonna happen to you."

"I got nothing to say, man."

They left Benny lying there for a while, in the rain. Then they put him in the back of a sedan, his hands cuffed behind his back. As he watched the SWAT team dressed in rain gear, with their search dogs and rifles, he figured they were searching for Sal. It took about a half hour, and then a gaggle of agents showed up with Sal in tow, cuffed and soaked to the bone. The agents put him in the back of a sedan parked next to Benny's.

They sat there for a while, with rain pounding the hood of those cars. Through the window, Benny could see a couple of agents, including Borah, talking to Fat George Lopez, who had also been in the house. He wasn't handcuffed. Benny got the impression they had brought George over near where he and Sal were so they could see the conversation. They couldn't hear anything, but Benny saw the lips moving. George was doing all the talking.

Benny could see Sal in the other sedan. They could both see George with Borah and the agents. Benny gave Sal a look: *This cocksucker. He's telling them everything, including where to find Willy Falcon.*

ON THE WAY HOME FROM the Chinese restaurant, Willy continued calling Sal's number on the cell phone.

Said Alina, "You're really worried, aren't you? Maybe you should stay at the beach house tonight until you find out what's going on with Sal."

Willy thought about it and said, "No, I'll stay at the Seminole house. He does this sometimes, you know? He's supposed to call, but he doesn't."

They got back to the house. There were no kids there; they had all been sent to live with their in-laws during the school year. It was safer that way. Investigators could not use the kids' coming and going to school as a way to track Falcon's whereabouts.

It was a massive house; when the kids weren't there, it felt empty. Both Willy and Alina headed upstairs to the master bedroom to get ready for bed. Alina went into the bathroom to remove her makeup, wash her face, and get ready to turn in. In the bedroom, Willy undressed and put on sweatpants and a black T-shirt with the Seahawk racing logo on the front.

He heard the distant sound of a helicopter. In Fort Lauderdale, or any city or town on the South Florida coast, the sound of a Coast Guard helicopter is not uncommon. It was almost like the sound of a police or ambulance siren in New York City. Every hour on the hour, helicopters cruise the surf looking for rafters or anything else out of the ordinary. But this helicopter sounded as if it was getting closer. Also, there was more than one. Willy thought, *Am I just being paranoid, or are those helicopters headed right here to my house?*

Before he could answer that question in his mind, the roof began to vibrate. The helicopters were over the house. Willy shouted, "Alina, it's them! They're here for me!"

Alina bolted out of the bathroom.

Said Willy, "Don't answer any questions they ask you."

They had talked about this, what to do or say when the law showed up. Basically, you say nothing. If the cops asked, "Is Willy here?" and you said, "Willy doesn't live here," you could be charged with harboring a fugitive. Keep your mouth shut.

They were banging on the front door with a battering ram.

Said Willy, "Go ahead, get dressed and go down there. Stall them if you can. Ask to see the warrant."

Alina left the room.

Hurriedly, Willy gathered up his six cell phones, his beepers, and a .380 pistol that he kept in the bedroom. He headed out on the second-floor balcony that overlooked the canal. It was his intention to throw everything into the water. What he saw made him feel as if a massive snort of coke had just hit his brainpan. There was a fifty-six-foot Coast Guard vessel, with the Coast Guard flag waving in the wind, and three or four speedboats. There were two helicopters circling overhead. Floodlights illuminated Willy on the balcony. Urgently, he went back inside and threw the phones and beeper onto the bed. He put the gun under the box spring mattress. He frantically grabbed papers, written notations—anything that might connect him to the cocaine business—and started flushing it down the toilet.

Over the bullhorn, they were calling for him to come downstairs with his hands up.

Willy walked out of the bedroom with his hands above his head. There were many commando cops with their guns raised. The first thing he noticed were the red dots on his black Seahawk T-shirt, all over his chest and stomach—their guns pointed in his direction.

As he came down the stairs, he saw Alina seated in a chair with a woman agent wearing a DEA jacket standing next to her. The agents grabbed Willy and cuffed him behind his back. As they led him toward the door, he looked at Alina and mouthed the words, "I love you. I'm sorry."

As soon as they brought Falcon outside, the agents gathered around. Somebody snapped a photo or two. A voice from the crowd said, "You got rabbit blood. We couldn't catch you, but we got you now."

Willy looked out over the agents. A light was glaring in his face, so he couldn't see much, but he said to the crowd, "Fuck all you bitches."

They put him in the back of a sedan with two US Marshals, Sean Convoy and Keith Braynon. Marshal Convoy turned to Falcon and said, "Don't worry, Willy. You're gonna be like any other drug dealer. You start cooperating with the government, you'll be out in three or four years."

Willy said, "You got me wrong, bud. If you think I'm a snitch, you're confused about life."

They drove Willy away to be arrested, booked, and processed at the federal detention center.

CHRIS CLARK WAS NOT ALONG on the raids at Willy's and Sal's homes. He was on the phone with David Borah, getting reports on the arrests effectuated by the US Marshals. As soon as those arrests were made, Clark and Borah appeared before the after-hours magistrate judge on duty and filed a search warrant to be executed immediately at both locations. The judge signed off on a handwritten affidavit and authorized the search of Falcon's and Magluta's properties.

It was a major night in the narco history of South Florida, back-to-back raids, arrests, and searches at the homes of two notorious cocaine kingpins. Helicopters filled the skies, and the agents, commandos, and cops came by land and sea.

Normally, prosecutors are not present at the scene of an arrest out of concern that they could be called as a witness. It was going to take hours for a team of agents, led by Borah, to search Willy's and Sal's homes. Clark would be on call throughout the night. For the next twelve to fifteen hours, nobody among the team was going to get much sleep. Even if they had wanted to, it might have been a physiological impossibility. The adrenaline was pumping, and the expectations were high.

After years of investigation, all the ups and downs, they finally had the tiger by the tail.

IV
DIRTY POOL

16

THE WHITE POWDER BAR

THE WAR ON DRUGS HAD become arguably the costliest domestic policy in the history of the US Department of Justice. In 1990, Attorney General Richard Thornburgh estimated that 42 percent of the DOJ budget had gone toward drug-related investigations and prosecutions. A sizable chunk of the system had been enlisted for this war. In South Florida, which had been the central theater of battle, there had been some noteworthy courtroom successes. In 1987, Carlos Lehder was convicted. Not only had the notorious Colombian narco's primary field of operation—the Caribbean islands—been greatly diminished as a smuggling route, but Lehder's conviction also led him to cut a deal with the US attorney's office. Lehder agreed to testify as a witness at the Southern District of Florida's other major narco prosecution, the trial of Manuel Noriega.

Proceedings for the Noriega trial had begun on September 5, 1991—five weeks before the arrest of Willy and Sal. Opening statements began on September 12. Assistant US Attorney Michael Patrick "Pat" Sullivan gave the opening statement for the government. Noriega's lawyer was Frank Rubino, who was no stranger to Los Muchachos. At the same time Rubino acted as legal advocate for the deposed Panamanian dictator, he was serving as counsel for El Cuño, Tony Garrudo, then incarcerated at the federal holding center in Miami.

For the US attorney's office in the Southern District of Florida, the prosecution of Falcon-Magluta et al. was the third in a series of major prosecutions, but to the media, the case, so far, had been inauspicious. The media had been programmed to expect a lawman's bounty—large amounts of seized kilos, guns, and cash laid out on a table at a press conference announcing dramatic arrests and seizures. With Willy and Sal, there were no kilos to show off, little weaponry, and even less cash. The case was mostly all on paper—trafficking figures and money-laundering transactions. There were no homicide counts in the indictment—no dead bodies—which tended to mitigate against coverage in the age of "if it bleeds it leads." The *Miami Herald* buried its article on the capture of Willy, Sal, and Benny inside the newspaper under the lackluster headline "3 Arrested in Cocaine Operation."

As far as AUSA Chris Clark was concerned, the lack of media attention was okay with him. He had begun to realize that it was far more effective to build a case behind the scenes, without the targets of the investigation knowing precisely what was happening. It had been crucial to the capture of Willy and Sal.

Few among Los Muchachos even knew that a key element in the investigation so far had been the arrest of the Deer (El Venado), Bernie Gonzalez, the organizer of the gang's powerboat smuggling operations.

It was through an interrogation of Juan Barroso that Clark and David Borah learned about Gonzalez, who was an essential member of Los Muchachos. The investigators were able to secure a conviction against Gonzalez on marijuana-smuggling charges.

When Clark and Borah approached Gonzalez in jail—only two weeks before the arrest of Willy and Sal—they explained the situation. New sentencing guidelines, passed as part of the Anti-Drug Abuse Act of 1986, established mandatory sentencing on federal narcotics convictions—including marijuana—that, in his case, all but guaranteed a life sentence. To the astonishment of Bernie Gonzalez, he was facing close to forty years behind bars. Said AUSA Clark, "Once this was pointed out for him, and made clear, getting him to cooperate was not difficult."

Not only did Bernie Gonzalez start talking, offering up detailed accounts of the gang's cocaine-smuggling routes through the Caribbean islands in the early 1980s, he agreed to help recruit others in the gang as informants. El Venado was used to befriend and make overtures to Jorge Valdés and Pegy Rosello, assuring them that Willy and Sal were finished, they were "going down," and if Valdés and Rosello were smart, they would cut a deal with the government before it was too late.

The approach to Pegy was especially important. Gonzalez first talked with Pegy at the North Dade holding pen a week after Rosello had been arrested. In the recreation area of the facility, off in a corner, he said to Pegy, "If you don't cut a deal with the feds, you're going away to prison for the rest of your life. *Entiende?* Don't be *una idiota*. You're a young man. You still have a life ahead of you. You gotta look out for yourself."

Pegy had once been a stand-up guy; indicted in Los Angeles as Luis Mendez, he stood his ground, and that case was dismissed. But times had changed. Pegy had been arrested the day before he was scheduled to be married to the woman of his dreams. His arrest had turned their lives upside down. El Venado was right: as the youngest of the entire group, he had the most to lose. He still had his best years ahead of him, and he didn't want to spend them locked away in a federal penitentiary.

Gonzalez was so effective in recruiting Pegy that when Clark and Borah came to see Rosello a few days later, he drew them a map to Sal Magluta's house at La Gorce Island. And that was before they had even ironed out the terms of a plea deal, or before they had debriefed him to find out what he had to offer. Pegy was eager to make a big impression; he let Chris Clark know, *I want in.*

That map was what led them to Sal's house, and Fat George was what led them to Willy Falcon.

The dual raids netted considerable evidence, some of which would lead to other charges. At Magluta's house, they seized a half dozen of Sal's false driver's licenses under aliases, and at least one false passport, which was a federal offense. At Willy's house they found nearly $1 million in cash and jewelry, a small amount of cocaine, and a kilo of gold. They also found one false passport, three fake driver's licenses, and one unlicensed .380 Browning handgun under the bed. These would be separate charges from the main indictment, smaller cases that would keep the Boys tied up in legal jeopardy for months and years to come.

By far, the biggest discovery was a briefcase found by David Borah in an office on the main floor of Sal's home. It was Sal's office, with a framed photo of him and his kids prominently displayed, and many triumphant photos from his time with the Seahawk racing team.

There was a safe in the office, but it wasn't being used. Next to the safe was a briefcase, stuffed with ledgers of some kind. Borah flipped through the pages. They were written in code, with nicknames and abbreviations and numbers written in longhand. Borah was pretty sure he knew what this was: ledger books detailing the gang's financial transactions going back to at least 1987.

The first order of business would be to send the ledgers out to an FBI forensic team to analyze and decode their content. But before he did that, Borah contacted Chris Clark and said, "You'll never believe what we came across."

For months, Willy Falcon, Benny B., and others had been telling Sal that he needed to find a separate place to secure those ledgers. There they were, out in the open: Magluta hadn't even locked them in the safe.

This may have been Clark's first big case, but even he knew how important the ledgers could be. In a complex case like the one they were pulling together, you needed witnesses, but you also needed a single piece of evidence that tied it all together, a single narrative with numbers, dates, names, and transactions. An accounting of the business, down on paper, in ink, irrefutable. If these ledgers were what he thought they were, the prosecution was off to a good start.

THE FIRST MEETING BETWEEN WILLY, Sal, Benny, and their attorneys took place in the legal conference area at Miami's Metropolitan Correctional Center. The Boys were wearing dark green, standard-issue prison jumpsuits. The lawyers were wearing suits and ties. Present were Mark Dachs, Marty Weinberg, Joe Oteri, and Jimmy Lawson, who was an attorney with the law firm of Weinberg and Oteri in Boston. It was two days after their arrest.

Since the arrest, Willy's biggest concern was Alina, who he had been told at their bond hearing was arrested for harboring a fugitive.

"What about Alina?" Willy asked Mark Dachs as soon as they sat down with the lawyers.

Said Dachs, "Your wife was released from federal custody yesterday afternoon under a one-hundred-and-fifty-thousand-dollar bond. She is now home with your children. She sends her love and says not to worry about her. She is fine."

Willy was relieved. Alina's fate had kept him awake the last couple of nights. Now he was ready to get down to business and fight.

Joe Oteri explained the situation: "Already, the government is playing their games. They have filed a motion that myself, Joe, and Mark be disqualified from representing you in this case."

Dachs interjected, "They say we are what's called 'house counsel.' Based on that, we can be removed as your attorneys."

It was another legal sidebar in the government's War on Drugs. In recent years, federal prosecutors had set their sights on the criminal defense bar. Lawyers in Miami who routinely represented cocaine cases were characterized as "the white powder bar." Those attorneys who had bolstered their careers by taking on cocaine-related cases would be made to pay the price. There were many thorny legal issues: preparing false affidavits; discouraging arrested criminals from cooperating with the government (obstruction of justice); using legal fees—proceeds from illegal activities—to move money around from one lawyer to another (money laundering). In the War on Drugs, the government argued that an attorney acting as house counsel was basically a member of the criminal organization. In some cases, prosecutors were even using forfeiture laws to confiscate fees paid to attorneys.

The defense bar was stunned by the aggressive tactics, but many in law enforcement who saw criminal defense lawyers as criminal enablers were encouraged. "I look upon these lawyers . . . as traitors," said the chief of the US Customs Service branch in Miami. "Hell, are we in a war or not? Why aren't these guys being charged with treason?"[1]

Dachs said to Willy, Sal, and Benny, "There will be a hearing about this. But we must tell you, judges have been looking favorably on these motions by the government. It's very likely there will be a ruling in favor of the prosecution. We will be prohibited from representing you, and you will need to find new lawyers."

The three Muchachos looked at each other. Okay, right off the bat, it was clear the prosecutors were playing hardball.

Said Willy, "Can you recommend some criminal defense lawyers for us, people who you think are the best?"

"Yes," said Dachs. "We'll consult with one another and make up a list." Then Dachs added, "There's another problem. Money. Your bank accounts and other assets have all been frozen under a protection order from a US district judge. The government plans on seizing those accounts. You have no cash flow."

Said Sal, "Then how are we supposed to pay for our legal defense?"

---

[1] Around the time of Willy's and Sal's arrests, the Miami US Attorney's Office launched a racketeering case that wound up netting six local criminal defense lawyers: Michael Abbell, William Moran, Donald Ferguson, Joel Rosenthal, Robert Moore, and Francisco Laguna. Eventually, an indictment was unsealed, and the lawyers were charged with various criminal acts such as preparing false affidavits or trying to discourage clients (cartel members) from cooperating with the government. Four of the attorneys pleaded guilty (Ferguson, Rosenthal, Moore, and Laguna), and two were found guilty at a trial in which the guilty lawyers were used as witnesses against them. The case stunned the local white powder bar and signaled a new level of hostile engagement between criminal defense lawyers in Miami and federal prosecutors. (Frederic Dannen, "The Thin White Line," New Yorker, July 31, 1995.)

"Well," offered Joe Oteri, "that is exactly how the US attorney's office wants it. It's part of their strategy that you be forced to use a public defender provided by the government. Given the nature of the charges against you, any public defender who takes on this case will be overwhelmed. You will be operating at a huge disadvantage."

Said Willy, "We're not going to use a court-appointed lawyer. No fucking way."

Said Dachs, "Okay. But the fees for any top-line attorney who takes on this case will be substantial. Possibly in excess of one million dollars. You will need to figure out a system for them to be paid—possibly through a patron in another country. Something like that would be time-consuming and therefore prohibitive for the prosecutors to trace."

The Boys looked at one another and nodded; they would need some time to figure it out.

Over the next hour, the lawyers and defendants discussed the case. The lawyers warned that the case was still evolving—the government would be using its arrests to recruit new snitches and add further counts to the indictment. It was clear that the case was a major priority for the US attorney's office in Miami, and they would be coming after the defendants with everything they had.

Said Willy to the lawyers, "We talked about this among ourselves last night. Listen, any lawyers who represent us, we want them to know—we want you to know—we've had years to think about this. We knew this day was coming. The government thinks we are defeated. They think that because we've been arrested and charged, this is the end for us. But it's not the end. It's the beginning. We are prepared to fight."

Sal and Benny nodded in agreement. Said Sal, "They're gonna come at us with all they got, well, so are we. We're gonna fight fire with fire, if that's the way it's gotta be."

"Good," said Dachs. "You're gonna need that kind of attitude to get through this."

Their time was up. As the guards came to cuff them and lead them away, they were brimming with confidence. Willy and Sal had been successful at nearly everything they had done—the boat races, the softball league, the construction of a business empire, and, at every level, the cocaine trade. As far as they were concerned, the government didn't know what it had gotten itself into. At least, this is what they told themselves.

Despite the bravado, they were immediately made aware of who held all the cards. They were taken to a room and strip-searched. Willy stood naked in the middle of an absurdly cold air-conditioned room. "Lift your balls, bend over, and spread your cheeks," said a guard, who proceeded to shine a mini-flashlight into Falcon's rectum.

After Willy, Sal, and Benny had been searched, they put their jumpsuits back on. They were recuffed and shackled and led back to the segregation wing of the facility.

As they passed through an intake room, with guards shepherding other inmates through the room, Willy noticed a corrections officer whom he recognized. The guy was buffed, with close-cropped hair, Cuban-looking. It took Willy a few seconds to place the face: Jorge Luis "George" Hernandez.

Willy and Sal had gone to high school with Hernandez, who at Miami High was known by the nickname "Hawaii 5-0." Hernandez had also been a groomsman at Willy's wedding. Willy had once heard that George had gone into corrections as a profession, but until then he hadn't known where he worked.

Willy whispered to Sal, "Two o'clock, Hawaii 5-0." Sal saw the corrections officer and his eyes opened wide.

At that moment, Hernandez looked at Willy and Sal and rolled his eyes. It was his way of letting them know: *Here we are, old classmates from Miami High, together again after all this time.*

OF ALL THE PROBLEMS THEY were facing, number one on the list was communications. Among other things, there was still a major shipment of kilos coming north via the Chilean freighters. The cocaine did not stop simply because somebody got arrested. Normally, Tavy Falcon, as third in command, would have taken control of the shipments, but Tavy had gone on the lam and was in hiding. So far, Willy had no idea where his brother was hiding out.

In this first week of incarceration, Willy and Sal were in an isolation wing of the MCC, locked down in individual cells. The cells were seven by nine feet, with a bunk bed and a stainless-steel toilet built into the wall. Soon, they would be moved to general population, they were told. Right now, the dominant mood was one of uncertainty and confusion. Willy and Sal weren't even able to communicate with one another, much less the outside world. Until they could talk privately, likely during one of their daily conference meetings with lawyers, there was no way they could monitor their business.

That night, around ten p.m., Willy was lying on his bed when he heard an unexpected knock at the door of his cell. He rose and stood peering through the slit in the door. It was George Hernandez. "Willy," said Hernandez, "sorry that it's under these circumstances, but it's great to see you."

"Hawaii 5-0. It's been at least five years since I've seen you. How are you?"

"I'm good, Willy. Listen, how are you doing so far? Is everything okay?"

"Yeah, I'm fine. But I wonder if you could do me a favor. Would you contact my wife, my mother, and my father and let them know that I'm doing okay?"

"Yes, Willy, I will do that. I will contact them."

The next night, Hernandez was at Willy's cell again, talking though the slit in the door. "Willy, I spoke with Alina and with your parents. Your father said to tell you everyone else in the family is doing good, they are safe." Hernandez emphasized this part, making it clear to Falcon that this was a reference to Tavy, who had likely contacted their parents and let them know he was okay.

"Glad to hear that," said Willy. He mentioned to Hernandez that he hoped that when he was eventually moved to a unit not on lockdown twenty-four hours a day, he might get his hands on a portable phone so he could contact his people on the street. "Can you help me with that?" he asked.

"Willy, listen, I'm willing to do anything for my friends and brothers, anything that you need."

"God bless you, *hermano*." Willy listened as Hernandez, keys jangling, walked down the hall to Sal's cell to talk with him.

Willy sat on his mattress and thought, *Damn, Sal was right. Miami. Where would we be without our network of Cuban exile brothers in Miami?*

THE FOLLOWING MORNING AT TEN A.M., Willy, dressed in his orange jumpsuit, was brought to the lawyer visitation area. Joe Oteri was there with another man, a formidable character in his midsixties, with a large, clean-shaven head, an expensive silk suit and tie, and the demeanor of someone who meant business. Willy was certain he'd seen the guy before, but he wasn't sure where.

Oteri said to Falcon, "Willy, I'd like you to meet criminal defense lawyer Albert J. Krieger, one of the best in the business. He's here to talk with you about possibly taking on your case."

Now Willy remembered: he'd seen the face on the television news. Albert Krieger represented the Mafia boss John Gotti in New York City.

They took a seat. For the next hour, Falcon interviewed the attorney to determine if he was the right man to hire. It turned out that Krieger had a license to practice law in both Florida and New York. "I have a strong desire to represent you, Willy. This is going to be a major case." Krieger mentioned some of the other cases he had handled, notably the Mafia boss Joseph Bonanno in the late 1960s, and, in 1973, a case of which Krieger said he was the proudest, his representation—pro bono—of members of the Lakota Sioux tribe who, as part of the American Indian Movement, had occupied Wounded Knee, South Dakota. Krieger helped win acquittals or dismissal of charges against nearly 150 defendants.

His most recent client, John Gotti, faced charges on multiple racketeering counts in the Eastern District of New York. That trial was scheduled to begin in the summer, five or six months away. It was believed that the Gotti trial would last four months. Krieger would not be available to represent Falcon at trial until the Gotti case was behind him, but in the meantime, his legal associates were fully capable of handling pretrial matters.

They talked about his fee, which would likely be in the $2 million range. Falcon assured Krieger that the fee would be paid, though the money would not be coming from him, since the district court, in furtherance of a motion filed by the government, put a restraining order on all of Falcon's and Magluta's assets. Payment could not come from them. It would come from a more round-about source. Said Krieger, "You are a lucky man to have friends who are willing to put up their own money to help you out in a time of need."

As a person who put a high premium on style and presentation, Willy was impressed with Krieger. He had gravitas, and he spoke in a resounding, mellifluous voice that sounded like something out of the Old Testament.

Krieger said to Willy, "If you ever decide to become a witness for the government, I will recommend another attorney to handle those negotiations with the prosecutors. I don't do those types of negotiations or representations."

Willy looked the lawyer straight in the eyes: "You will never have that issue with me as your client. The person you have in front of you would rather go to trial."

Willy told Krieger that he wanted to hire him as his attorney. The lawyer smiled and said, "I will give the court notice of my appearance on your behalf."

That same day, Sal was introduced to Roy Black, another heavyweight criminal defense attorney, whom he hired as his trial lawyer. Benny Lorenzo hired Jeffrey Weiner.

All of the lawyers agreed to a payment system for services rendered that would involve money orders and checks sent from a third party in another country, likely from banks in Venezuela, Panama, or Mexico.

After being locked up for one week, Willy was finally visited by his wife and his parents. It was an emotional morning in the visiting room. As direct family, they were allowed to embrace. Willy's mom and dad started to weep when they saw their son in his prison jumpsuit.

After they all sat down, Alina explained to Willy that, all things considered, the kids were okay. They were in school and staying with Alina's mother and father. She told Willy that, the previous day, she had gone with one of their lawyers to the house on Seminole Drive. The interior was practically destroyed. The government had seized pictures, exercise equipment, all of Alina's jewelry, and anything else of value. Alina was able to retrieve some of her clothes and had moved in with the kids at her parents' house.

Willy took Alina's hand, held her chin, and looked into her eyes. "*Mi amor*, I'm so sorry you've had to go through this."

Willy's father explained how the government had seized his and Marta's house at 8370 Southwest Second Street, in Dade County. They had moved into an apartment in Miami Beach. The US Marshals had also seized many of the properties that were in Arsenio's name.

Willy talked with them about his, Sal's, and Benny's case, trying to put a positive spin on things. He told them about taking on Albert Krieger as his attorney. "He's one of the best criminal defense lawyers in the United States," he said. "Krieger wouldn't take on this case unless he believed there was a chance we can beat these charges."

After about forty minutes, Willy pulled Alina aside and told her, "I need you to contact Miguel Vega." Vega was the manager of the organization, the go-to person now that the upper echelon of Los Muchachos was behind bars. "I need Miguel to take a cell phone and ten thousand dollars to George Hernandez. Remember him? He was a groomsman at our wedding."

Alina nodded.

"He works here as a correctional officer. George says that once we are transferred from segregation to a maximum-security unit, it will be more open. He will deliver the phone to us so we can communicate with people on the outside."

"Okay," said Alina, "I'll take care of that."

"I don't have to tell you, this is gonna be hard on our parents and maybe the kids. This is going to be a major test for us. We've had our issues, but nothing like this. We have to stay strong for everybody."

Alina nodded firmly. "Willy," she said, "my love for you has never been stronger than it is right now. Somehow, we will get through this."

As Willy was taken away, strip-searched, and led back to his cell, his eyes welled up when he thought about Alina and how strong she was being in the face of adversity. It was clearer to him now than ever before: he could have girlfriends, flings, even children with other women, but when it came down to it, Alina was the woman at his side. And if he had it his way, she would always be at his side, and he would make sure she was always taken care of, no matter what.

CHRIS CLARK RECEIVED WORD FROM the FBI's technical services division that, no doubt about it, the ledgers seized at Sal Magluta's house were indeed detailed financial records of Willy and Sal's cocaine business from 1987 to 1991. As exciting as that news was, it paled in comparison with what they had been getting from Pegy Rosello during ongoing debriefings. Rosello had given them the location of five separate stash houses in Little Havana. One stash house was in the home of Sergio Greco, a former minor-league baseball player (three seasons with the Triple-A affiliate of the Montreal Expos) whom Willy and Sal had first enlisted to play on their Seahawk softball team. Sergio was paid $25,000 to play for the team. That payment was eventually increased to $40,000.

One day, Sergio asked Willy if there was more that he could do for the organization than just play softball. Willy proposed that Sergio allow his modest home to be used as a stash house for kilos of cocaine. They would build a special compartment in the house—a clavo—where they could store as many as three thousand kilos at a time. They would pay him $40,000 a month, and no one would know about it except for Justo Jay, who oversaw the stash houses at the time.

Sergio thought it was a great idea. His home became one of the group's main stash houses.

In 1988, when Justo Jay was convicted and sent away to prison, Pegy Rosello took over as the manager of Sergio's stash house.

One month after the arrest of Willy, Sal, and Benny, David Borah and a team of DEA agents, along with a half dozen US Marshals, staged an early-morning raid on Sergio Greco's home. It was a major score. Not only did they confiscate three thousand kilos, which, at $15,000 per kilo, came to a total of $50 million worth of cocaine, but it seemed probable that Sergio would buckle and become a witness against the Falcon organization.

This bust gave the case something that it had been missing. The prosecutors now had plenty of kilos that they could showcase to a jury at trial. It was no longer only a cocaine case on paper. The prosecutors had the visual aids that were crucial to influencing a jury in court.

Clark was now working the case every day. US Attorney Dexter Lehtinen had entrusted the young neophyte with tremendous responsibility. Clark felt confident that he could handle the pretrial challenges, but he had known all along that when it came time to try the case in court, they were going to need an experienced trial lawyer. As he thought about who might be right for the case, there was only one prosecutor in the office who he thought was the perfect choice. He set his sights on star Assistant US Attorney Pat Sullivan.

Getting Sullivan to take it on was no sure thing. A fourteen-year veteran of the office, Sullivan was chief litigation counsel for the Southern District of Florida. Currently, he was embroiled in the Noriega trial, which had been ongoing for a couple of months and seemed likely to drag on until spring of the following year.

Well before he took on the Noriega prosecution, Sullivan had become a litigator whom Chris Clark and other AUSAs in the office viewed as a kind of North Star. Sullivan's upright, unfailing reputation made him a paragon of public service. He was an especially good choice for corruption cases, where there was no chance Sullivan might feel bad about prosecuting a fellow participant of the system—a cop, agent, judge, or government official on the take.

Starting in the mid-1980s, Sullivan had been lead prosecutor in a series of trials that had come to define the city's cocaine era. Corruption in law enforcement had become a major issue that undermined citizens' confidence in local Miami police. Criminals posing as police—like those who had kidnapped Marta Falcon back in 1981—had become a mini-epidemic in South Florida. That was why, in 1985, when a group of drug dealers were robbed by cops in uniform one night at a location on the Miami River, the detectives handling the case at first believed the perpetrators had to be bogus cops. During the robbery of four hundred kilos of cocaine, which took place on a boat called the *Mary C*, docked at the Jones Boat Yard on South River Drive, three dealers on the boat jumped into the river and drowned. The men in uniform absconded with $10 million in product.

An investigation of the robbery and the three deaths led prosecutors into a quagmire of corruption that stretched through many divisions of the Miami Police Department.

In 1986, AUSA Pat Sullivan became the lead prosecutor in what became known in the media as the "River Cops" case. It was a grueling prosecution, with hung juries and numerous trials that eventually led to guilty verdicts. Locally, it was a major news item, with daily articles in the *Herald* and reports on the nightly news.

It was a case that seemed to capture the mood of the times. The Noriega case, however, was international in scope, and it had raised Sullivan's profile to even greater heights.

Clark approached Sullivan in his office with a thumbnail explanation of the Falcon-Magluta case. He did not want to overburden him with too much background information while he was still in the middle of the Noriega case. Already, with the unavailability of Falcon's lawyer, Albert Krieger, and other scheduling issues, it had been determined that the trial would not begin for more than two years.

"Sounds interesting," said Sullivan, after Clark gave him the particulars. "The kind of case I would likely want to be involved with. But I can't give you an answer on that until we have a verdict in the Noriega trial."

Clark took that as a positive response. Having Pat Sullivan involved in the case would be a dream come true. He put that thought in his back pocket and continued his work on the case.

IN DECEMBER 1991, WILLY, SAL, AND Benny were finally transferred to E-Unit, which was a maximum-security unit elsewhere in the same facility. One hundred or so inmates were housed in this unit, which allowed for Willy, Sal, and Benny to leave their cells and circulate in common areas inside the building. There was a rec room with three television screens, two microwave ovens to heat up small food items, a wall lined with five collect-call telephones, and, outside, a cement surface, half-court basketball area for shooting hoops. The cells were tiered so that guards on various levels could also look down on the common gathering areas.

After having been in this unit less than forty-eight hours, Willy, Sal, and Benny one morning saw and made eye contact with George Hernandez. Part of the guard's duties involved searching the unit for weapons, alcohol, drugs, or any other contraband. Inmates and guards were not supposed to fraternize with one another. Willy got into one of the lines to use the phone so that he could approach his old neighborhood friend without being noticed.

Said George under his breath, "I see you guys are doing better. Now you have more freedom and you can move around a little."

"Yes," said Willy. "George, did you hear from my wife?"

"Yes, I did. I have the cellular phone at my house, and thank you for the money. You didn't have to do that. You know we are brothers and I'll do anything you guys need me to do."

Willy nodded his appreciation.

Said George, "Listen, tomorrow I will come into this unit around this same time. Part of my job is to search the trash cans. When I do that, that can over there by the stairs, in a brown paper bag I'm going to leave one cellular flip phone and two battery chargers. Wait until I leave the unit, then go over there and retrieve the package. Okay?"

Said Willy, "Got it. Thank you, brother. We will look for you tomorrow."

The next day, the three Muchachos awoke at seven a.m., along with every-one else, and sat in the rec area waiting for Hernandez to appear. Around eight a.m., George sauntered into the unit. He conducted his usual search, looking around the public areas in the unit and, casually, checking the trash cans with a wooden nightstick. Few inmates or other corrections officers paid much attention to Hernandez. When he got to the trash can by a metal staircase leading up to the various tiers, they saw him drop a package into the trash.

Even before they retrieved the package, Willy and Sal had spent the previous day deciding where they would store the phone and chargers once they had them. The cells were searched twice a day, once in the morning and once at night. The searches were thorough.

They came up with what they thought was a good plan. Using a nail clipper, Willy would carve out a brick from the wall in his cell. The empty space would be used as a clavo, or secret compartment. They chose a brick low on the wall and underneath the bed, not easy to spot. Once the flip phone and chargers were hidden in that space, they would then close it up by using toothpaste.

The toothpaste was white and stood out against the beige wall; this was a problem.

Out of sheer happenstance, some painters were on the unit that day painting the walls. The entire unit was painted in that same institutional beige color. Using his charms, Willy talked to one of the utility crew painters and convinced him to sell to Falcon a can of beige paint.

That morning, after Hernandez left the unit, Sal walked over to the trash can and discreetly retrieved the package. He took it to his cell and plugged one of the chargers into a wall socket (each cell had one) and connected the charger to the phone.

The Boys had to be patient. They wouldn't be able to use the phone until nine thirty that night, after the late-night count and then lockdown one hour later.

That night, the first call they made was to Miguel Vega. Sal held the phone, and Willy stood looking out the cell's small door window, making sure everything was clear. He could hear Vega's voice clearly.

Miguel was overjoyed to hear from them. They spoke in code, using their preferred terms "Betty" and "Martinez" in place of "cash" and "cocaine," and also an assortment of phrases and numeric codes designed to obscure the content of their conversation. Miguel explained that everything was going well outside in the real world. The big news was that Miguel Vega had heard from

Tavy Falcon, who was hiding out in the Florida city of Naples, on the Gulf of Mexico.

Said Willy, "Oh my God, you heard from my brother. That is amazing."

Miguel explained that Tavy was in good spirits. He was living under an assumed name with his wife, Amelia. He was living in Naples with Wilfredo Pino, a.k.a. Mata, his primary underling, who had also gone on the run and was hiding from the law. While in hiding, they were still able to manage aspects of the business. Tavy had been in touch with Mario Valencia. They were even discussing new routes. They were talking about bringing freighter shipments of kilos into Baltimore and Boston, where they had established new contacts.

"That's all positive news," said Willy. "I'm glad to hear it."

Miguel explained that Los Muchachos had received shipments of cash from Los Angeles and New York, as well as money that had been collected from clients in Miami. Miguel had already shipped $70 million in cash to Mario Valencia in Colombia in payment for a previous shipment. The money was carefully packaged inside stacks of paper and sent in the name of a paper company owned by the Valencia brothers in Colombia. The shipments were sent on a freighter from the Port of Miami.

"Beautiful," said Willy. "Even though we're locked up, we still make our payments. That's important."

Willy and Sal spoke with Miguel Vega for about half an hour, then they called Mario Valencia in Colombia.

Mario was amazed that they were able to call him from inside their prison cell. "Doctor, how are the feds treating you?" Mario asked Willy.

"Well, it's not exactly a five-star hotel," said Falcon, "but it's better than our accommodations last week, when they had us in the dungeon. We are holding up okay, and we are still taking care of business."

"Yes," said Mario. "We received your payment. Amazing. In prison, being harassed by the US government, and still you are able to fulfill your obligations. You, Sal, and your brother, Tavy, are the true gentlemen in this business."

Mario explained how he had been in touch with Tavy. They were moving forward with the new routes and shipments of cocaine from Cali, through Chile.

At times like these, with a narco partner facing problems with either other narcos or the law, partners sometimes felt the need to reaffirm their bond. Said Willy, "Mario, we have been at this for a while, and I hope you know how much me and Sal value our partnership. We want you to know that our operation has not been hindered at all. Now that we have open communications with you and all our people, everything will proceed as before."

Said Valencia, "The Cali Cartel is here for you, my friend, just as we always have been."

Willy had one last matter: he explained the situation with having to pay their lawyers through a third party in another country. They discussed how this might be done. Mario assured Willy that he would look into it and get back to him. Willy said he would call again the following night at this same time.

By the time Willy and Sal were finished talking with Mario, the battery was almost dead. They had to recharge it, which took one hour.

While they waited, quietly Willy and Sal talked about how gratifying it was to still have a functioning smuggling business even though they were locked up. The government thought that it could defeat them, but this was proof that they could not be defeated. For Willy and Sal, to still be trafficking kilos and making cash payments in the multiple millions of dollars meant that they were in control of their destiny. They were winning. And to them, winning was everything.

After the phone was recharged, Sal called his wife and spoke for thirty minutes. Then Willy called Alina. She was overjoyed to hear his voice. Willy reassured his wife that he was doing much better after having been moved out of the segregation unit. He felt strong, and now that he had a way to communicate with people by phone, he felt like he had his life back.

For most of the conversation, Willy let Alina do the talking. She spoke to him in calm and soothing tones about how everything was normal with the family. Though they had all lost their homes, many of their expensive belongings such as cars and boats, and had their lives turned upside down, Alina was determined to ease Willy's concerns. She seemed to understand intuitively what her role was in this situation: to help Willy settle his anxieties. She told him that within the next few days she would be visiting him at the prison with their two daughters, Aileen and Jessica. The idea of his daughters coming to visit him in prison brought moisture to Willy's eyes: partly, he would be embarrassed to have them see him in prison as a captured animal. But those concerns were overruled by the expectation of being able to embrace his kids for the first time in weeks.

It was two in the morning by the time Willy and Sal finished making all their calls. Willy took the phone and chargers back to his cell. After being locked in, he peered out through the small window in the door to make sure the coast was clear. Then he got down on his knees and used the nail clipper to pry the single brick from the wall. He placed the phone and chargers in the hiding place inside the wall, then he replaced the brick. Carefully, like a surgeon, he squeezed toothpaste from a tube to serve as mortar to hold the brick in place. Then, using his fingers, he dipped into his small can of beige paint and covered over the white toothpaste with a color that matched the preexisting grout. He leaned back and admired his work. Then he rose and slid his bed back into place. He put the toothpaste and paint away and washed his hands and face. He looked at himself in the mirror and thought, *You cannot fuck with Willy Falcon, you motherfuckers. Even behind bars, I will soar like a falcon.*

In bed, Willy stared at the ceiling. The adrenaline was still pumping from the various phone conversations he had had with associates and loved ones. He and Sal were in a maximum-security prison, and still they had the world by the balls. They had completed payment on a $70 million coke deal, and they had other major deals in the pipeline—including deals with new clients. They could not be stopped.

17

TRAIL OF DEATH

DETECTIVE RONALD "RON" ILHARDT, A twenty-two-year veteran of the Miami PD's homicide division, was the lead investigator at the scene when Juan Acosta was murdered in his law office. The crime scene was bloody and reeking of mayhem, but it did not appear to suggest an obvious motive. The gunmen had not previously known the lawyer, who was a real estate lawyer, not a criminal defense attorney (a more likely target of violence). It was not a robbery; the assailants did not ransack the office looking for valuables or legal files. In the account of the hit provided by Elizabeth Rodríguez, Acosta's secretary, the killers appeared to be hired hit men there to take out their target and then get the hell out. The secretary was Cuban. She determined from the accents of the killers that they were Colombian.

After some early, promising leads, the case had gone dormant, which is why Ilhardt was surprised when, in February 1992—two and a half years after the murder—he received a call from DEA Agent David Borah.

It was Borah who first provided the detective with a theory of the case. He had called Ilhardt the day after the murder and told the detective all about Acosta's upcoming date with a grand jury investigating Falcon and Magluta. "The lawyer was ready to talk," said Borah. "He knew all about their overseas accounts in the Caribbean and Panama. His testimony was going to blow it all wide open."

In homicide investigations, theories, like dreams, can be wonderfully instructive. But a detective still has a case to prove. He has to determine who pulled the trigger, and how it was done. It is all about the nuts and bolts of the act itself. Only then can a skilled investigator trace it up the chain of causation to determine who was the puppet master.

From the beginning, beyond the crime scene, Ilhardt had some leads. As one of the longest-serving detectives currently still active in the homicide division, he knew how to run a case. "It's like being the conductor of an orchestra," said Ilhardt. "As the lead investigator, I'm assigning my personnel to follow up on things. The killing took place in the middle of the day. I saw that there was a café nearby with outdoor seating. I sent a detective over there to interview everyone in the place. Right away, we had a witness, someone who had seen the getaway car. The witness gave us a description of the car. We checked with every used car lot in the city. Hired killers will often purchase a used car right off the lot, use it on their job, and then get rid of it. By that evening, we had what we figured was a positive ID on the car."

The getaway driver was a young Colombian named Juan Carlos Correa. The person who had purchased the car was Correa's older brother.

The detectives went to the apartment of Correa's brother. The brother was a legitimate, hardworking Colombian immigrant. He admitted that he had purchased the car for his brother, and he was stunned when he heard to what end it had been used. "I knew that maybe they were using it for something shady, a robbery or something like that. I never thought they were using it for murder." He explained that his brother, Juan Carlos Correa, was not a bad person. He was not a hardened criminal. But he had lately fallen in with some bad punks who regularly shuffled back and forth between Colombia and the United States. "They probably paid Juan a lot of money, and they used him because he was the only one who had a driver's license."

The next day, the detectives went to an apartment complex in Kendall, the address supplied by the brother. Parked outside the complex was the getaway car. Ilhardt called in a SWAT team, and they arrested Juan Carlos Correa. They brought him to the headquarters of the homicide division and put him in "the box," as the interrogation room was called.

Ilhardt had built his entire career on his skill at interrogation. As a detective, he made $120,000 a year. He was one of the highest-paid street cops in the Miami PD. He took great pride in his abilities: "I developed a skill set that was better than most, a reliability to interview and interrogate and get the information that you needed. How did I do it? I didn't care how long it took. I would sit in there twelve, fifteen hours interrogating people. And I wouldn't give up."

Juan Carlos Correa, age twenty-one, didn't take so long to crack. Within a few hours he confessed to having been the getaway driver. Partly, this was because Ilhardt threatened to also indict Correa's brother, since he was the one who had purchased the getaway vehicle. "My brother knew nothing about it," said Juan Carlos.

"Then you gotta come clean," said Ilhardt. "You gotta save your brother."

Correa did not immediately give up the names of his accomplices. He was shrewd enough to know he needed to use certain information to negotiate a deal for himself. He also understood that if he gave up the names, and his partners were immediately arrested, they would know he was the snitch. His life would be in danger.

Ilhardt and his partner, Detective Nelson Andreu, planned to let the kid stew overnight in jail. They put him in an isolation cell, on lockdown. They felt that if they left him in there for forty-eight hours, he would be ready to give up everything and everyone. As a psychological strategy, it usually worked.

Two days later, Ilhardt and Andreu came to pick up Juan Carlos Correa, and he was gone. One day earlier, agents from the US Marshals had come and picked up Correa. Acting on behalf of the US Immigration and Naturalization Service, they had seized the kid, put him on a plane, and sent him back to Colombia. He had been summarily deported.

Ilhardt was livid. He called around to find out what had happened. Unlike the time Sal Magluta had been mistakenly released from jail, which was the product of someone tampering with his record, this was simply a case of one hand not knowing what the other was doing. There had been a deportation order out on Juan Carlos Correa for more than a year. When he was arrested and incarcerated, it raised a red flag over at Immigration. They acted without ever thinking to notify the detectives involved in his arrest.

The Juan Acosta murder case became what detectives called a "dead fish." It lay there, lifeless, and gave off a bad stink. Then Willy and Sal got arrested.

Down south in Colombia, Juan Carlos Correa had seen a news report about Falcon and Magluta getting pinched in Miami—including the theory that they may have been behind the murder of Juan Acosta. Correa had been living in fear. When he was deported, he thought there was a good chance he was on somebody's hit list. That was the way it often worked: sicarios were sent to the United States to do hits. Afterward, they returned to Colombia and were paid for their services. For a while, they lived liked kings, spreading money in their barrio and among their friends. But the truth was, they knew too much. Whoever had given them the assignment to do the hit was part of a sequence of directives that went all the way up the chain of command. By doing a hit for the cartel, the sicario was now a potential threat to the organization.

Many sicarios, hired out of the worst slums in Medellín, Cali, and elsewhere, with no formal education, were not savvy enough to have thought it through. They never saw it coming.

Around the time that Willy and Sal were arrested, Juan Carlos Correa was stabbed—punctured eight times—on a bus in Medellín. He survived the attack and went into hiding. When he saw the report from the United States about the case against Falcon-Magluta, he called his brother in Miami and said, "Call that detective who was friendly with you. Tell him that I'm ready to tell everything I know. I'll give him names, including the connection not only to Falcon and Magluta, but to the Cali Cartel."

The brother called Ilhardt, who by then was in negotiations to retire from the Miami Police Department. "They were trying to get rid of all the old detectives with good salaries, so they could bring in younger people and pay them less. The negotiation went on for more than a year."

Ilhardt was "burned out," but he was not about to turn his back on an open case that nagged at his conscience. The detective picked up the phone and called Special Agent David Borah.

By now, Borah had been on the Los Muchachos beat for over five years. The Acosta murder alone had been an open case for a couple of years. Borah was used to getting tips and pieces of information about seemingly stale aspects of the case. But this one was exciting. Correa was promising to give them the entire Acosta murder. All the investigators had to do was come to Colombia and save his ass by getting him out of the country.

Ilhardt and Borah made plans to fly to Medellín's international airport. There they would be met by Juan Carlos Correa. They would bring him back to Miami, where he would be held in custody and debriefed about the case.

At least, that was the plan. But there were complications.

The immigration department told Ilhardt and Borah that Correa, as a violator of US immigration laws who had been deported as an undesirable, would not be allowed into the United States. He would be refused entry by US Customs.

Borah came up with an alternative plan. He said to Ilhardt, "How about if we take Correa to a neutral location. We'll fly him to Aruba and put him up there."

"Sounds good to me," said the detective.

Only problem was that when they checked with customs in Aruba, the investigators were told that the name of Juan Carlos Correa was on a list given to them by the US State Department. The names on that list, at the request of the US government, were to be denied entry.

It seemed that Ilhardt and Borah had hit a major roadblock. Then Ilhardt said, "Let me try something." He put in a call to a friend of his in the office of US Attorney General Janet Reno. Before she was appointed to her current post by President Bill Clinton, Reno had been the state attorney for Florida. Ilhardt's friend was able to make a plea on his behalf. Attorney General Reno allowed for Correa to receive a special one-day visa, so he could be brought to the United States for interrogation.

What Correa gave up to Ilhardt and Borah was worth the wait. He named the hit team, a Colombian assassin named Juan Velasco (a.k.a. Leopold Lopez), and the actual triggerman in the Acosta murder, an eighteen-year-old sicario named Manuel Mattos. The person who hired them for the hit was Javier Cadena, who was a known associate of the Cali Cartel. He was the one who could connect the killing of Juan Acosta to Willy and Sal.

The investigators now had the names of the entire hit team. Correa told them how the murder went down from his point of view as getaway driver. But they needed more. They needed to find at least one of the actual hit men and get him to confess to the crime. It was a tall order, maybe an impossible dream.

Once again, the case stalled. Ilhardt continued to negotiate with his employer of twenty-seven years over the terms of his retirement. Truthfully, he dragged his feet. He had no intention of leaving the job until he closed the Acosta murder case.

TAVY FALCON WAS UNDER A lot of pressure. As the only high-ranking member of Los Muchachos who had escaped capture, he was the de facto boss of what was now a scattered cocaine-trafficking organization. The kilos were still flowing, and it was Tavy's job to keep it that way.

The fact that he was still a free man was something of a miracle. At the time his brother was arrested, Tavy, his wife, Amelia, and their two children were living only a block away from Willy and Alina. They had only recently moved into that house, a massive ranch-style home with a large yard, located on the canals in Fort Lauderdale. On the night the raid occurred at Willy's place, Tavy and Amelia heard the sirens and saw the helicopters swirling nearby. They knew instinctively what was going down: Willy was being apprehended. They immediately gathered what they could in two small suitcases: mostly travel items and some clothes. They had two boats docked in the canal at their house, a large yacht and a smaller speedboat. In the dead of night, they got on the speedboat and pulled away from the house (their two kids were with Amelia's parents). They docked at a friend's place in Miami and stayed there for the night.

The next few days were chaotic. As they received information from Mark Dachs and other lawyers about who had been indicted, they made plans to flee. Tavy had been listed as a defendant in the indictment; he was a wanted man. They loaded up plastic garbage bags filled with millions of dollars in cash and, together with their suitcases, using whatever car was available at the time, they fled the city. They needed to go somewhere where they were not known at all, with no local connections, no potential informants. They wound up in the city of Naples on the Gulf Coast of Florida, a small, increasingly wealthy town with few Cubans, 127 miles due west from Miami.

Soon they were joined by Wilfredo "Mata" Pino. Mata was also a wanted man. He had been ratted out by Pegy. Authorities had no idea who Mata was until they debriefed Pegy, who kept saying "Mata this" and "Mata that," especially in relation to the stash houses. They showed Pegy a surveillance photo of someone they had seen frequently at the boat races. "That's Mata," said Pegy. An arrest warrant was issued for Wilfredo Pino. He gathered up his family and fled, heading for Naples to be with Tavy and his family.

Together, Tavy and Mata now composed the leadership of Los Muchachos. Though they were both wanted men, they were living in the free world and continued to function as decision makers and facilitators of Los Muchachos.

In Naples, Tavy and Amelia used the surname Reiss and claimed to be from Venezuela. Tavy occasionally spoke with Willy on his cell phone in prison, but not often. Willy and Sal were now mostly absorbed with formulating strategy for their legal defense. The cocaine business primarily revolved around terms that had already been set in stone. It was understood that Tavy had the authority to make decisions regarding the size and timing of shipments. He monitored the transference of kilos and cash.

Since the major cocaine bust in Southern California at the warehouse in Sylmar, the Boys had been exploring moving their initial point of entry into the United States from Los Angeles to Tucson, Arizona. Tavy met with Gilberto "Veci" Barrios, the leader of their trucking division, in Tucson to discuss the details of this move. Tavy also crossed the border from El Paso into Ciudad Juárez to meet with Amado Carrillo Fuentes, the Lord of the Skies, as Willy and Sal had done on numerous occasions. Along with the shipments using the Chilean freighters, Los Muchachos still had kilos coming from Amado's cartel in Ciudad Juárez.

Tavy respected Amado, but he had suspicions about the Mexicans in general. Amado had connected Tavy with his people in El Paso, Texas, which was the primary point of entry for his product. At a hotel in El Paso, Tavy met with the Mexicans, and he found them to be of dubious professionalism. Unlike the Colombians, who were businesslike and always reliable, some of the Mexicans were inclined to get high on their own supply. At another meeting with the Mexicans, in Houston, where Tavy was accompanied by Mata, one of the narcos was smoking crack from a pipe while doing business. Tavy was disgusted, but his organization was in deep with the Juárez Cartel. Later, Tavy made a point of telling Amado about it. "You need to surround yourself with better people," he advised.[1]

At times, Tavy felt overwhelmed. There were many decisions to be made and cocaine partners that needed to be cultivated and monitored. It was a lot of work for one person.

Back in Naples, Tavy, Mata, and their families sought to blend into the local culture. They rented a house, paying cash only. They had fake driver's licenses, fake passports, no credit cards, no bank account—nothing. Everything was paid for with cash. They pedaled bicycles everywhere they went, including to the grocery store to buy food. They rarely went to restaurants or public events. While out in public, they wore floppy hats and sunglasses. They befriended no one. Eventually, after they had been in hiding for four or five months, they

---

[1] Tavy Falcon would never see Amado Carrillo again. In July 1997, Carrillo, who by then was being pursued by Mexican and US authorities, died on the operating table as he underwent facial surgery to change his appearance. Some thought it might have been a hit, but there were two bodyguards in the operating room during the surgery. Four months later, the two surgeons who performed on the narco boss were found dead, encased in concrete inside steel drums, with their bodies showing signs of torture. (Molly Moore, "Dead Drug Lord's Doctors Found Embedded in Cement," *Washington Post*, November 7, 1997.)

arranged to have their two children come from Miami to live with them in Naples. The kids quickly learned the drill: they used the surname Reiss and were homeschooled by Amelia. They were cautious about making friends in Naples or revealing anything about their previous lives in Miami. As a unit, they became totally dependent on one another. Their universe contracted to contain two elements only: one, the family and their new lives as they had constructed them, making sure their existence was hermetically sealed and impenetrable; and two, for Tavy, the cocaine business and all that it presently entailed.

In Naples, Mata lived under the name Raúl Acosta. He opened a small karate school with a half dozen students. He taught them about knee kicks, elbow strikes, and knife hands. He showed them the modern style, using punching, grappling, throws, and attacking the vital strike points in an opponent's physique. When Mata wasn't teaching marital arts, he and Tavy would go golfing.

Tavy was a natural athlete and an effective teacher. He taught Mata how to golf. Later, Tavy also took Amelia to the golf course and taught her the basics. "He was so patient," she said. "That's the way he was."

Life underground was tough, but Amelia never lost faith.

I would have followed my husband to the ends of the earth. Whatever we needed to do to survive, I was ready to do it. And my kids felt the same way. We all became very close, very interdependent, much closer than we would have been had we been living a normal life. We were on the run, but we tried to make it normal. Though it was strange. It was definitely not normal. But whatever it was, we became such a tight family that you cannot imagine.

In March 1992, an event occurred that at the time did not look like anything major but turned out to be a kind of death knell. One of the truck drivers for the organization, a Cuban-born smuggler named Jorge Carnet, was hired by Manny Alonso to make a pickup of one thousand kilos from Jojo in Los Angeles. Six months earlier, unbeknownst to Manny or anyone else in Los Muchachos, Carnet had been busted while making a cocaine run for another organization. Using the threat of the government's new mandatory sentencing laws, federal prosecutors were able to compel Carnet to flip. Carnet told the prosecutors all about his work for the Falcon-Magluta organization. Carnet was sent back out on the street to work undercover and to gather information on Gilberto Barrios and Los Muchachos.

In short order, Carnet gave the prosecutors something that they did not have: inside information on Willy and Sal's extensive transportation system; and, even more important, he linked it all to Jojo Brito in Los Angeles and Manny Alonso in New Jersey–New York. These were the two essential bicoastal pillars of Los Muchachos. Brito and Alonso were, even after Willy and Sal were arrested, the ones who received kilos from the Mexicans and acted as central distribution points for the product as it made its way around the United States. They were the two most important vessels that kept the organization afloat.

Using information from the informant Carnet, federal agents moved in on Jojo Brito and Manny Alonso. Jojo was arrested in Los Angeles. Manny and six of his "secretaries" were arrested in New York. Both Jojo and Manny eventually pleaded guilty and were sent to prison. Later, this same investigation led to the arrest of Gilberto Barrios and Freddy Cruz, who also served time in prison.

It took Willy, Sal, and everyone else a while to realize the full impact of these arrests. With all the legal issues swirling around in their world, it seemed like just one more roundhouse left hook from the government. But Jojo's and Manny's operations formed the central arteries of Los Muchachos as a major national distribution network. Shut them down and the pipeline was effectively shut off. The game was over. This was it; this was the last kilo.

By the time the full parameters of this bust sank in with Willy and Sal, they were stunned. There were still 55,000 kilos out there in stash houses to be sold. There were multiple millions to be made. But their cocaine-distribution apparatus had been effectively disabled.

IT WAS AROUND THIS TIME that Willy and Sal began to discuss the possibility of a negotiated exit strategy. They brought in two lawyers—Neil Taylor and Martin "Marty" Raskin—whose sole job was to seek a deal with the Justice Department and the US attorney's office. The defendants raised the amounts of their previous offer before their arrests. They would pay $40 million and turn over three thousand kilos and plead guilty to cocaine-trafficking and money-laundering charges. In addition, Dominique Gonzalez, who was Willy's brother-in-law, would turn himself in from hiding, and so would Tavy Falcon. Tavy would surrender and plead guilty to the same charges as Willy and Sal. In exchange, the government would promise sentences of no more than fifteen years and a guarantee that Willy, Sal, and Tavy could not be hit with any additional criminal charges related to the case. Said Willy:

> We were offering them a way to settle the case and declare victory. The cocaine and money we would be obligated to pay was substantial. We were prepared to do fifteen years, which at the time seemed like a long sentence to both me and Sal. Tavy and Dominique would turn themselves in. There was no response for a long time. Then they came back and said the fugitives would first have to turn themselves in, then we could discuss a deal. Tavy said no, he was not going to turn himself in without a deal in place. I don't blame him. Eventually, they came back and said, "There is no deal." What happened was, in the middle of all this, a new US attorney took over as the top person in the office. Kendall Coffey became US attorney. He did not want, as one of his first decisions, to be known as the guy who cut a deal with Willy and Sal. We were told that he personally shut down the negotiation.

With no deal to be made, Willy and Sal turned all their attention and energy to beating their case in court.

Though Mark Dachs had been banned from serving as trial attorney for Los Muchachos, he was still able to work as part of their pretrial defense team. Willy and Sal referred to Dachs's law office as "the war room." The lawyer was authorized to employ a team of private investigators. On behalf of the defense, the investigators were able to identify people whom the government would likely be calling as witnesses at the trial. The PIs were to gather incriminating information on these people, to be used against them in court. Eventually, there would be more than one hundred files in the war room containing, in some cases, classified information on an assortment of potential snitches.

Like anyone who worked on behalf of Willy and Sal's defense, the investigators were well paid. Many of them were former Miami-area homicide detectives who had retired or been fired from their jobs as cops. They still had contacts in law enforcement, and that would be invaluable in their effort to undermine the many criminal informants who would be tripping over one another to "jump on the bus," as it was known when convicts and defendants sought a sentence reduction or favored treatment by testifying against one of the DOJ's high-value targets.

One of the PIs hired by Willy and Sal was Raul Diaz, the once famous Miami detective who, among other things, was the first cop to arrest Willy Falcon back in 1979 as part of the Video Canary case. Diaz was paid "off the books" by one of the many attorneys representing Los Muchachos.

In Miami, as in most American cities, former cops often became PIs and switched sides upon retirement, as did many prosecutors who became defense lawyers. This seemed to suggest that the system was not so much a case of good versus evil, but one of veteran civil servants building a résumé, then cashing in and offering their services to the highest bidder.

AT THE SAME TIME WILLY and Sal were dealing with their crumbling cocaine-distribution operation and the criminal case against them, they were paid a visit at the Miami Detention Center by Antonio Garcia Perez. Willy's nearly lifelong friend and main contact in the anti-Castro movement had stayed in touch with the Boys. There was a time, years earlier, when he and the others held simulated reconnaissance training sessions at the ranch in Clewiston, wading through water, firing at targets, pretending as if they were storming the beach in Cuba to overthrow Castro and take back the island.

All along, Falcon and Magluta had been sending money to Antonio and his organization, PUND, which had been actively enabling various anti-Castro operations around South America and the Caribbean. Through Miguel Vega, Antonio had requested a meeting with Willy in prison to discuss a current operation. Willy told Vega, "Miguel, please tell Antonio, respectfully, we have so much on our plate right now, we're not able to deal with this. Any money he needs, we will authorize that it be sent to him immediately. But we can't be directly involved right now."

Willy was surprised when Antonio came back with a response: "This is urgent. We need to meet. You will understand after we do so."

Through their lawyers, Willy and Sal were able to set up a meeting with Antonio and a companion that would take place in the lawyers' room at the facility, which afforded them the necessary privacy.

Willy and Sal were intrigued. Willy had not seen Antonio face-to-face since 1990, when they met in north Miami Beach one afternoon at the restaurant Sundays on the Bay. That day, his friend had introduced him to Frank Sturgis, the notorious Watergate burglar who was a longtime warrior in the anti-Castro movement. They were curious to see who Antonio would be bringing along this time.

In the lawyers' visiting room, they embraced and sat down. The man with Antonio was a Cuban older than all of them. He looked familiar, but Willy couldn't place the face until Antonio said, "Caballeros, I would like you to meet Justo Regalado Borges."

Regalado was another of those longtime anti-Castro militants who was legendary within the movement. He had served nearly twenty years in prison in Cuba as a political prisoner. Both Willy and Sal knew who he was. Currently, he was a high-ranking officer in PUND.

Justo Regalado explained to Willy and Sal how the recent collapse of the Soviet Union had changed everything in the anti-Castro efforts. After years of lack of focus and poor morale, the movement had been reenergized over the reality of Cuba losing its primary financial benefactor. The Cuban economy was reeling, and Castro had never been more vulnerable. "In fact," said Regalado, "we now have informants high in the Cuban directorate, higher in the Castro regime than we ever have before. We are able to track his movements, to know where and when he will show his face. We know, for instance, that he will be attending the gathering of Latin American leaders at the summit in Cartagena. This is more than a year away, but we have begun to gather intelligence and devise an action plan. We are putting together an assassination team whose sole task is to be ready when the opportunity presents itself. For this group to operate, we need the most modern technology—computers, tracking devices, communications equipment."

"I see," said Sal.

"This movement is no longer made up of guerrilla soldiers hiding in the swamps. The days of the Bay of Pigs invasion are long ago. This is high tech. If we are to take Castro out, it will be because we have the proper technology to do so."

"How much do you need?" asked Willy.

"One million dollars," said Regalado. "And that's just for starters. Until we go operational and will likely come to you again."

Willy and Sal looked at one another. They had been making these kinds of decisions for over a decade now. They knew where each other stood.

Said Falcon, "We will talk to Miguel Vega and authorize the payment. You will have that money whenever you need it."

They all embraced and said, "*Viva la lucha*" (long live the struggle).

Later, in the rec area of the jail, Willy and Sal talked about the situation. Wouldn't it be amazing, they agreed, that while their cocaine business was ending and their freedom was up in the air, in the middle of it all they would play a vital role in the elimination of the Great Satan? The assassination of Castro was something they had all dreamed about since they were teenagers. For Willy, the anti-Castro movement was how he had gotten involved in the cocaine business in the first place. There was a kind of poetic justice that this opportunity would present itself now, in what was, in some ways, their lowest moment. Even behind bars, they were playing a role as patriots, contributing to the cause. The idea that Castro might be killed, and that they would play a part in making that happen, made them positively giddy.

In the rec area that day, Willy and Sal strutted around as if they had just been given a release date, with a bounce in their step. Nobody else knew why.

IN THE ANNALS OF LOS Muchachos, violence had always been kept at bay. Within the group, it was a point of pride. But something had changed. It started with the murder of the lawyer Juan Acosta, which, if it had been intended to contain exposure of the lawyer's connections to Los Muchachos' bank accounts with Guillermo Endara in Panama City, had backfired miserably. Acosta's files laid out a paper trail that led from Willy and Sal's various shell companies directly to the man who was now president of Panama.[2]

---

[2] As a result of the Acosta murder investigation, *U.S. News & World Report* published an article in December 1991 titled "The Panama Connection," which detailed an alleged relationship between the new US-installed president of Panama and the Falcon-Magluta organization. Endara denied that he ever met or did business with the notorious narcos. Hernán Delgado also denied any money-laundering knowledge. (Linda Robinson, "The Panama Connection," *U.S. News & World Report*, December 9, 1991.)

In 1995, after his term as president of Panama, Guillermo Endara finally admitted that his law firm had a relationship with Falcon-Magluta. He pinned it all on Gabriel Castro, who was still director of PTJ at

Then, a few days after the murder of Acosta was the car bombing attack on Tony Posada.

More recently, in May 1992, Lazaro Cruz—a low-level member of the organization who had flipped and was scheduled to testify against Los Muchachos—was ambushed coming out of his house in Hialeah. Cruz was shot several times in the stomach and taken by ambulance to Jackson Memorial Hospital. He was in critical condition but expected to survive.

Three months later came the shooting of Juan Barroso. The coke dealer and speedboat operator for the organization had originally been indicted along with Willy, Sal, and the rest. But even at that time he was already in negotiations with prosecutor Chris Clark to become an informant. On August 5, while out on bail, Barroso was at a Shell gas station on Southwest Ninety-Seventh Avenue and Nineteenth Street fixing a flat tire when he was approached by a Latino male brandishing a TEC-9 machine gun. The guy opened fire with a spray of bullets, five of which hit Barroso. The gunman jumped into a getaway car and sped away. Barroso was rushed to Jackson Memorial. Like Lazaro Cruz, he arrived in critical condition but would survive the attack.

Somebody was taking potshots at potential witnesses against Willy and Sal. Though three out of the four had lived, and it had not yet been established whether these were actual murder attempts or merely warning attacks meant to intimidate other potential informants, the shootings cast a pall over the universe of Los Muchachos. It seemed possible that the carefully cultivated and fondly embraced image among the extended family of Cuban exile narcos—a mythology that held that even though the cocaine world was composed of many homicidal maniacs, they were not—was an illusion. Perhaps the indictment of Willy and Sal had altered the equation. Perhaps Willy and Sal were now descending to the same level as many other gangsters when their backs were against the wall and their liberty was at stake. They were attempting to eliminate witnesses.

Eventually, a version of the truth would come out, but at the time it was a mystery. Even Willy Falcon did not know precisely who was behind the various acts of violence. Willy always contended that the murder of Juan Acosta was a

the time. Endara claimed that, in 1987, Castro had taken over those accounts from attorney Juan Acosta, who was later murdered. Castro denied any wrongdoing. ("Endara rompe voto de silencio" [Endara breaks vow of silence], Inter Press Service (IPS), July 7, 1995.)

disaster for him and Sal. And the later attacks on Posada, Cruz, and Barroso didn't make much sense. Tony Posada and Lazaro Cruz were low-level members of the organization; any testimony they might have to give was not crucial. These attempted hits may have been a case of score-settling that had little or nothing to do with Willy and Sal's operation. On the other hand . . .

Falcon knew that the Cali Cartel had taken a special interest in their case. For more than a decade, Los Muchachos had composed the cartel's primary distribution network in the United States. As such, Los Muchachos had tremendous value. If it was true that the cartels in Colombia operated as the home office—a corporate management aspect of the business that sometimes made decisions based on its own needs, not the needs of its subsidiary partners—it was possible that the cartel could and would take matters into its own hands.

It was a fact that what was happening with the prosecution of Willy, Sal, and their organization was an existential threat to the Cali Cartel. At a trial, major aspects of the cartel's relationship with key distributors in the United States would be exposed.

This was a theory that was percolating among those who were thought to be in the know, including Willy Falcon. He could have asked Mario Valencia, specifically, who or what was behind the attacks, but he did not feel it was his place to do so. Which meant that he would remain somewhat in the dark, in a state of unknowing, which was a bad place to be when, on August 6—just one day after the attempted murder of Juan Barroso—an event occurred that stunned Willy Falcon, the city of Miami, and anyone in the free world or behind bars who dwelled within the darker corridors of the narcosphere.

THAT AFTERNOON, TONY GARRUDO—EL CUÑO—WAS in his car following Alina Falcon as she took care of some shopping on Miracle Mile in Coral Gables. It was a busy day for Alina. She had spent the afternoon at the office of attorney Frank Rubino, who was part of the Los Muchachos defense team. Rubino was handling the filing of a motion that would call into question the search and seizure of Willy and Alina's Fort Lauderdale house. It was Rubino's contention that the lawmen had entered the property with an arrest warrant but had begun searching the premises before they had a proper search warrant. He needed Alina to come by his office to create an affidavit describing what she saw, how the US Marshals and agents had immediately begun ransacking the house.

It took Alina one hour to complete the affidavit, then she got in her Jaguar and drove to Scruples, her ladies' clothing store located in Coral Gables.

Tony Garrudo met her at Scruples. Garrudo was out on bail. He was facing multiple cocaine-trafficking and conspiracy charges, but since he had no gun charges (unlike Willy), and he had not been a fugitive from the law (also unlike Willy, Sal, and Benny), he was able to post bond. The only condition was that he could not leave the Miami area.

It was traditional for members of Los Muchachos to serve as bodyguards for the women. Ever since the kidnapping of Willy Falcon's mother, a decade earlier, the men in the group took very seriously their role as protectors of the wives and children. El Cuño, as Willy's brother-in-law, married to Alina's sister, felt a special responsibility.

They were going to eat dinner at Tony and Ileana's house nearby in the Gables. At Scruples, Alina told Tony, "I'm going to stop by the hair salon to pick up some shampoo and conditioner. I'll meet you at your house."

Tony didn't like the idea. With the various shootings that had taken over the Los Muchachos universe, the general level of danger and paranoia had increased. Plus, in recent months there had been some random robberies and purse snatchings in Coral Gables. Alina was an attractive blond, clearly well off, with copious jewelry and expensive sunglasses, driving a Jaguar. By herself, she was a sitting duck.

"I can wait for you," said Tony.

"No, go on ahead. I'll only be a minute."

Reluctantly, Tony got in his car and drove the three or four blocks to the house.

In her Jaguar, Alina pulled up and double-parked in front of Clara Lorenzo 2000 Hair Designer salon at 1913 Ponce de Leon Boulevard. She grabbed her purse, got out, locked the doors, and hurried inside.

She was well known at the beauty salon. Everyone said hello. Alina purchased a bottle of shampoo and conditioner. One of the hairdressers tried to start up a conversation with Alina, but she said, "Sorry. I gotta go. I'm double-parked outside. I'll be back tomorrow."

She hurried back out to the car. It was rush hour, with lots of people on the street coming and going. Alina didn't notice that a sixteen-year-old Black kid, accompanied by two others roughly the same age, was following her every move. As she opened her car door and began to get inside, the kid stepped forward with a gun. He grabbed Alina's purse, but she held on. There was a tussle. "Give it to me," said the assailant.

"No," said Alina.

She managed to break free and slam shut the door, which she locked. The kid was now enraged. He took the butt of his gun and banged on the driver's side window. He was trying to shatter the glass. Frantically, Alina tried to start her car and drive away.

There were numerous witnesses in the street and passing cars who saw what happened next. The kid took one step back and aimed his gun at Alina.

Willy Falcon's wife looked at the gunman. The last thing she saw was the kid firing his weapon directly into her face.

A FEW BLOCKS AWAY, TONY Garrudo pulled up in the driveway outside his house. His wife, Ileana, came running out of the house. She screamed, "My sister! My sister! Somebody shot my sister!"

At first, for Tony, it did not compute. He had just left Alina two minutes earlier. What did Ileana mean that she had been shot? It didn't make sense.

Said Ileana, "They just called me from the salon. Quick, drive over there."

Tony didn't ask questions. Once Ileana was in the front seat next to him, he drove over to the salon.

They arrived at a chaotic scene. Alina had tumbled out of the car and was lying on her back in the street next to the Jaguar. There were pedestrians gathering around and the sound of approaching sirens. Tony stopped his car in the middle of Ponce de Leon Boulevard; he and Ileana jumped out and ran over to Alina. They bent down. She had been shot in the neck. There was blood everywhere, seeping down the car door and in the street. Alina's upper body was covered with blood. Her eyes were flickering.

From one knee, Tony cradled Alina in his arms. Ileana said, "Alina, who did this? Did you see who did this?"

Alina looked at her sister. Her eyes were vacant, uncomprehending.

For some reason, Ileana instantly thought of the time at the girls' home in Madrid, when they were children, how the nuns had tried to make her eat that awful gruel they were serving, and how, when she refused, they brought in Alina to convince her that she needed to eat the food. Ileana was stubborn; she refused. And then there was that image: Alina, so pretty, standing framed by the massive Spanish doorway, crying.

And now it was Ileana crying, the tears gushing from her eyes and running down her face, as she witnessed her sister in the ultimate state of distress, covered with blood, the life seeping from her body just a few buildings away from Scruples, her pride and joy, the high-fashion clothing store that was hers and hers alone.

Tony held Alina in his arms and looked into her eyes. He said, "Hold on, Alina. Stay strong. Stay with us." The eyes went blank. Tony was not a doctor, but he knew about vital signs. No pulse. She wasn't breathing. He was pretty sure that his sister-in-law had just died in his arms.

Not far away, a medevac helicopter landed in a Little League baseball field. The paramedics arrived and took over. They began pumping Alina's chest. They loaded her body onto a stretcher.

Tony and Ileana stood back and watched, helpless. Ileana crumbled into Tony's arms, weeping and convulsing.

Tony watched the body being loaded onto the helicopter. To one of the paramedics, a Latino, likely Cuban, Tony said, "*Yo soy el cuño.*"

"Meet us at Jackson Memorial emergency," said the paramedic.

The whirlybird rose in the sky; dirt and dust swept up and stirred around like a mini tornado. The helicopter headed in the direction of the hospital. Tony already knew that when Alina Rossique Falcon arrived at the emergency room, she would be declared DOA, dead on arrival.

WILLY FALCON HAD SPENT THE night in solitary confinement. He was there because, a few weeks earlier, prison authorities had received some incriminating information about a cell phone. Willy and Sal had smuggled in a second phone, which they kept stored in the cell of a fellow inmate named Billy "Tanky" Williams. That phone had come to them through the commissary, where a corrections officer had—for a price—allowed a visitor of Sal's to leave the phone in a shopping bag. That corrections officer later got busted for smuggling steroids into the facility. To create a better deal for himself, he snitched, telling investigators that he had smuggled a cell phone into the prison for Willy Falcon.

Prison authorities found the phone in Tanky's cell, but they did not yet know anything about the original phone in Willy's cell. That was fortunate. The phone in Willy's cell was the one he used for business matters. If they had found that phone, they could have accessed the call log that would have shown all the numbers he had contacted in Colombia and around the United States. The phone in Tanky's cell was used only for family calls and other nonbusiness-related matters.

One afternoon, as he was getting out of the shower, a dozen corrections officers descended on Falcon. A lieutenant from the Special Investigations Service (SIS) told Willy, "We know you had a phone smuggled in here. We found it."

Willy knew they had to be talking about the phone in Tanky's cell, which was a relief.

Falcon, Magluta, and Lorenzo were all put in separate solitary confinement cells in the lockdown unit. On one of the legal visits, Willy was able to pull aside a fellow Cuban inmate that he knew was on the same cell block as his cell with the phone. "I need you to do me a favor," he said to the guy. Willy explained that he needed him to bribe a guard and go into his cell. He explained where the cell phone was hidden under his bed and behind the brick in the wall. "I need you to get that phone and smash it into tiny pieces. Understand? Put those pieces inside an empty Coke can and throw it away. Throw it directly into the compactor. You will be well paid for this. I promise you."

"Okay, Willy, I will do that," said the guy.

"Good. Report back to me when you have taken care of that."

On the morning after Alina's killing, Willy was feeling pretty good. He had heard from the Cuban inmate the night before that the phone had been obliterated and thrown away without a trace. Disaster averted.

Around nine a.m. that morning, a guard came to Willy's cell in segregation. Willy put his hands through the slit in the door, and the guard clamped handcuffs to his wrists. Willy was then taken to a holding area, where two more guards brought Sal and Benny into the room. The three were handcuffed together on a chain, then they were brought to the lawyer-consultation room.

Waiting in the room was Albert Krieger, Willy's lawyer, and the attorney Frank Rubino. Also, there was Richard Ignacio Martinez, another lawyer who was Sal's brother-in-law, and Marilyn Bonachea, a longtime woman friend of Sal's whom he had enlisted as a key conduit and message carrier with associates on the outside. They had been able to register Marilyn as a paralegal.

Krieger stepped forward to give Falcon a hug. "Willy, I am so sorry. My condolences."

"What?" said Willy. "What happened?"

"Your wife, Alina, was shot and killed yesterday at the Miracle Mile shopping center in Coral Gables. Outside of a beauty shop."

Willy felt as if he had been smacked in the face. He blinked and said, "How could this have happened? Who shot her?"

"We only know what was reported on the news last night and this morning. You've been in isolation, so of course you don't know any of this."

Frank Rubino opened a copy of the *Miami Herald*. "This is from the morning edition," he said. He began reading from a long article. Willy could not believe what he was hearing.

A woman who stopped to buy a bottle of shampoo Thursday afternoon was fatally shot after she resisted two robbers who tried to snatch her purse outside of a Coral Gables beauty shop. Witnesses said that Alina Rossique Falcon managed to take her purse back after two robbers grabbed it, but she was shot through her window as she tried to flee in her car. . . . Falcon, 33 [*sic*], of Southwest Dade, was pronounced dead on arrival at Jackson Memorial Hospital. She is the wife of Augusto Guillermo Willy Falcon, the alleged leader of a large drug smuggling ring that shipped 75 tons of cocaine into South Florida in the late 1980s. He is in federal prison awaiting trial. Metro-Dade homicide detectives who are handling the case do not believe the slaying is related to Willy Falcon's alleged activities.

Willy tried to speak. He opened his mouth, but no words would come out.

Krieger spoke up and informed Willy that as soon as they left the prison, they would appear before the judge in his case and request from the court that the US Marshals escort him to the funeral home so he could see his wife for the last time.

Everyone stepped forward and hugged Willy. Even lawyers who were there to see other inmates stopped by their room to offer their condolences to Willy.

At one point, Sal pulled his friend and partner aside. He looked into Willy's eyes. "Willy, are you okay?"

"Honestly, no, I'm not, but I will be all right soon. Don't worry about me."

The legal visit ended. The inmates were handcuffed and escorted back to their cells in segregation.

For a while, Willy sat on his mattress and stared at the wall. He thought about Alina, her eyes, her aroma, the curve of her back, the sound of her voice. They had been together since they were teenagers. A wave of grief came over Willy, and he began to weep. Then the grief turned to rage. He stood up and began to swing at the brick wall in his cell. Pounding and pounding. He felt no pain at all, but then he noticed that his fists were shredded, his skin broken open. His knuckles were bruised and bleeding. He raged until he was exhausted; he fell on the mattress, curled up into the fetal position, and passed out.

It was pitch dark in the cell when he woke up.

Around six a.m., the guards came and told him to get dressed in his street clothes, as if he were going for a day in court. Then he was cuffed, complete with shackles around his ankles and an electric kidney belt placed around his waist. Escorted by seven marshals, including Sean Convoy, the marshal who had arrested him at his home in Fort Lauderdale, Willy was led out of the prison and put into the back of a corrections department van. Flanked by five or six escort vehicles filled with armed marshals, the entire cortege drove from the prison onto the I-95 expressway headed north. There were no windows in the van, but Willy could hear helicopters hovering overhead for the entire trip.

At the funeral parlor, Willy was removed from the van. The marshals did not take off the shackles or the kidney belt. They led him into the funeral parlor. There was an open casket in the middle of the room. No one else was there. No undertaker, no priest, nobody. The marshals stood off to the side and allowed Willy to step up to the casket.

Willy saw his beautiful wife looking serene and at peace. The embalmer had fixed her up. As he looked at Alina, Willy's knees buckled. He wept. Unlike back in his cell, where he had been overcome with tears of rage, here he wept quietly.

He apologized to Alina for not being there to protect her when she was shot. He asked for forgiveness for the many times that he let her down. He promised that he would take care of their children, and that his love for her would never die. He was allowed ninety minutes to spend alone with the body of his dead wife, then the marshals took him away.

He was loaded in the van and taken to the downtown federal courthouse. Again, the helicopters followed in the sky. At the courthouse, Willy was taken to the offices of the US Marshals and led to a conference room. He sat there alone for a while until a woman marshal entered, flanked by his three children, Aileen, Jessica, and Will Jr.

The children ran over to their father, and they all hugged. Willy told them that he had been able to spend time with Alina's body at the funeral parlor, to say goodbye. He assured his children that he loved them and would care for them as long as he lived. The kids were in shock, not yet fully comprehending all that had happened and was happening. Willy assured them that no matter what happened with his legal case, he would provide for them and keep them safe.

Aileen, the oldest at seventeen, was in mourning for her mother but also sad for her father:

> He was devastated, but I could see that he was trying to be strong for us. He wanted to reassure us that, as a family, we weren't going to fall apart. We were still going to be together; we would always be together. He said to us, "Remember what a beautiful person your mother was. She was special. She went down fighting. Let her memory give you strength."

Willy and the children were separated. He was taken back to the MCC and put in his isolation cell. He stared at the wall, and never felt more alone in his life.

Two and a half weeks after Alina Falcon's death, Hurricane Andrew hit South Florida. It was a category 5 storm, one of the worst ever seen in the area. Houses were flattened, highways knocked down, and power lines destroyed, causing a temporary blackout. Citizens hunkered down in their homes and waited for it to blow over.

For family and friends of Alina—Tony and Ileana, who were there when she died; Alina's parents, devasted at the loss of their oldest daughter; the kids; Willy—the storm seemed like a message from God. It was the Creator's way of saying, *Hear unto Me: In this place, on this day, make no mistake—all is not right with the universe.*

18

THE FIX

IT WAS HARD FOR PEOPLE to accept that Alina Falcon's murder was the result of a random act of violence. Even Willy had a hard time accepting it.

At the MCC, he asked around until he found out who was the leader of the preeminent African American gang in the Miami corrections system. Newspaper accounts had identified three young Black males who had gone on a purse-snatching and robbery spree in Coral Gables. Supposedly, they had come to Miami from Georgia with the intention of ripping off rich people. Willy wasn't so sure. He located and approached Kenneth "Boobie" Williams, who was the boss of a notorious Miami drug gang called the Boobie Boys. Williams was a major player in the cocaine trade at the street level in South Florida and was currently incarcerated on drug charges. Falcon and Williams had never met before.

In the MCC rec area, Falcon said to Williams, "Maybe you know who I am."

"Of course," said Boobie.

"You heard what happened to my wife?"

"I did." In his thirties, muscular, wearing a tight tank top, Boobie was no one to be trifled with. He was seated near the outdoor basketball court with a couple of underlings.

Said Willy, "Listen, I'm having doubts about what's been reported in the media about this. I will pay you one hundred thousand dollars—cash—if you can find answers for me. Ask around. I need to know if they were ordered to do this by someone higher up for whatever reason."

Boobie looked at Willy and said, "All right. I'll see what I can find out."

A week later, Williams came to Falcon and said, "I asked around. Nobody knows anything about those punks. It seems they are exactly what the papers say, assholes who came into the city from Georgia. Your wife was a target of opportunity."

Willy took in the information and said, "Okay, thanks. Where do I send your money?"

Said Boobie, "Falcon, you don't owe me nothing. Consider it a favor."[1]

THE DAMAGE FROM HURRICANE ANDREW was so severe that the National Guard was called in to help with the transfer of inmates from the MCC to other federal facilities. Led by armed federal soldiers, Willy Falcon, Sal Magluta, Benny Lorenzo, and one hundred others from E-Unit were rousted in the dead of night—around two a.m.—and led toward an awaiting bus.

But before that happened, there was another murder.

On the night of August 22—two days before Hurricane Andrew struck—Luis "Weetchie" Escobedo was shot dead in the parking garage outside Suzanne's, a Coconut Grove nightclub not far from where the Mutiny used to be located. He had been walking toward his car when somebody called out, "Hey, Weetchie." When he turned to look, he was riddled to death with bullets from a MAC-10 submachine gun.

Thirty-nine years old at the time of his death, Escobedo was a notorious Marielito who had come to Miami with nothing and, within a few years, was earning millions as a cocaine narco. He spoke no English. He was a low-level member of Los Muchachos, though central enough that he had been included as a codefendant in the indictment of Willy and Sal. Within months of his arrest, he had begun cooperating with the US attorney's office. It was well known that Weetchie would be testifying against Falcon and Magluta. He was out on bail at the time he was killed.

AUSA Chris Clark and his cocounsel, Pat Sullivan—who had by now officially joined the prosecution team—were outraged when they heard about the Weetchie Escobedo murder. They were especially angry considering information they received about how Falcon and Magluta had possibly smuggled a cell phone into prison. Although authorities with the Bureau of Prisons had

---

[1] In 1992, around the same time Boobie Williams was approached by Willy Falcon, he met Efrain Casada in that same facility. When they were released from custody later that year, Williams and Casada combined to form the largest street-level cocaine-distribution network the city had ever seen—also, the most violent. In the 1990s, the gang was believed to have played a role in at least thirty-five murders. In 2005, Boobie Williams, Casada, and nine other defendants were convicted on multiple cocaine-trafficking and conspiracy counts. Williams was given a life sentence.

withheld this information from them as they investigated the allegation, when the prosecutors were shown the report, they were apoplectic. The idea that Willy and Sal, while in federal prison, had been on the phone consummating coke deals and possibly ordering hits on potential witnesses made them sick to their stomachs. Plans were afoot to separate the defendants and bury them deep within the system by sending them to faraway, high-security, supermax facilities. Then Hurricane Andrew hit.

Seated on the prison bus, his hands cuffed and in leg shackles, Falcon looked out from the window at the devastation. As the packed vehicle pulled away from the prison, the prisoners craned their necks to get a view. A roof had been blown off part of the prison facility, and the barbed-wire fence had been flattened and spread around a large parking lot. Cars were turned over and power lines were down. In all his years in Miami, Willy had never seen anything this bad.

As the inmates pressed their faces to the bus windows, Willy noticed someone whom he recognized. There, in a green jumpsuit like everyone else, was none other than Manuel Noriega, the former Panamanian dictator.

Noriega's trial had ended earlier that year with a guilty verdict on eight counts of drug trafficking, money laundering, and racketeering. In July, he was sentenced to forty years in prison. He was appealing the verdict.

The prison bus drove through the night in near-total darkness. The inmates had no idea where they were being taken. As morning arrived, they spotted road signs showing that they were passing through the Deep South. Some of the inmates speculated on where they were headed. After driving for twenty-four hours straight, stopping only for gas, they arrived at the Federal Correctional Institution (FCI) in the town of Talladega, Alabama.

Chained together at the waist, the prisoners were brought off the bus and processed through the facility's intake procedures. Most of the group was led to a unit known as Alpha A, which was part of the prison's control unit. Composed of single, nine-by-seven-foot cells, this was a twenty-three-hour lockdown unit. The prisoners were allowed only one hour of recreation. They were allowed three showers per week. There were no televisions, but an inmate could order a Walkman radio from the commissary.

Falcon had been there nearly one week before he realized that housed in the cell next door to his was Noriega.

Late one night, Willy heard a tapping sound through the air-conditioning vent in his cell. "Psst, Willy. Willy Falcon, can you hear me?" It was Noriega.

Willy leaned closer to the vent. They spoke in Spanish. "General Noriega. Yes, I can hear you. How are you holding up?"

"Health wise, I am good, but lockdown like this is very difficult. Hey, I need you to do me a favor if it is possible. Are you having a legal visit tomorrow?"

"Yes, my lawyers are coming from Miami."

"I would greatly appreciate if one of your lawyers can get in touch with my lawyer, Frank Rubino. I know Rubino is a good friend of yours."

"Yes, he is. We even have him working in a supporting capacity on our case."

"Well, can somebody please let him know that I am here in Talladega, and I am doing fine. I need for Frank to request a legal phone call with me here at the prison. I also need him to call my wife and let her know where I am."

"Of course, I will do that. Also, if you give me your wife's phone number, I will pass it on to our paralegal tomorrow. She will call your wife and assure her that you are here and doing okay."

Noriega gave Willy the number. Then they bid each other good night and went to sleep.

Over the next few nights, after Willy had done the favor for the general, they talked regularly through the vent in their cells. Noriega seemed to be wistful and occasionally depressed. He reminded Falcon of the one time they met, at a party at the Hilton Hotel in Panama City to celebrate a boxing victory by Roberto Durán, who was a proud native of Panama. Durán was at the party, as were many celebrities. "I met you and your partner, Sal Magluta."

"Yes," said Willy, "I remember that."

Said Noriega, "I know that you were supporters of Guillermo Endara, who was a political rival of mine. I know that he managed your financial accounts and in exchange you helped finance his campaign. I have no hard feelings about that. I only wish that we had been able to spend real time together, and maybe this would have all turned out differently. . . . Strange, isn't it? We were once on top of the world, and now here we are in a lockdown cell, seven feet by nine feet, with a stainless-steel toilet and no access to telephone or TV or refrigerator or anything that we were once accustomed to having. Our lives have been turned upside down."

At times, Willy found himself annoyed listening to the once mighty dictator. For one thing, not once had Noriega offered condolences for the death of Willy's wife, which he must have known about. Also, Noriega was speaking as a man who had been humiliated and convicted. His attorney had filed for an appeal, which offered some hope, but Noriega was talking like a man who believed his life was over. Frankly, Falcon found it depressing.

Said Willy, "Listen, Noriega, life changes. That's the way it goes. We are on a path that we chose for ourselves. Maybe this is just another stepping stone before we can get back on top again. We have to keep our heads up and continue to fight back. You with your court appeals, and me trying to discredit the snitches that will be testifying against me and my codefendants at trial. Keep yourself together, man, be mentally strong and stay physically healthy. Your family and your people are expecting you to be strong for them."

Willy felt that it was absurd that he was having to bolster the morale of a man who had ordered his paramilitary goon squad—the Dignity Battalion—to assault his friend and lawyer Guillermo Endara. Noriega made life miserable for many people in Panama while he was in power. After a while, when Noriega called for him through the air-conditioning vent, Falcon did not respond.

By the early months of 1993, repairs to the MCC in Miami had mostly been completed. Of the one hundred inmates who had been moved from Miami to the prison in Talladega, the only ones remaining in Alabama were Willy, Sal, Benny, and Noriega. It was unusual to house defendants in faraway jurisdictions—much less entirely different states—as they were preparing for trial. It made it difficult to arrange meetings with investigators and attorneys on any kind of regular basis. In addition, there was the hardship of being separated from family by hundreds of miles. Attorneys for the three Muchachos filed a writ of habeas corpus with US Magistrate Judge Stephen T. Brown in the District of South Florida, demanding that they be returned to the MCC.

While Brown was considering this legal motion, he ruled on another matter that both sides, the defense and prosecution, had been waiting on for a long time.

At an earlier court hearing before Judge Brown, lawyers for Willy and Sal had argued in furtherance of their motion to suppress, which stated that the ledgers found at Sal Magluta's house should be declared inadmissible as evidence. The ledgers had been discovered while Special Agent David Borah was executing an arrest warrant, not a search warrant (the search warrant came a couple of hours later). At the hearing, all the arresting agents and marshals on the scene at Sal's house testified and were cross-examined by Sal's attorney, Roy Black. (It was at this hearing that Willy, Sal, and Benny, who were seated in court, learned officially and without doubt that it was Pegy Rosello who had ratted them out.)

Now, months later, Judge Brown had finally ruled that he agreed with counsel for the defense. The ledgers would be suppressed; they could not be used as evidence against Willy, Sal, and Benny.

It was a major victory for the lawyers. When told about it, the three defendants were ecstatic. "We felt we had won the case before it even started," said Benny.

By June, as they waited to hear if Judge Brown would again rule in their favor and authorize their return to Miami, Willy had a series of visits. In one, he met with his parents; in another, with his three children, who had been placed in the custody of their grandparents in South Florida.

It was the first time he had met face-to-face with his family since Alina was laid to rest. The pain of her death was still raw. Willy felt it was necessary for him to present a strong facade to his family, to help them with their own emotional trauma over the loss. It only made their interactions more agonizing, as if Alina's death was a terrible wound that could never heal.

Willy was carrying residual anger. He was angry at the people who killed his wife, and angry at the fates for allowing it to happen. He was especially angry at the criminal justice system that was holding him as a prisoner without bail, so that he had not been able to protect Alina and keep her safe. He was not able to grieve properly. There was a lot to process.

A convenient receptacle for his bitterness were the legal proceedings as they unfolded in the many months before the trial. A trial date had been set: October 3, 1994. By then, Krieger would be done with his representation of mafioso John Gotti in New York, and the two sides would be ready to begin the laborious process of jury selection. The fact the trial date was more than fifteen months away did not mitigate the sense of urgency felt by the defendants. At the visiting room in Talladega, the lawyers gathered: Susan Van

Dusen, who was a law partner of Albert Krieger; Roy Black, Sal's lawyer; Richard Martinez, who had switched from being an assistant district attorney to a defense attorney to take part in the Falcon-Magluta defense; Marty Weinberg; Jeff Weiner; and Benson Weintraub. All these lawyers, hired at considerable expense by Willy and Sal, were assigned to specific aspects of the defense.

Payment of the lawyers had involved its own elaborate criminal conspiracy. Luis Valverde, who was a cousin of Sal's wife, Isabel, handled the diversion of funds. Since there was a protective order in effect that prohibited use of money from either Willy's or Sal's accounts, it was arranged for suitcases filled with cash to be shipped to a rabbi in New York City. Using a fictitious name, Rabbi Harry Kozlik deposited the money in bank accounts in Israel, as well as in Venezuela, Colombia, and Zurich. The money was then transferred to the United States by wire transfers and checks from the rabbi's fraudulent accounts. The money was again transferred, this time to Mexican exchange houses for the issuance of foreign third-party checks.

In the United States, the lawyers, Krieger, Black, and the others, knew that whatever payment arrangements they had with Falcon and Magluta would be monitored closely by the government. They insisted that the checks that were delivered to them had to be delivered by an actual person—not a bank or wire transfer—and whoever that person was had to state verbally that they were making a payment on behalf of a private donor, and the funds did not come from any account associated with Falcon or Magluta.

So far, it had worked. The lawyers deposited their checks without issue. Eventually, in an article in the *Miami Herald*, it was estimated that over $25 million was paid to lawyers and private investigators for Los Muchachos using this method. Falcon suggested that with under-the-table payments to some of the lawyers and investigators, it was probably more like $50 million. (See appendix.)

In the visiting room at the prison in Talladega, Willy told the assembled legal team, "Make no mistake, we are at war with DEA, IRS, FBI, the Justice Department—whoever is involved in the case against us."

Sal concurred, adding, "We are treating this like one of our championship boat races. We only know one way: to give 100 percent. And we stop at nothing." Speaking to the high-priced legal talent seated around him, he offered what could have been digested, printed, and posted on the wall as their mission statement: "All who work for us as lawyers and investigators need to know, when Los Muchachos have their backs to the wall, that's when we are at our best. We play to win, and we will win—by any means necessary."

FOR THE PROSECUTORS, THE RULING by Judge Brown to suppress the ledgers was a setback, but it was not the end of the world. The US magistrate was not the court of last resort. AUSA Chris Clark filed a motion to appeal, and he felt the chances were good that Judge Brown's ruling would be overturned.

Meanwhile, Clark focused on the case. It wasn't the only case on his plate at the time. With the trial date so far off in the future, he was able to work other cases. But the Willy and Sal case began to generate heat in the press. The various murders and attempted murders of witnesses had changed everything. What had been solely a cocaine-trafficking and money-laundering case now took on the sinister aura of a mob trial, with potential witnesses at risk.

By June, it was ordered by the court that Falcon, Magluta, and Lorenzo be transferred back to the MCC in Miami. Within a few weeks, there was another killing.

The previous hits hadn't seemed to make much sense. The targets were minor players whose testimony against Willy and Sal was not crucial. Bernardo "El Venado" Gonzalez, on the other hand, was a major witness. He had been the organizer of the Boys' powerboat smuggling apparatus, and, after being convicted on drug-trafficking and conspiracy charges, he turned against Los Muchachos. He had been instrumental in getting other members of the organization to flip. Most notably, Jorge Valdés and Pegy Rosello had both agreed to inform against Willy and Sal after heart-to-heart conversations with Bernie Gonzalez.

Bernie's efforts on behalf of the prosecution were rewarded. In 1991, US District Judge Edward Davis reduced his sentence from fourteen to five and a half years. In November 1992, he was released on parole after serving forty-four months. At the time, he said to his family and attorney, "I am a marked man," though he declined to join the federal witness protection program.

On June 22, Bernie's younger brother, Humberto, had a meeting with three men to whom he was selling a boat. The previous day, he had taken these men on a test ride of the boat in Biscayne Bay. The men said they wanted to buy it.

Everyone agreed that they would meet the following day at the home of Bernie and Humberto's parents, at 12252 SW Forty-Sixth Street in Horse Country, where the boat would be held in the family garage.

When the men showed up, Bernie was out running an errand. In the garage, the men pistol-whipped Humberto and tied him up.

The house had a state-of-the-art security system, with electric gates, but the assassins were already on the inside. They waited for Bernie Gonzalez to show up. When he did, they opened the gate for him to enter the garage.

Humberto, bound and gagged, his mouth taped shut, was stuffed in a 150-gallon storage crate in the garage, out of view. Bernie pulled his car into the garage alongside the boat. When he rolled down the window of his car to speak with the men, he was shot multiple times in the face, head, and body.

One of the gunmen raised the lid on the storage crate and put a single bullet in the head of Humberto Gonzalez.

The three men fled, leaving behind a scene of mayhem and slaughter.

When Chris Clark heard about the double homicide, he was stunned. He had been working closely with Bernie Gonzalez and, for that matter, Weetchie Escobedo, both of whom had been taken out in professional hits in the last ten months.

Around the same time, prosecutors Clark and Sullivan took a call from Metro-Dade Detective Ron Ilhardt, who had received some startling information from detectives in New York City.

One of the most notorious open murder cases in New York was the assassination of a Latino journalist, which had taken place one year earlier in the neighborhood of Jackson Heights, Queens. On March 11, 1992, at rush hour, two gunmen entered the Meson Asturias Restaurant and shot Manuel de Dios Unanue, who was seated at the bar. The Cuban-born Dios was a former crusading editor in chief and columnist for *El Diario–La Prensa*, the city's preeminent Spanish-language newspaper. Recently, he had created two magazines, *Cambio XXI* and *Crimen*, which were dedicated to exposing the activities of the narcos, especially the Cali Cartel, which controlled the cocaine trade in New York.

To many, the murder of Dios was a new low. These kinds of professional hits of journalists may have been commonplace in the major cities of Colombia and Mexico, but this was the first time a journalist—specifically because of his writings on the narco war—had been murdered in the United States.

The New York City Police Department made the Dios murder one of its highest priorities, but the case stalled until officers arrested a young Colombian hit man for another murder he had committed. The sicario's name was Juan Velasco, a.k.a. Leopold Lopez, and he had begun to talk.

Velasco told the New York detectives that he was part of a team of assassins that had been sent from Cali to do several hits in the United States. One of those murders, which they had taken care of a few years earlier, was the murder of a lawyer in Miami named Juan Acosta.

Detective Ilhardt told Clark, "When the New York detective gave me that name, I jumped. Velasco, a.k.a. Leopold Lopez. Our guy, Juan Carlos Correa, gave us that name nearly two years ago. Said Velasco was part of the hit team. It all fits together."

Velasco could link the Acosta murder directly to the upper echelon of the Cali Cartel. He was saying that the hit had been organized by the Cali Cartel on behalf of the Falcon-Magluta organization. Furthermore, there was a list of other targets, some of whom had already been killed and some who were still out there as targets under open contracts.

To Clark, Sullivan, Borah, and any other representative of the government actively connected to the case against Willy and Sal, this information set off alarm bells.

Immediately, Ilhardt, Clark, Sullivan, and Borah made a trip to New York City in hopes of questioning Juan Velasco. But the prize informant in the Manuel de Dios murder case was currently being held at a secret location. Detectives and prosecutors in New York were not willing to allow access to Velasco until he had been thoroughly debriefed and prepared to testify in the Dios murder trial. This might possibly take a year or more.

Clark, Ilhardt, and the others went back to Miami empty-handed. But they were undeterred. In a multiagency effort, they launched an intelligence-gathering mission to find out what they could about the Cali Cartel's so-called hit list. A team of investigators canvassed all local prison facilities and the street, offering deals for information. What they found out was disturbing.

Yes, there was a hit list. The names on that list included Pegy Rosello, their primary informant against Willy and Sal, and it also included Special Agent David Borah.

The information about Borah was revealed at a joint task force meeting at the DEA regional headquarters in Fort Lauderdale. AUSA Chris Clark, who was there at the time, remembered:

> It was a threat that had originated in the prison system targeting Dave. I watched the agents around me; they all immediately get their automatic guns, and they lock and load. They were scrambling to get Borah and his wife. They took him to MacDill Air Force Base [in Tampa, Florida], where General [Norman] Schwarzkopf was being kept for safety reasons. On the way out the door, Dave turns to me and says, "You might want to look for a little help yourself." So, the next day, I called the marshals and said, "You know, yesterday, I witnessed a crew of your people take Dave Borah away and put him in hiding. Should I be concerned about my safety?" They said, "Has anybody threatened you?" I said, "Well, no." I was told, "Until that happens, don't worry about it."

The threat against Dave Borah was of such concern that he was taken off the case. "He wasn't happy about it," remembered AUSA Pat Sullivan. "It had been his case for six years, and now he was out." To replace Borah, DEA supervisors assigned to the case Special Agent Jane Anglestad, who was new to the Southern District of Florida.

REVELATIONS ABOUT THE COLOMBIAN HIT list threatened to derail the case. Clark and Sullivan went before US District Court Judge Federico A. Moreno, who had been assigned to *United States of America v. Augusto Guillermo "Willy" Falcon et al.* The prosecutors argued that Falcon, Magluta, and Lorenzo were a threat to the system. "We assert," Clark told the court, "that these defendants need to be separated and held in separate maximum-security facilities far away from one another. They have already demonstrated an ability to subvert the system by having cell phones smuggled into their facility. We need to put a stop to this before more potential witnesses are eliminated."

Lawyers for the defendants argued that Falcon and Magluta, with little evidence to support it, were now being blamed for every bad act that occurred in

Miami. Said attorney Roy Black to the judge, "There is no evidence that we know of, on the record, connecting my client to all these shootings and killings. To move the defendants to other facilities while we are at a crucial stage in preparing for trial puts an unfair burden on the defense."

The judge sided with the prosecutors. Falcon was bound, shackled, and shipped to a federal penitentiary in Atlanta, Georgia. Sal was transferred to the segregation unit at the MCC, where visitations were held behind plexiglass. Benny Lorenzo was moved to Broward County jail.

For Willy, the conditions were especially rough. He was incarcerated at United States Penitentiary (USP) Atlanta in a section known as Charlie Housing Unit, in what were referred to as "strong cells." These cells were the smallest allowed by law: five feet wide by nine feet long. There were only five strong cells, reserved for inmates who were believed to be violent and dangerous. Only the lieutenant for the segregation unit had a key to open the locked, chicken-wire gate to feed those in the strong cells. A bunk bed and a stainless-steel toilet took up nearly the entire cell. There was no air-conditioning, with only one standing electric fan in the hallway to service all five cells.

When Falcon arrived at the facility, it was July—midsummer. The temperature in the Charlie Unit, Falcon figured, had to be over one hundred degrees daily.

After he had been there for two and a half weeks, Willy was visited by attorney Mark Dachs.

In the lawyers' visiting room, Dachs noticed that the inmate was kept cuffed in a belly chain and leg shackles, which was unusual. Said Dachs to a corrections officer (CO), "Could you please unchain our client during the visit? We can't properly prepare for trial under these conditions."

The CO said, "These are orders from upstairs. I can't do anything about it."

Dachs and Willy sat down. The lawyer explained to Willy that another of their defenders, Benson Weintraub, had that day filed what was known as habeas corpus motion 2241 in Atlanta federal court. The motion was to request an emergency court hearing so it could be explained to a local judge how the Bureau of Prisons was treating a pretrial inmate attempting to prepare for trial.

"How are you holding up?" Dachs asked Falcon.

"It's fucking brutal in here," said Willy.

"They're playing hardball with you guys. They want to break you before this thing even goes to trial."

Said Willy, "If I can handle my wife getting killed by some punks in the street, I can handle this. Fuck them."[2]

Dachs paused to take in the full weight of that statement. "I've got some bad news," he said.

"Okay," said Willy. "*Dime*" (give it to me).

"Judge Brown's decision on the ledgers was overruled."

"Fuck." Willy was disappointed. "Is that it? Can we fight it?"

"Yes. We will appeal it all the way to the Supreme Court. But that's going to take time. The trial date is likely to be postponed again, possibly until early '95."

Willy sighed. "I trust you lawyers know what you are doing. We have the best that money can buy."

Dachs warned his client, "I have to tell you . . ." He explained that the chances of winning an appeal on the issue were slim. The ledgers would likely be used as evidence against them at trial. They would have to come up with a strategy that mitigated the damage from the ledgers.

For the next hour or so, lawyer and client discussed the possibilities of this and other matters. Then they said their goodbyes.

WILLY FALCON GOT HIS WISH: he was transferred from the federal prison in Atlanta, but it was a case of going from the frying pan into the fire. Beginning in September, his new domain of incarceration would be the federal penitentiary in Marion, Illinois, one of the most notorious supermax prisons in the system. Sal and Benny were also transferred, Sal to the prison in Atlanta, where Willy had been, and Benny to FCI Talladega.

It seemed to Falcon that the government was engaged in psychological warfare, moving them around in a kind of shell game. It made it impossible for them to communicate with one another, and preparation for their trial was greatly inhibited by their legal counsel's inability to visit them regularly. On top of everything else, the sense of isolation was compounded: far from home, no

---

[2] In January 1994, two of the killers of Alina Falcon—Charles Cheatham and Raymond Smith—were found guilty at a trial where a third member of the group testified against them. They were not affiliated with any criminal organization; they were merely armed, homicidal purse snatchers. Both Cheatham and Smith were sentenced to life in prison.

visits from family or friends—it all seemed to be designed to make an inmate wither and die on the vine.

What followed were months of incarceration that were harsher and more debilitating than anything Falcon had experienced so far. He was on lockdown twenty-three hours a day, living in an institutional world with no natural light, no physical recreation, with limited access to phones, television, and radio.

On Thanksgiving of that year, he was visited by his daughter Aileen. She was shocked by what she saw:

> He was so pale, his skin was a color I'd never seen before. His teeth were rotten, and his hair was turning white. He was a man who always kept himself in good shape, but clearly, he was not able to have much physical activity. It was like he was aging right before our eyes. I was concerned about mental deterioration. I talked to the lawyers. They filed motions trying to have him moved closer to home. That was all they could do.

In the first week of December 1993, Falcon was in the rec room for his one hour out of his cell. He'd just come from the shower room, where he had one of three showers he was allowed per week. Among the newspapers in the rec room was a copy of the *Miami Herald*. Willy caught a glimpse of the headline: "Pablo Escobar Killed in Medellín."

He picked up the paper, started to read, and sat down. He was stunned.

Despite Escobar's maniacal behavior, which over time had caused problems for Willy, Sal, and all the other narcos, Falcon felt a sadness wash over him. The last time he spoke directly with Pablo was in early 1991. Escobar had turned himself in to authorities. He was imprisoned, but in a "prison" of his own creation—La Catedral, a compound high in the hills above Medellín. Supposedly, he could not leave. In exchange for Escobar's turning himself in, the Colombian government suspended its extradition treaty with the United States.

At the time, Willy was on the lam. At the end of that cell phone conversation with Pablo, as always, he warned his friend to "take care, and watch out for yourself." Pablo had chuckled and replied, "Watch out for myself? Doctor, I'm already in prison. You're the one on the run. You are the one who needs to watch out and take care."

Willy enjoyed Pablo's droll sense of humor. He thought back to all the time they had spent together: in Colombia, Panama City, Aruba, Madrid, Las Vegas, Disney World in Orlando. It was typical of Pablo that on the day after Alina was murdered, he contacted his old friend through a prison messenger. Said Willy:

> Pablo let me know that if I needed his assistance, if it was necessary, he would send their people to take care of whoever did this to my wife. He assured me that all I had to do was give them the green light and the situation would be handled immediately. He had escaped from La Catedral. He was on the run again. But still he had time to make it known that he would be there for the Doctor if need be. That's the kind of partner he was.

In the paper, there was a picture of Escobar's dead body. He was on a rooftop in Medellín, after being hunted down by the Colombian Search Bloc and DEA agents. They were gathered around his corpse, smiling, like he was a trophy animal. Falcon was disgusted. Yes, Pablo had gone insane; he had started killing as a means to an end. He had entered into a war with Colombian society and gone down a road from which there was no return but death.

Willy thought about what Pablo had said to him many times—that he would rather be buried in a grave in Colombia than live in a cell in the United States. It appeared that he was going to get his wish.

Willy, on the other hand, did not want to die. He wanted to live. And he wanted to live in freedom, not in a godforsaken cell in America or any other country. He was going to do everything in his power to beat his case and free himself from incarceration.

Most of this rested in the hands of his lawyers.

In January, Falcon was visited at the prison in Illinois by Albert Krieger. By now, Krieger had devoted his full attention to Willy's case. Now that the ledgers had been ruled admissible as evidence, Krieger told Falcon, he and the other attorneys had arrived at a novel defense. They were going to admit that he and Sal had been distributing large kilo shipments of cocaine, but they had stopped doing so because of the kidnapping of Willy's mother.

Any trafficking crimes prior to 1984 could not be prosecuted under the statute of limitations. The lawyers felt that this was an ingenious strategy, in that it eliminated all the government's evidence for crimes before 1984. They were admitting to those crimes. Thus, the lawyers would restrict their defense to the later crimes, which the lawyers would seek to portray as an assortment of lies from criminal snitches looking to save their own necks by incriminating Willy and Sal.

A thought entered Willy's head: he wished he had stopped trafficking in 1984. That was three years after his mother's kidnapping, a bad omen if ever there was one. That's when he should have quit.

Krieger had another item on his agenda: lawyers for Falcon had filed a writ of habeas corpus in the Southern District of Illinois. Noting that Augusto Falcon had been moved from the MCC in Miami to FCI Talladega to USP Atlanta before arriving at USP Marion and was held under the most extreme conditions at each of these facilities, Falcon's lawyers argued that his treatment was unconstitutional. It would be one thing if the petitioner was a convicted inmate, Krieger had argued before a judge in US district court, but Falcon was a pretrial detainee. Moving him to a series of prisons far away from where he was charged, burying him in solitary confinement, was making it difficult for the defendant, together with his lawyers, to mount a cohesive defense. It was a violation of due process. They were requesting that he be returned immediately to a facility in the Southern District of Florida. Krieger wanted Falcon to know that their petition was now being deliberated on by an administrative review board, and they were awaiting a decision.

After the lawyer conference was over, and Krieger was getting ready to meet with another client, he said to Falcon, "Willy, I'd like you to meet one of my clients. John Gotti from New York."

Willy looked up, and there was the former *capo di tutti capi*, boss of the Gambino crime family. You couldn't mistake that face. During his 1992 trial in New York, Gotti's face was on national TV nearly every night. Willy admired Gotti's style—the silk suits, cashmere overcoats, and perfectly coiffed hair. He and Krieger had lost that case. Gotti was awaiting an appeal of his life sentence. That seemed like a long shot; he was likely in prison to stay.

"Hey," Gotti said to Willy, extending his hand, "Albert tells me good things about you."

Gotti and Falcon shook hands. Said Willy, "It's an honor to meet the God-father."

"I saw that thing on TV about you and your partner. On *60 Minutes*." Gotti was referring to a segment on *60 Minutes*, the highly rated CBS newsmagazine program, about his and Sal's upcoming trial. "You guys did well for yourselves," said Gotti, referring to the program's contention that Los Muchachos banked more than $2 billion in profits in their time as cocaine merchants.

"Those were the days," said Willy.

"Who knows," said Gotti, "once we get out of here, maybe we can do some-thing." He was smiling and chuckling. They were joking around. But they were, in a way, sizing each other up.

Willy wished that the circumstances had been different, that instead of orange jumpsuits they were on the street, or in a club, wearing their best suits and sharing a bottle of Dom Pérignon.

"First we gotta get out of here," said Willy.

"Yeah," said Gotti, "I'm working on that—on appeal. Good luck with your trial. I hope you beat the bastards."

Willy said thanks. Corrections officers approached and pulled him away. He left Krieger and Gotti behind in the visitors' room and was shuffled off back to his cell.

BY EARLY 1995, WILLY FALCON had been in solitary confinement in various penal facilities for over three years (his petition before the US District Court of Illinois had been denied). His last two years at the penitentiary in Marion were a special kind of hell that Falcon experienced as slow-motion state torture. Studies have shown that long-term solitary confinement can destroy a person's mind. The Vera Institute of Justice, a nonprofit think tank that studies incarceration in the United States, conducted a survey that determined even one week in solitary confinement can lead to "significant changes in electrical activity in the brain." The results are often "social pain" and profound levels of depression.[3]

---

[3] In *No Human Contact: Solitary Confinement, Maximum Security, and Two Inmates Who Changed the System*, his scalding book on the effects of solitary confinement, author Pete Early describes a dark day in 1983 when two corrections officers—in two separate incidents—were murdered by inmates at the Marion pen-itentiary. This led to a new and harsher form of solitary confinement at the prison than anywhere else in the system. That form of punishment was still in effect when Falcon became an inmate there.

Falcon's lawyers brought in a private doctor to examine their client, who was diagnosed as having severe sensory deprivation and mental deterioration. Willy believed he knew what the government was up to: they were trying to drive him insane, or even lead him to commit suicide—a not-uncommon response to solitary confinement. Falcon counteracted those urges by always keeping a photo of Alina on him. Sometimes, he would hold that photo of his late wife and stare at it for hours while mumbling a prayer.

In April, Willy was transferred back to Miami and brought before Judge Moreno. Said the judge, "Mister Falcon, I see that you have lost a lot of weight since the last time I saw you, and that could be attributed to your solitary confinement. You understand that you are being housed in solitary confinement because you are considered a flight risk by the BOP. I can't tell the BOP to move you out of solitary confinement, but now that you are here in FDC Miami, close to your attorneys and investigators, you will be able to adjust and be able to work with your defense team."

By then, most of the other defendants had fallen by the wayside. Benny Lorenzo, along with Victor Alvarez, had agreed to a plea deal. Their attorneys, Edward Shohat and Jeffrey Weiner, were able to negotiate a guilty plea in exchange for a sentence of fifteen years and seven months. Tony Garrudo, with Frank Rubino acting on his behalf, negotiated a plea deal of twenty years in federal prison.

By October, when jury selection finally rolled around, Willy had gained back some weight and seemed highly focused on the task at hand. He and Sal had been meeting nearly every day with their lawyers and private investigators. Millions of dollars had been spent securing incriminating information on some of the government's scheduled witnesses, including Jorge Valdés and Pegy Rosello. Willy and Sal, unbeknownst to the defense lawyers, had paid at least two inmates at FDC to take the stand and tell made-up stories about Pegy and other witnesses. Willy and Sal had no hesitations about "playing dirty." Their years of solitary confinement leading up to this moment had created within them an animosity toward the prosecutors that ate at their souls. "By any means necessary" was the phrase that Sal often used. It reflected a visceral response to what they saw as the government's desire to psychologically destroy them before the trial even began.

Jury selection is a key element in any trial, but it was especially crucial for US v. Falcon. Both sides knew they would be drawing from a local pool of prospective jurors. By then, in prosecutorial circles, Willy and Sal were legendary for their reputation among some Cuban exiles of their generation. Said AUSA Sullivan, "We knew they had the ability to corrupt a jury. We were aware of that. I guess we felt that the evidence we had was so strong that we felt we were on solid ground. It's a danger that a prosecutor runs into sometimes—overconfidence."

The prosecution was so secure in their case that they had decided to forgo any attempt to indict Falcon or Magluta on murder charges. They could possibly have added a count to include the Juan Acosta homicide, but they felt the case was not strong enough. The other violent acts, including the murders of Weetchie Escobedo and Bernie Gonzalez—which they believed had been perpetrated on behalf of Falcon-Magluta—presented nowhere near enough evidence to charge the duo.

It was Pat Sullivan who argued that their multiple-count indictment as a continuing criminal enterprise, which included twenty-three separate counts of cocaine importation, was enough to put the defendants away for life.

Sullivan had finally taken control of the case. Though Chris Clark was the primary investigator, Sullivan would be making many of the key legal arguments in court. He was thought to be tenacious, thorough, and tough. Raised in an Irish Catholic family (as was Clark) in Pennsylvania, Sullivan's first passion was football. He had started as a linebacker in grade school, excelled on his high school team, and eventually received a scholarship to play football at the University of Pennsylvania. At the same time, he entertained the idea of being a lawyer.

To Sullivan, football and being a lawyer had one thing in common. On the field, Sullivan, at two hundred pounds, was small for a linebacker. What he lacked in muscle, he made up for with comprehensive preparation. As a ballplayer, he was an overachiever. Similarly, as a law student, he was no intellectual or silver-tongued devil, as were some in his chosen profession. There may have been others who could outdo him in verbal gymnastics or soaring legal argument, but there were few who would ever be as well prepared.

Part of Sullivan's preparation involved a reputation for cautiousness. In the book, *The Big White Lie*, an insider's critique of the War on Drugs by former DEA special agent Michael Levine, the author called out Sullivan as an empty suit unwilling to make cases unless he was certain he would win. Levine's book was an attempt to show how drug cases made by brave, street-smart agents were undermined and even sabotaged by spineless, politically minded bureau-crats in positions of authority. "I never indict a case I'm not sure I am going to win," Levine quoted Sullivan as telling him. Levine looked down on it, but to Sullivan, it was the right approach—the smart approach—and he applied the same standard to the case against Willy and Sal. He was not going to indict them on murder charges if the prosecutors didn't have the goods.

TO FALCON, THE FIRST DAY of jury selection felt like a carnival. It took place in an auditorium at the old federal courthouse, which was across the street from a new courthouse building that, started in the wake of Hurricane Andrew, was in the finishing stages of construction. For a man who had spent years in sol-itary confinement, to suddenly be in a large room with many civilians coming and going—even some very attractive women among the jury pool—was like a day in the park.

Not much of consequence happened the first day. All those who had been summoned to appear for jury duty—well over one hundred people—were given questionnaires to fill out and told to return them the following week.

Later that afternoon, at a conference with the lawyers, Willy noticed that a paralegal working for Saúl Cimbler, one of their attorneys, was someone he recognized. It was José Fernández, an old friend from their Little Havana neighborhood. José Fernández had come from Cuba to Miami at the same time as Willy. He was a few years younger, but they had played together in the streets and grew up in the same cultural surroundings as the other exiles trying to make it in America.

When they saw each other, Willy and José embraced. Sal also came over and hugged José. "I work for Saúl Cimbler as a paralegal," said José. "Isn't that great? I'm working on your case."

"Amazing," said Willy. "Isn't it interesting how all of us from the old neighborhood are always brought back together for one reason or another? It's fate."

"Yeah," said José. He seemed excited about something, hardly able to con-tain himself. "Listen, I need to talk to you guys. You have a minute?"

"Sure," said Sal. They moved off to a corner of the room away from the attorneys, so they could talk privately.

In a lowered voice, José said, "Listen, it just so happens that a friend of ours from school, Raúl Sarraf, lives in the same building as one of the prospective jurors in your case."

Said Sal, "Raúl Sarraf, I remember him."

Continued José, "The potential juror's name is Gloria Alba. She received a summons to appear for jury duty. Raúl says that he knows Gloria Alba and her husband very well. If you guys are interested, he trusts them enough to offer them money if she is willing to vote not guilty at your trial."

"But the jury hasn't been selected yet," said Sal.

"Right," answered José. "First, she would have to get selected. But if she does, would she be willing to play along for the right price? Our friend thinks she would."

Willy and Sal looked at one another. Said Willy, "Hell yes. Tell Raúl to go for it. We would be willing to pay this lady one million dollars if she gets selected and votes not guilty."

José smiled. "Okay, I'll let Raúl know. I'll get back to you when I hear something."

That night, Willy and Sal discussed the possibilities. Having a plant on the jury would be tremendous. Having her vote not guilty would guarantee at least a hung jury. But this woman first had to get on the jury, and that would depend greatly on how she answered the questions on the questionnaire that each of the prospective jurors was required to fill out.

Through one of their attorneys, they got ahold of a sample questionnaire. After consulting with the lawyer, Willy and Sal filled out the questionnaire, providing answers that would be exactly what the prosecutors would want to hear.

The next morning, when Willy and Sal saw José Fernández in the conference room, they asked, "Anything?"

"No, not yet, but the offer has been made. They are thinking it over."

Said Willy to José, "Listen, we need you to deliver this questionnaire to Gloria Alba. She needs to fill out the paper in her own penmanship, but these are the answers that will help her get selected as a juror."

José took the paper. The next morning, he arrived with a big smile on his face. "Raúl Sarraf heard from the lady and her husband," he told Willy and Sal. "They're in."

"Here's how it's gonna work," said Sal. "The day she is selected to be on the jury, she'll receive a cash payment of five hundred thousand. At the end of the trial, when she votes not guilty, she gets the other five hundred thousand."

Willy said to his old friend, "José, this is exactly what we needed. We want you to know that we appreciate what you and Raúl have done. We will pay you and Raúl one million dollars as a finder's fee for this."

"Willy, Sal, I don't know what to say. You guys are the Robin Hoods of Miami. God bless you."

All that evening and into the weekend, the Boys were positively giddy. The jury hadn't even been fully selected yet and they already had a plant. They were the kings of their domain.

There was no discussion about morality, no questions about whether this was a violation of the law that could get them into deeper trouble. This was a chance to stick it to the prosecutors, to undermine their bogus, so-called system of justice and beat them at their own game. The thought that they could maybe pull this off and get away with it filled them with the kind of joy they hadn't experienced since they were snorting extra-hefty lines of yeyo off the backsides of beautiful blond models (aspiring actresses) in the Arabian Nights room at the Mutiny.

And then, on Monday, it continued.

This time it was Sal's cousin, Alfred Alonso, whom they had brought in to work as a legal assistant with another of their lawyers. Alfred was an accountant, just as Sal had been a long time ago. He was brought in to work on the money-laundering and tax-evasion counts in their indictment, and also to serve as a go-between with the outside world. Alfred had a story similar to what they had been told by José Fernández.

In the legal conference room at the jail, Alfred told Willy and Sal, "Miguel Vega sent me a message for you guys. He says that Eddie Guiterrez, who used to play softball on your Seahawk team, knows someone who received a summons to be a prospective juror in your trial. Vega said that this person is a good guy, and he has family members that were also involved in the cocaine business. Eddie had a conversation with this guy. The guy said to him, 'First of all, I believe that drugs in general should be legalized. It brings revenue into the city of Miami and creates jobs. Just look at the way Miami has progressed since the cocaine business took off in the nineteen seventies.' Then the guy says, 'In my heart, I could never vote to convict people like Willy and Sal, who helped a lot of people in Miami in their time of need.'"

"Damn," said Sal.

Continued Alfred, "Listen guys, Vega says this guy can be bought. He's ripe for the taking."

Said Willy, "Alfred, this is great news, but you need to tell Vega to tell Eddie to let this prospective juror know that he cannot say those things on the juror questionnaire. He cannot answer that he is for legalization of drugs, or that he thinks Willy and Sal are the Robin Hoods of Miami. You hear me?"

"Of course," said Alfred.

Sal said, "Have Vega tell Eddie to tell the prospective juror that we will pay him one million dollars for his vote of not guilty. But he first has to get on the jury. So, we'll give to him a mock questionnaire with all the answers he needs to write down to get selected. Because if he doesn't get selected, there's no payment."

Alfred said, "Right on. I'll let them know."

Within forty-eight hours, this prospective juror was all in. Not only did he agree to take the money in exchange for a not-guilty vote, but he made it clear to Willy and Sal's representative that he would take it upon himself to seek out and find other jurors who would be willing to take a secret payment. And he would seek to shape the direction of the trial. He would advocate for a not-guilty verdict among the other jurors, and he would argue on behalf of Willy and Sal once the jurors were in deliberation. He would control all these things by actively seeking to become the jury foreman, an influential position that would make it possible for him to tip the scales of justice. For the price of $1 million, he was determined to help Falcon and Magluta beat the system and walk out of court as free men.

The prospective juror's name was Miguel Moya.

19

"JUSTICE IS A BUZZARD"

IN THE YEAR OF OUR Lord Nineteen Hundred and Ninety-Five, Fidel Castro Ruz still walked among us. He had not yet been assassinated. It wasn't for lack of trying on the part of a generation's worth of Cuban exiles, who arose to the sound of the rooster somewhere in Little Havana, or wherever they were living, smelled the morning brew, and fantasized about Castro's death. Preferably, it would be violent and ugly, a car bomb or a bullet in the head at close range. Better yet, since it was a dream, and dreams were meant to be the manifestation of deeply held desires, they would get to strangle Fidel Castro to death with their bare hands, his eyes bulging out of his head, his mouth locked in a rictus grin, the air in his lungs ceasing to give sustenance to the lies, dastardly thoughts, and repressive dictatorial commandments that had characterized his Communist reign of power since it first began on New Year's Day 1959.

Willy Falcon had been doing whatever he could. The Contra struggle in Central America had come and gone, which, like the Bay of Pigs fiasco, constituted another defeat for the exiles. The Sandinistas remained in power, and the anti-Castro movement had been implicated in the Iran-Contra scandal. This may have damaged the movement's standing with the Republican Party. Republican presidents starting with Nixon and continuing with Reagan and Bush had been staunch allies, but the covert ops in Central America had been exposed—or at least partly exposed. Nobody was talking yet about how covert efforts to finance the Contras, under the direction of the CIA, had led to the beginnings of the cocaine business in America. That secret was safe—for now.

The new president, Bill Clinton, elected in 1992 and currently formulating plans for a reelection campaign in 1996, was, as a Democrat, not believed to be someone the exiles could trust. If they were to eliminate Fidel once and for all, it would not be with the help of the CIA under a Clinton administration. They would have to do it entirely on their own.

Falcon was willing. He estimated that he had paid somewhere around $15 million to the anti-Castro efforts over the last decade and a half. He and Sal had been major benefactors of the training camps in the Everglades, authorizing Miguel Vega to make payments of $200,000 every three months to PUND even after they were arrested.

Since being shuffled off to the supermax prison in Marion, Illinois, Willy had fallen out of touch with the movement. In that time, his lifelong friend and main contact, Antonio Garcia Perez, a.k.a. El Guajiro, had been convicted in early 1994 on cocaine-trafficking charges. This was a surprise to Willy. If he had known that El Guajiro was dealing coke, he might have taken the same tack he had with Ralph Linero, his pilot, when he told him, "You're not a dealer. That's not what you do. Stay in your lane." But it was too late for that now.

In the middle of jury selection, with Willy, Sal, and their representatives seeking to buy off at least two jurors so far, the defendants received an urgent message from Justo Regalado Borges, the legendary anti-Castro activist they had met through El Guajiro. Regalado was requesting a meeting with Willy and Sal as soon as possible to discuss something he characterized as "highly sensitive."

Sal was hesitant. "We got so much on our plate right now," he said. Willy suggested that someone of Regalado's stature would not be bothering them unless it was important. They could make time for the freedom fighter.

Arrangements were made for Regalado to accompany two of their attorneys on a legal visit. Present at this meeting was Alfred Alonso, Sal's cousin, who had become an important underling now that he was coordinating the situation with the juror Miguel Moya.

"Gentlemen," said Regalado, "I am most appreciative that you make time to see me right now. I know your trial is scheduled to begin soon; you must be extremely occupied. But what I have to tell you is something that simply could not wait."

Regalado mentioned that he was no longer with PUND. Since El Guajiro's conviction on cocaine charges, PUND had fallen apart as an organization. Regalado was now leader of a new anti-Castro group called United Command for Liberation (CLU). This group had acquired intelligence on Fidel Castro's plans for this year's Ibero-American summit meeting in the city of San Carlos de Bariloche, Argentina.

The annual gathering of Latin American leaders, which had been inaugurated in 1991, had for years been the apple of the eye of the anti-Castro movement, the perfect locale for a killing. Fidel would arrive to take a victory lap among the Latin American leaders, and the militant anti-Fidelistas would chop his head off. At least that was the plan. They had hoped to take out Fidel the previous year, when the Ibero-American summit was held in Cartagena, Colombia. The plan was to assassinate Castro with a rocket launcher as he was driving to the home of his good friend the Nobel Prize–winning author Gabriel García Márquez.

It never happened. Castro cancelled his trip to Colombia, perhaps because his people learned about the plot. Now the exiles hoped to take him out in Argentina.

"His itinerary is top secret," said Regalado, "nobody is supposed to know it, but we have a mole in Castro's inner circle. He will be arriving in Argentina in a matter of days. We have a team there already working on the logistics. We need five hundred thousand dollars immediately to facilitate this operation. If everything goes according to plan, the devil will be dead before your trial begins."

Willy and Sal were excited. Justo Regalado was a patriot who had spent twenty years as a political prisoner in Cuba. Since his release, he had devoted his life to *la lucha*. If Regalado felt the plan was solid, who were they to question it?

Said Willy, "Justo, we will authorize this payment with our people immediately. You will have the money within the next twenty-four hours."

They all stood. Regalado thanked Willy and Sal for having time for him even though they were in the midst of their own legal struggles. "You are true patriots," said Justo. "One day, the Cuban people will be eternally grateful. When Cuba becomes a free country, they will proclaim the names of Falcon and Magluta for helping the cause."

They all embraced. Regalado was led from the room by a corrections officer. Willy and Sal sat for a minute with Alfred Alonso. They were joined by Richard Martinez, who, along with Alonso, had become an important part of the inner circle. Long gone were the Tony Garrudos, Justo Jays, Tony Bembas, Benny Bs, and other street capos who kept the kilos flowing when Los Muchachos was in its heyday as the most successful cocaine-distribution network in America. They were all away in prison. Even Marilyn Bonachea, Sal's longtime paramour and gofer for Willy and Sal, had been prohibited by a federal judge from seeing the defendants.

In the years following Willy and Sal's arrest, Marilyn Bonachea had been Sal's closest friend on the outside. They had a bond that went back to their teenage years when they first dated. Marilyn felt a strong sense of loyalty to Magluta. In the 1980s, when her younger brother—who is deaf—was charged with and convicted of a double murder, Sal had lined up and paid for the brother's legal representation.

Marilyn assumed her role as Magluta's assistant and confidante with great fervor. She declared herself a paralegal for the attorney Mark Dachs in 1992 so that she could make regular legal visits to the prison. She brought in gourmet food for Willy, Sal, and Benny, and DVDs of current Hollywood movies for them to watch. She and Sal had sex in a conference room outside the view of corrections officers (this went on for three years in different prison institutions in different states).[1]

In April 1995, at the same time Willy and Sal were returned to prison in Miami, prosecutors Clark and Sullivan announced to Judge Moreno that they were thinking of calling Marilyn Bonachea as a hostile witness. The judge ruled that, as a potential witness at trial, she could no longer have any contact with the defendants.

With Marilyn and all the others no longer around, Willy and Sal's inner group of friends and enablers had fluctuated and dwindled. Now it was mostly new faces—with Sal, it was his brothers-in-law (Martinez and Eddie Lezcano) and cousin (Alfred Alonso). Willy leaned most heavily on old neighborhood friends like José Fernández, who would eventually take over Marilyn Bonachea's role as liaison with the outside world and sometimes paymaster. Then there were the private investigators (they had hired more than a dozen) and the attorneys, some of whom blurred the line between legal counsel and facilitator of their defendants' needs, legal and otherwise.

In the visiting area at the detention center, in the wake of Justo Regalado's visit, Willy said to Sal and Alfred, "That Cuban patriot is right. We should be proud of ourselves that with everything we have going, a trial coming up,

---

[1] Not to be outdone by Sal's amorous conquests, Willy fell into a relationship with a paralegal from Mark Dachs's office named Gloria "Cha Cha" Alfonso, age twenty. Cha Cha, whom Willy described as "the most beautiful woman I had seen in a long time," started coming to the prison in Miami with Dachs on legal consultations. Willy and Cha Cha were able to arrange sexual liaisons in one of the small conference rooms, with COs being paid to look the other way. (Gloria Alfonso confirmed that the relationship did take place, describing Willy Falcon as "the love of my life," but she declined to be interviewed for this book.)

having to defend ourselves, bribing jurors, we still manage to the best of our capabilities to support efforts to liberate our brothers and sisters in Cuba." The idea that this latest plot to kill Fidel might be successful, and that Castro would be assassinated right around the date of opening statements in their trial, was almost too good to believe.

Sal instructed his cousin to go directly to Luis Valverde, who controlled their remaining stash houses. "Get five hundred thousand dollars from Luis and deliver it to Justo right away."[2]

"Yeah," said Willy, "and after you do that, we need you to do us a favor. Go to Franco B's clothing store on Miracle Mile in the Gables. Tell our good friend Franco that Sal and me are going to need some new Brioni suits. Just like the ones we used to buy. But since our time in the free world, we've both lost weight and will need to be fitted. We will make arrangements with our attorneys to bring a tailor into the prison on a legal visit. Franco, or someone working for him, will need to come in here and take our measurements. You can pay Franco up front, whatever he says it will cost."

"Okay," said Alfred. He said goodbye and headed off to take care of Willy and Sal's financial expenditures, both counterrevolutionary and sartorial.

JURY SELECTION HAD TAKEN LONGER than expected. It was an arduous process, with the government exercising its right to block many more prospective jurors than they accepted. When it came to Miguel Moya, AUSA Clark expressed reservations to AUSA Sullivan, his cocounsel. Clark noted, "That guy looks just like Sal Magluta." Clark set his doubts aside, and Moya was selected.

With Gloria Alba, objections were expressed by Willy and Sal's team. Sandy Marks, a veteran jury consultant hired by the defense, felt that Alba's questionnaire showed that she had a bias in favor of the government. Unbeknownst to the jury consultant, Willy and Sal had provided Alba with her answers on the

---

[2] The Ibero-American summit took place in Argentina on October 17–18, 1995. Fidel Castro was in attendance. He was not assassinated. Once again, either details of the plot were leaked, or through an abundance of caution Castro's team changed his itinerary from what had been publicly announced. As with all the plots to assassinate Fidel—634, according to the Cuban state intelligence agency—this one remained nothing more than a costly fever dream among a group of men whom Castro derisively referred to as "*los gusanos.*"

questionnaire. They could not tell the jury consultant that they were the ones who had filled out Alba's questionnaire, but they argued that she was a good choice because she was Cuban and would understand guys like them.

So far, things were going as planned for the defendants. Both Alba and Moya managed to get themselves chosen as jurors, and Moya had successfully asserted himself as jury foreman. It was almost too good to be true the way things were unfolding. Willy and Sal had authorized payments of cash to both jurors. Every day, they met with their lawyers to deal with pretrial matters, which included a potential witness list submitted by the government that totaled over one hundred people. Their team of private investigators was digging up dirt on the government's witnesses. The buildup was intense, to the point where Willy and Sal were looking forward to the proceedings with heightened expectations.

Before the trial started, they landed another juror. Through Miguel Vega, Willy and Sal were notified that they had made contact with another potential juror, a woman whom Willy and Sal only knew by the code name "Pretty Woman." "You will have no trouble spotting her amongst the prospective jurors," Vega told Willy. "She's in her late twenties, and she's a knockout."

Through Pretty Woman's boyfriend, Vega was told that she was an admirer of Willy and Sal, and that she would vote not guilty whether they paid her or not.

Willy and Sal were startled. All these people coming forward and offering to throw the case was not something they had planned on. It was as if God—or at least the Miami Cuban exile community—was firmly on their side. There was some discussion between Willy and Sal that the more jurors there were on the take, the higher the possibility of a leak ("loose lips sink ships"), but those concerns were countered by the excitement that not only might they engineer a hung jury but maybe they could also even bring about a not-guilty verdict, which had previously seemed impossible.

The hard part was that they could not tell the jury consultant or their attorneys what was going on. It was their little secret.

AUSA Clark had reservations about the selection of Pretty Woman as a juror. He said to Pat Sullivan, "She looks like the kind of woman who would date a drug dealer." Nonetheless, she was chosen as one of the jurors.

On the day before opening statements, as the government finally prepared to present its case to a fully selected jury, US Attorney Kendall Coffey stood on the steps in front of the federal courthouse in downtown Miami. Coffey, age forty-three, had been appointed by President Bill Clinton in 1993 to head what had become the largest US attorney's offices in the country, overseeing 235 prosecutors in four locations in a South Florida jurisdiction that stretched from Vero Beach to Key West. Coffey had signed on to the Justice Department's War on Drugs with great fervor. He understood that his office was at the center of that war.

In his two years on the job, Coffey had become friendly with Chris Clark and his prosecutorial team. He monitored their case closely, announcing to media outside the courthouse, "This is the largest and most important narcotics case put forth by this office since I've been in charge. This is part of our ongoing federal effort to impede the smuggling of cocaine into South Florida, and to score another major victory in the War on Drugs. We think we have a strong case and look forward to presenting the evidence to a jury."

On the same day the US attorney gave his press conference, in a final meeting with their legal team, the jury consultant Sandy Marks explained to the Boys that it was important that they did not dress like gangsters in the courtroom. "Wear something simple," Marks said to Willy and Sal. "Present yourself as two people the jurors can identify with."

Willy and Sal looked at one another. The previous day their custom-fit Brioni suits had arrived at the prison. The suits cost $3,000 apiece (they ordered five, one for each day of the week).

Said Willy, "Look, Mister Sandy, I'm sure you are very good at what you do. You are known to be the best jury consultant in the business. But there's something you should know—when me and Sal walk into court, in front of a jury of our peers, we are going to look the best that we can. It's always been that way with us, and it always will be that way. We will be wearing the best suits money can buy, and we will hold our heads high."

Marks saw that this was not an argument he could win. Stubbornness in a defendant was one of the hazards of the job. Sometimes, it was a prescription for disaster.

October 23, 1995
That morning, Willy and Sal were awakened at four thirty a.m. and taken by corrections officers to a room where their prefitted Brioni suits were in garment

bags waiting for them. Their waist and ankle cuffs were removed, and they were allowed to get dressed: brand-new underwear and socks, white silk shirt under a black suit, with a matching tie, black shoes, black belt. Said Falcon:

It was strange. It had been four years since I had worn any kind of street clothes, much less a brand-new, expensive suit. I felt a sense of freedom in those clothes. Me and Sal looked at each other. It was like we were putting on our uniforms to go into battle. We felt secure about ourselves.

Once fully garbed, they were again cuffed and shackled and put into a special cell, where they waited nearly three hours. Eventually, a gaggle of US Marshals came for Willy and Sal and led them down a long underground tunnel that connected the jail with the courthouse building. They were put in a freight elevator that led to the tenth floor. They were taken off the elevator by the marshals and led to an antechamber outside the courtroom. Their cuffs were removed, and they were escorted by the marshals into the courtroom, which was well lit and already packed with people.

It seemed fitting that the trial of Willy and Sal was the first major case to take place in the newly constructed federal courthouse. The courtroom was impressive. Shiny mahogany wainscotting and high ceilings, lit up like a Broadway stage. The room reminded Willy of when he and Alina had lived in New York and frequently went to see plays at one of the historic theaters near Times Square. When greeted by his attorney, Albert Krieger, Willy could have sworn he was wearing stage makeup. The entire event was like a theatrical production.

Judge Federico Moreno, in a black robe and under an American flag, sat like a potentate on what is called his bench, an elevated perch from which he could survey the prosecution and defense tables, and the spectators' gallery, with wooden benches lined like church pews all the way to the back door of the courtroom.

After a bang of the gavel called everyone to attention, and some preliminary introductions, Judge Moreno gave his instructions to the jury, which meant that he explained the charges and reminded the jurors of their obligations to carefully listen to the testimony and consider the evidence. The judge had no way of knowing that three of the twelve jurors were already on the take.

AUSA Clark gave the government's opening statement: "Ladies and gentlemen, may I present to you the case of the United States of America versus Augusto Guillermo Falcon and Salvador Magluta. Willy and Sal. Los Muchachos. The Boys."

And so the trial began. For the next fifteen weeks, the courtroom became a showcase for the expansive evidence gathered by a small army of government investigators. A distinguished team of defense lawyers sought to poke holes in the evidence, through aggressive, sometimes brutal cross-examination of the government's witnesses, and by entering into the record counterevidence—documents, private correspondence, sworn statements, and criminal records of those on the stand.

For the prosecution, it was a carefully curated presentation of witnesses designed to take in the full scope of the Falcon-Magluta cocaine operation. There was DEA Special Agent David Borah, who described how he first learned about Los Muchachos in 1986 and, in what seemed like an impossible dream at the time, opened a criminal case that would go on for years. FBI Special Agent Ken Paulin of the bureau's Racketeering Record Analysis Unit testified about the ledgers, which had been a source of fierce pretrial maneuvering before finally being declared admissible. Agent Paulin broke down the coded language of the ledgers and explained how they were an accounting of transactions worth hundreds of millions in cocaine profits. And then came the "snitch" witnesses from inside the organization: Jorge Valdés, who had been with the Boys almost from the beginning; Jack Devoe, their star pilot; Sermon Dyess Jr. and Butch Reddish, who explained the operation in Clewiston; Keith Eickert, who testified as to how KS&W (the K stood for Keith), the powerboat-engine-building company, had been started as a way to launder cocaine proceeds; Sergio Greco, who ran the stash house where three thousand kilos had been confiscated, his appearance on the stand making it possible for the prosecution to enter into evidence the kilos that had been seized. A few of those kilos were passed among the jurors, the kind of show-and-tell exhibit that is worth its weight in gold.

And then there was Pegy Rosello, brother of Tavy Falcon's wife, a blood relative, whose insider account of Willy and Sal's cocaine operation was the single-most-devasting testimony in the entire trial. Willy, watching Pegy from the defense table, was stunned; he had held out hope that Rosello would change his mind before taking the stand, but there he was, still in his late twenties, fresh faced, surprisingly calm and poised, as he delivered testimony designed to destroy Los Muchachos once and for all.

There were other witnesses and more evidence, the kind of massive accumulation of evidentiary firepower that can make a prosecutor cocky, which was the case with Chris Clark, whose supreme confidence rankled the family members of Falcon and Magluta who attended the proceedings nearly every day.

For Willy and Sal, the trial was a complex ritual that required an almost cosmic level of attention on their part. For one thing, in the beginning, they sought to figure out who their friendly jurors were and establish some kind of hidden communication with them. They were able to make eye contact with Miguel Moya, but they needed to be discreet so that no one else in the courtroom recognized what was going on. They nodded toward Gloria Alba, who nodded but preferred not to make eye contact with the defendants. Willy frequently made contact with Pretty Woman.

Sandy Marks, the jury consultant, who sometimes sat at the defense table, saw Willy and Pretty Woman making what he interpreted as "goo goo eyes" at one another. "Yes," Willy remembers Marks saying to him. "Good. Make her fall in love with you. Seduce her with your eyes."

Eventually, Willy and Sal were able to open up a correspondence with Miguel Moya. Sal wrote a letter that was delivered by Alfred Alonso to Moya. They asked him to write back and let them know how things were going with the jury. What were their opinions of the evidence and how were they interpreting the testimony?

Right away, Moya wrote back. Off in a corner of the lawyers' conference room, Sal read the letter to Willy: "To my friends, don't worry about anything. I got you guys covered. As you know by now, I was selected to be jury foreman, and I am beginning to control things in the jury room." Moya explained that there were two women jurors he had gotten to know on the lunch breaks. He felt they could be reached. "I would like to have your permission to approach these two ladies and offer them money for their vote of not guilty. I am positive that they will be happy to make some money for themselves, and by us paying them we will guarantee that they will do the right thing for you guys at the end of the trial."

Willy said to Sal, "Coño. This guy Moya is really on a mission."

Over the course of the trial, Moya wrote more letters. He was so forward in his plans to control the jury that Willy and Sal had to occasionally talk him down. Sal wrote in a return letter, "Don't be so aggressive or trusting of every juror. Don't make them suspicious of you."

Throughout the days of testimony, the defense did not have many high-water marks. One good day was when a man named Nestor Galleano, a Colombian, took the stand. Galleano had been a cocaine pilot for Manuel Garces in the 1970s, flying shipments of kilos from Colombia into the Caribbean islands and Miami. He explained how Garces—the Godfather—met Willy and Sal and introduced them to Pablo Escobar in Medellín and the Valencia brothers from Cali. Galleano was on the stand to establish a link between the Colombian suppliers and Los Muchachos.

In the mid-1980s, Galleano had been busted in New York at a time when he was working with the Ochoa family of the Medellín Cartel. From the stand, he admitted that he had been convicted and given a sentence of thirty years. He was currently residing in federal prison serving his sentence.

In his direct testimony presented by AUSA Clark, Galleano was on the stand for the better part of the day. Afterward, Marty Weinberg came forward to conduct cross-examination. Acting as cocounsel for Sal Magluta, Weinberg had an ace in the hole. Weeks earlier, the defense had been contacted by Manuel Garces all the way from Medellín. Garces let the defense lawyers know that he had received several letters from Nestor Galleano that they might find interesting. Galleano was writing from prison, where he had learned that prosecutors were fishing for information on Willy and Sal. Galleano wrote Garces asking if he could supply him with any dirt that he might have on the two. Wrote Galleano, "The stars appeared to me and made me an offer I couldn't refuse. They asked me, are you with us or against us? Imagine another indictment for racketeering or organized crime with the minimum of thirty years to life prison sentence without parole. Me without a lawyer, broke and more cooked than a fish in a pan. In other words FRIED."

Not only did Weinberg confront an unsuspecting Galleano with the letters, he had them blown up on a screen in the courtroom.

"In this case," the defense attorney asked the witness, "when you say the stars came to you, what or who are you referring to by that?"

"The stars are the prosecutors who came to me and the DEA agent David Borah."

"They came to you and offered you a deal."

"Yes."

Weinberg produced more letters and had Galleano read them out loud: "Dear Old Man, this is the Willy and Sal festival. There are over one hundred potential government witnesses here with me on the thirteenth floor of this federal prison building. We are all here in the same place trading stories about Willy and Sal. These people are doing this to help themselves. . . . The eagle of justice is a buzzard in a prison desert which threatens to slowly devour the bravest person to their death. . . . The truth of the matter is, you have to dance to the gringo beat. . . . Because out of a thirty-five-year sentence, I have to do thirty years. I am forty-one years old, a rather old man, not even a Galapagos tortoise could complete that sentence."

In another letter, Galleano wrote: "Dear Old Man, if you assist me in this matter, I won't even have to mention your name to the DEA agents about my dealings with you. I don't want to see you here, and whenever it is, I want to be there in my beloved and sorely missed Medellín, since my heart remains with you in those mountains."

Not only had Garces not provided Galleano with anything incriminating of Willy and Sal, unbeknownst to the aspiring informant, his letters were passed along to the defense team.

The reading of the Galleano letters in court was a humiliation to the witness and an embarrassment to the prosecutors, but, for the defense, the joys were transitory. Overall, the trial was an embarrassment of riches for the prosecution.

In February 1996, after four months of testimony, closing arguments from the government and the defense, and a closing charge from the judge, the jury received the case. One day into deliberations, in a total surprise, the jury foreman, Moya, announced to the judge that the jury wanted to be sequestered. This was strange; most juries do not want to be cooped up in a hotel while deliberations drag on. Moya explained it all in a letter to Willy and Sal, as he noted that having the jury sequestered would make it easier for him to control the situation and aggressively convince any holdouts that Falcon and Magluta should be found not guilty.

The jury was sequestered at the less-than-glamorous Everglades Hotel in downtown Miami.

On February 16, they were ready. As jury foreman, Moya announced to the court that the jury had reached a verdict.

By now, unbeknownst to everybody except Moya, Willy, Sal, and a small handful of coconspirators, there were a total of five jurors on the take (four regular jurors and one alternate).

Years later, AUSA Clark remembered the day like it was yesterday:

Our hangout was Tobacco Road [a bar near the downtown courthouse]. The jury had been deliberating for less than a week. It was me, Pat, Jane, and Dave Borah. Even though Dave was no longer on the case, we felt he deserved to be there for the verdict. Suddenly, we all get beeped. We're wanted back at the courthouse. It's not a hung jury; that would have been reported to the judge already. They've reached a verdict. This has to be good news, right? Because there's no way a jury is going to acquit these guys. They could have convicted them on one count, or on eighteen counts. Under the sentencing guideline, that has no impact; they would have gotten the same sentence—life. We headed back to the courthouse. It was dusk, around seven p.m., and it was getting dark. We were feeling pretty confident.

Back in the courtroom, everyone gathered, including a SWAT team protective detail of armed marshals. Willy and Sal were brought into the courtroom. Clark noticed that they were "ashen. They looked like they were going to the gallows. Whatever their arrangement was with Moya and the other jurors, they looked like they didn't believe it was possible."

Clark was approached by Albert Krieger, who said, "You know, let's do the forfeiture hearing down the road, okay? Let's not deal with that tonight, if it's okay with you."

Krieger was conceding a guilty verdict, acknowledging that there would be forfeiture issues to deal with as a consequence. Clark took note: even the top defense lawyer assumed they were guilty.

Though the courtroom was packed with legal eagles, marshals, media, and a legion of spectators, the room was hushed. Pat Sullivan leaned over to Clark and said, "Listen. Even if they acquit on those first few counts, the kingpin counts, don't freak out. We'll convict on the other counts."

The jury filed into the courtroom. Everyone stood, until the judge asked everyone to sit.

Miguel Moya stood to read the verdict. Remembered Clark:

So they read the first count. As to Augusto Guillermo Falcon, not guilty. Okay. That's what Pat warned me about. Salvador Magluta, count one, not guilty. Then they get to count two, conspiracy to import cocaine. Not guilty. Then count three, conspiracy to possess or intent to distribute cocaine, not guilty. And then count four. And count five. I'm just looking at the foreman like, What is this?

Willy, Sal, and their supporters all erupted. The defendants embraced, and the lawyers slapped each other on the backs. The judge banged his gavel, but to no avail. It was celebration time in the universe of Los Muchachos.

Outside the courthouse, with media lights set up to illuminate the scene for television cameras, US Attorney Kendall Coffey stood with Chris Clark, Pat Sullivan, and Jane Anglestad. They all looked as though they had been clubbed in the head with baseball bats. A cloud of gloom hung over them like a tropical depression. Coffey, barely able to speak, said into a microphone, "I can't recall a case with this much evidence that was this well presented. I am shocked by the result."

It had been a stressful verdict for Coffey. He was the one who had personally shot down a plea deal with Willy and Sal, in which they would have pleaded guilty to cocaine charges and turned over three thousand kilos and $40 million in narcotics proceeds. That would have gotten the prosecutors the conviction they wanted and constituted an impressive seizure of funds for the government. A lost opportunity.

That night, the prosecutors all went back over to Tobacco Road. They ordered drinks, and then more drinks. A Jimmy Buffett song played over and over on the jukebox. They were too stunned to yet consider the possibility of a fixed jury. Everyone was despondent, but most especially Kendall Coffey. He grabbed his car keys and, without even saying goodbye, left Tobacco Road.

It would be a few days before Clark and the others heard what happened to Kendall Coffey that night. He had gone straight from the bar to the Lipstik Adult Entertainment Club, a strip club located in south Miami-Dade. There he drank more alcohol and got into an altercation with a dancer. He bit her on the arm, breaking the skin, and was thrown out of the club by bouncers.

In the days that followed, a boyfriend for the dancer approached Kendall Coffey and demanded a payment or insisted they were going to press charges. Coffey let it be known that he was not going to pay. The boyfriend went to the media, and the case exploded in the pages of the *Miami Herald*, and elsewhere. Coffey at first denied everything, even that he had been at Lipstik. But he had paid his bill that night using his official US attorney's office credit card, so it was easy to trace. Coffey came under investigation by the US Justice Department under Attorney General Janet Reno.

The inquiry lasted three months. Coffey was given a choice: resign or be fired. In May, the good family man, married with two kids, resigned as US attorney for the Southern District of Florida. At yet another press conference on the outdoor steps of the federal building, Coffey announced, "This is the most painful and difficult decision of my life. But leave I must because my family has already paid too great a price for the sacrifices that accompany public service."

Decades later, still troubled by Coffey's fall from grace, Chris Clark said, "He had a beer with us, and he took off and went to Lipstik. All Kendall had to do was say, 'Chris, come with me.' I would have kept him out of harm's way. I would have said, 'Kendall, you can't use your government credit card.'"

When Willy and Sal heard how it played out for Kendall Coffey, they were almost as ecstatic as they had been on the day of their verdict.

NEITHER WILLY NOR SAL WAS released immediately upon the return of their stunning not-guilty verdict. Both were still facing other charges. On some of those charges, they had already gotten lucky.

Before the trial, when the government was feeling confident about *US v. Falcon-Magluta*, the Florida district attorney allowed that the prison time Willy and Sal owed on the Video Canary case—fourteen months—be counted as "time served." That case was finally closed. Then, in Los Angeles, where they had been indicted in 1985 on charges of cocaine possession and conspiracy to sell, that case fell apart. It was revealed in a sensational corruption scandal known as "the Ramparts scandal" (after the precinct in South Central LA where the scandal was centered) that a crew of renegade police officers had been robbing and extorting cocaine dealers. Some of the police who arrested the Boys at the Marina del Rey condominium were part of that crew. Subsequently, the charges against Willy and Sal were dropped.

The Boys were still facing a money-laundering indictment in the Middle District of Florida related to the KS&W powerboat-engine-building business. Sal was facing indictment on fraudulent passport charges stemming from the fake passports that had been confiscated when his house on La Gorce Island was raided. Willy was facing two illegal gun possession charges.

Within days of their acquittal, Willy and Sal's high-priced legal talent filed motions requesting that they be released pending trials in their outstanding cases. Falcon's motion was denied. Magluta's motion—on the lesser charge of false passport versus the illegal possession of a gun—was granted. Sal posted a bond of $500,000 and was released from jail.

At the press conference outside the federal building, Sal, speaking to reporters, thanked "the Lord for watching over us." From the windows of the nearby prison could be heard clamoring and shouting. It took a while to figure out that the noise coming from the prison was that of inmates cheering for Salvador Magluta.

SAL WAS FREE, AND IT should have been a good time for the released narco, but the following months and years were instead a time of self-destruction. The seeds of Sal's downward spiral could be traced to his arrest at La Gorce in 1991. Being careless with the ledgers, after he had been warned often by both Willy and Benny B., was a source of humiliation on Sal's part. He had fucked up in a big way. Then there was his having brought Fat George to Willy's house in Fort Lauderdale, a screwup that had led directly to Willy's apprehension.

Many times, after their arrest, while they were incarcerated together at the same facility, Sal was nearly in tears telling Willy that he blamed himself for their problems. Willy told Sal, "Forget it. It's not your fault." But Sal felt guilty.

Guilt had became a regular companion for Sal. Marilyn Bonachea, his long-time friend and lover, once visited Sal in the lawyers' conference room at the Miami Detention Center. Marilyn noticed that Sal was in a somber mood. She asked, "Sal, what's wrong with you today?"

He began to cry. He was sobbing, and he said, "'I did a bad thing.' We were all Catholics, you know. That's how we were raised. He was feeling guilty. That's when he admitted that he played a part in the murder of Juan Acosta, the lawyer."

The murders didn't stop with Juan Acosta. Marilyn would later testify that Sal told her he was involved in other murders, and that he was planning to murder other potential witnesses who were going to testify at his trial.

The murders were the elephant in the room, reported in newspaper headlines and on the television news, but not charged against Willy or Sal. Following their acquittal, law enforcement got serious about pinning the murders and attempted murders of witnesses on Los Muchachos. Federal prosecutors had convicted the three Colombian sicarios in the murder of Juan Acosta, but they had not yet connected it to Willy or Sal. That came later, when, after the convictions, detectives and prosecutors approached one of the Colombian hit men with a picture of Eddie Lezcano. "That's the guy," said the gunman. "He's the one who showed us the photos and gave us the guns."

Lezcano, Magluta's brother-in-law and the owner of HoneyComb Paging and Cell Enterprises, which had for years provided Los Muchachos with pagers and cell phones, had, according to prosecutors, become a key conduit in the conspiracy to kill potential witnesses. With Lezcano now having been identified, he, along with two Colombian accomplices, was indicted on murder charges. At a trial in front of Judge Joan A. Lenard, some of the Colombian hit men—including Juan Carlos Correa and Juan Velasco—testified against the defendants. The witnesses were vigorously cross-examined. After a two-month trial, the jury found Eduardo Lezcano guilty along with his codefendants, Jairo Castro and Judy Ramirez. They were convicted on three counts for each murder, although they were not accused of firing the fatal shot. They were found guilty of providing weapons, money, addresses, and other information to help the assassins hired to kill the witnesses between 1989 and 1993. The three defendants—Lezcano, Castro, and Ramirez—received life sentences in prison.

At the same time all this was happening, another startling sequence of events unfolded in the Willy and Sal universe. Weeks after their acquittal, AUSA Pat Sullivan received a call from a man who identified himself as having been on the jury. Said Sullivan, "The guy was distraught about how the trial had turned out. He felt that Falcon and Magluta should have been found guilty. He told me about the jury foreman, Miguel Moya, how he had browbeaten many of the jurors into voting not guilty. 'That guy was up to something,' said this juror. 'You should look into that guy.'"

Sullivan and AUSA Clark talked it over. Even before the phone call, they had begun to discuss the possibility of the jury having been tampered with. The more time that passed, the more obvious it seemed. They did not want to be seen as being vindictive because they had lost their case, so they contacted the FBI and IRS, who initiated an investigation of Miguel Moya.

It was supposed to be a secret investigation, but rumors spread. IRS investigators were looking into Moya and his family. Moya had been spending conspicuously since the Falcon-Magluta verdict, buying a new house and a boat.

Sal Magluta, who was still out on bail, heard the rumors: the feds were on to Miguel Moya. It was only a matter of time before Moya got arrested.

Meanwhile, Sal had a trial coming up. In February 1997, he was scheduled to go on trial on false passport charges. The trial took place in the same federal court where he and Willy had been tried. He was facing a sentence of three to four years. Midway through the trial, Sal told his attorneys that he was going out to the car for something. He never came back. Just as he had done in Los Angeles years ago with Willy, he skipped bail. The judge issued a warrant for his arrest.

Many who knew Sal could see that he was becoming increasingly unhinged. He was making bad choices. Attorney Mark Dachs once referred to Magluta as "a genius." But now, Sal was like an engine with a loose fan belt; his mind was slipping.

On April 16, federal investigators received a tip that Sal Magluta was living under a false identity at the Ritz-Carlton hotel in Palm Beach, one hundred miles from Miami. A team of US Marshals was sent to stake out the hotel. That night, at eleven thirty p.m., they pulled over a Lincoln Town Car driving near the hotel. It was Sal Magluta, wearing a cheesy sandy-blond wig. When he stepped out of the car, his wig fell off; his head was shaved bald. Inside the car, marshals found a canvas bag containing $20,000 in fifty- and hundred-dollar bills and a cell phone. Sal was carrying a passport under the name Juan Manuel Alonso, a current driver's license under that name, as well as a social security card, a Dade County voter registration card, and credit cards from Visa, American Express, Mastercard, and Macy's.

Magluta was taken into custody.

Just one year earlier, Willy and Sal had defied the odds with their seemingly miraculous acquittal. Now their world was collapsing from within.

IN OCTOBER, SAL RETURNED TO US district court and was put on trial again. This time, he was facing additional charges for jumping bail and once again using false identifications. Security in the courtroom was reinforced with an extra-large contingent of armed US Marshals. Magluta was found guilty and given a sentence of nine years.

Not long after Sal's apprehension, the other shoe dropped. Miguel Moya was arrested and charged on fourteen criminal counts, including bribery, bribery conspiracy, witness tampering, and tax charges.

In what was seen as a vindication for the Southern District of Florida, Moya went on trial in February 1999. It was not an open-and-shut case. Though, during their investigation, FBI investigators had a recording of Moya partially admitting to an undercover agent, Jack Garcia, that he had taken money from representatives of Willy and Sal, it was not conclusive. The first trial ended in a hung jury. Moya was retried in July and found guilty. As was the custom, the prosecutors celebrated at Tobacco Road.

Meanwhile, from prison, Falcon took in news of these various legal fiascos like a fighter fading in the late rounds, the accumulated blows leaving him punch-drunk. He had his own legal matters to deal with, which involved two separate trials on gun-possession charges. In 1996 and 1997, Falcon sat through those trials. One lasted three weeks, and he was found guilty and received a prison sentence of 120 months. The other trial, involving the .38-caliber Colt pistol seized when Falcon was arrested at his home in Fort Lauderdale, lasted two weeks and resulted in a guilty verdict, with a sentence of 47 months.

As substantial as these convictions were, for Willy and Sal, they were minor compared with what they knew was waiting around the corner. Ever since it had been discovered that Miguel Moya had been on the take, it was a foregone conclusion that the US attorney's office would retry Willy and Sal on cocaine, money-laundering, and tax-evasion charges. Rumor was that the government was preparing a massive prosecution under the RICO statute (Racketeer Influenced and Corrupt Organizations Act) that would include not only Willy and Sal but also a whole new round of codefendants.

In August 1999, when this new indictment was announced in the media by the Department of Justice, it was as if an atom bomb had hit at the heart of the Los Muchachos universe. Prosecutors had gone back to the origins of their case and dug deeper into the evidence against Willy, Sal, and their crew. There were the expected additional counts related to the bribing of jurors (investigators had by now found out about Gloria Alba and Maria Penalver as well). But they were startled to see that two lawyers—Mark Dachs and Richard Martinez—were also included as codefendants in the indictment. And finally, most sobering of all, were the numerous counts of murder and attempted murder in furtherance of the racketeering conspiracy.

The indictment was comprehensive, detailed, and seemingly insurmountable.

Buried within the indictment was a surprise for Willy Falcon. Back in 1996, not long after their acquittal, Marilyn Bonachea had been pulled over on a rainy night while driving to the office of lawyer Richard Martinez. Police stopped her for speeding and searched her car. In the trunk were several ledger books that Marilyn had been using to log covert financial transactions, including $7.7 million from the stash houses to make under-the-table payments to lawyers and private investigators and other fellow travelers of Los Muchachos.

Bonachea was held in the back of a squad car while the police contacted DEA Special Agent Jane Anglestad, who came to the scene and examined the ledgers. She ordered that they be confiscated and Bonachea placed under arrest.

Ledgers.

Again.

When Willy heard about Marilyn's ledgers being found, he almost thought it was a joke. He wanted to throttle Sal for allowing this to happen again.

Bonachea was arrested and then released on bond. Sal arranged for Marilyn to flee the state and hide out at a motel in upstate New York. Within a year, her whereabouts were discovered by FBI Special Agent Mario Tariche and an apprehension team. Bonachea was taken into custody. She was facing charges of obstruction, money laundering, and tax evasion stemming from the illegal payments she had made on behalf of Sal. Once the mandatory sentencing guidelines were explained to her, and she realized she was facing twenty-five years or more in prison, she flipped and told prosecutors all about her work for the Falcon-Magluta organization. She was sent back to the streets to work undercover for the FBI to gather more information on various associates of Los Muchachos.

The pressures were building, and with pressure, Falcon, being a gambler, felt a need to raise the ante. Now that his former attorney Mark Dachs had been indicted and was no longer representing him, Willy had lost contact with Cha Cha Alfonso, his temporary paramour. In 2001, he began a sexual relationship with a new partner, Katherine Ferro, age twenty-six, who was an attorney in the law office of one of his partners. These encounters, which took place at Miami FDC, had to be carefully orchestrated. Falcon would reserve a conference room at the far end of the hallway next to a coffee and vending machine area. He hired a fellow inmate to serve as a lookout while he and the lawyer engaged in sexual intercourse.

It was risky on several levels. An inmate was not allowed to have physical contact at all with a visitor, much less full-on copulation. For Ferro, a licensed attorney, it was against ethics as put forth by the Florida Bar to have sex with a client, especially one locked up behind bars. If it became known, Ferro would be fined or possibly lose her license to practice law.

For Willy, it was like a game of baccarat. The higher the stakes, the more he needed to take chances; it was part of his psychological makeup.

In October 2001, Ferro discovered that she was pregnant with Willy's child. In a visit to the prison, she told Falcon that she wanted to bring the pregnancy to term. Willy agreed that he would help take care of the child financially. But, they both agreed, Willy's role as the father would have to be kept secret, or Ferro's career as a lawyer might be over.

On May 16, 2002, Katherine Ferro gave birth to a healthy female child.[3]

---

[3] In support of the child, Arsenio Falcon, Willy's father, delivered monthly cash payments to Katherine Ferro. In 2017, when Arsenio Falcon passed away (Willy's mother passed away one year earlier, in 2016), the payments were delivered by Will Jr., Willy's son with Alina. Those payments continued until the child of Falcon and Ferro reached adulthood.

A new round of attorneys came into Falcon's life. They told him this new indictment was a beast. There was one strategy that might potentially help. If they could sever the counts against Willy from the counts against Sal, they could ask for a separate trial. This made sense. The murder counts in the indictment did not include Willy Falcon. The lawyers could argue that it would be prejudicial to try Falcon under the taint of those charges. It was a long shot, but it might work.

At first, Willy was against the idea. He and Sal had been partners for so long that it was impossible to conceive of their being tried separately, mostly on the same counts. Separating the cases basically would bring an end to Willy and Sal as a team. As disappointed as Willy was with Sal and his many screwups, there was that thing known as Cuban loyalty. *Uno para todos y todos para uno.* In the end, so many seemingly sacred values in their world had been trashed or destroyed on the long march to the penitentiary that being tried separately no longer seemed like a violation of Willy and Sal's partnership.

In August 2002, Sal Magluta went on trial. One of the key witnesses against him was Marilyn Bonachea, who was now living under the protection of WITSEC, otherwise known as the federal witness protection program.

When the trial was over, the surprise was that Magluta was found not guilty on the murder counts. The witnesses against Sal on these charges were an assortment of Colombian assassins looking to lessen their time in prison. The jury did not find their testimony conclusive. On most of the other charges— eight counts of money laundering, obstruction of justice, and bribery—Sal was found guilty.

At his sentencing before US District Judge Patricia Seitz, on January 19, 2003, Magluta pleaded for mercy. He said to his family, who was present in the courtroom, "I have failed you in every way possible and for that I am sorry."

Judge Seitz imposed on Magluta fines totaling $63 million and handed down a sentence of 2,460 months—205 years—in federal prison.

20

SHAME

WILLY FALCON SAW THE PROVERBIAL writing on the wall. The sentence given to Sal was a warning as much as it was a punishment. Falcon was facing a similar sentencing Armageddon if he went to trial. He discussed the possibility of a plea deal with his team of lawyers. Albert Krieger, his trial lawyer, had moved on. His primary counsel, Jeff Weiner, thought it was worth exploring with the US attorney's office what the terms of a plea deal might be. Could Willy get a reasonable sentence in the twenty- to twenty-five-year range, something in which he might walk out of prison one day while he was still capable of having a meaningful life? And what would he have to give up in return? Falcon made it clear that he was not willing to testify as a witness against anyone.

After months of negotiation, the US attorney's office and lawyers for Falcon reached a deal. The defendant would change his plea from "not guilty" to "guilty" on one count of money laundering. He would pay a fine of $1 million. As part of the plea agreement, he would admit that his crime—money laundering—played a major role in the financing of a large-scale cocaine-distribution conspiracy, and that it fueled the obstruction of justice by underwriting the bribing of jurors.

For the prosecutors, this was no small matter: Falcon's guilty plea would be a validation of the government's theory of prosecution underlying the pursuit of Willy and Sal. In exchange for this plea, the government would drop the jury-bribing count and forty-one additional counts of money laundering.

The plea deal had to be accepted by Judge Patricia Seitz. There was no guarantee that she would accept the terms. In sentencing Sal Magluta, Seitz—perhaps reflecting the views of many in the criminal justice system in the Southern District of Florida—let it be known that she was determined to slam the door on the era of Willy and Sal. For more than a decade, cases related to Los Muchachos had clogged the courts and cost taxpayers millions. A final comeuppance for Willy Falcon, something blunt and punitive, might just be a necessary statement of justice.

On June 16, 2003, at a change-of-plea hearing, Judge Seitz had questions about how and why the government had agreed to the deal. Present at this hearing were AUSA Pat Sullivan and AUSA Michael Davis, who had negotiated the deal not only with Falcon's attorneys but also with senior prosecutors in the US attorney's office. For the defense, along with Falcon, was his legal team, which included Weiner, Richard Diaz, Kenneth Kukec, and Katherine Ferro, with whom the defendant had recently—and secretly—had a child.

Judge Seitz asked the prosecutors how and why this day had come to be. Ironically, the man who stood to advocate on behalf of the deal was Pat Sullivan, one of Falcon's primary nemeses in the criminal justice system. "Your honor," said Sullivan, "this defendant's guilty plea to drug money laundering contains substantial benefits for the government and the public. First, it brings finality to the government's long pursuit of this defendant. There won't be a two-month trial. There will be no further prosecutions, no appeals from such prosecutions. . . . It obviates any doubt whatsoever for members of the public about the need for the extraordinary expenditure by the government of significant resources over a number of years to investigate and prosecute these acts of obstruction. The plea agreement allows the government and the public to obtain these results without the costs and risks of a lengthy trial."

In answer to further questions from the judge, Sullivan continued his defense of the agreement, speaking for nearly a half hour. At the core of his position was an acknowledgment that the case against Willy and Sal and their many underlings, associates, and coconspirators had become, for the Southern District of Florida, a crucial battlefront in the War on Drugs. The government had invested multiple millions of dollars in the many prosecutions related to the Falcon organization. Its pursuit had been relentless, spanning many years. Sullivan noted that back in 1992, before Willy and Sal's trial, there had been negotiations about a plea deal. "Different lawyers took part in those negotiations. They were before my time [on this case]. I have often thought back to why it couldn't have been in '92 or '93 that an extra step couldn't have been taken by someone, both sides or one side, to make this work back then. It would have prevented ten years of further litigation and the commission of new crimes and the expenditure of much more effort." Even Sullivan, one of the most respected prosecutors in the Southern District of Florida, was acknowledging the missed opportunities, and he was waving the white flag of surrender. "After everything we have been through, we are now in agreement to end it and not continue with another twelve, thirteen years of attack and counter-attack."

Still, there was the issue of a sentence. Judge Seitz was curious how a defendant who was facing criminal charges that, according to sentencing guidelines, would have brought him a sentence ranging from 292 to 365 months was receiving what some might consider a light sentence.

To which Weiner, one of the defense lawyers, answered, "Your honor, I have often suggested at times of sentencing that it would be a worthwhile experience for lawyers and judges to actually not just visit penitentiaries but spend a day or two or three in them, all of us in the system, probation officers, everyone, agents and others. Because with these guidelines and the terms that we talk about, actually experiencing the incarceration, not in general population but in the hole and in the SHU [Special Housing Unit], I think then one can fully appreciate and vindicate the community's interest in seeing that punishment is meted out here for the crime that Willy Falcon is pleading to. This was serious incarceration; incarceration that I have said to the United States Attorney, and to Pat and Mike, and to virtually all the US attorneys, I am not sure of many people I know who could actually endure the conditions of confinement that Willy Falcon has endured and come out with any semblance of sanity. And yet he comes out not only with his sanity, but with politeness, courteousness, genuine remorse, and the willingness to accept full responsibility for his acts and to plead guilty. And I think all of those are factors that I ask your honor to consider."

Weiner also noted that with the twelve years in prison that Falcon had already served, the twenty-year sentence was more like thirty-two years.

After Weiner spoke, Judge Seitz accepted Willy Falcon's change of plea.

One month later, at a sentencing hearing in the same courtroom, Seitz imposed a punishment of twenty years, in accordance with the recommendation of the prosecution. Then she addressed the defendant: "Mister Falcon, I wish you and your family all the best. May today begin a day of moving forward in a very positive way. It is never too late. Each day is the beginning of the rest of your life. Use the talents that God gave you to leave this a much-better world. God bless you."

AND SO, WILLY FALCON WAS jettisoned from the last remnants of civilian life further into the bowels of the federal prison system as a convicted felon. In being sentenced once and for all, he joined the ranks of his fellow Muchachos who had already been sentenced and sent away. These men, who had grown up together mostly in Little Havana as a generation of exiles, who had come to represent an entire generation of Cuban Miamians who were seduced by the glamour and riches of the cocaine era, now wore prison jumpsuits; awoke in a cell; circulated in prison to the extent that they were allowed; and went to bed according to a rigidly defined routine. They dreamed of a far-off day when they would be released. Each one was made to ponder the nature of his crimes and deal with the consequences for his loved ones on the outside.

Tony "Bemba" Garcia, having once been, along with Willy, the co-originator of the entire operation, thought he had left the cocaine business for good in 1980, when he cashed out of Los Muchachos. He was paid $8 million, which he thought would last him a lifetime, but it did not. "The problem with money," said Garcia, "is if you have what seems like an unlimited amount, you don't think about how to manage your money, because you think you don't have to." Even though he was no longer a part of the cocaine business, Tony Bemba was still very much a part of the Los Muchachos social circle. He served as a navigator on the speedboats during races, and he attended most of the parties for their daughters' quinceañeras, weddings, birthdays, and other events.

Eventually, Garcia got seduced back into the business, and that cost him his freedom. In 1987, he was sentenced to sixty years in prison.

What depressed him the most was that, as a child in Cuba, when he used to go visit his father in prison at the Isle of Pines, enduring seasickness and the trauma of seeing his father as a caged animal, he swore he would never wind up in a similar situation. And now he was.

Disappointment can be a motivator. Tony always felt bad that he didn't finish high school, and so in prison he not only attained his GED high school equivalency, but, after five years of study, he also attained an associate's degree in business management from Illinois Central College. "I think that was a great accomplishment for me," said Garcia.

Loneliness was the bête noire of prison life; it would stalk you like a hungry animal.

Only one time in his years of incarceration did Garcia see an actual animal. At the Beacon Correctional Facility, in Dutchess County, New York, a prison in the hinterland surrounded by woods, through a slit in the wall that served as a window to the outside world, Tony saw a deer or an antelope or something peering through the trees at the prison building. He froze, mesmerized by the sight of something alive and free. He thought, *That creature is free; I am the one caged like an animal.* It could not get any worse than this.

And, yet, every day Tony Bemba would awake and say, "Thank you, God, for another day of life on this planet."

Garcia's wife could not wait for him. They were divorced not long after his incarceration. Tony had a five-year-old daughter who would sometimes be brought by relatives for a visit. It was a thirty-hour drive from Miami, so the visits were rare—once a year or every eighteen months. The visits were a high point, but they also sent Tony on a downward spiral of despair.

And then, twenty-seven months into his sentence, his father died. The loss of his father hit Tony hard. The failure to liberate Cuba from Fidel Castro had haunted Tony even before his incarceration, but now he equated it with his father's passing, and the fact that he was behind bars only made it worse. It was a dark cloud that would not go away.

It was at this point that the government, in the person of AUSA Diane Fernandez, came calling. The pressure to testify against Willy and Sal was intense. Garcia was dragged into the courtroom and asked questions. He always took the Fifth. Fernandez added two years to his sentence for contempt.

In 2003, around the same time that Willy Falcon was sentenced, Tony Bemba, having served seventeen years behind bars, was released on parole. The first thing he did was go to the beach:

The thing I missed the most was the water, the sound of the waves, the seagulls overhead. In prison, you dream about these things. I went to the beach and stood there looking out at the sea. It was hard to make up for lost time.

If you get sent away for five years, that's one thing. Your wife sticks by you through the trial or the proceedings to pass, and then you only have two or three years left. The wife waits for you. Your dog might still be around. Your kids, maybe they were five, now they are ten. The difference is not so much. But when you are talking seventeen years, or twenty-something like Willy got, there's no dog that is alive after seventeen years. In most case, your kids are now grown up. It's a big difference. In some cases, your woman might wait for you, but in other cases they don't because it's a long time.

At the time of his release, Tony's daughter was twenty-two, a grown woman. Trying to pretend like the seventeen-year gulf in lost time was not an issue was an act of magical thinking. In many ways, they were strangers, but strangers with a strong blood connection. It was a prescription for sadness over the way things could never be.

Tony went to work as an accountant for his brother, who was a doctor. Then he transitioned into flipping houses in the always-developing Miami area, working with real estate agents and contractors. He was happy to be working, happy to be free, and even happier to be alive.

THE DAY THAT WILLY AND Sal's acquittal was announced in February 1996, Benny Lorenzo was in the hole at a penitentiary in Pennsylvania. It wasn't until a few days later, when Benny received a legal visit, that his lawyer told him, "Guess what? They got acquitted."

For weeks leading up to the verdict, Lorenzo had been telling the assorted mafiosi inmates he saw during his one hour of rec time, "Hey, my friends are gonna win. You watch, they're gonna win." They would say, "Get the fuck outta here. You fucking Cubans think you are all the shit." It was good-natured ribbing, but Benny B. was serious. "Way back when we first got arrested, we used to talk about how we could reach a juror. That was always in our back pocket." And then there was Lorenzo's inherent confidence in the power of Los Muchachos: "We were champions of softball, champions of racing, champions at smuggling. We were champions of everything."

After the not-guilty verdict, Benny told the imprisoned mafiosi, "See, I told you guys. Don't fuck with the Cubans."

When it was learned that it had been a tainted verdict, Benny did not lose any standing with his fellow inmates. In fact, everyone was in awe that Willy and Sal had managed to buy off a total of five jurors.

Early in his incarceration, Lorenzo realized that he would have to transform himself from the pretty boy he was known to be into a man whom no inmate would fuck with. He worked out in the gym every day and built up his physique until his body was almost unrecognizable. He developed a prison attitude, so that no one would test him. He hardened himself until that innocent kid he used to be, the basketball star out of Miami High, was a distant memory.

Back in the day, in civilian life, Benny had been the Muchacho most likely to get laid. He was good looking, and a ladies' man. In prison, things were different. Benny was not in the Miami Detention Center or any other South Florida facility where he might have used local contacts to arrange a way for him to have sex with a visitor, à la Willy and Sal. He was buried deep in the federal system, where one of the only options for sexual gratification was "Fifi."

Fifi was a simulated vagina. It was constructed from an empty toilet paper roll, or tube, which was lined with a surgical glove of polyurethane. The roll was wrapped in a towel. Sometimes Vaseline was rubbed on the entrance to the tube, and sometimes the entire contraption was placed in a microwave to give it warmth. An inmate could then penetrate the tube with his member, as if Fifi were, in fact, a warm, moist vagina. To some, it was viewed as the poor man's version of simulated sex. To others, it was an imaginative and slightly more satisfying version of jerking off.

For Benny B., it was a far cry from the seemingly unlimited number of sexual options he had when he was in the world as a member of Los Muchachos, but it was better than nothing.

Benny Lorenzo was released from prison on parole on December 24, 2003. In early 2004, a friend gave him a job selling high-end cars at Warren Henry Auto Group, located on 151st Street in North Miami. They sold Range Rovers, Jaguars, Infinitis, and Lamborghinis. One day, near the end of the shift, a coworker of Benny's made a sale of a Ford Escort. The car needed to be shipped overseas. The coworker asked Benny if he could handle the shipment the following day, as he would not be in. "I will have everything ready for you—the completed paperwork, an extra set of keys, the car cleaned and ready to go. All you have to do is submit it all to the tow truck driver when he arrives to pick up the vehicle and deliver it to the port."

The next day, Benny was there to complete the transaction. The tow truck showed up, and the driver was none other than Pegy Rosello.

The man who snitched on Benny and the entire Muchachos family saw Benny B., and his eyes lit up. He walked over and tried to give Benny a hug. Remembered Benny:

> I stepped away from him and said, "I'm probational." My eyes got watery. I wanted to at least spit on him, or something. But I was on probation. I was afraid to say or do anything or he might say to a parole officer, "Hey, this guy threatened me."

Benny never saw Pegy again, except on documentaries and podcasts, where Pegy sought to explain or justify his testimony against his former friends.

In 2007, Rosello was arrested for having sex with a minor and was sentenced to twelve years' probation. Five years later he was arrested for violating his probation and sent to jail. After his release, in 2018, Pegy was arrested after attempting to sell five kilos of coke to an undercover DEA agent. Rosello was again sentenced to prison.

"I feel bad for his kids," said Benny B. "Pegy was always a bad accident waiting to happen. I'm not even angry. You got to be at peace. Otherwise, you can't live. Whatever happened, happened. That's all behind me now. Time to move forward and enjoy the time I got left here."

FOR TONY AND ILEANA GARRUDO, the stigma of having been part of one of the most public and notorious criminal scandals in recent Miami history was a heavy burden. Add to that the hardship of criminal proceedings, incarceration, and postprison life as a convicted felon, and life was reduced to the level of a faulty premise or a broken toy, where all the parts were there but none of them worked.

Tony and Ileana had the added trauma of having witnessed the murder of Alina Falcon: the sight of Ileana's older sister helpless, covered in blood, the life seeping from her body as Tony held her in his arms.

Cubans did not often talk about post-traumatic stress disorder (PTSD), not even those who had been held as political prisoners by a tyrant back in Cuba, or those abruptly forced off the island because of their political beliefs or desire for free expression, or those who climbed onto rickety boats, rafts, and inner tubes and set out to sea in the hope of creating a better life.

PTSD was for the gringos, a financial luxury based on intellectual concepts. According to some Cubans (not all, but some), the best way to overcome trauma was to be tough, or to eat, drink, dance, get high, or fuck—not necessarily in that order.

For Ileana, her husband's arrest brought for her a different type of imprisonment. "It was like he was incarcerated by the Bureau of Prisons, and I was incarcerated in the city of Miami. Because when you have a loved one in your life who goes to prison, you are also incarcerated, in a way. Your life totally changes. I'm out here dealing with everything, and my relationships totally changed."

One issue was their son, Anthony, who was five years old when Tony was arrested and sent away to prison. As he grew older, Anthony came to resent having a father who was never there for him. He acted out, causing major problems for Ileana, who never planned on being a single parent.

On occasion, she brought Anthony along to visitations to the prison. In the visiting room, father and son hashed it out. Tony would say, "You have to stop making things difficult for your mother." The son would say, "What do you care? You're not even there. You don't care."

"It's not that I don't care," said Tony. "It's that I'm locked up in here and there's nothing I can do about that. I'm still your father. I still love your mother, and I want what's best for you."

The back-and-forth often got heated. Tony would almost burst with frustration. "Here I was, someone who had immigrated, struggled, then found success, but with an illegal business, a very stressful kind of success. I handled all that [he was El Cuño, the guy who could solve problems and get people out of jams], but I could not handle my own son."

For Tony Garrudo, doing time was hellish, not so much because of the realities of life behind bars, but because it separated him from his obligations as a husband, a father, and a man. "I felt guilty," he said. "From our group, everybody's in jail. And the kids on the outside, all of our kids, they're all going through psychological problems. And I feel the blame, myself."

The years of incarceration were torturous: time passed like a sloth on quaaludes. Tony did fifteen years. In 2010, he was released to a halfway house in Fort Myers, Florida. He was close to the finish line.

The halfway house was structured like a dormitory, with small rooms shared by two prisoners. Garrudo was put in a room with a big Black guy. Right away, there were problems. The guy told Tony, "Listen, I want my side of the room cleaned every day. You're gonna do that for me. I want my bed made. I want my clothes hung up and put away."

Tony said to the guy, "My friend, you are making a mistake. I'm not some stupid white guy, you understand? I may be white, but I'm Cuban. I am not a gringo. Do not think that you can fuck with me. Do not make that mistake."

The guy continued with his harassment. Every day. It was relentless.

Tony had a part-time job at a nearby mechanic's shop. It was the only time he was released from the facility. There were no weekend furloughs. He was trapped with that roommate every day. He spent most of his time in the rec room watching TV, or outside in the yard. But every time he returned to his room, the roommate started up: "I told you, you dumb motherfucker, make my bed. Take my dirty clothes to the laundry."

Tony understood that this was never going to stop unless he made it stop. At the mechanic's shop, he found a large screwdriver and filed it down to a sharp edge. He wrapped the weapon in cellophane so that it would not trigger the metal detector at the halfway house, and he strapped it to his leg inside his pants.

Back at the house, after a long day of work at the shop, Tony returned to his room. The guy was there, lounging on his bed like a big, fat sea lion on a rock in the sun. Tony told himself that he would give the roommate a chance; he would not attack unless the guy started in on him. Sure enough: "What did I tell you about my dirty laundry. I told you to take that to the wash, you dumb white motherfucker."

Tony ripped the screwdriver from his leg, and he pounced. With a fury, he stabbed the guy twice. The guy jumped up and tried to run. He stumbled out of the room into the hallway. Tony caught up with him, and he pummeled the guy with the screwdriver, again and again and again.

Security guards came from everywhere. Tony was locked down and sent back to Coleman Penitentiary, where he had been until he was released to the halfway house. There was a disciplinary hearing. The guy recovered, and he did not press charges, but Garrudo was punished. He had to give back his "good time" and serve an additional thirteen months in solitary confinement at Coleman.

When Garrudo was finally released, in 2012, the transition was awkward. It was like everything was out of synch. Tony and Ileana had to become re-acquainted. "He was different," said the wife. "He had been through things I could never understand. His emotions were locked up inside, and then he would explode. It took a lot of patience for both of us to reconnect."

With Anthony, it was even more difficult. Said Tony:

My son look at me as a monster, a hit man, a killer, because of all the things in the media about our group over the years. He say to me, "Where were you when I needed you most? Where were you when my mother take me to the baseball game and all the other kids were there with their father? I have to go with my mother. You left me, you coward, you traitor. You left me all alone." I had to take all that. I said, "Son, I never left you in all of my life."

In public, Ileana was hyperaware of the stares and comments:

Our first outing after Tony was back, we went to my son's graduation. People were like, "Oh, here he is, the big mobster." All of a sudden, you see people's demeanor and face change. You go to school, they don't want their children with my son. "Oh, you used to come to my birthday parties, now you don't want your children coming with mine."

Said Tony, "They don't want to be next to you. They don't want to talk to you. No birthday parties, no baseball. We would go to the baseball game, and everybody would isolate our kid. At karate classes, the parents would keep their kids away. Mean people, judgmental. People with no heart."

Finally, after five years of patience and talking, Tony felt that he and his son had begun to understand one another. The future was not so dark. But the past, that was always going to be bad: memories of late-night arrests, the legal problems, the wasted years doing hard time, the stabbing at the halfway house. Ugly, all of it.

"Me and my wife, we made a decision to bury the past. If you want to continue a new life and have a future, you have to forget about the past."

For a long time, Tony could not find meaningful work. But eventually he was hired by a law firm as an investigator. He investigates criminal cases and facilitates civil litigation and has become highly knowledgeable on the inner workings of the law.

LIFE ON THE RUN MEANT being attuned to any possible danger of discovery. Tavy Falcon was surprised that he was still able to conduct business. It was true that by the late 1990s, what was left of Los Muchachos had contracted almost to nothing. There were no kilos of cocaine being imported anymore. What was left of their stock from the stash houses was in the process of being sold off. For Tavy, the main obligation now was to safeguard and occasionally distribute cash as payment to lawyers and family members of incarcerated Muchachos, of which there were many. The only one left still operating in civilian life was Tavy Falcon.

In 1999, when Willy and Sal were indicted for the second time, Wilfredo "Mata" Pino was named as a codefendant. Somehow, authorities found out where he was, and an arrest was made in Naples. Decades later, Mata still had no idea who it was who snitched on him.

Mata's sudden arrest spooked Tavy and his wife, Amelia. While on the run, you had to be ready to move on a moment's notice. Tavy, Amelia, and their kids gathered up everything they had and moved to Orlando. They rented a house near Disney World. Amelia paid the deposit and first and last months' rent in cash under the last name Reiss. The children used the surname Lopez.

The theory was to hide in plain sight. The neighborhood near Disney World was busy, with people coming and going all the time. It was easy to be anonymous.

For a while, Tavy and Amelia tried to keep their predicament from their kids. They told the kids that they were on the run for not having paid taxes—which was true but not the whole story. The kids knew that something was strange about their life, but they didn't ask many questions. Then, one day, after they had been in hiding for more than a decade, David, the son, came to Amelia. He had Googled the name "Willy Falcon."

"Mom," he said, "I read some things about Uncle Willy on the internet. I think we need to talk."

Tavy was also standing in the kitchen at the time. Amelia looked at her husband and said, "I can't handle this. You deal with it."

That night, Tavy and Amelia sat the kids down and, for the first time, explained the true nature of their lives. Amelia said to the kids, "Whatever you hear about your uncle Willy, what you need to know is that man has a heart of gold. He helped out so many people in his life, friends and family. Just because somebody is found guilty of a crime, that doesn't make them a bad person. Your uncle is a good man, never forget that."

After decades, it was possible to forget that you were living life on the run. Sooner or later, the abnormal becomes normal. The concerns about being discovered become suppressed, and the illusion of normalcy becomes like a medication that you take every day on a regular basis. But the truth can be like a virus. It remains dormant deep inside until suddenly, on a moment's notice, for some reason it is activated. Maybe somebody—a stranger or even an acquaintance—asks a question, and you stumble with the answer. They become suspicious, and so you pull away. It might be a neighbor, or, for the children, a prospective boyfriend or girlfriend. It is in these moments that you realize that there is nothing normal about your life, no matter how hard you try to make that the case. Ultimately, you are constantly in a state of withdrawal, distrust, circumspection. Your world remains small, your circle of love limited to the tight parameters of your nuclear family. This creates a burden, a weight on your shoulders that seeps into your muscles and your bones. And at the core of it all is fear—fear that you will be found out or exposed, that something you do or say will trigger a set of circumstances that will pull the mask off your carefully managed fake existence, and that this will lead to the destruction of your family, your life, and the world as you know it.

In 2008, Gustavo Falcon was profiled on the highly touted television program *America's Most Wanted*. The segment aired four times between 2008 and 2012. Although the show often congratulated itself for fugitives being caught or turning themselves in, Tavy simply grew a beard, or shaved off an already existing beard, or put on sunglasses and a floppy hat, and went on with his clandestine existence.

INCARCERATION IS THE GREAT LEVELER for many people who are un-lucky enough to have the experience. It can exacerbate weaknesses in a person's character, or it can present challenges that bring to the fore an instinct for sur-vival. Willy Falcon sought to see prison life as an extension of what he had been doing since he was a young man—maximizing opportunities, getting ahead, and bringing out the best in people.

Before long, Willy devised a contraband system in prison that provided drugs, cigarettes, food, medicines, and other items that the average inmate could not access. He also had a bookmaking operation, in which inmates came to him to place bets on sports, political elections, two cockroaches running up a wall, or whatever else men behind bars were willing to wager on. In prison, Willy always carried a homemade shank, but his intention was to survive by making himself indispensable. He had been a leader of men on the outside, and he remained so on the inside, not through force or coercion or superior intellect, but by showing his authentic self and leading others to trust that he was a man of his word.

His post-conviction sentence began at the federal penitentiary in Lewisburg, Pennsylvania, in the middle of the state, 1,224 miles from Miami. Though it was an epic journey to get there, his family regularly visited. Aileen, Jessica, and Will Jr. staggered their visits so that their father received the maximum number possible. Willy even received a visit from Lourdes Castellon and his two twin sons, Angelo and William, who were now nineteen years old. Falcon had not seen the boys since they were babies, and he was struck by how much they looked like him.

On the occasions when Falcon was visited by his parents (at least once a month), he felt a special sense of guilt about the plight of Tavy. Though his parents rarely brought it up, Willy knew that they held him responsible for his brother's predicament. While living as a fugitive, Tavy was unable to visit or even have much communication with his parents. The parents were being mon-itored by the US Marshals; it was a common belief in law enforcement that the best way to catch a fugitive was to surveil his family. For Arsenio and Marta Falcon, it was a worst-case scenario: they had lost both sons, one to prison and one to life on the run. They carried with them a sadness that Willy absorbed as a rebuke of his life as a notorious narco.

The years passed. Willy was transferred from the federal penitentiary at Lewisburg to one in Allenwood, Pennsylvania. It was in Allenwood that Falcon was brought up on disciplinary charges for running a contraband operation behind bars. Willy had to smile when, in the report on his activities, his network of inmates and crooked COs was referred to as "the Falcon organization," just as Los Muchachos had been on the outside. Falcon was given a punishment of eight additional months behind bars and extended time in solitary confinement.

Eventually, in 2008, Falcon was shipped out to USP Victorville, located in the California desert near Barstow. For someone from the tropical environments of Cuba and South Florida, it represented the asshole of the universe, as it was likely intended to.

In Victorville, Falcon had an experience that conjured up his years of dedication to the cause of eliminating Fidel Castro and liberating Cuba. Among the prisoners incarcerated at Victorville was Gerardo Hernández, who was one of the "Cuban Five." Among the many spies whom the Castro government had inculcated into the Unites States, the Cuban Five were renowned. Hernández had been part of the Cuban spy initiative known as the Wasp Network. In 1998, he and the four others who composed the Cuban Five were arrested, charged, and put on trial for conspiracy to commit espionage, conspiracy to commit murder, and acting as an agent of a foreign government. They were all found guilty.

At Victorville, there were not many inmates of Caribbean descent. The prison population was mostly a witches' brew of Mexicans and white supremacists. The Mexicans were divided along lines of *sureños* and *norteños*, gang members affiliated with groups from either Southern or Northern California.

The Caribbean inmates, of which there were maybe one dozen, would gather in the rec yard to play dominos. One day, Falcon was late to the domino game. When he arrived, he saw Gerardo Hernández. Falcon and Hernández had already had words once before. One time, when Willy saw Hernández showing images of Cuba to some other inmates, he butted in:

He was showing photographs of hotels and tourist attractions in Cuba. He was telling [the inmates], "Look, this is Cuba. This is what the Communists have to offer"—you know, bragging about it. . . . I got upset and told him, "Listen, you know very well that the only people who could visit those attractions, those fancy hotels, propaganda hotels, are the tourist people that visit the country that bring dollars. The Cuban people are not allowed to walk into those places, and if they try to get into those places, they would be arrested. So don't be lying."

Hernández mostly kept quiet that day. Victorville was neutral ground; the convicted spy had no way of knowing who would have been for or against him among the inmates.

On the day Willy arrived late for dominos, Hernández was explaining to the other players how, even though dominos was popularized in Miami, it got its start in Cuba. Falcon, who was feeling frisky, offered his two cents:

I said, "But the only difference between Cuba and the United States, Miami, is that in Miami you could say anything you want about the president, and you don't get into trouble. In Cuba, you say something about your regime, and you get tortured for it or put in a firing squad. That's the only difference."

This time, Hernández lost his cool: "Augusto Falcon! We knew all about you. We had intelligence about you and your anti-Castro beliefs. We know you were a patron of Guillermo Endara in Panama. As soon as we learned that, we reported back to our intelligence service that Fidel Castro and Raúl should avoid traveling to Panama or having any dealings with the new president there."

Willy thought, *Yeah, but did you know that I was smuggling thousands of kilos through Cuba with the knowledge of Raúl Castro?* He was pretty sure Hernández did not know that and would likely deny it if he did.

At Victorville, Falcon and the Cuban spy mostly stayed away from each other.

A few years later, Falcon was transferred first to a prison in Colorado, and then to McCreary Penitentiary in McCreary, Kentucky. In 2014, in the rec room at the prison, Falcon saw a report on CNN television news that the Cuban Five had been released by President Barack Obama as part of a prisoner exchange with Cuba. Willy watched images of Gerardo Hernández and the others being received in Havana as heroes by Raúl Castro, who had taken over as *líder máximo* since Fidel had become sick a few years earlier.

It crossed Willy's mind: *Knowing what the Cuban government has on me, imagine the danger I would be in if I were ever to return to Cuba. If they didn't execute me for my anti-Castro activities, they would most surely hang me for my knowledge of how Cuba under the Castros allowed their country to be used as a transshipment point for cocaine smuggling.*

More years passed. By late 2016, as Falcon's release date first came into view, there was the issue of his legal status. Willy had no one to blame but himself that he had never taken the time to become a US citizen. Tony Bemba, among others, had often pleaded with Willy to get his citizenship papers. Said Tony: "He always told me, 'Tony, we are only renting here. We will go back to Cuba one day. And the fact that we are still Cuban citizens will put us in a position to open businesses and buy property. We will be ahead of the game.'"

Tony knew that this was not the reason that Willy demurred. He knew that Falcon, like so many Cuban exiles, feared that to become a US citizen would represent a final severing of the umbilical cord between themselves and *la patria*, the homeland. Willy feared that by becoming a US citizen, he would lose Cuba forever.

Even Tony Bemba, whose father had been thrown into a dungeon on the Isle of Pines by Fidel Castro, who, along with Willy Falcon, swore as a young man that he would one day return to a free Cuba, had gotten his US citizenship (at the behest of his wife at the time).

In 2017, Falcon received a letter from the US Department of Homeland Security informing him that as soon as he was released from prison (he had a release date of June 16), he would be taken into custody and deported from the United States. The letter was not a surprise. What was a surprise was the country that they were announcing they were going to deport him to: his country of origin, Cuba.

Never in his mind had Falcon considered that the United States would deport him to Cuba. The United States had no diplomatic relations with Cuba. How could they possibly send him to a place where it was known that he was hostile to the very existence of the government in power? Falcon was convinced that to send him to Cuba would be a death sentence. Upon arrival there, he would either be thrown in prison as an enemy of the state, or he would be summarily executed.

A new cast of lawyers came into Falcon's life. He was being forced to contest the decision, which would now be decided by the DOJ Executive Office for Immigration Review.

Since being discharged from the prison in Kentucky, Falcon had been in custody at an immigration facility in Oakdale, Louisiana. It was a prison, much like any other, except that the detainees were Mexicans, Haitians, Chinese, and others with outstanding immigration matters. Willy was held there for six months before he was granted a hearing before immigration judge Agnelis Reese.

On January 24, 2018, in a makeshift courtroom at the immigration facility, Willy was placed under oath and seated before Judge Reese; a prosecutor representing the Department of Homeland Security; and his two Miami-based attorneys, Ada Beatriz Pozo and Steven A. Goldstein. Falcon's daughter Jessica, and her husband were present as spectators.

It was an unusual proceeding. In the interest of convincing a judge that by deporting him to his place of birth the government would be sentencing him to imprisonment or death, Willy found himself in the position of having to reveal facts that he had mostly kept secret all his life. Neither his wife nor his parents nor many of his closest associates knew the details of his involvement in the anti-Castro movement of the previous forty years. It was a covert enterprise that involved many of the leading lights of the Miami anti-Castro exile movement. Never had Falcon talked openly about this subject, especially while under oath in what was essentially a court of law. Now his future depended on it.

Falcon's attorney elicited testimony from Willy regarding the earliest days of his involvement in the movement, how he first became friendly with Antonio Garcia Perez, a.k.a. El Guajiro, who introduced him to major players in *la lucha*. Willy described a mission that he undertook in 1981 on behalf of Eduardo Arocena, leader of Omega 7, the underground anti-Castro organization. Using his own fifty-four-foot yacht, Willy sailed to Cayo Sal, located between Florida and Cuba, to pick up a load of guns and explosives—including several bazookas—and a Cuban "freedom fighter" and transported the shipment through various barricades that had been set up during the Mariel Boatlift. The arms were offloaded to another boat in Key West and shipped to Cuba.

While under oath, Willy told of meeting with Jorge Mas Canosa, leader of the Cuban American National Foundation (CANF), the most powerful and politically influential anti-Castro exile organization in Miami. As a lobbying group, CANF had no comparison in the South Florida exile community. Politicians running for office, including Ronald Reagan and George Bush, as well as Republican Party candidates for governor and senator, kissed the ring of Jorge Mas Canosa and his organization, which had the ability to deliver votes on Election Day. As a legally licensed nonprofit, CANF claimed to be nonpartisan, but its financial enabling of secret anti-Castro cells like Omega 7 and Alpha 66, and its connections to the CIA, were a source of much speculation in the Cuban exile community and beyond.

In 1982, Mas, accompanied by Gaspar Jimenez, a notorious anti-Castro operative and drug trafficker, came to see Willy and Sal at the CMM Ranch. Said Willy:

> They presented a plan to overthrow Fidel Castro, the Castro regime. . . . [Mas] told me that Cuban American National Foundation, most of the people that belong to this anti-Castro group are ex–CIA agents, veterans of Bay of Pigs. They were training at the time in Honduras with the Nicaraguan Contras. . . . They needed financial assistance. They also needed me to help them establish themselves in the country of Panama. They needed the banking. . . . That same day I called Guillermo Endara in Panama, and I instructed him to give Jorge Mas Canosa and CANF a large sum of financial support that they needed for their operation. Also to assist them with the army in the Republic of Panama, to purchase a large arsenal of weapons that was needed for the cause. And also to form two registered front companies, to register two ships that could be used for the planned invasion into Cuba.

Most tellingly, Willy told the story of the cocaine shipments through Cuba as authorized by General Arnaldo Ochoa—shipments of kilos from Pablo Escobar, through Cuba and into the United States, all of it, Falcon had been told, with the knowledge of Raúl Castro.

The hearing lasted four days and included testimony from not only Falcon but also others who had recently served time as political prisoners in Cuba. It was a rare tribunal, highly secretive, that revealed much about the underground history of the anti-Castro movement in the United States.

When it was all over, the judge ruled against Falcon. Judge Reese had a history of denying torture petitions such as Falcon's and ordering deportations.

The legal battle was not over. Falcon was held in custody while his lawyers appealed the judge's ruling.

Eventually, an appellate court judge sided with Falcon, citing a 1984 United Nations treaty that forbade nations to transport people to any country where there was reason to believe they would be tortured. Augusto Guillermo Falcon could not be forcibly deported to Cuba. He was given several days to find a country that would take him. His attorneys went hat in hand to a number of countries. The government of the Dominican Republic (DR) agreed to allow entry to Falcon.

November 6, 2018, was an exciting day for Falcon and his family. Willy was officially deported to the DR, taken by plane, and dropped at Aeropuerto Internacional Las Américas, near the capital city of Santo Domingo. After passing through customs, he met his children from his marriage to Alina, and his grandchildren (both Jessica and Aileen now had two kids). He was housed at the home of a friend in a suburb of Santo Domingo. Though he was a free man, Falcon was kept under armed guard until the paperwork could be completed for him to live in the Dominican Republic as a legal resident.

After a week or so on the island, news of Willy Falcon's presence exploded in the local media. A politician running for office declared that the ruling political party should be condemned for allowing the country to become a "sanctuary for drug traffickers." Over the next few weeks, Falcon and his family were moved three times to different living quarters, as the notorious ex-narco became a political hot potato in the Dominican Republic. Said Willy:

> I was thinking, Why does everything in my life have to be a trauma? I felt bad for my children, who were now caught up in this drama. But I had come too far to turn back now. After so many years in maximum-security prisons, I kept telling myself, "At least you are a free man." Though it didn't really feel like it at the time.

Eventually, the minister of foreign relations informed Falcon's lawyers that he could not stay in the Dominican Republic. He would have to leave.

Who would take in Willy Falcon? What nation would allow legal residency to the former Cocaine Cowboy?

A minister with the United States embassy in the DR came to Falcon with a list of seven or eight countries. These are the nations that will take you, he was told. Willy looked over the list and decided where he needed to be.

On December 10, after Willy had been in the DR for thirty-three days, the headline in *Alternativas Noticiosas*, a leading newspaper on the island, read: "*Willy Falcon, el líder del cartel de 'Los Cowboys de la cocaine,' abandono el pais* (Willy Falcon, the leader of the 'Cocaine Cowboys' cartel has left the country)."

In the dead of night, Falcon flew with his daughter and lawyer to the country where he would now be living. It was a Latin American country known for its tropical beauty. Willy arrived around three a.m. and passed through customs under cover of darkness. He had found a new home.

In the months that followed, he had some visitors from the Unites States, family members and long-lost friends. But soon the COVID-19 crisis settled in, and world travel became complicated.

Like everyone else, Willy went on lockdown, and when he did venture out in public, he wore a mask. In his new home, no one knew who he was. Unlike in the DR, there was no media attention upon his arrival. Now a man in his midsixties, he blended in with his surroundings. He settled down in a midsize city and sought to adjust to life outside prison walls, behind which he had spent the previous twenty-seven years.

In 2019, Falcon met a new lady friend, and, on October 15, 2022, they were married.

His new country of residence was not unlike the land of his birth. A lush tropical landscape, with palm trees, rolling hills, country roads, jacaranda, and much verdant vegetation greeted Falcon from a veranda in his modest apartment. Every morning, with a cup of coffee, he sat on the veranda and looked out over this gorgeous, peaceful landscape. Memories and images from his life came to him in a rush, like a movie with the scenes shown out of sequence. He remembered his idyllic upbringing in the town of Alquízar, in La Habana Province, as a kind of tropical paradise. And then the dark cloud of Fidel Castro blew in seemingly from out of nowhere. Then there was early Miami, where shell-shocked Cuban exiles arrived to reinvent themselves as the most capitalist of the capitalists. Almost as a gift to their exiled parents, Falcon and his generation sought to excel in America, to make their parents proud in a way that might lessen their pain at being chased out of paradise. There were the years of unparalleled success, epitomized by the bacchanalia that was the Mutiny, and the other nightclubs, and the championship powerboat races, and the transformation of Miami from a swampy backwater to the most glistening real estate gold rush in the Americas. There were the years of legal combat in court, the final showdown in the War on Drugs, the illusory not-guilty verdict, and the inevitable crash that came afterward. Finally, there was the long blur of half a lifetime behind bars, the negation of everything that had come before, and the bitter pill that mostly what remained in the end was shame.

And at the core of it all was yeyo, perico, tootie, blow. The white powder had seduced a certain type of American hedonist, a generation of chemical thrill seekers, and the industry it created was massive enough to engulf the value system of the modern world. Narco dollars controlled nations, corrupted the weak, and fueled a party scene that seemed as though it would never end. But it did end. It ended with a whimper and not a bang, a long slow fade into, if not oblivion, then something like postapocalyptic stasis, a quiet, simple life stripped of all its glamour, a state of mind where all that mattered was love and the comfort of knowing there was still life to be lived.

Willy Falcon sat on his veranda amid the tropical splendor, and he thought, *Did all that really happen, or was it just a dream?*

EPILOGUE

ON APRIL 12, 2017, TWO MONTHS before his brother, Willy, was scheduled to be released from federal prison, Tavy Falcon, together with his wife, Amelia, was coming home from an epic bike ride. Two years earlier, Tavy and his family had moved to a rental home in Kissimmee, Florida, just 28 miles south of Orlando and 217 miles from Miami. They had been living in the Orlando area for twenty years as Maria and Luis Andres Reiss, an attractive couple with two kids who mostly kept to themselves. They were avid bike riders, and on this day they were approaching the end of a nearly forty-mile sojourn.

What they did not know was that they were being tailed by a team of US Marshals and FBI agents.

One week earlier, an anonymous sketch artist for the government had come across a photo ID of Luis Andres Reiss that also included an address in Kissimmee. The sketch artist had been enlisted to create a series of sketches of Tavy Falcon as he might look as an older man. When the sketch artist came across the photo of Luis Reiss on the internet, he was struck by the similarities to his subject. He contacted the DOJ, which sent a team of US Marshals to conduct surveillance on the house.

In the back of his mind, Tavy had been feeling a lingering concern. Four years earlier, in May 2013, he'd had a fender bender while driving his Chevrolet Impala on Livingston Road in Osceola County. Accidentally, he bumped a bicyclist. No medical assistance was needed; there was no damage to the car and minimal damage to the bike. A Florida Highway Patrol trooper arrived on the scene and asked to see Tavy's identification. He looked at the ID for Luis Andres Reiss, wrote down the information, and sent everyone on his way. It would have ended there, but the cyclist later filed an insurance claim for the fifty dollars' worth of damage to his bike. He submitted a photo of Tavy's license to the insurance company; they filed a claim. That was how that photo had wound up in an online government database.

Being on the run for a total of twenty-six years, Tavy had become hyper attuned to how any small irregularity might be a danger to his life as a fugitive from the law. This one bothered him, but there had been other concerns over the years that always turned out to be nothing, so he wasn't going to let this one ruin his day.

As Tavy and Amelia peddled through Kissimmee toward their house, they were feeling pleasantly exhausted after such a long ride. As they rounded a corner, numerous vehicles from three different directions suddenly screeched to a halt, blocking their way. Armed US Marshals, with guns drawn, flooded out of the vehicles and surrounded Tavy and Amelia.

"Down on the ground!" several marshals shouted at Tavy.

Tavy lay face down on the ground. A marshal stepped on his back and slapped on a set of handcuffs.

A woman marshal pulled Amelia aside and clipped onto her wrists a set of pink handcuffs. "What's your name?" said the marshal.

"Maria Reiss," said Amelia.

"You know you're not Maria Reiss."

"Oh yes. My name is Maria Reiss."

A male marshal came over and said, "You know, we could take you to jail right now for aiding and abetting a fugitive."

Said Amelia, "He's my husband. Do what you got to do."

By now, Tavy had been brought to his feet and was standing near his wife. Said the marshal, "I'm going to ask you again, what is your name?"

Amelia looked at Tavy, who shrugged and nodded his ascent.

"My name is Amelia Falcon," she said.

"Thank you," said the marshal. "Are your kids, Jennifer and David, at home?"

They know the name of my kids, thought Amelia. "Yes, sir," she said.

"Are there any guns in the house?"

"No, sir."

"Then here's what we're going to do," explained the marshal. "Your husband is under arrest. We're taking him away with us. We will be sending a team to search your house, but we will first allow you to go home. We don't want to terrify your kids. You go home and tell your kids what happened to their dad. We will be there shortly thereafter."

"Thank you," said Amelia. She picked up her bike and walked it the short distance to her house. She knocked on the front door. Her daughter, Jennifer, opened the door and looked at her mother, who was alone and looking frazzled. The daughter instantly knew without the mother having to utter a word: *Dad's been apprehended.*

When Willy Falcon received word in prison that Tavy had been caught in Kissimmee, he was startled. First of all—*Kissimmee?* Willy hadn't known that Tavy was now living in Kissimmee. This small town outside Orlando was where Willy had received his very first load of cocaine by air forty years earlier. That was a weird coincidence. And then there was the fact that Willy was on the verge of release after twenty-six years behind bars. He was anticipating a legal struggle with Homeland Security and US Citizenship and Immigration Services. Was this a ploy to somehow weaken his case?

It was like when Alina was murdered: a set of circumstances so unreal that it was hard to accept it as mere coincidence.

When word of Gustavo Falcon's capture and arrest hit the news in South Florida, it touched off a tidal wave of posts and links on social media. CNN led off its nightly broadcast with a report on "the last of the Cocaine Cowboys" being captured. It became an occasion to dust off all the old tropes about the cocaine era in Miami, with clips from *Scarface* and *Miami Vice* accompanying nearly every report. Said Amelia, "For three straight days there was a horde of media people outside my house, knocking on the door, with cameras."

Tavy was transported to Miami, to be booked and held at the Miami Detention Center. A week later, Amelia loaded up the kids and moved to the city, the place of her upbringing, where she had not set foot in twenty-six years. Said Amelia:

> I felt like I was picked up from one planet and dropped on another planet. I couldn't remember anything about Miami. I couldn't remember the people or the places. It was like I had locked the door and threw away the keys. . . . I moved in with my dad. He had a three-bedroom apartment. And my daughter and her boyfriend lived with my sister for a while, until I was lucky enough to find a house where nobody asked me for a credit check. Because in Miami, I no longer existed. I had no credit whatsoever.

Amelia and her kids moved into a house in Kendall. By then, the story of Gustavo was in the news and online. Since she was again using her real name—Amelia Falcon—some people recognized who she was. Some were supportive. When she called the manager of the house in Kendall, she said, "Joe, this is Maria."

The manager said patiently, "No, you're not Maria. From now on, you are Amelia."

One day, Jennifer and David, the children, called for an Uber. They were going to the Miami jail for a visitation with their father. The Uber driver saw the name—Jennifer Falcon.

"Falcon?" he said. "Are you related to the Falcon Cocaine Cowboys?"

"Yes," said Jennifer. "Gustavo Falcon is my father."

The driver smiled. "Man, tell your dad and your uncle thank you. They gave us Miami. They made Miami."

One year after Tavy Falcon had been captured and pleaded guilty to charges of cocaine conspiracy, in federal court in the Southern District of Florida, he was brought before Judge Federico Moreno, the same judge who had presided over the original Willy and Tavy trial twenty-two years earlier. Tavy was there for his sentencing. He had provided the judge with a five-page letter expressing his remorse for his years as a narco. "I regret that I did not develop my own identity as a teenager. When my brother asked me to help him in the cocaine business, I did. I should have had the courage to say no. But I loved and looked up to him." It was ironic, given that Tavy was the one who convinced his brother to bring him in as a partner, but the convicted narco knew what the judge needed to hear if he were to look favorably on the repentant felon.

Tavy's defense lawyers asked for a sentence of nine years; the government suggested fourteen. Judge Moreno gave Falcon a sentence of eleven years.

Tavy was sent off to prison. In the world of remaining Muchachos, it was another weird coincidence. After twenty-six years, Tavy was being brought into the penal system just as Willy Falcon was being released into the outside world. If freedom were a large body of water, Willy and Tavy passed one another like two ships in the night.

In prison, Tavy was often received as a celebrity. One day, when Amelia was there for a scheduled visit, her husband told her, "Some of these inmates, they just bow at my feet. I swear to God. I tell them, 'Man, get up. I'm nobody.'"

Tavy told Amelia, "There was this one day, here in the visiting room, an inmate was being visited by his mom. The mom looked at me and said to her son, 'Oh, don't get close to that guy. That guy is bad.' The son, who I know, said, 'No, Mom, he's good. I want you to meet him.' So, he introduced me to the mom. We talked for a little bit, and she said, 'Wow, you're nothing like I've heard in the news.'"

In August 2021, the six-part documentary series *Cocaine Cowboys: Kings of Miami* debuted on Netflix. The series was all about Willy and Sal. Based mostly on calcified reporting about the story that had been in the public arena for decades, *Kings of Miami* trafficked in cocaine-era tropes and stereotypes that had become standardized almost to the point of cliché.

Tavy watched the series on television in prison, and Willy watched from his home. There were few on-camera sources from inside Los Muchachos, though the snitches were well represented. Willy was especially annoyed by the interview with Jorge "George" Valdés, who for decades had been promoting himself as the most successful cocaine kingpin who ever was and claiming that he was the one who had launched Willy and Sal in the business.

Living outside the United States, far from his old stomping grounds in Miami, Los Angeles, and New York, Willy fretted over the way Los Muchachos were portrayed in the media. Though he often expressed regret about those years—especially the way his children and family had been made to carry the burden of his reputation as a notorious criminal—it was a legacy of sorts. On one level, Willy, Tavy, and most of the others were, down deep, proud of what they had created with a minimum of violence and mayhem.

Tavy was sanguine about it all. Mostly, he laughed at *Kings of Miami*, which he saw as a continuation of *Scarface*, *Miami Vice*, and all the other depictions of crazed Latinos with Uzis looking to terrify the masses.

In prison, after a screening of the Netflix doc, a Caucasian corrections officer said to Tavy, "So, you wanted to be like Scarface, huh?"

Tavy replied, "No. He wanted to be like me."

Tavy and Willy spoke on the phone whenever they could. Tavy was able to call from the jail, and because of his status among the inmates, nobody ever sought to cut in on his phone time. Tavy also spoke with his partner Wilfredo "Mata" Pino, and with Benny, Tony Bemba, Ralph Linero, and others who had done significant stretches of time in prison and were now out on the streets.

For those among the group formerly known as Los Muchachos who might have blamed Sal for his numerous tactical mistakes (most notably his carelessness with the ledgers, which provided the government with incriminating evidence that led some of them to serve long prison sentences), even they felt that Sal was as much a blood brother as the rest of them. The idea that he would waste away forever in prison while everyone was now free was a source of sadness.

Hopes were raised in September 2021 when attorneys for Magluta filed a motion seeking a reduction of sentence based on compassionate release grounds. Magluta was now sixty-six, had been in prison for close to thirty years, and, according to his motion, was suffering from "cognitive impairment" brought on by dementia. His lawyers also cited the COVID-19 pandemic, which made incarceration a potentially perilous situation for inmates with health issues.

Magluta's motion was brought before Judge Patricia Seitz, the same judge who'd given him a 205-year sentence back in 2003.

Seitz denied the motion, noting that even though Magluta had taken part in a couple of "rehabilitation programs" cited in his motion, he also had been cited in 2013 for smuggling two cellular phones into his cell.

With Seitz's ruling, it seemed unlikely that Magluta would ever see the light of day outside prison walls.

The months passed. Winter came, and then in accordance with lunar patterns came spring, summer, and fall. Willy and the other former narcos became more accustomed to their postincarceration lives of freedom. Though Willy was far away, they spoke often among themselves by phone and the newfangled technology of Zoom.

In late October 2022, to the surprise of most everyone, it was announced that Tavy was being released from prison after having served five years. He was being released under what was known as the Cares Act, a new law passed in 2020 to address the financial consequences of the COVID-19 pandemic. Tavy also received time off for good behavior. On November 9, he walked out of prison and rejoined his family in civilian life, to finish the rest of his sentence in home confinement.

Freedom was like the love of a soulmate: to be fully aware of its power, you had to have it, then lose it, then regain it. For thirty years, Tavy Falcon had been on the run or in prison. He had never been a truly free man. And now he was.

Bound by the terms of his parole, Tavy could not leave the state of Florida. He had a monitoring device on his ankle, and he had to speak with his parole officer at least once a day. None of that felt like a hardship after what he had been through. The projected date for Falcon to complete his sentence was November 12, 2024.

In 2023, Tavy and Amelia became grandparents of twin girls, and their family all moved in together in a house in Miami.

Willy spoke with his brother almost every day after his release. They did something they had rarely been able to do over the previous three decades—talk aimlessly with no restrictions on privacy or time. Most often, they reminisced about the cocaine business. There was much that had gone on that one or the other of them was not aware of. There was much that Tavy did not know about Willy's activities with the anti-Castro movement, the CIA, and the Contras. Tavy did not fully know about his brother's dealings with the Colombian cartels, his friendship with Pablo Escobar, the full extent of his involvement with world leaders like Guillermo Endara, Raúl Castro, and Manuel Noriega.

Willy knew little about Tavy's frantic efforts to keep the operation in gear after the arrests in 1991, how Tavy had continued meeting with the Mexicans and monitoring the shipments by freighter from Chile, through Mexico, and into the United States.

It was almost beyond comprehension, what they had pulled off. There were many unanswered questions and hazy memories. It helped to talk about it, especially with someone who was connected by blood and had been there from early on.

Often, the brothers talked about their parents. Both felt guilty that they had not been able to be there for their funerals or burials. In the end, the way it all played out had created emotional hardship for Arsenio and Marta Falcon. Willy knew that his father had been disapproving of how he achieved his success because he often said so. But Willy also believed that his dad had to have had a modicum of pride.

He and his brother had seized on a phenomenon that was not of their making, but they had made something of it that was unprecedented in the annals of history. A distribution network composed mostly of a generation of Cuban exiles who saw an opportunity and seized it with vigor, imagination, and, yes, a sense of honor such as it was from the streets and in the narcosphere.

There were others who saw it differently. The prosecutors, Assistant US Attorneys Chris Clark, Pat Sullivan, and others, were still dismayed decades later that Willy and Sal had been able to buy off five members of the jury at their trial in 1996. To them, what Falcon and Magluta had done was a stain on something sacred, the sanctity of the jury-selection process, a principle at the core of the justice system. It was a violation of almost incalculable magnitude. Decades later, because Willy and Sal had achieved their not-guilty verdict through fraudulent means, AUSA Clark was still haunted by it. He took it personally. "A loss is a loss," he said. "So, I have the distinction of having lost the biggest drug case in the country. I have the distinction of bringing down the US attorney [Kendall Coffey]. I mean, I've got a lot of weight on my shoulders."

History is alive in the hearts of those who lived it. In their long phone conversations, Willy and Tavy reminisced. Their memories ran the gamut of emotions. Whenever Willy would get on his high horse, expressing his recollections with vigor and righteousness, all Tavy had to say was, "I know, Willy, I was there. Remember?"

One day, they would get to meet face-to-face. Once Tavy fulfilled the terms of his parole and had his ankle monitor removed, he would fly to Willy's country of residence, and they would embrace. Their family members would all be there, children and grandchildren. They would all say a prayer for the souls of Arsenio and Marta.

Every time Willy and Tavy spoke on the phone, they reminded each other about their plans. They spoke about it often. It gave them reason to hope.

ACKNOWLEDGMENTS

MOST BOOK PROJECTS HAVE A life all their own. This one grew out of contacts and sources I have in Miami, a city that never ceases to dazzle me with the complexity and storied nature of its criminal history. For a crime writer, Miami is the gift that keeps on giving.

First and foremost, thank you to Willy Falcon's children, Jessica, Will Jr., and Aileen, all of whom to one degree or another facilitated the development of this project.

Working with Willy Falcon was one of the more interesting collaborations I have had in my career writing about the criminal underworld. I have never spent so much time with one source. Falcon never became overwhelmed or frustrated or lost patience. He understood that his role was to communicate his story to me and not intrude on my process as the writer. I am grateful for his generous nature and sense of responsibility, which allowed for us to get through what was at times a project that seemed as though it might never end. Falcon's commitment to it was an inspiration.

Thanks to the esteemed Jay Weaver of the *Miami Herald* for sharing his files, which is a gracious thing for a fellow journalist to do. Roben Farzad, the author of *Hotel Scarface*, was kind enough to take my phone calls and respond to emails and even provide contact information for one important source, Humberto "Bert" Becerra. Also helpful in Miami were Bruce Fleischer, Esq., Tony Gonzalez, and Jaydee Freixas.

Marc Johnson led me to Lourdes Castellon, who was an important and helpful source. Owen Band, who was interviewed for this book, was also a great help by putting me in touch with Mollie Hampton, a former waitress at the Mutiny.

Manuela Garces was a wonderful assistant when I needed it most in a foreign land. It was a pleasure to meet and interview her father, Manuel Garces, who provided insights and knowledge in Medellín, Colombia.

In another part of the world, Sandra Osorio Falcon facilitated my connecting with Willy Falcon in ways that made it not only possible, but enjoyable.

Many friends and family members helped by providing camaraderie and support. For this I would like to thank the following people: Michael Becerra; Tom Dreeson; Stuart Deutsch; Teresita Levy; Christina Lorenzatto; Suzanne and Chris Damore; LaSherma Grant; Mike and Stefanie English; Ed English; Eric Eisner; Bill Nevins; Deryle Perryman; Fran and Kevin Hopper.

In the sources section, I list all the people who were interviewed for this book. A special thank-you to all of them for sharing their stories, but some deserve special mention for also helping lead me to other sources or to relevant pieces of information. Special credit to Tony and Ileana Garrudo, Benny Lorenzo, Tavy and Amelia Falcon, and Tony Garcia for their assistance.

For a couple of decades now, the folks at Sobel Weber Associates have been my rock of support in our dealings with the publishing world. A heartfelt thank-you to Nat Sobel and Judith Weber for staying the course. This book is my eighth with William Morrow/HarperCollins. Thanks to David Highfill, who initiated this project, and my new editor, Nick Amphlett, who helped guide it into print.

Music is an important source of sustenance for me as I grapple with the challenges of creating a work of literature. For me, there is added joy when the music and the subject matter find a place of connection. The soundtrack to the writing of this book included the great Cuban percussionists Chano Pozo and Mongo Santamaria, the dramatic vocal stylings of La Lupe, and a hip-hop song that I listened to over and over while writing, honing, and shaping this tome: "Pure Cocaine," by Lil Baby.

APPENDIX

$25 Million Cocaine Defense

It was said of the Falcon-Magluta organization that they were the best thing that ever happened to the criminal defense bar in Miami. Federal prosecutors reported that these attorneys and private investigators received fees totaling more than $25 million during the first Falcon-Magluta trial in 1995–96. These fees also include legal work that was done for other members of Los Muchachos around the same time. The totals are those the lawyers were required by law to report as their payment. Willy Falcon estimates that there may have been another $25 million in under-the-table payments to some of the lawyers and investigators.

ATTORNEY	FEE PAID
Roy Black	$3,754,955.00
Albert Krieger	$3,620,119.40
Martin Weinberg	$3,483,837.50
L. Mark Dachs	$2,826,667.12
Benson Weintraub	$1,500,790.00
Richard I. Martinez	$1,415,930.00
Jeffrey Weiner	$847,912.00
Scott Srebnick	$647,500.00
Donald Ferguson	$566,540.00
Jon May	$546,000.00
Susan Van Dusen	$492,650.00
Edward Shohat	$449,330.00
Frank Rubino	$447,091.43
Scott Furstman	$350,000.00
Fred Salazer	$333,867.45
Neil Taylor	$275,000.00
Martin Raskin	$260,000.00
Neil Schuster	$215,000.00

Akerman Senterfitt	$213,142.46
Saúl Cimbler	$197,000.00
Paul Petruzzi	$125,000.00
Paul Friedman	$90,000.00
Stuart Adelstein	$75,000.00
Joel Kaplan	$73,500.00
David Fechheimer	$69,970.00
David Garvin	$50,000.00
William Riley	$50,000.00
Galberson law office	$42,500.00
Michael Blacker	$40,000.00
Vincent Flynn	$36,000.00
Robert Wells	$35,000.00
Carlos Canety	$32,650.00
Melvin Black	$30,000.00
Jack Fernandez	$30,000.00
Charles Lembcky	$26,200.00
Zwerling & Kemler	$25,000.00
Bridget Moyer	$20,000.00
J. C. Eslo	$8,000.00
Sam Rabin	$7,500.00
PRIVATE INVESTIGATOR	**FEE PAID**
Juan Cayado	$353,966.65
Kim Homan	$336,354.83
Rene Silva	$294,789.00
Manuel Sires Jr.	$215,960.00
Jorge Hernandez	$193,000.00
Aldo Gonzalez	$141,000.00
Diego Adama	$134,000.00
Leif Fernandez	$36,000.00
Lourdes Gonzalez	$20,000.00
GRAND TOTAL	**$25,062,844.65**

(Source: *Miami Herald*, September 10, 2000)

NOTES

Introduction
Ascendance of cocaine in the 1980s: Michael Demarest, "Cocaine: Middle Class High," *Time*, July 6, 1981.
Los Muchachos at screening of *Scarface*: Interview with Orlando Begnino "Benny B." Lorenzo, May 7, 2021; interview with Augusto Guillermo "Willy" Falcon, March 10, 2021.[1]

Prologue
Kidnapping of Marta Falcon: Interview with Willy Falcon; interview with Gustavo "Tavy" Falcon, November 19, 2022; interview with Antonio "Tony Bemba" Garcia, March 25, 2021.

1. Freedom Flight
Young Willy Falcon in Cuba: Memoir manuscript by Augusto Guillermo "Willy" Falcon, hereafter known as "Falcon manuscript"; interview with Willy Falcon.
Revolutionary Cuba: Ada Ferrar, *Cuba: An American History* (Scribner, 2021); T. J. English, *Havana Nocturne: How the Mob Owned Cuba . . . And Lost It to the Revolution* (William Morrow, 2008); Aviva Chomsky, *A History of the Cuban Revolution* (Wiley-Blackwell, 2015).
"The location where the invasion occurred": Interview with Willy Falcon.
Fidel Castro in power: Sebastian Balfour, *Castro: Profiles in Power* (Routledge, 2015); Betty Viamontes, *Waiting on Zapote Street: Love and Loss in Castro's Cuba* (Zapote Street Books, 2015).
Economic embargo of Cuba: Proclamation 3447—Embargo on All Trade with Cuba, President John F. Kennedy, February 3, 1962 (presidency.ucsb.edu).
Cuban Missile Crisis: "Forty Years Ago: The Cuban Missile Crisis," *Prologue* 34, no. 3 (Fall 2002), National Archives (https://www.archives.gov/publications/prologue/2002/fall/cuban-missiles.html).
Freedom Flights: Miguel Gonzalez-Pando, *Development Stages of the "Cuban Exile Country,"* ASCE, 1997; Louis A. Perez Jr., *On Becoming Cuban: Identity, Nationality and Culture* (Eco, 1999).
Development of Cuban Miami: Gonzalez-Pando, *Development Stages of the "Cuban Exile Country"*; David Rieff, *The Exile: Cuba in the Heart of Miami* (Simon & Schuster, 1993); Susan Jacoby, "The 350,000 Cubans in South Florida Make a Remarkable Success Story," *New York Times*, September 29, 1974; Lourdes Arguelles, "Cuban Miami: The Roots, Development, and Everyday Life of an Emigré Enclave in the U.S. National Security State," *Contemporary Marxism*, no. 5 (Summer 1982): 27–43.
First meeting of Willy and Tony Bemba: Interview with Willy Falcon; interview with Tony Garcia.
"They called me *mojón*": Interview with Tavy Falcon.

---

[1] In instances where more than one interview was conducted with a subject, the date of the first interview is used.

Anti-Castro movement in Miami: Antonio Veciana, *Trained to Kill: The Inside Story of CIA Plots against Castro, Kennedy, and Che* (Skyhorse, 2017); Joan Didion, *Miami* (Weidenfeld & Nicholson, 1988); Justo Regalado Borges, *Rebeldía* (Agata, 2014); T. J. English, *The Corporation: An Epic Story of the Cuban American Underworld* (William Morrow, 2018).

Rafael "Chi Chi" Quintero and Armando Lopez Estrada: Don Bohning, "Rafael Quintero, Cold War Warrior: From the Bay of Pigs to Iran-Contra," *International Journal of Intelligence and Counterintelligence* 21, no. 4 (2008): 726–47; Tim Weiner, "Rafael Quintero, 66, Secret Agent Who Stalked Castro for C.I.A., Dies," *New York Times*, October 19, 2006; Felix Rodriguez and John Weisman, *Shadow Warrior: The CIA Hero of a Hundred Unknown Battles* (Simon & Schuster, 1989), 101–4; Spartacus Educational, www.spartacus-educational.com; interview with Willy Falcon; Falcon manuscript.

Origins of Falcon-Quintero alliance: Interview with Willy Falcon; Falcon manuscript; interview with Tony Garcia.

First cocaine shipment: Interview with Willy Falcon; interview with Tony Garcia; Falcon manuscript.

Jack Devoe: Interview with Willy Falcon; Falcon manuscript; written statement from Jack Devoe, *President's Commission on Organized Crime and Cocaine Trafficking*, November 1985; testimony of Jack Devoe, *US v. Falcon-Magluta* (transcript), 1995.

Meeting with Isaac Padron's widow: Falcon manuscript; interview with Willy Falcon.

2. Alina

Sigmund Freud and cocaine: Sigmund Freud, *Cocaine Papers*, ed. Robert Byck (Stonehill Publishing, 1974).

"Woe to you, my princess": Ibid., 10.

"The natives of South America": Ibid., 50.

Background on Alina Rossique Falcon: Interview with Ileana Rossique Garrudo, March 27, 2021; interview with Willy Falcon.

"Ever since we were little girls": Interview with Rossique Garrudo.

"At dinner in the cafeteria": Ibid.

Salvador Magluta background: Jim DeFede, "Willy and Sal," *Miami New Times*, February 12, 1992; Roben Farzad, *Hotel Scarface: Where Cocaine Cowboys Partied and Plotted to Control Miami* (New American Library, 2017), 72, 79, 82, 97.

Willy and Alina wedding: Interview with Willy Falcon; interview with Rossique Garrudo.

Griselda Blanco: Richard Smitten, *The Godmother: The True Story of the Hunt for the Most Bloodthirsty Female Criminal of Our Time* (Pocket Books, 1990); *Cocaine Cowboys 2: Hustlin' with the Godmother*, Billy Corben (dir.), documentary, Netflix, 2008.

Jorge "George" Valdés: Interview with Manuel Garces, April 27, 2021; interview with Willy Falcon; Falcon manuscript; testimony of Sermon Dyess Jr., *US v. Falcon-Magluta* (transcript); testimony of Butch Reddish, *US v. Falcon-Magluta* (transcript); Jorge L. Valdés, with Ken Abraham, *Coming Clean: The True Story of a Cocaine Drug Lord and His Unexpected Encounter* (Xlibris, 2008); Valdés podcasts: George Valdés talks frequently about his cocaine years on his own podcast and as a guest on many other podcasts. He rarely misses an opportunity to denigrate Willy Falcon and claim that he, Valdés, was the biggest cocaine kingpin in the United States in the late 1970s. Evidence to support this claim is sketchy.

George Ordoñez: Falcon manuscript; interview with Willy Falcon; interview with Garces.

Stash houses: Interview with Willy Falcon; Falcon manuscript; interview with Wilfredo "Mata" Pino, March 24, 2021; interview with Tavy Falcon; testimony of Pedro "Pegy" Rosello, *US v. Falcon-Magluta* (transcript).

Violence in Miami: Interview with Detective Pat Diaz, May 6, 2021; interview with Detective Al Singleton, May 4, 2021; interview with Detective Ron Ilhardt, February 6, 2023; Carl Hiaasen and Al Messerschmidt, "Shoot-Out at the Cocaine Corral," *Miami Herald*, July 8, 1979; George Volsky, "Killings in Florida over Drug Use on the Rise," *New York Times*, July 22, 1979; Edna Buchanan, *The Corpse Had a Familiar Face: Covering Miami, America's Hottest Beat* (Random House, 1987); Nicholas Griffin, *The Year of Dangerous Days: Riots, Refugees, and Cocaine in Miami, 1980* (37 Ink, 2020).

Manuel Garces: Interview with Garces; interview with Willy Falcon; Falcon manuscript.

Colombia smuggling history and culture: Interview with Garces; Lina Brito, *Marijuana Boom: The Rise and Fall of Colombia's First Drug Paradise* (University of California Press, 2020).

Ray Corona: Interview with Willy Falcon; Farzad, *Hotel Scarface*, 69–71, 78, 80, 197–99; Brian Duffy, "U.S. Bankers Helped Smuggler Hide Drug Profits," *Miami Herald*, June 3, 1985.

Origins of Seahawk and KS&W: Interview with Tavy Falcon; interview with Willy Falcon; Falcon manuscript; testimony of Keith Eickert, *US v. Falcon-Magluta* (transcript).

3. Makin' It

Alina-Willy relationship: Interview with Willy Falcon.

The Mutiny: Interview with Willy Falcon; interview with Mollie Hampton, November 15, 2022; interview with Tony Garcia; interview with Antonio "Tony" Garrudo, March 27, 2021; interview with Ralph "Cabeza" Linero, March 24, 2021; interview with Owen Band, October 28, 2022; Sean Rowe, "Glorious & Notorious," *Miami New Times*, February 27, 1997; Murray J. Brown, "Florida Hotel Offers Exotic Rooms," *Rochester Democrat and Chronicle*, December 28, 1980; Farzad, *Hotel Scarface*.

Anti-Castro royalty: John Rothchild, "The Informant," *Harper's*, January 1982; Associated Press, "Warren Report Incomplete, Says Former Guard of JFK," *Washington Post*, January 20, 1967; FBI Memorandum, "Subject: Assassination of President John Fitzgerald Kennedy, November 23, 1963, Dallas, Texas," February 20, 1967; Farzad, *Hotel Scarface*, 19–20, 24, 28, 33, 102–6, 112–16.

"In a suite at the Mutiny": Farzad, *Hotel Scarface*, 35.

Laney Jacobs: Interview with Willy Falcon; Falcon manuscript; Steven Wick, *Bad Company: Drugs, Hollywood and the Cotton Club Murder* (Harcourt Brace Jovanavich, 1990); Ann Bardach, "Blond Widow: Seven Husbands, Two Murders, a Sea of Cocaine and other Tales," *Buzz*, November/December 1991.

Alina Falcon–Carlene Quesada relationship: Interview with Humberto "Bert" Becerra, November 8, 2022; interview with Hampton; interview with Willy Falcon.

Jack Devoe and Profullo "Prof" Mondal: Testimony of Devoe, *US v. Falcon-Magluta* (transcript).

Clewiston, Florida, operations: Falcon manuscript; interview with Willy Falcon; testimony of Dyess Jr., *US v. Falcon-Magluta* (transcript); testimony of Reddish, *US v. Falcon-Magluta* (transcript).

Dyess Jr. takes $700,000 payment: Falcon manuscript; interview with Willy Falcon; Jeff Testerman, "Former Hendry Sheriff Indicted," *Tampa Bay Times*, January 5, 1993; Jeff Testerman, "Former Sheriff Pleads Guilty in Cocaine Case," *Tampa Bay Times*, February 9, 1993; testimony of Dyess Jr., *US v. Falcon-Magluta* (transcript).

Tony Fandino: Falcon manuscript; interview with Willy Falcon.

Pablo Escobar background: Interview with Garces; Jenna L. Bowley, "Robin Hood or Villain: The Social Construction of Pablo Escobar" (master's thesis, University of

Maine, May 2013), accessed online; Juan Pablo Escobar, *Pablo Escobar: My Father* (Thomas Dunne Books, 2016); Roberto Escobar, *Escobar: The Inside Story of Pablo Escobar* (Hodder, 2010); Mark Bowden, *Killing Pablo: The Hunt for the World's Greatest Outlaw* (Atlantic Monthly Press, 1994).

Falcon and Magluta meet the Valencia brothers: Falcon manuscript; interview with Willy Falcon; interview with Garces.

Jojo Brito: Interview with Jojo Brito, March 23, 2021.

4. Viva Las Vegas

Video Canary case: Interview with Willy Falcon; Falcon manuscript; interview with L. Mark Dachs, June 1, 2022.

Birth of the Contras: Glenn Garvin, *Everybody Had His Own Gringo: The CIA and the Contras* (Brassey's, 1992); Jonathan Marshall, *Drug Wars: Corruption, Counterinsurgency and Covert Operations in the Third World* (Cohen & Cohen, 1991); "Drugs, Law Enforcement and Foreign Policy," *Report of the Subcommittee on Terrorism, Narcotics and International Operations*, Committee on Foreign Relations, US Senate, John Kerry, chairman, December 1988.

CIA, the Contras, and cocaine: In the late 1990s, there was a brief attempt in the US media to come to terms with allegations about the CIA's involvement in the early days of the cocaine business. A series of articles in the *San Jose Mercury News* titled "Dark Alliance: Behind the Crack Explosion" uncovered a connection between the Los Angeles–based drug operation of a twenty-year-old dealer name Ricky Ross and two Latinos, Oscar Danilo Blandon and Norwin Meneses. Blandon and Meneses were active in anti-Sandinista efforts in Nicaragua, especially with the Fuerza Democrática Nicaragüense (FDN), a group affiliated with the Contras. Over many months, Blandon and Meneses sold tons of cocaine to Ross, who converted it to crack and sold it on the streets of Los Angeles and other cities. The newspaper articles suggested that the US government, in the guise of the CIA, protected Blandon and Meneses, who were selling the drug to raise money to purchase arms for the Contras.

The articles touched off a fierce controversy, with mainstream publications like the *New York Times* and *Los Angeles Times* declaring that the journalism behind the articles was shoddy. The reporter responsible for most of the article was Gary Webb, who later committed suicide.

The crux of those articles, and later investigations by other journalists and authors, coincides with the scenario described by Willy Falcon in this book. The only difference is the element of the anti-Castro movement and how that might have shaped the relationships that made it all possible.

Antonio Garcia Perez: Interview with Willy Falcon; testimony of Willy Falcon, US DOJ Office of Immigration Review, "In the Matter of Augusto Guillermo Falcon," January 24, 2018 (transcript); interview with Tony Garcia; Falcon manuscript; Terence Cullen, "'Cocaine Cowboys' Used Drug Profits to Fund CIA-Tied Efforts to Assassinate Castro," *Daily News* (New York), September 30, 2017.

Powerboat racing scene: Interview with Tavy Falcon; interview with Willy Falcon; testimony of Juan Barroso, *US v. Falcon-Magluta* (transcript); interview with Linero; John Crouse, *Searace: A History of Offshore Powerboat Racing* (Crouse Publications, 1989); Thomas Burdick, *Blue Thunder: How the Mafia Owned and Finally Murdered the Cigarette Boat King Donald Aronow* (Simon & Schuster, 1990). Aronow, the inventor of the Cigarette boat, was a legend in Miami boating circles. On February 3, 1987, he was gunned down while sitting in his car on Thunder Road. The murder remained unsolved for two decades until a local hit man, shortly before he died, admitted to pulling the trigger at the behest of Ben Kramer, the winner of the 1986 APBA Offshore Championship. Kramer had a business dispute with Aronow. By the time the crime was solved, Kramer was already in prison on a life sentence for drug smuggling, gun possession, and attempted escape from prison.

Mandy Campo at Caesars Palace: Interview with Willy Falcon.

Las Vegas: Interview with Linero; interview with Tony Garcia; interview with Tavy Falcon; interview with Willy Falcon.

Frank Ocando Paz: Interview with Willy Falcon; interview with Tony Garrudo.

Holiday season for Los Muchachos: Interview with Willy Falcon; interview with Tavy Falcon; interview with Linero; interview with Tony Garcia; interview with Lorenzo; interview with Tony Garrudo.

Pablo in Vegas: Interview with Willy Falcon; interview with Tavy Falcon; Falcon manuscript; interview with Lorenzo.

The Houston Livestock Show and Rodeo: Testimony of Dyess Jr., *US v. Falcon-Magluta* (transcript); testimony of Jorge "George" Valdés, *US v. Falcon-Magluta* (transcript); interview with Willy Falcon; interview with Garces; Falcon manuscript.

Dyess Jr. snorts cocaine: Interview with Willy Falcon; Falcon manuscript.

Meeting at Sonny's Real Pit Bar-B-Q: Testimony of Dyess Jr., *US v. Falcon-Magluta* (transcript); testimony of Reddish, *US v. Falcon-Magluta* (transcript); interview with Willy Falcon; Falcon manuscript. The author visited Sonny's in Clewiston, Florida, to verify the location and the quality of the ribs.

Dyess Jr. and Reddish monitor incoming flights: Testimony of Dyess Jr., *US v. Falcon-Magluta* (transcript); testimony of Reddish, *US v. Falcon-Magluta* (transcript).

Anti-Castro training activities at the ranch: Interview with Willy Falcon; Falcon manuscript.

5. Miami Rising

Melvyn Kessler: Interview with Dachs; Philip Smith, "Drug Suspects' Lawyer Heavy on Candor, Cash," *Washington Post*, March 21, 1985; Donald Goddard, *Easy Money: The High-Rolling, Superflying, Drug-Powered World of the Spanish and Black "Mafias"* (Farrar, Straus and Giroux, 1978), 57–59, 71; interview with Willy Falcon; Falcon manuscript.

"Kessler schooled me on things like conspiracy": Interview with Willy Falcon.

George Valdés in Panama: Testimony of Valdés, *US v. Falcon-Magluta* (transcript); Valdés, *Coming Clean*, 91–114.

Introduction to Juan Acosta: Interview with Willy Falcon; Falcon manuscript.

Guillermo Endara and Hernán Delgado: Falcon manuscript; interview with Willy Falcon; Linda Robinson, "The Panama Connection," *U.S. News & World Report*, December 9, 1991; Frederick Kempe, *Divorcing the Dictator: America's Bungled Affair with Noriega* (Putnam, 1990), 231–33, 311, 322–26, 401–2. The Endara-Delgado money-laundering relationship with Los Muchachos would become a major aspect of the federal government's case against Willy and Sal, as detailed in the trial testimony of Keith Eickert, co-owner of KS&W; and Leticia Gonzalez, an employee at the Endara Firm in Panama who was subpoenaed and gave testimony in *US v. Falcon-Magluta*.

Falcon-Magluta shell companies at Endara Firm: The companies are listed in the indictment of *US v. Falcon-Magluta*; Falcon manuscript.

Gabriel Castro (PTJ): Interview with Willy Falcon; Falcon manuscript; José Quintero De León, "Fallece exministro Gabriel Castro Suarez," *La Estrella de Panama*, July 5,

2017; "Endara rompe voto de silencio" (Endara breaks vow of silence), Inter Press Service (IPS), July 7, 1995.

Birth of the DEA and War on Drugs: Dan Baum, *Smoke and Mirrors: The War on Drugs and the Politics of Failure* (Back Bay Books, 1997); Michael Levine, *The Big White Lie: The Deep Cover Operation That Exposed the CIA Sabotage of the Drug War* (Thunder's Mouth Press, 1991).

David Borah: Testimony of Special Agent David Borah, *US v. Falcon-Magluta* (transcript). Borah declined to be interviewed for this book, as he has for most books, podcasts, and documentaries since the era of Willy and Sal. It is unusual for a long-since-retired lawman to not talk about his past cases, especially one that was as central to an agent's career as the Falcon-Magluta investigation was for Borah. Among the former cops, agents, and prosecutors interviewed for this book, there was much speculation about Borah's silence, ranging from fear brought on by threats of retribution for his involvement in the case, or lingering resentment from how he was abruptly removed from the case right before trial. His unwillingness to be interviewed about the case remains a mystery.

Crime in Miami: Gregory Jaynes, "Miami Crime Rises as Drugs Pour In," *New York Times*, August 12, 1981; Jeff Leen, "S. Florida's Cocaine Toll Skyrockets," *Miami Herald*, July 13, 1986; Griffin, *Year of Dangerous Days*; Buchanan, *Corpse Had a Familiar Face*.

Miami real estate development: Interview with real estate agent Esther Percal, June 2, 2022.

Willy and Sal's financial diversification: Falcon manuscript; interview with Willy Falcon; DeFede, "Willy and Sal."

Purchase of CMM Ranch: Interview with Willy Falcon; Falcon manuscript; interview with Dachs; opening statement of AUSA Chris Clark, *US v. Falcon-Magluta* (transcript), 1995.

Party night, from the Mutiny to the ranch: Interview with Willy Falcon; Falcon manuscript.

6. New Sheriff in Town

Alina and the fashion business: Interview with Rossique Garrudo; interview with Willy Falcon.

The Mariel Boatlift: "U.S. Agrees to Admit Up to 3,500 Cubans from Peru Embassy," *New York Times*, April 15, 1980; Victor Andres Triay, *The Mariel Boatlift: A Cuban American Journey* (University of Florida Press, 2019).

Arrest of Richard Passapera: Interview with Willy Falcon; Falcon manuscript; interview with Lorenzo.

Sheriff Dyess Jr. at the Mutiny: Interview with Willy Falcon; Falcon manuscript.

Murder of Sermon Dyess Sr.: Sheriff Earl Sermon Dyess Sr. memorial page, Officer Down Memorial Page, n.d., https://www.odmp.org/officer/4434-sheriff-earl-sermon-dyess-sr.

Dyess Jr. asks for campaign contribution: Interview with Willy Falcon; Falcon manuscript.

"I own this damn county": Interview with Willy Falcon; Falcon manuscript.

Aftermath of Marta Falcon kidnapping: Interview with Willy Falcon; interview with Tavy Falcon; "Ex–Police Officers Charged as Members of Lucrative Kidnap Ring," *Tampa Bay Times*, April 9, 1981; "Police Tie-In Is Alleged in Kidnappings in Florida," United Press International, April 10, 1981. Eight months after the kidnapping of Marta Falcon, there was within the Los Muchachos universe another kidnapping attempt, this one of Willy himself. This time, Willy was departing a safe house apartment that Los Muchachos kept in Coral Gables specifically for counting money, when he was accosted by two gunmen, one of whom was dressed as a woman. Falcon literally jumped out of his flip-flops and ran through a series of backyards, where he cut himself while jumping over a chain-link fence. Bleeding profusely, he pounded on doors until someone allowed him to use their phone and call the police. Weeks later, a police sergeant at the local Coral Gables police department called Willy into the station to listen to a tape recording they had of a notorious Miami narco named Mario Tabraue swearing that he was going to kidnap and kill someone named Willy. Tabraue was a serious criminal; he would soon be suspected in the murder of his wife but never charged. When Tabraue heard that local police were trying to implicate him in the attempted kidnapping or killing of Falcon, he called Willy, whom he knew, to make clear that he was talking about an entirely different Willy in the taped phone conversation. Falcon and Los Muchachos never did find out who tried to kidnap Willy. Falcon thinks they were attempting to kidnap Alina, his wife, who sometimes stayed at the Coral Gables apartment when she and Willy were feuding. Mario Tabraue, after spending twelve years in prison on cocaine-trafficking charges, became something of a celebrity in 2020 as the star of a popular Netflix docuseries called *Tiger King*.

David Earl Rogers: UPI, "Cop Arrested in Kidnapping-Extortion Ring," *South Florida Sun Sentinel*, April 9, 1981; "Ex–Police Officers Charged"; "Police Tie-In Is Alleged."

Jack Devoe becomes a *basuco* junkie: Interview with Willy Falcon; Falcon manuscript; testimony of Devoe, *US v. Falcon-Magluta* (transcript).

Willy nurses Jack back to health: Interview with Willy Falcon; Falcon manuscript.

Jack Devoe background: Testimony of Devoe, *US v. Falcon-Magluta* (transcript).

Passapera found not guilty: Interview with Dachs; interview with Willy Falcon; Falcon manuscript.

7. War on Drugs

Mainstreaming of cocaine: Michael Demarest, "Cocaine: Middle Class High," *Time*, July 6, 1981; Colin Campbell, "Trade in Drugs Thriving in Office-Tower Shadows," *New York Times*, April 25, 1981; Thomas O'Toole, "Cocaine: America's 'Drug of Choice,'" *Washington Post*, October 27, 1981; Ena Naunton, "Cocaine and the Quest for Death," *Miami Herald*, August 8, 1982; *Cocaine Use in America: Epidemiologic and Clinical Perspectives*, Department of Health and Human Services/National Institute of Drug Abuse, 1985; Baum, *Smoke and Mirrors*.

For a stellar exploration of the politics of cocaine as it became an economic force in South and North America, see Rensselaer W. Lee III, *The White Labyrinth: Cocaine Politics and Power* (Transaction Publishers, 1989).

South Florida Drug Task Force: "Statement Announcing Establishment of a Federal Anti-Crime Task Force for Southern Florida," The White House, Office of the President, January 28, 1982 (https://www.reaganlibrary.gov/archives/speech/statement-announcing-establishment-federal-anti-crime-task-force-southern-florida); David K. Willis, "Hunting Down the Drug Smugglers," *Christian Science Monitor*, December 21, 1983.

"We didn't have no competitors": Interview with Willy Falcon.

"For example, John in San Francisco": Ibid.

"Drugs already reach deeply": "Text of President's Speech on National Drug Control Strategy," *New York Times*, September 6, 1989.

Tavy and Amelia: Interview with Tavy Falcon; interview with Amelia Rosello Falcon, March 24, 2021.

George H. W. Bush and the Contras: Garvin, *Everybody Had His Own Gringo*, 186, 243–47, 255.

Meeting with Nigel Bowe and Lawrence Major: Interview with Willy Falcon; Falcon manuscript. For background on both Bowe and Major, see Paul Eddy, with Hugo Sabogal and Sara Weldon, *The Cocaine Wars* (W. W. Norton, 1988).

Kilos shipped through Grand Harbor Island: Interview with Willy Falcon; Falcon manuscript.

Seahawk boats retrofitted for smuggling: Interview with Lorenzo; Falcon manuscript.

Carlos Lehder background: Eddy, with Sabogal and Weldon, *Cocaine Wars*, 147–48, 150–54, 156–57, 162–63, 171, 189, 286–87.

MAS (Death to Kidnappers): Guy Gugliotta and Jeff Leen, *Kings of Cocaine: Inside the Medellín Cartel, an Astonishing True Story of Murder, Money, and International Corruption* (Simon & Schuster, 1989), 103–112, 115; Bowden, *Killing Pablo*, 54–57, 89, 101, 105.

Meeting with Escobar in Aruba: Interview with Willy Falcon; interview with Tavy Falcon; Falcon manuscript.

Tony Garrudo, a.k.a. El Cuño: Interview with Tony Garrudo.

"When you are bringing new people": Interview with Willy Falcon.

Tony G. creates Aviation Cleaners: Interview with Tony Garrudo; interview with Willy Falcon.

Willy dumps Jack Devoe: Interview with Willy Falcon; interview with Tony Garrudo; Falcon manuscript; testimony of Devoe, *US v. Falcon-Magluta* (transcript).

8. Pablo in Disney World

Coca processing in Colombia: Itayosara Rojas Herrera and Joost Dessiein, "'We Are Not Drug Traffickers, We Are Colombian Peasants': The Voices and History of *Cocaleros* in the Substitution Programme of Illicit Crops in Colombia," *Geoforum*, vol. 141 (May 2023); *Drug Wars: Inside the $400 Billion Global Business*, Frontline PBS, 1987.

Willy and Sal visit Cauca Valley: Interview with Willy Falcon; Falcon manuscript.

"Willy and Sal were so close": Interview with Fernando Garcia, November 18, 2022.

HoneyComb Paging: Falcon manuscript; interview with Willy Falcon.

Flashiness of Los Muchachos: Interview with Tony Garrudo; interview with Willy Falcon; interview with Lorenzo.

Pedro "Pegy" Rosello: Rosello manuscript, written by Michelle Salom. In the early 2000s, Rosello created an eighty-eight-page outline for a book, film, or television project that never got off the ground.

Purchase of Lear 55: Interview with Willy Falcon; Falcon manuscript; interview with Tavy Falcon.

Escobar and family visit Disney World: Interview with Willy Falcon; Falcon manuscript. Pablo's fascination with Disney World is commented on in most of the Escobar biographies, and it is mentioned in the television series *Narcos* (Netflix), which dramatized the kingpin's criminal career.

Falcon introduces Escobar to Guillermo Endara: Interview with Willy Falcon; Falcon manuscript.

President Reagan visits Homestead Air Force Base: David Hoffman, "President Examines Florida Crime Booty, Vows to Widen War," *Washington Post*, November 18, 1982.

Devoe borrows money from Willy: Testimony of Devoe, *US v. Falcon-Magluta* (transcript).

Los Muchachos transition to Mexico: Falcon manuscript; interview with Willy Falcon; interview with Linero; testimony of Devoe, *US v. Falcon-Magluta* (transcript). In interviews and testimony, the pilots Devoe and Linero noted how the transition away from the Caribbean islands to Mexico as the group's primary smuggling route was a major blow to their moneymaking opportunities.

Mario Valencia introduces Willy and Sal to Juan Ramón Matta-Ballesteros: Interview with Willy Falcon; Falcon manuscript.

Matta-Ballesteros's background: "Drugs, Law Enforcement and Foreign Policy."

Willy, Benny Lorenzo, and Victor Alvarez travel to Los Angeles: Interview with Willy Falcon; Falcon manuscript; interview with Lorenzo; interview with Brito.

Benny B. as "chick magnet": Interview with Willy Falcon; interview with Lorenzo.

Meeting with Pepe in San Bernardino: Interview with Willy Falcon; Falcon manuscript; interview with Lorenzo.

Meeting at Bonaventure Hotel: Interview with Willy Falcon; interview with Lorenzo; interview with Brito; Falcon manuscript.

9. "It's a Boy(s)!"

Lourdes Castellon: Interview with Lourdes Castellon, November 4, 2022; interview with Willy Falcon.

"They were a bunch of bullies": Interview with Castellon.

Lourdes becomes pregnant: Interview with Castellon; interview with Willy Falcon.

Confrontation between Lourdes and Alina: Interview with Castellon.

L. Mark Dachs's background: Interview with Dachs.

Meeting with Gallardo, Quintero, and Fonseca Carrillo in Mexico City: Interview with Willy Falcon; Falcon manuscript.

Meeting with Endara and Castro in Panama City: Interview with Willy Falcon; Falcon manuscript.

"The next day came": Interview with Willy Falcon.

Ralph Linero in Colombia: Interview with Linero; interview with Willy Falcon.

"That's why I'm with him": Interview with Linero.

Falcon moves to Los Angeles: Interview with Willy Falcon; Falcon manuscript; interview with Brito.

Social life in Los Angeles: Interview with Willy Falcon; Falcon manuscript; interview with Lorenzo; interview with Brito.

Meeting the Rat Pack in Las Vegas: Interview with Willy Falcon; Falcon manuscript.

10. LA Blues

Meeting Escobar et al. in Panama City: Interview with Willy Falcon; Falcon manuscript.

Memory from Willy and Sal's childhood: Falcon manuscript.

Willy wins his first powerboat championship race: Joe Leary, "Sizzling Speed Leads 'Seahawk' to Marathon Win," *South Florida Sun Sentinel*, May 4, 1986.

Raymond (Ramón) "Manny" Alonso: Interview with Raymond "Manny" Alonso, April 28, 2021.

"It was a Cuban social club": Ibid.

Falcon puts Manny to work: Interview with Willy Falcon; Falcon manuscript; interview with Alonso.

Falcon says no to dealing with Sandinista government: Interview with Willy Falcon; Falcon manuscript.

Escobar suggests Cuba: Interview with Willy Falcon; testimony of Willy Falcon, "In the Matter of Augusto Guillermo Falcon."

George Morales: Associated Press, "Cocaine Dealer Tells Panel He Smuggled Contra Drugs," *Los Angeles Times*, July 16, 1987; Keith Schneider, "Iran Contra Hearings:

Smuggler Ties Contras to U.S. Drug Network," *New York Times,* July 16, 1987; Joe Leary, "Champion Boat Racer Gets 16 Years on Drug Charges," *South Florida Sun Sentinel,* April 18, 1987. George Morales was one of the star witnesses at the US Senate subcommittee hearings on drugs, the Contras, and the CIA, chaired by Senator John Kerry of Massachusetts, in 1988.

Smuggling kilos through Cuba: Interview with Willy Falcon. This was a topic that Falcon initially did not want to discuss. He left any mention of it out of his manuscript.

Los Muchachos expand in Los Angeles: Interview with Willy Falcon; Falcon manuscript; interview with Brito; interview with Lorenzo; testimony of Rosello, *US v. Falcon-Magluta* (transcript).

Willy, Sal et al. busted in Marina Del Rey: Interview with Willy Falcon; Falcon manuscript; interview with Lorenzo; interview with Tony Garrudo.

Devoe becomes a snitch: Testimony of Devoe, *US v. Falcon-Magluta* (transcript).

Devoe meets DEA Special Agent Borah: Ibid.

11. White Dude with a Camera

Mutiny closes: Dory Ownes, "Peninsula Forecloses on Mutiny Hotel," *Miami Herald,* April 24, 1985; Howard Cohen, "Sex, Drugs and Disco: Mutiny Hotel's Visionary, Burton Goldberg, Dies at 90," *Miami Herald,* November 19, 2016; Farzad, *Hotel Scarface,* 201–4, 211, 214–15.

Murder of Margarita Eilenberg: Farzad, *Hotel Scarface,* 128–30, 132–33, 137, 151.

Willy Falcon birthday party: Interview with Willy Falcon; Falcon manuscript.

Escobar war on Colombian society: The campaign of terror, bombings, and assassinations of public officials and journalists is a major part of all the biographies on Escobar, including, but not limited to, the following: *Killing Pablo* by Mark Bowden, *Escobar vs. Cali* by Ron Chepesiuk, *Pablo Escobar* by Juan Pablo Escobar, *Escobar* by Roberto Escobar, *The Accountant's Story* by David Fisher, and *Kings of Cocaine* by Guy Gugliotta and Jeff Leen.

Mario Valencia wants Willy-Sal to intercede with Escobar: Interview with Willy Falcon; Falcon manuscript.

Agent Borah opens case in 1986: Testimony of SA Borah, *US v. Falcon-Magluta* (transcript).

Agent Borah at the powerboat race: Testimony of SA Borah, *US v. Falcon-Magluta* (transcript); interview with Willy Falcon; Falcon manuscript.

Search warrant executed at KS&W: Interview with Willy Falcon; Falcon manuscript.

Meeting in Mexico City, summer 1986: Interview with Willy Falcon; Falcon manuscript.

Tavy Falcon takes on larger role: Interview with Tavy Falcon.

"This was always a problem": Ibid.

Meeting with Pacho Herrera in Aruba: Interview with Willy Falcon; Falcon manuscript. Falcon disputes what he calls "a myth in the drug trade," found in many written histories, that Escobar acceded New York to the Cali Cartel. Says Willy: "I can assure you, that never happened. No deal was ever made with Pablo allowing Pacho and the Cali Cartel to control New York. Whoever had the best cocaine quality and best price controlled the marketplace."

Endara solicits campaign contribution: Interview with Willy Falcon; Falcon manuscript.

Willy and Sal skip bail in Los Angeles: Interview with Willy Falcon; Falcon manuscript.

Muchachos group meeting in Orlando: Interview with Willy Falcon; interview with Tavy Falcon; interview with Lorenzo.

12. New York State of Mind

Iran-Contra hearings: The historical significance of the Joint Hearings before the House Select Committee to Investigate Covert Arms Transactions with Iran and the Senate Select Committee on Secret Military Assistance to Iran and the Nicaraguan Opposition are now the subject of various online archives, including the entire transcript of the hearings at the National Archive (www.archives.gov).

Willy and Alina in NYC: Falcon manuscript; interview with Willy Falcon; interview with Rossique Garrudo.

"It was amazing": Interview with Willy Falcon.

Escobar confronts Willy-Sal about Cali Cartel: Interview with Willy Falcon; Falcon manuscript.

"In our organization": Interview with Willy Falcon.

Unloading financial assets: Interview with Dachs; interview with Willy Falcon; Falcon manuscript.

Incident at Tunnel nightclub: Interview with Willy Falcon.

Incident with Manny, Monito, and police tail: Interview with Alonso; interview with Willy Falcon; Falcon manuscript.

The crack epidemic: Craig Reinarman and Harry G. Levine, "Crack in Context: Politics and Media in the Making of a Drug Scare," *Contemporary Drug Problems: A Special Report* (1990); David Farber, *Crack: Rock Cocaine, Street Capitalism, and the Decade of Greed* (Cambridge University Press, 2019); Baum, *Smoke and Mirrors*, xiv, 213, 219–21, 235, 251, 254–56.

"When I started making money": Interview with Lorenzo.

Tony Garrudo and his father: Interview with Tony Garrudo.

13. Sal as Zorro

Meeting with Félix Gallardo in Mexico City: Interview with Willy Falcon; Falcon manuscript.

Pegy Rosello visited by aliens: *Don't Blink Podcast*, episode 90, guest: Pedro "Pegy" Rosello, September 13, 2022.

"We were driving back": Ibid.

Pegy and Justo Jay: Rosello manuscript.

Pegy in LA: Ibid.

Pegy's social life in Miami Beach: Ibid.

The concept of "Green Eyes": Interview with Willy Falcon. To Willy, the term simply meant money, which made you desirable to the ladies. But to others, the term was open to various interpretations.

Creating new cocaine route: Falcon manuscript; interview with Willy Falcon.

"Our first night in Vegas": Interview with Willy Falcon.

The seizure and then repurchase of CMM Ranch: Interview with Willy Falcon; Falcon manuscript; interview with Lorenzo.

Willy and Alina move to Fort Lauderdale: Interview with Willy Falcon; Falcon manuscript.

Meeting in Medellín with Garces and Captain Zuluaga: Interview with Garces; interview with Willy Falcon; Falcon manuscript.

Conversation with Escobar: Interview with Willy Falcon; Falcon manuscript.

Owen Band and Bernardo de Torres: Interview with Band.

"Rick was living in North Hollywood": Ibid.

"James got out of the jacuzzi": Ibid.

Sal in Zorro outfit: Ibid.

Arrest and release of Magluta: Interview with Willy Falcon; Falcon manuscript; interview with AUSA Christopher "Chris" Clark, May 5, 2021; interview with AUSA Michael Patrick "Pat" Sullivan, May, 20, 2021; arresting officer Jorge Plasencia, interview for *Cocaine Cowboys: Kings of Cocaine*, Netflix, 2021.

14. Mexican Hat Dance

Christopher Clark background: Interview with AUSA Clark.

AUSA Clark and SA Borah attempt to recruit informants: Ibid.

"I tried to tell them that": Interview with Tony Garcia.

Asset forfeiture as a tool in the War on Drugs: Eric Blumenson and Eva Nilson, "Policing for Profit: The Drug War's Hidden Economic Agenda," *University of Chicago Law Review* 65, no. 1 (1998): 35–114; DEA Asset Forfeiture, United States Drug Enforcement Administration (www.dea.gov). The use of civil asset forfeiture is now viewed as one of the more onerous legacies of the drug war and has come under legal challenge.

Endara assaulted after being elected president of Panama: Linsey Gruson, "3 Top Opponents of Noriega Assaulted in the Street Melee; Disputed Election Nullified," *New York Times*, May 11, 1989.

Willy and Sal meet with Endara in Panama: Interview with Willy Falcon; Falcon manuscript.

Meeting with Amado Carrillo Fuentes ("Lord of the Skies") in Ciudad Juárez: Interview with Willy Falcon; Falcon manuscript.

Escobar asks Willy and Sal to meet with Amado Carrillo: Interview with Willy Falcon; Falcon manuscript.

George H. W. Bush and the War on Drugs: Jefferson Morley, "Bush's Drug Problem—and Ours," *The Nation*, August 27, 1988; Michael Isikoff, "Drug Buy Set Up for Bush Speech: DEA Lured Seller to Lafayette Park," *Washington Post*, September 22, 1989.

"Our most serious problem today": Statement from President George H. W. Bush, The White House, Office of the President, September 6, 1989 (accessed online).

William Bennett as drug czar: The appointment of Bennett was one of the more provocative gestures of the Bush administration during the War on Drugs. Bennett seemed to believe it was his role to stir the pot and turn the issue of drugs into a major tenet of the country's culture wars, which he detailed in a bestselling book titled *The Book of Virtues*.

National Drug and Crime Emergency Act: This law has been renewed every few years by every president, Republican and Democratic, since it was enacted under President H. W. Bush—including, most recently, by President Biden, in 2022.

US intelligence and General Manuel Noriega: Stephen Englelberg with Jeff Gerth, "U.S. Worry: What Damage Can Noriega Do?," *New York Times*, January 6, 1990; David Johnston, "U.S. Admits Payments to Noriega," *New York Times*, January 19, 1991; Elida Moreno, "Panama's Noriega: CIA Spy Turned Drug-Running Dictator," Reuters, May 30, 2017.

Murder of Juan Acosta: Interview with Detective Ilhardt; Donna Gehrke, "Lawyer Gunned Down in His Office," *Miami Herald*, September 19, 1989; Jim DeFede, "In Pursuit of Willy and Sal," *Miami New Times*, February 25, 1999.

Willy rebuffed by Hernán Delgado: Interview with Willy Falcon; Falcon manuscript.

"The apartment was extremely small": Interview with Willy Falcon; Falcon manuscript.

15. Tiger by the Tail

Watching TV report on Panama invasion: Interview with Willy Falcon; Falcon manuscript.

Willy and Sal meet Frank Sturgis: Interview with Willy Falcon; Falcon manuscript.

Gilberto "Veci" Barrios: In November 1999, Barrios was found guilty at trial on three counts: conspiracy to possess cocaine with the intent to distribute, conspiracy to import cocaine, and possessing cocaine with intent to distribute. He was given a sentence of twenty-seven years in prison. After losing appeals to have his sentence reduced, Barrios agreed to cooperate with the DOJ and testified against Sal Magluta at his trial in 2002.

Jorge Valdés becomes informant: Testimony of Valdés, *US v. Falcon-Magluta* (transcript). Valdés, *Coming Clean*.

Attempted murder of Tony Posada: Interview with Tony Garrudo; interview with Willy Falcon.

Willy and Sal have words: Interview with Willy Falcon; Falcon manuscript.

Conversations with Tony Bemba and Justo Jay: Interview with Willy Falcon; Falcon manuscript.

Revisiting the CMM Ranch: Interview with Willy Falcon; Falcon manuscript.

Attempt to reach a plea deal with DOJ: Interview with Willy Falcon; Falcon manuscript. As part of bartering with the US attorney's office, in which they would plead guilty to cocaine-trafficking charges in exchange for a reduced sentence, Willy and Sal offered an affidavit detailing their dealings with the Cuban government of Fidel Castro. This information led directly to the creation of an indictment in the Southern District of Florida naming Raúl Castro as the leader of an international cocaine-trafficking conspiracy. This indictment became something of a local urban legend among prosecutors and intelligence operatives. Because of its explosive political implications, the indictment was never unsealed, and Raúl Castro was never charged. Interview with AUSA Dick Gregorie, March 26, 2021; David Lyons, "Feds vs. Willie Falcon, Round 2," *Miami Herald*, July 8, 1996.

Arrests on May 17, 1991: Interview with Tony Garrudo; interview with Rossique Garrudo; interview with Willy Falcon.

Frank Rubino represents Noriega: David Margolick, "Win or Lose, Noriega Case Means Victory for Lawyer," *New York Times*, January 12, 1990.

Benny B. on Pegy Rosello: Interview with Lorenzo.

"While I'm pumping gas": Ibid.

Account of Sal's and Benny B.'s arrests at La Gorce: Ibid.; testimony of SA Borah, *US v. Falcon-Magluta* (transcript).

"The restaurant was excellent": Interview with Willy Falcon.

Account of Falcon arrest: Ibid.

AUSA Clark and SA Borah obtain search warrant: Interview with AUSA Clark; testimony of SA Borah, *US v. Falcon-Magluta* (transcript).

16. The White Powder Bar

Willy-Sal-Benny arrest in the media: David Lyons, "3 Arrested in Cocaine Operation," *Miami Herald*, October 16, 1991.

Bernie Gonzalez's role in recruiting informants: Testimony of Valdés, *US v. Falcon-Magluta* (transcript); testimony of Rosello, *US v. Falcon-Magluta* (transcript); Don Van Natta Jr. and Davis Lyons, "Slain Informant Recruited Drug-Case Witnesses," *Miami Herald*, June 25, 1993.

Pegy Rosello cooperation: Testimony of Rosello, *US v. Falcon-Magluta* (transcript).

First meeting in jail with lawyers: Interview with Willy Falcon; Falcon manuscript; interview with Lorenzo.

DOJ's war on criminal defense attorneys: Fredric Dannen, "The Thin White Line," *New Yorker*, July 31, 1995; Jim DeFede, "The Best Defense Money Can Buy," *Miami New Times*, December 14, 1995.

Corrections Officer George Hernandez, a.k.a. Hawaii Five-0: Interview with Willy Falcon.

Falcon meets Albert Krieger: Ibid.

Falcon visitation with his wife and parents: Ibid.

Sergio Greco's stash house: Testimony of Sergio Greco, *US v. Falcon-Magluta* (transcript); testimony of Rosello, *US v. Falcon-Magluta* (transcript).

AUSA Clark approaches AUSA Pat Sullivan: Interview with AUSA Clark; interview with AUSA Sullivan.

Miami River Cops case: Pete Hamill, "White Line Fever," *Village Voice*, August 26, 1986; Staff, "Officer Convicted in River Cops Trial," *South Florida Sun Sentinel*, September 24, 1987; Staff, "Cops the Villains in This Miami Vice; Renegades with Uniforms, Badges Targeted Drug Dealers, Stole Cocaine," *South Florida Sun Sentinel*, November 8, 1987.

Falcon-Magluta receive cell phone in jail: Interview with Willy Falcon; Falcon manuscript; interview with Lorenzo.

First round of calls to partners and family: Interview with Willy Falcon; Falcon manuscript.

17. Trail of Death

Acosta murder investigation: Interview with Detective Ilhardt; DeFede, "In Pursuit of Willy and Sal."

Tavy Falcon on the run: Interview with Tavy Falcon; interview with Amelia Falcon.

Joined on the lam by Wilfredo "Mata" Pino: Interview with Tavy Falcon; interview with Pino.

"I would have followed my husband": Interview with Amelia Falcon.

Jorge Carnet becomes informant: Testimony of Jorge Carnet, *US v. Falcon-Magluta* (transcript); interview with Willy Falcon; interview with Alonso.

Second attempt at plea deal: Interview with Willy Falcon; Falcon manuscript; interview with AUSA Clark.

"We were offering": Interview with Willy Falcon.

Meeting with El Guajiro and Justo Regalado Borges: Interview with Willy Falcon; Falcon manuscript.

Violence against potential witnesses: Manny Garcia, John Lantigua, and Don Van Natta Jr., "Are the Relatives of Key Witnesses Being Targeted?," *Miami Herald*, October 16, 1993.

Killing of Alina Falcon: Interview with Willy Falcon; interview with Tony Garrudo; interview with Rossique Garrudo; Falcon manuscript.

Falcon learns about his wife's murder: Interview with Willy Falcon; Falcon manuscript.

Falcon taken to funeral parlor and meets children: Interview with Willy Falcon; Falcon manuscript; interview with Aileen Falcon, March 24, 2021.

"He was devastated": Interview with Aileen Falcon.

18. The Fix

Falcon meets with Boobie Williams: Interview with Willy Falcon; Staff, "Jury Convicts 11 Members of Drug Gang," *Tampa Bay Times*, March 3, 2000; Seth Ferranti, "The Boobie Boys," *Gorilla Convict*, October 29, 2011.

Killing of Weetchie Escobedo: Farzad, *Hotel Scarface*, 294–96.

Transfer to FCI Talladega: Interview with Willy Falcon; Falcon manuscript.

Encounters with Manuel Noriega: Interview with Willy Falcon; Falcon manuscript.

Legal implications of the ledgers: Interview with AUSA Clark; interview with AUSA Sullivan; interview with Dachs. Given their importance as evidence, the ledgers became the linchpin of the prosecution's case.

Paying the lawyers: Interview with Willy Falcon; Falcon manuscript.

Role of Richard Martinez: On July 14, 2000, Martinez entered a plea of guilty before Judge Patricia A. Seitz on charges that he received approximately $1 million in "proceeds obtained from the distribution of a controlled substance," and that he did "corruptly endeavor to influence, obstruct and impede the due administration of justice" by knowingly violating a protective order when receiving money from Falcon and Magluta. *Florida Bar v. Richard Ignacio Martinez*, Supreme Court of Florida, 2001.

Killing of Bernie Gonzalez: Don Van Natta Jr. and David Lyons, "Slain Informant Recruited Drug-Case Witnesses," *Miami Herald*, June 25, 1993; Peter Slevin, Manny Garcia, and Don Van Natta Jr., "A String of Witnesses, a String of Violence," *Miami Herald*, July 18, 1993.

Murder of Manuel de Dios Unanue in NYC: Ginger Thompson, "Suspect in Journalist's Slaying Is Arrested," *New York Times*, April 19, 1999; Joseph Fried, "Man Is Sentenced to 18 Years in Killing of Anti-Drug Writer," *New York Times*, May 11, 1996.

Juan Velasco: Interview with Detective Ilhardt; interview with AUSA Clark; DeFede, "In Pursuit of Willy and Sal."

Hit list: The belief that there was a hit list stemmed from information provided by Lazaro Diaz, a low-level Miami narco who, to cut a deal for himself, regaled investigators with stories about hit teams and prospective targets. It was Diaz who told prosecutors that the same hit team that gunned down Bernie Gonzalez was out to kill DEA Special Agent David Borah, among others. Prosecutors were alarmed: Diaz's stories became the basis for AUSAs Clark and Sullivan arguing before a judge that Falcon and Magluta, by court order, be moved from Miami to maximum-security facilities in Atlanta and Marion.

Eventually, the prosecutors rejected Lazaro Diaz and even indicted him for providing false information, though, in the end, some of what he told them about the Colombian hit teams turned out to be true. Don Van Natta Jr., "U.S. Prosecutors: Drug Witness Made Up Tales of Hit Teams," *Miami Herald*, January 2, 1994.

"It was a threat that": Interview with AUSA Clark.

Willy, Sal, and Benny transferred to maximum security: Interview with Willy Falcon; Falcon manuscript; interview with Lorenzo.

Visit with lawyer Dachs in Atlanta prison: Interview with Willy Falcon; Falcon manuscript; interview with Dachs.

"He was so pale": Interview with Aileen Falcon.

Death of Pablo Escobar: Interview with Willy Falcon; Falcon manuscript. Escobar's death was a major international news story, with coverage on all major media outlets.

"Pablo let me know": Interview with Willy Falcon.

Falcon petition of BOP: *Falcon v. US Bureau of Prisons*, US District Court, Southern District of Illinois, May 10, 1994.

Falcon meets John Gotti at FCI Marion: Interview with Willy Falcon; Falcon manuscript.

Solitary confinement: Kayla James and Alana Vanko, "The Impacts of Solitary Confinement," (evidence brief), Vera Institute of Justice, April 2021. Conditions at Marion Penitentiary figure prominently in Pete Early, *No Human Contact* (Citadel Press, 2023), 62–65, 95–98, 108–11, 119–20, 123–24.

Statement from Judge Moreno: Falcon manuscript.
"We knew they had the ability": Interview with AUSA Sullivan.
AUSA Sullivan background: Interview with AUSA Sullivan; "Goodbye to Big-Gun Prosecutor Who Took On Some of Miami's Most-Infamous Criminals," *Miami Herald*, September 2, 2017.
Sullivan in *The Big White Lie*: Levine, *Big White Lie*, 64–67; interview with AUSA Sullivan.
Jury-selection process: Interview with Willy Falcon; Falcon manuscript; interview with AUSA Clark; interview with AUSA Sullivan.
José Fernández: Interview with Willy Falcon; Falcon manuscript. Fernández eventually pleaded guilty to charges of bribery, bribery conspiracy, and violation of the restraining order against Falcon and Magluta.
Bribery of Gloria Alba: Interview with Willy Falcon; Falcon manuscript.
Bribery of Miguel Moya: Interview with Willy Falcon; Falcon manuscript.
Role of Alfred Alonso: In 2000, Alonso pleaded guilty to charges of bribery, bribery conspiracy, and violating a restraining order by receiving illegal payments from Willy and Sal. He accepted a plea deal, in which he agreed to testify against his cousin, Sal Magluta, in court in exchange for a reduced sentence.

19. "Justice Is a Buzzard"
Plots to assassinate Fidel: Fabian Escalante, *634 Ways to Kill Fidel* (Seven Stories Press, 2022).
Willy and Sal finance Castro assassination attempt: Interview with Willy Falcon; Falcon manuscript.
Magluta-Bonachea relationship: Marilyn Bonachea interview, *Cocaine Cowboys*; Bonachea interview, *The Streets Don't Love You Back* podcast, hosted by Rob and Lucinda Boyd, September 11, 2021.
"That guy looks just like Sal Magluta": Interview with AUSA Clark.
"It was strange": Interview with Willy Falcon.
The trial: Manny Garcia, "Security Tight as Big Drug Trial Begins," *Miami Herald*, October 4, 1993; interview with Willy Falcon; Falcon manuscript; interview with AUSA Clark; interview with AUSA Sullivan. Among the revelations at trial was the testimony regarding Guillermo Endara, the current Panamanian president, and Hernán Delgado, his former law partner. Neither man was called to testify, but Leticia Gonzalez, a clerk in the Endara law firm, did testify about how Falcon and Magluta's accounts were handled by the Endara Firm. And Keith Eickert, the co-owner of KS&W Offshore Engineering who turned against Willy and Sal, testified about how Endara and Delgado once visited him at the business headquarters in Saint Augustine to coordinate the books for money-laundering purposes. Testimony of Leticia Gonzalez, *US v. Falcon-Magluta* (transcript); testimony of Eickert, *US v. Falcon-Magluta* (transcript).
Moya's letters to Willy and Sal: Falcon manuscript; interview with Willy Falcon.
Nestor Galleano's letters to Garces: Interview with Garces; interview with Willy Falcon; Falcon manuscript; testimony of Nestor Galleano, *US v. Falcon-Magluta* (transcript).
"Our hangout was Tobacco Road": Interview with AUSA Clark.
"So they read the first count": Ibid.
The verdict: Interview with AUSA Clark; interview with AUSA Sullivan; interview with Aileen Falcon; interview with Willy Falcon; Jim DeFede, "The Impossible Victory," *Miami New Times*, February 29, 1996.

US Attorney Kendall Coffey at Lipstik: Mireya Navarro, "U.S. Attorney in South Florida Quits after Inquiry into Reported Altercation," *New York Times*, May 18, 1996; "Stripper Allegations Fell Coffey," *South Florida Sun Sentinel*, May 18, 1996; Staff, "Florida U.S. Attorney Quits amid Biting Dispute," *Los Angeles Times*, May 18, 1996; Jake Tapper, "Love at First Bite," *Salon*, November 13, 2000.

KS&W Offshore Engineering money-laundering indictment: Eventually, the acquittal of Falcon and Magluta would lead to the dismissal of charges in the Middle District of Florida on "double jeopardy" grounds. After Falcon and Magluta were tried and found not guilty, US Attorney Charles Wilson announced, "We did not feel it was an appropriate expenditure of taxpayers' resources and judicial resources for us to proceed with what is left on the case." "New Charges Dropped," *South Florida Sun Sentinel*, April 18, 1996.

Magluta and the murders: Manny Garcia, "Police: Killings Tied to Kingpins," *Miami Herald*, May 13, 1995; Slevin, Garcia, and Van Natta Jr., "A String of Witnesses, a String of Violence"; Marilyn Bonachea interview, *Cocaine Cowboys*; testimony of Justo Jay, *US v. Mario Valencia-Trujillo* (transcript); testimony of Eduardo Lezcano, *US v. Valencia-Trujillo* (transcript).

"I did a bad thing": Marilyn Bonachea interview, *Cocaine Cowboys*. It should be noted that Bonachea's testimony regarding the murders, in *US v. Magluta*, 2002, was not enough to convince a jury of Sal's guilt.

Role of Eduardo Lezcano: David Kidwell, "Six Alleged Hitmen for Drug Lords Indicted," *Miami Herald*, May 19, 2000; Associated Press, "Trial Opens for 3 Accused in Drug Witness Deaths," *Pensacola News Journal*, October 3, 2001; Catherine Wilson, "Trio Convicted in 'Hit' Killings on 3 Witnesses," *South Florida Sentinel*, November 8, 2001; interview with AUSA Clark; interview with AUSA Sullivan. Altogether, there were three trials with six convictions for the various hits. Lezcano was found guilty of his role in the murders of Juan Acosta, Luis "Weetchie" Escobedo, and the Gonzalez brothers, Bernardo and Humberto. Lezcano was given what was essentially a life sentence. In 2005, he sought to lessen his sentence by testifying in a trial against Mario Valencia, in Tampa, Florida. Prosecutors assured Lezcano that he would be given "consideration" for his cooperation. Said AUSA Pat Sullivan, "[The prosecutors] made some promises, but myself and Chris Clark had to approve that. We said no way."

Moya's bribery discovered: Interview with AUSA Sullivan; interview with AUSA Clark; Jim DeFede, "In Pursuit of Willy and Sal, Part Two," *Miami New Times*, March 4, 1999.

Magluta skips bail, goes on the lam: Jim DeFede, "The Last Dance," *Miami New Times*, April 24, 1997.

Alba and Penalver plead guilty: "Jurors Plead Guilty in Bribery," *Orlando Sentinel*, September 20, 2003.

Maria Penalver: Interview with Willy Falcon; Falcon manuscript.

Bonachea arrested with ledgers: Marilyn Bonachea interview, *Cocaine Cowboys*.

Legal travails for L. Mark Dachs: Interview with Dachs. In 2000, Dachs pleaded guilty to an obstruction of justice charge and a charge that he knowingly received $1.8 million in fees that had been obtained from the distribution of a controlled substance. He was sentenced by Judge Patricia A. Seitz to six months in prison, and, in 2001, he was disbarred by the Florida Bar. After serving his sentence, Dachs applied to have his law license reinstated. Eventually, his license was restored, and, as of 2023, he actively practiced law in Miami.

Relationship with Katherine Ferro: Interview with Willy Falcon. I was unable to reach Ferro for comment.

Further prosecutions of Magluta: Interview with FBI Special Agent Mario Tariche, June 3, 2021; DeFede, "In Pursuit of Willy and Sal"; DeFede, "In Pursuit of Willy and Sal, Part Two"; Jay Weaver, "Colombian 'Homicide Factory' Took Aim at Government Drug Witnesses," *Miami Herald*, June 3, 2002; Weaver, "Magluta Murder Trial Begins," *Miami Herald*, May 15, 2002; Weaver, "Jury Hears Details of Ordered Hits," *Miami Herald*, June 3, 2002. A consequence of Magluta's downfall was that his father, Manuel, and son, Christian, were both sentenced to prison for helping Sal conceal and launder his cocaine proceeds.

August 2002 Magluta trial: Along with Marilyn Bonachea, a devastating witness against Sal was Jorge Luis "George" Hernandez, a.k.a. Hawaii 5-0. Back when it was first discovered that Hernandez, as a prison guard at FDC, had played a role in supplying Falcon and Magluta with a smuggled cell phone, he resigned from his job and went to work for Los Muchachos. Specifically, he served as an intermediary in the bribery of two jurors. In 1998, Hernandez was implicated by Bonachea, who by then was working as an undercover informant for the FBI. Bonachea wore a wire and recorded Hernandez discussing the bribing of a juror. At first, he was indicted along with Sal in 1999, then he negotiated a plea deal with the US attorney's office in exchange for his testimony against Sal. "Second Juror in 1996 Trial Got Paid to Acquit Alleged Drug Kingpins," *The Ledger*, August 22, 1999; interview with Willy Falcon; interview with AUSA Michael Davis, April 9, 2021.

Magluta's sentence: Magluta's sentence was eventually lowered by a judge to 195 years.

20. Shame

Willy pleads guilty: *US v. Augusto Guillermo Falcon*, Change of Plea Hearing before Hon. Patricia A. Seitz, Southern District of Florida, June 16, 2003 (transcript); *US v. Augusto Guillermo Falcon*, Sentencing Hearing before Hon. Patricia A. Seitz, Southern District of Florida, July 22, 2003 (transcript); Ann W. O'Neill, "Trafficker Sentenced to 20 Years in Prison," *Sun Sentinel*, July 23, 2003.

Adjusting to prison and life afterward as convicted felons: Interview with Tony Garcia; interview with Lorenzo; interview with Tony Garrudo; interview with Rossique Garrudo; interview with Amelia Falcon; interview with Tavy Falcon.

"The thing I missed the most": Interview with Tony Garcia.

"I stepped away from him": Interview with Lorenzo.

"My son look at me as a monster": Interview with Tony Garrudo.

"Our first outing after Tony was back": Interview with Rossique Garrudo.

Encounter in USP Victorville with Gerardo Hernández: Testimony of Willy Falcon, "In the Matter of Augusto Guillermo Falcon."

Falcon immigration hearing: Ibid.

"He was showing photographs of hotels": Ibid.

"I said, 'But the only difference'": Ibid.

"They presented a plan to overthrow Fidel Castro": Ibid.

Saga of Willy Falcon's release/deportation: Interview with Willy Falcon; interview with Aileen Falcon; Jay Weaver, "'Cocaine Cowboy' deported to Dominican Republic after His Bid to Stay in U.S. Fails," *Miami Herald*, November 20, 2018; "Cuban Kingpin Makes Dominican Republic the 'World's Latrine,'" *Dominican Today*, November 13, 2018.

Epilogue

Capture, sentencing, and release of Tavy Falcon: Interview with Tavy Falcon; interview with Amelia Falcon; interview with Willy Falcon; Tim Elfrink, "Cocaine Cowboy

Gustavo Falcon Captured in Orlando after 26 Years on the Run," *Miami New Times*, April 13, 2017; Tony Pipitone, "Routine Traffic Crash Report Helped Lead Authorities to 'Cocaine Cowboy' Fugitive," NBC 6 South Florida, April 13, 2017 (https://www.nbcmiami.com/news/local/routine-traffic-crash-report-helped-lead-authorities-to-cocaine-cowboy-fugitive/11243/); Jay Weaver, "After 26 Years on the Lam, 'Last' Miami Cocaine Cowboy Arrested Near Orlando," *Miami Herald*, April 14, 2017; Weaver, "Once a Fugitive, Gustavo Falcon Imprisoned 11 Years for Past as 'Cocaine Cowboy,'" *Miami Herald*, April 25, 2018.

Cocaine Cowboys: Kings of Miami: Billy Corben (dir.), documentary series, Netflix, 2021.

"Calcified reporting": No disrespect to Jim DeFede, a reporter for the *Miami New Times* who owned the Willy and Sal story for several years in the late 1990s. His reporting was groundbreaking, but by the time the documentary was made twenty years later, the information and insights had grown stale. The primary fresh source for the documentary series was Marilyn Bonachea, who became a central focus of the narrative, even though she was not a member of Los Muchachos or a significant part of its inner circle during its years of operation.

"A loss is a loss": Interview with AUSA Clark.

Personal legacy of Los Muchachos: Interview with Willy Falcon; interview with Tavy Falcon.

In mid-2017, I was first approached by the family of Willy Falcon—specifically, his daughter Jessica and her husband. Jessica informed me that her father was soon coming to the end of his long prison sentence, and he was exploring the idea of having a book written about his life and career. Years earlier, Falcon had read the first book I published, *The Westies* (1990), and more recently he had read an advance-publication copy of *The Corporation* (2018), which touched on some of the same Cuban exile history that is presented in this book. At this first meeting in Miami, Falcon's daughter told me, "He thinks you might be the right person to collaborate with on a book."

I was intrigued but also skeptical. What was most interesting was that Willy Falcon would have paid his debt to society, so to speak. This put him in an unusual position to be truthful in a way that many professional criminals are not. But I could not commit to working with Falcon until I had a chance to meet him, to take the measure of him as a person, to get a sense of how honest he was willing to be, how precise his memory might be, how capable he was of being thoughtful and reflective about his life.

I suggested to Jessica two things: One was that Falcon begin to create a manuscript of his own, sort of a memoir or autobiography of everything that he could remember. This could be the basis for whatever he chose to do with a writer in the future, whether it was me or someone else. The other thing was that I needed to visit him in prison so that we could meet face-to-face.

I began the process of applying to visit Falcon in prison. Eventually, my request was denied. Prison authorities cited security concerns.

In the many months that followed, Falcon became caught up in immigration matters surrounding his release from prison, which are touched on in the final chapter of this book. His priorities became consumed by the uncertainty about the conditions of his deportation from the United States. The idea of doing a book drifted into the background. He wasn't available to do it.

I moved on to work on another book (*Dangerous Rhythms: Jazz and the Underworld*, 2022) and figured I had likely heard the last of Willy Falcon. If he did get around to cooperating on the writing of a book about his experiences, it would be with a writer whose availability jibed with his complicated and somewhat uncertain future.

Then COVID hit. Falcon's representatives and I were out of touch. I completed my book.

In 2021, I received a call from someone representing Falcon, who told me that Willy had explored the possibility of working with another writer, but it hadn't worked out. If I wanted to revisit the idea of working together, Falcon was game.

Three years had passed since the initial overture from Jessica Falcon. Willy was free from incarceration and had finally found a place to live outside the United States.

I asked if Willy had continued working on his manuscript. Oh yes, I was told, he completed it. It was over two thousand pages long.

I said that I needed to read the manuscript. If it seemed like something that might lead to the creation of a legitimate book, I would be interested in coming on board.

Falcon is not a writer, and the King's English is not his first language. He had assistance in compiling his manuscript from a cellmate who typed the pages. Some of the narrative in his pages was derived from memory, but many details were to be found in the dozens of boxes of discovery material that Falcon kept from his criminal trial in 1995–96, and from other legal matters pertaining to his case, or cases. The manuscript was dense with information and difficult to read but remarkable in its detail, with dates, locations, time frames, and other pertinent bits of ephemera culled from financial ledgers, police reports, DEA files, and logs that Falcon kept of his travels in South America and the United States consummating cocaine deals and facilitating shipments.

The Falcon manuscript was a mother lode of information. In it were Willy's thoughts and opinions on the events in his life.

As comprehensive as it was, I did not accept the manuscript at face value. Over more than two years, Falcon and I engaged in extensive interviews. Some of these interviews were via Zoom. A few were conducted at Falcon's place of residence, which involved travel and secrecy on my part. These interviews were at least two hours and sometimes over three hours in length. I burrowed deeper into subjects covered in the manuscript and challenged Willy on his views, feelings, and memories. It was an exhaustive process.

Our understanding was that the book was mine to write. Though Falcon's contributions were central to the project, I told him I would be gathering my own intelligence. The book would be composed of my research, interviews, thoughts, peccadillos, and interpretations. It would not be a book by T. J. English and Willy Falcon; it would be a book by T. J. English. I had the final say on everything. It says a lot about Willy Falcon that he accepted these terms and adhered to them throughout the process. We had our ups and downs, but Falcon never once sought to assert a false version of the facts or insist that his interpretation was the only one that mattered. Yes, he had a lot to get off his chest; he had been thinking about finally telling his story as he saw it for nearly thirty years. He was ready to talk. But he was also open to the concept of a writer taking his story and applying it to the larger framework of history. We both felt that his life story deserved that.

Falcon's willingness to tell his story opened the door for others from the world of Los Muchachos. This required many more interviews, which took me into the lives of others associated with the group. The story expanded beyond Falcon and his life to take in an entire generation of Cuban exiles who became caught up in the cocaine era. Their life stories were remarkable. Many were talking about these experiences to an outsider for the first time in their lives. It was sometimes emotional, and it afforded me an opportunity to cross-check information that I was receiving from Falcon and other firsthand sources.

In addition, I interviewed people in law enforcement who worked on the many criminal cases involving Willy, Sal, and the rest. These conversations were also occasionally emotional, as matters related to the War on Drugs, or the cocaine era in Miami and elsewhere, had come to dominate their lives as cops, agents, and prosecutors throughout the course of their entire careers.

The relationship between a writer and a source is, to me, a kind of sacred pact. In this case, people were telling me the details of their lives knowing that I would be using this information however I saw fit. A profound level of trust is required; the leap of faith a source takes when they reveal to me things about their life that they would not normally reveal to anyone is not something that I take lightly. Even so, sometimes the shock of seeing aspects of their life depicted on the page, with re-created scenes and reconstructed dialogue, is enough to drive someone to drink. It should be noted that although this book was thoroughly researched and is presented via many firsthand points of view, there are interpretations, historical reconstructions, thoughts, asides, biases, and viewpoints that are entirely mine.

INTERVIEWS
Augusto Guillermo "Willy" Falcon (3/10/21; 4/21/21; 4/30/21; 5/1/21; 5/2/21; 5/31/22; 12/13/22; 7/3/23; 9/14/23); Jojo Brito (3/23/21); Amelia Rosello Falcon (3/24/21); Aileen Falcon (3/24/21); Wilfredo "Mata" Pino (3/24/21); Ralph "Cabeza" Linero (3/24/21); Antonio "Tony Bemba" Garcia (3/25/21); Assistant US Attorney Dick Gregorie (3/26/21); Antonio "Tony" Garrudo (3/27/21; 6/3/22); Ileana Rossique Garrudo (3/27/21; 6/3/22); Assistant US Attorney Michael Davis (4/9/21; 4/19/21); Manuel Garces (4/27/21); Raymond "Manny" Alonso (4/28/21); Detective Al Singleton (5/4/21); Assistant US Attorney Christopher "Chris" Clark (5/5/21); Detective Pat Diaz (5/6/21); Orlando Begnino "Benny B." Lorenzo (5/7/21); Assistant US Attorney Michael Patrick "Pat" Sullivan (5/20/21); L. Mark Dachs (6/1/22); Esther Percal

(6/2/22); FBI Special Agent Mario Tariche (6/3/21); Owen Band (10/28/22; 11/7/22); Lourdes Castellon (11/4/22); Roben Farzad (11/6/22); Humberto "Bert" Becerra (11/8/22); Mollie Hampton (11/15/22); Fernando Garcia (11/18/22); Gustavo "Tavy" Falcon (11/19/22); Detective Ron Ilhardt (2/6/23).

COURT DOCUMENTS

The 1995–96 trial *United States of America v. Falcon-Magluta* was a primary source of information for this book. Testimony from that trial and other relevant legal proceedings are cited in the notes section of this book. The other major legal proceedings cited are:

- *State of Florida v. Augusto Guillermo Falcon et al.* (Video Canary case), 1980.
- *State of California v. Augusto Guillermo Falcon and Salvador Magluta*, 1987.
- *United States v. Miguel Moya* I, 1999.
- *United States v. Miguel Moya* II, 1999.
- *United States v. Eduardo Lezcano*, 2001.
- *United States v. Salvador Magluta*, 2002.
- *United States v. Joaquin Mario Valencia-Trujillo*, 2005.
- *United States Department of Justice (DOJ), Executive Office for Immigration Review re: Augusto Guillermo Falcon*, January 24, 2018.

PERIODICALS AND BOOKS

Dozens of newspapers, magazines, government reports, and academic thesis papers were used as research in the writing of this book. The primary newspapers and magazines are: *Miami Herald, New York Times, Washington Post, Tampa Tribune, South Florida Sentinel, Naples Daily News, Tallahassee Democrat, Pensacola News Journal, Los Angeles Times, Wall Street Journal, The Atlantic, U.S. News & World Report, Life, Time*, and *Newsweek*.

Numerous books provided historical and cultural context on a variety of subjects, including the Cuban Revolution; the Cuban exile experience; the anti-Castro movement in the United States; cocaine, its cultural history and development as an illegal business; the cartels in Colombia and Mexico; the War on Drugs; professional powerboat racing; the Iran-Contra scandal; and biographical information on many of the characters in this story, including narcos, federal agents, and presidents. The pertinent books and authors are cited in the notes section.

INDEX